THE UNIVERSITY OF CALIFORNIA: History and Achievements

THE UNIVERSITY OF CALIFORNIA: History and Achievements

DEAN C. JOHNSON

Printed in the United States by UC Printing Services, University of California

©1996 by The Regents of the University of California, All Rights Reserved

Deep appreciation is extended to the William and Flora Hewlett Foundation and IBM for their generous support of this project.

The University of California: History and Achievements is the first reference book about the University to be published in some thirty years. A previous work, the *Centennial Record of the University of California*, was published in early 1967 to commemorate UC's 100th anniversary.

Like its predecessor, this new volume describes the institution's many outstanding scholarly and scientific accomplishments in teaching, research and public service.

The book acknowledges the contributions of thousands of dedicated men and women throughout the University whose efforts help advance the goals of higher education. In addition, the book pays tribute to the millions of Californians who have supported and sustained the institution from its inception to the present. They have always been extremely proud of their University as a center of learning which is renowned throughout the world.

The past 30 years represents one of the most important periods in the University's history. This era has seen a host of unprecedented changes that will leave an indelible mark on the future of higher education past the turn of the century.

In view of these changes, this new volume is intended to do the following:

1) Provide a record of the University of California as a single institution consisting of a community of highly individualized campuses, each with its own distinctions and strengths.

2) Document the achievements and contributions of the University as a statewide, national and international academic institution of the highest rank—indeed, as leader in many fields—by including pertinent information that conveys a wealth of scholarly and intellectual activities at UC.

3) Provide the University community with a historical reference source that, at the same time, looks ahead to the turn of the century.

In supporting this approach, the text includes information about Universitywide, multicampus, Office of the President and Regental matters.

First is a narrative section and chronology about the University's growth and development as a single institution. This section describes major programs, issues and changes that have taken place within the University.

The section is followed by campus profiles which provide text about major aspects of each of the campuses.

Following these profiles is the book's encyclopedic section.

Topics therein contain narrative and other information relating to UC, listed in alphabetical order and accompanied by a documentation of sources. These are extensively cross-referenced.

Topics within the encyclopedic section include:

(1) Highly significant academic and research achievements, (2) new academic and research programs and significant changes in existing programs, (3) national, international and other major recognitions, (4) growth, development and changes in administrative programs, (5) changes in Regental, OP and Universitywide structures, and (6) actions and programs undertaken by UC in response to issues affecting higher education.

In some instances, highly significant achievements or discoveries in critical areas of importance to society, sometimes of a statewide nature, but particularly of national or international significance, will be included even if they took place on a single campus.

Lists, tables and graphs may be used to provide additional important data to amplify the narrative.

Background

While every effort was made to gather as much pertinent detail possible about each major topic, there are gaps in some of the information because of incomplete records. Therefore, some topics receive more attention than others since more in-depth information was available through official documents or first-hand interviews.

Another caveat should be mentioned. Some UC programs and activities changed or grew between the time the book was undertaken and the time all its text was completed. In addition, for a variety of reasons the book took considerably longer to prepare than originally intended, not only in the earlier phases of research, writing, rewriting and review, but in the later stages of pre-printing and printing. As a result, not all the information is completely up to date; however, such information does retain considerable value as a record of recent history, one that is not available in other publications.

Finally, the information in this book is inevitably selective because the extraordinarily wide range of programs and activities at the University could not easily be encompassed in a book of this size in any great detail, as the larger *Centennial Record* was able to do. As a result, certain decisions had to be made in preparing the text, particularly in view of staffing and budgetary considerations, in order to reflect the University's major achievements and contributions within a limited space.

Nevertheless, descriptive material in the brief history at the beginning of the book, in the profiles of UC's nine campuses and in the encyclopedic section (with references) should provide an extremely valuable overview for readers and researchers.

Documentation

The references at the end of each topic usually include the most comprehensive documents and other informational sources that were available during the preparation of the book. For later information, the offices identified in the text or in the references can be contacted. While the name of each office was the one in use when the text was prepared, some names were later changed to reflect a restructuring of responsibilities. Information in University directories or assistance from an appropriate public information office at UC may prove useful in finding a current name or designation.

Authorship

In most instances, the text was written by the author and then reviewed, and sometimes revised, by one or more individuals who had in-depth knowledge about a particular subject. A few articles on specialized subjects were prepared by specific writers and reviewed by the author. In some cases, the text was based solely on an official publication or University report.

Overall, the goal was to be certain that information was as complete and accurate as possible. It is hoped that any errors have been kept to an absolute minimum.

Acknowledgments

Appreciation is extended to all those who helped in the preparation of the book through their advice and guidance or through providing invaluable material. The compilation of this book required the assistance of hundreds of people, as information sources, as reviewers, as consultants, and as staff.

The publication could not have been completed without their input, particularly when they were extremely busy with their own demanding responsibilities. They were all consummate professionals and a credit to the University.

Specifically, deep appreciation should be extended to David P. Gardner, 15th President of the University, who saw the importance of a book which would describe UC's history, achievements and contributions and would demonstrate how UC serves higher education and, ultimately, the people of California. It was his vision that brought about this new volume, and throughout its preparation he provided substantial encouragement and support.

In addition, Vice President William B. Baker and Assistant Vice Presidents Edwin Crawford and Celeste Rose should be recognized for their patience, encouragement and continued kindness, especially during difficult times. Their support, both personal and professional, was essential to the completion of this project.

Special thanks also goes to the following for their unwavering professional assistance and advice: Ronald Kolb, Mike Lassiter, Laurie Itow, Paul West, Sondra Hopson-Smith, Rose Barksdale, Davis Krauter and

Linn Lee. The assistance of Richard West, who provided vitally needed work space and computer support, is also much appreciated.

UC Printing Services rendered invaluable assistance as well during the book's preparation. Among those who played critical roles in the pre-printing phases were George Craig, the Director of UCPS, Georgette Salazar, Ronald Banister and Charles Scribner.

Recognition should also be given to Georgina Edwards and Amy Foster, two outstanding, conscientious editorial assistants who were thorough professionals in every way.

In addition, Robert Eustachy, who designed the book, deserves credit for his deep dedication and great sense of creativity in fulfilling his exacting responsibilities. His work demonstrates the finest skills that a graphic artist can bring to his profession.

Recognition should be extended to a group of approximately two dozen colleagues within the University community who provided sound advice and guidance at the outset of the project. As members of a blue ribbon editorial board, they helped immeasurably in getting the book properly under way. Their names appear toward the end of the book.

The project owes a debt of gratitude to Verne Stadtman, Editor of the 1967 *Centennial Record*. He was generous in giving substantial time in providing information about his editorship, as well as insights about the University and its history. His views were extraordinarily valuable and much appreciated.

Finally, the names of other members of the University community, both active and retired, who played important roles in this project appear in the final pages of the book.

Contents

THE UNIVERSITY OF CALIFORNIA is widely recognized for its exceptional programs of teaching, research and public service.

Such programs result from the dedication and hard work of thousands of outstanding people within the University community who, day after day, serve the needs of higher education and of society itself.

Throughout each year, the men and women who teach and conduct research, the faculty and students who work on crucial public service projects within their communities, the agricultural specialists who seek to bring the best from the land, the health sciences practitioners who help Californians live healthier, longer lives, and many others within the University family all have a substantial impact on the lives of everyone they reach.

In addition, the University of California's achievements and contributions provide invaluable benefits for California's economy and its quality of life.

Intellectual Capital

UC's objective continues to be to provide only the highest level of education to its students.

Now more than ever, California needs the bright, creative minds that drive society. And UC's graduates are among California's leaders.

For example, in the recent past, alumni and faculty from two of UC's nine campuses have founded over 50 companies in California, employing over 106,000 people and generating over $14 billion in revenue.

UC's international reputation continues to attract leading educators from every field. Among the University's distinguished faculty members are 18 Nobel Prize winners and 254 members of the National Academy of Sciences, more than at any other college or university in the United States (the figures are as of 1995).

But scholarship isn't the whole story. UC's vital role in everyone's life is more than strictly academic.

Industry's Partner

Nuclear physics started at UC. Biotechnology originated there as well. Agriculture was revolutionized there. The movie industry grew up there. All are now multi-billion-dollar industries.

UC research attracts over a billion dollars annually from government and hundreds of millions from private sources. It's students and faculty help industry find answers, while industry's funds help build classrooms and furnish scholarships.

It's a partnership that's vital to the economic health of industry and the state.

A Community Lifeline

UC public school programs provide tutoring, counseling and workshops, motivating youngsters to excel and to go on to college.

At UC's five teaching hospitals, more than 110,000 people are treated annually. And a remarkable 1.5 million visits are made to UC clinics and emergency rooms for treatment.

UC museums, aquariums, concerts and creative events enrich the quality of everyone's lives.

Experts agree that without a healthy, vibrant UC system, the leadership role California has played in the arts, sciences and industry in this generation would disappear for the next generation.

In a state as rich and diverse as California, the University of California is an extraordinarily valuable resource.

But in order to fully understand the University of California, it is necessary to go back in time, to an era full of hope and expectation.

The University of California: A Brief History of Its Growth and Achievements

The hope for a University of California was expressed at the first Constitutional Convention in Monterey in 1849.

This was a year after the discovery of gold at Sutter's Mill and a year before California's admission to the union.

But the new state, for all of its apparent wealth, lacked the means to support government and education. To fill the vacuum, private schools and academies sprang up.

Among the founders was a handful of churchmen sent by the American Home Missionary Society of New York to minister to human souls in the mining camps and boom towns.

They opened the Contra Costa Academy in Oakland in 1853. Two years later, it was incorporated as the College of California.

Through a transfer of its buildings and lands to the state, this institution gave impetus to the creation of the University of California.

Among the supporters in those early days was the Rev. Henry Durant, of Yale. He was to become head of the College of California and first president of the University.

The Start of a Dream

Debt stalked the College of California from the beginning, and bill collectors routinely waylaid Durant in the streets of Oakland.

Despite intense dedication of the part of Durant, the students, trustees and friends of the college, the future remained doubtful.

However, in 1853, Congress had bestowed upon the state 46,000 acres of public lands. The proceeds of the sale of these lands were to be used for a "seminary of learning."

Then in 1862, the Morrill Act offered a grant of public lands to each state that would establish a college teaching agriculture and the mechanic art. California's share was 150,000 acres.

Taking advantage of this grant, the legislature in 1866 established an agricultural, mining and mechanical arts college.

The new college had funds but no campus. The College of California had an adequate site, but limited funds.

Therefore, in 1867, the college offered its buildings and lands to the state on condition that "a complete university" be established to teach the humanities as well as agriculture, mining and mechanics.

The legislature accepted. The act of 1866 was repealed, and a new act passed. Signed by Governor H. H. Haight on March 23, 1966 (Charter Day), the new act created the University of California.

The property for the University included, in addition to the Oakland site, land for a new campus four miles to the north, among oak trees and open fields.

After prolonged deliberation by leaders of the university movement, the surrounding townsite was named for George Berkeley, Bishop of Cloyne, who had visited America in 1729 in hope of founding an educational institution. He never did, but he provided the model for Columbia University and endowed three scholarships at Yale.

The University started here at the College of California, located in downtown Oakland.

The University's Class of 1873 poses for a portrait. This group of UC's first graduates was known as the "Twelve Apostles," and all eventually made significant contributions to society.

A Tiny Band of Scholars

The Organic Act of establishing the University entrusted its organization and government to a corporate body, the Regents of the University of California.

When the University opened its door in Oakland in 1869, a tiny band of scholars was on hand. They included 40 students and 10 faculty members.

Durant was named the first UC president in 1870. Classes began at Berkeley in 1873.

The Organic Act provided that, "for the time being, an admission fee and rates of tuition such as the board of regents shall deem expedient, may be required of each pupil. . . . As soon as the income shall permit, admission and tuition shall be free to all residents of the State."

Thus, three months after opening the University, the Regents abolished tuition.

A different type of charge, called an incidental fee, was levied to cover the cost of student services. This fee has risen through the years as the variety and cost of such services has increased.

The University's original plan to admit men only was changed by the Regents in 1870, and 17 women registered that fall.

In 1872, Durant resigned, and the Regents named Daniel Coit Gilman of Yale to succeed him. He served for three turbulent years.

Dissension rose on every side and, for a time, the critics and enemies of the University jeopardized its very existence.

Criticism centered on the relative emphases to be given to the literary, agricultural and scientific departments, as well as on the use of funds. Competing segments of the state's young economy pressed their interests.

In addition, a legislative investigation of alleged mismanagement of the University's land-grant funds was undertaken.

Although it resulted in the return of a clean ledger, it affirmed that there had been a lack of clear understanding both as to the grant and the management of the University.

Because of these frustrations, Gilman offered his resignation as president in 1874, but was dissuaded by the Regents. However, the following year he accepted the presidency of Johns Hopkins University.

In the perspective of history, Gilman's ability to articulate the role of the University stands out.

Between 1874 and 1899, the University had five presidents: John LeConte, 1874–81; William T. Reid, 1881–85; Edward S. Holden, 1885–87; Horace Davis, 1888–90; and Martin Kellogg, 1893–94 (acting, 1890–93).

During much of this time, the University's financial problems seemed endless.

In 1887, the legislature levied a cent of tax on every $100 of taxable property in the state. A decade later, the tax advanced to two cents; yet, in the early years, it was seldom easy to get the necessary appropriations for the University.

In addition, many years were to pass before the citizens of California gave large donations to their University. However, as Californians began to feel a personal pride in the University, there began a tradition of generous private support that has made possible the steady climb to eminence.

A New Century Begins

The approach of a new century brought a quicker tempo and a broadening responsiveness by the University to the needs of the state and the nation. In addition, scholars and scientists of international reputation were being attracted to Berkeley.

Although the first two years of undergraduate study continued to be general in nature, the variety of upper division courses rapidly increased to meet the requirements of a developing society.

Isolated by geography from the great eastern centers of learning, the University was developing the distinctive Californian characteristics of restlessness and vigor. As a result, agriculture, the humanities and engineering were to form the bases of the University's early claims to fame.

Its fame began to grow in other fields, as well, including architecture, languages, economics and the sciences.

The state, particularly the San Francisco Bay Area, was eager to develop trade with Asia, and commerce became an important disciplinary area for Berkeley scholars and students. Industry and business throughout the state also wanted college graduates with education and skills that would be valuable in those fields of endeavor.

The University's Boom Years

In 1899, Benjamin Ide Wheeler came to the University as its eighth president. He served in that capacity for 20 years. They were the University's boom years.

Although Wheeler saw the intimate relation of the University to the state, the importance of research, the necessity of a great library and spacious buildings, he regarded the primary role of higher learning as the development of character.

Before his tenure, in 1887, self-government by the student body had begun. Wheeler initiated a new system that proved so effective that the faculty, in practice, gave up all but an advisory role.

Then the faculty itself demanded a freer rein in the control of its affairs, on the premise that if students could be trusted with self-government, so could their elders.

This action won for the Academic Senate the right to set its own rules, select its own members, and appoint its committees.

During Wheeler's tenure, the University began the growth that accelerated in subsequent years.

For example, the University established the University Farm School at Davis, the Citrus Experiment Station at Riverside, and the Scripps Institution for Biological Research at La Jolla.

The Southern Branch of the University at Los Angeles was just coming into being. University Extension, established in 1892, matured rapidly. Graduate work expanded.

Emergence of a Major University

By 1923, the University led the universities of the U.S. and the world in enrollment, with 14,061 fulltime students.

By the end of the 1920s, it had conferred more than 40,000 degrees. Its alumni included four governors of California and several members of Congress. Other graduates were occupying positions of responsibility in all avenues of life and in many parts of the world.

In terms of academic and scientific achievement, the University was not yet among the vanguard of the nation's great centers of learning, but it was getting there, and rapidly.

Westward migration was swelling the population of California, and the University was hard-pressed to keep pace.

Primarily because of rapid development of the Southern Branch, Professor David Prescott Barrows, who succeeded President Wheeler, signaled his induction into office by presenting the University with its first red-ink budget, to the extent of half a million dollars.

The reaction from the Regents was, "It doesn't seem enough." Thereupon, the president increased the deficit to $670,000. His action received the Board's approval.

An initiative measure that would have provided an income from the state of more than $4 million was submitted to the voters in 1920. Although failing to pass by a narrow margin, it paved the way for financial aid by legislative act a few months later.

William Wallace Campbell, a professor of astronomy and for many years director of Lick Observatory, served as president from 1923 to 1930.

His administration was characterized by steady growth and rising enrollments. The enrollment increase continued even when the onset of the Depression foreshadowed a curtailment of physical development.

Until the 1930s, the University remained a lively place, but it was still a predominantly regional institution.

If one year can be said to have marked a turning point, it was 1934. That year, the American Council of Education asked 2,000 leading U.S. scholars to analyze the graduate schools of the nation's universities.

For the first time, the Ivy League was compelled to acknowledge serious competition in the west, as the result of ratings given to California's academic institutions, including the University.

Depression, War and the Nuclear Age

In 1930, Robert Gordon Sproul became the first native Californian and UC alumnus to serve as its president.

He was to guide its fortunes longer than any of his predecessors, or those who succeeded him in the next decades.

His tenure lasted through three cataclysmic decades that included the Depression, World War II and the birth of the atomic bomb.

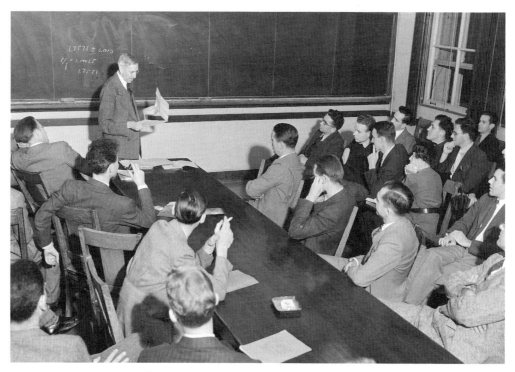

Here is a moment between two major eras, as caught by the camera in 1938. UC's internationally renowned physicist Raymond T. Birge (standing) speaks to a group of faculty and graduate students at a meeting of the Journal Club, consisting of a group of leading scientists and brilliant graduate students. At the far left is Ernest O. Lawrence, who had invented the cyclotron just a few short years before; to his immediate right is J. Robert Oppenheimer, who would lead a team of scientists in developing the atomic bomb during World War II.

And he was to see the University attain world renown for scientific achievement in a period when the body of scientific knowledge began to expand at an unprecedented rate.

When Sproul assumed office, the University had become the first major institution in the country to expand to a multi-campus plan. The problem of maintaining unity of purpose and spirit among the diverse segments had assumed major proportions.

For many years, Sproul spent about half of his time at Berkeley, a third at Los Angeles, and the rest among the other campuses. In 1936, he and his family transferred their main residence to Los Angeles for a year.

The burden of his tasks was somewhat lightened in the early 1950s when considerable local autonomy was granted to the chancellors at Berkeley and Los Angeles and to the chief campus officers on the other campuses.

With a view to ensuring academic excellence, Sproul hammered away at a single theme: the University must be able to compete for top faculty members, not merely with other universities in California but with the leading institutions in the nation.

During his tenure, UC was able to match, in salaries and in the facilities for teaching and research, the best that the eastern universities could offer.

Over the years, Sproul attracted a brilliant array of talent in virtually every branch of learning. Thus, it was possible for the University, while expanding horizontally, to maintain quality.

In 1929, Ernest O. Lawrence had invented the cyclotron at Berkeley, the first of a succession of "atom smashers." For his invention, he was awarded the Nobel Prize. This award was the first of a succession of Nobel Prizes to come to members of the faculty.

With the advent of World War II, every campus became a center of research and training. Thousands of members of the academic community were granted leave to engage in war work, to join the armed forces, or to devote full time to scientific research.

The University-operated Los Alamos Laboratory produced the first atomic bombs, whose use toward the end of World War II came as a shocking revelation of the power to destroy. However, research began to focus on the peaceful uses of this vast source of energy, and the nation looked to the universities to lead the way.

During Sproul's 28-year tenure, many honors came to the faculty at the University for their outstanding scholarship, the libraries continued to grow in size and quality of its collections, and campuses began to expand.

Physical development had lagged during the Depression and the war years. However, it seemed to explode during the late 1940s and into the 1950s.

The campuses had to grow, because the University anticipated an immediate peak in the form of huge veteran enrollments and a subsequent period of sustained growth.

Between 1944 and 1958, the University the Santa Barbara campus and developed liberal arts colleges at Davis and Riverside.

The medical school at Los Angeles was begun during that period. Meanwhile, graduate programs were expanding rapidly, and there was great demand for postdoctoral training in the medical and physical sciences.

In California and throughout nation, a new tide was running in student demand for college admission.

At the beginning of Sproul's long presidency, new state and junior colleges (the forerunner of today's community colleges) had started springing up everywhere. Each session of the California legislature brought greater pressure and competition for new campuses and budgets.

Sproul recognized that, unless means could be found for their orderly development, the institutions of public higher education faced a potentially disastrous course of competition. He saw this as national problem, but one that held particular urgency for rapidly growing California.

In 1931, he had persuaded the Regents and the legislature to provide matching funds for a study by the Carnegie Institute. The result was one of three studies during ensuing decades that led, finally, to the *Master Plan for Higher Education in California, 1960–75.*

Sproul retired in 1958. He was succeeded by Clark Kerr, formerly the chancellor at Berkeley.

The Master Plan for Higher Education

By 1958, the University had 44,000 students and foresaw that its enrollment would rise to almost 120,000 by 1975. (This turned out to be a modest projection.) Facilities would need to be tripled in that period.

The state and junior colleges also needed new classrooms and campuses and larger facilities.

The problem might have daunted California, which soon was to become the most populous state. However, there was early recognition of the need for planning.

In 1959, the legislature requested the Liaison Committee of the Regents and the California State Board of Education to develop a long-range plan.

A survey team under the direction of the two boards produced the *Master Plan for Higher Education in California.* The Master Plan was approved in principle by the Regents and the state board in December 1959.

A special session of 1960 legislature passed the Donahoe Higher Education Act, incorporating most of the Master Plan recommendations. The legislature also approved other legislation to implement the plan.

Thus, the state was able to move forward with expansion of all segments of public higher education without wasteful duplication.

In order to provide for new campuses and enlargement of others, the public voted large construction bond issues in 1956, 1958, 1962 and 1964.

Under the plan, the University continued to meet its traditional obligations: university-level instruction and professional teaching, research and public service.

New admissions standards were introduced in 1962 under which the top 12.5 percent of California high school graduates were eligible for the University.

The plan provided for the University's lower division enrollment to be somewhat decreased relative to upper and graduate division enrollments.

Certain lower division curricula were abolished, since increasing numbers of students would do their lower division work at junior colleges.

The University and the state colleges established a Joint Graduate Board to develop procedures for a cooperative doctoral program and the awarding of joint doctorates in selected fields.

Achievements of the 1960s

By 1960, UC's enrollment was almost 50,000. Its seven campuses and many research stations were spread across thousands of acres. The whole enterprise cost $360 million a year to run, and the cost (like enrollment and everything else) was skyrocketing.

As a complement to sheer size, however, the University offered a diverse academic and cultural fare, as well as opportunities for research that could be matched by few other institutions.

President Kerr's approach to mass education was to decentralize administrative authority to the campuses and, in academic planning, make the large seem small and personal, to the extent it was possible.

The Regents early adopted his recommendation for a major administrative reorganization under which much of the daily operating responsibility for the campuses was decentralized to the chief campus officers.

Throughout the first half of the 1960s, decentralization continued by stages, resulting in a substantial reduction of the Universitywide administrative staff and a greater autonomy for the campuses.

In 1961. the Regents adopted a University Academic Plan outlining the needs of the foreseeable future and emphasizing the theme of "unity with diversity."

New general campuses at San Diego, Irvine and Santa Cruz offered University planners a rare opportunity for innovation and experiment. As the first campuses to be designed from the start with a view to eventual large enrollments, they were encouraged to evolve along lines that would foster individuality, while meeting UC's traditional standards of excellence.

At the time, administrators had in mind enrollments of some 273,000 by the year 2000. In their planning, the administration was planning potential future campuses. Areas under consideration were the San Joaquin Valley, the San Gabriel or San Fernando Valley, the North Bay or North Coast area, and the Northern Sacramento Valley.

In the first half dozen years of Kerr's administration, the "knowledge explosion," along with society's efforts to keep abreast of it, demanded more kinds of classes at higher instructional levels and at a constantly growing range of research.

Ten new schools or colleges were created, with 80 new programs leading to master's degrees and 68 to the doctoral degree.

Many of these advanced programs were established at Davis, Riverside and Santa Barbara, and several others were established at San Diego.

The Regents approved a long-range plan guaranteeing access to outstanding research libraries for the new and smaller campuses. Berkeley and Los Angeles continued to develop their collections as primary research sources, while their catalog cards were given Universitywide distribution. Vehicles began plying daily between small and large campuses to facilitate intercampus borrowing.

This plan encouraged the smaller campuses, in addition to building up their basic libraries, to acquire collections unique within the University. Substantial economies were achieved by having the San Diego campus buy and catalog books, not only for its own new undergraduate library but, simultaneously, for those at Irvine and Santa Cruz.

Growing Roster of Honors

By the mid-1960s, both faculty and students reflected credit on the institution with a growing roster of honors.

For example, the University had 12 Nobel Prize-winners, and more and more faculty members throughout the institution were being elected to the prestigious National Academy of Sciences and winning coveted Guggenheim Fellowships, among other forms of recognition.

As for students, they ranked high in Woodrow Wilson and National Science Foundation Fellowships and in Rhodes Scholarships to Oxford University.

In the early 1960s, the Regents created a special scholarship program for outstanding students needing financial aid, and made available a number of tuition scholarships for exceptional students from other countries, thus supplementing programs that had been supported for many years by alumni and the State.

The Regents also provided matching funds to campuses undertaking Special Opportunity Programs designed to encourage qualified high school students from disadvantaged backgrounds to attend the University.

During this period, the University accelerated and broadened its services to the people and government of California.

For example, institutes of governmental and public affairs were conducting research on metropolitan, regional and state problems, and scientists continued to work toward solutions to problems such as smog control, water conservation, desalinization of sea water, traffic and airport safety, sewage disposal, forestry conservation, and the assurance of adequate food for a growing population.

And the demand for "lifelong learning" was reflected in the expansion of offerings by University Extension. A high proportion of the state's lawyers, doctors and dentists were availing themselves of continuing education programs.

In addition, engineers, scientists, teachers and business people were returning to the extension classrooms at intervals throughout their careers to enhance their professional capabilities.

Thus, as the University reached the mid-point in the 1960s, it could be proud of the fact that its impact on society was substantial and enduring.

A Time of Trouble

When 1967 began, Clark Kerr had been serving as UC president for eight and a half years. His hope was to be president when the University celebrated its centennial in 1968.

However, on January 20, 1967, in the midst of political and social turmoil that was seriously affecting the University, the Regents relieved Kerr of the presidency by a vote of 14–8.

Throughout the last two years of his administration, student unrest and disturbances on the Berkeley campus drew criticism of the University's management from many citizens and public officials in California.

As chief executive of the University, Kerr was held responsible for the restoration of order. On the methods to be used in dealing with the situation at Berkeley and on other matters, Kerr was often in disagreement with some of the Regents. In March 1965, he submitted his resignation from the presidency, but was requested by the Regents to withdraw it a few days later.

Thereafter, rumors of Kerr's impending resignation or dismissal reoccurred periodically. They were particularly persistent after November 1966, when three ex officio members of the Board were replaced as a result of a change in party control of the State administration.

In announcing the actions of the Regents on January 20, 1967, Theodore Meyer, chairman of the Board, said that the Regents had decided "that the state of uncertainty which had prevailed for many months concerning the President's status should be resolved without further delay."

The dismissal of Kerr from the presidency evoked expressions of gratitude and confidence for his service and leadership and criticism of his dismissal from student bodies and divisions of the Academic Senate throughout the University.

Kerr's immediate successor was Vice President Harry R. Wellman, who had served as second in command throughout Kerr's administration. He was named Acting President until a permanent successor could be found.

During this time, and in the immediate years ahead, the University's stability was severely tested by turmoil on some of its campuses and by consequent negative public and political opinion. A good many Californians saw UC as an institution of turbulence rather than tranquility, particularly as strikes and marches continued and as confrontations with administrators and police intensified.

Disruptions at the University were fueled by disaffection with the purposes of higher education, as well as by concerns over racism, deteriorating urban environments and other societal issues, and eventually by growing opposition to the Vietnam war. (Of course, UC was not alone in these concerns; student unrest had become a fact of life at colleges and universities across the country.)

Many Californians sought to punish the University, particularly by supporting budget cuts, because they thought UC was not taking sufficiently strong action against those threatening it. People wanted students who were responsible for disruptions at UC severely disciplined.

However, one important point often was overlooked during these difficult times. Many of the young people causing the disruptions were not UC students, and most UC campuses were not involved in the continuing turmoil. In addition, those involved who were enrolled at UC were a distinct minority among the thousands of responsible, dedicated students who continued year after year to go to classes and take advantage of the outstanding education offered by the University.

Achievements Amid Turmoil

The year 1965 had seen tension and unrest spread from Berkeley to other UC campuses. It also had marked the arrival of Charles J. Hitch, newly appointed Vice President—Business and Finance and professor of economics.

Hitch, a graduate of the University of Arizona, had undertaken graduate study in economics at Harvard and had been with the Rand Corporation before joining the Department of Defense as Assistant Secretary of Defense (Comptroller) under the late President John F. Kennedy. Hitch also had behind him many years of teaching and research, particularly at Oxford University. (He was the first American Rhodes Scholar to become an Oxford don.)

In 1966, in a new position as Vice President of the University for Administration, Hitch had considerably expanded responsibilities. By 1967, because of his exemplary work, he was regarded as a logical choice to succeed Clark Kerr as UC president. The Regents made it official in September when they accepted the unanimous recommendation of a special committee appointed to select a president.

Confrontations between police and demonstrators were a common sight on campuses in the late 1960s and early 1970s. Often, demonstrators might express their views in non-violent ways, but clashes were inevitable when negotiation and compromise failed, or when mobs took over.

On January 1, 1968 Hitch became the University's 13th president.

By the end of the decade, the University showed itself to be a success in carrying out its mission of higher education. By then, UC was enrolling more than 100,000 students, proving it was possible to provide education of the highest quality for large numbers of young men and women.

Large numbers of these students showed they were capable of achieving high academic distinction. Many were winning major competitive honors, such as National Science Foundation Fellowships and Woodrow Wilson Fellowships. In addition, more National Merit Scholars chose to enroll at the University than at any other institution because of its academic stature.

Scientists and scholars at all of UC's campuses kept earning national and international distinction, as well. For example, UC moved from second to first place in membership in the prestigious National Academy of Sciences, and it continued to lead the nation in the number of Nobel laureates. Its membership in leading national societies and associations grew apace.

While all this was happening, the University continued to play a major role in agricultural research and service to farmers in the state, and also served a demand for lifelong learning by more and more adults throughout California through its extension courses.

In addition, UC's medical researchers continued to make advances against an array of human illnesses, and advances in all scientific fields continued unabated.

While Hitch could point with pride to these and other major accomplishments at the University, Californians recognized that much of UC's intellectual stature was the result of his steady leadership. He was known as a president who protected the excellence and integrity of the University and finally brought it together as one institution at a highly critical time in its history.

During his tenure, Hitch believed that the University should play a major role in helping society meet some of its most urgent problems. For example, in 1968, he directed that all UC campuses mobilize their resources to help deal with the needs of cities and the growing urban crisis in America.

Among other priorities was the enhancement of energy resources and the environment. For example, one

Clark Kerr: A New Era of National and International Achievements

Four days after Clark Kerr's dismissal as UC's president in January 1967, The Carnegie Foundation for the Advancement of Teaching announced that he had accepted the chairmanship of a long-term study on the future, structure and financing of American higher education.

The purpose of the study, known as the Carnegie Study of Higher Education, was to analyze how Americans could afford the quantity and quality of the higher education they were likely to demand in the years to come. During the period of the study, Kerr held the position of chairman of the Carnegie Commission on Higher Education (1967–73).

National educator Waldemar Nielsen made this observation in a 1985 work of his own about the commission's work:

"In breadth of coverage, quality, objectivity, and impact on public policy the work of the commission constituted probably the most important body of descriptive and analytical literature about American higher education ever produced."

From 1974 to 1979, Kerr served as chairman of the Carnegie Council on Higher Education. He retired officially as a UC faculty member early in 1974 and became a professor emeritus.

During this time, the Regents also bestowed on him the title "President Emeritus of the University." When

the honor was announced, then-UC President Charles J. Hitch praised Kerr as "one of the giants of American higher education. The University—and particularly the new campuses he helped create—will always bear his mark and be in his debt. Nothing could be more appropriate than that he should have the honored title of President Emeritus."

Over the years, Kerr has continued to be recognized in important ways for his many contributions to higher education.

In 1967, for example, the Clark Kerr Award for Extraordinary and Distinguished Contributions to the Advancement of Higher Education had been established by the Academic Senate at Berkeley as the faculty's ongoing tribute to him.

The award is granted by the campus to individuals who have demonstrated distinguished service to higher education. In 1968, Kerr became its first recipient.

In 1978, Kerr received the Academy for Educational Development award for Distinctive Contributions to the Solution of Critical Problems of Higher Education, and in 1980 he was named an Academy Fellow.

Also in 1980, he received the American Council on Education's First Annual Award for Outstanding Lifetime Contributions to American Higher Education. The following year, he was given The Carnegie Foundation

of the major environmental programs of his presidency was the institution of Project Clean Air.

Hitch strengthened the University's approach in meeting these and its other challenges by effective planning and management and by bringing academic planning and fiscal planning into a closer relationship.

Early in the Hitch administration, it had been apparent that a turning point was at hand. Massive growth throughout most of the 1960s had dominated the University's fiscal planning processes; to meet the unprecedented enrollment demand, emphasis in planning had focused on developing adequate programs and facilities.

In the next few years, with gradual but significant reductions in the rate of enrollment growth (a nationwide pattern), and relatively constrained state and federal funding, emphasis shifted to specific aspects of development of each campus.

The University's new Growth Plan, adopted in 1972 and the new University Academic Plan, adopted in 1974, defined these shifts in direction.

Wherever it could be done, Hitch told a legislative committee in 1973, the University would seek to "develop and capitalize on academic specialization and strengths" of the campuses.

Concentration of rare and costly resources would be a major objective, while the students would be offered core options in academic style and content to guide their choice among campuses.

Already diverse, the unique nature of each campus would be further developed so that each would have special academic strengths as well as distinct approaches and environments—in other words, "one University comprised of many."

In his inaugural address, Hitch called upon the University to help all minority groups gain access to higher education. By 1973, minority group enrollment rose to more 20 percent, compared to less than 9 percent in 1968.

During about the same time, there also was a substantial increase in the employment of minorities and women, as well as a commitment to improve representation of these groups in higher levels of responsibility.

Another focus of the Hitch administration was the attention centered on extending the benefits of higher ed-

---

for the Advancement of Teaching Award for Distinguished Service to Higher Education.

In 1986, the Clark Kerr campus, part of UC Berkeley, was named in his honor. The site is a 47-acre complex of Spanish-style buildings and landscaped grounds containing student housing, dining services and recreation facilities. It has been placed on the National Register of Historic Places and in the State Historic Resources Inventory.

Kerr's other honors have included 38 honorary degrees and appointment to many special lectureships around the world.

Throughout the past two decades, opinion polls have identified him as a major educational leader.

For example, U.S. News and World Report twice named him "the most influential" person in the nation in the field of education. The magazine also named him, more years than anyone else, as being among the five most influential persons in education during the 1970s.

In addition, he was listed by Change magazine in 1975 as the person who contributed "most significantly to the thoughts and actions of American higher learning" and again in 1985 as one of two persons "most influential in American higher education" and "most admired for creative and insightful thinking."

Kerr also has continued to serve in a variety of public service functions, both nationally and internationally.

For example, from 1967 to 1972 he was chairman of the National Committee for a Political Settlement in Vietnam. He also was a member of the U.S. Delegation to Observe the El Salvadoran National Election in 1982.

In addition, he was chairman of Global Perspectives in Education (1976–85) and of the Study Commission on Global Perspectives in Education (1985–86).

He also served on the Board of Directors of the Association of Governing Boards of Universities and Colleges and in other capacities with the association. From 1975 to the present, he has been chairman of the Board of Trustees of the Work in America Institute.

Kerr also has continued to be a prolific writer, with works that cover both higher education and his academic specialty of industrial relations.

Recent books include *Education and National Development* (1979), *The Future of Industrial Societies* (1983, 1984), *The Great Transformation in Higher Education, 1960–1980* (1991), *Troubled Times for American Higher Education: The 1990s and Beyond* (1994), *Higher Education Cannot Escape History: Issues for the Twenty-first Century* (1994).

He also was co-editor of and contributor to *Labor Economics and Industrial Relations: Markets and Institutions* (1994).

His many books have been published by major university presses and translated into a number of foreign languages.

In 1993, Kerr was at work on a personal memoir on the University of California during the years he was Chancellor at Berkeley and President of the University (1952–1967).

ucation to a greater number of Californians, making it easier for working men and women to upgrade or even change their lifework.

With the support of the 1970 All-University Faculty Conference, the University initiated the Extended University, an experimental program that offered part-time students the opportunity to study for degrees on and off campus.

In particular, it was intended to benefit individuals previously denied access to the University because of location, work schedules and demands, home responsibilities, and similar impediments to fulltime, residential study.

The Extended University concept was tested through a series of pilot programs designed to uncover possible solutions to the educational fiscal, organizational and related problems associated with widening access to students wishing to study at different times. It permitted the University to experiment with unconventional forms and modes of instruction and to try new approaches to the educational process. (The program eventually ended as UC's budget grew tighter.)

The Demands of Change

During his administration, Hitch considered handling the demands of change one of the University's major tasks.

In his words, "it is difficult to look back over the history of the University without being impressed—even astonished—at the dramatic changes both in form and function which have occurred since its chartering little more than a century ago. During the brief period of the 1960s, the University added three new campuses, three new medical schools, and literally doubled in size in terms of students enrolled and number of faculty.

"Although the demands of growth will cease for the most part, the years to come also will be dominated by change; in technology, in how we shape our lives together, in how we use and conserve the very finite resources of the planet.

"Some awesomely large questions will be asked of us, but the men and women who together are the University of California have a century-long tradition of developing right answers. This is an immensely resourceful institution, and I feel sure it will respond with excellence to whatever the future holds."

In 1975, Hitch announced his retirement from the presidency. He subsequently became president of Resources for the Future, a nonprofit corporation for research and education in the development, conservation and use of natural resources.

As he left the University, he was widely praised, both within and outside the University, for his extraordinary level of public service. A resolution passed unanimously by the Board of Regents noted that "he put new meaning into the phrase, the academic community, and in so doing he earned the admiration, profound respect, and lasting esteem of all who love the University."

The Saxon Years

In 1975, David S. Saxon, who was University Provost in the Office of the President, was appointed to the presidency of the University.

His appointment as UC's 14th president was the apex of a noteworthy 28-year career with the University.

He had started as an assistant professor of physics at UCLA in 1947. He left in 1950 and returned the following year. He became a professor in 1958 and, after that, a dean and a vice chancellor. In the latter capacity, he supervised a major review of academic and budgetary matters that led to changes in UCLA's academic program.

In 1974, he was appointed Executive Vice Chancellor at UCLA, as well as Provost in the Office of the President. As Provost, he was responsible for relating long-range academic planning to available budget resources for UC as a whole.

In undertaking all these responsibilities, Saxon had distinguished himself as a scholar of the first rank, an outstanding teacher (earning a coveted Distinguished Teaching Award), a noted researcher, a respected educational leader, and a tireless, devoted administrator.

Not only that, to those who remembered their University history, he was an authentic hero, a man who exhibited courage and stood by his convictions during one of the University's most troubled eras.

It happened back in the early, and politically turbulent, 1950s. Saxon and 30 other faculty members at the University, as a matter of principle, refused to sign a loyalty oath sanctioned by the Regents. As a result, they were all dismissed from the University. However, some two years later the courts ruled that the Regents' oath was unconstitutional, thus opening the way for the faculty members' reinstatement.

In 1975, people who remembered Saxon's courage at that earlier time knew that his strength of character and his commitment to principle would serve the University well during its presidency. And it did.

By the time Saxon assumed the presidency, the force of student protest had largely, but not entirely, spent itself. However, another threat had emerged: an unprecedented diminution of state financial support for the University, which resulted, in turn, from a lack of political support for UC and even continued political hostility toward it.

In an era of serious inflation, the University had to cope with revised state priorities and a "smaller is better" philosophy. Like his predecessor, Saxon laid aside ambitious plans in an effort to safeguard the scholarly course that UC had always followed. However, this did not stop him from moving forward in areas where he knew there were critical needs.

In confronting the challenges facing the University during this period of severe financial crises, Saxon stood as an eloquent spokesman for the institution's integrity. He staunchly defended its vital academic and research programs and maintained his conviction that higher education provides immeasurable benefits for society.

He fought especially hard to improve faculty salaries during his presidency, which had slumped to such an extent that they were not adequately competitive with other major academic institutions, and UC was in danger of losing some of its best faculty to other universities.

In taking a stand in support of the University and higher education in general, Saxon traveled a long, hard road during much of his tenure. At times, he seemed a lone voice (but an effective one) as he stumped the state to remind Californians of their obligations in support of education and the benefits that education produces for the betterment of society.

In particular, he spoke out vigorously against Proposition 9, a major tax-cut initiative (another such initiative, Proposition 13, had been passed earlier by the voters). Saxon warned that "government by initiative" favoring large tax cuts could impair the state's ability to support higher education adequately. Not only that, as a concerned citizen, he stated that the repeated use of the initiative process could seriously undercut representative government.

In taking his stand on Proposition 9, Saxon failed to gain support from the Regents for what appeared to be an unpopular stand, and political experts in Sacramento told him he was wasting his time. Nevertheless, he continued to speak out against the initiative, along with other concerned citizens around the state, and Proposition 9 went down in defeat.

Outstanding Achievements

As a result of Saxon's hard-fought advocacy of the University during his presidency, the institution could point to a number of outstanding achievements.

For example, UC reached the highest enrollment in its history during his tenure, won national acclaim for its distinguished academic programs and scholarly accomplishments, and confirmed its reputation as an invaluable resource for the people of California and the nation.

During his tenure, Saxon strongly supported the improvement of academic standards in high schools, the preparation of minority and low-income students for college, and increased access to education.

He was highly supportive of UC's active outreach program which cooperated with community colleges and high schools in encouraging and assisting as many students as possible to extend their educational horizons.

The advantages of a higher education in California had been extended to thousands of youngsters who had not enjoyed such opportunities in the past, and the overwhelming majority were doing well. Under Saxon's leadership, the University continued to seek ways to provide students more adequate levels of financial aid and to give them the academic services they needed to succeed in their college work.

Increasingly, however, UC administrators realized that the University had to reach out to more disadvantaged students sooner in their early schooling, in order to get them motivated to start on college-preparatory courses as soon as they entered high school.

As a result, Saxon initiated UC's Partnership Program, to be conducted in cooperation with the state's junior high schools.

By the end of the 1970s, UC was working with some 250 junior high schools and about 10,000 young students around California. It was reputed to be the largest program of its kind in the nation, and it was still growing in reputation and size.

In another area of education, UC found that students who met all its formal criteria for admission were found to be sadly lacking in writing skills.

Saxon put his support behind the growth of UC's California Writing Project (formerly the Bay Area Writing Project), which trains teachers in the newest techniques of teaching English composition to all levels, elementary school through university.

This program proved so successful at its home site in the San Francisco Bay area that the National Endowment for the Humanities provided grants to help set up centers in other parts of California and in other states. Saxon also supported the further development of a similar project in mathematics.

His deep commitment to education was accompanied by a desire to see that learning and knowledge were available to youngsters from a wide variety of personal

Students gained greater access to higher education in the 1970s.   Photo by Jane Scherr

and demographic backgrounds, and as a result he fostered a commitment by the University to opening up its resources to student diversity.

Saxon also continued to stress the importance of a strong liberal education in a technological age. At the same time, he knew the importance of technology, science and related fields to the economic health of California, and he guided UC in developing innovative research in microelectronics, energy, astronomy and space, the medical and health sciences, agriculture and other major areas of research and development.

A New, Centralized System

To reach some of his goals, Saxon had to bring the University into the 20th century in one respect, by helping to create a new centralized program of information systems that would be efficient and cost-effective in serving an array of administrative needs throughout the University. This pioneering effort was a lengthy and complex process that needed the advice of a committee consisting of top-flight administrators from throughout the University.

By the time the system was in place, it was capable of serving a variety of campus and corporate data needs through information systems such as computing, telecomputing and other sophisticated means of communications. With such a system in place, all major University offices could have access to an array of critical information, including extensive data for campus and Universitywide payroll, budget and staffing operations and corporate functions, as well as statistics to help UC respond to the official reporting requirements of state, federal and other external agencies.

Saxon also played a substantial role in the development of a comprehensive Universitywide plan to develop and maintain the library collections, facilities and services of the nine campuses in such a way that they would serve the essential academic needs of the entire University in an efficient, coherent and dependable way. A major goal was to improve the methods of library acquisitions, operations and access to holdings while reducing the rapid rise in library costs.

To achieve these goals, the University emphasized increased cooperation among the University's libraries and creation of a system that would serve all UC users regardless of campus or location. Such an approach would utilize, among other innovations, enhanced intercampus exchange, an online union catalog, a shared acquisitions program, and increased automated equipment. Librarians also began to emphasize the preservation of library materials that would otherwise become unusable over time as a result of chemical deterioration, environmental damage and wear.

Of particular importance to Saxon in making the entire enterprise successful was the creation of two regional libraries, one in the northern part of the state and one in the south, to act as central repositories of books that could be easily available to any campus library or user on an as-needed basis.

In addition to all these and other contributions as president, Saxon initiated cooperative endeavors with other segments of education and the State, as well as with business and industry and minority firms. In 1981, he appointed a special task force to study UC's business opportunities for both minorities and women.

In the early 1980s, Saxon brought together leaders from all levels of education in California, as well as civic and minority groups by establishing a California Round Table on Equal Educational Opportunity.

The Round Table was a public interest coalition dedicated to improving opportunity for low income and minority students. Special emphasis was placed on improving elementary and secondary schools that served low income students and underrepresented students from minority groups, in order to enhance academic achievement and provide them with new opportunities to succeed in postsecondary education.

A number of other issues were important during the Saxon administration.

For example, in the famed Bakke case that was resolved by the U.S. Supreme Court in 1978 , the Court ruled that colleges and universities could continue to take account of race as one among a number of factors to be considered in admissions; however, the Court ruled that race cannot be the sole or exclusive factor.

The ruling allowed UC to continue its commitment to the enrollment of substantial numbers of minority students in its medical and other schools. As Saxon noted in a news conference following the court ruling, "we can and we shall go forward under the law to bring into the learned professions those who have been underrepresented, and that means particularly minorities."

Debate Over the Labs

Saxon also provided a forceful, eloquent voice during the serious debate over the University's continued management of the three national laboratories at Berkeley, Livermore and Los Alamos for the federal government. While the debate grew in intensity, the management contracts were renewed. The UC community also focused its attention on whether or not the Board of Regents should divest itself of all investments in companies doing business in South Africa. These issues would continue to be addressed during the succeeding presidency.

Other issues continued to gain Saxon's attention as the 1980s got under way.

At that time, the state was experiencing near-disastrous financial troubles, which meant that the University faced tremendous financial stresses as well.

However, even though UC's budget prospects looked grim, Saxon remained unwavering in his commitment to the critical role the University could play in the advancement of knowledge. Therefore, Saxon initiated the first steps toward involving the University in the construction of the world's largest and most advanced telescope.

Saxon's optimism sprung from his deep and abiding faith in the University and its future. His faith was ultimately justified when the Keck Telescope, the world's largest, was built several years later.

However, in 1983 the state had serious financial problems. Given the economic situation and the tax structure that was in place, there simply was no enough money to go around. As a result, UC was faced with the possibility of cuts so substantial that they would force it to reduce programs significantly and, further, to put at risk the thoroughly documented excellence of the University's programs.

As he looked toward retirement from the presidency, Saxon saw that the reductions in the State budget for UC over the previous years had finally brought the University to a crossroad. It would be a time for a new president to prove himself.

Nevertheless, Saxon had built a solid base for the new president through his many contributions to higher education. These contributions, as well as his distinctive strengths in protecting and preserving the University, were recognized by the Regents in a special resolution before he left office.

The Regents praised him "as a man of steady principle and firm convictions, of integrity, staunch character, and vision; as a caring human being whose reflective manner and quiet humor illuminate the lives of many; as a friend and colleague with a deep concern for the University and

Libraries have remained a priority for UC through the years.

a heartfelt belief in its capacity to serve California; and as a concerned individual dedicated to the search for peace."

Upon his retirement, Saxon assumed further leadership responsibilities in the academic world as chairman of the Corporation of the Massachusetts Institute of Technology.

MIT was not new territory for Saxon. He had received a bachelor of science degree there in 1941, as well as a Ph.D. in 1944. During World War II, he had been a research physicist at MIT's wartime Radiation Laboratory, the center of radar development during World War II.

As Saxon headed east for his new responsibilities, his successor prepared to face the University's latest challenges.

The Gardner Years

In 1983, David Pierpont Gardner became the University's 15th president.

At the time of his appointment, Gardner was nationally recognized as an eloquent champion of academic quality and educational reform, as well as a highly dedicated and innovative educator and administrator whose approach to educational issues was characterized by intellectual vigor, exacting academic standards, and a keen intellect.

He had been closely associated with the University since the late 1950s. While earning master's and Ph.D degrees at Berkeley, he was Field and Scholarship Director of the California Alumni Association. In the mid-1960s and early 1970s, he was a vice chancellor and faculty member at UC Santa Barbara, during the years of student unrest and dramatic growth of that campus. From 1971 to 1973, he served as a UC vice president, responsible for the Extended University and University Extension. During this time he pioneered new approaches to adult education.

In 1973, Gardner was named president of the University of Utah. During his 10-year presidency there, he also served as chairman of the National Commission on Excellence in Education. In this capacity, he was principally responsible for authoring "A Nation at Risk," the commission's groundbreaking 1983 report that helped launch a national effort to improve schooling in America.

When Gardner arrived at UC in 1983, the University had experienced nearly two decades of dwindling financial support, internal turmoil, major student unrest, periods of public alienation, and nearly ruinous inflation.

It was readily apparent that relationships between the University and State government were strained, and UC's fiscal health was in a precarious position.

The new president's first priority was to restore confidence in the University, both within the institution and outside, and to revitalize UC's financial health.

He persuaded the newly elected Governor George Deukmejian and the Legislature to approve a one-year

30 percent increase in UC's state operating budget, including a 14 percent increase in faculty salaries.

This single augmentation by the State for 1984–85, as well as subsequent budget support, gave the University the jump start it needed to set in motion a period of growth and development virtually unmatched in the history of California higher education.

By 1984, the state's economic environment was improving, and public confidence in higher education was rising from the low point of the late 1960s and early 1970s.

Gardner's leadership during this period of dramatic recovery in state and public support of the University resulted in a number of new records in growth and development.

For example, when Gardner arrived at UC in 1983, student enrollment on the nine campuses totaled 141,000. By fall 1992, when he left, that figure had increased by about 26,000 students.

Another Dramatic Upturn

The Gardner years also saw a dramatic upturn in private support. In 1983, annual gifts to UC totaled $157.5 million; by the beginning of the 1990s, the annual figure was $414.7 million. Over $2.5 billion in gifts and endowments were received by UC during Gardner's presidency.

Federally sponsored research increased dramatically, as well, during the Gardner years. Federal research money stood at close to $900 million a year by the time he left the presidency in 1992, compared to $355 million in 1983. (Federally sponsored research represented about 10 percent of federal research at all American colleges and universities.)

State support for the University also increased steadily through the 1980s, averaging about 10 percent a year. (However, in the 1990–92 period, the State's fiscal crisis adversely affected UC's general fund allocation, and the crisis continued to deepen.)

During Gardner's tenure, UC experienced a building boom greater than at any other time in its history—$3.7 billion in capital projects, with annual capital funding from the State alone growing from about $16.5 million in 1983 to $232 million in 1990–91.

At the same time, the University experienced growing enrollment pressures as the percentage of students in the eligible pool choosing to attend UC increased significantly, from about 5.2 percent of all high school graduates in 1983 to about 7.6 percent in 1991.

At least one factor was the increasing attractiveness of UC to historically underrepresented minority students. Their numbers steadily increased during Gardner's presidency, particularly at the undergraduate level, and a new and widely respected fellowship program for minority and women graduate students was put into place to increase the number of such students preparing for academic careers.

The increase in undergraduates resulted mostly from a wide range of successful affirmative action programs that UC sponsored in the junior and senior high schools.

For example, when Gardner arrived in 1983, African-Americans represented about 4 percent of the undergraduate student body, Hispanics represented 6.4 percent, and Asian-Americans comprised about 16 percent of the total.

In eight years, African-American enrollments increased by 38.8 percent, Hispanics by 108 percent, and Asian-Americans by 65 percent.

These trends convinced Gardner that the University would have to reassess its long-range planning assumptions, in order to ensure that it could maintain its historic commitment to enroll all eligible California students who chose to attend.

Consequently, he commissioned a two-year study of campus plans, culminating in the Regents' approval of Long Range Development Plans for all nine UC campuses and a 1988 decision to plan for up to three new UC campuses into the next century.

Paralleling this institutional growth, faculty awards and honors also continued to grow. For example, five more Nobel Prize laureates were added to the faculty roster, and UC memberships in the highly prestigious National Academy of Sciences, the American Academy of Arts and Sciences and the National Academy of Engineering increased substantially.

Other Achievements

Many other achievements also marked the Gardner years.

For instance, Gardner's concern about educational quality, particularly at the undergraduate level, and especially at the lower division level, manifested itself in several UC reports and their resultant activities.

Among them was the Smelser Report on Lower Division Education in 1986 and the Pister Task Force Report on Faculty Rewards in 1991. (Both reports were named after two prominent UC faculty members who at Gardner's request chaired the respective task forces.)

Gardner also convened the first All-University Faculty Conference in 15 years. Held in 1990, it was devoted to faculty and graduate student affirmative action issues. The second such faculty conference, in February 1992, focused on undergraduate education.

In addition, in keeping with his continuing concern about American education in primary and secondary schools, he authorized a series of UC research initiatives with California schools. Designed to improve classroom instruction, the partnerships have applied principles developed in research settings to real-life teaching situations.

Gardner also was instrumental in authorizing the creation and development of several major research facilities and Organized Research Units.

In addition, he personally shepherded an initiative to enhance research and teaching in the humanities, which featured the establishment of a Universitywide Humanities Institute at the Irvine campus, as well as the provision of new graduate fellowships and faculty support, in 1987.

And he forged a UC partnership with the California Institute of Technology that resulted in the construction of the world's two largest optical telescopes at the W. M. Keck Observatory atop Mauna Kea in Hawaii.

Among Gardner's other significant legacies were his accomplishments and leadership in international education.

A specialist on Pacific Rim issues and cooperation, he fostered the expansion of UC's Education Abroad Program, especially into the Asia/Pacific Region, and dramatically increased scholarship support for UC students wishing to study abroad.

During his service, 43 additional overseas centers were established in collaboration with distinguished foreign universities, accommodating another 710 UC students studying abroad.

Gardner also encouraged and supported the establishment of the Graduate School of International Relations and Pacific Studies at UC San Diego in 1986. In addition, Organized Research Units focusing on Pacific Rim projects were developed on several campuses, and funding for research on this region of the world was increased.

On the European continent, Gardner's acquaintance with Chancellor Helmut Kohl of Germany helped facilitate the establishment of the Center for German and European Studies at the Berkeley campus in 1990.

Gardner's international experiences attracted renowned scholars and statesmen to the University as part of the Tanner Lectures on Human Values, an endowed international lectureship on whose board he served and at one time chaired.

Gardner also shared his expertise with foreign governments. For example, he served as a member of the board and special advisor for the new Hong Kong University of Science and Technology.

Other Educational Enterprises

Stateside, he served as co-chair with former Harvard President Derek Bok on a national College Board task force studying the use and effectiveness of the Scholastic Aptitude Test, which resulted in significant changes being made in the SAT. The changes included the provision for certain Asian languages to be offered along with Western languages in the Board's array of national language examinations.

Gardner also served a two-year term as chairman of the Business-Higher Education Forum, a national consortium of corporate chief executives and university presidents.

Finally, in addition to the Graduate School of International Relations at San Diego, three other professional schools were added to UC's catalog during the Gardner years: the School of Engineering at Riverside, the School of Environmental Science and Management at Santa Barbara, and the School of Architecture at San Diego.

Despite his many achievements and contributions while leading the University, Gardner also had to confront a variety of daunting and complex issues.

At one point, for example, South Africa occupied a good part of his and the University's attention.

In 1985–86, the practice of apartheid in South Africa was the target of protest throughout the world. The stormy, sometimes violent debate over this issue within the University culminated in demands that the Regents divest themselves of all UC investments in companies doing business in South Africa.

The Regents and the State eventually voted to do so after two years of protest and acrimonious debate. However, Gardner disagreed with the action on grounds that the University, acting in its corporate or collective capacity, should not be taking political positions, especially using UC funds, including UC's retirement funds. His controversial stand put him at odds with many students and faculty, the governor and eventually the majority of Regents.

He also found himself on an unpopular side of a debate, especially with some faculty, arising from UC's management of the U.S. Department of Energy labora-

Supercomputers began playing a major role in scientific investigation in the 1980s.   Photo by Mickey Phleger

tories at Livermore and Los Alamos, the sites where nuclear weapons have been designed since World War II.

Gardner's position was that UC's management was an invited public service to the nation and had been performed at the explicit request of the U.S. government for nearly 50 years. Others believed that UC should cease managing the labs. The Regents reaffirmed UC's management of the labs each time the issue came to the Board during Gardner's presidency.

Gardner's skill and his will also were tested as he confronted UC's budget prospects. During tough budget deliberations he was faced with unpopular choices such as student fee increases, prospective enrollment limits, faculty and staff salary freezes, and cuts in the UC administration, in order to preserve institutional quality and UC's fiscal stability.

At the same time, Gardner could point proudly to steady progress in improving ethnic representation among key undergraduate student groups, together with consistently improving levels of academic achievement among the University's entering classes.

He also recommended, and the Regents appointed, the first two women and the first Asian-American in UC history to hold the chancellor's title. They were among the seven campus chancellors he recommended to the Regents for appointment during his service.

However, efforts to ethnically diversify other areas of the University came slowly. Nevertheless, Gardner's commitment to encompass the changing face of California within the entire UC community was unqualified and consistent.

A Bitter Challenge

Gardner faced one last, bitter challenge at the end of his presidency. At that time, he and the Regents were the target of criticism by the news media, some politicians, and others for the size of the retirement package triggered by his departure from the University. Although he weathered these criticisms, the Regents eventually made changes in the methodology and form of funding compensation and retirement packages for UC's senior officers.

Gardner stepped down as UC's president on October 1, 1992 after nine years and two months of service in that post.

In a personal letter to Board of Regents Chairman Meredith Khachigian, Gardner indicated that his decision arose because of the death earlier in the year of his wife, Libby Fuhriman Gardner, who had played a major role as a close and caring member of the University community.

In his letter, Gardner explained:

"As you know, I have been struggling since Libby's death of last February to reconcile the reality of her passing with my ongoing life and work. Friends and colleagues, both within the University of California community and beyond, and of course members of my own family, have been constant in their support, encouragement, and love as I have tried to hold together what has

been so central a fact in Libby's adult life and my own, that is, serving the University of California for over twenty years and the University of Utah for ten.

"We served together because we chose to do so. It was a partnership that brought both of us immense personal pleasure, challenge, accomplishment, and satisfaction, enriched by a unique regard and respect for what each contributed.

"Death has now dissolved our partnership, at least for this life, although according to our faith not forever, and it has become clearer with each passing month since Libby's death that without her I cannot remain as President of the University of California."

He stated, therefore, that he intended to step down as President of the University on October 1, 1992.

By that date, Gardner as UC president had guided the University longer than any of his predecessors except Benjamin Ide Wheeler (1899–1919) and Robert Gordon Sproul (1930–1958).

Worldwide Recognition

During that time, his record of scholarship and educational achievement and his dedicated service to the University and to society had been recognized many times over.

Among such recognitions was his selection as a member of the National Academy of Education and of the American Philosophical Society, a Fellow of the National Academy of Public Administration, a Fellow of the American Academy of Arts and Sciences, and a Fulbright 40th Anniversary Distinguished Fellow (as such, he presented his Fulbright Lecture in Japan). He also was knighted by the German government and is a member of the French Legion of Honor.

Gardner's tenure came to a close as the University prepared for its 125th anniversary. Just prior to leaving on October 1, he accepted the presidency of the William and Flora Hewlett Foundation of Menlo Park, California, one of the nation's 20 largest foundations. His appointment was unanimously approved by the Foundation's Board of Directors, to be effective January 1, 1993.

As he moved on to his new career, Gardner was accorded wide recognition for his many accomplishments as an ardent and eloquent champion of the University. Specifically, he was recognized for his many contributions in helping the University regain the national and international recognition it deserved in teaching, research and public service.

The Regents summed up his substantial achievements in a resolution expressing their appreciation for his service to the University and to higher education. The resolution stated that he "staunchly fought to preserve the University's excellence above all else, addressing every question strategically and analytically and displaying an eloquence in discourse and clarity of thought that illuminated the most difficult and complex of issues, seeking in all possible instances consensus and compromise through the generous application of warmth, grace, and reason."

The Peltason Years

In April 1992, the University chose one of its own to become UC's 16th president.

He was Jack W. Peltason, chancellor of UC Irvine since 1984. His appointment was effective October 1.

An internationally respected political scientist and higher education administrator, Peltason actually began his affiliation with UC in 1964.

As vice chancellor for academic affairs, he helped assemble the faculty for the fledgling Irvine campus that would open a year later.

In 1967. he began a 10-year tenure as chancellor at the University of Illinois at Urbana-Champaign, and from 1977 to 1984, he served as president of the American Council on Education (ACE) in Washington, D.C.

In announcing Peltason's appointment as UC president in 1992, UC Regents' Chairman Meredith Khachigian stated:

"His international stature, his integrity, his credibility, are all qualities that Jack Peltason will bring to the position of President." The chairman further stated: "We discovered a deep respect for him among colleagues, with the faculty and students, and with all who have worked with him over the years."

Khachigian cited Peltason's knowledge about the political process and his experience working with legislative and governmental constituents, adding that, with his intense knowledge of UC and the difficult economic environment of the state, Peltason's ability to represent UC's interests in an effective, articulate way "will be essential to our mission and to the preservation of our excellence."

Peltason not only had a hand in designing the blueprints for UCI's academic development in the 1960s, under founding Chancellor Daniel Aldrich; he also directed, as the second chancellor, its dramatic surge in growth during the 1980s and its emergence as a world-class public research institution.

At one point, more than $350 million in new buildings were under construction or being planned. Paralleling the physical growth of the campus was a growth in private support from about $10 million, the year Peltason arrived, to a high of $32.8 million in 1988–89. Much of this fund-raising was credited to Peltason's strong personal relationships with community and business leaders in Orange County.

Enrollments during Peltason's tenure at UCI increased from 12,600 in 1984 to nearly 17,000 students by 1992. And with that growth came a broadening of the curriculum and the emergence of several programs of academic distinction, including geosciences, neurosciences and the Universitywide Humanities Research Institute, centered at UCI.

Peltason had established his national reputation during his seven years with the prestigious ACE, the platform for higher education interests in Washington. As president, he represented the viewpoint of public and private colleges and universities whenever and wherever government policies and laws were being formulated.

Peltason was a Phi Beta Kappa graduate of the University of Missouri. He did graduate work there as well as at Princeton University, where he was awarded the Ph.D. in 1947. In addition to his administrative service, he was a member of the faculty at the University of Missouri, Princeton, Smith College and the University of Illinois. He also taught selected classes at UCI.

The recipient of numerous honorary degrees, Peltason is a fellow of the American Academy of Arts and Sciences and is a past president of the National Council of Pi Sigma Alpha, a national honorary political science council. At the time of his UC appointment, he was a trustee of the Carnegie Foundation for the Advancement of Teaching and the American College Testing Program, as well as vice president of the American Political Science Association. He also is the author of numerous publications on U.S. government, including two widely used political science texts that focus on constitutional law.

In 1993, as he completed his first year in office, Peltason reported to the Regents on the state of the University, saying that it had been "a year of major challenges."

And yet, Peltason said, it was important to remember that during the year, difficult as it had been, "students got educated, faculty discovered and created new knowledge, and staff took care of the thousands of tasks necessary to keep our doors open."

The president noted that the University was "experiencing the most difficult economic retrenchment in its history." He said it would be "foolish to say that the consequences haven't been wrenching for everybody. Students are paying more and faculty and staff are working harder for less pay. We have had to make many choices that were neither easy nor painless.

"But we have done what stewards of the public trust must do. We have tried to protect high-quality instruction, we have continued our commitment to diversity, we have maintained a distinguished faculty and a talented and dedicated staff, and we are streamlining our operations on every campus and in the Office of the President."

Despite the problems, 1992–93 had been positive, because it had been a year of reorganization and strategic planning, and much had been accomplished.

Among the accomplishments was the appointment of a transition team, headed by UCLA's chancellor, to recommend ways the University could preserve its standing as one of the world's great centers of learning despite the virtual certainty of diminished support from the State through the mid-1990s and perhaps beyond.

Some of the transition team's more than 85 recommendations, with Regental concurrence, had been or were being implemented. In essence, what these recommendations accomplished was, among other things, to reorganize UC's administration in ways that better reflect the centrality of its academic mission, clarify responsibilities and decentralize functions to campuses where appropriate.

"Taken together," Peltason explained, "these actions represent a fundamental rethinking of how the University reorganizes itself, one of the most far-reaching we have done in many years."

The work of the transition team was a first step toward preparing the University for a tougher financial environment. The next was the University's four strategic initiatives, which Peltason had announced the previous December.

The aim of these initiatives has been to focus on improving management, preserving academic quality, finding new sources of support for UC, and helping the State get the economy moving again.

At the time of Peltason's presentation to the Regents on his first year, here was the status of each initiative.

• "We have not just reorganized administration, we have made the entire University a leaner and meaner organization," Peltason said. "In this era of reinventing government and improving the operation of public agencies, the University has been a leader, as it is in so many other areas as well. We are doing more with fewer people, and I am proud of the intelligence, ingenuity and dedication with which the University community has responded to the need to use our resources more effectively and efficiently than we have ever done before."

• "We are working hard on preserving the University's high academic quality despite a stringent fiscal environment," Peltason stated. "Academic planning under way on the campuses has already brought us closer to our goal of achieving relative stability during the next four years, while enrollments are not expected to increase and we have a chance to put together plans for the future.

"The chancellors and the campus communities have done a remarkable job in a remarkably short time, and they deserve congratulations," Peltason said, adding that discussions would soon be held at the University-wide level on the values and goals the University should pursue as it moves into the 21st century. He said the discussions were expected to provide clear and explicit principles that would serve as guidelines for future academic planning and help the University make the most of precious resources.

• Under Peltason's leadership, the University was actively pursuing new sources of support. Private giving to UC had reached a new high during the past year, Peltason said, and this was an encouraging sign. In addition, UC was stepping up its fundraising efforts. The University also was working with other colleges and universities and with the business community to secure stable funding for higher education.

• The University was moving ahead in its efforts to put its brainpower more directly at the service of California, particularly through UC's highly successful technology transfer activities. In addition, over the past few months, discussions had been held with UC faculty about the best ways to organize UC's economic development initiatives, and particularly how to capitalize further on UC's success in technology transfer.

This area was becoming even more important in light of the economic development opportunities that were expected to flow from the Clinton Administration's defense conversion and base conversion activities.

In this connection, UC's campuses and the Lawrence Berkeley Laboratory had submitted 60 proposals to the Clinton Administration, for a total of about $113 million, to be considered by the Administration in awarding contracts. This involvement by the University in defense and base conversion represented just one of the ways UC was working to speed California's economic recovery.

In addition to work on the strategic initiatives, the University had been spending the year on building and renewing partnerships. In this connection, the California Business-Higher Education Forum, consisting of college and university heads and leaders in the business community, had forged a common agenda in two areas.

One was to alert California to the risks facing higher education and the importance of doing something about them. Another was to propose ways of reversing business flight from the state and promoting economic development.

"The Forum is working simultaneously on these two goals because it is clear that the future of the economy and the future of education are inseparable," Peltason said.

Also, the Regents and the California State University trustees held a historic, and first, joint meeting in October 1993 to look at higher education within a framework that is larger than the perspective of any single institution. They discussed, among other matters, California's changing demographics and population growth, short- and long-term prospects for financing higher education, and the role of the Master Plan at this point in higher education's history.

Peltason had told The Regents soon after his appointment that the biggest challenge was to do more than simply react to economic adversity. "We need to try to anticipate what we will face in the next decade and to get ahead of the game," he said. As 1994 began, Peltason approached this challenge from several different directions.

Within the University, administrators were planning and building a business system that focuses on improving quality, productivity, and service. Peltason also began a careful re-examination of the University's five teaching hospitals, which were struggling with the realities of a rapidly changing and increasingly competitive health-care marketplace.

He encouraged the campuses to make greater use of information and other technologies and to explore new ways of delivering education to students. Peltason was especially concerned to see that the University weathered its fiscal crisis with its ability to serve California intact. Some proposals, for example, called for curtailing or even abolishing the University's research mission on several campuses as a way of diverting resources to undergraduate education. Peltason argued that it made no sense to dismantle selectively the University's capacity to generate new knowledge, a capacity that contributes tremendously to the strength of California's economy and every year brings more than a billion dollars into California from federal contracts and grants alone.

Throughout 1994, Peltason traveled the length and breadth of California to bring home the message that California's superb system of higher education was in jeopardy. Neither the Governor nor the Legislature wanted this to happen, he said; both were making heroic efforts to support the University despite California's staggering fiscal problems. But the end of the recession would not bring the end of higher education's fiscal crisis. A variety of structural and constitutional problems would continue to erode California's capacity to support higher education at the levels that have made it great.

Several groups in California recognized the problem and were searching for solutions. One of them was the California Business-Higher Education Forum, the organization Peltason had established to build a partnership between the business and higher education communities. CBHEF's Task Force on Fiscal Reform issued a report in April 1994 calling for major structural reform of California's finances and a reinvestment in the education and other infrastructure that powered California's phenomenal economic growth in the 1950s, 60s, and 70s. The Task Force's report was one of the first items considered by a constitutional revision commission appointed by the Governor to propose alternatives for governmental reform in California.

While the future of such reform remains uncertain, January of 1995 brought welcome news. The Governor's proposed budget for 1995–96 included a new compact with higher education in California. He proposed a 2 percent increase for the University in 1995–96, to be followed by annual increases averaging 4 percent for the next three years. While far short of the University's needs, this compact held out two important possibilities: a stable framework within which the University could plan for its future, and the opportunity to restore competitiveness to faculty salaries over time.

In that same month, Peltason announced his decision to resign as President, effective October 1, 1995. "I'm happy to say that the work I signed on to do is essentially completed," Peltason wrote Chairman of the Board Howard Leach. "The California economy is now recovering and the Governor has given us welcome indications that sufficient funding will be available to enable the University to carry out its current programs. . . . I believe the University is now positioned to meet both its responsibilities and its potential as it moves ahead to the new century, and that now is the time to bring a new leader aboard to head that effort."

Peltason could point to a number of accomplishments during his tenure as the University's sixteenth President. He instituted significant reforms in executive compensation. He took the first steps toward a major restructuring of the University's administration, including the Office of the President, in response to the challenges of the 1990s. He guided the University through the worst budget crisis in its history, and despite the necessity of student fee increases and a budgetary shortfall over four years approaching a billion dollars, he succeeded in protecting its accessibility and its essential academic quality.

A 1994 study on the performance of 300 American research universities since World War II shows that UC's nine campuses outstrip all other public universities in its research. UC is now at the very top of the nation's

Despite budgetary and other problems, UC's research and teaching achievements, and its contributions to society, still shine through. Even in the uncertain 1990s, graduates can express hope and optimism as they look forward to their new challenges.

most successful technology transfer programs, with annual patent revenues of $47 million. In the fall of 1994 the University received the largest number of applications from California high school seniors in its history, impressive testimony to the continuing quality of a University of California education. Private giving in the past few years has reached the highest levels in the University's history as well.

Peltason summed up the challenge facing the University in a message to the University community in the fall of 1994:

> We dared to dream of a great public university, a university for all the people, and more, we made that dream real. We need to recommit ourselves to the land-grant tradition that has so enriched California not just with material wealth but with opportunity

for its people. We didn't do that by settling for a university that was just good enough. We did it by insisting on a great public university.

Our challenge is to make sure the University is positioned to achieve its potential, to make it even better than it has been, to get it safely from what it was to what it must be.

The University of California has made many contributions to the state and the nation in its 125-year history, but its most remarkable achievement may well be the University itself. UC is a vast and creative intellectual enterprise, an enterprise that has never been more important to California than it is today. One thing is certain. The University's seventeenth President will have the privilege and opportunity of leading one of the great public universities of the world.

University Milestones

1853 – Contra Costa Academy opens in Oakland.

1855 – College of California chartered.

1860 – College of California trustees dedicate Berkeley site.

1866 – Agricultural, Mining and Mechanical Arts College created by the legislature.

1868 – Legislation creating the University of California signed by Governor Henry H. Haight.

1869 – University opens its doors in Oakland.

1870 – Henry Durant named first UC president.

1872 – Daniel Coit Gilman accepts the presidency of the University.

1873 – Medical School founded as a result of a gift by Dr. H. H. Toland.

California Pharmaceutical Society is affiliated with the University.

First Commencement is held at Berkeley.

1874 – Lick Observatory is established by a gift from James Lick; it is accepted by the Regents as the Lick Astronomical Department of the University in 1888.

1875 – John LeConte becomes UC president.

1878 – Hastings College of the Law opens in San Francisco.

1881 – W. T. Reid becomes UC president.

Los Angeles State Normal School established.

College of Dentistry established at San Francisco.

1885 – Edward S. Holden named UC president.

1888 – Horace Davis named UC president.

1890 – Martin Kellogg named UC president *pro tempore*.

1891 – University Extension inaugurated.

1893 – Martin Kellogg named UC president.

1898 – Medical Department and Colleges of Pharmacy and Dentistry moved from privately owned buildings in downtown San Francisco to buildings on Parnassus Heights (present site of the San Francisco campus).

1899 – Benjamin Ide Wheeler inaugurated as UC president.

1900 – Summer School begins.

1901 – Marine Station at La Jolla (now Scripps Institution of Oceanography) endowed by Ellen B. and E. W. Scripps; it becomes part of UC in 1912.

1905 – University Farm School at Davis created by the legislature.

1907 – Citrus Experiment Station established at Riverside.

1909 – University Farm School at Davis begins operation.

1912 – Extension Division established.

1914 – Agriculture Extension Service is supported jointly by UC and the U.S. Department of Agriculture.

1919 – David Prescott Barrows named UC president.

Los Angeles State Normal School becomes the Southern Branch of the University.

1923 – William Wallace Campbell named UC president.

1929 – Robert Gordon Sproul named president of the University.

Los Angeles campus moves to Westwood site.

1939 – School of Nursing established at San Francisco.

1943 – Davis campus taken over by the Army Signal Corps (1943–45).

1944 – Santa Barbara State College becomes a UC campus.

1952 – Clark Kerr named first chancellor at Berkeley.

1954 – Santa Barbara campus moved to Goleta site.

1958 – Clark Kerr named UC president.

Santa Barbara designated a general campus of the University.

1959 – Regents declare Davis and Riverside general campuses of the University.

Regents approve development of site at La Jolla as a general campus (named University of California, San Diego in 1960).

Site on the Irvine Ranch in Orange County tentatively selected for a new UC campus.

1960 – The Irvine Company offers 1,000 acres as a gift to the University for the site of a new campus.

1961 – Cowell Ranch property at Santa Cruz designated by the Regents as the south central coast site for a general campus of the University.

1965 – Irvine campus opens.

Cowell College begins instruction at Santa Cruz.

1967 – Regents fire UC President Clark Kerr; Acting President Harry R. Wellman succeeds him as head of the University system.

1968 – Charles J. Hitch becomes UC's 13th president.

UC celebrates its centennial.

1970 – Protests erupt over Vietnam War, invasion of Cambodia and killing of four students at Kent State University. Governor closes all State-funded campuses for two days. Many classes are canceled, taught off-campus, or "reconstituted" to focus on ending the war.

1974 – Amendments made to the California Constitution affecting the length of Regental terms and the composition of the Board.

1975 – David S. Saxon named UC's 14th president.

1976 – UC participates in celebrating the nation's Bicentennial Year.

1978 – Bakke affirmative action decision handed down by the U.S. Supreme Court.

1979 – Tomás Rivera is named UC's first Hispanic chancellor; he is appointed by the Regents to head the Riverside campus.

1981 – MELVYL™ comes on line with links to computer terminals throughout UC's libraries. The system enables users to determine by computer what books are held by any UC library.

1983 – The Regents name David P. Gardner to be UC's 15th president.

UC receives the first of annual allocations from the State to fight AIDS and sets up a task force to allocate funds to researchers trying to learn more about cause and treatment of the deadly syndrome.

The third Monday in January, beginning in 1984, is designated as a University holiday in honor of Dr. Martin Luther King, Jr.

1984 – The President's Fellowship Program is established. It is believed that this is the largest program of its kind sponsored by a major university. The program offers more than $1 million in postdoctoral fellowships for minority and women scholars.

1985 – Review of the California Master Plan for Higher Education undertaken.

In response to unprecedented enrollment, the University adopts a new multiple filing system allowing students to use a single application form to apply to as many UC campuses as they want.

1986 – President Gardner supports the establishment of the Graduate School of International Relations and Pacific Studies at UC San Diego, the first of its kind to concentrate on the importance of the Pacific Rim.

UC Regents take a final vote on the issue of UC investments in companies with business ties to South Africa, with regard to apartheid; at this time, the Board adopts a policy of phased full divestment.

UC opens a regional office in Fresno to ensure that Central Valley students have ready access to information about UC campuses.

Smelser Report on Lower Division Education is issued.

1987 – Regents approve the historic appointments of four new chancellors all at once, two of them—Rosemary S. J. Schraer, at UC Riverside, and Barbara Uehling, at UC Santa Barbara, are UC's first women chancellors.

President Gardner shepherds an initiative to enhance research and teaching in the humanities, featuring the establishment of a Universitywide Humanities Research Institute at UC Irvine.

1988 – UC launches planning for up to three new campuses to meet the state's growing college enrollment demands.

Groundbreaking ceremony held for Keck Observatory to house the world's largest telescope.

1989 – UC awards its one-millionth degree.

UC is named a host institute for the Tanner Lectures on Human Values, joining institutions such as Cambridge, Oxford and Harvard.

UC begins a phased move of Office of the President employees from Berkeley to the Kaiser Center in Oakland.

1990 – Chang-Lin Tien is the first Asian-American to be named a UC chancellor; he is appointed by the Regents to head the Berkeley campus.

The first All-University Faculty Conference since 1976 is convened to discuss faculty and graduate student affirmative action.

1991 – The Pister Task Force Report on Faculty Rewards is issued.

1992 – Jack W. Peltason, chancellor of UC Irvine since 1984, becomes UC's 16th president.

1993 – The University celebrates its 125th anniversary.

Sources: Various. Other UC milestones may be found in the Brief History, Campus Profiles, and each subject heading.

Presidents of the University

John LeConte, acting president, 1869–70

Henry Durant, 1870–72

Daniel Coit Gilman, 1872–75

John LeConte, 1876–81

W.T. Reid, 1881–85

Edward S. Holden, 1885–88

Horace Davis, 1888–90

Martin Kellogg, acting president, 1890–93

Martin Kellogg, 1893–99

Benjamin Ide Wheeler, 1899–1919

David Prescott Barrows, 1919–23

William Wallace Campbell, 1923–30

Robert Gordon Sproul, 1930–58

Clark Kerr, 1958–67

Henry R. Wellman, acting president, 1967

Charles J. Hitch, 1968–75

David S. Saxon, 1975–83

David P. Gardner, 1983–92

Jack W. Peltason, 1992–95

Presidents of the University—1967–1995

CLARK KERR
1958–1967

HARRY R. WELLMAN
Acting President
1967

CHARLES J. HITCH
1968–1975

DAVID S. SAXON
1975–1983

DAVID P. GARDNER
1983–1992

JACK W. PELTASON
1992–1995

Photos of previous UC presidents may be found in *The Centennial Record of the University of California,*
printed in 1967 and available in UC libraries.

BERKELEY • DAVIS • IRVINE • LOS ANGELES

Campus Profiles

THROUGHOUT ITS HISTORY, the University of California has built an international reputation for excellence in teaching and scholarship. It boasts outstanding academic programs, research facilities, libraries, public service enterprises and other strengths that make it a leader in higher education.

Each of the eight general UC campuses—Berkeley, Davis, Irvine, Los Angeles, Riverside, San Diego, Santa Barbara and Santa Cruz— offers a well-balanced educational program of undergraduate study. In addition, each campus has academic programs that make it unique. While four of the general campuses also have medical schools, the ninth campus—San Francisco—is special because of its total emphasis on the health sciences and related fields.

Here, then, are profiles of the nine campuses, showing how each plays a distinctive role within one University system.

• RIVERSIDE • SAN DIEGO • SAN FRANCISCO • SANTA BARBARA • SANTA CRUZ

The Berkeley campus and the Campanile, looking west toward the Golden Gate Bridge.

BERKELEY

Facts at a Glance

Chancellor: Chang-Lin Tien. *Opened:* 1873. *Acres:* 1,232.

Students: Undergraduate, 21,841, Graduate, 8,781, total, 30,622.

Students living on campus: 4,966.

Majors with largest enrollments: English, electrical engineering and computer science, psychology, business, political science. *Degrees:* Bachelor, 6,002, Masters, 1,845, Ph.D., 798, other postgraduate degrees, 412.

Academic staff (includes academic administrators, Cooperative Extension personnel, researchers, student assistants and faculty): 7,576. *Total employees:* 18,179. *Budget:* $811 million.

Source: Director of Public Information, UC Berkeley. Figures as of Fall 1992.

THE UNIVERSITY OF CALIFORNIA AT BERKELEY is known internationally for academic excellence.

By any standard, Berkeley ranks as one of the world's leading intellectual centers, renowned for the size and quality of its libraries and laboratories, the scope of its research and publications, and the distinction of its faculty and students.

A few facts help tell the story.

The campus ranked at the top among the nation's graduate schools in the most recent survey by the Conference Board of the Associated Research Councils.

UC Berkeley's nationally recognized academic programs include business, environmental design, public health and education.

Its distinguished faculty includes eight Nobel laureates. Of its academic staff, 81 have been commended by the National Science Foundation as Presidential Young Investigators, more than any other university since the award started in 1984.

The campus also leads the country in the number of prestigious Guggenheim Fellowships its faculty has received. It has had a total of 420 since 1964.

In addition, 109 members have been named to the National Academy of Sciences, and 68 members have been appointed to the National Academy of Engineering

Ethnic minorities represent about half of the student enrollment, making the campus one of the most ethnically diverse in the country.

UC Berkeley awards more doctoral degrees to ethnic minorities and more total doctoral degrees than any other university nationwide.

Berkeley's current achievements match its proud past.

The campus had its beginnings in Oakland in 1867. There, the small College of California had been teaching students for more than a decade.

However, while it had an adequate site, its funds were limited. To help the situation, it offered its buildings and lands to the State of California on condition that a "complete university" be established to teach the humanities, as well as agriculture, mining and mechanics.

The State Legislature accepted, and on March 23, 1868, Governor H. H. Haight signed the charter creating the University of California. That date is celebrated each year at Berkeley as Charter Day.

The property of the College of California, in addition to the Oakland site, had included land for a new campus among the oak trees and open fields four miles to the north of Oakland.

The surrounding townsite eventually was named Berkeley, after England's George Berkeley, Bishop of Cloyne, who had once visited America in hope of founding an educational institution.

He was the author of a poem that begins with the words "Westward the course of empire takes its way,"

a poem which inspired the founders of the new UC campus.

Classes for the new university initially were held at the College of California site in Oakland. Classes began at Berkeley in 1873 on completion of North and South Halls (the latter building still stands).

While the campus at the base of the Berkeley hills has grown considerably since that time, it has retained much of the tranquil beauty of its rural past and is now a park-like oasis in an urban setting.

Students study, work and relax among buildings of varied architectural styles and amid wooded glens and parklands spread across 1,232 scenic acres overlooking San Francisco Bay.

With more than 30,000 graduate and undergraduate students, a distinguished faculty, nearly 300 degree programs, and alumni in positions of national and international leadership, Berkeley today is a large and complex institution, offering students a vast range of scholarly endeavor and a wide arena for personal growth.

UC Berkeley is internationally renowned as a major research university. From that one site have come many of the great discoveries of the past several decades.

Research accomplishments include the development of the first cyclotron, the discovery of the first cancer-causing oncogene, and landmark studies based on the world's largest collection of Mark Twain materials.

Among UC Berkeley's most exciting new research projects is a pioneering effort to develop microtechnology, tiny gears, motors, sensors and other mechanical devices that would fit into the period at the end of this sentence.

The campus has 51 research centers. The range of research projects there and elsewhere on the campus is wide-ranging, complex and highly important, reflecting the diversity of disciplines represented.

However, at a large institution often known more for its outstanding research, teaching is still highly important. Consequently, at Berkeley, students have the benefit of learning from world-renowned theorists and researchers who often are distinguished teachers.

And every year, the campus honors several of its outstanding faculty members by presenting them with the Distinguished Teaching Award. In addition, departments annually nominate many of their faculty as distinguished teachers.

Nearly 150 faculty members in 45 departments have been recognized in this way for their outstanding teaching.

The quality of Berkeley's student body complements the stature of its teaching and research faculty.

The student body can best be characterized by its diversity. Nearly half of the students are minorities, helping to produce the wide range of opinion and perspective essential to a great university.

Most students are Californians, but every state and 100 foreign countries are represented.

Many programs, such as African American, Asian American, Chicano and Native American Studies, reflect the diversity, as does the opportunity students have to design their own major if their interests do not match any of the 100 majors offered.

The Berkeley campus is divided into 14 colleges and schools, most of which are subdivided into departments.

Colleges accept students directly from high school or as transfers from other institutions and offer undergraduate instruction, normally as a four-year program, leading to the bachelor's degree.

Schools usually begin instruction at the upper division level and provide students with preparatory training for specific professions.

Each of the colleges and schools has its own regulations for earning degrees and is headed by a dean who has final authority for all academic decision making.

At the same time, there are several possibilities for studies of an interdisciplinary nature at Berkeley. The Division of Undergraduate and Interdisciplinary Studies develops and administers innovative and interdisciplinary courses and programs in the College of Letters and Science that do not belong to a single department.

For example, it has administered the field major in the social sciences and the group majors in Celtic studies, cognitive science, environmental sciences, film, mass communications and religious studies. It also offers special interdisciplinary courses, such as Topics in Western Civilization and The Development of World Civilization.

In addition, courses in Special Studies provide credits directly applicable to a University degree. They are established through interrelationships among colleges, schools and departments, and, in certain cases, in conjunction with community groups, other UC campuses and other universities.

The following are designated as Special Studies programs:

Programs in Asian American Studies, Chicano Studies and Native American Studies in the Ethnic Studies Department; Energy and Resources Group; International Education; and the Military Officers' Education Program (ROTC), which includes Military Affairs courses and programs in Aerospace Studies (Air Force ROTC), Military Science (Army ROTC) and Naval Science (Navy ROTC).

Berkeley also is noted for its international teaching programs.

International issues are the focus of six undergraduate and two graduate interdisciplinary majors offered by the International and Area Studies Teaching Programs.

Through the undergraduate group majors in Asian studies, development studies, Latin American studies, Middle Eastern studies and political economy of industrial societies, students can focus their education on a variety of geographical or issue-oriented areas and topics.

Sather Gate is a memorial to Peder Sather, San Francisco banker and trustee of the College of California.

Students also can enjoy the advantages of close relationships with many of the centers of research affiliated with International and Area Studies, including the Mathematical Sciences Research Institute, the Institute of East Asian Studies, the Electronics Research Laboratory, and the Institute of Urban and Regional Development.

A special word should be reserved for the Western Hemisphere's first earthquake recording system, the 19 Seismographic Stations operated by the Berkeley campus.

The Seismographic Stations celebrated a centennial in 1987. The occasion was marked by starting a new network to record an unprecedented range of quake-produced ground motion.

The system is known as the Berkeley Digital Seismographic Network (BDSN). It extends the amplitude and frequency of quake-produced motion recordable on one seismograph.

As a result, it provides a far more complete picture of earthquake mechanisms and the effects of ground wave movement through the earth.

Scientists can record, on the same seismograph, ground movement throughout the West, ranging from zero magnitude on the Richter scale to a major earthquake measuring 8.6.

The data is expected to aid mathematical analysis of the form of ground motion waves, the mechanisms of fault movement, and an overall improved understanding of the dynamics of earth movements.

Between their inauguration in 1887 and the 100th anniversary, the seismographic stations had recorded more than 150,000 quakes.

These are listed in widely distributed catalogs used for work on earthquake risk mapping, studies of geologic movements, and the structure of the earth.

To support its important teaching and research activities, UC Berkeley has the leading library west of the Mississippi River.

Its library system, which contains one of the best research collections in the country, consists of the Main (Doe) Library, the Moffitt Undergraduate Library, the Bancroft Library, 22 branch libraries and many special libraries.

The combined holdings of the libraries total more than 7,854,600 volumes, 88,300 current serial publications, 55,000,000 manuscripts, more than 4,580,800 microform items, 398,500 maps and 60,000 sound recordings.

Most of the Berkeley humanities and social sciences materials are located in the Main Library.

In addition, an open stack core collection of 170,000 volumes and 300 serial titles, designed to provide a convenient entry into the library system for Berkeley's 21,000 undergraduate students, is available in the Moffitt Undergraduate Library.

The Bancroft library, devoted primarily to the documentation of western North America, maintains the largest collection of Mark Twain writing and photographs in the world.

The Berkeley collection is also distinguished for its East Asiatic Library, which contains rare editions of early manuscripts, scrolls, woodblock and engraved maps, stone rubbings and bronze inscriptions.

Special collections elsewhere in the library system include some of the rarest books and illuminated manuscripts in the world.

The library system also includes 15 affiliated libraries that contain specialized research collections of unique and often difficult-to-locate materials associated with organized research units, academic departments and professional schools at Berkeley.

Another campus resource is the Lawrence Hall of Science (LHS). It is both a public science center and a research unit in science education.

To increase public understanding of science, LHS's programs are designed to involve participants actively in science.

For example, visitors play logic games on computers, participate in interactive planetarium shows, conduct do-it-yourself experiments and observations in the biology and physics discovery laboratories, and explore a myriad of other exhibits on everything from dinosaurs to lasers.

LHS also offers public lectures; science and general interest videos; numerous special events; workshops for school groups and after-school classes in biology, chemistry, physics, astronomy, computers, robotics and math; and summer science camps.

Science curricula developed at LHS are used throughout the world and teacher-training workshops actively involve participants in curriculum development.

Another major resource is the Phoebe Apperson Hearst Museum of Anthropology, which facilitates scholarly research and education for undergraduate and graduate students in numerous disciplines.

Teaching exhibits are installed to assist faculty and students with ongoing instruction and individual study.

The museum also maintains a program of changing exhibits in its exhibit hall and at other points on campus to meet the varied educational and aesthetic interests of the University community and general public.

There are 645,000 catalogued specimens in the museum's holdings.

Also at Berkeley is the University Research Expeditions Program (UREP), which allows students, staff and members of the general public to join domestic and foreign field research projects sponsored by the University.

Participants become short-term members of field research teams engaged in projects such as wildlife habitat studies, botanical collecting expeditions, ethnographic field work, ecological surveys, fossil excavations, and historical studies.

Among UC Berkeley's cultural assets is the University Art Museum, a major resource that serves the University community.

Facilities include galleries, a fine arts bookstore, a sculpture garden and a film theater and film library.

The museum annually offers about 15 exhibitions. Some are nationally circulating and others originate at the museum. A permanent collection of Western and Asian art is on display on a rotating basis. The MATRIX program is a changing exhibition of contemporary art.

Special study collections are available to students and faculty, works in storage are made available for study upon request and various exhibitions are prepared for and by University classes and seminars.

In addition, the museum has an internship program in which advanced students receive practical experience by assisting in museum work.

Lectures on art by artists and art historians are regularly held.

Sometimes on a nice day, a class might be held outdoors. The Campanile appears behind this particular group of Berkeley students.

The museum's Pacific Film Archive (PFA) is one of the major film exhibition centers in the country, offering programs of international cinema to the public each evening.

PFA maintains a study collection of 6,000 prints and 4,000 books and provides a media information service and facilities for both film study and research screenings.

Monthly film programs are scheduled for preschool through high school classes as well.

The Botanical Garden was established in 1890 and transferred to its current location on 34 acres in Strawberry Canyon in the 1920s.

Although relatively small in area, the garden ranks with the world's leading gardens in the variety and quality of its plants.

There are 12,000 different species, and something is in bloom every month of the year.

So, at Berkeley, there is something for everyone every day of the year, whether that someone is a student, a faculty member, a member of the wider university community, or the general public.

It has been that way for 125 years, and as the campus looks to the 21st century, it is confident that its resources for teaching, research and public service can match any of the challenges it will face.

However, there is much to be done before this century is over. The Berkeley campus will be doing whatever is needed, and it will be doing it in the same way it has always carried out its missions: in an outstanding manner and with great pride.

Chancellors

Clark Kerr, 1952–58
Glenn T. Seaborg, 1958–61
Edward W. Strong, 1961–65
Martin E. Meyerson (Acting Chancellor), 1965
Roger W. Heyns, 1965–71
Albert H. Bowker, 1971–80
Ira Michael Heyman, 1980–90
Chang-Lin Tien, 1990–present

UCB Milestones

1868 – Governor Henry Haight signs act creating the University on March 23—Charter Day.

1869 – A "tiny band of scholars"—10 faculty members, 40 students—are on hand when the University opens in Oakland, with "Colleges" of Agriculture, Civil Engineering, Letters, Mechanics, and Mining.

1870 – Henry Durant, Congregational minister and Yale alumnus, becomes the first president of the University.

The first women students (17) enroll.

1872 – Daniel Coit Gilman becomes the second president, incorporating an influence of European universities.

Regent Edward Tompkins' gift establishes the first "chair of learning" in Oriental languages and literature.

Graduates, most from the College of California, form an alumni association.

1873 – Twelve young men, thereafter known as the "12 Apostles," receive the first UC diplomas.

Classes begin at Berkeley for 199 students on completion of North and South Halls. (South Hall still stands.)

1887 – Student self-government becomes organized as Associated Students of the University of California (ASUC).

1893 – UC Press publishes its first book.

1896 – The Regents call for an international competition to provide an architectural plan for the University. Phoebe Apperson Hearst (later the first woman Regent) funds the competition.

1898 – The College of Commerce, later the School of Business Administration, opens. It is the first of its kind in the U.S.

1899 – Benjamin Ide Wheeler, from Cornell, becomes UC's eighth president, ushering in a golden age of growth and consolidation.

1903 – John Galen Howard begins executing UC Berkeley's architectural plan and establishes the Department of Architecture. His legacy includes Sather Gate and Sather Tower (the Campanile), Hearst Greek Theatre, Hearst Memorial Mining Building, Wellman Hall, Doe Library, California Hall, Gilman Hall, LeConte Hall, Wheeler Hall and California Memorial Stadium.

1905 – The University purchases a collection of western Americana and Spanish-American historical materials from Hubert Howe Bancroft to be installed in the fledgling Bancroft Library, now one of the world's outstanding collections.

Serious injuries prompt presidents of Cal and Stanford to abolish football. From 1906 to 1914, the two universities play rugby instead.

1919 – The University establishes the "Southern Branch" in Los Angeles.

The faculty begins a "revolt" against the Regents' power, gaining over the next few years increased power for itself and UC's president in academic areas.

1928 – Cal crew wins the first of three Olympic gold medals in Amsterdam.

1929 – The first residence hall for students, Bowles Hall, opens, funded by private gifts.

1930 – Robert Gordon Sproul, '13, becomes the 11th president of the University.

International House opens. A gift from John D. Rockefeller, Jr., funds the purchase of the land and construction. UC enrolls almost 10 percent of all international students in the U.S.

1931 – Ernest O. Lawrence conducts the first successful operation of a cyclotron.

1933 – In the midst of the Depression, UC cuts programs and reduces salaries in response to a one-third cut in the budget.

1939 – Ernest O. Lawrence becomes Berkeley's first Nobel laureate, winning the prize in physics for inventing the atom-smashing cyclotron.

1941 – Professors Glenn Seaborg and Edwin McMillan participate in the discovery of plutonium and in 1951 share the Nobel prize for chemistry.

1942: The campus turns its energy to war work, and the curriculum is revised to include "national service courses." During the war, male enrollment drops more than 50 percent, and many males are Army and Navy members in officer training programs.

1943 – UC officially takes over operation of the government laboratory at Los Alamos, N.M., that is continuing the work of Berkeley faculty and others in the development of the atomic bomb. Berkeley physics professor J. Robert Oppenheimer, who led earlier LeConte Hall discussions about the bomb, is the director.

1945 – Berkeley completes $57 million worth of government-sponsored World War II research. Its partnership with the federal government sets the stage for continued high levels of research sponsored by the government and, later, industry, transforming Cal into a major research university.

1946 – Returning GIs double Berkeley enrollment to more than 25,000, severely straining facilities.

1952 – Clark Kerr, professor of industrial relations, is named Berkeley's first chancellor.

1958 – Kerr becomes UC's 12th president, and Nobel laureate Glenn Seaborg succeeds him as Berkeley chancellor.

1961 – A new student union opens, now called the Martin Luther King, Jr., Student Union.

1962 – President John F. Kennedy addresses 90,000 people in Memorial Stadium on Charter Day. This event represents the largest public event in UC history.

1964 – Students demonstrate against rules that prohibit certain political activities on campus, leading to what later became the Free Speech Movement.

1966 – In a comparative study of graduate departments, the American Council on Education names Berkeley the "best balanced distinguished university in the country." Harvard is second.

1968 – The campus celebrates its centennial.

1969 – Student protests take place over use of three-acre lot later called People's Park, leading eventually to action by the National Guard.

1973 – Enrollment in the fall quarter exceeds 30,000 for the first time.

1982 – Berkeley is rated the strongest graduate institution across the board in a national study by four academic organizations.

1986 – Clark Kerr Campus opens in honor of the UC president emeritus and first Berkeley chancellor.

1988 – For the first time, no ethnic group forms a majority among undergraduates.

1989 – The Berkeley faculty approves the American Cultures requirement: students must take a course that examines the experiences in, and contributions to, American culture of a mixture of ethnic groups.

1990 – Chang-Lin Tien becomes chancellor.

Berkeley's "Keeping the Promise" capital campaign ends, having raised more money, $470 million, than that raised by any other public university.

1992–93 – Berkeley celebrates the 125th anniversary of the founding of the University.

Mrak Hall overlooks Putah Creek, which is bordered by a two-mile footpath through the campus's arboretum, home to one of the best collections of dry land plants in the country.

DAVIS

Facts at a Glance

Chancellor: Larry N. Vanderhoef. *Opened:* 1959. *Acres:* 5,200.

Students: undergraduate, 17,508, graduate, 5,381, total, 22,889.

Students living on campus: 4,720. *Majors with largest enrollments* (in ranked order): biological sciences, psychology, international relations, biochemistry, English, political science, human development, agriculture and managerial economics. *Degrees:* Bachelor, 4,125, Master, 646, Ph.D., 284, Law, 168, Doctor of Veterinary Medicine, 112, M.D., 94.

Academic staff (includes academic administrators, Cooperative Extension personnel, researchers, student assistants and teaching staff): 5,716. *Total employees:* 20,310. *Budget:* $912 million.

Source: Director of Public Communications, UC Davis. (Information from fall 1992, the most current data available at the time of the encyclopedia's preparation.)

Founded as the "University Farm" in 1905 amid the fertile fields of the state's Central Valley, UC Davis has emerged an acknowledged leader in agricultural, biological and environmental sciences and is gaining similar recognition for excellence in the arts, humanities, social sciences, engineering, health sciences, law and management.

Twenty-four of the undergraduate programs at UC Davis recently ranked among the top 10 in the country, and the campus stands among the top 20 universities in research funding.

Its School of Veterinary Medicine, the only such school in the state, consistently holds top recognition nationally among its peers.

Two years ago, *U.S. News & World Report* identified the campus as one of five "up-and-coming" national universities and has since named the UC Davis School of Medicine among the top comprehensive medical schools emphasizing the education of primary-care physicians.

In 1993, the magazine reported that academics ranked the graduate program at the UC Davis College of Engineering as among the top 20 of public engineering schools in the country.

The campus owes much of its strength to its deep traditional roots in agriculture, the impressive diversity of academic programs that emerged from this foundation, a distinguished faculty of scholars and scientists, a treasured sense of community and a dedication to the land-grant values of creative, responsive and innovative teaching, research and public service.

Providing a rich and challenging learning experience for undergraduate and graduate students is critical to UC Davis' mission and is a cherished commitment and hallmark of the campus.

Several programs support this aim, including a $25,000 prize awarded to a faculty member each year in recognition of outstanding teaching and scholarly achievement.

Research is an integral part of teaching at UC Davis. Faculty members share their research findings in the classroom, and students learn firsthand about discovery while working with professors in the laboratory and field.

Research at Davis also supports California's economic, intellectual and social development.

The campus's varied research programs explore and seek solutions to problems in agriculture, resource management, the environment, health, medicine, engineering, business, the economy and public policy.

UC Davis is the northernmost of the UC campuses—15 miles west of Sacramento and 72 miles northeast of San Francisco—and its proximity to the state capital places the campus resources and scholarship within easy reach of those shaping public policy.

UC Davis scholars also explore the intellectual frontiers of the physical, biological and social sciences, as well as in the humanities.

Recently established teaching and research centers at UC Davis include:

• A bioengineering center—one of 25 science and technology centers established by the National Science Foundation—for investigating new ways to protect plants against disease

• A center for environmental health sciences

• A center for studying the health of ecosystems in the state and throughout the nation

• An agricultural health and safety center

• An institute for transportation studies

• A center for neuroscience

• A center for the study of state and local tax policy

• A center for population biology

• An internship and career center in Washington, D.C.

• A computer center for image processing and interactive computing

The largest of the UC campuses, UC Davis occupies almost 5,200 acres adjacent to the city of Davis (the campus ranks second among the UC campuses in budget and third in enrollment).

The campus's open and engaging environment reflects the collegial nature of its culture.

Large shade trees, an eclectic blend of architectural styles and a network of bike paths dominate the interior of the campus.

Bright-red London double-decker buses, operated by Associated Students of UC Davis, ferry students and employees to and from town.

Thousands of visitors flock to the campus each year for its annual Picnic Day celebration, an event that dates back to 1909.

Home to a number of past and present internationally recognized faculty artists, UC Davis continues to build and treasure its cultural arts programs and activities.

Throughout each year audiences enjoy numerous musical and dramatic events as well as lectures by nationally known figures.

Six campus galleries are devoted to displaying a range of visual arts, and a growing outdoor gallery of art found throughout the campus grounds includes sculptures by the late artist and faculty member Robert Arneson.

UC Davis owes its world-renowned reputation for its agricultural programs to its early days when "Cal Aggie" students came to the "University Farm" to study agriculture.

Since initiating its first four-year degree program in 1922 in conjunction with the UC Berkeley College of Agriculture, the campus has increased substantially the breadth of its academic programs.

Recognized as a comprehensive campus in 1959, UC Davis now offers nearly 100 undergraduate majors and more than 70 graduate programs in the College of Agricultural and Environmental Sciences, the College of Engineering and the College of Letters and Science.

In addition, UC Davis has four professional programs: the School of Law, the Graduate School of Management, the School of Medicine and the School of Veterinary Medicine.

The UC Davis Medical Center—the main clinical education site for the UC Davis School of Medicine and the only level-1 trauma center in interior Northern California—operates a teaching hospital, a regional burn center, cardiac services including open-heart and transplant surgery, and an eye and tissue bank.

It recently celebrated the opening of a new cancer center.

The diversity of teaching and research programs at UC Davis stems from its colleges and schools and their varied histories.

The College of Agricultural and Environmental Sciences, established in 1952, continues to recognize contemporary trends and the future needs of agriculture while also expanding the breadth of the College programs to embrace human and natural resources and the environment.

The primary thrust of the College's key programs is in environmental and resource sciences and policy, plant sciences, animal biology, and human health and development.

Through a vast array of programs, the College prepares students for advanced studies and leadership in areas such as public policy, research and development, managerial and natural resource economics, agricultural systems, environmental protection, safety and design, human nutrition, health and development, and food, fiber, textile and apparel industries.

Recognized as a college in 1962, the College of Engineering at UC Davis, with its highly regarded programs in basic sciences and engineering, produces graduates who are greatly valued in industry and research.

Its programs focus on biological and agricultural engineering, applied science, chemical engineering and materials sciences, civil and environmental engineering, computer science, electrical and computer engineering, and mechanical and aeronautical engineering.

Undergraduate education in engineering at UC Davis is intended to serve as a sound basis for beginning professional practice in engineering design and development, as a general preparation for careers in corporate or governmental operations or as a foundation for graduate study.

The College of Letters and Science, founded in 1951 and currently the largest of the three undergraduate colleges at UC Davis, offers thousands of courses per year in the fine arts, humanities, life sciences, physical sciences, social sciences and mathematical sciences.

The tree-shaded Davis campus is a place of beauty conducive to community gatherings, contemplative thought and recreational pursuits.

With a commitment to liberal education, rather than specialized vocationally-oriented training, the College seeks to expose students to the world of human experience, of ideas and of artistic accomplishments.

Students are encouraged to explore a variety of academic fields, engage in the pursuit of fundamental knowledge and gain the capacity for independent study and thought.

By learning to think carefully and critically, students will be able to continue the ongoing process of education that begins in the classroom but continues over a lifetime.

The Division of Biological Sciences, which coordinates biological teaching and research programs across the campus, focuses on continuing to build and strengthen one of the key areas of academic strength at UC Davis.

Major themes of modern biology are found within the Divisions' five principal programs: evolution and ecology, microbiology, neurobiology, physiology and behavior, molecular and cellular biology and plant biology.

Nearly 17 percent of undergraduates at Davis select a major offered through the Division.

In addition to the above, UC Davis is home to four highly regarded professional schools.

Having held its first classes in 1966, the School of Law has grown into an accomplished institution.

Its achievements include a nationally recognized immigration law clinic, graduates who rank among the top three of 60 law schools in California in their passage rate of the bar examination, and recognition as the only law school in California to win the National Moot Court Competition.

The Graduate School of Management opened its doors in 1981 and is gaining recognition with its maturity.

Entry-level and mid-career students develop an understanding of management approaches to problem solving and an awareness of the environment within which public and private management decisions are made.

The School's programs emphasize international management and ethics throughout the curriculum, while offering concentrations in agricultural management, and environmental and resources management.

Founded in 1966, the School of Medicine is California's northernmost medical school and is the only one serving the state's expansive Central Valley.

Recognized for its teaching and research programs, the school ranks among the country's best comprehensive medical schools in its education of primary-care physicians.

Students, residents, interns and faculty work closely together in the classroom and at UC Davis Medical Center in Sacramento, the School's main clinical education site.

The School's and Center's biomedical research programs continue to gain in stature.

For instance, the School has one of seven national AIDS research centers in the country and is one of 16 centers participating in a decade-long medical trial as part of the national Women's Health Initiative.

The School of Veterinary Medicine welcomed its first students in 1948 and has graduated veterinarians every year since 1952.

The only such school in the state, it consistently ranks top among veterinary schools across the country.

Students learn their profession in the classroom and laboratory, as well as at the Veterinary Medicine Teaching Hospital on campus, which also supports faculty research.

Contributing substantially to the School's reputation is its large and diverse research program focusing on animal diseases and the maintenance of animal health.

An impressive array of academic resources support the teaching and research programs at UC Davis. These include:

• Bodega Marine Laboratory, a facility located along the coast 100 miles west of the campus that is dedicated to teaching and research in marine biology and related fields. It is surrounded by a 362-acre reserve with remarkably diverse habitats, including a rocky intertidal zone, sand beaches, salt marsh, lagoon tidal flats, freshwater marsh, coastal prairie and dunes.

• California Regional Primate Research Center, one of seven national primate centers supported by the U.S. Department of Health and Human Services. During its more than 30 years of existence, the Center has been the site of studies in AIDS, respiratory diseases, developmental and reproductive biology, behavioral biology, immunology and virology.

• Collections and museums that include the Anthropology Museum, Botany Collection Greenhouse, Environmental Horticulture Herbarium, Foundation Seed and Plant Materials Service, Geology Museum, John M. Tucker Herbarium, R. M. Bohart Museum of Entomology, Nematode Collection, and Wine Yeast and Bacteria Collection.

• Crocker Nuclear Laboratory, a teaching and research facility focused on the operations of a medium-energy particle accelerator (a 76-inch cyclotron). For more than 25 years, the laboratory has supported basic and applied research in areas that include nuclear physics and chemistry, air pollution analysis, biology, neutron damage studies, the effect of background radiation on computers, and historical studies.

• General Library, ranked among the top research libraries in North America and comprising five units: the Peter J. Shields Library, the Physical Sciences Library, the Loren D. Carlson Health Sciences Library, the Agricultural Economics Library and the library at

Students studying at Shields Library. Collections in agricultural technology, viticulture and enology, bee biology and nematology are unequaled worldwide.

the UC Davis Medical Center in Sacramento. Collectively, these libraries contain over 2.5 million volumes and receive about 51,000 periodical and journal titles annually. In addition, there are more than 2.6 million items on microform, 224,000 maps, 595,000 pamphlets and 13,400 sound recordings.

• Information Technology, a campuswide service unit that provides a range of computing, communications and media services to the campus, in addition to academic access to microcomputing, workstation computing and supercomputing.

• Natural Reserve System, a collection of more than 30 teaching and research reserves located across the state. UC Davis manages six of these reserves: Bodega Marine Reserve, Eagle Lake Field Station, Donald and Sylvia McLaughlin Reserve, Jepson Prairie Reserve, Stebbins Cold Canyon Reserve and Quail Ridge Ecological Reserve.

• Special facilities that include the Antibody Engineering Laboratory, Bee Biology Facility, Center for Geotechnical Modeling, Early Childhood Laboratory, Electron Microscopy Laboratory, Facility for Advanced Instrumentation, Human Performance Laboratory, Hybridoma and Cell Engineering Laboratory, Limnology Labs at Lake Tahoe and Castle Lake, Mann Laboratory, Monoclonal Antibody Laboratory, Nuclear Magnetic Resonance Facility, Plant Science Growth Chamber Facility, Protein Structure Laboratory, Student Experimental Farm, Transgenic Mouse Laboratory, Veterinary Genetics Laboratory, Veterinary Medicine Teaching and Research Center in Tulare and X-ray Crystallographic Facility.

• University Arboretum, a living museum that covers 125 acres along the southern edge of the campus. Home to one of the best collections of dry plants in the world, the Arboretum contains 2,000 different kinds of trees, flowers and shrubs, including more than a dozen rare or endangered species.

Chief Campus Officers

Stanley B. Freeborn, Provost 1952–58/Chancellor 1958–1959

Emil M. Mrak, Chancellor 1959–1969

James H. Meyer, Chancellor 1969–1987

Theodore L. Hullar, Chancellor 1987–1994

Larry N. Vanderhoef, 1994–

UCD Milestones

1909 – University Farm School opens in Davisville.

1909 – More than 2,200 come to the first Picnic Day.

1911 – First graduates number four.

1914 – First regularly enrolled female students arrive in the spring.

1922 – Four-year degree program initiated.

1928 – Celeste Turner (Wright) is the first regular woman faculty member and the first Ph.D. in the humanities to teach at Davis.

1935 – Courses in winemaking offered for the first time at Davis.

1940 – Division of Chemistry holds the first patents for the entire University of California.

Library and administration building (later to be named Shields Library) is completed.

1943 – Instruction is discontinued and the Davis campus is converted to a training school for the Army Signal Corps. Regular students will not return until 1945.

1948 – Groundbreaking day for the School of Veterinary Medicine.

First commencement on the Davis campus; 300 students receive degrees. University acquires Straloch Farm, which becomes the first and only university-owned airport in California.

Fred Bixby begins the Bixby Work-Learn Program with a $250,000 grant. This is the beginning of what has become the Internship and Career Center.

1950 – In the 1950s, Royce S. Bringhurst and Victor Voth develop new methods for planting strawberries. They improve varieties, tripling California's annual yield (which is 75% of the U.S. output).

1955 – The Memorial Union is dedicated commemorating 128 Cal Aggie students lost in military service during WWII. The $1 million cost was paid by alumni, students, faculty, friends.

1959 – Regents declare UC Davis a general campus.

Alumni leaders form the Cal Aggie Alumni Foundation as a non-profit entity to raise private funds for campus.

1960 – Undergraduate enrollment in Letters and Sciences equals that of the College of Agriculture.

1962 – TIME Magazine recognizes UC Davis as the M.I.T. of California Agriculture.

1965 – Crocker Nuclear Lab is completed and incorporates part of the cyclotron from Berkeley.

Academic Senate passes resolution endorsing students' freedom of speech.

1966 – Experimental College begins.

Institute of Ecology is formed.

A grant from the Cowell Foundation finances a hospital addition to the Student Health Center—serving as the only hospital, in-patient facility in Davis.

1967 – Under a $1 million grant from the Ford Foundation, the Center on Administration of Criminal Justice is established.

1968 – Project Involvement is launched by Chancellor Mrak to bring students, faculty and staff together to solve campus problems.

1969 – First in a series of planned ethnic studies programs is approved.

First Resort, a student-staffed, peer-advising center, opens.

Women's Center opens.

1975 – Veterinary School ranked first in the nation.

1976 – Doctoral program in agricultural economics ranked No. 1 nationally.

1979 – Davis Chancellor's Club established.

1980 – A total hip prosthesis for dogs is developed at the Vet School.

Annual Fund established at UC Davis with two donor support groups: the Davis Chancellor's Club and the Century Club (Pacesetters, Gold, Silver).

1986 – A team of UC Davis physicists develop an air pollution monitoring network using a particle accelerator.

1987 – First UC Davis Prize for Teaching and Scholarly Achievement presented; at $25,000 it is believed to be the largest of its kind in the nation.

1989 – UC Davis researchers pioneer first robot-assisted surgery (Robodoc) used to perform hip implants on dogs. Human surgery is expected within two years.

UC Davis is named one of seven national centers for AIDS research and will share a 5-year grant of more than $30 million.

Seventy-fifth anniversary of Cooperative Extension.

1990 – A cross-cultural center is established, to open in 1992.

1991 – Law school's 83.3% Bar passage rate is highest in state among accredited schools.

Total number of alumni reaches and exceeds 100,000.

Davis has the highest graduation rate among the UC campuses.

1992–93 – The first 125 years of UC excellence in teaching, research and public service is celebrated.

Students study, relax and dine at UCI's Student Center, a popular gathering spot.

IRVINE

Facts at a Glance

Chancellor: Laurel L. Wilkening. *Opened:* 1965. *Acres:* 1,489.

Students (Fall 1992): undergraduate, 13,888, graduate, 3,251, total, 17,139.

Students living on campus: 4,589. *Majors with largest enrollments:* biological sciences, social sciences, humanities, engineering, social ecology and physical sciences. *Degrees* (Spring 1993): Bachelor, 3,111, Master, 427, Ph.D., 162, M.D., 82, Teaching Credentials, 339.

Academic staff, Fall 1992 (includes academic administrators, Cooperative Extension personnel, researchers, student assistants and teaching staff): 2,342. *Total employees:* 8,759. *Budget:* $600 million.

Source: Director of Communications, UC Irvine.

FROM THE TIME IT OPENED its doors in 1965, UC Irvine has remained dedicated to providing a learning environment responsive to changing technologies and social issues.

In 1990, UCI emerged from its 25th anniversary as a full partner in the education, culture and development of its region and of California as a whole.

In fact, *U.S. News and World Report's* 1991 survey named UCI as one of the nation's top five "up and coming" campuses.

The mid-1980s in particular saw the addition of many internationally known scholars and scientists, including Francisco Ayala in evolutionary biology, Ricardo Asch in obstetrics and J. Hillis Miller in critical theory.

These recent recruits joined such noted faculty as atmospheric chemist F. Sherwood Rowland, who co-discovered that Earth's protective ozone layer is threatened by chlorofluorocarbons.

The campus also is home to several prestigious research centers.

Among them is the Bonney Center for the Neurobiology of Learning and Memory, one of several research facilities at UCI focusing on the neurosciences.

Notably, a recent report on scholarship in neuroscience and behavior ranked UCI sixth in the nation in this field. Conducted by the Institute for Scientific Information, the ranking is based on the number of citations in science journals.

In addition, UCI's Beckman Laser Institute and Medical Clinic is a leader in medical laser technology, providing advanced treatment in cancer, ophthalmology and cardiovascular disease.

UCI has made equally strong strides in the arts and humanities as well. The campus is home to the UC Humanities Research Institute and Thesaurus Linguae Graecae, the world's only computerized data bank of all existing Greek manuscripts.

And the graduate writing program in fiction, is considered one of the top two in the country.

Housing UCI's academic programs are some of the UC's most distinctive architectural projects, such as Frank Gehry's engineering complex, Charles Moore's University Extension building and Robert A.M. Stern's Fine Arts Studio Four.

UCI's location offers the cultural and economic resources of an urban area along with access to the scenic, recreational areas of Southern California.

Located 40 miles south of Los Angeles, five miles from the Pacific Ocean, and nestled in coastal foothills, UCI lies amid rapidly growing residential communities and a dynamic national and multinational business and industrial complex that affords many employment opportunities.

Cultural opportunities include repertory theatres, orchestras, choral groups, dance companies, galleries and museums.

Even in the midst of all this, however, the campus remains an oasis of green, a natural arboretum planted with trees and shrubs from all over the world.

Adjacent to the campus, lies the San Joaquin Freshwater Marsh Reserve, part of the University's natural land reserve system and home to a wide variety of migratory and nonmigratory waterfowl and other wildlife.

The Western Center of the American Academy of Arts and Sciences is located on the campus, and the Arnold and Mabel Beckman Center of the National Academies of Sciences and Engineering is adjacent to the campus.

University Town Center, a commercial center, is linked to the campus by a pedestrian bridge.

It's all a far cry from the open ranchland that once occupied the site of this vibrant, thriving campus.

Since its inception in 1965, the campus has attained national, and even international, distinction for its outstanding teaching and research programs and for the quality of its faculty.

Instruction and research programs focus on fundamental areas of knowledge, and at the same time provide for interdisciplinary and professional study.

Since research is an integral part of all schools and departments, it has a positive impact on both undergraduate and graduate education.

At the undergraduate level, UCI's research programs provide students with access to a faculty made up of researchers at the forefront of their fields. Research is critical to graduate education because of the research-oriented nature of doctoral study.

Five basic Schools represent five fundamental areas of knowledge: Biological Sciences, Fine Arts, Humanities, Physical Sciences and Social Sciences.

The School of Biological Sciences is UCI's largest academic unit. There, undergraduates have access to a faculty made up of researchers at the forefront of their fields. As a consequence, the knowledge received by UCI students is the latest available.

The School's faculty engages in research areas that include, for example, neural plasticity and behavior (which in part encompasses the development of the nervous system, memory, response to injury and degenerative brain diseases such as Alzheimer's), the nature of cell-cell interactions, the organization and expression of genes; biomolecular structure, and cell biology.

Elsewhere on campus, the School of Fine Arts teaches the creative as well, as the academic and critical sides of the arts.

The School is concerned with the vitality of the arts in society. Faculty energies are directed toward the refinement, enhancement and encouragement of students' artistic and creative talents and toward the development of the students' understanding of related theory and history.

The School offers programs which emphasize extensive studio and workshop experiences, essential theoretical and historical background studies and exercises in criticism.

The School of Humanities faculty, the largest at UCI, has been repeatedly honored for its teaching and scholarly excellence.

Included in the faculty's more than 100 research specialties are literary criticism, film studies, Southern history, the philosophy of science, women's studies, East Asian languages and literatures and bilingual education.

The School houses the renowned Rene Wellek Special Collection of Literary Criticism and the Thesaurus Linguae Graecae Project, the unique computerized databank of all existing Greek literature, from its Homeric beginnings to A.D. 1453. The Project has made UCI a major source of classics research activity.

The School of Physical Sciences is another vital area for student education.

There, students learn from faculty who are conducting investigations in critical areas such as atmospheric chemistry (including the discovery of the adverse impact of manmade chlorofluorocarbon compounds on the earth's ozone layer), biogeochemistry and climate, synthetic chemistry, laser spectroscopy, elementary particle physics (including the discoveries of a new subatomic particle, the neutrino, and a rare subatomic event, the double beta decay), and plasma physics.

The School of Social Sciences is the second largest academic unit at UCI.

The faculty's expertise covers a wide range of specific social science topics, several of which are nationally recognized: the mathematical modeling of perception and cognitive processes; the economic analysis of transportation; the examination of the impact of society's political system on its economy and vice versa; and the exploration of authority structures and inequality in society.

In addition to these several academic programs on campus, programs covering interdisciplinary and professional studies are offered in the Department of Information and Computer Science, the School of Social Ecology, the School of Engineering, the Graduate School of Management and the Department of Education.

The Department of Information and Computer Science (ICS) is dedicated to teaching and research in the rapidly expanding fields of information management and use, as well as the technologies that support those fields.

ICS is a national leader in research into the social and economic aspects of the emerging global information society. A major focus is the field of computer science, which covers computer system architecture and design, mathematical aspects of computation, software design and development, and artificial intelligence.

The School of Social Ecology, a multidisciplinary unit established in 1970, is unique to UCI.

The School's central objectives are the application of scientific methods to the analysis and resolution of societal problems and the development of theory and knowledge pertinent to environmental and social phenomena.

An informal study group meets outside the Social Sciences Laboratory.

Research and teaching are organized in three areas of specialization.

The Department of Psychology and Social Behavior is concerned with human development, health psychology and mental health.

The Department of Environmental Analysis and Design focuses on design, environmental health and science and planning.

The Department of Criminology, Law and Society covers criminal behavior, social processes and legal systems.

The School of Engineering focuses on the analysis and design of physical systems applying modern scientific principles to the development of technology for society.

The major disciplines are civil, mechanical and aerospace, electrical and computer, biochemical and environmental engineering.

Research issues include earthquake engineering, water resources, transportation, parallel and distributed computer systems, intelligent systems and neural networks, image and signal processing, opto-electronic devices and materials, fluid mechanics, combustion and jet propulsion, materials processing, and robotics and modern control theory.

The Graduate School of Management offers studies in organizational behavior, management information systems, finance, marketing, real estate, managerial economics, accounting, decision sciences, operations management, strategy, public policy and health care management.

In addition, the School has an Executive M.B.A. Program and a Fully Employed M.B.A. Program.

UCI's Department of Education offers credential programs for teachers and administrators in California's public elementary and secondary schools.

These programs are enriched by an emphasis upon teachers' use of computers in school classrooms, the teaching of writing, and the prevention of abuse of alcohol and other drugs among school children.

The Department has one of the largest, credential programs within the UC system. It is recognized throughout California for its leadership in the development of innovative programs to improve education in grades K-12.

The UCI College of Medicine is another major and distinctive facility at UCI.

It provides educational programs for medical and health sciences graduate students, medical residents and practicing physicians.

It also offers one of the country's largest residency training programs in primary care and internal medicine.

In addition, it houses some of the most advanced equipment in medical imaging and laser medicine available in the world (including a positron emission tomography scanner and an ultrasound microscope, which is one of only two such machines in the U.S. and the only one used in biomedical research).

The College's faculty conduct innovative research in areas such as bioethics, biomolecular structure, oncology, cardiovascular and pulmonary diseases, geriatric medicine, immunology, molecular and human genetics, the neurosciences and perinatology.

Another major resource at UCI is the Laser Microbeam Program (LAMP), established in 1979 as a national facility in the area of laser microbeam biotechnology.

LAMP functions as a research, training and service facility, and provides interaction between the laser industry and the academic biomedical research community.

It serves as a resource to promote research in cell biology, developmental biology, neurobiology, genetics, oncology and clinical medicine. Microsurgery is performed at subcellular, cellular and tissue levels.

The program is conducted in the Beckman Laser Institute and Medical Clinic and is funded through a grant from the Biotechnology Resources Program of the National Institutes of Health.

Because of the activities of all its schools, colleges and other academic endeavors, UCI provides an atmosphere conducive to creative work and scholarship at all levels, to the exploration of the accumulated knowledge of humanity, and to the development of new knowledge through basic and applied research.

In so doing, UCI offers programs designed to provide students with a foundation on which to continue developing their intellectual, aesthetic and moral capacities.

Programs and curricula are based on the belief that a student's collective University experience should provide understanding and insight which are the basis for an intellectual identity and lifelong learning.

An important aspect of the educational approach at UCI is the emphasis placed on student involvement in independent study, research and the creative process as a complement to classroom study.

Independent research in laboratories, field study, involvement in writing workshops and participation in fine arts productions are normal elements of the UCI experience.

In addition, in many departments special programs and courses which involve students in original research and creative activities are integrated into the curriculum.

Along with these objectives, UCI has a serious commitment to public service.

The campus generates research expertise which may be applied to regional and national social issues, and seeks to provide humanistic understanding of the problems of society.

The UCI Library, at the heart of the campus, supports all UCI's educational, research and public service programs.

Established in 1963, the UCI Library collection has been carefully selected and developed in conjunction with the campus academic plan.

Actually, there are several libraries: the Main Library, the Physical Sciences Library, the Biomedical Library, the Biological Sciences Library and the Medical Center Library (in Orange) and a new Science Library scheduled for completion in 1994.

The libraries have more than 1.5 million volumes and more than 19,000 currently active serials subscriptions that are available for study, teaching and research.

UCI's Main Library, designed by noted architect William Pereira, is home to more than 1.5 million volumes and some 19,000 active subscriptions.

In addition, campus users may request library materials, including periodical articles, from other libraries throughout the world.

UCI is the home of another special set of resources. Several sites there are part of UC's land and water reserve system containing areas that are representative of the state's habitat and geographic diversity.

Reserves at UCI include the San Joaquin Freshwater Marsh Reserve and the Burns Pinon Ridge Reserve. These serve as outdoor laboratories for students, faculty and staff, and are intended primarily for education and research. The reserves are administered by a campus management committee.

A highly important facility and resource for campus and community is the UCI Medical Center, one of five teaching hospitals owned and operated by the University.

The Medical Center, located in Orange 13 miles from the campus, serves as the principal clinical facility for teaching and research programs for the College of Medicine. College of Medicine faculty and resident physicians are the professional staff for medical services at the Center.

The hospital maintains inpatient and outpatient services in virtually all medical specialties and is fully accredited by the Joint Commission on Accreditation of Hospitals.

In addition, the Medical Center is the only designated Level I tertiary trauma referral center in Orange County.

The availability of advanced technology and the widely recognized expertise of members of the staff have made UCI Medical Center a regional referral center for the diagnosis and treatment of many medical problems.

The hospital is nationally recognized for its burn center and expertise in the surgical replantation of severed limbs.

In addition, the Medical Center offers special programs for high-risk pregnant women and critically ill newborns.

Other services include multidisciplinary cardiology and oncology programs and a comprehensive psychiatry program for adults, adolescents and children.

Basic research in neurobiology combined with clinical expertise in neurology and neurosurgery are placing College of Medicine faculty in the forefront in the understanding and treatment of many neurological disorders, including epilepsy, cerebral palsy and Alzheimer's disease.

The Medical Center also is one of the primary centers for the comprehensive management of diabetes.

In addition, the Medical Center has received federal approval for the use of lasers in the treatment of cancers of the head, neck and female reproductive system, and for cardiovascular disease.

Programs in research and patient care using laser technology are coordinated by the Beckman Laster Institute and Medical Clinic, located on the campus.

In 1980, the University established occupational health centers in Northern and Southern California to train occupational health professionals, conduct research on occupational health issues, provide clinical evaluation of the worker/patient for work-related disease, and to be linked to a hazardous chemicals alert system.

The centers also have strong ties to the University's Schools of Medicine and Public Health.

The Irvine Occupational Health Center (IOHC) is comprised of health professionals from UCI. Faculty research is concerned with identification of causal association between disease and occupational exposure as a basis for prevention of occupational disease and injury.

In summary, all the educational, research and public service programs at UCI are there for a major purpose: to seek and transmit knowledge in ways that will benefit and advance society to the greatest extent possible.

In the short number of years that UCI has been serving the needs of higher education, it has become an academic star. Its contributions and achievements have been impressive in a relatively short span of years. What has been accomplished in this time is a source of great pride to the entire UCI community.

More than that, they know that the next quarter century will bring even greater contributions and achievements. They know, too, that the world will be a better place because of what they are doing.

Chief Campus Officers

Daniel G. Aldrich, Jr., 1962–84

Jack W. Peltason, 1984–92

Laurel L. Wilkening, 1993–Present

L. Dennis Smith served as acting chancellor, October 1, 1992–June 30, 1993.

UCI Milestones

September 30, 1960 – The official founding date of the Irvine campus is on the deed transferring the 1,000-acre gift of land from the Irvine Company to the University; an additional 510 acres was purchased for $3.3 million in January 1964.

January 19, 1962 – University Dean of Agriculture Daniel G. Aldrich, Jr., is appointed chancellor.

June 20, 1964 – The campus site is dedicated in conjunction with the first meeting of the Regents at Irvine; a crowd of 15,000 attends the ceremony in Gateway Plaza and hears remarks by President Lyndon Johnson, Governor Edmund G. Brown, UC President Clark Kerr, Chancellor Aldrich and others.

October 4, 1965 – Enrollment for the first day of classes totals 1,589, including 958 freshmen, 215 sophomores, 254 juniors, 2 seniors, 20 limited special students and 140 postgraduates.

April 23, 1968 – Edmund A. Steinhaus, dean of biological sciences and considered the "father" of modern invertebrate pathology, is elected to membership in the National Academy of Sciences (he is the first UCI faculty member to be elected); Steinhaus was UCI's first faculty member, hired in May 1963 as dean of biological sciences.

October 21, 1969 – KUCI, the student-operated campus radio station, broadcasts for the first time at 7 p.m. with the program "The Problems of the World Solved Tonight."

November 28, 1970 – Ferdy Massimino scores an 18-foot overhead lob shot into the far corner of the UCLA goal in the second overtime to give the Anteaters a 7–6 victory and the NCAA water polo championship; Coach Ted Newland's squad complied a 27–2 season record in winning UCI's first division title (Newland also led the Anteaters to NCAA championships in 1982 and 1989.)

June 1974 – An article in the British journal *Nature* publishes findings by F.S. Rowland, professor of chemistry, and Mario Molina, postdoctoral researcher, that release of chlorofluorocarbons into the atmosphere is depleting the Earth's ozone layer; the research prompted the 1978 ban on most aerosols containing CFC propellants in the U.S., as well as the Montreal Protocol, signed by 31 countries in September 1987, which calls for a 50 percent phaseout of five CFCs by the year 2000.

July 1, 1976 – A new University of California, Irvine Medical Center sign is unveiled at a ceremony commemorating the transfer of ownership of the Orange County Medical Center and Community Clinic of Orange County to the University.

December 4, 1979 – The Department of Energy announces support for a $2 million project to test the stability of matter. Frederick Reines, professor of physics, is co-director; his neutrino research is UCI's largest research project, with record funding of more than $31 million. (In February 1985, Reines received the National Medal of Science in ceremonies at the White House.)

January 1980 – Plans are announced to establish a federally funded facility, the Laser Microbeam Program; directed by Michael Berns, the $2.3 million program eventually developed into the Beckman Laser Institute and Medical Clinic.

October 21, 1981 – The UCI Library celebrates acquisition of its millionth volume, "De Nuptiis Philologiae et Mercurii," donated by the UCI Friends of the Library.

July 25, 1982 – UCI senior Greg Louganis wins both the springboard and platform diving competitions at the National Sports Festival in Indianapolis, an accomplishment he would repeat at the 1984 and 1988 Olympic Games; with his double victory in the 1988 Games, he became the first male diver ever to win double gold in consecutive Olympic Games.

February 18, 1983 – UCI and Nelson Research and Development Co. enter into a lease agreement providing for the construction of facilities at UCI to be used for research by Nelson and for teaching and research by UCI faculty; it is the first time that a private firm has

been given permission to build its research facilities on UCI land.

March 15, 1984 – The Regents name Jack Peltason, president of the American Council on Education and UCI's first vice chancellor for academic affairs, as successor to Chancellor Aldrich, effective, September 1, 1984.

July–August 1985 – The first 81 families move into University Hills, the new UCI faculty and staff housing development; with the completion of Phase 5 in October 1990, the community will contain 431 homes.

September 18, 1987 – UCI is selected as the site for the UC Humanities Research Institute, a major center for humanistic inquiry; the institute's first director is Murray Krieger, UCI's only University Professor (University Professor is a title bestowed on some 14 faculty in the UC system).

April 8, 1988 – Richard Ott, professor of cardiology, performs the first heart transplant in Orange County at the UCI Medical Center; the recipient is a 26-year-old Huntington Beach man.

August 2, 1988 – Irvine Company officials announce they will lift the deed restrictions on 510 acres of land purchased by UCI in 1964; the modification of the agreement between the company and UCI will allow the construction of income-producing buildings at UCI.

Irvine Company Chairman Donald Bren announces he will donate $1.5 million to UCI to establish a fund to support the academic pursuits of a distinguished group of scholars drawn from UCI and other institutions.

November 30, 1988 – The College of Medicine receives an $8.5 million trust, its largest gift ever, from Edra E. Brophy, whose father, William Cheney, co-founded Farmers Insurance Group.

February 15, 1990 – Jenny Doh, a senior majoring in political sciences, becomes the first UCI student appointed to serve on the Board of Regents; she was one of 65 UC students who applied for the position.

October 19, 1990 – A public celebration is held to begin a year of 25th anniversary celebration activities. Honored are campus founders Jean Aldrich, widow of Daniel G. Aldrich, Jr., the founding chancellor; former Regent Edward Carter; Irvine Ranch heiress Joan Irvine Smith; former Governor Edmund G. Brown; and former UC President Clark Kerr.

April 3, 1992 – Chancellor Jack Peltason is named UC's president, succeeding David P. Gardner; his appointment is effective October 1.

January 15, 1993 – Laurel L. Wilkening, academic provost at the University of Washington, is named UCI's third chancellor.

Students relax and study under the gracefully arched cloisters of Royce Hall, UCLA's signature landmark. One of four original buildings which opened on the Westwood campus in 1929, it contains a concert hall which ranks as one of Los Angeles's premier performance venues.

LOS ANGELES

Facts at a Glance

Chancellor: Charles E. Young. *Opened:* 1919. *Acres:* 419.

Students: Undergraduate 22,911, Graduate 11,442, Total 34,353.

Students living on campus: 5,945. *Majors with largest enrollments:* Economics, psychology, political science, biology, history, English. *Degrees:* Bachelor's, 5,673. Masters, 2,204, Ph.D., 613, Law, 281, M.D., 171, D.D.S., 78, Engineering, 13, C.Phil., 261.

Academic staff (includes academic administrators, Cooperative Extension personnel, researchers and teaching staff): 4,878. *Total employees:* 20,473. *Budget:* $1.615 billion.

Source: Public Information Office, UCLA

O N MAY 23, 1919, California Governor William D. Stephens signed Assembly Bill 626, transferring the Los Angeles State Normal School's 25-acre site to the Regents of the University of California. With that act, UCLA was born.

The "Southern Branch" of the University opened in September of that year, offering a two-year program in undergraduate instruction to 250 students in letters and science and 1,125 students in the Teachers College.

As UCLA celebrated its 75th anniversary, the campus spanned 419 acres and enrolled nearly 35,000 students—the largest enrollment in the UC system. It is consistently ranked among the best research universities in the United States and as one of the two leading public university campuses. And UCLA is distinguished as the only campus among the nation's top 10 research universities that was established in the 20th century.

Analysis of the results of a comprehensive 1982 study by the Conference Board of Associated Research Councils placed UCLA among the top five American universities overall, with 17 of its academic departments rated in the top 10 nationally.

UCLA also ranks among the world's largest research institutions, with some two dozen organized research units and more than 5,000 funded research projects in progress at any given time. The campus receives more than $300 million a year in extramural contracts and grants to help finance its research activities, placing it first among the UC campuses in research support.

Students carry out their studies in the College of Letters and Science—the largest academic unit in the UC system with 23,000 students and nearly 1,000 faculty—and 13 professional schools. The College offers programs leading to both undergraduate and graduate degrees, as do the School of the Arts, School of Engineering and Applied Science, School of Nursing and School of Theater, Film and Television.

The other professional schools, which offer graduate programs exclusively, are the Graduate School of Architecture and Urban Planning, Graduate School of Education, School of Law, Graduate School of Library and Information Science, John E. Anderson Graduate School of Management, School of Social Welfare and, in the health sciences, the schools of Dentistry, Medicine and Public Health.

Of the many factors that go into the making of a great university, no single factor is as important as its faculty. UCLA's faculty members have consistently received national and international academic recognition in many forms.

The faculty roster includes two Nobel laureates: chemist Donald Cram and physicist Julian Schwinger. There are dozens of John Simon Guggenheim fellows and Fulbright scholars in all fields. And faculty membership in the most illustrious academic societies in the country, the American Academy of Arts and Sciences and the National Academy of Sciences, places UCLA on a par with the leading universities. Five distinguished

faculty also have been awarded the prestigious National Medal of Science, America's highest scientific honor.

UCLA faculty are equally dedicated to disseminating their findings in the classroom, and the Harriet and Charles Luckman Distinguished Teaching Awards are highly prized. By the same token, UCLA students pride themselves on academic excellence. Freshman classes usually average above a 3.90 high school GPA, with average SAT scores topping 1,100 out of a possible 1,600.

The undergraduate student body is among the most ethnically mixed and culturally diverse—both in total students and as a percentage of enrollment—of any major U.S. university. Ethnic minorities comprise 59 percent of the undergraduate and 34 percent of the graduate student population. International students and scholars number some 1,700, making UCLA one of the most popular American universities for students from abroad.

Undergraduate education is a special priority at UCLA, and the campus has developed several innovative programs by which these students can enrich and personalize their college experience. They have opportunities to do research with professors in their labs, take cluster programs that combine introductory courses with small seminars, or enroll in an honors program where rigorous interdisciplinary courses teach them to think creatively and critically.

And they can enhance their experience even further by living at Sunset Village, UCLA's new residence community where students are totally immersed in an academic environment that includes classrooms, tutorial labs, computer facilities, faculty offices and recreation areas.

A long-established tradition at UCLA is community service. Students serve the Los Angeles area in dozens of ways through their internships and broad-based volunteer activities. The annual Mardi Gras carnival raises funds for UniCamp, a student-staffed summer camp for financially underprivileged youth. Design for Sharing makes it possible for these young people, as well as disadvantaged senior citizens and handicapped persons, to attend cultural and performing arts events on campus.

In addition, UCLA Alumni Association volunteers advise high school students, mobilize to clean up Los Angeles, rehabilitate homes for elderly and disabled citizens, and act as reading tutors for adults in the award-winning "Target: Literacy" program.

The community also benefits greatly from the campus's vast resources. With more than 6.2 million volumes, UCLA's library is rated among the five finest in the country. Its athletic teams have made the campus an acknowledged leader in intercollegiate sports. Its Center for the Performing Arts ranks as the largest, most comprehensive program of its kind in the nation. And UCLA Extension, serving more than 100,000 adult students through 4,500 courses each year, is one of the largest single-campus continuing higher education programs worldwide.

Also, UCLA is an important center for health care. The UCLA Center for the Health Sciences (CHS), which includes nearly all of the campus's patient care, clinical education and biomedical research facilities, has achieved an international reputation for its health care programs and scientific advancements.

Contained within the CHS are the professional schools of dentistry, medicine, nursing and public health; the UCLA Medical Center; UCLA Medical Plaza; the Neuropsychiatric Institute and Hospital; the Jules Stein Eye Institute and the Doris Stein Eye Research Center; the Jonsson Comprehensive Cancer Center; the Gordon and Virginia MacDonald Medical Research Laboratories; and an extensive network of research institutes. UCLA physicians are noted for their pioneering work in heart and liver transplants, cardiac surgery, oncology and other vital fields.

The scope of research carried out at UCLA is as infinite as the cosmos. Medical scientists, using some of the most sophisticated facilities and technology available, are at the forefront of research into heart disease, AIDS, cancer, and genetic engineering. Political scientists and economists assess the implications of international events, while engineers work to perfect water desalination membranes. An art department professor reconstructs a lost notebook on painting by Leonardo da Vinci . . . an archaeologist unearths a 2,400-year-old Mayan city . . . a dentist discovers that teeth may be excellent candidates for transplantation . . . an education professor conducts the largest study of college and university students in the country.

Providing an interdisciplinary approach to the search for knowledge at UCLA is a group of 24 organized research units. ORUs are study centers and research institutes consisting of groups of faculty and students from various departments, engaged in continuing interdisciplinary research of particular subjects.

One of the newest ORUs, for example, is the Center for the Study of Women, which sponsors conferences, publications and programs dealing with women's issues and addresses public policies affecting women's lives.

At the same time, UCLA has four major ethnic study centers—in Afro-American, American Indian, Asian American, and Chicano studies—which collectively analyze and illuminate issues related to our multicultural society.

Addressing issues of global concern, the Office of International Studies and Overseas Programs coordinates UCLA's international and foreign area studies. Under its aegis are four major interdisciplinary research centers that rank among the best in the nation: the Coleman African Studies Center, the Latin American Center, the von Grunebaum Center for Near Eastern Studies, and the Center for Russian and East European Studies.

Other specialized organized research units include the Institute of Plasma and Fusion Research, the Institute of Archaeology, the Molecular Biology Institute, and the Institute of Industrial Relations. And in the Humanities, the Center for Medieval and Renaissance Studies deals with the development of civilization between

A.D. 300 and 1650, while the Center for Seventeenth- and Eighteenth-Century Studies focuses on the early modern period.

In the health sciences, the Jules Stein Eye Institute is devoted to the study of vision, the care of patients with eye disease, and ophthalmological education. Its sister facility, the Doris Stein Eye Research Center, houses new research and training programs concentrating on major eye diseases worldwide.

The center for neuroscience research and education at UCLA is the highly-respected Brain Research Institute. There, in a huge and far-reaching investigative program, scientists are involved in every aspect of research on the nervous system from molecular organization of neural cells to human behavior.

Other important ORUs in the health sciences include the Dental Research Institute, the Mental Retardation

Astride the sturdy back of UCLA's Bruin mascot, a graduate rejoices. She is one of some 8,500 students who receive bachelor's and advanced degrees from the University each year. The bronze statue was a gift to the campus from the UCLA Alumni Foundation in 1984.

Research Center, and the Crump Institute for Biological Imaging.

Integral to research of any kind, of course, are academic resources such as the library system. Consisting of the University Research Library, the College Library and 11 specialized libraries, the UCLA Library is among the country's largest and most renowned. The Department of Special Collections, housed in the Research Library, contains rare books and manuscripts including such holdings as the Sadleir Collection of 19th-century fiction, the Ahmanson-Murphy Collection of Early Italian Printing, and the Tom Bradley Archive.

Also of significance is the William Andrews Clark Memorial Library, with its collection of 86,200 volumes and nearly 19,000 manuscripts concentrating on English culture of the 17th and 18th centuries. The holdings include one of the finest institutional collections of Oscar Wilde manuscripts and texts in the world, and a nearly complete collection of early Dryden works.

Another resource respected by industry and scholars alike is the UCLA Film and Television Archive, which makes its vast collections of original film, newsreel and television materials available to students, faculty and many other constituencies. Activities are dedicated to the preservation, research and study, and public programming of the moving image.

Other major resources at UCLA include its outstanding art galleries and museums. The Wight Art Gallery, for example, is a multi-faceted museum which both responds to the needs of the academic community and makes an important contribution to the cultural life of Southern California by offering several major exhibitions each year.

Included in the Wight complex is the Grunwald Center for the Graphic Arts, with its growing collection of more than 35,000 works of art on paper including prints, drawings and photographs dating from the 13th century. And the Franklin D. Murphy Sculpture Garden, the Wight's "open-air museum," showcases more than 70 works by Rodin, Matisse, Miro, Noguchi, David Smith and many other late 19th- and 20th-century masters.

The Fowler Museum of Cultural History, considered one of the four leading university-based anthropological museums in the United States, exhibits art and artifacts in a cultural context. Its permanent collection of more than 750,000 objects represent contemporary, historic and prehistoric cultures primarily from Africa, the Americas, Oceania and Asia. The Fowler's textile and Latin American folk art collections are among the most outstanding in the world.

UCLA's two major gardens fulfill the dual purposes of serious study and contemplative enjoyment. The Mathias Botanical Garden, used for botanical and ornithological teaching and research, contains some 4,000 species of native and exotic plants. And the beautiful Carter Japanese Garden, an authentic Kyoto-style garden in nearby Bel-Air, was designed and constructed by Japanese artisans and architects using native plants and objects.

Across the "Quad" from Royce Hall sits the stately Romanesque facade of the Powell Library Building, another of UCLA's four original buildings. It houses the principal collections for undergraduate study.

Any list of UCLA's cultural treasures would be incomplete without reference to the campus's landmark and symbol, Royce Hall. Its 1,900-seat auditorium is a vital cultural center for the campus and the entire Los Angeles community. Virtually every major artist and ensemble of the last six decades has performed under its proscenium arch, and dignitaries including Albert Einstein, Vaclav Havel, John F. Kennedy and Carl Sandburg have spoken there.

Resources such as those included here are vital in the support of UCLA's vast academic and research enterprise, and ensure its ability to make a positive impact on society.

Throughout UCLA's 75-year existence, its laboratories have seen major breakthroughs in scientific and medical research; its study centers have helped foster understanding among the various cultures of the world; ongoing pursuits of new knowledge in a myriad of vital areas continue the quest to improve the quality of life for people around the world.

Ernest Carroll Moore, one of UCLA's founders, predicted in 1920 that "This University . . . is certain to be greater, far greater, than the imagination of any of us can foresee."

The dream of Moore and his colleagues has been surpassed many times over, and the future holds the promise of yet unfulfilled achievements for this renowned campus.

Chief Executive Officers

Provost Ernest Carroll Moore, 1919–36
Provost Robert Gordon Sproul, 1936–37
Provost Earle R. Hedrick, 1937–45
Provost Clarence A. Dykstra, 1945–52
Chancellor Raymond B. Allen, 1952–59
Chancellor Vern O. Knudsen, 1959–60
Chancellor Franklin D. Murphy, 1960–68
Chancellor Charles E. Young, 1968–Present

UCLA Milestones

1919 – On May 23, Governor William D. Stephens signed Assembly Bill 626 titled, "An Act of the Legislature of California Transferring the Los Angeles State Normal School to the Regents of the University of California."

On June 10 the 25-acre site on Vermont Avenue was approved by the Regents, who voted to call their new campus the "Southern California Branch"—soon to be shortened to "Southern Branch." Ernest Carroll Moore was named Provost.

On September 15, the Southern Branch of the University of California opened its doors. Two years of undergraduate instruction were offered to 250 Letters and Science students and 1,125 students in the Teachers College.

1922 – A four-year curriculum in the Teachers College was established.

1923 – First degrees were awarded at the Southern Branch commencement in June; 26 students received Bachelor of Education degrees.

College of Letters and Science founded.

1924 – Third- and fourth-year curriculum added to Letters and Science.

1925 – In March, the Regents named Westwood as the site of a new Southern Branch campus.

In June the first Bachelor of Arts degrees were awarded in the College of Letters and Science to 100 women and 24 men.

1926 – Founders' Rock was brought from Perris Valley for the dedication of the new campus site at Westwood.

1927 – Construction began on the new campus with the bridge over the arroyo.

The Regents adopted the name "University of California at Los Angeles," soon to be widely known as UCLA.

The Bruin mascot was adopted (replacing the Grizzlies) when UCLA joined the Pacific Coast Conference.

1929 – On Monday, March 18, before the official opening of the campus, the first class at Westwood was held in the not-quite-completed Chemistry Building.

Official first day of classes on the Westwood campus: Monday, September 23. First four buildings were Royce Hall, the Library (now Powell Library), the Chemistry Building (Haines Hall), and the Physics-Biology Building (Kinsey Hall). Number of students: 5,500.

1930 – Kerckhoff Hall was built as the first Student Union Building.

The University Residence, official home of UCLA's chief administrator, was completed and first occupied by Ernest Carroll Moore.

1933 – Graduate study was authorized for the Master of Arts degree with an initial enrollment of approximately 125 students. Programs for the M.A. degree were offered in 16 fields, and 42 degrees were awarded at the end of the first year.

First UCLA Homecoming Parade rolled through the streets of Westwood.

1934 – Graduate Division established.

UCLA Alumni Association founded.

William Andrews Clark Library is a gift to UCLA.

1935 – College of Business Administration founded.

Unicamp, a student-run summer camp for underprivileged and handicapped youth, was adopted as UCLA's official charity.

1936 – Robert Gordon Sproul became Provost, succeeding Ernest Carroll Moore.

Doctoral degrees were added to the graduate studies program, and doctoral programs were approved in three departments.

1937 – Earle R. Hedrick became Provost, succeeding Robert Gordon Sproul.

Enrollment topped 7,000—men exceeding women at UCLA for the first time.

1938 – Kenneth P. Bailey became the first recipient of a Ph.D. degree from UCLA, awarded by the Department of History.

1939 – School of Education founded.

College of Applied Arts founded.

1943 – UCLA made its first Rose Bowl appearance (January 1).

1944 – College of Engineering founded.

1945 – Clarence A. Dykstra became Provost.

Great post-World War II campus expansion began.

1946 – UCLA enrollment almost doubled from the prewar level of 7,000 to 13,800.

School of Medicine founded.

1947 – Establishment of the UCLA Progress Fund, forerunner to The UCLA Foundation, as the campus's private fund-raising arm.

School of Law founded.

1949 – School of Nursing founded.

Thirty-four acres of Veteran's Administration property (now known as the Southwest Campus) was transferred to UCLA by the federal government, bringing total campus acreage to 419.

UCLA won its first NCAA athletic championship (men's tennis).

John Wooden became head coach of UCLA men's basketball.

1950 – School of Social Welfare founded.

College of Business Administration renamed the School of Business Administration.

1952 – Raymond B. Allen became UCLA's first Chancellor.

1953 – Number of volumes in the UCLA Library reached one million.

1954 – UCLA Medical Center Hospital opened.

1955 – School of Business Administration renamed Graduate School of Business Administration.

Following UCLA's developmental work on electronic computers in the late 1940s, IBM donated more than $1 million to help establish the Western Data Processing Center.

1958 – The word "at" was replaced by a comma in the name University of California, Los Angeles.

School of Dentistry founded.

School of Library Service founded.

1959 – Vern O. Knudsen succeeded Raymond B. Allen as Chancellor.

1960 – Franklin D. Murphy succeeded Vern O. Knudsen as Chancellor.

College of Applied Arts replaced by College of Fine Arts.

1961 – School of Public Health founded.

1962 – UCLA enrollment exceeded 20,000.

1963 – Franklin D. Murphy Sculpture Garden established on North Campus.

1964 – The UCLA basketball team won the first of 10 NCAA championships under Coach John Wooden.

1965 – Japanese Gardens in Bel Air were donated to UCLA by Regent Edward W. Carter.

1966 – School of Architecture and Urban Planning founded.

School of Education renamed Graduate School of Education.

The UCLA football team won its first Rose Bowl game, against #1-ranked Michigan State.

1967 – Franklin D. Murphy Sculpture Garden dedicated.

1968 – Charles E. Young replaced Franklin D. Murphy as Chancellor.

1969 – Charles E. Young official inaugurated as Chancellor on May 23, the 50th anniversary of UCLA's founding.

College of Engineering renamed School of Engineering and Applied Science.

1971 – The UCLA Library contained more than 3 million volumes.

Graduate School of Business Administration renamed Graduate School of Management.

1973 – UCLA enrollment exceeded 30,000 students.

School of Library Service renamed Graduate School of Library and Information Science.

1975 – Men's basketball team won tenth NCAA championship; Coach Wooden retired.

1981 – School of Architecture and Urban Planning renamed Graduate School of Architecture and Urban Planning.

1982 – The UCLA Campaign, first campuswide fundraising effort to support academic programs, was launched.

The Conference Board of Associated Research Councils evaluated the quality of faculty in more than 150 American research universities. Of the 32 disciplines studied, 17 of UCLA's academic departments were rated among the top 10 in the country, and 30 were in the top 16. UCLA's ranking is said to be second in the nation among public universities and in the top five overall.

The Rose Bowl in Pasadena became the Bruin's home football stadium.

1983 – The UCLA Library contained more than 5 million volumes.

1984 – The UCLA campus served as a 4,000-athlete Olympic Village and hosted gymnastics and tennis competitions during the Summer Olympic Games in Los Angeles.

Royce Hall renovation completed; auditorium opens to rave reviews.

1985 – UCLA hosted the General Conference of the International Association of Universities (IAU), held for the first time in the U.S. It was attended by 1,000 top administrators from 800 universities around the world.

1987 – Graduate School of Management renamed Anderson Graduate School of Management after a $15-million gift to the school by alumnus John E. Anderson.

1988 – The UCLA Campaign ended with a total of $373 million in private donations—exceeding its goal by $73 million.

Pauley Pavilion served as the site of a presidential debate between then-Vice President George Bush and Massachusetts Governor Michael Dukakis.

1989 – In a major reorganization of the arts at UCLA, the School of the Arts and the School of Theater, Film and Television were established, replacing the College of Fine Arts.

1990 – As part of a campus development boom, several new facilities were completed, including the Doris Stein Eye Research Center, Engineering IV, a new child care center and the UCLA Medical Plaza.

A professional study showed that UCLA's impact on the national economy exceeds $4 billion.

1992 – A major earthquake safety program got under way in the heart of campus, with seismic work beginning on Moore Hall, Powell Library, Math Sciences, Bunche and Kerckhoff Halls.

Sunset Village, a new student residential/academic complex, opened on the northwest campus.

The Fowler Museum of Cultural History opened to the public.

The UCLA Library contained more than 6 million volumes.

1994 – Yearlong celebrations commemorate the 75th anniversary of UCLA's founding.

Colonnade of the Tomás Rivera Library.

RIVERSIDE

Facts at a Glance

Chancellor: Raymond L. Orbach. *Opened:* 1954. *Acres:* 1,200.

Students: undergraduate, 7,217, graduate, 1,588, total, 8,805 (Fall 1992).

Students living on campus: 2,600. *Majors with largest enrollments:* biology, psychology, political science, business administration, biomedical sciences. *Degrees:* Bachelor, 1,678, Masters, 231, Ph.D., 104.

Academic staff (includes teaching faculty, academic administrators, Cooperative Extension personnel, researchers and student assistants): 1,623. *Total employees:* 4,773. *Budget:* $198 million.

Source: Director of University Relations, UC Riverside.

WHAT BEGAN IN RIVERSIDE in 1907 as the Citrus Experiment Station has evolved into one of the nation's most dynamic campuses.

UC Riverside is recognized for its remarkable record in educating undergraduate students who go on to obtain doctorate degrees.

In a mid-1980s nationwide survey, UCR was one of four universities, including the University of Chicago and Harvard University, cited for the large percentage of students who go on to earn doctorates in the sciences and humanities.

Currently, three out of four students go on to graduate or professional school.

Today, UCR offers the quality and rigor of a major institution while assuring its undergraduates personal attention and a sense of community. Faculty members have a strong commitment to excellence in undergraduate instruction.

UCR offers 54 undergraduate majors and 33 minors, 28 Ph.D. programs, 35 master's programs and seven teaching and administrative services credential programs. Colleges and professional schools are the College of Engineering, the College of Humanities and Social Sciences, the College of Natural and Agricultural Sciences, the Graduate School of Management, and the School of Education.

The campus is at the center of an important and growing area of the state, in the heart of California's "Inland Empire," which encompasses parts of Riverside, San Bernardino and Los Angeles counties.

The 1,200-acre campus is located some 60 miles east of Los Angeles and within easy driving distance to most of the major cultural and recreational offerings in Southern California, as well as to major transportation hubs.

The area, one of the fastest growing in the nation, has contributed to UCR's enrollments over the last several years and is expected to continue to do so well into the 21st century.

The roots of the campus date back to 1907 when, by act of the State Legislature, the Citrus Experiment Station was established to conduct research in the agricultural problems of Southern California.

The Citrus Experiment Station was the outgrowth of a lobbying effort launched by Riverside citrus growers in 1899 under the community leadership of pioneer orange grower John Henry Reed, who is recognized as its founder.

The Experiment Station began operations in 1906 on a small site at the foot of Mount Rubidoux, where its original research emphasis was on citrus and subtropical horticulture.

In 1914, the Regents approved expansion of the Experiment Station, and a new site was purchased at the base of the Box Springs Mountains, where the campus lies today.

The corridors of the earliest buildings on the site, first occupied in 1917, are rich in associations with pioneer scientific discoveries and the early researchers who made them.

Those headquarter buildings are today marked by a Riverside County Historical Landmark plaque.

Graduate work was conducted early in the Experiment Station's history, and today, graduate education is central to its mission.

As the Experiment Station grew and contributed to agricultural growth and development in California, the site began to assume a new importance.

In 1948, the Regents approved the establishment of the College of Letters and Science at UCR.

Necessary legislation was passed by the Academic Senate in 1951.

The College opened for classes in February 1954.

By act of the Regents, the Riverside campus in 1959 was declared a general campus with a mandate to develop appropriate areas of study.

In 1961, the Graduate Division was established, and graduate and professional programs began being added.

In 1961, the name of the Citrus Experiment Station, which was the forerunner of the campus, was changed to the "Citrus Research Center and Agricultural Experiment Station" to reflect the increasingly broader scope of research.

Today, UCR's academic divisions include the College of Natural and Agricultural Sciences, the College of Humanities and Social Sciences, the College of Engineering, the School of Education, the Graduate School of Management, the Graduate Division, and the Summer Session.

The campus, with its modern classroom and office buildings, its beautiful University Commons and its 161-foot Carillon Tower, is designed to accommodate the academic and research programs which are part of its assigned mission as a general campus in the University system.

Its University Library is the focal point for research and study. The Library collections are arranged and staffed to support undergraduate and graduate programs and faculty research.

The collections are housed in the Tomás Rivera Library, Bio-Agricultural Library, Physical Sciences Library, Music Library and in a Media Resources Library.

Among the major collections are the Rupert Costo Library of the American Indian and the J. Lloyd Eaton Collection of Science Fiction and Fantasy.

The Library makes use of the latest technological developments in providing automated circulation, reference acquisition and cataloging services. For example, computer terminals for access to the University's MELVYL On-line Union Catalog are located in each of the libraries.

Also at UCR, the California Museum of Photography represents a resource that is unique among institutions of higher learning.

Since its inception in 1973, the Museum has grown into a major photography study center for the West Coast, with one of the largest and finest collections of photographs, cameras and related material anywhere in the world.

The museum offers exhibits, lectures and other activities to enrich the cultural atmosphere of UC Riverside and all of Southern California, as well as to further the study of history, art and society through photographic images.

Art can be appreciated in another form across from the main campus.

At the University Art Gallery, students, faculty, staff and the community can enjoy, as well as learn from, collections of works by both European and American artists. Both contemporary and historical works are on display.

The Art Gallery, open since 1963, develops and presents exhibitions through the year. The exhibitions, publications, educational programs, and collections form one of the most important elements of campus-community interaction.

The Gallery also functions as a laboratory for training future museum and other professionals by working with faculty members from various academic departments to sponsor special courses and internships on topics, including historical research and exhibition installation.

The Botanic Gardens are another major resource for the campus and city community.

The Botanic Gardens are divided into two main parts.

One part is the landscaped area around the campus buildings, demonstrating the use of a wide assortment of plants that grow well in Southern California. The second part comprises more than 39 acres along the eastern boundary of the campus, which is available to the public.

The gardens were established primarily for teaching and for serving a wide assortment of plant materials for courses such as anthropology, biology, ecology, morphology, ornamental horticulture, and taxonomy.

Not only are the gardens used by UCR classes, but they are visited by classes from a variety of educational institutions in the vicinity, as well as by other groups.

Other important functions are to provide plant materials for various research projects and to serve for the testing and exhibition of plant species introduced from all over the world.

UCR offers other services to campus and community.

For example, the campus is the home of the regional headquarters of Cooperative Extension and a branch of University Extension.

Scotty the Highlander Bear, UCR's mascot.

In addition, UCR is administratively responsible for eight of the sites in the University's Natural Reserve System, including the Philip L. Boyd Deep Canyon Desert Research Center.

Another important program at UCR is the University of California Institute for Mexico and the United States (UC MEXUS).

The Riverside campus is the headquarters for this program. It focuses the resources of the nine campuses as they relate to Mexico, U.S.-Mexico relations, Mexicans and people of Mexican descent in the United States, as well as a wide variety of scientific issues of importance to both countries.

Important programs for students include the Education Abroad Program, which offers an opportunity to study abroad while earning UC credit.

Another student program, launched in 1983, is the Education at Home Program. This offers students a chance for a quarter's study of early American history and culture on the East Coast. Students reside for two months in Williamsburg, Virginia, taking classes on the campus of the College of William and Mary.

Research is important to good education at UCR, and the campus is nationally known for its many research centers and special resources, has a number of outstanding organized research facilities.

Among the major ones is the Citrus Research Center and Agricultural Experiment Station (CRC-AES).

CRC-AES is a branch of the University's Statewide Agricultural Experiment Station, which is the nation's largest land grant experiment station and the research arm of UC's Division of Natural and Agricultural Sciences.

Over the years, research at the facility has been expanded to cover every commercial crop grown in Southern California, and today it conducts both basic and applied studies of more than 230 crops.

The role of the CRC-AES is to meet the unique basic and applied research needs of Southern California relating to agriculture, natural resources and the consumer.

The facility's research covers a broad, diverse number of topics which help in solving various agricultural problems. Information about this research is disseminated to other scientists, farmers and the general public.

Emphasis currently is placed on innovative research that will lead to development of new technologies, such as those involving recombinant DNA and other genetic engineering techniques.

As a result, the facility has formed interdisciplinary research units in biotechnology, toxicology, plant stress/productivity (including space biology), energy and waste management and analytical chemistry.

Another major facility at UCR is the Statewide Air Pollution Research Center, established in 1961.

Its principal mission is to conduct fundamental and applied research in atmospheric chemistry and plant sciences related to air pollution topics.

These studies include such phenomena as airborne toxic substances, hazardous gases and acidic materials.

Research results are translated into recommendations for cost-effective air pollution control strategies and into assessments of economic losses due to the pollutants.

Still another facility is the Dry Lands Research Institute.

The Institute was established in 1963 as a Universitywide organization with headquarters at Riverside to promote, coordinate and support interdisciplinary research and training in the sustained and productive use of the physical, biotic and cultural resources in the world's dry lands.

The research program has placed special emphasis on agricultural and environmental relationships, conserving and adapting the resources of the dry lands to human needs, as well as adapting human activity to the resources and the region.

Another major research unit is the UCR branch of the Universitywide Institute of Geophysics and Planetary Physics (IGPP), established in 1967. The IGPP has other branches on the Los Angeles and San Diego campuses and at the Los Alamos and Lawrence Livermore National Laboratories.

The UCR facility conducts research in astrophysics, space sciences, earth sciences, radiocarbon dating, and other fields of study.

Research in the earth sciences includes a wide range of geophysical, geological and geochemical investigations.

Since 1968, the IGPP at UC Riverside has explored and assessed areas that are potential sources of geothermal energy, particularly the Imperial Valley and Coso Hot Springs of Southern California and Cerro Prieto in Northern Mexico.

In 1988, the Geothermal Resources Program was reorganized into the Geothermal Resources Center within the IGPP.

In addition, research on earthquakes includes studies of the structure and physical properties and field studies of earthquake phenomena.

Additional studies encompass groundwater studies, fault zone characterization and regional tectonics.

UC Riverside also was once home to the Water Resources Center, a Universitywide organized research unit charged with coordinating water resources research on the various UC campuses.

The Water Resources Center recently moved to UC Davis; however, UC Riverside continues to operate a satellite.

The facility supports selected research in areas such as agricultural sciences, biographical sciences, economics, engineering, history, geography, law, meteorology, physical sciences, and political science.

A number of other research units at UCR provide valuable insights into areas of interest to the University and to society at large.

For example, the Center for Social and Behavioral Science Research encourages, facilitates and coordinates interdisciplinary social science research on a variety of topics of interest to the faculty.

In addition, the Center highlights for the wider campus community the specific contributions that social science research can make to research and development projects.

The California Educational Research Cooperative (CERC), founded in 1988, is a partnership between county offices of education, local school districts and the School of Education.

It is designed to serve as a research, development and graduate training center for members and the School by combining the professional experience and practical wisdom of practicing professional educators with the theoretical interests and research talents of UCR's education faculty.

Carillon Tower at the Riverside campus.

CERC provides a cooperative forum for systematic study and joint action to resolve pressing problems facing public schools.

Also at UCR is the Center for Ideas and Society, which is a comprehensive program to address current and future needs in the humanities.

It was established in 1989 in response to the Humanities Initiative of the Office of the President and the reports of the Chancellor's Task Force on Planning.

The Center's purpose is to promote and advance humanistic research and study at UCR, as well as nationally and internationally.

In view of all these resources and many others that UC Riverside has to offer, few university campuses in the U.S. can match it for its potential as an outstanding academic institution. As a result, the campus looks forward to the 21st century with confidence and great optimism.

Chief Campus Officers

Gordon S. Watkins, Provost, 1949–56

Herman Spieth, Provost, 1956–58/ Chancellor, 1958–64

Ivan Hinderaker, Chancellor, 1964–79

Tomás Rivera, Chancellor, 1979–84

Daniel G. Aldrich, Jr., Acting Chancellor, 1984–85

Theodore L. Hullar, Chancellor, 1985–87

Rosemary S. J. Schraer, Chancellor, 1987–92

Raymond L. Orbach, Chancellor, 1992–Present

UCR Milestones

1907 – Citrus Experiment Station is given final approval by the Regents; it is established to conduct research on the agricultural problems of Southern California (graduate work was conducted early in the Station's history, and today graduate education is central to its mission).

1948 – California Governor Earl Warren signs a bill appropriating funds to create a four-year liberal arts branch of the University at Riverside.

1949 – Gordon S. Watkins is appointed chief campus officer.

1951 – Groundbreaking for the new campus takes place early in the year.

1954 – UCR established as a liberal arts college on the site of the Citrus Experiment Station, and the College of Letters and Science opens for classes in February.

1955 – The University purchases a Canyon Crest housing development, which previously had served March Air Force Base personnel, for student and faculty housing.

1956 – Herman T. Spieth appointed provost; post subsequently redefined as chancellor (1958).

1958 – Fall enrollment tops 1,000, with 1,006 students.

1959 – The Regents announce that UCR will become a general campus, expanding the curriculum, and the Aberdeen-Inverness dormitory is completed.

1961 – A Graduate Division with master's and doctoral programs is established.

1961–70 – UCR experiences rapid and broadly spread development of the general campus in all areas of science, humanities, social science and fine arts at the undergraduate and graduate levels.

1961 – The College of Agriculture is established.

1962 – Fall enrollment tops 2,000, with 2,173 students.

1963 – Lothian dormitory is completed.

1964 – Ivan Hinderaker is appointed chancellor, and fall enrollment tops 3,000, with 3,109 students.

1966 – The UCR Carillon Tower is built.

1967 – The Student Commons opens. Enrollment tops 4,000 (4,183)

1969 – The School of Education is established, and fall enrollment tops 5,000, with 5,361 students.

1970 – The Graduate School of Administration is established.

1970–84 – Period of consolidation, with programs redirected toward the needs of the 1980s.

1971 – Fall enrollment tops 6,000, with 6,176 students (UCR's all-time high until fall 1987, when enrollment hit 6,554).

1978 – The fall enrollment decline bottoms out at 4,574 (enrollment stayed between 4,600 and 4,800 until fall 1985).

1979 – Tomás Rivera is appointed chancellor.

1984 – Following Rivera's death, UCI Chancellor Emeritus Daniel G. Aldrich, Jr., is appointed acting chancellor at UCR.

1984–early 1990s – A period of new development and growth takes place.

1985 – Theodore L. Hullar is named chancellor, and the fall enrollment of 5,227 is the highest at UCR since 1973.

1987 – Rosemary S. J. Schraer appointed chancellor following Hullar's appointment as chancellor at UC Davis, and fall enrollment of 6,554 students sets another record; Chancellor Schraer is the first woman chancellor to be inaugurated in the UC system.

1989 – New College of Engineering enrolls its first freshman class.

1990 – In July, the Regents approve UCR's Long Range Development Plan providing for an estimated student population of 18,050 by the year 2005–06.

1992 – Raymond L. Orbach becomes chancellor on April 20.

UNIVERSITY OF CALIFORNIA
RIVERSIDE

Students gather at the Price Center for lunch and music.

SAN DIEGO

Facts at a Glance

Chancellor: Richard C. Atkinson (named President of the University in 1995). *Opened:* 1960. *Acres:* 2,040.

Students (spring 1993): undergraduate, 13,672, graduate, 2,120, Scripps (510), 163, School of Medicine, 973, total 16,928.

Students living on campus: 4,650. *The 10 most popular undergraduate majors in order:* general biology, psychology, political science, biochemistry and cell biology, economics, communication, animal physiology, sociology, history, bio-engineering/pre-med. *Degrees:* Bachelor, 2,677, Masters, 357, Ph.D., 185, M.D., 131.

Academic staff (includes academic administrators, Cooperative Extension personnel, researchers, student assistants, and teaching staff): 5,000. *Total employees:* 16,000. *Budget:* $1,010,584 million.

Source: Director of University Communications, UC San Diego.

SINCE ITS FOUNDING in 1960 as a general campus of the University, UC San Diego has grown into one of the nation's leading teaching and research institutions.

The campus also has become one of America's major centers for high-technology electronics and biomedical research.

UCSD is well recognized throughout the academic world both for the eminence of its faculty and for the quality of its graduate and undergraduate programs. Its distinction as an academic institution can be measured in many ways.

For example, UCSD annually attracts a total of $235 million in federal research funds, reflecting its international reputation for scholarship in natural sciences, engineering, oceanography, medicine, social sciences, arts and humanities.

In addition, UCSD's faculty includes six Nobel laureates, numerous members of the National Academy of Sciences, a 1989 Pulitzer Prize winner in music, and a recipient of the Fields Medal, the highest honor in mathematics.

At both the undergraduate and graduate levels, UCSD's curricula and programs have been singled out for high rankings in recent surveys of American higher education.

Among the nation's public universities, UCSD ranks first in the percentage of undergraduates who enroll in medical and graduate schools.

And the campus ranks eighth nationally in its postdoctoral science and engineering enrollments, reflecting its international reputation for scholarship in these fields.

With its La Jolla campus located on a 1,200-acre wooded site overlooking the Pacific, in a setting of scenic beauty and superb climate, UCSD is one of the newest of UC's nine campuses.

Although it enrolled its first undergraduates in 1964, it can trace its origins as far back as the late 1800s when Berkeley zoologists found La Jolla a desirable site for a marine field station.

The facility they established became part of UC in 1912 and was eventually named the Scripps Institution of Oceanography.

In the late 1950s, when the Regents decided to situate a general campus in the San Diego region, Scripps Institution and its small but distinguished staff of scientists formed the nucleus around which the new campus was to grow.

Today, UCSD is a full-fledged, four-year undergraduate campus, as well as a major graduate and research university site. Graduate and undergraduate programs, offered in a wide range of disciplines, lead to the bachelor's, master's, M.D. and Ph.D degrees.

UCSD's undergraduates enjoy the benefits of a great university without the disadvantages of the large size found in many of today's huge universities.

To achieve this balance, the master plan conceived by UCSD's planners borrowed from the Oxford and Cambridge concept to provide a "family" of colleges, each with its own special academic and social ambiance. UCSD's students gain a sense of "belonging" through affiliation with one of the semi-autonomous colleges on the campus.

Currently there are five colleges: Revelle (the first one, founded in 1964), John Muir, Thurgood Marshall, Earl Warren, and Eleanor Roosevelt.

Each of the five is independent, yet all are interrelated: all university academic and support facilities are available to all students, regardless of their college affiliation.

Each college is designed to accommodate approximately 2,500 students. Each has its own residence halls, commons (which include dining facilities and meeting rooms) and classrooms. And each college has its own educational philosophies and traditions, its own administrative and advising staff.

The objective is to give students and faculty the advantages of a small, liberal-arts college combined with the best features of a major university.

Each of the five colleges at UCSD has a distinctive philosophy.

Revelle College stresses the broad character of general education.

During the first two years there, a student spends roughly one-third of the class time in mathematics and the natural sciences and the other two-thirds in social sciences, humanities, foreign language and the fine arts.

These two years of structured liberal-arts courses help establish a strong educational foundation. In the final two years, students concentrate on developing professional competence in one academic discipline and a basic understanding of another unrelated academic field.

John Muir College has established a flexible set of general-education and graduation requirements that ensures breadth and depth of learning and encourages students to take an active role in their own intellectual development.

Students complete four year-long sequences drawn from the social sciences; the natural sciences or mathematics; and the humanities, fine arts or foreign languages.

Thurgood Marshall College is a liberal arts and sciences college dedicated to the development of the scholar and citizen. Students pursue majors in the social sciences, natural and physical sciences, mathematics, engineering, humanities and the fine arts.

The college's educational philosophy is guided by the belief that regardless of a student's major, a broad liberal arts education must include an awareness and understanding of the diversity of cultures and the variety of ways culture enables people to fashion lives of dignity.

Warren College emphasizes curricula and programs that assist students in making a close connection between their undergraduate education and their personal and professional goals for their postbaccalaureate years.

This approach applies to all students, whether their career aspirations lie in the professions, the arts or the sciences. As a means of supplementing curricular requirements, the college encourages students to take advantage of academic internships and career-life planning programs to sharpen their skills and test their career choices.

Eleanor Roosevelt College faculty believe that to be truly educated in today's world, students must learn about their own cultural heritage as well as the cultures of other major countries in the world.

Therefore, the general-education requirements of the college have an international orientation designed to instill in students, regardless of major, a global perspective that can involve both Western and non-Western cultures.

Each of the five colleges has a provost, a faculty member who acts as the chief administrative officer and academic dean. In addition, each college has a director of academic advising and a dean of student life.

The campus fosters undergraduate and graduate education in a number of distinctive ways.

For example, its Graduate School of International Relations and Pacific Studies, approved in 1986, is the only school of international affairs in the UC system and the only school of its kind in the nation to focus exclusively on the Pacific Rim.

The school's programs have been developed in response to the increasing participation of the U.S. in global economic an political affairs.

In other endeavors, UCSD faculty and scholars are continually involved in an array of research and developmental projects that put the campus at the forefront of advances in science, technology, the humanities and the arts (particularly music, theater and visual arts).

UC San Diego was named the site of a Supercomputer Center by the National Science Foundation in 1985. Its research supports the work of many of the programs in science and technology.

Scripps Institution of Oceanography is a prime example of one of the outstanding programs of education and research at UCSD.

Scripps is one of the oldest, largest and most important centers for marine and global climate research, graduate training and public service in the world.

Its prominence in the marine sciences is reflective of its preeminent programs, distinguished faculty and outstanding facilities.

Revelle College fountain.

Research at Scripps encompasses physical, chemical, biological, geological and geophysical studies of the oceans.

Ongoing investigations include the topography and composition of the ocean bottom, waves and currents, and the flow and interchange of matter between seawater and the ocean bottom or the atmosphere.

Scripps' research ships are used in these investigations throughout the world's oceans.

The educational program at Scripps has grown hand in hand with its research programs. Instruction is on the graduate level, and students are admitted as candidates for the Ph.D. degree.

In addition, Scripps' Stephen Birch Aquarium-Museum provides a wide variety of educational courses in the marine sciences for students from primary grades to high school level.

Another of UCSD's strengths is its School of Medicine, which has won national acclaim for excellence.

The School of Medicine's distinctive interdisciplinary approach to medical education enables students to benefit from a diversity of laboratory facilities, clinical opportunities and faculty talent and knowledge.

UCSD's health sciences program includes the UCSD Medical Center-Hillcrest and the UCSD Medical Center-La Jolla, plus specialized clinical facilities and research centers throughout San Diego County which serve as a national resource for clinical care and biomedical research expertise.

Also at UCSD, organized research institutes and centers carry out advanced research projects that often span the areas of knowledge encompassed by several academic departments. At the same time, they provide opportunities for graduate student support in broad disciplines.

There are many of these research institutes and centers, and their work is fascinating, complex and critical to an understanding of the world around us.

One of the major facilities is the California Space Institute. CalSpace conducts and supports space research, both pure and applied, with special emphasis on the opportunities created by space science and technology in the applied field.

Also at UCSD, the Institute of Geophysics and Planetary Physics (IGPP) makes its facilities available to graduate students from various departments who have chosen to write their dissertations on geophysical problems.

The Institute on Global Conflict and Cooperation studies the causes of international conflict and the means of its attenuation.

Elsewhere on campus, the Institute of Marine Resources (IMR), headquartered at Scripps, enhances understanding of the marine environment and human interactions with it by supporting research programs and stimulating interchange among the campuses.

In addition to its regular research programs, IMR administers the California Sea Grant Program.

On UCSD's main campus, structural research engineers from the Charles Lee Powell Structural Research Laboratories conduct seismic studies on full-scale highway bridges, columns and buildings to assess their ability to withstand earthquake stresses. Information obtained from these studies are being used as a basis for new earthquake standards for such structures.

In addition to these and other research facilities, there are a number of campuswide institutes.

A major one is the Biomedical Engineering Institute, which provides an academic research unit for interdisciplinary interactions among faculty and students aimed at promoting and coordinating bioengineering research and education at the interface of engineering, biology and medicine.

The Institute for Nonlinear Science promotes interdisciplinary research and graduate education in the development and application of contemporary methods in the study of nonlinear dynamical systems.

The Institute for Pure and Applied Physical Sciences, which is an interdisciplinary research unit, brings together members of departments in the sciences and engineering, and Scripps Institution of Oceanography. The institute is concerned with fluids and materials.

The Sam and Rose Stein Institute for Research on Aging encourages interdisciplinary research into an array of phenomena and changes in body function associated with aging. These range from the basic nature of the biological process of aging to the clinical disorders that occur in greater frequency with advanced age.

There also are a number of major centers at UCSD.

One of them is the UCSD Cancer Center, which is a National Cancer Institute-designated Clinical and Research Cancer Center.

Elsewhere at UCSD, the Center for Astrophysics and Space Sciences brings together academic and research staff from various departments to conduct studies on a number of scientific areas related to the skies.

In another part of UCSD, the Center for Iberian and Latin American Studies coordinates and promotes Latin American and Iberian research, teaching and service activities for faculty and students in all departments at the university.

One of the most important facilities in recent years has been the Center for Magnetic Recording Research. This is a national center devoted to multidisciplinary teaching and research in areas of science and engineering related to magnetic recording.

The Center for Molecular Genetics promotes molecular genetic research and the training of graduate students and postdoctoral fellows in biological and biomedical sciences.

The Center for Research in Computing and the Arts fosters collaborative working relationships among artists, scientists and technologists by identifying and promoting projects in which common research interests may be advanced through the application of computer-mediated strategies.

Revelle College breezeway.

And another important facility is the Center for U.S.-Mexican Studies, established in 1979. It is the nation's largest program devoted exclusively to the study of Mexico and U.S.-Mexican relations.

In addition to all these and its many other educational and research facilities, UC San Diego also is noted as the site of several theaters and galleries, as well as the nationally acclaimed Stuart Collection of outdoor sculpture. These and other campus facilities provide a major cultural resource for San Diego.

It is true that UCSD's reputation as an academic institution of outstanding distinction and quality in all its endeavors did not happen by accident. Its rise to distinction resulted from wise and careful planning by visionary faculty and administrators.

To accomplish the objective of creating a first-rate university in a short time, these planners sought from the outset to attract the best scholars the academic world could offer and to build the new campus around them.

Today, the vision of UCSD's planners is being fulfilled, and the future looks bright to faculty and students alike.

Chancellors

Herbert F. York, 1961–64
John S. Galbraith, 1964–68
William J. McGill, 1968–70
Herbert F. York, Acting Chancellor, 1970–71
William D. McElroy, 1971–80
Richard C. Atkinson, 1980–95

UCSD Milestones

1903 – Marine Biological Association (MBA) established.
1912 – Marine Biological Association deeds 174 acres and one building to UC Regents.
1925 – MBA name changed to Scripps Institution of Oceanography.
1954 – Institute of Marine Resources established.
1958 – Regents establish Institute of Technology and Engineering (ITE) at La Jolla.
1959 – ITE name changed to UC School of Science and Engineering.
1960 – First students enrolled: graduate students in physics.
1961 – Herbert F. York named first chancellor.
1963 – School of Science and Engineering renamed First College.
1964 – Dr. Joseph Stokes, III named dean of School of Medicine.
1965 – First College renamed Revelle College.

1966 – Center for Human Information Processing established.
1967 – Clifford Grobstein appointed dean of School of Medicine.
1968 – William J. McGill named third chancellor.
1969 – Center for Research in Language established.
1970 – Central University Library opened.
1972 – Center for Music Experiment established.
1973 – First Board of Overseers meeting.
1974 – First students enroll in Fourth College.
1975 – Mandeville Center opened.
1976 – Center for Iberian and Latin American Studies established.
1977 – Fourth College renamed Warren College.
1979 – UCSD Cancer Center established.
1980 – Richard C. Atkinson named fifth chancellor.
1981 – UCSD purchases University Hospital from County of San Diego (renamed UCSD Medical Center).
1984 – Center for Molecular Genetics established.
1985 – San Diego Supercomputer Center building opened.
1986 – Institute for Nonlinear Science established.
1988 – Ida and Cecil Green Faculty Club opened.
1989 – Price Center opens.
1990 – Center for Interfact and Materials Science established.
1991 – Shiley Eye Center opened.
Mandell Weiss Forum Theatre dedicated.
Institute for Biomedical Engineering established.
Clinical Sciences Building opened.
Cellular and Molecular Medicine Building opened.
1992 – Early Childhood Education Center opened.
University Extension's Downtown Center opened.
Steven Birch Aquarium-Museum dedicated.
1993 – Visual Arts Facility opened.
Central Library expansion completed; library rededicated.
Sciences Building opened.
Third College renamed Thurgood Marshall College.
John M. and Sally B. Thornton Hospital and Perlman Ambulatory Care Center opened.
1994 – Structural Testing Laboratories dedicated.
Fifth College renamed Eleanor Roosevelt College.
Institute on Environmental Technology established at Scripps Institution.

University of California,
San Diego

Airview of UC San Francisco

SAN FRANCISCO

Facts at a Glance

Chancellor: Joseph B. Martin, M.D., Ph.D. *Opened:* UC San Francisco officially became an independent campus with its own chancellor in 1964. Before that date, it was allied closely with the Berkeley campus. *Acres:* 107 at its main campus on Parnassus Heights.

Students: Graduate: 3,712. *Living on campus:* 400. *Degrees* (annual): Bachelor, 105; Master, 243; MD, 138; Doctor of Dental Surgery, 79; Doctor of Pharmacy, 118; Ph.D., 52.

Academic Staff: (includes academic administrators, Cooperative Extension personnel, researchers, student assistants and teaching staff) 1,438. *Total employees:* 15,338 *Budget:* $1.2 billion.

Source: UCSF Annual Report 1992/93.

IN BOTH SIZE AND NUMBER of students, UC San Francisco is the smallest of the nine UC campuses. But its relative size belies its distinction as one of the leading biomedical research and health science education centers in the world.

Such distinction does not come without a long history of achievement and excellence, something that few could have predicted in 1873 when the financially troubled Toland Medical College—begun by San Francisco physician Hugh H. Toland nine years before—and the brand new California College of Pharmacy agreed to affiliate with the fledgling University of California across the bay.

With the addition of the College of Dentistry in 1881, coupled with the move to Parnassus Heights in 1898 on 13 acres donated by former San Francisco Mayor Adolph Sutro, UC San Francisco assumed the geographical outlines of today's 107-acre main campus just above Golden Gate Park.

Over the last century, that original nucleus of Schools has grown to include a School of Nursing (1939) and Langley Porter Psychiatric Institute (1942), which contained the city's first psychiatric hospital, and a Graduate Division (1961) which functions as an administrative unit for the more than 2,000 doctoral students and postdoctoral fellows at this graduate level institution.

With more than 15,000 employees and an operating budget over one billion dollars, UCSF also is home to 11 research institutes, 1,500 laboratories, more than 2,000 ongoing research projects and a new library whose state-of-the-art computing and communications infrastructure is making it a 21st-century temple of knowledge management.

Although the move to the comparatively remote Parnassus Heights was somewhat controversial in 1898, it proved fortuitous eight years later when the great 1906 earthquake and fire left many of the city's hospitals—not to mention the former home of Toland Medical College—destroyed or unusable.

UCSF's location enabled it to offer emergency services to city residents in a makeshift space within the College of Medicine building. The following year, two floors of the building were set aside for hospital services. Ten years later, the first UC Hospital opened at the west end of campus; a clinics building followed in 1934.

Today's UCSF Medical Center includes two acute care hospitals (Moffitt and Long) with 560 beds and an Ambulatory Care Center with more than 20 faculty practice and outpatient clinics that together tally more than 325,000 patient visits per year. This is not to mention UCSF-staffed clinics in Santa Rosa, Fresno and Salinas.

More than 400 faculty physicians admit and care for patients at the Medical Center each year, as well as supervise approximately 1,300 residents on the main campus, at Mount Zion (which became part of UCSF in 1990) and the affiliated San Francisco General Hospital and Veterans Affairs Medical Center.

Always a center for excellence in such medical specialties as neurological surgery, neurology, transplant surgery, pediatrics, obstetrics/gynecology, ophthalmology, otolaryngology and cardiology, UCSF also is known for the quality and diversity of its student body—more than half are women and over 40 percent are members of minority groups—and for producing large numbers of primary care physicians, nurse practitioners, clinical pharmacists and dentists.

All have benefited from the accelerated pace of discovery that in the last 25 years has solidified UCSF's reputation as an innovator and pioneer. Among the many examples.

It was UCSF cardiologist Melvin Scheinman who developed a technique called catheter ablation which uses catheters and high-frequency radio waves to correct abnormally fast and life-threatening heart rhythms; pediatric cardiologist Abraham Rudolph and colleague Michael Heymann who discovered that an aspirin-like drug could save the lives of thousands of premature infants with a structural abnormality in the heart; and a team led by physiologist John Clements which found a cure for respiratory distress syndrome in infants and later developed a synthetic substance that prevents the often fatal lung condition altogether.

UCSF also figured prominently in the near eradication of newborn pneumonia when epidemiologist Julius Schacter discovered that the common sexually transmitted bacteria, chlamydia trachomatis, was responsible and that antibiotic treatment of infected mothers would prevent its transmission.

Virologist Jay Levy also was one of the first to isolate the virus, later named Human Immunodeficiency Virus (HIV), responsible for AIDS and part of the first team that developed a heat treatment process for clotting factors that protected hemophiliacs from HIV infection.

In 1981, UCSF was the site of the world's first successful fetal surgery, during which a surgical team led by Michael Harrison, Mitchell Golbus and Roy Filly corrected a defect that would have damaged or killed the fetus before birth. This success presaged the opening of the internationally respected Fetal Treatment Center.

UCSF is the home of the Brain Tumor Research Center, which under the direction of neurosurgeon Charles Wilson, has become the largest surgery and research center of its kind in the world.

Add to this the first operations to relieve chronic debilitating pain by inserting electrodes deep in the brain; the development of the first successful multichannel cochlear implant, which gives the deaf the ability to understand human speech; the world's first bladder pacemaker; the world's first inpatient ward for AIDS patients at San Francisco General Hospital; the world's oldest and largest kidney transplant program (more than 4,000 kidney transplants in 30 years); and, after just five years, one of the world's most successful liver transplant programs, it is clear what underlies UCSF's medical renown.

That renown is of long standing. Earlier in UCSF's history, Herbert Evans and colleagues discovered vitamin E

(1923); Chauncey Leake developed new treatments for dysentery and introduced new types of anesthetics (1928); and Karl F. Meyer began mass production of the plague vaccine given U.S. military personnel in World War II. UCSF also opened one of the country's first cancer research institutes in 1948 and, in 1966, was the first in the U.S. to develop a clinical pharmacy program.

While these discoveries and medical advances were helping patients live longer and healthier lives, achievements of another sort were sparking one of the most profound scientific revolutions in history.

Known as the recombinant DNA revolution, it began simply enough with a sketch drawn on delicatessen napkin in 1972. From that first brainstorming session, UCSF's Herbert Boyer and Stanford University's Stanley Cohen went on to devise a technique called DNA cloning.

In essence, DNA cloning allowed scientists to chemically "cut" a fragment of DNA from one source and splice it—or recombine it—with the DNA of another cell that reproduces rapidly. The rapid reproduction allowed for the creation—and study—of billions of identical copies of any DNA segment so desired.

Within 10 years, genetically engineered insulin and human growth hormone, which occur naturally in only minute quantities, became widely available, marking the official birth of the biotechnology industry.

The fruits of biotechnology are now part of our everyday life and the promise part of our future. From a hepatitis B vaccine and powerful new drugs, which do everything from save the lives of heart attack victims to battle multiple sclerosis, to transgenic mice and gene therapy, which hold the key to curing such diverse scourges as cystic fibrosis, melanoma, diabetes and AIDS, the biotechnology bonanza is forever tied to UCSF and its spirit of discovery.

What the DNA revolution accomplished in the world of ideas was just as momentous as the creation of the computer. Like the universal language of bits and bytes, the DNA revolution created a common language than enabled scientists from different disciplines to breach the invisible walls of academia, to talk to each other, to share information, to excite and inspire.

As a result, cell biologists interested in how cells specialize into muscle or heart tissue, or brain and bone, could now help biochemists and immunologists understand ways to outwit a virus, just as psychiatrists interested in the possible causes of manic depression and schizophrenia could talk to geneticists about where in the human genome to search.

UCSF was quick to exploit these intellectual breakthroughs, adding faculty like Y.W. Kan, who later developed the first genetic tests for sickle cell anemia and the inherited blood disease beta thalassemia; Ira Herskowitz, whose molecular analysis of common baker's yeast revealed how yeast genes are turned on and off and offered important clues as to how the same process worked in humans; and Christine Guthrie, whose discoveries about messenger RNA have given us a better idea of how a gene's protein-building message is received outside the nucleus.

This clock tower is a landmark at UCSF.

They joined a group that already included future Nobel Prize winners J. Michael Bishop and Harold Varmus. Their collaboration in 1976 led to the discovery of oncogenes, the seeds of cancer in our genetic dowry.

Twenty years later, the results of this collaborative ethic are everywhere to be seen at UCSF.

In the brand new Keck Center of Integrative Neurosciences, for example, researchers from such specialties as anatomy, neurology, pharmacology, physiology and otolaryngology are linking cellular studies of the brain with those focusing on sense, reflex and pain networks.

Molecular biologists, biochemists and pharmaceutical chemists, many with joint appointments in both the Schools of Medicine and Pharmacy, also have joined forces with high-powered computers in a strategy called rational drug design. Their goal: to determine the three-dimensional shape of large molecules and then create drugs that protect the molecules from attack by agents of disease. This approach already has produced new lines of attack on such world killers as malaria, schistosomiasis, hepatitis A and AIDS.

At the same time, neurologist Stanley Prusiner and colleagues have discovered a novel infectious agent called prions which differ markedly from viruses and bacteria. Their work has shown prions to be the cause of the rare and lethal Creutzfeld-Jakob disease in humans as well as several animal diseases—including the "mad cow" infection in Great Britain. Initially greeted with skepticism, the research has led to Prusiner's selection to the prestigious National Academy of Sciences, only the third neurologist in the 20th century to be so honored.

More wonders are still in the early stages. UCSF basic scientists continue to make progress deciphering the secrets of the cell cycle and, with that, perhaps the underlying principle of cancer growth; to discover the biochemical processes that explain how a single sperm fertilizes an egg and by implication, suggest new techniques for conception and contraception; to find ways to "light up" the chromosomes in cancer cells and, by so doing, change the way that cancer is diagnosed and treated; to unravel the cellular basis of alcoholism; and to expose the role of platelet-derived growth factor in heart attack and stroke.

Apart from its research interests, UCSF also takes seriously its role as public servant. From a medical clinic for the homeless and low-cost dental programs for the poor to home therapy services to recently discharged patients and special programs for the aging and troubled adolescents—UCSF is intimately involved in the health of the community.

It is a community educator as well. Since 1987, UCSF has been bolstering science education in San Francisco public schools with a partnership program between teachers and UCSF scientists that consists of cooperative classroom projects, laboratory visits, science update lectures and student science classroom teaching contest. That effort was broadened four years later with an intensive continuing education program for public school science teachers in the primary and secondary grades.

UCSF's involvement in community education has proven to be an important weapon in the continuing battle against scientific illiteracy. Still another has been to teach well the science and art of medicine, dentistry, nursing and pharmacy to UCSF's own 4,000 graduate-level students. By every measure—independent ranking reports, accrediting evaluations, numbers of applicants and ratio of acceptances, student critiques, clinic visits, teacher status and faculty morale—the four schools and their students are excelling.

Using their knowledge of drugs and drug interactions, for example, pharmacy students and residents have become an integral part of hospital health care teams. Traveling dentistry residents have become a critical resource for the homebound and the nursing school an important training ground for nursing deans and directors all over the U.S.

UCSF has spearheaded the educational reform movement as well, shifting to more problem-based learning and smaller classroom sizes and reorganizing and rewriting courses and clinical clerkships to reflect the changing

One of the many major UCSF buildings devoted to the health sciences.

demands of the health care marketplace and the changing needs of its students.

Whatever the shifting circumstances and bedeviling details of the moment, what has remained consistent about UCSF is the zest for learning and service. That has been UCSF's signature for this century and its anticipated imprint on the next.

As more than one UCSF chancellor has remarked, UCSF's past is only prologue. Like Columbus, UCSF is on a quest for discovery. It is not always sure of the destination or even the route. But it believes that in the end the labor, risk and imagination invested in the search will benefit and ennoble us all.

Chancellors

Prior to 1954, deans of various schools reported directly to the President of the University.

On June 6, 1955, an administrative advisory committee was formed, composed of deans of schools, with the Dean of the School of Medicine serving as Chairman.

On September 19, 1958, the Chairman's title was changed to Provost.

On January 24, 1964, the title of Provost was changed to Chancellor. The following have served as Chancellors since then:

J.B. de C.M. Saunders, M.D., 1964–66

Willard C. Fleming, D.D.S. (interim appointment), 1966–69

Philip R. Lee, M.D., (effective 9/30/72), 1969–72

Francis A. Sooy, M.D., (Acting Chancellor),
    10/1/72–11/17/72
Francis A. Sooy, M.D., 1972–82
Julius R. Krevans, M.D., 1983–93
Joseph B. Martin, M.D., Ph.D., 1993–Present

UCSF Milestones

1864 – Hugh H. Toland starts the Toland Medical College in North Beach, the oldest medical school in the West in continuous operation.

1873 – Toland Medical College becomes the Medical Department of the University of California under Dean R. Beverly Cole. California College of Pharmacy, organized the year before, affiliates with UC.

1874 – UC adopts policy to admit women and all other qualified applicants. Two years later, Lucy Wanzer becomes the first woman to graduate from a California medical school.

1895 – Governor James Budd signs $250,000 appropriation for the Affiliated Colleges buildings. Mayor Adolph Sutro donates 13 acres of land on Mount Parnassus to UC's Medical, Dental and Pharmacy departments, and the School of Veterinary Medicine.

1898 – Affiliated Colleges open at their new location on Parnassus.

1906 – UCSF sets up makeshift hospital on the Parnassus campus and in Golden Gate Park to care for those injured in the earthquake.

1909 – First nurse graduates from UC wearing the unique white mortarboard cap and square blue and gold pin.

1912 – Ishi, last survivor of Yahi Indian tribe, comes to Parnassus.

1917 – New UC Hospital is completed.

1918 – School of Dentistry promotes the first course for dental hygienists. First class of graduates accredited by the state in 1920.

1923 – Herbert Evans and colleagues discover vitamin E. He also discovers animal pituitary growth hormone and succeeds in purifying it in the 1940s.

1925 – Karl F. Meyer completes studies underlying protective measures that save the canning industry from botulism. He also discovers that plague resides naturally in the state's wild rodent population and later isolates the virus responsible for Western equine encephalitis.

1928 – Chauncey Leake establishes department of pharmacology. Over the next 15 years, he and his colleagues develop new treatments for dysentery, discover amphetamines and introduce new types of anesthetics.

1934 – Nobel Prize goes to George Whipple, former director of the Hooper Foundation, for work he started at UCSF.

1939 – UC Hospital Training School officially becomes UC School of Nursing.

1941 – Former Medical School dean Robert Langley Porter persuades the state to build a neuropsychiatric institute, completed in 1942 and named after him.

1952 – Basic sciences division returns from Berkeley, reuniting the entire medical school and initiating the integration of basic and clinical sciences.

1958 – Medical Sciences building opens. With new Moffitt Hospital, UCSF becomes the largest health sciences teaching facility on the West Coast.

1964 – Kidney transplant program begins under John Najarian. Sam Kountz takes over as director in 1967, and helps make the service the world's largest.

1965 – Doctor of Nursing Science degree, first in the country, approved by Regents.

1966 – Health Science towers constructed.
School of Pharmacy tests the use of clinically skilled pharmacists in a patient care area for the first time. From this, clinical pharmacy program develops.

1967 – Hormone Research laboratory moves from Berkeley to Parnassus under C.H. Li. Four years later, Li synthesizes human growth hormone.

1969 – John Clements, William Tooley, Roderic Phibbs and George Gregory pioneer work in the treatment of infant respiratory distress syndrome and develop a technique, called CPAP, which dramatically improves babies' survival rate. Ten years later Clements, Phibbs and colleagues develop synthetic surfactant.

1970 – The campus is renamed the University of California, San Francisco.

1974 – Herbert Boyer and Stanford colleague Stanley Cohen develop recombinant DNA technique that revolutionizes biology and spawns the biotechnology industry.

1976 – J. Michael Bishop and Harold Varmus discover genes, called oncogenes, that can lead to cancer.

1976 – Y.W. Kan develops the molecular techniques and Mitchell Golbus the clinical techniques that lead to the first fetal test for sickle cell anemia and other genetic blood diseases.

1977 – William Rutter and UCSF colleagues achieve the first major triumph of genetic engineering by isolating the gene for rat insulin and transplanting it into bacteria.

1978 – Abraham Rudolph and Michael Heymann develop drug therapy for patent ductus arteriosis, a potentially fatal heart defect in premature infants.

1981 – Team of Michael Harrison, Mitchell Golbus, and Roy Filly performs the first successful in-utero surgical procedure.

1983 – Joseph M. Long Hospital opens.
UCSF clinicians and researchers develop the country's first outpatent AIDS clinic and inpatient ward at SFGH and mount an enormous multidisciplinary effort to fight the disease.

1986 – FDA approves genetically engineered hepatitis B vaccine created by William Rutter and colleagues.

1989 – J. Michael Bishop and Harold Varmus win Nobel Prize for Medicine. UCSF's first.

1990 – UCSF acquires Mount Zion Hospital.

1991 – UCSF's Millie Hughes-Fulford, a research scientist at the UAMC is part of space shuttle Columbia crew that conducts experiments on bone density loss.

1993 – Gladstone Institute of Virology Immunology opens at SFGH.
Harold Varmus named NIH director.

University of California, San Francisco

Storke Tower, officially called the Thomas M. Storke Student Publications Building. It houses the editorial and business offices of the student newspaper and yearbook and the campus radio station, as well as a 61-bell carillon.

SANTA BARBARA

Facts at a Glance

Chancellor: Henry T. Yang. *Opened:* 1958. *Acres:* 815.

Students: undergraduate, 16,297, graduate, 2,222, total, 18,519.

Students living on campus: 3,867. *Majors with largest enrollments:* psychology, political science, communication studies, biological sciences, English, electrical engineering. *Degrees:* Bachelor, 3,194, Master, 475, Ph.D., 174.

Academic staff (includes academic administrators, Cooperative Extension personnel, researchers, student assistants and teaching staff): 2,563. *Total employees:* 8,018. *Budget:* $333 million.

Source: Assistant Vice Chancellor, Public Affairs, UC Santa Barbara.

Bordered by the Pacific Ocean and backed by the Santa Ynez Mountains, UC Santa Barbara combines an extraordinarily beautiful setting with academic programs of national and international renown.

UCSB is a major research institute offering undergraduate and graduate education in the arts, humanities, physical and social sciences and engineering.

Long recognized for its distinction in undergraduate teaching, UCSB has been a pioneer in the disciplines of environmental studies, materials science and public history.

And the high quality of research undertaken by scholars at UCSB has been acknowledged by the National Science Foundation, which has established three major research centers on campus: the Institute of Theoretical Physics, the Center for Quantized Electronic Structures, and the National Center for Geographic Information and Analysis.

The campus has two professional school, the College of Engineering and the Graduate School of Education.

They are being joined in the 1994–95 academic year by the School of Environmental Science and Management.

The new school's curriculum is designed to provide students with the cross-disciplinary skills and training required to assess and solve the many environmental problems of the modern world.

The School will stimulate interaction among scientists and policymakers. It constitutes the first program of its kind in the Western United States.

UCSB provides other distinctive opportunities within the University of California.

It is home to the College of Creative Studies, designed for talented students with the ability to do advanced, independent work in the sciences and humanities.

The campus confers UC's only master's and doctoral degrees in musical performance, and it is the only campus to offer advanced degrees in Religious Studies.

Among the UC campuses in Southern California, only UCSB offers a program in Asian Studies.

UCSB is also home to the Coleccion Tloque Nahuaque, one of the premier collections of Chicano studies materials in the U.S., and the Thoreau Edition, a long-term editing project by scholars who are producing an authoritative multi-volume edition of the writings of Henry David Thoreau.

The UCSB faculty includes recipients of the National Medal of Science, members of the National Academy of Sciences and the National Academy of Engineering, numerous Guggenheim fellows, Fulbright scholars, and fellows of the National Endowments for the Arts and for the Humanities.

As a result of all these resources and more, UC Santa Barbara is large enough to offer world-class academic opportunities, but small enough to ensure a strong sense of community. It provides a learning environment that has made it one of UC's most popular campuses among freshmen applicants.

UCSB's origins date back to the Santa Barbara State Normal School, created by the State Legislature in 1909. The school became Santa Barbara State College in 1935.

It became a UC campus in 1944 following the transfer of the facilities of Santa Barbara State College to the University.

In 1953, graduate study leading to the Master of Arts degree was authorized.

In 1958, UCSB was designated a general campus of the University, authorized to award the Doctor of Philosophy degree.

The campus is situated on an 815-acre promontory on the Pacific coast. It is bordered on two sides by the ocean and on the third by the community of Isla Vista. On the fourth side, the campus faces the Santa Ynez mountain range across Goleta Valley.

The main campus contains most of the 300 buildings that house the University site.

The outlying Storke campus includes playing fields and a family student housing complex.

The west campus is largely undeveloped, containing an ecologically significant expanse of dunes that has been set aside as a natural preserve.

At the heart of the campus is the UCSB library, a major research facility which participates in cooperative programs and policy development with other major research libraries to provide collections and services for the UCSB community.

The library has about 2 million books and bound journals. The collection grows by about 60,000 volumes annually. In addition, the library has an excellent collection of maps, technical reports, satellite imagery, government documents, manuscripts and microformat materials.

The UCSB library collection is housed in two buildings: the Main Library and the Arts Library.

The main building houses the general collection, as well as several specialized units and services.

Here can be found the Science and Engineering Library, the Government Publications Department, the Map and Imagery Laboratory, the Curriculum Laboratory, the Black Studies Unit and the Coleccion Tloque Nahuaque.

Also located in the Main Library is the Department of Special Collections, which houses rare books and manuscripts as well as several distinguished collections, including the Wyles Collection on the American West and the Skofield Printers' Collection.

The University Art Museum is another major resource for the campus.

It is nationally renowned for its changing exhibition program, which is balanced between historical and contemporary art.

It features artists of diverse cultural origins. Exhibitions complement academic programs, particularly art history and art studio, and interdisciplinary projects are encouraged.

The permanent collections include more than 6,000 art objects, ranging from ancient terra cottas to old master drawings to contemporary sculpture. Collections include work produced in Europe, America, Africa and Asia.

The Sedgwick Collection of 15th-, 16th- and 17th-century European paintings and the Morgeroth Collection of Renaissance medals and plaquettes are examples of works on permanent exhibition.

One of the most distinctive resources in the University system is UCSB's College of Creative Studies.

It enrolls undergraduate students with demonstrated talent for independent work in the arts, mathematics and the sciences.

Emphases are offered in art (painting, sculpture and book arts), biology, chemistry, literature, mathematics, music composition and physics.

The College of Engineering, one of the two professional schools on campus, offers professional undergraduate education in five disciplines: chemical, electrical, mechanical and nuclear engineering, and computer science.

The Graduate School of Education, the other professional school, prepares researchers, teachers and administrators in education.

Two-thirds of the students are working on their Doctor of Philosophy or Master of Arts degrees, and one-third are enrolled in the teaching credential program to qualify for elementary and secondary school teaching.

The largest undergraduate college on campus is the College of Letters and Science, which enrolls more 15,000 undergraduates.

The college offers nearly 80 majors, including a number of interdisciplinary programs. It awards four degrees: Bachelor of Arts, Bachelor of Science, Bachelor of Fine Arts and Bachelor of Music.

Through the Graduate Division, UCSB offers advanced programs of study and research leading to the Master of Arts, Master of Music, Doctor of Musical Arts, Master of Science and Doctor of Philosophy degrees.

It also awards the Master of Fine Arts in studio art subjects and Master of Education degrees, as well as various credentials and certificates.

UC Santa Barbara is especially noteworthy as the headquarters of the Universitywide Education Abroad Program (EAP). Participating students remain registered on their home campuses while studying abroad. They receive full academic credit for their work. As part of EAP, international students attend the University, with scholarships provided through UC and their home institutions.

UCSB is well recognized not only for its commitment to quality education through its colleges, schools and

Broida Hall, the physics building. On any given day, there are 10,000 bikes on campus.

special programs, but to its dedication to the advancement of knowledge through research.

It has been recognized for its research potential and capabilities through its selection as the home of three national research centers.

These centers offer specialized research opportunities and a multidisciplinary environment for study at the undergraduate, graduate and postdoctoral levels.

The first is the Center for Quantized Electronic Structures (QUEST). It was one of 11 national Science and Technology Centers established by the National Science Foundation in 1989.

QUEST emphasizes the study of microelectronics, the investigation and development of semi-conducting materials containing features known as quantum structures. Such microstructures show promise as a basis for revolutionary new electronic devices.

Recently renewed by NSF for funding to 1997, the center consists of faculty from the departments of chemical and nuclear engineering, chemistry, electrical and computer engineering, materials and physics.

To enhance linkages with relevant industry, government and other university research facilities, QUEST maintains programs such as a distinguished lecturer program, a scholar-in-residence program and summer workshops.

The center conducts education programs to involve K-12 students in advanced science and to provide research opportunities for high school students, teachers and undergraduates.

The second national facility at UCSB is the National Center for Geographic Information and Analysis (NCGIA).

NCGIA was established in 1988 with NSF funding. It is a consortium consisting of UCSB, the State University of New York at Buffalo and the University of Maine in Orono.

Faculty at the three institutions are broadly interdisciplinary including researchers in geography, surveying engineering, computer science, economics, linguistics and psychology.

The Center's efforts focus on developing and promoting the use of geographical information systems (GIS) in the natural and social science and in the applied, planning and engineering sciences.

In 1990, the Santa Barbara Center was named the David Simonett Center for Spatial Analysis.

The third national facility is the Institute of Theoretical Physics.

The Institute for Theoretical Physics, initiated in 1979, brings together physicists from all over the world to collaborate on cross-disciplinary problems.

Areas of study include elementary particles and nuclei, condensed-matter physics, astrophysics and cosmology.

Approximately 45 researchers are in residence at the Institute at any given time.

To support other advanced studies, UCSB has a number of research facilities that focus on areas of critical interest in today's world. They provide unusual opportunities for faculty researchers, as well as students, to conduct basic and applied research in a variety of disciplines.

One highly important facility is the Center for Chicano Studies, which supports and conducts basic and applied research on the history and contemporary condition of Chicanos/Latinos in the United States. It also organizes and promotes a variety of special public-service events designed to improve upon the understanding and appreciation of Chicano/Latino society and culture.

Such areas include archeology in the Americas, the economics of criminal justice, the linguistics of almost extinct and modern languages, the sociology of religion, and the issue of how health care data are acquired and used in research.

Another research facility is the Computer Systems Laboratory/Center for Remote Sensing and Environmental Optics (CSL/CRSEO).

It conducts basic and applied research using the tools of remote sensing and environmental optics, which depend on computers and digital image-processing technology. Research is conducted in areas such as oceanography, hydrology, land vegetation, limnology and meteorology.

The Institute for Crustal Studies was established to increase the understanding of the earth's crust and lithosphere, including the portions below the sea floor. Technical approaches to issues involving the earth's crust are being explored through collaborative research projects between university, government and industry.

The Institute for Polymers and Organic Solids is an interdisciplinary effort involving physics, chemistry and polymer science. It draws upon expertise from these fields to conduct fundamental research on a new class of materials.

The materials are conjugated organic polymers with delocalized electronic conductivity, aniostropic linear and nonlinear optical properties and novel electrochemical properties. To better understand these novel materials, the Institute has capabilities in experimental physics, synthetic chemistry and polymer processing and characterization.

The Intercampus Institute for Research at Particle Accelerators (IRPA) has aided the experimental work of the high-energy physics groups at other UC campuses and at the Stanford Linear Accelerator Center.

The Marine Science Institute (MSI) is the focus of marine research and program development. MSI administers and supports research projects involving faculty and graduate students from 14 disciplines. Much of the research activity focuses on the resources of the California coast, although an increasing amount of effort is being directed toward an understanding of the world's oceans.

The Neuroscience Research Institute (NRI) is concerned with fields that relate function of an organism to the changing environment. Its primary purpose is to further basic fundamental research of an interdisciplinary nature in cellular and molecular neuroscience.

The Quantum Institute is an interdisciplinary research unit in which the Center for Free Electron Laser Studies (CFELS) and the Center for Nonlinear Sciences (CNLS) are housed.

CFELS offers opportunities for research in the biological, chemical, physical and material sciences, using the unique properties of the UCSB free-electron laser in the far infrared red—particularly nonlinear and non-equilibrium studies.

CNLS promotes interactions between researchers who share common interests in nonlinear problems and encourages undergraduate and graduate education in the nonlinear sciences.

View of UCSB from Isla Vista, showing San Nicholas Residence Hall.

UC Santa Barbara also has a number of important affiliated units.

One of the major ones is the Center for Black Studies. The Center conducts research on the social, historical, political, economic and cultural meanings that have affected peoples of African heritage throughout the world.

Another facility is the UCSB Global Change Program, initiated in 1990 to formalize the long standing commitment of the campus to education and research on global change issues. The program consists of a campuswide consortium of more than 40 faculty representing nine departments and several research institutes.

The Interdisciplinary Humanities Center, established in 1987, is part of the University's initiative to encourage humanities education and research in the curriculum.

The Center promotes innovative forms of collaborative research and teaching, including projects that overlap traditional disciplines. Participants at the center include UCSB faculty and students, as well as distinguished visiting scholars from around the world.

One of the other important facilities at UCSB is the Linguistic Minority Research Project (LMRP). This is a Universitywide project based on the campus. It is part of the Graduate School of Education.

It was established to conduct research on the education of language minority students in the K-12 education sector with the long-range goal of improving these students' access to college. An emphasis is placed on the collaborative research with schools and school systems.

All of these educational and research activities at UC Santa Barbara demonstrate an important point about the campus.

It is involved to a major extent in helping to advance and transmit knowledge, not only to its students but to the world at large. Because this world is statewide, national and international, UC Santa Barbara is realizing its potential as a major academic resource for the University of California.

With all its educational and research strengths, and with its strong commitment to academic quality and public service, UC Santa Barbara is confident that it has the capacity to meet the many challenges of the 21st century.

Chief Campus Officers

Clarence L. Phelps, Provost, 1944–46 (also president of antecedent institutions from 1918)

J. Harold Williams, Provost, 1946–55

Clark G. Kuebler, Provost, 1955

John C. Snidecor, Acting Provost, 1956

Elmer R. Noble, Acting Provost, 1956–59

Samuel B. Gould, Chancellor, 1959–62

Vernon I. Cheadle, Chancellor, 1962–77

Robert A. Huttenback, Chancellor, 1977–86

Daniel G. Aldrich, Jr., Acting Chancellor, 1986–87

Barbara S. Uehling, Chancellor, 1987–94

Henry T. Yang, Chancellor, 1994–

UCSB Milestones

1891 – Anna S.C. Blake Manual Training School founded.

1909 – School becomes State institution: Santa Barbara State Normal School of Manual Arts and Home Economics. Miss Ednah Rich, President.

1919 – Name of institution changed to Santa Barbara Normal School.

1921 – Name changed to Santa Barbara State Teachers College. A.B. degree authorized.

1935 – School becomes Santa Barbara State College.

1944 – Santa Barbara College of the University of California established by Board of Regents of the University of California.

1954 – College moves from Riviera and Mesa Campuses to new 408 acre site, portion of WW II Marine air base. 200 acres subsequently purchased.

1959 – On Sept. 19, Regents designated this as a "general campus" offering the highest degrees. Name changed to University of California, Santa Barbara.

1958 – First Chancellor appointed: Dr. Samuel B. Gould (1959–1962).

1962 – Dr. Vernon I. Cheadle appointed Chancellor.

1964 – Department of Religious Studies opens.

1967 – College of Creative Studies founded.

1966–67 – New organized research units: Institute of Religious Studies; Community and Organizations Research Institute.

New doctoral programs: German Language and Literature: Mechanical and Environmental Engineering.

1967–68 – New Buildings: Library Tower (September); Stadium (May); Faculty Club (June); Centennial House.

1968–69 – New organized research institute: Marine Science Institute (April).

Doctoral degrees: Art, Art History, Religious Studies.

Black and Chicano Studies programs and research centers authorized.

Campus ombudsman's office created to give students means of mediation and direct access outside established lines of authority.

1969–70 – Fall enrollment: 13,254 (2037) graduate students): 650 students in Educational Opportunity Program; minority presence on campus growing significantly.

New organized research units: Institute for Behavioral Sciences (July); Quantum Institute (December); Center for Black Studies (fall); Center for Chicano Studies (fall).

Black Studies Department opens.

B.A. program in Environmental Studies established, second in nation.

Isla Vista riot, Bank of America building burned (February 25, 1970); state of emergency declared; more than a hundred arrested.

Student newspaper, *El Gaucho,* renamed *Nexus* to establish new identity.

1970–71 – Chicano Studies Department opens.

Fall enrollment: 13,009 (reduction of 250 students) (1846 graduate students).

1971–72 – Fall enrollment: 12,239 (1750 graduates).

New doctoral programs: Speech and Hearing Sciences.

New organized research unit: Computer Systems Laboratory (February).

1972–73 – Fall enrollment: 11,828 (1771 graduate students); represents loss of 1500 students over three years.

New doctoral programs: Biochemistry-Molecular Biology; Individualized Doctorate authorized.

1973–74 – Fall enrollment: 11,928.

New organized research unit: Institute for Interdisciplinary Applications of Algebra and Combinatorics (July).

M.A. program in Nuclear Engineering authorized, First in UC.

1974–75 – Fall enrollment: 12,297 (1 out of five of ethnic minority identity).

New organized research unit: Social Process Research Institute (November), formed by merger of Bureau of Educational Research and development, and Institute for Behavioral Sciences.

1975–76 – Fall enrollment: 14,135 (largest to the point).

New doctoral program: Hispanic Language and Literature

Total bachelor's degrees conferred, 1962–77: 28,223; total M.A. degrees conferred 1962–75: 3,365; total Ph.D. degrees, same period: 844 (675 within years 1970–75).

1976–77 – Fall enrollment: 14,691.

Total FTE faculty positions: 1038; ladder rank faculty, 490.

B.A. programs: 80; M.A. programs: 44; Ph.D. programs: 29.

New M.A. programs and Ph.D. program initiated: The Graduate Program in Public Historical Studies, the first in the nation.

Robert A. Huttenback announced as choice for third Chancellor of the campus (April) Vernon I. Cheadle retires (June).

1977–78 – Fall enrollment: 14,588 (1882 graduate students).

Resignation of Vice Chancellor-Academic Affairs Alec P. Alexander (May).

1978–79 – Robert S. Michaelson appointed the Vice Chancellor (February).

Robert A. Huttenback formally inaugurated as third Chancellor of UCSB (June 7, 1979).

1979 – Institute for Theoretical Physics, sponsored by the National Science Foundation, was founded.

1982 – Presidential Chair established.

1984 – Aaron and Cherie Raznich Chair established.

King Saud Chair established.

1985 – Dehlsen Chair established in Environmental Studies.

Chancellor Huttenback Chair established.

Essam Khashoggi Chair established in Physics.

Donald W. Whittier Chair established in Electrical Engineering.

1986 – ALCOA Chair established in Materials.

Corwin Chair established in Music.

1988 – National Center for Geographic Information and Analysis created; sponsored by the National Science Foundation.

Louis Lancaster Chair established in International Relations.

J.F. Rowny Chair established in Comparative Religions and in the Religion and Society Department.

1989 – Maxwell and Mary Pellish Chair established in Economics.

1990 – Center for Quantized Electronic Structures established; sponsored by the National Science Foundation.

1992 – Materials Research Laboratory established; sponsored by the National Science Foundation.

1993 – Jose Manuel de Barandiaran Chair established in Basque Studies.

Luis Leal Chair established in Chicano Studies.

Koichi Takashima Chair established in the Japanese Cultural Studies Program.

UNIVERSITY OF CALIFORNIA
SANTA BARBARA

McHenry Library was named in honor of the founding chancellor, Dean E. McHenry.
UCSC Photo Services.

SANTA CRUZ

Facts at a Glance

Chancellor: Karl S. Pister.* *Opened:* 1965. *Acres:* 2,000.

Students: undergraduate, 9,320; graduate, 853; total, 10,173.

Students living on campus: 4,231. *Majors with largest enrollments:* psychology, biology, literature, economics, computer engineering and environmental studies.

Degrees awarded in a recent year: Bachelor, 1,915, Master, 150, Ph.D., 67.

Academic staff (includes academic administrators, Cooperative Extension personnel, researchers, student assistants and teaching staff): 1,543. *Total employees:* 4,746. *Budget:* $197 million.

Source: Acting Director of Public Information and Publications, UC Santa Cruz.

*Resigned 1996.

THE CAMPUS OF UC SANTA CRUZ OPENED IN 1965 as an innovative campus offering a personalized, small-college atmosphere with the resources of a major university.

From its inception, UCSC has been highly regarded as an institution that emphasizes undergraduate education. Today, 92 percent of its students are undergraduates.

At the same time, the graduate student population continues to grow and is expected ultimately to represent 15 percent to 20 percent of enrollment, reflecting the increasing stature of graduate offerings at the campus.

From its inception, UCSC has won a distinctive position within the University system as an academic institution devoted to excellence in undergraduate and graduate studies and in research.

Today, the campus occupies 2,000 acres of meadow and forest on the west side of the city of Santa Cruz.

Overlooking Monterey Bay, it lies about 75 miles south of San Francisco and 35 miles southwest of San Jose. Expansive meadows at the campus entrance gradually slope up to a redwood forest that covers most of the site.

The residential college is an important part of the Santa Cruz experience. Each college is within easy access of the central core of the campus.

The center of the campus includes an extensive library, science laboratories, lecture halls, art studios, a performing arts center, a student center and athletic facilities.

The site for the campus was well-chosen. The city of Santa Cruz is a well-known recreational area and center for the arts. Mild weather, miles of beaches and many cultural opportunities combine to make the area an enjoyable place to study and live.

Among the faculty and emeriti who have been attracted to Santa Cruz by the opportunity for creative teaching and scholarship are 13 members of the National Academy of Sciences and 19 members of the American Academy of Arts and Sciences.

Some 40 faculty members have been awarded Guggenheim Fellowships, and several have been honored with national awards for distinguished teaching.

Furthermore, one faculty member and two former graduate students have been named MacArthur Fellows, and since 1972 when UCSC began participating in the program, 79 Fulbright scholarships have been awarded to UCSC students.

The campus has eight "residential colleges," each including housing and classrooms, as well as faculty and administrative offices.

These colleges divide a large university campus into smaller academic communities, each serving as a social and intellectual gathering place for 900–1,300 students and 30–100 faculty fellows from a variety of academic disciplines.

Every undergraduate is affiliated with a particular college while participating in a campuswide academic program.

All academic programs are open to students from all colleges.

Each college has a distinctive quality derived from its core course and extracurricular programs, its faculty and their academic disciplines and its architectural style.

The faculty, or fellows, of each college come from a variety of academic disciplines. Some of the colleges have faculty from nearly all the liberal arts and sciences, while the faculty in other colleges are more concentrated in particular disciplinary interests. Most faculty, except those in the natural sciences, have their offices in the colleges.

In undergraduate education, the campus offers a full range of major programs within the arts, humanities, natural sciences and social sciences, as well as a considerable number of interdisciplinary-major programs.

The major programs are administered by boards or committees of studies, which are similar to departments at other universities.

In most cases, boards and committees are composed of faculty in the same field, but the interdisciplinary programs draw on faculty from several fields.

In addition to established major programs, individual majors are available.

Students can take advantage of innovative academic planning combined with the research and scholarship strengths of the University.

A strong program of general education is coupled with outstanding opportunities for both undergraduate and graduate students to pursue their academic specialties.

To personalize grading, UCSC professors provide students written evaluations of their work. Letter grades are offered as an option in most upper division and some lower division courses.

Undergraduate education at Santa Cruz is focused on the individual student.

UCSC's college core courses give each freshman a small seminar experience, providing close contact with faculty; intensive work on writing, speaking and critical reasoning; and an orientation to academic life.

To fulfill UCSC's unusually rigorous comprehensive requirement, every senior must pass a comprehensive examination or, in some majors, complete a senior thesis or project.

The campus strongly encourages undergraduate students to take advantage of the many opportunities for public service such as those provided through field programs, colleges and the Career & Internship Services Center.

Individual studies, apprentice teaching, field studies and internships are important parts of the undergraduate curriculum.

Bike path at the Santa Cruz campus, overlooking Monterey Bay.   Photo: Don Kenny.

More than 1,000 students participate in campus field programs each year.

Furthermore, individual research is encouraged, and hundreds of research papers coauthored by Santa Cruz undergraduates and their professors have been published in recognized journals.

Based on a survey of students who graduated in 1988, one-third of UCSC graduates continued their education in advanced-degree programs.

Ninety-four percent of the UCSC students applying to graduate school were accepted into a program.

Popular career choices included law, media and communications, computer sciences, health sciences, natural sciences, marketing, engineering, architecture, art, music, and education and teaching.

In graduate education, the UCSC campus offers 22 graduate programs, including new programs in computer engineering, international economics, anthropology and environmental studies.

Within the graduate programs, there are numerous paths of study leading to advanced degrees or graduate certificates, many offering a range of options for concentrated study within a specialized field.

Graduate study emphasizes close interaction between faculty and students, independent student research, supervised teaching experience and interdisciplinary work.

UCSC is nationally recognized as a multi-discipline research center.

For example, in 1990–91, its 25th anniversary year, the campus received a $6.5 million grant from the U.S.

Office of Education to coordinate the National Center for Research on Cultural Diversity and Second Language Learning.

It also has been designated as one of eight collaborating institutions of the Southern California Earthquake Center.

UCSC is recognized in particular for its astronomy program and for the research achievements of its Lick Observatory on Mount Hamilton in Santa Clara County. Its summer workshop on astronomy and astrophysics has drawn scholars from throughout the world.

The UC Observatories, which include Lick Observatory in Santa Clara County and the Keck Telescope in Hawaii, is headquartered at UCSC.

Other highly regarded programs include the Institute of Marine Sciences, the Santa Cruz Institute for Particle Physics, the Institute of Tectonics, and the Center for Nonlinear Science.

The campus also supports numerous other important organized research endeavors.

The Center for the Molecular Biology of RNA brings together an interdisciplinary group of researchers whose common interest is the structure and function of RNA. Many molecular biologists believe that RNA may have preceded both protein and DNA in the early molecular evolution of life.

In addition, the campus is the home of Shakespeare Santa Cruz, a professional theater company that unites theatrical experience with academic endeavor. Each summer, the company offers courses, tours, presentations and theatrical productions featuring members of the Royal Shakespeare Company of London.

UCSC also is the site of the Dickens Project, which brings together scholars from universities nationwide and abroad to study the work of Dickens and Victorian culture.

Currently, many new facilities are being built to meet current and future needs and to diversify educational and research opportunities for undergraduate and graduate students alike.

For example, the Robert L. Sinsheimer Laboratories (named after a former chancellor and completed in 1989) provide UCSC with an additional laboratory and science-related floor space.

The Science Library, opened in 1991, has quadrupled the space available in the previous building. Renovations to the older building created new classrooms and offices for the University of California Observatories/Lick Observatory.

The Earth and Marine Sciences Building opened in 1994.

Construction of College Eight residence halls, apartments and academic facilities is complete. Social Sciences 1 (the academic building for the planned College Nine), opened in 1994. Social Sciences 2 (the academic building for the planned College Ten), is under construction, as is a campuswide Music Center.

The Student Center, opened in time for the 1989–90 academic year, provides a focal point for campuswide student activities.

The campus is accredited by the Commission for Senior Colleges and Universities of the Western Association of Schools and Colleges (WASC), the regional accrediting association.

In addition, UCSC is a member of the Association of American Colleges and other professional and academic organizations.

These memberships are indicative of UCSC's high standards of academic achievement and performance.

Taken together, UCSC's resources and achievements hold great promise for the future. The reasons are many.

UCSC has been fortunate to recruit a faculty committed to teaching and undergraduate education as well as to graduate instruction and research.

This commitment, along with a tradition of innovation, makes it possible for UCSC to take a leading role in defining the university of the 21st century.

In its second quarter century, UCSC is dedicated to sustaining and enhancing its reputation for excellence and to carrying out its mission to serve the state's increasingly diverse population.

As the century draws to a close, the population of the state continues to grow at a rapid pace, becoming more varied ethnically and racially. UCSC is committed to planning for these future students.

The campus also is committed to expanding educational opportunities for all students, as well as to a full expression of intellectual and human diversity that will reflect the state's increasingly pluralistic society.

Chancellors

Dean E. McHenry, 1961–74

Mark N. Christensen, 1974–76

Angus E. Taylor, Acting Chancellor, 1976–77

Robert L. Sinsheimer, 1977–87

Robert Stevens, 1987–91

Karl S. Pister, 1991–Present

UCSC Milestones

1965 – UCSC's first college, Cowell College, opens with 652 students, most in trailers on the East Field. History professor Page Smith is founding provost. S.H. Cowell Foundation helps fund college construction.

University Library, under Donald Clark, opens with 75,000 volumes.

1966 – Construction of Cowell and the second college, named for Adlai E. Stevenson, completed.

Graduate Division established under acting dean and government professor Karl Lamb.

Lick Observatory astronomers and technical personnel plan move from Mt. Hamilton to campus as UCSC's first Organized Research Unit.

Charles Page is founding provost of Stevenson College, UCSC's second college.

Interior of the Robert L. Sinsheimer Laboratories at UCSC, named for the fourth chancellor. Photo: Joel Leivick.

1967 – Campus holds first commencement in Upper Quarry Amphitheater, awarding 80 bachelor's degrees, two master's, and one Ph.D.

Crown College opens with biological sciences professor Kenneth V. Thimann as provost and construction funding provided by Crown Zellerbach Foundation.

1968 – Merrill College opens with economics professor Philip W. Bell as provost and construction partially funded by Charles E. Merrill Trust.

1969 – College Five opens with literature professor James B. Hall as provost. (In 1981, the college is renamed Benjamin F. Porter College in recognition of additional construction funding from the Porter-Sesnon family.)

1971 – Kresge College, under provost and biology professor Robert Edgar, accepts first students and sets up operation in the Family Student Housing complex.

Kresge Foundation funds construction of the college.

1972 – Oakes College and College Eight established. A college endowment and support for the construction of Oakes is provided by the San Francisco Foundation, using funds from the Roscoe and Margaret Oakes Foundation.

Sociology professor J. Herman Blake appointed provost for Oakes; environmental planning professor Paul Niebanck, for College Eight. Institute of Marine Sciences established.

1974 – Founding chancellor Dean E. McHenry retires; UC Berkeley geology and geophysics professor Mark N. Christensen named UCSC's second chancellor.

1976 – Chancellor Christensen resigns and University Provost Angus E. Taylor named acting chancellor.

1977 – Robert L. Sinsheimer, a genetic biologist from Caltech, becomes UCSC's fourth chancellor.

1978 – First phase of Joseph M. Long Marine Laboratory completed on oceanside site given by Santa Cruz residents Marion and Donald Younger.

1980 – Santa Cruz Institute for Particle Physics founded. UCSC teams enter Division III of NCAA.

1981 – Dickens Project established at UCSC as an intercampus research group to further academic investigation and teaching of the author's works in the context of Victorian society.

1982 – Shakespeare Santa Cruz's first season, featuring outdoor performances of A Midsummer Night's Dream in the Festival Glen and King Lear in the Performing Arts Theater.

1985 – Elena Baskin Visual Arts Studios dedicated.

1986 – Institute of Tectonics established.

Baskin Center for Computer Engineering and Information Sciences, named for Santa Cruz philanthropist Jack Baskin, dedicated in a remodeled wing of Applied Sciences Building.

1987 – Robert Stevens, legal history professor and president of Haverford College, becomes fifth chancellor of UCSC.

Center for Nonlinear Science established.

1988 – Construction of Earth and Marine Sciences Building approved.

Regents establish University of California Observatories (UCO) at Santa Cruz to manage both Lick Observatory and UC's component of the new Keck Observatory in Hawaii, housing the world's largest optical telescope.

1989 – UC Regents approve campus's Long-Range Development Plan, projecting a campus population of 12,000 undergraduates and 3,000 graduate students by 2005.

1990 – Dedication of Robert L. Sinsheimer Laboratories, housing biology and biochemistry.

UCSC begins 25th anniversary year. Fall enrollment exceeds 10,000 students.

U.S. Department of Education establishes National Center for Research on Cultural Diversity and Second Language Learning at UCSC.

1991 – Dedication of facilities for College Eight.

UCSC celebrates University Library's one-millionth volume and dedicates new Science Library.

Chancellor Stevens leaves to practice law with a London firm. Karl S. Pister, former dean of UC Berkeley's College of Engineering, succeeds Stevens as interim chancellor.

Regents approve site and design of a Music Center with 400-seat hall.

1992 – Center for the Molecular Biology of RNA founded with grant from Lucille P. Markey Charitable Trust.

Construction begins on academic building for the planned College Nine.

Agroecology Program's Garden celebrates 25th anniversary.

UCSC—a major sponsor—joins in the dedication of the Monterey Bay National Marine Sanctuary.

Karl S. Pister inaugurated as UCSC's sixth chancellor, with a Colloquium on Diversity with Unity.

1993 – University celebrates its 125th anniversary.

Topical References

A

Academic Computing: In recent years, computers and data communications systems have made available information and tools of scholarship that are revolutionizing the fields of teaching, learning and research for students and faculty throughout the nation's academic institutions.

The University has become a full participant in what is literally an information revolution, one that is made possible by rapid advances in computer and telecommunications technology.

While funds for computer development often have been scarce in recent years, support nevertheless has been provided from varied sources, and sometimes increased, to help UC keep pace with the opportunities available.

In 1977, a report by a Universitywide Computer Task Force found that the academic use of computers at UC had benefitted from lower equipment costs, greater opportunities for interactive access to computers, decentralization of use, and decentralization of funding.

By the early 1980s, the 1977 analysis of computer trends had proven correct in other important respects. By then, computers had become integral parts of laboratory equipment for collecting data and controlling experiments, and telecommunications networks had become essential to access resources both on and off campus.

To learn still more about current academic uses of computers at UC, another Universitywide task force was formed in 1984. Its goals were to consider how computing should fit into the fabric of the University, to identify computing needs, and to recommend academic computing policy objectives.

After surveying the campuses and after considerable deliberation, the task force in its report issued in 1986 concluded that, in the future, universities will be ranked to a large extent according to their facilities for computing and data communication and their ability to use that technology.

Therefore, the task force report noted, the University's goal should be to make access to computing and the transmission of information "non-limiting to the tasks of research and instruction."

The task force also addressed Universitywide strategies that would further the effective use of academic computing at the University. Two of these strategies were the Instructional Use of Computing (IUC) model and program and development of the UC Intercampus Telecommunications Network (ITN). These eventually were put in place at the University, and other strategies evolved later based on various task force recommendations.

The report showed that computing and interest in computing from all UC sources surveyed had greatly increased. No longer limited to the sciences, the computer had become a useful tool throughout the University.

By then, computer use was increasingly tied to academic excellence in a variety of ways and in a broadened number of disciplines. For example, computers were being used to support an array of scholarly activities, such as literature and data base searches, maintaining scholarly reference data, and analyzing bodies of data to explore and understand trends and circumstances.

Simulation, modeling and precise computerization were enabling enhanced understanding of complex phenomena in a variety of fields such as the physical, mathematical, biological, social and engineering sciences. In many fields, computers had become essential to the effective conduct of empirical investigation— for example, to control experiments and to collect and analyze experimental data.

In music, in the graphic arts and in dance, computers had found increasing value in processes of artistic creation. In addition, computers were tied to improvements

Computers are a valuable learning tool at the University of California.

in the efficient exchange of information in the scholarly community via new developments in computer networking, telecommunications, and remote file transfer.

By 1986, computers could be used in limited, yet important, circumstances to reduce labor-intensive, repetitious, dull aspects of teaching, as in drilling students on vocabulary and verb forms in foreign languages. Computers also could be used to improve faculty productivity for grading and student record-keeping.

Finally, computer graphic systems were being used in disciplines, such as engineering, architecture and computer science, to aid in the creative process of system design, as well as in many classes of complex phenomena such as weather systems, national economies, and biological systems.

In late 1993, another report by the Universitywide Task Force on Academic computing was being prepared. Its charge was to review academic computing support in the University in relation to UC's academic mission and to develop strategies for the further development of academic computing capabilities over the next five years, including strategies for short- and long-term funding.

The new report in draft form showed that the objectives and recommendations of the 1986 task force report had served the University well. In particular, the State had accepted the Instructional Use of Computing (IUC) model developed by the task force and provided budgetary support for its implementation.

However, the pace of technological change, as well as changing needs and demand placed on instructional and research programs of the University have introduced new issues that could not be foreseen in 1986.

Among these has been the growth in demand for supercomputing and the establishment of the San Diego Supercomputing Center in 1986, as well as the growth in size, complexity and expense of high-speed communications networks, which have become indispensable for scientific and scholarly research and communication.

However, of more importance than these issues is the manner in which the mid-1980s understanding of academic computing had evolved in response to change in the technological environment.

In 1986, the vision of the future of academic computing at UC was of "computers linked by networks." In 1993, this vision had been transformed into one of "networked computing."

The 1986 report asserted that "if our computers are connected by networks, extraordinary important academic functions can be performed." It was possible at that time to conceive of numerous applications of academic computing for which network connectivity might not be needed (e.g., basic word processing) or might be supplied via occasional low-speed dial-up access to a campus mainframe computer (e.g., searching of library catalogs).

However, with extensive changes in network technology and academic use of computer networks, it is no longer possible for UC faculty, students and staff to effectively perform academic computing functions without high-speed access to the information resources and communications facilities provided by academic networks.

As a result, computing and networking can no longer be planned and implemented independently, but have become inextricably merged into what is called a "networked information technology infrastructure."

This transformation has been brought about by several important technological trends:

(1) The phenomenal growth in the speed, sophistication and accessibility of networks at all levels, from the campus department to the nation and beyond, (2) the rapid increase in the performance (and accompanying fall in price/performance ratios) of personal computers and workstations, which has made network-capable computing technology affordable and available to an ever-larger number of users), (3) the rapid proliferation of computing applications and information sources available through networks; (4) the advent of new hardware and software technologies, such as client-server software architecture, that are explicitly designed to take advantage of the networked computing environment, and (5) the emergence of multimedia applications, integrating text, data, sound, images and video, which will require both higher-performance workstations and greater network bandwidth.

In looking to the remainder of the 1990s, the University anticipates a communications revolution, one that will stress communication rather than computation.

Specifically, the University sees a future that emphasizes a "networked information technology infrastructure." This infrastructure will provide a number of innovations to do the following, among other innovations:

• Provide network connectivity for faculty, students and staff

• Offer the network services required to support communication, access to information, and access to computing resources needed for teaching, research and academic administration

Computers have proven to be essential in UC's libraries.

• Support network-compatible computing equipment, peripheral devices, and software capable of providing the networked computing services needed by users

• Make available the network-connected computing and information resources needed to support the academic program

• Provide a reliable mechanism for delivery of network services to the campus and Universitywide community

For UC, the shift in strategic emphasis needed to achieve this vision means that the greatest attention, at both campus and Universitywide levels, must be devoted to the following:

1) Completing the physical network infrastructure by extending network connectivity to locations where it is not yet available and assuring that all members of the academic community have ready access to network-connected computers and workstations of sufficient power and appropriate configuration to meet their needs

2) Supporting the users of the infrastructure with hardware, software and consulting services that promote full and effective use of the system

3) Sustaining the infrastructure with planning and budgeting mechanisms that take account of the life cycles of equipment and software and provide support for expanding future needs and uses

4) Providing access to the information resources available through the network

5) Financing the networked computing environment by developing equitable methods for funding the costs of networked equipment, services and information resource

Throughout, the University's goal will be to provide support services that will enable the full potential of computer systems throughout the institution to help fulfill UC's crucial missions of teaching, research and public service.

REFERENCES: Reports of the Task Force on Academic Computing, Office of the President; 1991 Profile of Campus Academic Computing Plans and Strategies, a Universitywide survey designed and conducted by the Office of the President; surveys of UC students conducted in 1985–86, 1986–87, 1987–88 and 1988–89 under the auspices of the Instructional Use of Computing Evaluation Group, and a similar survey of UC faculty.

CROSS-REFERENCES: Subjects cited in the above text.

Academic Planning and Program Review Board:

In 1972, UC President Charles J. Hitch announced the establishment of a board to integrate UC's academic, fiscal and physical planning.

The Academic Planning and Program Review Board (APPRB) replaced three separate groups which had handled aspects of UC planning.

The three were the Program Review Board, the Growth Plan Task Force, and the New Initiatives in Planning Group.

The new board was formed to sharpen UC's planning and budget review processes in view of UC's severe budgetary problems.

During the 1960s, the major issues in program planning for UC had involved questions like the following:

How many campuses should UC have, what core programs should a campus require for effective education, and what resources are needed for high-quality programs.

However, the issues facing UC in the early 1970s were different in kind as well as degree. The times had changed, and UC's planning mechanism had to change as well.

The new era raised such questions as:

How should UC allocate scarce resources? How should it best justify its budget requests as competition increased with other programs for public resources?

As a coordinating agency for campus and Universitywide planning, the new board was given the responsibility for:

• Developing guidelines for its coordination activities.

• Reviewing and coordinating campus academic plans and proposals for new programs.

• Preparing UC's Academic Plan.

• Preparing and revising growth plans.

• Reviewing UC's academic and professional offerings.

• Preparing the operating and capital outlay budget recommendations to the president.

Under the new system, the campuses continued their role in initiating academic planning and in proposing academic programs.

In response to changing needs, the Board's role and responsibilities have evolved gradually since its establishment in 1972.

Owing to the deterioration of the state's economic and fiscal situation in the early 1990s, UC's budget sustained substantial cuts.

Consequently, the University and the Board have had to face some very difficult planning issues. These have included possible reduction, discontinuance, disestablishment or consolidation of programs, together with early retirement programs for faculty and staff.

By Spring 1993, prospects for rapid improvement in the budget were considered poor; at the same time, substantial enrollment increases have been projected to begin by the end of the century.

The role and responsibilities of the Board were being re-examined in order that it be as well prepared as possible to address the complexities of future planning issues.

The Academic Planning Council (APC) was established in Fall 1993 to succeed the Academic Planning and Program Review Board (APPRB). Its purpose is to enable the University better to respond and plan in an era of severe fiscal constraints, taking into account likely social and economic changes in the future.

The APC is a joint faculty-administration body with membership drawn from the Academic Senate, campus administration, faculty, and the System Office.

The APC is charged to advise on Universitywide strategic academic planning and coordination, and to foster innovative approaches to the academic enterprise. Accordingly, it will provide guidance on such issues as rapid changes in existing programs, planning for new programs in a constrained environment, and issues of quality.

The APC had its first meeting on January 24, 1994, at which it identified seven action items and issues that it will address.

REFERENCES: "President Hitch Establishes New Academic Planning and Review Board," *University Bulletin*, Vol. 20, No. 11, January 10, 1972; information from Academic Affairs, Office of the President.

CROSS-REFERENCES: Budget Capital Improvement.

Academic Senate.

From its beginning, the University has operated on the theory that matters of faculty business are best dealt with by a system of faculty government.

This government is exercised by the Academic Senate. It was established in the Organic Act which was the University's founding document.

The Senate's powers are stated in the Regents' Standing Orders.

Within the provisions of the Standing Orders, the Senate determines its own membership and organizes and chooses its own offices and committees in such a manner as it may determine.

The Senate has a number of major responsibilities that are delegated by the Regents.

These include, for example, control over UC's academic program, curriculum, the awarding of degrees, and conditions for admission to the University.

Another responsibility involves consultation with the University administration.

For example, the Senate is consulted by the administration on issues such as the personnel process, educational and research policies, budget allocations, library policies, the academic calendar, the awarding of prizes and fellowships, and other areas.

The Senate also has the related responsibility inherent in "discretionary consultation."

This form of consultation applies to issues where there is no Regental mandate for the administration to consult with the Senate.

However, the administration does consult with the Senate in most of these circumstances, even though it is not required to do so.

Other Senate responsibilities include its quasi-judicial function on matters involving charges by and against faculty. In those instances, the Senate's Privilege and Tenure Committees sit as hearing committees.

Finally, the Senate serves to express the views of faculty on current issues. It is the one vehicle through which UC faculty members as a whole, by resolution or memorial, may express views on current issues they believe are important.

In 1961, special committees considered reorganizing the Senate as it was then constituted.

One committee studied the question of reorganizing the Senate so that Universitywide issues could be dealt with more effectively. At the same time, consideration was given to granting as much autonomy as possible to the campuses.

This committee recommended abolishing the two Academic Senate sections in effect at the time.

These two sections, the Northern and Southern Sections, had been established to accommodate a university that had grown from a small institution to encompass growing campuses and major research sites in both Northern and Southern California.

The Northern Section consisted of the Berkeley, Davis and San Francisco campuses, as well as Mt. Hamilton, where Lick Observatory is located. The Southern Section consisted of UCLA, Riverside and La Jolla.

The earlier creation of northern and southern sections had meant the development of an elaborate set of local, parallel and combined committees, all devised in an attempt to adapt to a growing and changing university.

However, despite the system that had been devised, faculty government was still exercised, in fact if not in theory, from Universitywide headquarters in Berkeley.

The special committee established in 1961 recommended abolishing the northern and southern sections and establishing a Universitywide Assembly of the Academic Senate.

Senate Faculty and Assembly Members, 1992–93

Listed below are the number of Academic Senate members at each campus for 1992–93 and the resulting number of Assembly representatives.

The Academic Senate's Universitywide Assembly is reapportioned each year.

Campus	Academic Senate Members	Assembly Representatives
Berkeley	2,158	7
Davis	1,845	6
Irvine	978	3
Los Angeles	2,850	9
Riverside	659	2
San Diego	1,233	4
San Francisco	1,083	4
Santa Barbara	896	3
Santa Cruz	489	2
TOTAL	12,191	40

Source: Notice, April 1992.

This new body's duties, in general, would be to hear and debate reports from its own committees and from the Academic Senate divisions at each campus and major research site.

The Universitywide Academic Senate also would be responsible for enacting legislation applicable to the University as a whole. Matters of divisional import would be reserved to the divisions.

Another special committee was appointed during this time to rewrite the Senate's bylaws to reflect details of the reorganization.

In the debates preceding the final reorganization, many amendments were introduced. As a result, the power of the Universitywide Academic Senate Assembly, as reflected in the bylaws, became rather less than originally proposed. At the same time, the powers of the divisions were increased.

Today, the Senate structure is as follows.

First, there is the Universitywide Assembly, which is the legislative arm of the Universitywide Academic Senate.

All Senate resolutions that affect academic programs of the University as a whole go through the assembly.

The six Universitywide committees represented in the Assembly are as follows:

The University Committee on Academic Personnel, the University Committee on Educational Policy, the Board of Admissions and Relations with Schools (BOARS), the Coordinating Committee on Graduate Affairs, the University Committee on Faculty Welfare, and the University Committee on Planning and Budget.

The Assembly's executive arm is the Academic Council, which also advises the University's president.

The Council includes its own chair and vice chair, the chairs of six important Universitywide committees, and the chairs of the nine campus senates, as well as 40 campus representatives chosen proportionally from all nine campuses.

The Council is a pro-tem assembly. This means that, when the Assembly does not meet, the Council is empowered to approve provisionally proposed Divisional Regulations which are at variance with Universitywide Regulations until the Assembly convenes. Its jurisdiction extends to all matters of Universitywide concern.

Although the Assembly meets no more than three times a year, the Council meets almost monthly.

Every meeting starts with a visit by UC's president and vice presidents, who report on matters of concern. At this time, members of the Council can exchange views with the administration and ask questions.

Each campus has a Senate structure that mirrors, for the most part, the Universitywide Senate. In addition, the chairs of the campus divisional committees often serve as members of the Universitywide committees.

With respect to matters that are campuswide, or local, in nature (that is, matters that do not raise issues of Uni-

versitywide concern), the local divisions have whatever authority the Universitywide Senate generally has.

REFERENCES: Centennial Record; "Commentary: Explaining the Academic Senate. What It Does. How It Works," by Murray L. Schwartz, chair of the Academic Council (and later interim vice president—academic affairs), *Notice*, Vol. 12, No. 2, November 1987, based on a presentation to the Regents; Regents' Standing Orders.

CROSS-REFERENCES: Faculty Representation on the Board of Regents.

Administration of the University: The University comprises nine campuses, each with distinctive qualities.

Four campuses are in Northern California: Davis, Berkeley, San Francisco and Santa Cruz.

Five campuses are in Southern California: Santa Barbara, Los Angeles, San Diego, Irvine and Riverside.

Under the State Constitution, the government of the University is entrusted to the Board of Regents.

The Regents appoint UC's president and, with the president's advice, appoint the chancellors, directors of major laboratories, provosts, and deans who administer the affairs of the individual campuses and other divisions of the University.

Authority in academic matters is delegated by the Regents to the Academic Senate. The Senate consists of faculty and certain administrative officers.

UC's president is executive head of the nine-campus University system. The Office of the President, located in Oakland, is the University's central administrative headquarters.

Each campus has a chancellor as its chief administrative officer. The chancellor is responsible for the organization and operation of the campus, including academic, student and business affairs.

Students participate in policy-making at both the campus and Universitywide levels.

REFERENCES; University Relations files, Office of the President.

CROSS-REFERENCES: Subjects in the above text.

Administrative and Corporate Headquarters: In 1991, the Office of the President completed its historic move from its Berkeley headquarters to the Kaiser Building in Oakland.

The move was part of a plan to consolidate all administrative units within the Office of the President at one site and make available to the Berkeley campus critically needed office space.

Prior to the move, approximately 1,100 Office of the President staff were housed at University Hall, a UC building across the street from the Berkeley campus, and in six leased locations in downtown Berkeley.

University Hall had been the site of the Universitywide headquarters since the late 1950s, when it had been built. However, over the years, some of the offices had been forced to move to nearby buildings in Berkeley as space became restricted.

By the mid 1980s, the Office of the President recognized it needed to reconsolidate as many of its offices in a single location as possible, in order to gain more administrative efficiency and to cut costs.

Discussions with the City of Berkeley regarding the possibility of expanding University Hall did not lead to any agreement. Following those discussions, the first steps in connection with the move from Berkeley began in 1986.

In May of that year, the Office of the President undertook a process to identify developers that might build a new headquarters facility.

Four developers were selected to present designs and financial proposals.

However, the Regents rejected the plans because of budget uncertainties and funding priorities in the system.

(Costs for a new building would have ranged from $35 million to $47 million.)

Instead, in March 1987, the Regents directed UC officials to seek ways to consolidate Office of the President activities in the various leased facilities by moving to a single existing location.

In April 1987, UC issued its request for lease proposals.

On May 13, 1987, a total of 23 proposals from developers were received, including six from Oakland, nine from San Francisco, two each from Alameda and Richmond, and one each from Berkeley, Emeryville, Concord and Martinez.

Kaiser Center, Inc., in Oakland, was found to be the most responsive to the requirements as set forth in UC's request for proposals.

In June 1987, UC entered into negotiations with Kaiser.

On November 23, 1987, the University and Kaiser Center, Inc. announced a 10-year lease agreement.

In addition, UC accepted a gift of 10 years free rent to move its Patent, Trademark and Copyright Office from leased space in Berkeley to the Harbor Bay Business Park in Alameda.

The initial move to Oakland took place in 1988, when the first Office of the President employees moved to Oakland in two phases, the first in February and the second in June.

This move involved 450 employees in the Division of Agricultural and Natural Resources, the Benefits Office, Information Systems and Administrative Services, the University Auditor's Office, and Materiel Management.

When the long, complex move to Oakland was finally completed in June 1991, the University had come full circle.

Just a few blocks away from the new headquarters in the Kaiser Building is the original site of the College of California, where the University had first opened its doors more than a century before. The site is now occupied by a public garage.

In 1968, when UC celebrated its centennial, the University and the City of Oakland installed a plaque on the brick wall of the garage to commemorate the place where an important part of California's history began.

REFERENCES: Informational materials, Information Systems and Administrative Services, and University Relations, Office of the President.

CROSS-REFERENCES: All topics related to Administration.

Admissions: The foundation of the University's undergraduate admissions policy is the Master Plan for Higher Education in California.

The Master Plan mandates that the top one-eighth of the state's public high school graduates, as well as those community college transfer students who have successfully completed specified college work, be eligible for admission to the University.

To implement these Master Plan provisions, the University's eligibility requirements specify the course work, grade point average and standardized test scores needed for admission.

These requirements also serve to communicate to students and to schools the basic level of academic preparation required for students to succeed in the University.

Eligibility requirements for freshmen have been strengthened five times in the past 12 years (1981 to 1993). During the same period, eligibility requirements for transfers have remained basically the same.

The most recent change for freshmen, adopted in May 1990 and effective beginning with applicants to the Fall 1994 term, increases the requirements for laboratory science and history/social science.

Changes in freshman requirements have been proposed primarily to strengthen the academic preparation of entering students.

However, they also have been introduced to bring the eligibility rate into compliance with the 12.5% mandated by the Master Plan.

The most recent study on eligibility rates, which was conducted by the California Postsecondary Education Committee (CPEC) on 1990 public high school graduates, found that the rate for fully eligible high school graduates was 12.3%.

A small percentage of newly enrolled undergraduate students can be admitted in exception to University eligibility requirements.

The current provision for this exception, adopted in May 1990, allows up to 6% of new enrolled freshmen and up to 6% of enrolled transfer students to be admitted by exception to the eligibility requirements.

The current policy allows the University to admit students by exception within the following categories:

- Disadvantaged (those from underrepresented minority and/or low-income or educationally disadvantaged backgrounds)
  - Athletes
  - Special Talent or Other (those who have demonstrated exceptional ability in certain areas or have shown marked improvement in academic performance)

Inherent in the University's admissions policy is the commitment to offer a place within the University to every California resident applicant who applies on time and meets the eligibility requirements.

(However, admission to the campus and program of students' choice is not guaranteed.)

Meeting this commitment has become increasingly difficult in recent years due to the growth in the number of applicants.

From 1979 through 1992, the number of California freshman applicants to the University increased by more than 28%.

During that time the percentage of California high school graduates choosing to enroll at the University increased, from 5.8% to 7.5%.

Quick Summary of High School Courses Needed to Meet Subject Requirements in Applying to UC

- History/Social Science
  2 years required
- English
  4 years required
- Mathematics
  3 years required, 4 recommended
- Laboratory Science
  2 years required, 3 recommended
- Language other than English
  2 years required, 3 recommended
- College Prep Electives
  2 years required

Note: If the grade point average in these subjects is 3.3 or higher, the student has met the minimum requirement for admission to UC.

If the grade point average is below 3.3 but above 2,81, the student must achieve a certain score on the college entrance exams to meet the minimum requirement for admission.

In addition, all students are required to submit scores from a specified battery of college entrance examinations.

Source: Introducing the University, 1994–1995, Academic Affairs, Office of the President.

Also, during a five year period (from Fall 1988 to Fall 1992), California transfer applicants increased by 19%.

In choosing their entering classes, campuses that cannot accommodate all eligible applicants employ selection criteria beyond the minimum eligibility requirements.

This selection process is governed by guidelines which were first developed in the early 1970s following recommendations in the Master Plan.

These early guidelines were revised further in 1988, following adoption of the Policy on Undergraduate Admissions by the Regents in May 1988.

The policy articulates the University's commitment to serve the people of California and the needs of the state within the framework of the Master Plan.

In addition, the policy emphasizes UC's commitment to maintain high academic standards and to enroll a student body that encompasses the state's cultural, racial, geographic and socio-economic diversity.

In accordance with the policy and revised guidelines, campuses select approximately half their students entirely on the basis of test scores, course work and grades.

The remainder of the class is selected from the full range of the eligible applicant group using factors that, in combination with coursework, test scores and grades, contribute to the makeup of a vigorous and diverse intellectual and social environment at the University.

Enrollment pressures have resulted in a number of changes in admissions practices.

More campuses now close to new applications immediately after the priority filing period in November, and fewer campuses open to new applicants in winter and spring terms.

While enrollment pressures were first felt in the 1980s at the freshman level, transfer applications increased significantly in recent years.

As a consequence, at some campuses and in some majors the academic qualifications for admission have increased well beyond the basic eligibility requirements for transfer students.

Consistent with the Master Plan, priority is given to California Community College transfers in cases where the number of qualified applicants exceeds the space available.

Also, except in hardship cases, campuses require that general education requirements and lower division major preparation be complete, or nearly so, before transfer.

These requirements are implemented in consultation with the community colleges to help promote a smooth transition to the University.

REFERENCES: "Report on University of California Admissions and Enrollments," Item 306 for Discussion, Regents' Committee on Educational Policy, May 20, 1993.

CROSS-REFERENCES: Master Plan; sections relating to education.

Statistical Overview of Admissions at the University

The following is based on a UC report released in May 1993. It summarizes UC's Fall 1992 undergraduate application flow of applicants, admitted students and enrolling students.

It also compares 1992 figures with trends during a five year period.

The emphasis is on California students, who make up 94.3% of new undergraduates. Just over 4% of new Fall 1992 students were from other states, and 1.5% were international students.

California students

• During the previous five years, the number of California freshman applicants to the University decreased by 2.9%. This was due to fewer high school graduates in the state; the percent of high school graduates who apply to the University actually increased slightly.

• In Fall 1992, 14.8% of 1991–92 California (public and private) high school graduates applied to UC, 12.2% were admitted and 7.5% enrolled.

• The last five years had seen a steady increase in the percent of California high school graduates who apply (from 14.3% to 14.8%) and are admitted (from 11.6% to 12.2%). The percent enrolling decreased from 7.7% to 7.5%.

• California transfer applicants increased by 19.0% in the previous five years due to a nearly 50% increase in California Community College applicants. Community college transfer entrants now make up 88.6% of new California transfers, compared to 76.5% five years ago.

• For California freshmen, there is no longer a majority ethnic group among either applicants, admits or

enrolled students. In Fall 1992, whites comprised 47.3% of applicants, Asian Americans 24.5%, Chicanos 9.8%, African Americans 4.8%, Filipino Americans 4.2%, Latinos 3.9%, and American Indians 0.8%.

• California transfer applicants are somewhat less ethnically diverse than freshmen. Proportionately speaking, there are more whites and American Indians among transfers than among freshmen.

• At the freshmen level, the size of the entering class fell by 6.9% in the previous five years. Ethnic groups with larger than average decreases were African Americans (30.1%), American Indians (25.2%), whites (21.6%) and Latinos (14.4%). Groups that increased were Asian Americans (30.7%) and Chicanos (6.3%).

• The size of the entering transfer class increased by 20.0%, and all ethnic groups increased in number.

• Students who apply to many campuses are far more likely to be admitted to the University than students who apply only to one or two campuses. For instance, 57.5% of freshmen who apply to only one campus are admitted, compared to 90.8% of those who apply to five or more campuses.

While the above information covers only fall terms, winter and spring terms also are significant.

For example, in the 1991–92 academic year, 13.2% of new undergraduates entered in winter or spring, including 27.7% of the year's new transfer students and 24.6% of new students from underrepresented minority groups.

Source: Report on University of California Admissions and Enrollments," Item 306 for Discussion, Regents' Committee on Educational Policy, May 20, 1993.

Underrepresented Students At the University

Underrepresented minority students belong to ethnic groups whose UC eligibility rates are below the statewide average of 12.3%.

Underrepresented groups are African American, Chicano, Latino and American Indian.

CPEC's Eligibility Study in 1990 found that the eligibility rates for African American public high school graduates was 5.1% and for Chicanos/Latinos (a composite group in that study) 3.9%.

Although no eligibility data are available for American Indians, the University has traditionally included this group because the numbers of American Indian students at UC is low.

Because these ethnic groups are served by the University's Student Affirmative Action (SAA) programs, they are referred to as SAA students.

Admissions Applications: Students interested in applying to the University can obtain an Undergraduate Application packet from their student counselor or at any of the UC campus Admissions Offices.

The packet explains the application process, fees and all the items that a student must submit with his or her application. A student may apply to as many campuses as he or she wishes using one application form.

Because the University has received an increasing number of applications in the last few years, most campuses are not able to accept applications after a filing period ends. A campus will accept applications after the filing period only if it still has space for new students.

Some schools, colleges and majors do not accept applications for admission to the winter and spring terms. Students are directed to check with the campus Admissions Office to find out if the college to which they want to apply has any filing restrictions.

REFERENCES: "1994–1995: Introducing the University," informational booklet, Student Academic Services, Office of the President.
CROSS-REFERENCES: Admissions.

**California Freshman Applicants
Fall 1979-1992**

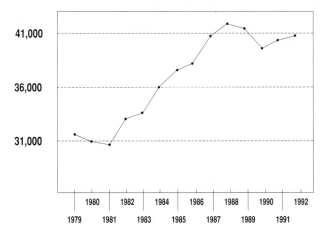

Affirmative Action Programs for Undergraduates:

The University's policy on undergraduate admission, adopted by The Regents in May 1988, states UC's intent to enroll students who both meet high academic standards and who encompass the broad cultural, racial, geographic, economic and social diversity of California.

This policy is based on the idea that a diverse student body, one that represents all segments of society and, therefore, differing points of view and experiences, is fundamental to enhancing the quality of education received by all students.

For nearly three decades the University has supported programs designed to contribute to the diversity of its undergraduate student body.

The first of these efforts was the Educational Opportunity Program, established in 1964.

The success of this program led to steady growth in underrepresented student enrollment at the University during the late sixties and early seventies.

In 1973, however, enrollment of Chicano students began to level off, while that of African American students began to decline.

In 1974, to reverse this trend, the University organized a series of Universitywide Task Groups to assess the status of educational opportunity within the University and to review relevant University practices.

These practices have included student recruitment, admissions, financial aid, academic support services, and non-academic support.

An important recommendation of these groups was that the University initiate large-scale programs to encourage ninth and tenth grade students to strive for UC eligibility and admission.

In 1975, the University requested and received a budgetary augmentation from the State of California to establish developmental student affirmative action programs.

In spring 1976, the University began the Early Outreach Program, focusing on junior high school students.

In 1978, UC initiated a second component of that program to continue at the high school level the activity begun with junior high school students.

These efforts have since been organized as the Early Academic Outreach Program (EAOP).

The Immediate Outreach Program, the recruitment aspects of the University's SAA effort, also began in 1978.

The Immediate Outreach Program identifies students interested in the University and encourages them to apply and enroll.

Also in 1978, a program of support services designed to help students succeed academically once they are enrolled at the University was established.

Collectively, these outreach efforts form a "pipeline" from junior high school to a baccalaureate eduction at the University, as well as to enrollment at the California State University and other postsecondary institutions.

The University's graduate and professional SAA programs build on these undergraduate efforts with the goal of increasing the diversity of the graduate student body and eventually of the faculty.

The following provides details about student affirmative action programs.

• Early Academic Outreach Program

The major issue confronting the University in diversifying its undergraduate population is, and has been, inadequate academic preparation of underrepresented students at the elementary and secondary school level.

Among certain ethnic groups there have been relatively few students who meet the University's eligibility requirements.

In 1990, an eligibility study by the California Postsecondary Education Commission (CPEC) estimated that only 5.1% of African American and 3.9% of Chicano/Latino public high school graduates are fully eligible for UC, compared to 12.7% for White and 32.2% for Asian American students.

The Early Academic Outreach Program aims to increase the number of underrepresented students graduating from California high schools who are academically eligible for a baccalaureate program.

Working with junior high/middle school students, program staff identify potential participants, encourage them to aspire to a college education, and inform them of relevant admission requirements.

As participants progress toward high school graduation, program services are concentrated increasingly on students' academic needs.

Academic tutorials provide help in developing study skills necessary for success in college and assist with academic coursework; in the 12th grade, participants receive help with admissions applications, university enrollment and financial aid processes.

Each UC campus serves a limited number of schools located within its geographical region.

The schools selected are among those with a higher than average proportion of underrepresented students enrolled, and a higher than average proportion of students from families receiving Aid to Families with Dependent Children (AFDC).

In 1991–92, the Early Academic Outreach Program served 54,077 students enrolled in 488 schools.

• Immediate Outreach Program

The goal of the Immediate Outreach Program is to recruit to the University academically qualified underrepresented freshmen and transfer students.

Outreach officers present information at high schools, community colleges and parent conferences.

Admissions counseling also is provided in most of the schools and community colleges in the state, including private and parochial schools.

Budgetary reductions have forced the campuses to reduce the scope of recruitment activities. Examples of these reductions include fewer organized visitations to the campuses by prospective students, reductions in visitations to schools by recruitment personnel, participation in fewer parent programs, and decreased Spring outreach activity.

Yield activity (activity to enroll admitted students) is often carried out largely by Immediate Outreach personnel.

A recent initiative is the UC Admissions Preparation Program (UCAPP).

Participating in a series of day-long events throughout the state, promising underrepresented juniors are brought together with UC Immediate Outreach personnel to begin the recruitment process.

By thoroughly reviewing the academic record of each student, UC recruiters are able to provide advice for increasing the academic competitiveness of these prospective applicants.

By beginning interaction while students are still juniors in high school, the University has effectively expanded the recruitment season.

In the past, UC outreach personnel interacted with prospective students mostly during the Fall prior to the application filing period.

UCAP provides the campuses six more months to work with these prospective applicants prior to the application filing.

• SAA Support Services

SAA support services have proven to be valuable in enhancing students' academic performance, personal growth and social integration into the University.

Enhancing graduation rates for an increasingly diverse student population has been recognized nationally as one of the critical issues confronting undergraduate education.

Learning assistance, such as tutoring and basic learning skills, has a positive, short-term impact which increases a student's academic performance and likelihood of graduation.

Activities such as advising, orientation, summer bridge programs and career planning also have effects upon academic success and simultaneously help students cope with personal problems such as low self-esteem and stress.

All of the campuses offer a wide range of both academic and non-academic student services.

While all programs are essential pieces of the student support network, learning skills centers and summer bridge programs are the most widely used and most thoroughly evaluated support programs.

Learning skills centers typically offer tutoring, academic workshops, computer literacy, student skill training, preparation courses for graduate school examinations, and training programs for tutors.

Tutoring and workshop programs consistently receive high marks from students for their immediate impact on improved academic performance.

Campus studies show that these programs do improve academic performance; students who regularly use tutorial and workshop programs outperform those of similar backgrounds who do not use such services.

Progress in the affirmative action programs in this section is described in the informational material in the text and in the references.

The following provides information about enrollments and related issues.

• Overall Undergraduate Enrollment

Among all undergraduates within UC, the number of underrepresented students increased by 166% between 1976, when SAA efforts began, and 1992.

During the same time period, the overall undergraduate population increased by 36.6%.

While underrepresented students comprised 9.9% of all undergraduates in Fall 1976, they represented 18.5% of all undergraduates in Fall 1992.

Most of this gain was due to increases among new underrepresented freshmen.

Details are provided in relevant reports related to affirmative action.

By 1995, affirmative action nationally and at the state level was being re-examined.

REFERENCES: "Report on University Undergraduate Student Affirmative Action Programs," Item 1 for Discussion, Regents' Committee on Affirmative Action Policies, May 20, 1993.

CROSS-REFERENCES: All subjects relating to affirmative action, as well as programs mentioned in the text.

Changing Demographics Mean New Challenges for UC

Recent data from the State Department of Finance indicate that dramatic and far-reaching changes are taking place in the size and ethnic makeup of California's K-12 population.

These changes will have a dramatic effect on future demand for the University.

Between the academic years ending 1992 and 2006, the number of public high school graduates is projected to grow by 67%, from 246,966 to 411,387 graduates, with the principal growth among the non-white population.

From 1992 to 2006, white graduates will increase by 15%, but the rate of growth among non-white groups will be much higher.

The percentage increases among the groups range from a low of 51% for African Americans to a high of 132% among Chicanos/Latinos.

The projected numerical changes will have a significant impact on the proportional make-up of public high school graduates overall.

By 2005, the percent of graduates who are American Indians and Filipinos will remain approximately the same.

African Americans will decline from 7.3% to 6.6%.

Whites, who currently represent 50.3%, will decline to 34.8%.

Asian American graduates will increase from the current 11.3% to 15.4%.

Numerical and proportional growth among Chicano/Latino graduates far exceeds that of any other group.

Chicanos/Latinos currently represent 27.4% of public high school graduates, but will represent 38.2% by 2006.

UC's challenge is clear.

The University must maintain its efforts, in partnership with the schools, to raise the rates of full eligibility for students from underrepresented groups, which remain substantially below the 12.5% rate called for by the Master Plan.

If 94%–96% of African American and Chicano/Latino graduates continue to be ineligible for admission to UC, the principal barrier to access will remain unchanged, and will negatively affect many more young Californians.

A number of issues need to be addressed.

Three strategies are seen to have the most significant impact on the problem of underrepresented student enrollment.

They are as follows:

1) Budget reductions have impacted negatively on the ability of the Early Academic Outreach Program to continue developing large numbers of qualified underrepresented students and to meet increased demands for services in the schools.

In response, the Council of Chancellors recently agreed to arrest the decline in budgetary resources committed to the Early Academic Outreach Program.

2) Financial aid awarding practices have been identified as a factor leading underrepresented students to enroll at other institutions.

Some private institutions are able to provide information about the amount and composition of financial aid awarded to a student well before the student must make a final decision about which campus to attend.

Despite the fact that total cost of attending UC remains far lower by comparison, students often believe that the aid package offered by private institutions is superior to that of UC.

There also is evidence that many underrepresented students opt to continue living at home to minimize costs, thereby eliminating UC options which would require living in on-campus housing.

In addition, program officers report an increasing sensitivity on the part of underrepresented students to taking out student loans, particularly when their families believe that borrowing is for those unable to live within their means.

In response, the President has stated that he will work with the Chancellors to increase the amount of grant funding available for needy students.

3) Recent media attention on the increasing cost of attendance has reinforced a commonly held belief among parents in low-income families that the University is not a realistic option for their children.

Generally, parents of underrepresented students have the same concerns and aspirations for their children as other parents; they hope their children do well in school and that they continue their education at the postsecondary level.

Unfortunately, these parents, who generally lack postsecondary education themselves, believe the decision to attend college is to be considered by their students as they prepare for high school graduation.

In response, the President's office is developing a comprehensive media campaign which, through the airing of public service announcements on relevant topics, will communicate broadly the availability and accessibility that will continue to exist for needy eligible students.

Other strategies include establishment and enhancement of new technologies in recruitment and increased collaboration between the California Subject Matter Projects and UC's Early Academic Outreach Program.

Other efforts include further innovations by the Puente Project and MESA. These programs are described elsewhere in the book.

Source: "Report on University Undergraduate Student Affirmative Action Programs," Item 1 for Discussion, Regents' Committee on Affirmative Action Policies, May 20, 1993.

Affirmative Action Programs for University Academic Employees and Graduate and Professional Students: The University seeks to identify and encourage students, postdoctoral fellows and faculty whose participation in higher education is low and to assist them to progress to the next stages of the educational pipeline.

California's population is among the most ethnically diverse in the nation. About 43% of Californians are now African Americans, Chicanos, Latinos, American Indians, Filipino Americans or other Asian Americans. That percentage is projected to increase to more than 53% by the year 2005.

This diversity is increasingly reflected in the University's undergraduate enrollments; increases in UC's graduate programs and among the faculty, while more modest, have been steady as well.

Participation remains low, however, in certain disciplines and among certain groups. The programs described below are designed to increase the flow of minority and women students into graduate and postdoctoral study at the University and to develop a pool of individuals who will become candidates for UC faculty positions in the near future. This need is particularly acute as uncommonly large numbers of faculty are expected to retire by the turn of the century.

In close consultation with campus administrators, the programs described below promote development of the interest, skills and credentials necessary for academic advancement. They also provide the financial support and faculty mentorship that are crucial to success along an academic career path.

UC Pregraduate Programs

In 1989, the University initiated two pregraduate programs designed to assist UC undergraduates in the transition to graduate and doctoral study. The goal of the University's pregraduate programs is to expand the pool of minority and women undergraduates who are interested in and prepared to undertake graduate study.

The Undergraduate Minority Scholars Program is intended to help students develop collaborative study skills and group learning techniques in faculty-directed, small-group sections. The Pregraduate Mentorship Program provides undergraduates with academic enrichment through faculty mentorship and active participation in faculty research projects.

In both programs, participating faculty on each campus work with individual students to:

(1) Strengthen their academic skills, (2) involve them in structural research projects, (3) arrange for supplemental academic assistance through academic support services, and (4) provide an understanding of the opportunities that graduate school and an academic career can offer.

All UC campuses have the opportunity to participate in a five-year, $1 million-a-year Alliance for Minority Participation grant from the National Science Foundation. Focusing primarily on promoting science careers, the California Alliance for Minority Participation (CAMP) seeks to identify and address barriers to participation for minorities and women at key transition points in the science and engineering educational pipeline. The alliance is a consortium of UC campuses, the California State Universities (CSU), California Community Colleges, and independent universities, as well as corporations and national laboratories.

Intersegmental Outreach and Recruitment

In its effort to enlarge the pool of minorities and women in its graduate programs, the University seeks to draw upon the large numbers of underrepresented undergraduate and master's students in the California State University who have the potential to succeed in UC doctoral programs. In 1989–90, the Office of the President and the campus graduate divisions joined with CSU to coordinate the California Pre-Doctoral Program.

Program funds enable 75 minority and women students to participate in disciplinary conferences and to travel with CSU faculty to visit UC graduate programs. The Pre-Doctoral Scholars may participate in UC's Summer Research Internship Programs or, in the case of CSU master's students, work independently with UC faculty members on the student's research interests.

Representatives of the graduate divisions of UC, CSU and several California independent colleges and universities have established the California Minority Graduate Education Forum. Held each spring, the Forum provides 600-800 students with information on financial support opportunities, how to select and apply to the right graduate school, and how to prepare for the Graduate Record Examination, as well as tips on succeeding in graduate school.

Students also attend discipline-based workshops, in which faculty members discuss course requirements, workload expectations, research opportunities and other aspects of doctoral study. Students also meet individually with outreach representatives from about 100 of the nation's leading graduate schools.

Graduate Outreach and Student Support

To encourage minorities and women at the graduate level to prepare for academic careers, UC has developed an integrated program of support designed to provide opportunities to prepare for, enter and complete doctoral degree programs. The enterprise, the Academic Career Development Program, has four components.

1) The Graduate Outreach and Recruitment Program enables UC graduate divisions and departmental representatives to make contact with minority and women students by visiting campuses and attending forums throughout the country and by bringing potential students to UC campuses for departmental visits and for participation in summer research internship programs.

A key feature of these summer programs is the involvement of faculty members. Faculty serve as instructors, career counselors and research preceptors, as well as encourage and support students in their applications to graduate programs.

2) The Eugene Cota-Robles Fellowship Program was established in 1989–90 to provide mentoring and two years of financial support to outstanding minority and women students entering doctoral programs at UC. The program supports 67 new Fellows each year.

3) The Graduate Research Assistantship/Mentorship Program was established in 1984–85 to provide minority and women graduate students in their second, third or fourth year with up to two years of support as half-time research assistants. This program is intended to reduce students' reliance on loans and employment in order to devote more time to improving the quality and breadth of their graduate work and engage in intensive research under faculty guidance and supervision.

4) Since 1989, the Dissertation-Year Fellowship Program has provided one year of support to minority and women Ph.D. degree candidates to enable them to complete their doctoral theses and to assist them in preparing for faculty teaching positions.

Other support opportunities for women and minority graduate students include the Graduate Opportunity Fellowship Program, which provides each qualified recipient with a stipend, plus fees and nonresident tuition if applicable.

Each campus also has its own minority student financial support programs, some involving federal funds. On several campuses, the Graduate Divisions have extended the Eugene Cota-Robles Fellowship Program to a four-year support package, with the third and fourth year funded with campus resources.

Postdoctoral Program

The President's Postdoctoral Fellowship Program was established in 1984–85 to enhance talented Ph.D. recipients' prospects for securing faculty positions.

Particularly in the sciences, a postdoctoral research appointment is the normal and expected transition step that precedes a ladder-rank faculty appointment. The UC program is designed to increase the competitiveness of women and racial and ethnic minority Ph.D. degree recipients for faculty appointment at UC and other major institutions of higher education.

Administered directly by the Office of the President, the program offers up to two years of support for postdoctoral research for each of 23 new Fellows per year. Each Fellow has a faculty sponsor who provides mentoring and guidance and who helps promote the Fellow's visibility among colleagues on other campuses.

In addition to providing a unique research opportunity, the President's Postdoctoral Fellowship Program's annual orientation day and two-day professional development retreat provide Fellows with the opportunity to meet peers and faculty in their respective fields of research. On more than one occasion, these events have directly resulted in the recruitment of a President's Fellow to a ladder-rank faculty position at UC.

Faculty Development

Since 1978–79, the University has provided support for minority and women faculty and staff through the Employee Affirmative Action Development Program.

Faculty awards support research for junior faculty that assists their promotion to tenure. The program also provides a break from the high level of advising and other commitments that minority and women junior faculty members typically assume.

Campus experience with this program has shown that substantial release time—a minimum of one quarter and preferably two quarters—produces the greatest benefits. This knowledge resulted in the establishment in 1986–87 of the Pre-Tenure Award Program.

Awards under the Pre-Tenure Award Program are made to minority and women junior faculty prior to the mid-career review (which normally takes place two years before a departmental decision on tenure). Typically, the Awards provide support to conduct research and to pursue and complete projects for publication.

REFERENCES: "Report on Affirmative Action Programs for University Academic Employees and Graduate and Professional Students." Item 2 for Action, Regents' Special Committee on Affirmative Action Policies, May 14, 1992; "Continue the Journey" publication and President's Post-doctoral Program brochure, Office of the President.

CROSS REFERENCES: All subjects related to affirmative action and education.

Affirmative Action for University Staff and Management:

In response to California's changing society, the University is engaged in actively recruiting minorities and women in all areas of staff employment.

By April 1992, University officials were reporting steady progress in increasing the number and percentages of minorities and women employed at UC.

A report to the Regents in September 1992 showed that minorities and women represented almost 79 percent of UC's 94,110 employees in executive, management, professional and staff positions.

Of this number of employees, 41.4 percent were minority, and 62.5 percent were women (25.4 percent were minority women).

The minorities identified in the UC report were Blacks/African Americans, Hispanics, Asians and American Indians.

The report's data, covering 1988 to 1992, showed that the numbers of minorities and women in all UC personnel programs had increased.

Statistical analyses of personnel data for this four-tier personnel program system were conducted for the first time in 1989. Data covered calendar year 1988.

Tables showing the growth in numbers and percentages of minorities and women in detail, as well as other valuable information, may be found in the material cited under REFERENCES.

The figures reveal a number of changes in the demographic composition of racial and ethnic minorities and women in each tier.

The University attributes the successful growth reflected in the figures to the affirmative action plans, goals and outreach activities that it has developed since 1988, including the following:

1) Establishment of the position of director of affirmative action for employment and business programs, within the Office of the President.

2) Creation of a Universitywide affirmative action advisory committee, reporting to a senior vice president, to identify new strategies and programs to improve the representation of minorities and women among UC management.

3) Development of seminars for UC administrators to increase their understanding of issues concerning disabled employees.

4) Creation of a successful advertising campaign to promote opportunities for minorities and women in UC administrative, managerial and professional jobs.

5) Training and career development programs for minority and women staff.

While development programs have been in place since 1978–79, the University has intensified its efforts in recent years. Currently, such programs include the following:

• The Management Fellowship Program, which provides career development opportunities and a UC Executive-level mentor for underrepresented minority and women staff to help them successfully compete for campus management jobs.

• The Management Skills Assessment Program, which provides minority and women employees at mid-level in administration with an assessment of their management potential.

• The Professional Skills Assessment Program, which is modeled after the Management Skills Assessment Program. It provides support employees with an assessment of their potential for professional careers.

• The Professional Internship Program, which provides mentors for minority and women employees, who take on assignments that enhance their experience and skills. The internships are designed to help employees better compete for professional and senior administrative jobs.

• The Computer Software Training Program, which is provided to specific administrative and support employees who require specialized computer skills. The on-the-job training and other special courses give employees basic technical skills and help them qualify for promotion.

• The Staff Affirmative Action Development Program, which provides funds to develop programs that assist underrepresented minorities and women in enhancing their job and career development skills to improve their opportunities for advancement. "Seed money" is also provided for model pilot programs that can be utilized at other UC locations.

As the 1990s proceed, the University maintains a strong commitment to affirmative action through programs such as these, in order to ensure the continued recruitment and promotion of underrepresented groups at all levels.

REFERENCES: Report on University Staff and Management Affirmative Action Programs, September 1992, Business and Employment Affirmative Action, and associated news releases, University Relations, Office of the President.

CROSS-REFERENCES: Other Affirmative Action.

A Four-Tier Personnel Program For University Employees

Beginning in 1986, the University instituted a four-tier personnel program system for staff and management employees.

The system was fully implemented at all campuses in July 1988.

Currently, the four programs are:

• The Executive Program, which includes positions which provide campus or Universitywide leadership and which are responsible for setting policy and program direction. Such positions include Officers of the University and senior-level administrators.

• The Management and Professional (MAP) Program, which includes management positions below the Executive level, together with senior-level professional positions, at the nine campuses, the Office of the President, and the Principal Officers of the Regents.

• The Administrative and Professional Staff (A&PS) Program, which includes positions that provide high-level administrative and professional support for UC's administrative offices, departments, programs and fields of study.

• The Staff Personnel Program, which includes employees throughout UC in a wide variety of occupational areas encompassing secretarial and clerical, service and maintenance, and various technical and paraprofessional job classifications.

Staff Personnel is the largest category of employees. It is comprised of persons in the Staff Personnel Program and those in the various collective bargaining units.

Affirmative Action—Business: As part of its affirmative action efforts, the University offers small businesses an opportunity to compete equally with larger companies for UC contracts in the areas of purchasing, construction, design and other professional services.

Within the Office of the President, the Office of Business Affirmative Action Programs is responsible for overseeing the progress of the Universitywide effort.

Since its inception in 1985–86, the program has focused on disadvantaged business enterprises and enterprises owned by women.

As of January 1992, the program also has included disabled veteran-owned business enterprises.

Each of UC's principal locations, including its nine campuses, five hospitals and several agricultural facilities, as well as the national laboratories managed by UC for the federal government, have coordinators who serve as UC liaisons for small businesses.

UC has developed a number of activities to promote business relationships with disadvantaged, minority, women, and disabled veteran contractors. These activities include the following:

Trade Fairs: Annual trade fairs are held at each of UC's principal locations, where small businesses owned by disadvantaged, women, and disabled veterans are invited to promote their products and services to UC buyers.

Buyer Training: UC has more than 100 buyers who receive training in developing relationships with disadvantaged, women, and disabled veteran vendors, and who attend seminars and workshops on issues such as negotiating techniques and identifying business opportunities.

Construction Workshops: These sessions are conducted for businesses owned by disadvantaged, women, and disabled veterans to help them better understand how to compete for UC construction contracts.

By 1990, UC also was planning to develop a computerized directory of small businesses that have been certified Universitywide as being owned by disadvantaged, women, or disabled veterans.

The University has been so successful in its business affirmative action efforts that it received a Special Award for Minority Business Development from the U.S. Department of Commerce, Minority Business Development Agency, San Francisco Regional Office, in 1992.

UC's business affirmative action program had its inception in November 1984 when the Regents adopted a policy on Affirmative Action in University Business Activities.

The program formally got under way in January 1985.

As amended in September 1991, the Regents' policy on Affirmative Action in University Business Activities reads as follows:

"It is the policy of the University of California, consistent with State and Federal law, to take affirmative action to optimize opportunities for business contracting with small business enterprises, particularly small disadvantaged, women's, and disabled veteran business enterprises, in areas of purchasing, construction, and design and other professional services provided to the University, and to ensure the placement of a fair proportion of business contracts with such enterprises."

Under this policy, procedures have been developed to ensure the placement of a fair proportion of UC contracts with small business enterprises. These procedures (which are consistent with state and federal law) include, but are not limited to, the following:

1) Establishment of annual targets for such enterprises, including subcontracts for construction.

2) Preparation of annual statistical reports on the participation of such enterprises.

3) Provision for allowing the award of a construction contract to such enterprises if a bid from one of them is substantially equal to the lowest bid of a majority-owned firm and it is in UC's best interest to make such an award.

4) Preparation of directories of disadvantaged business enterprises, women's business enterprises, and disabled veteran-owned business enterprises.

5) Establishment of outreach programs.

REFERENCES: Regents' Policy on Affirmative Action in University Business Activities, November 1984, revised September 1991; Annual Reports on University Business Affirmative Action Programs, Business and Employment Affirmative Action, Office of the President.

CROSS-REFERENCES: All topics related to Affirmative Action.

Business Affirmative Action: Looking at the Bottom Line

In the 1991–92 fiscal year, total Universitywide expenditures in the areas of purchasing, construction and design with respect to all large and small businesses reached $1.55 billion.

The previous year, the figure was $1.51 billion.

Of this total, small business enterprises (SBEs) received $515.59 million (33.33%).

Contract awards specifically to disadvantaged business enterprises (DBEs) totalled $129.21 million (8.32%). This represented a decrease from the previous year.

▶ DBEs include those owned by minority men and women.

▶ Contract awards to woman-owned business enterprises (WBEs) totalled $81.3 million (5.2%). This represented an increase over the previous year.

▶ WBEs are those owned by white females.

▶ Awards to disabled veteran-owned enterprises (DVBEs) totalled $127.41 thousand.

▶ The national laboratories managed by UC for the U.S. Department of Energy had $1.21 billion in combined expenditures in purchasing, construction and design in 1991–92.

▶ DBEs received $146.66 million (12.33%), and WBEs received $25.85 million (2.13%). (DVBE expenditures were not reported for 1991–92, since the national laboratories are exempt from having to meet state of California DVBE targets.)

Agriculture and Natural Resources: For more than a century, the research and extension programs of the University's Division of Agriculture and Natural Resources (DANR) have helped create a better life for Californians.

These programs have produced tangible benefits that touch everyone, including abundant, low-cost food supplies, improved nutrition, better management of natural resources and the environment, and high-quality educational opportunities for rural and urban youth.

In the tradition of land-grant universities, people in the Division are problem-solvers. DANR programs extend over a broad continuum, ranging from basic research in the laboratory, to applied research in the field and to the dissemination of practical, science-based information to farmers, ranchers, consumers, public officials and other decision-makers throughout California.

The Division is the leading organization of its kind in the nation. The Agricultural Experiment Station (AES), the Division's primary research arm, draws from 54 departments on the Berkeley, Davis and Riverside campuses.

DANR scientists form a world-respected team of basic and applied researchers, working to solve problems related to food, nutrition, agriculture, natural resources and the environment, veterinary medicine, and human and community resource development.

More than 1,100 research projects are underway in the Division at any one time, and AES scientists also help teach 8,000 graduate and undergraduate students at the campuses.

Cooperative Extension, the most visible public service arm of the University, serves Californians through county offices from Alturas in the north to San Diego on the U.S.-Mexican border. Campus-based specialists and county-based farm, home and youth development advisors work as teams to extend the results of UC's research to the public and to bring local research needs back to the campuses.

In addition, two dozen statewide programs—including integrated pest management, 4-H youth development, sustainable agriculture, water and wildland resources, small-scale farming, and nutrition education for low-income families—focus on areas of special concern.

The Division also operates the Natural Reserve System (NRS) and 10 research and extension centers. The 32-site NRS preserves a cross-section of California's natural habitats for research and instruction purposes. The off-campus research and extension centers provide labor, land and equipment in support of basic and applied research. They also help deliver a wide range of UC public service programs to local communities.

Among its many recent activities, the Division:

• Implemented biological control research programs to combat the ash and the silverleaf whiteflies, which are non-native pests that threaten California's agricultural and urban ornamental industries

• Published a widely circulated study revealing that agriculture anchors California's economy, generating about a tenth of all jobs and personal income in the state

• Was selected by the U.S. Forest Service to play a key role in a study of the Sierra Nevada ecosystem that promises to be one of the most significant science-based assessments of resource options ever conducted

• Expanded the 4-H Youth Development Program to serve more than 130,000 California youth, from rural counties to inner cities.

• Helped more than 10,000 California youngsters—many from underrepresented groups—gain a better understanding and appreciation for science through a UC program that has been adopted by 28 other states

• Expanded programs to improve farm and worker safety

• Established the Center for Pest Management Research and Extension to coordinate the work of UC scientists grappling with pest problems across the state

• Developed a quality after-school program for latchkey kids that has been implemented in some of California's most impoverished areas and replicated in 40 other states

• Organized a communitywide direct relief program for farm workers left jobless by a devastating freeze in the San Joaquin Valley

• Continued to advance the frontiers of basic biology, from which an array of agricultural and environmental biotechnologies will emerge in the coming decades

The Division is proud of its many accomplishments and its contributions to Californians in all walks of life and to the nation. As the 21st century approaches, however, new challenges and opportunities confront California and the Division.

These challenges include continuing California's abundance of food and fiber by maintaining a productive, internationally competitive agriculture; wisely managing the increasingly scarce natural resources of a rapidly growing society; protecting and enhancing the natural environment for future generations; improving opportunities for youth to play full and productive roles in California's future.

The people of the Division—dedicated to the principle of using science and education to help Californians help themselves—will be a vital resource for meeting these challenges.

REFERENCES: "Extending the Bounty of Research" and "A Harvest of Knowledge," informational brochures, Division of Agriculture and Natural Resources, 1992.

CROSS-REFERENCES: Research Achievements; subjects cited in the text.

DANR: A Sampling of Accomplishments Over the Years

• UC researchers led the first large-scale biological control effort conducted in an urban setting. Using a tiny stingless wasp that feeds on ash whiteflies, they controlled this non-native pest, which devastated urban ornamentals in the early 1990s and threatened California's nursery and agricultural industries.

• UC researchers unlocked the secrets of a key chemical that controls critical plant processes, from seed germination to the ripening of fruit. This work prolonged the shelf life of fruits, vegetables and flowers and provides consumers with better quality produce year-round.

• Before the 1940s, California produced only enough strawberries for its own consumers. Today, the state produces 80 percent of the nation's crop, thanks to UC scientists who developed strawberry varieties suited to California climates and soils, and cultural practices that maximized the yields of these varieties.

• The loss of a million acres of native oak woodlands—a rich habitat for wildlife—prompted UC scientists to seek better methods of oak regeneration. In a cooperative venture with state agencies, UC implemented a statewide oak regeneration research program, trained landowners and conservation groups in oak-planting techniques, and provided 100,000 seedlings for restoration projects in fire-ravaged areas.

• Millions of people in Africa were fed and famine was averted in the 1980s by a black-eyed bean developed by UC.

• For five decades, UC scientists have advanced the basic understanding of important livestock diseases and developed vaccines and other preventive measure to combat milk gland bacterial disease, rinderpest, blue tongue virus and Newcastle disease.

• UC scientists coined the term "integrated control," the forerunner of "integrated pest management" and pioneered the development of these innovative principles. The Division's IPM program, established in 1979, has contributed significantly to the reduction of pesticide and chemical use in California agriculture and is a model for similar programs across the nation.

• UC scientists have found a way to remove toxic levels of selenium in soil, using microbes that consume and neutralize the trace element. Ongoing large-scale field tests show promise for cleanup of contaminated soils and water and restoration of natural habitats.

• Since the 1930s, UC researchers and Cooperative Extension (CE) county advisors have helped make California wines among the best in the world by developing new grape varieties and new winemaking techniques.

• The SERIES (Science Experiences and Resources for Informal Education Settings) Program, developed by Cooperative Extension, stimulates young people's understanding and appreciation for science. More than 10,000 California youngsters have taken part in the program, which teaches high school students to guide pre-teens through a variety of hands-on science projects.

• Cooperative Extension specialists developed a practical family education program that teaches low-income families to stretch their household dollars. CE home economists teach the course in many counties, and the military has embraced the program for lower ranking military personnel.

• UC plays a significant role in developing seafood and fish farming in California. UC scientists have made important advances in oyster, trout and striped bass culture, in creating a viable sturgeon industry, and in finding the cause of "summer mortality" disease in shellfish.

• Tissue culture techniques developed by UC scientists established the foundation for plant biotechnology and are now used worldwide.

All Californians Benefit From "Programs for People"

"Programs for People" is a motto of the Division of Agriculture and Natural Resources.

The Division undertakes a number of special programs that serve particular needs, in addition to those conducted by the Agricultural Experiment Station, Cooperative Extension, and the Natural Reserve System (all described in their own sections of the book).

These special programs include:

• Agricultural Issues Center, which brings together experts from many disciplines to focus on significant public policy issues

• Agricultural Personnel Management Program, which fosters sound personnel management practices in California agriculture

• Aquaculture and Fisheries Program, which conducts research and educational programs relating to water plants, animals and fisheries

• Center for Cooperatives, which helps California's 30,000 rural and urban cooperatives prosper

• Center for Pest Management Research and Extension, which provides statewide leadership for the Division's pest management work

• Expanded Food and Nutrition Education Program, which strives to improve the nutrition of low-income families

• Farm Safety Program, which helps farmers and workers reduce deaths and injuries

• 4-H Youth Development Program, which helps some 120,000 young Californians become responsible adults

• Genetic Resources Conservation Program, which works to conserve the state's biological diversity

• Giannini Foundation, which encourages development of useful information in agricultural economics

• Integrated Hardwood Range Management Program, which helps California preserve its native oaks

• Integrated Pest Management Project, which helps farmers manage pests with economically and environmentally sound agricultural practices

• IR-4, which is a federally funded program generating registration data for minor crop use of pesticides

• Kearney Foundation of Soil Science, which conducts research in soil, water and plant sciences

• Mosquito Research Program, which helps control mosquitoes and mosquito-borne diseases

• Pesticide Impact Assessment Program, which conducts research and generates benefit assessment data on registered pesticides

• Pesticide Information and Coordination, which provides liaison between UC and state and federal agencies for pesticides

• Renewable Resources Extension Act Program, which assesses educational needs in managing California's forests and rangelands

• Salinity/Drainage Task Force, which focuses on drain water problems in the San Joaquin Valley

• Sea Grant Extension Program, which develops solutions for marine resource concerns in California

• Elvenia J. Slosson Endowment, which supports work in environmental horticulture

• Small Farm Program, which supports limited-resource farming efforts

• Sustainable Agriculture Research and Education Program, which helps agriculture move toward environmentally and economically sound production systems

• Urban Garden Program, which encourages community development and gardening for low-income people in Los Angeles

• Water Resources Center, which conducts research on the effective use of the state's water resources

• Wildlands Resources Center, which focuses on the conservation, management and use of wildlands

Sources: "Extending the Bounty of Research" and "A Harvest of Knowledge," informational booklet and folder, Division of Agriculture and Natural Resources, 1992.

The Agricultural Experiment Station: Projects from A to Z

The Agricultural Experiment Station (AES) has nearly 700 basic and applied scientists in nearly 60 disciplines working on more than 1,100 research projects from agronomy to zoology.

In seeking environmentally sound practices to produce reliable food supplies, these scientists contribute to the state's increase in farming productivity.

Their contributions to research have resulted in safe, abundant, inexpensive food for Californians.

Scientists also teach 8,000 graduate and undergraduate students in the Division's three colleges and one school.

These are the College of Natural Resources at Berkeley, the College of Agricultural and Environmental Sciences and School of Veterinary Medicine at Davis, and the College of Natural and Agricultural Sciences at Riverside.

The Agricultural Experiment Station is the oldest college-created experiment station in continuous operation in the nation.

It was founded in 1874, well ahead of the passage of the Hatch Act in 1887, which led to the establishment of agricultural experiment stations all across the nation.

REFERENCES: Centennial Record; "Extending the Bounty of Research" and "A Harvest of Knowledge," informational booklet and folder, Division of Agriculture and Natural Resources, 1992.

CROSS-REFERENCES: Agriculture and Natural Resources; Cooperative Extension; Natural Reserve System.

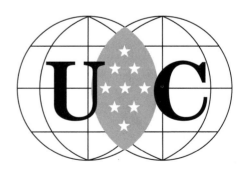

AIDS Research Program: In 1983, the California Legislature augmented the University's research budget so that UC could solicit and support important research in the fight against AIDS (Acquired Immune Deficiency Syndrome).

During the same year, UC's Office of the President established the Universitywide Task Force on AIDS to provide advice on utilization of AIDS research funds, program development, future direction, and policy emphasis.

The Task Force consists of scientists from UC's campuses and other academic institutions in California who are engaged in AIDS research. In 1992, outside non-faculty individuals with considerable expertise in AIDS issues were included to bring community-based members into the decision-making processes, along with the clinicians, basic scientists, and social scientists.

The Office of Health Affairs within the Office of the President is responsible for a component called the Universitywide AIDS Research Program (UARP).

UARP administers the funds allocated to this program, provides a point of contact for all interested parties, and acts as liaison between the Universitywide Task Force on AIDS and the State of California.

The UARP staff also coordinates the merit review of all applications by peer groups and ensures effective use of the funds.

Investigators whose work is funded by UARP have made progress in a number of major areas, including the following:

• Elucidating the processes involved in the disease.

• Developing drugs to benefit HIV-infected individuals.

• Evaluating the efficacy of drugs, in many cases speeding their licensing for use as treatment for AIDS and AIDS-associated diseases, thus extending survival time and quality of life for victims.

• Developing AIDS prevention strategies through education and behavior modification of groups at high risk for HIV infection.

• Developing models for clinical and social services.

• Improving the quality of patient care.

• Providing enhanced information to service providers and those responsible for program design and policy-making.

The search for new methods of treatment for AIDS virus infection and AIDS-associated opportunistic infections continues to be a high priority at the University and elsewhere.

Equally urgent is the development of a safe, effective vaccine to prevent the spread of AIDS virus infections.

While progress had been made during the decade since AIDS was first identified, it still remained a fatal disease that had yet to be controlled and eliminated.

However, victims have been living longer because of drugs developed to fight the disease.

AIDS was first recognized as a clinical entity in 1981.

It is characterized by a defect in a body's natural immunity that leaves a patient vulnerable to certain infections and malignancies. Such infections are not a threat to individuals whose immune system functions normally.

The disease is thought to be caused by a retrovirus called human immunodeficiency virus (HIV).

This retrovirus, or AIDS virus, infects primarily certain white blood cells which play a key role in the body's immune response to foreign substances.

It also can infect macrophages and other immune system cells and, occasionally, brain cells.

Thus, infection can lead to profound disturbances in immune function and may account for the neurologic symptoms seen in some patients with AIDS.

The diagnosis for AIDS is made only when a patient's condition meets certain clinical criteria established by the Centers for Disease Control of the U.S. Department of Health and Human Services.

These include more than 23 clinical conditions, such as the presence of unusual opportunistic infections, for example, one form of pneumonia, or unique malignancies (e.g., Kaposi's sarcoma).

In 1993, the case definition was expanded to include HIV-infected persons with certain T cell counts below 200 cells per microliter, pulmonary tuberculosis, recurrent pulmonary bacterial pneumonia, and invasive cervical cancer.

In patients who have not progressed to full-blown AIDS, the early symptoms, which are known as AIDS-related complex (ARC), persist for variable lengths of time.

In the U.S., the great majority of AIDS patients falls into certain high-risk groups. At first, AIDS had been identified mainly as a disease of gay men.

However, AIDS quickly began to spread among other groups.

These have included intravenous drug abusers, recipients of blood transfusions and blood products (particularly before the screening of blood was instituted), persons with hemophilia and other coagulation disorders, heterosexual partners of AIDS victims or members of high-risk groups, and children born of mothers who have AIDS or who are members of high-risk groups.

In 1993, the epidemic was spreading most rapidly among people of color, women, and sexually active adolescents.

As of February 1, 1993, some 253,443 cases of AIDS had been reported in the U.S. Corresponding cases in California totalled 49,135.

Nationwide, about one million people, including 200,000 Californians, were estimated to be HIV-infected.

The World Health Organization (WHO) reported that AIDS cases worldwide would continue to rise rapidly. It was estimated that 40 million people worldwide would be

Continued on page following chronology

From the Beginning: AIDS Treatment and Research

1981: Early reports point to a puzzling disease afflicting gay men: five cases in Los Angeles, six in San Francisco and 20 in New York are cited.

UCLA immunologist Michael Gottlieb co-writes the first national report on the disease.

1982: The disease gets the name AIDS, for Acquired Immune Deficiency Syndrome.

Pediatric immunologists at UCSF discover that the AIDS virus can be transmitted via blood transfusions.

1983: AIDS is declared the nation's top health priority by the U.S. Department of Health and Human Services.

A heat treatment for blood, developed by UCSF researchers, ensures the safety of the nation's blood supply against AIDS.

1984: UCSF scientists become one of three groups of researchers in the world to identify the AIDS virus.

1985: UC Davis scientists link a virus found in monkeys with AIDS, providing a laboratory model to develop a vaccine.

1986: Studies at UCLA, UCSF and UCSD lead to the approval of AZT for AIDS treatment.

1987: Research at UCSD shows that the AIDS virus impairs the brain.

Scientists at UCLA show that HIV strains isolated from a single individual have unique properties for growth in different cell types.

1988: The School of Nursing at UCSF becomes the first in the country to offer a graduate curriculum in AIDS and a minor in AIDS care.

1989: The death toll from AIDS tops more than 84,000 nationwide, according to the Centers for Disease Control in Atlanta.

A new drug, aerosolized pentamidine, gains federal approval after UCSF researchers show it curbs pneumocystis pneumonia, a leading cause of death among AIDS patients.

1990: The sixth International Conference on AIDS, hosted by UCSF, draws more than 12,000 scientists and health care workers and 2,000 reporters.

Researchers at UC Irvine find a similarity between cancer cells and HIV-infected cells, a link that could help overcome a resistance to AZT.

Testing for an experimental AIDS vaccine begins at UC-affiliated San Francisco General Hospital, the first trial in California involving people not infected with HIV.

1991: U.S. News & World Report ranks San Francisco General Hospital No. 1, the UCSF Medical Center No. 2 and the UCLA Medical Center No. 4 for AIDS treatment nationwide.

UCLA scientist identifies resistance to caring for HIV positive patients among primary care physicians.

UC Berkeley scientists find evidence that genetics determine why some HIV-infected people succumb quickly to AIDS while others fight off the disease for years.

In recent years, questions are being raised about the importance of cofactors in AIDS.

1992: Testing for experimental AIDS vaccines and searching for new drugs are underway at the Davis, San Francisco, Los Angeles, and San Diego campuses.

In the absence of an effective drug or vaccine for AIDS, research continues on prevention of HIV transmission via sexual and other risk-taking behaviors.

Scientists at UC San Francisco develop a blood test to detect HIV infection in infants younger than three months, a group difficult to diagnose with standard HIV testing.

A UC San Francisco study suggests that HIV transmission from infected mothers to newborns occurs through new HIV strains resistant to maternal antibodies.

Homeless adults in San Francisco show high rates of tuberculosis and HIV infection.

HIV antibody is detected in nine percent of blood-contaminated needles obtained from an intravenous drug abuse needle exchange program in San Francisco.

The bacillus Hemophilus ducreyi, which causes genital ulcer disease, is highly associated with risk of HIV transmission among heterosexuals.

AT UC San Diego, studies with an animal model show that local treatments with a water soluble drug (HPMC) are nontoxic and effective in controlling retinitis, common in AIDS patients, for a prolonged period.

UC Irvine scientists and others in the U.S. and abroad report an "AIDS-like" disease (now called idiopathic CD4+ T lymphocytopenia, or ICL) in persons not infected with HIV. Studies suggest that ICL may not pose a public health threat.

UCLA investigators observe that erythropoietin, a blood cell stimulating factor, reduces AZT-induced anemia in AIDS patients, leading to FDA approval for use of this compound.

UCLA scientists find that the drug foscarnet is effective in treating acyclovir-resistant herpes simplex virus infection in AIDS patients.

1992/93: Physicians at UCLA show that the simple measurement of acid dissociated p24 antigen makes possible the diagnosis in infants born of HIV positive mothers at birth and within the first few days of life.

Presence of autologous neutralizing antibody to HIV in maternal serum was shown by scientists at UCLA to be associated with the prevention of transmission of virus from mother to fetus.

A UCLA study shows that AZT treatment of mothers with low CD4 counts during gestation and at the time of delivery significantly reduces HIV transmission to infant.

AIDS *(Cont'd)*

infected with HIV by the end of this decade. Some 90 percent would be in developing countries.

Because the virus mutates into different strains, it has been extremely difficult to find a vaccine that will work against the disease.

Even detecting the virus in an individual has not been a simple matter.

However, the presence or absence of infection could be assessed by an AIDS antibody test. (Antibodies are proteins made by the immune system cells in response to foreign substances, such as the AIDS virus.)

And by 1993, scientists were hopeful that medical advances eventually could reach the point where doctors would know how to suppress the AIDS virus and keep it in check, thus allowing patients to live a normal life.

Until a vaccine and more effective drugs are developed, social/behavioral research aimed at prevention of HIV transmission continues to be a high priority.

REFERENCES: "Facts About AIDS," informational document for the Regents, October 1986, "A Decade of Despair and Discovery," *UC Focus,* September/October 1991, "UC AIDS Research Program Making Progress," news release, October 31, 1991, University Relations, Office of the President, and annual reports, Universitywide AIDS Research Program, Office of Health Affairs (all sources within the Office of the President). Also, Das NK, CL Hopper, M Jencks, J Silva. A University of California State-supported AIDS research award program—A unique State and university partnership in AIDS research. J. Clin Immunol 11:65–73, 1991. Lewis D, NK Das, CL Hopper, M Jencks. A program of support for AIDS research in the social/ behavioral sciences. MIRA $\underline{5}$ (3), September 1991.

CROSS-REFERENCES: Health Sciences.

All-University Faculty Conferences: University of California President Robert Gordon Sproul initiated the first All-University Faculty Conference in 1944.

When the first conference was being planned, there was no thought of repeating the event.

However, before it was over, many delegates expressed a desire for future meetings.

The second conference was held in 1947.

Further conferences, all convened by the president of the University, were held each year or every other year through 1976, when the 30th All-University Faculty Conference was held.

After that, for budgetary and other reasons, the annual assembly was discontinued until 1990.

The conferences have been designed to:

• Stimulate broad faculty consideration of University-wide problems.

• Give faculty members an opportunity to discuss these problems freely, frankly and thoroughly, with other faculty members, the president and Regents.

• Foster a sense of unity among delegates who come from all the campuses.

Recommendations about study topics, delegates and general arrangements are made by a Faculty Steering Committee appointed by the president.

Between 125 and 200 or more delegates have participated in the conferences, which usually have been held over a three-day period in the spring.

Although such conferences do not produce policy, their resolutions are recognized as important guides to planning and action.

Conference proceedings are published each year. They incorporate the initial study committee reports, summaries of the conference discussions, and the resolutions passed by the conferees.

The first All-University Faculty Conference since 1976 was held Feb. 8–10, 1990.

The subject of this 31st conference was "Graduate Student and Faculty Affirmative Action."

More than 150 leading UC faculty, senior administrators and Regents attended the gathering to consider strategies for meeting the challenges of changing demographics and cultural diversity at UC.

During the conference, participants considered how the faculty could improve the rates by which students from various ethnic groups qualify for UC.

Participants also pondered means of improving the percentage of minorities in UC's graduate and professional schools, as well as approaches that the faculty could develop to help achieve such a goal.

The faculty deliberations eventually were assembled into a final report that contained a number of recommendations.

In February 1992, more than 200 UC faculty members, administrators and Regents gathered for the 1992 All-University Faculty Conference.

The topic was "The Role of the Department in Shaping and Delivering Undergraduate Education at the University of California."

A large number of ideas emerged from the conference's small group sessions, panel discussions and keynote addresses.

From these, conference participants and Office of the President staff formulated a report on strengthening UC's undergraduate education.

All-University Faculty Conferences

1. Postwar University Conference, November 3–5, 1944 (the first conference, which was general in nature).

2. "The Relation of the University to the State," February 8–10, 1947.

3. "How Can the Educational Effectiveness of the University Be Improved?", February 9–11, 1948.

4. "The University of California in the Next Ten Years," April 28–30, 1949.

5. "Problems and Opportunities of the Large University," April 27–29, 1950.

6. "The Graduate Academic Function of the University," April 26–28, 1951.

7. "The Function of the Upper Division in the University," May 1–3, 1952.

8. "The Faculty and the Educational Policies of the University," April 30, May 1–2, 1953.

9. "How to Appraise the Value of the University to Society," April 29–30, May 1, 1954.

10. "The University of California Student, 1945–65," April 28–30, 1955.

11. "The Role of the University in Higher Education in California," April 27–29, 1956.

12. "Quality of Education in Relation to Numbers," April 4–6, 1957.

13. "University of California: Retrospect and Prospect," April 2–4, 1958.

14. Autonomy and Centralization in the State-Wide University," April 2–4, 1959.

15. "The Research Function of the University," April 12–14.

16. "The University in a Period of Growth," March 27–29, 1961.

17. "New and Continuing Problems in an Expanding University," April 16–18, 1962.

18. "The Student and the Quality of His Intellectual Environment in the University," April 7–10, 1963.

19. "The University of California 1944–64–84: Responses and Responsibilities," March 22–25, 1964.

20. "Undergraduate Education and Its Relation to High School and Junior College," April 11–14, 1965.

21. "The Arts and the Humanities in the University," April 3–6, 1966.

22. "The University as a Major Influence in the State," March 20–23, 1967.

23. "The University as It Enters Its Second Century," (the Centennial Year Conference), March 19–21, 1968.

24. "The Urban Crisis," March 23–25, 1969.

25. "Problems and Opportunities of the Extended University," March 25–27, 1970.

26. "The Future of Graduate and Professional Education in the University," March 23–25, 1971.

27. "The University in the Seventies: The Impacts of Changing Circumstances," March 26–28, 1973.

28. "Applied and Public Service Research in the University of California," March 26–28, 1974.

29. "The Entering Undergraduate Student: Changes and Educational Implications," March 24–26, 1975.

30. "Undergraduate Education in the University of California," March 25–27, 1976.

31. "Graduate Student and Faculty Affirmative Action," February 8–10, 1990.

32. "Undergraduate Education at the University of California," September, 1992.

REFERENCES: Centennial Record; Reports of All-University Faculty Conferences, Office of the President.

CROSS-REFERENCES: Admissions; Affirmative Action; Arts; Public Service and Community Relations; Education; Humanities; Research Achievements.

Alumni Associations of the University of California: In 1975 the alumni associations from the University's nine campuses joined together to create an association representing all UC alumni.

The entity was named The Alumni Association of the University of California (AAUC). The name was changed to The Alumni Associations of the University of California in 1988.

The constitution and bylaws of the group became effective on June 15, 1975, having been approved in principle by the respective presidents on April 3, 1975 and formally approved by the member associations in the period of mid-April to early July.

(The original constitution, effective June 15, 1948, had been approved by a vote of the majority of the members of the councils of the California Alumni Association, representing Berkeley, and the University of California, Los Angeles Alumni Association.)

The AAUC encompasses representatives from each of UC's nine independent alumni associations.

As an umbrella organization, it links all of UC's alumni and friends for one primary purpose: to promote the welfare of UC by fostering goodwill among public officials and the general public.

Membership includes these campus-wide alumni associations (the first two named are the associations at Berkeley and Davis, respectively): California Alumni Association, California Aggie Alumni Association, UCI Alumni Association, UCLA Alumni Association, UCR Alumni Association, UCSB Alumni Association, UCSC Alumni Association, UCSD Alumni Association, and Alumni Association of UCSF.

The purposes of the umbrella association are to:

• Create an organization representative of all UC alumni.

• Promote UC's welfare through legislative advocacy.

• Provide for the selection of the member(s) of the Board of Regents to represent the alumni, as provided in the State Constitution.

• Provide for the selection of a secretary and a treasurer invited to attend meetings of the Regents pursuant to its bylaws (these two are commonly referred to as "Regents-Designate.")

• Provide for the selection of a UC alumnus to serve on the governor's advisory committee on the selection of Regents, as provided in the State Constitution.

(The Constitution stipulates that seats on the Board be held by "the president and the vice president of the alumni association of the University.")

• Facilitate an exchange of ideas, experiences and resources among constituent members.

• Promote and conduct activities of mutual benefit to the constituent members of the University.

In the fiscal year commencing July 1, 1975, the offices of president, vice president, secretary and treasurer were to be held for a term of one fiscal year by the president or other duly designated representative of the member associations.

REFERENCES: Constitution and Bylaws of The Alumni Association of the University of California, April 11, 1975 (rev.), and "AAUC, The Alumni Associations of the University of California," folder for alumni, University Relations, Office of the President.

CROSS-REFERENCES: Regents.

Alumni of the University Who Have Made a Difference

From the first graduating class in 1873 to the present, many UC alumni have been acclaimed as leaders and innovators in their respective fields.

They have contributed in diverse ways to the state, the nation or the world in fields as wide-ranging as science, public service, education, the arts, entertainment, business, philanthropy, the environment, athletics and other areas of endeavor.

An early outstanding alumnus was James H. Budd, California governor from 1895 to 1899. He had been one of the 12 men in UC's first graduating class (B.A. 1873).

Another of the early alumni was Rose L. Scrivener, first woman graduate of UC and the only woman in her graduating class (B.A. 1874). She and eight women of the 1876 class chose blue and gold as UC's colors.

The following roll call of alumni is only a representative sample of other notable individuals, selected from among the scores who have achieved public stature (their year of graduation is noted in parenthesis).

Julia Morgan (B.S. 1894), California's pioneering woman architect, gave the state a rich legacy of impressive buildings that remain renowned and admired to this day. In the arts, there have been luminaries such as Agnes DeMille (B.A. 1926), choreographer who brought ballet form to the musical theater.

Alice Waters (B.A. 1967) became an internationally noted chef who helped create California cuisine.

In the field of literature, Irving Stone (B.A. 1923), was a widely read novelist and biographer. Also known for distinguished and incisive works is Joan Didion (B.A. 1956 UCB), novelist, poet and playwright. Maxine Hong Kingston (B.A. 1962), a UC professor, is the best-selling author of books including "Woman Warrior" and "China Men."

Among those dedicated to our natural environment have been Horace Albright (B.A. 1912), the noted conservationist who served with distinction as director of the National Parks Service from 1929 to 1933; Roger Revelle (Ph.D. 1936), internationally known oceanographer, father of the greenhouse warming theory; and Julie Packard (B.A. 1974, M.A. 1978), executive director of the Monterey Bay Aquarium, one of the nation's most innovative aquariums.

Leading University figures have been Robert G. Sproul (B.A. 1913), first UC president, who served from 1930 to 1958; Clark Kerr, (Ph.D. 1939), UC president from 1958 to 1967 and a national leader in higher education; and David P. Gardner (M.A. 1959, Ph.D. 1966), UC president from 1983 to 1992, president of the William and Flora Hewlett Foundation, and a leader in national higher education. Other noted educators have included John B. Slaughter (M.S. 1961, Ph.D. 1971), president of Occidental College in Los Angeles since 1988, director of the National Science Foundation from 1980 to 1982, who was named the first "Black Engineer of the Year" by *U.S. Black Engineer* magazine in 1987.

Nobel laureates have included William F. Giauque (B.S. 1920, Ph.D. 1922), 1949 Nobel Prize winner in chemistry, who was recognized for his work to determine the properties of matter and its transformation; Harold C. Urey (Ph.D 1923), 1934 Nobel Prize winner in chemistry; Willard F. Libby, (B.S. 1931, Ph.D. 1933), 1960 Nobel Prize winner in chemistry; and Glenn T. Seaborg (B.A. 1934, Ph.D. 1937), Berkeley chancellor from 1958 to 1961, co-discoverer of plutonium, 1951 Nobel Prize winner in chemistry.

Other Nobelists have been R. Bruce Merrifield (B.S. 1943, Ph.D. 1949), 1984 Nobel laureate in chemistry; William Sharpe (B.A. 1955, M.A. 1956, Ph.D. 1961), Stanford University professor who shared the 1990 Nobel Prize in economics; Yan T. Lee (Ph.D. 1965), UC Berkeley chemistry professor, 1986 Nobel laureate in chemistry; Susumu Tonegawa (M.D. 1968), 1988 Nobel Prize winner in medicine for research on the immune system.

Other alumni on the international scene have included Ralph Bunche Jr. (B.A. 1927, L.L.B. 1950), United Nations undersecretary general who in 1950 became the first African American to win the Nobel Peace Prize; Robert McNamara (B.A. 1937), U.S. Secretary of the Defense from 1961 to 1966 and president of the World Bank from 1968 to 1981; and Barbara Bodine (B.A. 1970), first woman to serve as a U.S. embassy deputy chief in an Arab country when assigned in 1989 to Kuwait, where she served during the 1990 Persian Gulf War; she went on to be associate coordinator for counter-terrorism in the U.S. State Department.

Other UC alumni have been recognized throughout the world for their outstanding professional skill in meeting awesome challenges. Among them have been Marguerite Higgins (B.A. 1941), 1949 Pulitzer Prize winner for international news for her reporting in Korea, and Kathryn Sullivan (B.A. 1973), the first American woman to walk in space.

Among individuals distinguished by their public service have been Earl Warren (B.A. 1912, J.D. 1914), California governor from 1945 to 1953 and chief justice of the U.S. Supreme Court from 1953 to 1969; John A. McCone (B.A. 1922), businessman, presidential adviser and director of the CIA during the Kennedy and Johnson administrations, from 1961 to 1965; and John Kenneth Galbraith (M.A. 1932, Ph.D. 1934), adviser to President John F. Kennedy and ambassador to India from 1961 to 1963.

Others who served in important capacities have been William French Smith (B.A. 1939), former UC Regent who served as U.S. Attorney General from 1981 to 1984; Edwin Meese III (L.L.B. 1958), U.S. attorney general, 1985–88; and Yvonne Brathwaite Burke (B.A. 1954), lawyer, former UC Regent, Los Angeles County supervisor, former California assemblywoman, former U.S. representative, and first African American woman elected to Congress from California (1972).

Leading California public servants have included Edmund G. "Jerry" Brown Jr. (B.A. 1961), California governor, 1975–82; Pete Wilson (J.D. 1962), California governor, elected in 1990; March Fong Eu (B.S. 1948), California secretary of state, former California assemblywoman, and first Asian American elected to the State Legislature, in 1966; Rose E. Bird (M.S. 1962, J.D. 1965), chief justice of the California Supreme Court, 1977–87, the first woman in that post; and Willie L. Brown Jr. (J.D. 1958), California assembly speaker, 1980–present, the first African American to be elected to the post.

Other leading figures on the public scene in California have been Tom Bradley (attended UC 1939–40), Los Angeles mayor, 1973–93; Elihu Harris (J.D. 1972), mayor of Oakland since 1991, former California assemblyman; and Michael Woo (B.A. 1973), the first Asian American elected to the Los Angeles City Council.

National and internationally renowned sports figures have included Helen Wills Roark (who attended UC 1923–1926), one of the all-time great tennis players who won eight Wimbledon singles championships from 1927 to 1938, a record equaled only by another tennis great a half century later; Archie F. Williams (B.S 1939), California's first individual Olympic gold-medal winner in track and field, who in 1936 set a world record in the 400-meter run; Jackie Robinson (who attended UC 1939–41), the first African American to play Major League baseball; and Rafer Johnson (B.S. 1959), Olympic decathlon gold medalist in 1960.

Equally renowned and admired have been Arthur Ashe Jr. (B.S. 1966), first African American to win a Wimbledon championship, in 1975; Kareem Abdul-Jabbar (B.A. 1969), all-time scoring leader in the National Basketball Association and six-time NBA Most Valuable Player; Greg Louganis (B.A. 1982), four-time 1988 Olympic gold medalist in diving; Donna E. de Varona (B.A. 1986), double 1964 Olympic gold medalist in swimming; Jackie Joyner-Kersee (B.A. 1986), 1988 Olympic gold medalist in both the heptathlon and long jump; and Matt Biondi (B.A. 1988), winner of 11 Olympic medals (eight gold, two silver and a bronze) in swimming from the 1984, 1988 and 1992 games; he tied with two others for the most Olympic medals won by an American.

Leaders in the business community have included Dean Witter (B.A. 1909), founder of one of the nation's largest stock brokerage firms, as well as members of the Haas family who were executives of Levi Strauss & Co. The following helped build that firm into the world's largest apparel company: Walter A. Haas, Sr. (B.S. 1910) and sons Walter A., Jr. (B.A. 1937) and Peter E. (B.A. 1940).

Other business leaders have been Stephen D. Bechtel, Sr. (attended UC 1919–21), chairman, 1936–69, of the world's largest privately held construction and engineering company; Edgar F. Kaiser (attended 1926–30), industrialist who, with his father Henry J., established the first health maintenance organization and the first planned living communities; and Edward W. Carter (B.A. 1932), former UC Regent and co-founder of a major retail chain.

Also notable have been the Ahmanson brothers: Robert (B.S. 1949), president of one of the nation's largest charitable foundations, and William H. (B.S. 1950), chairman, 1969–86, of the parent company of one of the nation's largest savings and loan.

Finally, the field of entertainment has been enhanced by the presence of noted actor Gregory Peck (B.A. 1942); Carol Burnett (A.A. 1954), actress, comedienne, five-time Emmy-award winner; and Michael Douglas (B.A. 1968), Academy-award winning actor and producer.

Source: Communications Services, Office of the President, from a list of 125 outstanding alumni (June/July 1993), based on information provided by UC's campuses.

American University of Armenia:

American University of Armenia: In the summer of 1991, the University took its first steps to help develop the first American university in Armenia.

In July 1991, the Regents approved UC's proposal to assist in establishing the new academic institution, and in August, UC representatives arrived in the Soviet Republic of Armenia. At the time, students were being selected for admission.

The UC representatives continued into very early September working out arrangements for the new university.

On September 5, 1991, UC President David P. Gardner signed the affiliation agreement approved earlier by the Regents, and the American University of Armenia was formally established in Yerevan, the capital of Armenia.

At the time, the plan was to move the site to facilities to be completed three to four years hence in nearby Abovian.

Under the terms of the agreement, UC agreed to:

(1) Train Armenians as faculty for the new university through the UC's normal graduate education process, (2) develop a curriculum and an administrative plan, (3) design the campus, and (4) develop an exchange and cooperation program between UC and the new university.

The development of the new university was expected to provide an ongoing, cooperative student and academic exchange program that would enhance learning, research and teaching at both institutions.

The new institution is being funded by the Republic of Armenia and the Armenian General Benevolent Union, a philanthropic organization with headquarters in the U.S.

The organization had asked UC to help develop an institution based on American models because of UC's noted academic reputation.

The undertaking was a joint venture between the Republic of Armenia's Ministry of Higher Education and Science and the American University of Armenia Corporation.

UC's participation in the project is based on its affiliation with the American University of Armenia Corporation, a nonprofit California corporation founded by a group of private individuals, including several UC administrators and faculty.

There is no cost to UC for the development of the new university. The Armenian General Benevolent Union provided initial funding and is primarily responsible for fund-raising.

UC had been interested in the joint venture, because it would give it a presence in an important area of the (now former) Soviet Union, provide opportunities for teaching and research, and raise its public service role to an even greater international level.

Mihran S. Agbabian, an Armenian-American and chair of the department of civil engineering at the University of Southern California, was appointed the first president of the new university.

Armen Der Kiureghian, UC Berkeley professor of civil engineering, was appointed dean of the new university's College of Engineering, and Stepan Karamardian, former UC Riverside dean, was named dean of the College of Business Management.

The Armenian University received 102 applicants for its first semester. The academic program began in spring 1992 with graduate programs in earthquake engineering, industrial engineering, and business management.

About 80 percent of the applications were for the business management program, which was the first of its kind in the Soviet Union.

(Despite major earthquake damage in Armenia before the new university opened, the numbers of applicants for studies in earthquake engineering were the fewest among the three programs. The greatest interest was in

---

The University That Could, And the Coup That Couldn't

Almost as soon as UC representatives arrived in the Soviet Republic of Armenia, a major event posed a possible threat to their plans to help develop the first American university there.

At the time, in August 1991, students were being selected for admission to the new academic institution.

One day all the radio and television stations in the country abruptly started playing classical music in place of their regular programs.

This shift in programming indicated that the stations had imposed a news blackout.

From experience, the Armenian people knew that a major event was in the making, maybe even a change in power within the Soviet Union.

Rumors, including those of a massed Soviet army, assassination and civil war were widespread; but, no one, including the UC representatives, could learn what was actually happening.

During this time, a coup attempt was made to topple Soviet President Mikhail Gorbachev and Russian President Boris Yeltsin.

But within three days the coup leaders lost their gamble, and the two leaders regained power. (Ultimately, however, the Soviet Union would break apart.)

After the coup was over, the UC representatives continued through the rest of August and early September working out arrangements for the new university.

---

the study of joint business ventures, particularly with the U. S.)

Classes in the three graduate programs are taught in English by American-trained instructors, primarily from UC and the University of Southern California, in a building that previously housed a communist youth education program. Each program takes two years to complete.

The academic calendar is March through November, primarily so that the American professors can teach classes on their summer breaks.

(However, weather is also an important factor. It is very cold in the winter, and the supply of fuel is not assured.)

A new campus is planned for construction by the mid-1990s.

REFERENCES: "American University Gets Off the Ground During Coup," *Intercom*, September 1991, and related news releases, Office of the President; related Regents' items.

Animals in Research and Teaching, Use of: On October 15, 1984, the president of the University issued a policy on the use of animals in research and teaching, effective as of that date.

Before and after the policy was issued, animal activist groups demonstrated and, in some instances, carried out illegal acts in opposition to the use of animals in research and teaching.

The University suffered some of the earliest and most destructive actions against research facilities, including criminal break-ins of laboratories, vandalism and the destruction by arson of a $3 million building at UC Davis.

Such violence subsequently spread throughout the U. S. and eventually led to the passage of a federal anti-break-in bill in 1992.

The University's position is that it has a mandate to promote the best biomedical research, and it has strongly supported the animal research of its faculty. For example, research and teaching activities in a large number of scientific fields, from basic physiology to applied veterinary medicine, require the use of live animal models.

The University's policy sets forth common procedures that assure not only the humane use of animals, but the continued maintenance of high standards of animal care.

The preamble to UC's policy on the use of animals in research and teaching states:

"The University of California recognizes the importance of the use of animals in its research and teaching programs. Animals are vital both for understanding basic biological processes and in developing treatment for human and animal diseases.

"The University, committed to maintaining high standards for the care and use of animals in research and teaching, therefore adopts as its own principles the National Institutes of Health (NIH) 'Principles for Use of Animals.'"

A further statement notes: "The University, including its investigators and researchers, accepts responsibility for determining that research and teaching involving the use of animals fulfill these principles."

The policy requires UC facilities to be in compliance with all state and federal laws and regulations affecting animals.

The University's institution animal care and use committees, which include members from outside UC, review and approve research proposals. These committees have the authority to suspend animal research activities that do not conform to federal law and regulations.

The committees also are required to conduct inspections of animal research facilities.

REFERENCES: Information, State Legislative Issues, Office of the President.

CROSS-REFERENCES: Animal Research and Teaching Alternatives.

Animal Research and Teaching Alternatives: A
program to promote the use of alternatives in animal research, teaching and testing was developed at the University in 1991.

UC already had been doing a great deal with alternatives to animal research. In addition, much was being done nationally.

Specifically, the program was designed to provide information about alternatives in order to promote what commonly have been known as "the three R's."

These refer to "replacement, reduction or refinement" of animal use in research, teaching and testing.

"Replacement" means the use of research methods that do not require animals.

Replacement can be achieved in some situations by the use of cell or tissue cultures, and physical, chemical and computer models that mimic bodily functions.

"Reduction" means the use of fewer animals, which can be achieved through improved animal care methods and the use of sophisticated statistical methods.

"Refinement" of animal care and use can include use of new veterinary procedures to improve the well being of research animals.

The program assists all UC campuses by organizing and managing:

• A computerized database containing material on animal alternatives, including information on innovative research models.

• A reference library with materials on animal alternatives.

• A clearinghouse for new software, videotapes and other educational materials for use in teaching.

• Outreach and educational activities such as conferences and workshops.

The UC alternatives program was the result of efforts begun in 1988.

In response to a report that year by UC's Animal Alternative Study Task Force and a subsequent request from the State Legislature, the Office of the President studied the development of a program to promote alternatives.

An advisory committee appointed by UC's president in 1989 included representatives from UC, animal welfare groups, industry, government and other universities.

This committee recommended that UC create an alternatives program.

The program has been conducted with the assistance of an executive committee consisting of representatives from each campus and the Department of Energy laboratories operated by UC.

The executive committee has helped set the priorities of the program and has reviewed the performance of the director's office.

REFERENCES: Joint news release, December 18, 1991, Public Information Office, UC Davis, and University Relations, Office of the President.

CROSS-REFERENCES: Animal Research and Teaching; Medical and Health Sciences.

Anniversary Commemoration: The University
celebrated its 125th anniversary in 1993.

The anniversary marked the first major Universitywide celebration of its years of service to California and the nation since UC's centennial in 1968.

The occasion commemorated the University's achievements in teaching, research and public service and its contributions to California higher education.

Throughout the University, anniversary events commemorated the vision of UC's founders, its accomplishments over the past 125 years, and the state's heritage of cultural diversity, all of which have contributed to making UC a premier public institution of higher learning.

During the commemoration, UC reassessed its founders' goals in the light of the contemporary and future needs of the state, the nation and the world.

In so doing, the University community recognized that it faced critical challenges unlike any that it had experienced in its history.

At the same time, the University reaffirmed its deep trust in the capacity of the institution to meet those challenges, with the strong support of its many alumni, friends and supporters.

As the anniversary celebrations around the University came to a close, UC's leaders and the University community pledged to continue making the institution a valuable resource to the state and the nation into the next century.

(For the 125th anniversary, UC created a logo and slogan to link the various events and publications associated with the occasion. The logo appears below.)

The Arts: Notable Programs Across the Campuses

Each campus of the University has notable programs in the arts.

Within the Office of the President, a coordinator for intercampus arts (ICA) works with the Intercampus Arts Committee, which represents music, dance, visual arts, theatre, galleries, museums and the presenting organizations, to encourage artistic endeavors across the campuses.

("Presenting organizations" are those that are responsible for the presentation of musical, dramatic, artistic, dance and other cultural offerings at the campuses.)

The Intercampus Arts Committee's responsibilities include promoting the visual and performing arts at the University, fostering artistic interaction among the campuses, and supporting collaboration and exchange of artistic activities throughout UC.

Any faculty or staff member or any UC organization may initiate a proposal for ICA funding by applying to the coordinator's office.

These are the four funding categories available to applicants:

• Touring Artists, which is designed to help support tours by UC performing and visual artists to other campuses.

For performers, this category supports faculty, staff and student artists who perform individually or in ensemble.

For visual artists, including film and video, this category supports both solo and group exhibitions.

Funds are available for travel and, in the case of faculty artists, for an honorarium.

• Intercampus Travel, which funds transportation costs for student groups to attend performances and exhibitions at other UC campuses. Such groups may be organized by faculty in conjunction with a class or sponsored by a campus organization.

• Special Projects, which funds collaborative projects involving at least three campuses. These include, but are not limited to, festivals, conferences, joint productions and exhibitions, and other projects not covered by the preceding categories.

In Fall 1990, ICA established advisory committees in the major arts disciplines (music, visual arts, theatre, dance) to develop and recommend collaborative projects for ICA consideration.

The projects may be generated within the committees (which consist of faculty representatives from the various campuses) or be the result of proposals made by any faculty or staff member.

• Residencies and Masterclasses, which is a category of funding that may be used by UC faculty or guest artists from outside UC to work with students in a teaching capacity.

ICA does not fund individual faculty research, travel for individual faculty or student artists outside UC, or the creation or commission of new works by UC faculty or students.

REFERENCES: "ICA Intercampus Arts," 1991–92 folder, ICA Program Coordinator, Academic Affairs Office, Office of the President.

CROSS-REFERENCES: Humanities.

On the next page are some of UC's artistic endeavers.

THE ARTS

The world of the arts at UC attracts many students who demonstrate energy and versatility, as well as exceptional talent.

As shown on these pages, their range of talent extends, for example, to music, painting and dance.

Outstanding students also are engaged in opera, film-making and drama.

Many of the students go on to make their mark as artists in the professional world, while others use the skills they learned at UC to enrich their personal lives.

Associate of the President/Chancellor: In 1987, a University policy provided for the designation of an "Associate of the President/Chancellor."

The policy states that, upon the recommendation of a chancellor, the president may approve the appointment of the chancellor's spouse as "Associate of the Chancellor."

In addition, upon consultation with the Regents' chairman, the president may authorize the appointment of the president's spouse as "Associate of the President."

The appointments are without salary and do not convey employee status.

The two designations are intended to reflect and recognize the contributions and services to the University of those spouses under two circumstances: when hosting UC events in an official capacity or when acting officially for UC or the president or chancellor at various activities.

These include meetings, workshops, conferences, UC and community activities, alumni and fund-raising events, or gatherings of faculty, students or staff.

In addition, the appointment acknowledges each Associate's oversight responsibilities in planning and arranging many of the above functions and in managing an official UC residence.

This appointment is not automatic; it is conditional on the spouse's being significantly involved in the above activities and functions.

The following is provided to each individual when acting in the capacity of an Associate, in accordance with UC policy and procedures:

An identification card for libraries and other UC facilities; reimbursement for travel and travel insurance coverage; workers' compensation coverage; automobile allowance; business cards; and courtesy parking permits for UC sites.

In September 1990, as additional recognition of the services provided to UC by the Associates, the Regents approved a special augmentation to the Executive Program severance pay plan for Associates of the President/Chancellors.

However, in November 1992, the Regents suspended the augmentation because of the impact of the continuing state budget crisis on UC.

The contributions and responsibilities of the eligible spouses of the president and chancellors continue to be recognized by appointment as Associate on a without-compensation basis, but with all other benefits that have been approved for the appointment.

REFERENCES: "Policy on Associate of the President/Chancellor," November 1, 1987, Office of the President; "Amendment of Policy on Executive Program Severance Pay Plan to Suspend Special Augmentation for Associates of the President/Chancellors," Item 506 for Action, Regents' Committee on Finance, November 18, 1992.

CROSS-REFERENCES: Chancellors.

Auxiliary Enterprises: Auxiliary enterprises are non-instructional support services provided primarily to students in return for specified charges.

Auxiliary enterprises generate sufficient revenues to cover all direct and indirect operating costs.

During 1992–93, it was anticipated that $385,453,000 would be generated through auxiliary enterprises and expended approximately as follows: 59 percent, residence and dining services; 12 percent, parking operations (including van pools); 6 percent, intercollegiate athletics; 17 percent bookstores; and 6 percent, other.

The largest element in this budget program is student housing, which consists of approximately 27,100 residence hall spaces and 9,800 apartments with associated dining and recreation facilities.

These facilities housed about 43,300 students in 1992–93. They are available to single students and student families and, in addition, may be used as conference and visitor housing during the summer months.

A subset of the student housing element is faculty rental housing. Approximately 616 faculty units are available at four campuses: Irvine, Los Angeles, San Diego and Santa Cruz.

The units are self-supporting without subsidy from student rental income, and are made available to newly appointed faculty on the basis of criteria established by each campus.

Another major element of auxiliary services is the parking program with approximately 91,462 spaces for students, faculty, staff and visitors.

No State funds are provided for auxiliary enterprises. The annual budget is based upon income projections. Any budget increases are matched by corresponding increases in revenue.

REFERENCES: "1993–94 Budget for Current Operations," November 1992, Office of the President.

CROSS-REFERENCES: Budgets; Faculty Housing; Parking Policy; Student Housing.

Astronomy: See Lick Observatory.

B

Biodiversity: A concept called "biological diversity," or "biodiversity," began to emerge in the 1970s.

According to the California Department of Fish and Game: "In the simplest of terms, biological diversity (biodiversity) is the full variety of life and its associated patterns and processes. It includes the variety of living organisms, the genetic differences among them, and the communities and ecosystems in which they occur."

The concept is a complex one involving the close interaction of biological, geographical and ecological areas of knowledge and activity.

From the 1970s to the present, it has become obvious that the extremely rapid growth of California's human population is affecting the state's biodiversity, resulting in the accelerated deterioration of the state's natural environment and placing its natural resources under increasing stress.

In addition to the state's problems with impaired air and water quality, there has been mounting evidence of damage to California's diverse biota: plants, animals and microorganisms.

A major danger of this environmental deterioration has been the extinction of native animals and plants, many of which are found only in California.

The causes of the damage are complex. They include invasions and introductions of exotic species, fires, drought, and loss of habitat for wildlife due to urban development and agricultural, forestry and grazing practices.

Recently, farmers, forest and grazing land managers, as well as industrial and urban developers, have been confronted with growing public concern and an array of public policies and interest group activities aimed at protecting native habitats.

As a result, work toward gaining a more complete understanding of California's unique biodiversity has been started in earnest by various agencies within the state. Consequently, there has been a strong need to coordinate the many complex issues and concerns involved.

To that end, a special coordinating council was developed in 1991. The council, of which the University is a part, is called the California Council on Biological Diversity.

In 1991, UC and nine federal and state groups, which formed the initial membership of the council, signed a memorandum of understanding on "California's Coordinated Regional Strategy To Conserve Biological Diversity." Its purpose was to establish ways to facilitate communication among its members and to integrate programs for the "protection of biological diversity and the maintenance of economic viability throughout California." (County government organizations are now included.) Rather than focusing on individual species, the council has emphasized a wide-ranging "bioregional"

approach, to better reflect the inner workings and multiple levels of nature.

Scientists at the University's campuses in a wide range of disciplines conduct numerous major studies in the area of biodiversity. Some of the research is conducted within UC's Natural Reserve System.

REFERENCES: "NRS Represents UC on New Council to Protect State's Biodiversity," *Transect*, Vol. 10, No. 1, Spring 1992; "Integrated resource management: new coalitions, familiar clientele," Kenneth R. Farrell, Vice President—Agriculture and Natural Resources, *California Agriculture*, Vol. 47, No. 1, January–February 1993.

CROSS-REFERENCES: Agriculture and Natural Resources.

The UC Systemwide **Biotechnology Research and Education Program** is California's initiative to support the continued development of biotechnology in the state.

Since 1985 the program has provided more than $10 million in creating 61 new research and training projects throughout UC.

It also has established public education and public policy initiatives that are improving the understanding of biotechnology's many roles in society.

The program's activities are sustaining California's international prominence and competitiveness in biotechnology research and commercialization, as well as providing an essential driving force for economic growth in the state and the nation.

Since 1985, UC's Biotechnology Research and Education Program has supported the training of more than 450 new scientists and engineers.

Nearly 200 have already entered permanent, independent research positions in companies or universities—a conversion rate much higher than the national average for scientific and engineering training.

These young scientists and engineers have been trained in the kinds of broad interdisciplinary, collaborative research programs that uniquely support biotechnology investigations.

The success of California's biotechnology efforts are based on the interaction of three factors: basic university research, transformation of new knowledge into technologies and products, and economic development.

Researchers involved in the field are at the threshold of whole new biomedical, environmental and agricultural industrial advancements. Sales of biotechnology products in pharmaceuticals alone are projected by some analysts to grow from $5.6 billion in 1993 to $50 billion in 1999.

California has more biotechnology companies and produces higher sales and more jobs in the field than any other state in the nation or any other country in the world.

The University of California and Stanford University are the birthplace of recombinant DNA technology, the seminal discovery that launched the biological revolution of the 1970s.

Subsequently, the University's Biotechnology Research and Education Program was created to sustain its early developments in biotechnology. The program has helped immeasurably in supporting new ventures in research and training, in order to produce the knowledge and highly skilled personnel that are critical to success.

The University's researchers continue to make fundamental contributions of scientific, commercial and, ultimately, social value in all sectors of biotechnology. For example, UC research has been a factor in the development of most major biotechnology therapeutic products of the 1980s.

These include the development of human insulin and growth hormone, alpha interferon, hepatitis B vaccine, tissue plasminogen activator (tPA) and erythropoietin.

In addition, the University's biotechnology patents are among UC's top royalty income earners.

California's lead in biotechnology derives in large part from decades of state and federal investment in UC's research infrastructure, faculty and trainees. In turn, California's intellectual resources have provided the quality of research needed to attract investment from the private sector.

However, many issues may influence the further development of California biotechnology.

Many of these issues are related to university-government-industry relationships, which will have an impact on funding constraints, redirection of public funding priorities and regulation of research and products.

Responding to these problems, the University's Biotechnology Research and Education Program has strengthened the competitiveness of UC faculty in the federal funding arena.

In so doing, UC campuses have significantly leveraged their Biotechnology Program seed grants against substantial federal funding.

This process has aided in the establishment of important facilities, including the Marine Biotechnology Center at UC Santa Barbara, the Center for Engineering Plants for Resistance Against Pathogens at UC Davis, and the drug design group at UC San Francisco.

Beyond funding concerns, public policies that affect research or the commercialization of developments from publicly funded research are proving to be an equally powerful determinant of California biotechnology's future.

In this regard, the Biotechnology Program supports an active policy analysis effort, informing policy discussions and responding to legislative and regulatory proposals.

This includes providing legislative seminars and briefings on emerging issues and controversies, ranging from DNA fingerprinting to food safety.

Ultimately, realization of the potential benefits of publicly funded research and of the rapid growth of the biotechnology industry in California depends upon public understanding and acceptance.

Since 1985, the Biotechnology Program has developed and supported a broad spectrum of innovative educational activities aimed at enhancing public awareness and participation in decision-making.

In addition, the program serves as a statewide information clearinghouse on biotechnology. It also is a respected educational resource for California policymakers, journalists and educators.

The Biotechnology Program promotes professional training programs for California's traditional communicators in cities and counties throughout the state.

What does the future hold?

Goals for the Biotechnology Program include enhanced emphasis on the support of engineering training and molecular sciences.

In the public arena, the program will continue to contribute to governmental decision-making and will move towards greater coordination of the state's vast public policy and education resources.

In addition, it will continue to serve as a catalyst and focal point for raising public awareness of the potential that biotechnology holds for meeting some of California's pressing economic and social needs.

REFERENCES: Adapted from information provided by the Biotechnology Research and Education Program.

CROSS-REFERENCES: Research Achievements; Technology Transfer.

Black Eligibility Study: In 1986, the University embarked on an in-depth study of factors affecting the academic preparation of African American high school students.

The purpose was to identify ways to increase eligibility rates among African Americans for admission to higher education.

The study was conducted by a task force consisting of UC scholars and administrators whose expertise bore on the subject of educational attainment among African American students.

The Task Force on Black Student Eligibility did the following:

• Reviewed current research on the factors influencing and determining the academic preparation and eligibility rates of African American students.

• Decided on the kinds of investigations needed to further understand the reasons for low educational achievement among such students.

• Identified educational models that have proved successful and could guide research resulting from the study.

In issuing its report in March 1990, the task force found a clear and urgent problem that represented a disturbing educational and social concern.

The report noted that the University's "alarmingly low" rate of African American student enrollment had to be addressed by UC in collaboration with other interested parties in order to generate public discussion.

Such parties, the report suggested, should include members of the African American community, other educational institutions, state and national organizations concerned with education, community groups, public officials, and civic and business leaders.

The report said UC alone could not resolve the problem, but it could help reverse the trend by participating in collaborative, comprehensive efforts.

The 65-page report, "Making the Future Different," called on UC to initiate reforms to address the issue of college enrollment among African-Americans.

Some of the recommendations called for UC to expand programs to increase the number of African American students transferring from community colleges to UC and to establish a multi-campus research unit to conduct research and disseminate information about the academic achievement of African American students. Another recommendation suggested hiring more African American faculty members.

The report also called on UC to help community-based programs improve the academic performance of African American children and to collaborate with state and local agencies to improve the public school curriculum and teacher training.

In addition, the report urged UC to work with corporations and government agencies to support community development in African American neighborhoods.

Such efforts could help broaden the perceptions of African American youth about their occupational opportunities and the value of educational achievement, the report stated.

"The implementation of these recommendations would put California in a unique position to initiate serious reforms, which might serve as a model to the nation." said Troy S. Duster, professor of sociology at Berkeley, who chaired the task force.

By the time the report was issued in March 1990, a study by the California Postsecondary Education Commission (CPEC) showed that only 4.5 percent of African American high school graduates in California were eligible for admission to UC.

This compared with 14.1 percent of all public high school graduates in the state.

According to the data, African American students had the lowest eligibility rate among all the minority groups in the study.

Over the period 1991–92, in keeping with the recommendations of the Black Student Eligibility Study, a number of statewide conferences were held to discuss issues involved.

For example, in 1992, a statewide conference was held in Berkeley to discuss collaborative efforts that had taken place to improve the educational and socio-economic circumstances of African American and other disadvantaged young people.

The conference was sponsored by UC's Urban Community-School Collaborative. Director of the Collaborative was Hardy Frye, in the Office of the President.

Conferees learned that pilot programs were under way at UC and elsewhere in Northern and Southern California as a result of efforts facilitated by the UC Urban Community-School Collaborative.

One program in Southern California, for example, involved cooperative efforts by a UC campus with local school districts and county offices to provide comprehensive health, social and educational services (including tutoring and health and family counseling) to a cluster of local schools.

A similar field-based field station was being developed at a middle school in Northern California. It focused on curriculum and teacher development and the formation of health, social and educational services at the site which is a pilot program to serve the high school, middle schools and elementary schools in the immediate area.

REFERENCES: Black Student Eligibility Study, March 1990; "Report: Increase black enrollment," *UC Focus,* Vol. 4, No. 6, May 1990, and media advisory, October 13, 1992, University Relations, Office of the President.

CROSS-REFERENCES: Affirmative Action; California Postsecondary Education Commission; Diversity.

Blake House and Blake Garden,

located in the Kensington hills overlooking San Francisco Bay, were given to the University by Mr. and Mrs. Anson Stiles Blake in 1957.

In 1969, it was restored and modernized and became the President's House.

Blake House was planned and constructed between 1922 and 1924. (The architect was Walter Bliss.) In deeding the property to the University in 1957, the Blakes reserved "unto themselves and the survivor of them the right to occupy the property for life."

The Blake family had a long association with the University. Mr. Blake's grandfather, Anson Gale Stiles had been a trustee of the College of California, which later became the University of California. Stiles Hall, the Berkeley campus YMCA, was named for him.

Mr. and Mrs. Anson Stiles Blake were both UC alumni.

As a Berkeley student, Mr. Blake was active in Stiles Hall and served as chairman of its advisory board from 1902 to 1952.

During his lifetime, Anson Stiles Blake was involved in his family quarry business in nearby Richmond. He also was interested in California history. In addition, he shared his wife's interest in the garden and in Asian and European art objects and antiques. Many of these are in the house today.

Mrs. Blake, who was an enthusiastic horticulturalist, assembled in the 10-acre garden some 2,500 different species of plants from all over the world.

A view of Blake House

Her sister, Mabel Symmes, who lived with the Blakes, was one of the first students at Berkeley to study landscape design. She was largely responsible for the planning of the formal gardens.

From the beginning, individual faculty members and their students used the garden. Since 1957, the garden has been maintained and used by the Department of Landscape Architecture at Berkeley as a teaching laboratory.

Mr. Blake died in 1959, and Mrs. Blake passed away in 1962.

From 1962 to 1964, the house served as a residence for women graduate students. In 1967, the Regents decided that Blake House should be restored for use as the President's House.

Today, the furnishings are part Blake bequests and part purchases made by the University. Many other furnishings have been dispersed to the libraries, art departments and chancellors' houses at the nine campuses.

In addition to having been a UC president's home, Blake House has been used for official University meetings, conferences and other appropriate functions.

REFERENCES: "The President's House and Blake Garden, Kensington, California," official folder, Office of the President; Policy for Use of Blake House, December 12, 1983, Office of the President.

Bonds: General obligations bonds are a form of long-term financial financing for major construction projects, such as schools, water systems, parks and prisons.

Much like mortgage loans, bonds enable the State to borrow money and pay it back over several years.

To raise funds, the State sells bonds to investors, who can earn interest on the money they loan to the State.

In 1986, Californians for Higher Education (CHE) was formed as a California nonprofit corporation. Its purposes are to educate the citizens of California regarding the needs of higher education in the state and to provide solutions for those needs through literature and public forums.

The Board of Directors of CHE consists of six voting members, two from each of California's three segments of public higher education. University and community college staff members provide assistance to the Board relating to non-political activities.

Between 1986 when CHE was formed and 1992, five general obligation bonds for higher education were placed on the ballot (a number of bond issues had been placed on the ballot before those years, as well, including a major medical and health sciences bond issue in the 1970s).

(A table appears below with information about the general obligation bonds.)

General Obligation Bonds, 1986–92

Date	Measure	Results		Amount
November 1986	Prop. 56	**Passed**	59.5%	$400,000
November 1988	Prop. 78	**Passed**	57.7%	$600,000
June 1990	Prop. 121	**Passed**	55.1%	$450,000
November 1990	Prop. 143	**Failed**	48.7%	$450,000
June 1992	Prop. 153	**Passed**	50.8%	$400,000

Each of the three systems of public higher education received approximately one-third of the total amount of the general obligation bonds approved by the voters since 1986.

REFERENCES: Adapted from CHE background material.

CROSS-REFERENCES: All subjects related to education.

Budget for Current Operations: Over the past quarter century, the University has worked with the State to gain the support it requires for its operating budget in order to carry out its crucial missions of teaching, research and public service.

The adequacy of State support has varied depending upon the economy.

For example, during the late 1960s and early 1970s, the University experienced budget reductions of about 20 percent in real dollars.

Faculty positions and research funding were cut, and the student/faculty ratio deteriorated by about 20 percent.

In the late 1970s and early 1980s, the University again experienced a number of budget cuts.

By the early 1980s, faculty salaries lagged far behind comparison institutions and top faculty were being lost to other institutions; buildings needed repair; classrooms, laboratories and clinics were poorly equipped; libraries suffered; and the building program came virtually to a halt.

The situation improved significantly in the mid-1980s when a period of rebuilding was initiated. Faculty and staff salaries were returned to competitive levels; funds became available for basic needs such as instructional equipment replacement and building maintenance; and research efforts expanded.

The capital budget also improved dramatically. In addition, there was significant growth in private giving, and the University once again became highly competitive for Federal research funds.

By the late 1980s, however, the situation began to change.

A complicated mix of political and demographic forces, and fiscal problems at the State level, led to a growing erosion of gains made during the mid-1980s.

In just three years, the University's share of the total State General Fund budget dropped from a high of 5.8 percent in 1986–87 to 5.1 percent in 1989–90. By 1989–90, the University was already struggling with the early stages of a fiscal problem that subsequently turned into a major crisis.

One way to convey the magnitude of the problem is this:

The University's 1993–94 budget was less than its 1987–88 budget—even though inflation has been over 25 percent, and enrollments have grown by about 6,500 students during the six years.

Another way to convey the magnitude:

The University's budget would have been about $900 million greater in 1993–94 if the State had maintained the base and funded normal cost increases and workload growth over the past four years.

The University has coped with the shortfall in ways that reflect the limited nature of its options in the short term.

Cuts to campus and Office of the President budgets accommodated about half of the budgetary shortfall, and another quarter was accommodated through student fee increases.

Most of the remaining quarter was handled by providing no salary and benefit cost-of-living increases for employees—and a temporary salary reduction, with a much smaller amount reflected in unfunded workload, especially planned enrollment growth at the graduate level and in the health sciences which had to be deferred.

The University is aware that it cannot recoup most of this loss, and it is in the process of making the necessary adjustments to a permanently reduced resource base.

By 1994–95, campus and Office of the President budgets will have been cut by $433 million, which is roughly 20 percent of the University's State-funded budget in 1989–90 just prior to the period of severe budgetary shortfalls.

The University has attempted to protect the instructional program to the extent possible by making deeper cuts in other areas, such as administration, research, public service, student services, and maintenance.

Administration, especially, has been assigned heavy cuts both on the campuses and on a Universitywide basis. Core administrative activities in the Office of the President are receiving substantially greater cuts than campus budgets.

In addition, purchase of scholarly journals for the libraries has been severely curtailed; the backlog of deferred maintenance projects has grown to nearly $350 million, with about $140 million considered critical; and the budget for instructional equipment replacement is now only about half of the amount needed.

Although instructional resources have been eroded by the budget cuts, the University has honored the California Master Plan for Higher Education by continuing to offer a place to all eligible California resident students seeking admission at the undergraduate level.

In another area related to the budget, faculty and staff received no cost-of-living salary increase for two years in a row (1991–92 and 1992–93), and in the third year (1993–94) salaries were cut by 3.5 percent for one year.

In addition, in 1991–92, staff received no merit increase, and faculty merits were delayed for one year.

In 1994–95, even assuming the best possible outcome with respect to salaries (restoration of base salaries, a 5 percent cost-of-living adjustment, and normal merit increases), UC faculty salaries were expected to lag about 7 percent behind salaries at the eight institutions traditionally used for comparison purposes.

Also, student fees increased by about 125 percent in just four years (1989–90 to 1993–94). For a resident undergraduate, UC fees in 1993–94 are about $400 less than projected average fees at the University's four public salary comparison institutions and about $500 above fees at 23 public institutions nationwide. For nonresident students, UC fees are somewhat higher.

The University has maintained its commitment to provide sufficient financial aid to cover fee increases for needy students. For example, financial aid grants from University funds have increased by about $95 million on a permanent basis over the four-year period. For 1993–94, it is estimated that about half of all UC students will have their fee increase covered by financial aid.

The measures taken by the University to address the operating budget losses represent short-term responses. A planning process has been under way to identify ways in which UC can permanently adjust to a reduced resource base.

For example, review of academic programs has been accelerated with the goal of setting priorities and focusing resources selectively. There likely will be reduction, consolidation or elimination of some programs while other programs are strengthened.

The University also is exploring new ways of sharing resources among the campuses and capitalizing on the most recent educational technologies. Opportunities to achieve further cost-savings and management efficiencies will also continued to be explored.

As it looks ahead, the University is not planning to seek funds for enrollment growth for most of the next four years. Enrollments are expected to be essentially stable over the near term, through 1997–98, with a small dip in the early years followed by a return to slightly above the 1993–94 level.

The University hopes to achieve fiscal stability during this period.

Given the current outlook for economic recovery in California, the University's near-term goal is simply to stay even with inflation and fixed cost increases—to avoid losing further ground.

Beginning in 1998–99, there will be a dramatic increase in the number of eligible students wishing to enroll. If the University continues to maintain access under the Master Plan, and allowing for modest growth in graduate students consistent with earlier enrollment plans, a total of 45,000 additional students will be enrolled by the year 2005.

A major issue for the future is whether State resources will be available to accommodate such tremendous

Where the University of California Gets its Funding

The percentage of UC's operating budget derived from the state is declining, but state funding still provides the core support for academic programs and is the key to attracting other revenue.

Almost all other UC revenue is restricted to specific uses and cannot replace the shortfall in state funds.

Building programs are funded separately by bonds approved by voters and the state Legislature.

Revenue from these bonds cannot be used for any other purpose.

State general fund   28%

Funds earmarked for the general support of UC including teaching, research and public service programs and activities mandated by the state Legislature.

UC General Fund   2%

Funds collected primarily from nonresident tuition and from a share of federal research grants to cover indirect costs. Like the state general fund, this revenue is earmarked for the general support of teaching, research and public service and other mandated activities.

Teaching hospitals   22.1%

Fees for patient services at UC's five teaching hospitals, which must support the continuing operation of those facilities.

Federal Government   15%

Funds from federal agencies, which are restricted to support specific research projects and other programs.

Student fees & tuition   8.6%

Fees support student activities, financial aid, health centers and libraries. Tuition includes fees charged by self-supporting programs such as UC Extension and summer session.

Service activities   7.4%

Funds generated by activities such as educational workshops and treatment at medical, dental and veterinary clinics. Generally, the revenue must be used to defray the cost of operations.

Auxiliary enterprises   6.6%

Money collected from operations such as parking lots, student housing and dining facilities. These funds must be used to support their continued operations.

Private gifts, grants & contracts   4.9%

Funds from private foundations, groups and individuals which almost always are earmarked for specific purposes.

Endowments   1.1%

Income earned on funds donated to UC and invested. In almost all cases, donors specify how income is to be used.

Local governments   0.9%

Funds received from contracts and grants to perform services for local governments. For example, UC San Francisco receives revenue from the city of San Francisco to manage San Francisco General Hospital.

Other sources   3.4%

Funds from sources such as publication sales, or fees charged for the use of facilities and services. Generally, the revenue must be used to defray the cost of operations.

Source: University and External Relations, Office of the President.

growth. The University's intent and goal is to continue to honor the Master Plan, but this will require significant budget increases beginning in 1998–99 if quality and access are to be maintained in the face of rapidly accelerating enrollment demand.

The University intends to continue working with the State, with the other segments of higher education, and with business and industry in a long-term effort to determine whether a mechanism for financing higher education can be developed so that access is assured for the coming generation of students.

REFERENCES: "1994–95 Budget for Current Operations," October 1, 1993, Office of the President.

CROSS-REFERENCES: Master Plan; Retirement; Student Fees; Student Financial Aid; other subjects mentioned in the text.

UC Current Operations General Fund Budget ($000)

The first column shows the total of the State's General Fund for the years indicated, the second column shows how much of this amount the University received, and the third column shows the percentage of what UC received in relation to the State's General Fund Budget.

	Total State General Fund	UC State General Funds	UC's % State General Fund Budget
1970–71	4,853,860	337,079	6.94%
1971–72	5,027,300	335,578	6.68%
1972–73	5,615,684	384,705	6.85%
1973–74	7,299,436	445,910	6.11%
1974–75	8,348,642	514,566	6.16%
1975–76	9,518,436	585,461	6.15%
1976–77	10,466,097	683,742	6.53%
1977–78	11,685,643	737,498	6.31%
1978–79	16,250,774	767,050	4.72%
1979–80	18,534,148	901,951	4.87%
1980–81	21,104,852	1,074,584	5.09%
1981–82	21,692,782	1,097,293	5.06%
1982–83	21,751,413	1,125,425	5.17%
1983–84	22,869,226	1,110,012	4.85%
1984–85	25,721,660	1,457,144	5.67%
1985–86	28,841,313	1,641,741	5.69%
1986–87	31,469,006	1,788,304	5.68%
1987–88	33,020,822	1,888,872	5.72%
1988–89	35,897,298	1,970,047	5.49%
1989–90	39,455,870	2,076,662	5.26%
1990–91	40,263,581	2,135,733	5.30%
1991–92	43,326,985	2,105,560	4.86%
1992–93	40,821,871	1,878,547	4.60%
1993–94	37,333,038	1,743,570	4.67%

Except for 1992–93 and 1993–94, which are "Current Year" and "Budget Year," respectively, data are from the "Actual Year" column of the Governor's Budget (Schedule #3 through 1983–84 Governor's Budget; and Schedule #9 thereafter).

Information as of 1/29/93, obtained from UC's Budget Office.

The University Budget And State Funding

UC's Growing Budget Shortfall

Since 1991, state funding for the University has fallen about $900 million below normal funding increases for inflation, fixed costs and workload growth.

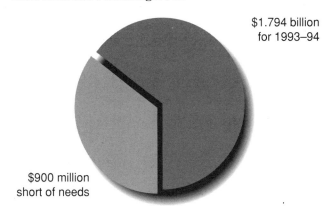

$1.794 billion for 1993–94

$900 million short of needs

UC's Shrinking State Budget

UC's 1993–94 state budget is slightly less than it was in 1986–87. In that seven-year period, inflation went up 32% and UC enrollment grew by 10,000 students.

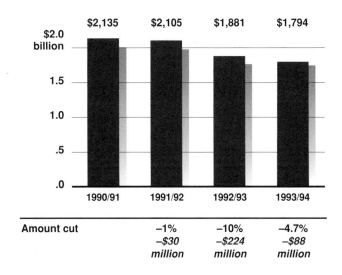

Amount cut		–1% –$30 million	–10% –$224 million	–4.7% –$88 million

How UC Has Coped with Funding Cuts

- Faculty and staff have gone two years without a general salary increase and will receive a one-time annualized pay cut of approximately 3.5% in 1993–94.
- The University has eliminated funding for over 6,000 jobs.
- Deep cuts have been made in budgets for libraries, equipment, maintenance and other non-salary items.
- Student fees have increased 125% in four years, defraying 26% of UC's $900 million shortfall during that period.

Source: University and External Relations, Office of the President.

UC's Funding Going Down

Roughly 85 percent of the state budget is statutorily or constitutionally guaranteed to certain protected programs and correctional programs. UC is not among these protected programs.

If present policies and growth trends are unchanged. UC's share of state dollars will decline each year. By the year 2000 UC would receive no state general funding.

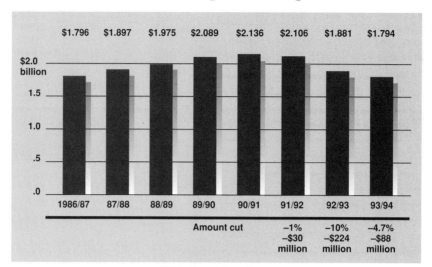

UC's State Funding

The Practical Effect of the State's Budgeting System

A look at the state-funded areas of government that have shown the largest numerical changes in employees since 1939 illustrates the plight of higher education in California.

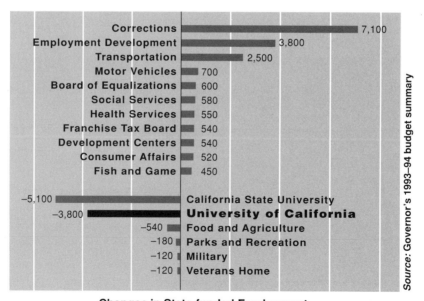

Changes in State-funded Employment
1989–90 to 1992–93
(numbers are in full-time equivalent)

Source: University and External Relations, Office of the President.

Buildings: The following section provides a list of major structures at the University which are devoted to teaching, research and other educational or related activities.

The list is not all-inclusive; rather, it is intended to provide an overview of structures at each campus that are of permanent construction (e.g., brick, concrete, steel or stucco).

The information was generated from a central computer source, based on data provided by each campus. While the names of the structures are in a shortened computerized form, most of the names are readily identifiable. A set of campus maps follows the list which will aid the reader in identifying these structures, as well as others that are not on the list. The maps were taken from official sources available at the time the book was being prepared.

The buildings on the following list were constructed beginning in the mid-1960s. Information about buildings constructed prior to that time may be found in the *Centennial Record*. Copies of the *Centennial Record* are available in campus libraries, archives, public information offices, offices responsible for capital programs, and other central locations at UC.

The headings in the list below show the name of the structure, the year it was built, the outside gross square feet, or OGSF (size of the structure) and the assigned

square footage, or ASF (the space devoted to teaching, research or other activities).

In addition to the large list, a separate and shorter list appears on this page indicating overall figures for each major UC site.

University of California
Corporate Equipment and Facilities Data System
Total ASF, OGSF 100 Excluding Hastings

Year	Campus	Total Buildings	Total Rooms	Outside Gross@100%	Assignable Square Feet	Eff Ratio
1992	Berkeley	606	21,450	13,373,979	7,760,356	.58
	Davis-AgFldSta	210	210	210	210	1.00
	Davis	1,286	19,895	9,428,486	6,282,929	.67
	Irvine	436	12,603	6,218,363	3,858,461	.62
	Los Angeles	286	26,018	19,226,096	8,752,069	.46
	Riverside	503	6,279	3,329,000	2,201,248	.66
	San Diego	535	19,394	9,762,897	5,604,458	.57
	San Francisco	175	11,178	5,761,941	3,429,004	.60
	Santa Barbara	354	9,279	4,604,385	3,044,113	.66
	Santa Cruz	462	7,380	3,293,438	2,186,212	.66
	SW-Los Angeles	1	35	134,962	101,521	.75
	Systemwide	19	1,727	940,770	748,815	.80
TOTAL	1992	4,873	135,448	76,074,527	43,969,396	8.03

Building Name	Date Constructed	OGSF	ASF
BERKELEY			
BARKER	1964	95,072	53,979
BARROWS	1964	203,142	106,259
BECHTEL CNTR	1980	51,025	35,538
BIRGE	1964	98,329	53,188
CALVIN LAB	1964	44,971	23,718
ESHLEMAN	1965	48,840	26,678
ETCHEVERRY	1964	204,100	108,534
EVANS	1971	293,166	157,083
FOOTHILL 1	1990	47,219	34,760
FOOTHILL 4	1990	39,357	25,135
FOOTHILL 7	1990	33,877	23,329
FOOTHILL 8	1990	37,025	27,081
G&PB TEACH	1990	30,585	15,123
HASTE 2417	1992	72,666	28,143
HILDEBRAND	1966	146,206	86,698
KOSHLAND	1990	154,257	91,617
LATIMER	1963	195,575	115,134
LAW	1966	175,030	117,547
LAWRENCE	1968	134,388	77,839
LSB ADDITION	1988	205,390	122,022
MANVILLE	1966	34,284	23,680
MINOR ADDITN	1978	56,120	30,572
MOFFITT	1970	145,390	86,701
NW AN FACIL	1991	52,845	29,018
PARKING A	1967	141,290	0
PARKING H	1971	121,000	0
PARKING NW	1989	98,539	357
R 280	1963	35,800	33,174
REC SPRT FAC	1984	254,457	84,416
RH3 DINING	1964	37,638	30,828

Building Name	Date Constructed	OGSF	ASF
RH3 NORTON	1964	45,390	31,291
RH3 PRIESTLY	1964	40,851	27,315
RH3 SPENSBLK	1964	40,851	27,315
RH3 SPROUL	1964	47,924	31,063
SILVER LAB	1966	45,932	27,979
UNIV ART CEN	1970	108,872	58,247
WURSTER	1964	217,355	147,660
ZELLERBACH	1968	156,620	86,963
DAVIS			
ACADMC SURGE	1992	126,029	83,739
ART	1966	56,045	36,824
BAINER	1966	172,821	121,329
BRIGGS	1971	199,005	122,178
CHEM	1966	128,483	76,616
CHEM ANX	1971	104,788	55,642
DRAMA	1966	48,653	34,641
HUTCH	1963	120,160	68,083
KERR	1969	54,923	32,189
KING	1968	95,917	66,140
LEACH	1970	59,775	33,078
MED SCI I A	1977	257,508	151,168
MED SCI I B	1976	57,527	43,464
MEYER	1987	216,631	121,737
MRAK	1966	93,680	64,951
OLSON	1963	57,468	31,030
PHY SCI LIB	1971	34,033	22,416
PHYGEO	1971	122,604	62,393
REC HALL	1977	151,552	92,926
SEG RYERSON	1963	46,514	24,938
SPROUL	1963	50,956	27,108

Building Name	Date Constructed	OGSF	ASF
STORER	1968	92,936	52,136
SURGE 3	1966	58,447	40,195
TEC COMMUNIT	1967	37,600	24,149
THOREAU	1989	56,603	37,658
UMC ADMN SPT	1987	45,174	32,706
UMC CNCR CTR	1990	55,265	36,090
VET MED 2	1979	46,165	28,590
VMTH	1969	83,824	54,542
WELLMN	1969	49,670	29,478
IRVINE			
ADMIN BLDG	1973	103,274	66,346
BIO SCI 2	1991	213,717	128,225
BREN EVENTS	1987	102,392	65,829
COMMONS	1965	31,115	18,079
COMP SCI BLD	1970	74,670	33,490
CRAWFORD HAL	1965	68,177	47,550
ENGINRNG LAB	1987	36,764	22,719
ENGR BLDG 1	1970	142,706	79,166
GSMANAGEMENT	1988	41,455	26,641
HUM OFF BLDG	1965	44,060	27,344
HUMANITIES H	1965	61,848	29,091
LIBRARY BLDG	1965	155,031	125,115
MC BLDG 1A	1981	101,156	57,511
MC BLDG 22A	1982	37,845	17,414
MC BLDG 22C	1986	39,832	11,749
MC BLDG 23	1991	75,559	44,240
MC BLDG 72	1978	87,000	0
ME ALDOR ROH	1989	30,100	18,139
ME BAL HARR	1989	30,100	18,139
ME GOND SNOW	1989	30,100	18,139

Building Name	Date Constructed	OGSF	ASF	Building Name	Date Constructed	OGSF	ASF	Building Name	Date Constructed	OGSF	ASF
IRVINE				SLICHTER	1965	76,597	33,874	THIRD APT I	1975	61,805	52,060
ME GREYH CAL	1989	30,100	18,139	SO PRKG HSC	1977	557,428	60,963	THIRD APT II	1980	103,817	83,812
ME SHAD ELR	1989	30,100	18,139	SRLF	1987	134,962	101,521	TIOGA HALL	1968	96,460	74,182
ME WOODH WW	1989	30,100	18,139	TOWELL TENT	1992	36,993	32,059	UH BACH CYN	1988	321,521	936
MED SCI 1	1978	159,844	98,942					UH OUTPT CTR	1977	66,126	31,542
MED SURG 2	1969	61,210	41,805	**RIVERSIDE**				UREY HALL	1963	196,483	102,775
MEDICL PLAZA	1988	44,202	16,948	BATCHELOR	1965	120,259	58,342	WAR LEC HALL	1990	69,298	41,220
MESA CEN SER	1968	39,672	22,039	BOOKSTORE	1991	34,200	24,990	WARREN APTS	1984	371,688	195,802
PARK STRUC 1	1990	321,000	1,000	BOYCE	1974	112,187	61,595	YORK HALL	1966	144,476	69,104
PHYS SCI 1	1968	197,248	112,392	LOTHIAN HALL	1963	250,412	148,352	**SAN FRANCISCO**			
PHYS SCI 2	1990	160,274	98,072	OLMSTED	1963	96,545	46,919	DENTISTRY	1979	128,403	69,399
SOC ECOLOGY	1983	55,230	30,466	PHYSICS	1965	98,662	55,434	HSIR EAST	1966	209,948	133,592
SOCSCI LAB	1971	55,147	29,768	PIERCE	1966	114,180	65,026	HSIR SERV CR	1966	42,774	464
SOCSCI TOWER	1971	94,606	46,870	SPROUL	1965	81,861	44,506	HSIR WEST	1966	193,627	119,931
STEINHAUS H	1965	118,192	73,615	STAT COMP	1974	42,096	24,208	LIBRARY	1991	122,764	97,262
UCI STU CNTR	1990	175,962	107,418	UNIV COMMONS	1965	100,716	53,239	LONG HOSP	1982	372,469	208,087
								NURSING	1972	89,406	45,589
LOS ANGELES				**SAN DIEGO**				UC CLINICS	1972	607,618	144,191
ACOSTA T CTR	1965	32,526	28,305	AP M BLDG	1969	196,029	101,121	VISION RSCH	1986	45,160	24,479
BUNCHE	1964	222,065	126,446	BAS SCI BLDG	1969	328,299	196,799				
C SERV BLD 1	1977	51,897	38,393	BIOLOGY BLDG	1970	78,432	47,062	**SANTA BARBARA**			
CANYON POINT	1991	100,985	64,968	BONNER HALL	1964	142,745	60,339	BIOLOGY 2	1966	133,413	71,616
COURT SIDE/P	1992	317,246	57,894	CENT MOL MED	1990	80,063	48,678	BROIDA HALL	1967	158,334	78,696
DELTA TERR	1991	117,555	69,835	CENT UNI LIB	1970	428,977	273,252	CHEADLE HALL	1963	71,453	44,918
DENTISTRY	1966	216,580	121,583	CHEM RES BLD	1976	52,030	25,544	CHEMISTRY	1964	101,584	61,995
DICKSON	1965	153,130	94,439	CLIN SCI BLD	1991	107,795	63,231	ELLISON HALL	1967	119,717	65,440
ENGR BLDG 4	1990	298,554	164,638	CMRR	1985	49,824	29,270	ENGINEERING	1965	104,470	64,972
EXTENSION	1971	99,938	66,168	COG SCI BLDG	1976	57,954	31,702	ENGR 2	1986	140,585	88,167
FAC APTS-LVG	1983	122,390	60,656	CTF	1978	127,273	82,715	EVENTS CNTR	1980	64,986	51,527
FOWLER MUSM	1990	101,995	64,720	CTRL MESA	1975	196,274	139,776	HARDER STAD	1966	59,336	22,261
GRIFFIN COMM	1992	119,831	60,320	ECKART LIB	1976	49,702	32,139	KERR HALL	1975	44,895	31,270
GUEST HOUSE	1984	36,926	18,318	ENG UNIT 1	1988	221,128	131,686	MAR BIO LAB	1963	37,585	22,507
HEDRICK HALL	1964	206,451	122,184	FACULTY APTS	1981	59,070	49,490	PHELPS HALL	1965	146,198	87,971
J WOODEN/PS4	1983	279,953	68,433	GALBRTH HALL	1965	146,390	68,526	PSYCHOLOGY	1963	52,916	27,573
JD MORGAN CT	1965	35,014	30,298	GYMNASIUM	1968	56,544	37,615	SAN NICOLAS	1964	85,999	50,625
JE WST A CTR	1976	33,962	24,795	H SS BLDG	1970	98,072	51,486	SAN RAFAEL M	1967	60,182	40,282
JS EYE INST	1967	96,067	52,388	HUBBS HALL	1976	95,040	39,947	SAN RAFAEL W	1967	75,119	41,831
KNUDSEN	1963	152,476	85,018	IGPP	1963	43,448	32,403	SNIDECOR HLL	1963	59,182	34,865
L FACTOR HSC	1981	200,342	108,830	LITERATURE	1990	50,429	31,338	SOUTH HALL	1969	135,542	80,151
LAUNDRY FAC	1969	58,547	52,542	MANDEVILLE	1974	131,663	70,656	STDNT HLTH	1968	47,818	24,365
LIFE SCI 3	1976	134,368	71,510	MATTHEW APTS	1980	87,659	67,620	UNIV CENTER	1964	112,336	72,797
MACDONALD RL	1991	148,372	84,735	MAYER HALL	1963	145,197	56,525				
MACGOWAN	1963	90,500	65,144	MCGILL BLDG	1970	111,022	61,946	**SANTA CRUZ**			
MED PLAZA200	1990	366,834	198,769	MEDIA CTR	1975	37,275	14,193	APPLIED SCI	1971	183,938	107,665
MED PLAZA300	1990	102,470	69,187	MOL BIO BLDG	1987	44,553	25,153	CL COLL COM	1966	47,740	27,486
MELNITZ	1967	63,478	38,125	MTF	1978	110,801	56,532	COMMO BLDG	1968	38,412	25,387
NCISF1	1991	30,214	24,436	MUIR APTS	1971	83,949	58,185	FIELD HSE E	1965	30,833	21,888
PARKG STR E	1967	70,652	0	MUIR COMMONS	1970	30,158	19,787	HAHN STUD SV	1965	35,993	22,915
PARKG STR RC	1989	47,545	0	MULTIPURPOSE	1988	56,237	47,655	KERR HALL	1973	80,755	45,046
PARKG STR 1	1989	858,246	0	NIERENBERG	1984	48,643	28,890	MCHENRY LIB	1966	167,357	115,281
PARKG STR 14	1963	465,315	0	PEP CYN APTS	1988	180,832	146,514	ME HOUSE A	1968	44,073	28,129
PARKG STR 2	1969	699,622	0	PRICE CTR	1989	164,171	125,645	NAT SCI 2	1969	88,753	50,565
PARKG STR 3	1964	354,716	0	RCRH ARGO	1968	76,183	52,544	PA THEATRE	1971	43,200	17,087
PARKG STR 6	1980	251,334	0	RCRH BLAKE	1968	37,417	27,462	PORTER ACAD	1971	35,706	20,773
PARKG STR 8	1967	872,288	22,755	REV COMMONS	1966	34,307	27,289	PORTER HSE A	1971	52,687	31,985
PARKG STR 9	1966	636,813	3,200	ROBINSON 1	1990	31,798	21,933	PORTER HSE B	1971	74,884	47,476
PAULEY	1965	190,787	116,472	SHILEY EYE	1991	34,473	26,596	SCIENCE LIB	1991	78,500	55,160
PS 32	1986	249,875	0	SIO AQUARIUM	1992	34,151	27,523	SINSHEIMR LB	1989	99,774	62,098
PV UEBERROTH	1982	66,180	51,766	SOUTH MESA	1981	229,000	191,670	ST ACAD BLDG	1966	30,849	16,591
REED RES CTR	1970	71,388	36,658	SUPERCOMPUTR	1985	60,685	30,116	THIMANN LAB	1966	91,047	56,010
REHAB CENTER	1965	127,728	68,032	TC RES HALLS	1988	134,899	88,224				
RESEARCH LIB	1964	309,119	247,916	TENAYA HALL	1968	73,780	57,032	**SYSTEMWIDE**			
RIEBER HALL	1963	208,090	126,839	TGCF	1982	38,451	20,974	NOR REG LIB	1982	98,305	90,586
SCHOOL PUB H	1968	144,381	76,201								

Maps

On the following pages are maps, available at the time of publication from UC's General Catalogs, showing major buildings at each campus.

BERKELEY CAMPUS

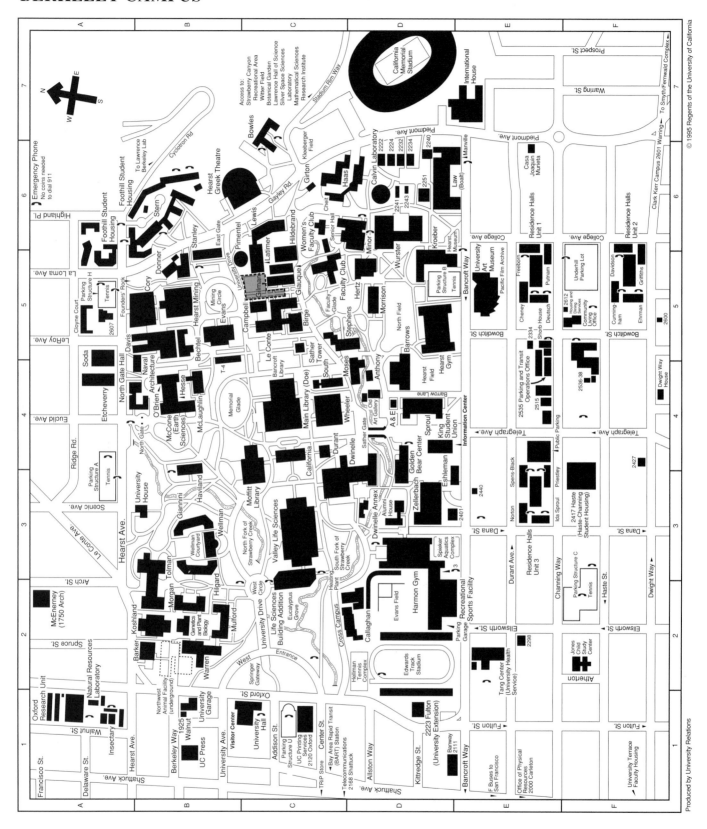

Key

122

DAVIS CAMPUS

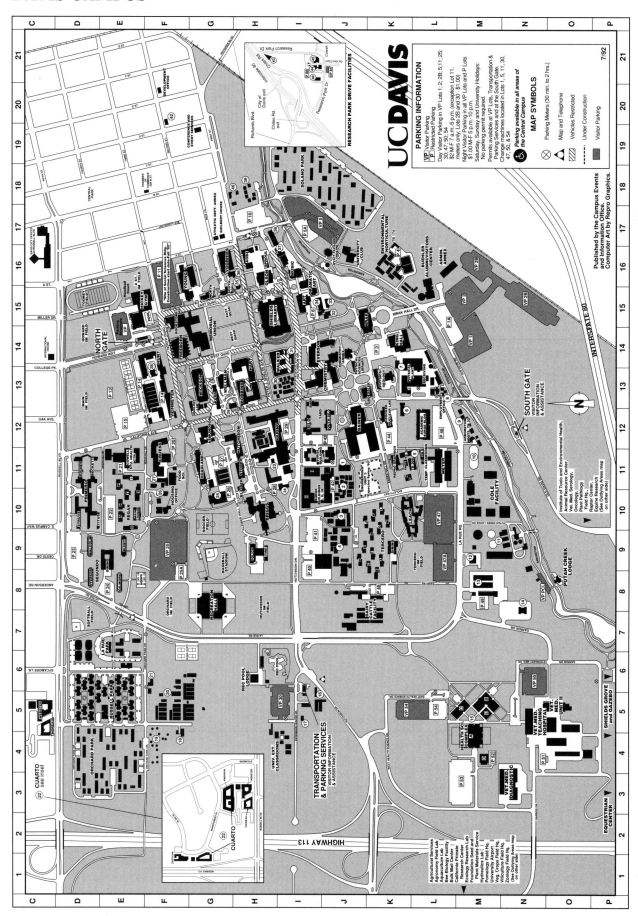

Key

FACILITIES, DEPARTMENTS, SERVICES
(*Refer to Outlying Areas Map)

IRVINE CAMPUS

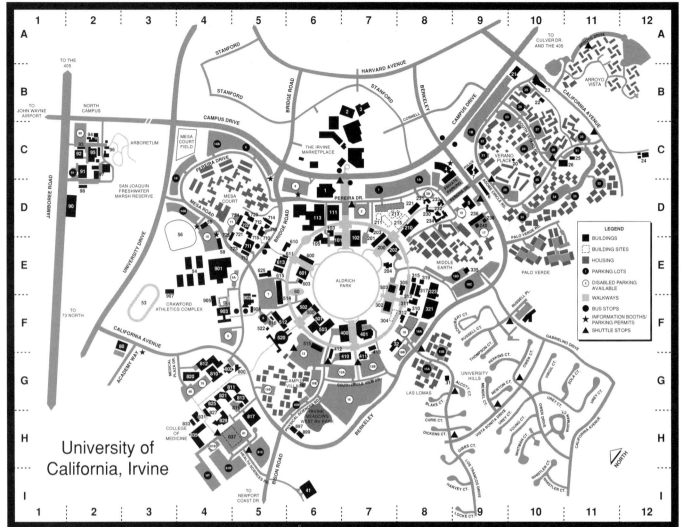

Map grid columns 1–12 (top and bottom), rows A–I (left and right).

Labels visible on map: TO CULVER DR. AND THE 405, ARROYO DRIVE, ARROYO VISTA, CALIFORNIA AVENUE, STANFORD, HARVARD AVENUE, BRIDGE ROAD, BERKELEY, CORNELL, CAMPUS DRIVE, TO THE 405, TO JOHN WAYNE AIRPORT, NORTH CAMPUS, ARBORETUM, MESA COURT FIELD, THE IRVINE MARKETPLACE, PEREIRA DRIVE, PEREIRA DR., VERANO PLACE, PRIVATE PARKING, MIDDLE EARTH, PALO VERDE RD., PALO VERDE, JAMBOREE ROAD, SAN JOAQUIN FRESHWATER MARSH RESERVE, MESA COURT, MESA ROAD, UNIVERSITY DRIVE, ALDRICH PARK, RUSSELL PL., RUSSELL CT., SCHUBERT CT., THOMPSON CT., PERKINS CT., OWEN CT., VIRGIL CT., GABRIELINO DRIVE, ZOLA CT., TO 73 NORTH, CALIFORNIA AVENUE, ACADEMY WAY, MEDICAL PLAZA DR., CRAWFORD ATHLETICS COMPLEX, CAMPUS VILLAGE, SOUTH CIRCLE VIEW DR., LAS LOMAS, UNIVERSITY HILLS, ALCOTT CT., MENDEL CT., NEWTON CT., VISTA BONITA DRIVE, UREY CT., YOUNG CT., OWEN DRIVE, WHITMAN CT., URET CT., FACULTY/STAFF HOUSING OFFICE, BLAKE CT., CURIE CT., DICKENS CT., GIBBS CT., WHITMAN CT., WHISTLER CT., COLLEGE OF MEDICINE, IRVINE MEADOWS WEST RV PARK, PHYSICAL SCIENCES RD., HEALTH SCIENCES RD., BISON ROAD, BERKELEY, HARVEY CT., LOS TRANCOS DRIVE, WHISTLER CT., LOCKE CT., TO NEWPORT COAST DR.

University of California, Irvine

LEGEND
- BUILDINGS
- BUILDING SITES
- HOUSING
- PARKING LOTS
- DISABLED PARKING AVAILABLE
- WALKWAYS
- BUS STOPS
- INFORMATION BOOTHS/ PARKING PERMITS
- SHUTTLE STOPS

NORTH

NOVEMBER 1994

Key

DEPARTMENTS/OFFICES

Administration Building (D6) **111**
Admissions:
    College of Medicine (G4) **821**
    Graduate (D6) **111**
    Undergraduate (D6) **111**
Air Pollution Labs (C2) **94**
Alumni House (D8) **233**
American Academy of Arts and
    Sciences (C8) **4**
American Heart Association (B10) **21**
Arboretum (C2) **96**
Arnold and Mabel Beckman Center
    of the National Academies of
    Sciences and Engineering (F3) **80**
Athletics Complex:
    Pool (F4) **51**
    Track (F3) **53**
    Tennis Courts (E4) **54**
    Anteater Field (D4) **56**
    Bren Events Center (E4) **901**
    Crawford Hall (F4) **903**
    Handball/Racquetball Courts (F4) **905**
Beckman Laser Institute (H5) **817**
Berkeley Place (C8) **4**

Biological Sciences I (Steinhaus Hall)
    (F6) **502**
Biological Sciences II (F6) **503**
Biological Sciences Administration (F6)
    515
Biological Sciences Lecture Hall
    (F6) **501**
Bookstore (The UCI Store, Market-
    place) (B7) **3**
Bookstore, The UCI (D6) **113**
Bren Events Center (E4) **901**
Cancer Research Institute (F6) **502**
Career Planning and Placement
    Center (E6) **105**
Center for Research Information
    Technology and Organizations (C8) **4**
Center for the Neurobiology of
    Learning and Memory (Bonney
    Center) (F5) **512**
Central Plant (F5) **902**
Chancellor's Office (D6) **111**
Child Care Centers:
    Children's Center (C10) **26**
    Early Childhood Education Center
    (B10) **23**

Extended Day Center (C11) **25**
Infant/Toddler Center (B10) **22**
University Montessori School (F10) **30**
Verano Preschool (C10) **20**
Child Development Center (D2) **90**
Civil Engineering Facility (E8) **317**
Computer Science (F7) **302**
Computer Science/Engineering
    (F8) **312**
Computer Sciences Annex (site)
    (F8) **304**
Concert Hall (D5) **710**
Counseling Center (E6) **105**
Crawford Hall (F4) **903**
Cross-Cultural Center (D6) **103**
Disability Services (E5) **615**
Electrical Substation (I6) **41**
Engineering Tower (E7) **303**
Engineering Gateway (F8) **321**
Engineering Instructional Facility
    (E9) **335**
Engineering Laboratory Facility (E8) **323**
Engineering Lecture Hall (E8) **305**
Facilities Management Shops (C2) **97**

Faculty Research Facility (C2) **95**
Faculty/Staff Housing Office (G8) **31**
Family Fitness Center (C8) **4**
Farm School/Barn (C12) **24**
Fine Arts Village (D5) **710-725**
Food Facilities:
    B.C.'s Cavern on the Green (F6) **500**
    Bonjour Café, (D8) **233**
    Cafe Med (G5) **800**
    Olive Grove (D5) **Fine Arts Village**
    Phoenix Grille (E7) **204**
    UCI Student Center (D6) **113**
Founders' Court (E6) **60**
Gallery, Fine Arts (D5) **712**
Gateway Commons (E6) **101**
Graduate School of Management
    (D8) **221**
Graduate Studies and Research
    (D6) **111**
Greenhouse (E5) **514**
Grounds Maintenance Facility (H6) **897**
Handball and Racquetball Courts
    (F4) **905**
Health Policy and Research (C8) **4**

Housing Administrative Services (D9) **6**
Human Resources, Staff (C8) **4**
Humanities Annex (E5) **610**
Humanities Hall (E6) **601**
Humanities Interim Classroom Facility (E5) **611**
Humanities Office Building (E6) **600**
Humanities Office Building 2 (E5) **625**
Humanities Research Institute (D6) **111**
Humanities Trailer Complex (E5) **613**
ICS Trailers (E8) **313**
ICS/Engineering Research Facility (F8) **310**
Information, Campus (D9) **6**, (D6) **111**, (D6) **113**
Information and Computer Science (F7) **302**
Institute for Surface and Interface Science (F7) **400**
Institute of Transportation Studies (C8) **4**
Interfaith (E8) **319**
Interim Classroom Facility (E8) **315**
Interim Office Building (C2) **92**
Irvine Barclay Theatre (D6) **1**
Irvine Hall (H4) **835**
Libraries:
  Main (E7) **102**
  Science (F5) **520**
Little Theatre (E6) **601**
Mailroom (C2) **93**
McDonnell Douglas Engineering Auditorium (F8) **311**
Media Services (E6) **603**
Medical Education Building (G4) **802**
Medical Plaza (G4) **820**
Medical Sciences A (G5) **813**
Medical Sciences B (G5) **811**
Medical Sciences C (G4) **821**
Medical Sciences D (G4) **825**
Medical Sciences E (H4) **827**
Medical Sciences F (H4) **831**
Medical Sciences Classroom Facility (H4) **833**
Medical Surge I (G4) **810**
Medical Surge II (G4) **812**
Mesa Arts Building (E4) **58**
Mesa Office Building (D4) **59**
Neuroscience Research Facility (site) (H5) **837**
Nixon Theatre (D5) **722**
Parking and Transportation Office (C9) **7**
Physical Sciences I (F7) **400**
Physical Sciences II (F7) **401**
Physical Sciences Classroom Building (F7) **413**
Physical Sciences Graduate Offices (F6) **412**
Physical Sciences Lecture Hall (G7) **411**
Physical Sciences Research Facility (G7) **410**
Physical Sciences Trailers (F6) **412**
Plumwood House (Hitachi) (H4) **829**
Police (C9) **7**
Public Services (C9) **7**
Purchasing (C9) **7**
Rachel Long Morgan Building (D8) **231**
Radioactive and Chemical Waste Handling Facility (F5) **522**
Receiving (C2) **91**
Recycling Center (D2) **98**
Registrar:
  College of Medicine (H4) **827**
  Main Campus (D6) **111**

Rockwell Engineering Center (F8) **311**
Social Ecology (D8) **210**
Social Science A (site) (D7) **211**
Social Science B (site) (D7) **213**
Social Science C (site) (D8) **215**
Social Science Hall (E7) **200**
Social Science Laboratory (E7) **202**
Social Science Tower (E7) **201**
Social Science Trailer (D7) **203**
Steinhaus Hall (Biological Sciences) (F6) **502**
Storehouse (C2) **91**
Student Center (D6) **113**
Student Health Center (D9) **5**
Student Services I, II (E6) **105**
Teacher Education (C8) **4**
Thesaurus Linguae Graecae (C8) **4**
Theoretical Neurobiology Facility (F5) **516**
Ticket Offices:
  Bren Events Center (E4) **55**
  Fine Arts (E5) **711**
  Irvine Barclay Theatre (D6) **1**
Tours (D6) **111**
UC Conference Center (D4) **59**
University Club (F8) **32**
University Extension A (D8) **231**
University Extension B (D8) **230**
University Extension C (D8) **232**
University Extension D (D8) **234**
University Extension H (D9) **236**
University Extension I (D9) **238**
University Extension J (D9) **240**
University/Industry Research Technology (B7) **2**
University Tower (B7) **2**
Village Theatre (E5) **711**
Vivarium Administrative Offices (G5) **815**
Women and Gender Education, Center for (E5) **610**
Women's Opportunities Center (D8) **231**

BUILDINGS

1 Irvine Barclay Theatre (D6)
2 University Tower (B7)
3 Bookstore (The UCI Store, Marketplace) (B7)
4 Berkeley Place (C8)
5 Student Health Center (D9)
6 Housing Administrative Services (D9)
7 Public Services (C9)
20 Verano Preschool (C10)
21 American Heart Association (B10)
22 Infant/Toddler Center (B10)
23 Early Childhood Education Center (B10)
24 Farm School/Barn (C12)
25 Extended Day Center (C11)
26 Children's Center (C10)
30 University Montessori School (F10)
31 Faculty/Staff Housing Office (G8)
32 University Club (F8)
41 Electrical Substation (I6)
51 Pool (F4)
53 Track (F3)
54 Tennis Courts (E4)
55 Bren Events Center (E4)
56 Anteater Field (D4)
58 Mesa Arts Building (E4)
59 Mesa Office Building (D4)
60 Founders' Court (E6)

80 Arnold and Mabel Beckman Center of the National Academies of Sciences and Engineering (F3)
90 Child Development Center (D2)
91 Receiving/Storehouse (C2)
92 Interim Office Building (C2)
93 Mailroom (C2)
94 Air Pollution Labs (C2)
95 Faculty Research Facility (C2)
96 Arboretum (C2)
97 Facilities Management Shops (C2)
98 Recycling Center (D2)
101 Gateway Commons (E6)
102 Main Library (E7)
103 Cross-Cultural Center (D6)
105 Student Services I, II (E6)
111 Administration (D6)
113 Student Center (D6)
200 Social Science Hall (E7)
201 Social Science Tower (E7)
202 Social Science Laboratory (E7)
203 Social Science Trailer (D7)
204 Phoenix Grille (E7)
210 Social Ecology (D8)
211 Social Science A (site) (D7)
213 Social Science B (site) (D7)
215 Social Science C (site) (D8)
221 Graduate School of Management (D8)
230 University Extension B (D8)
231 Rachel Long Morgan Building/ University Extension A (D8)
232 University Extension C (D8)
233 Alumni House (D8)
234 University Extension D (D8)
236 University Extension H (D9)
238 University Extension I (D9)
240 University Extension J (D9)
302 Information and Computer Science (F7)
303 Engineering Tower (E7)
304 Computer Sciences Annex (site) (F8)
305 Engineering Lecture Hall (E8)
310 ICS/Engineering Research Facility (F8)
311 Rockwell Engineering Center (F8)
312 Computer Science/Engineering (F8)
313 ICS Trailers (E8)
315 Interim Classroom Facility (E8)
317 Civil Engineering Facility (E8)
319 Interfaith (E8)
321 Engineering Gateway (F8)
323 Engineering Laboratory Facility (E8)
335 Engineering Instructional Facility (E9)
400 Physical Sciences I (F7)
401 Physical Sciences II (F7)
410 Physical Sciences Research Facility (G7)
411 Physical Sciences Lecture Hall (G7)
412 Physical Sciences Trailers (F6)
413 Physical Sciences Classroom Building (F7)
500 B.C.'S Cavern on the Green (F6)
501 Biological Sciences Lecture Hall (F6)
502 Biological Sciences I (Steinhaus Hall) (F6)
503 Biological Sciences II (F6)

512 Center for the Neurobiology of Learning and Memory (Bonney Center) (F5)
514 Greenhouse (E5)
515 Biological Sciences Administration (F6)
516 Theoretical Neurobiology Facility (F5)
520 Science Library (F5)
522 Radioactive and Chemical Waste Handling Facility (F5)
600 Humanities Office Building (E6)
601 Humanities Hall (E6)
603 Media Services (E6)
610 Humanities Annex (E5)
611 Humanities Interim Classroom Facility (E5)
613 Humanities Trailer Complex (E5)
615 Disability Services (E5)
625 Humanities Office Building 2 (E5)
710 Concert Hall (D5)
711 Fine Arts Village Theatre (E5)
712 Fine Arts Gallery (D5)
713 Studio Theatre (E5)
714 Music Building (D5)
715 Drama and Art History (D5)
718 Orchestra Rehearsal Hall (D5)
720 Sculpture and Ceramic Studios (D5)
721 Fine Arts Dean's Office (D5)
722 Art and T.V. Studios (D5)
723 Fine Arts Production Studio (E5)
724 Fine Arts Student Affairs (D5)
725 Studio Four (E5)
800 Cafe Med (G4)
802 Medical Education Building (G4)
810 Medical Surge I (G4)
811 Medical Sciences B (G5)
812 Medical Surge II (G4)
813 Medical Sciences A (G5)
815 Vivarium Administrative Offices (G5)
817 Beckman Laser Institute (H5)
820 Medical Plaza (G4)
821 Medical Sciences C (G4)
825 Medical Sciences D (G4)
827 Medical Sciences E (H4)
829 Plumwood House (Hitachi) (H4)
831 Medical Sciences F (H4)
833 Medical Sciences Classroom Facility (H4)
835 Irvine Hall (H4)
837 Neuroscience Research Facility (site) (H5)
897 Grounds Maintenance Facility (H6)
899 Keyshop (H6)
901 Bren Events Center (E4)
902 Central Plant (F5)
903 Crawford Hall (F4)
904 Electronic Communications Services Trailer (F5)
905 Handball/Racquetball Courts (F4)
907 Track and Field House (E3)

HOUSING COMPLEXES

Arroyo Vista (B11)
Campus Village (G6)
Irvine Meadows West RV Park (H6)
Las Lomas (G8)
Mesa Court (D4)
Middle Earth (E8)
Palo Verde (E10)
University Hills (G9)
Verano Place (C10)

LOS ANGELES CAMPUS

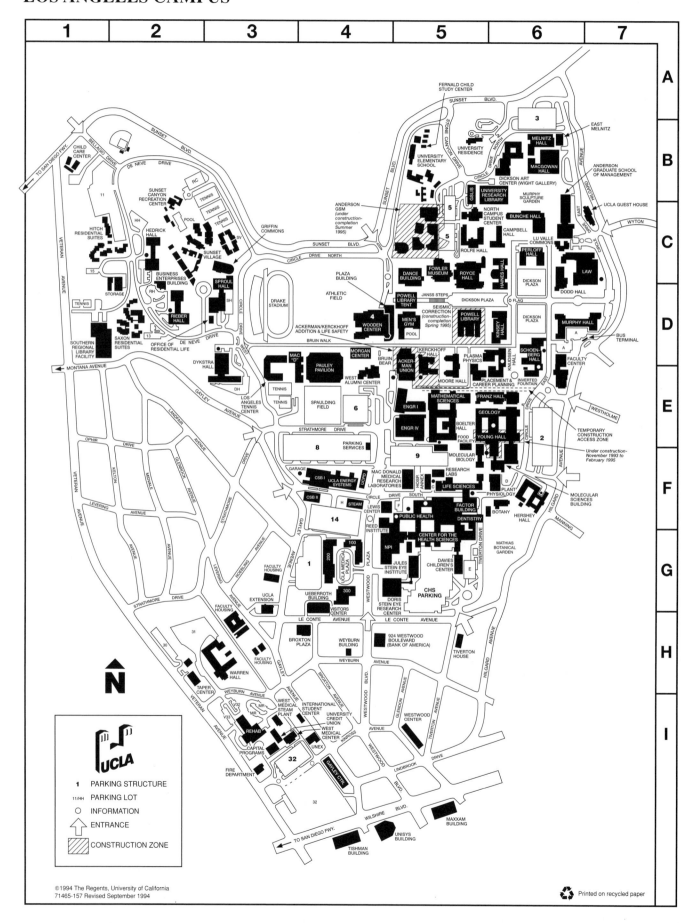

Printed on recycled paper

Key

Building	Grid No.
Ackerman Student Union	E5
Anderson Graduate School of Management	C6
Belt Library (Dickson Art Center)	B6
Boelter Hall	E5
Botany	F6
Broxton Plaza	H4
Bunche Hall	C6
Business Enterprises Building	C2
Campbell Hall	C6
Campus Services Buildings I and II	F4
Capital Programs Building	I3
Center for the Health Sciences	G5
Biomedical Cyclotron	G5
Brain Research Institute	G5
Davies Children's Center	G5
Dentistry, School of	F5
Doris Stein Eye Research Center	G5
Factor Health Sciences Building	F5
Jules Stein Eye Institute	G5
Lewis Neuromuscular Research Center	F4
MacDonald Medical Research Laboratories	F5
Medical Center	G5
Medicine, School of	G5
Neuropsychiatric Institute and Hospital	G5
Nursing, School of	F5
Public Health, School of	F5
Reed Neurological Research Center	G4
Child Care Center	B1
Court of Sciences Food Facility	F5
Dance Building	C5
Dickson Art Center	B6
Dodd Hall	D6
Drake Stadium	D3
Dykstra Hall	E3
East Melnitz Building	B6
Engineering I	E5
Engineering IV	E5
Faculty Center	E6
Fowler Museum of Cultural History	C5
Franz Hall	E6
Garage	F4
Gayley Center	I4
Geology	E6
Griffin Commons (Sunset Village)	C3
Grunwald Center for the Graphic Arts (Dickson Art Center)	B6

Building	Grid No.
Haines Hall	C6
Hedrick Hall	C2
Hershey Hall	F6
Hitch Residential Suites	C1
International Student Center	I4
Kerckhoff Hall	D5
Kinsey Hall	D6
Knudsen Hall	E6
Law, School of	C7
Library and Information Sciences (GSLIS)	B5
Life Sciences	F5
Los Angeles Tennis Center	E3
Lu Valle Commons	C6
Macgowan Hall	B6
Mathematical Sciences	E5
Mathias Botanical Garden	G6
Maxxam Building	I5
Melnitz Hall	B6
Men's Gymnasium	D5
Molecular Biology Institute	F5
Molecular Sciences Building	F6
Moore Hall	E5
Morgan Intercollegiate Athletics Center	D4
Murphy Hall (Administration)	D6
Murphy Sculpture Garden	B6
924 Westwood Boulevard (B of A)	H4
North Campus Student Center	C6
Parking Services (Lot 8)	F4
Pauley Pavilion	E4
Perloff Hall	C6
Physical Plant Office	F4
Placement and Career Planning Center	E6
Plant Physiology	F6
Plasma Physics	D5
Plaza Building	D4
Police, Campus	F4
Powell Library	D5
Powell Library Tent (Towell)	D5
Rehabilitation Center	I3
Residential Life Building	D3
Rieber Hall	D2
Rolfe Hall	C5
Royce Hall	C5
Saxon Residential Suites	D2
Schoenberg Hall	D6
Slichter Hall	E6

Building	Grid No.
Southern Regional Library Facility	D1
Sproul Hall	D3
Sunset Canyon Recreation Center	B2
Sunset Village	C3
Taper Center	I2
Tishman Building	I4
Tiverton House	H5
UCLA Extension Building	G3
UCLA Guest House	C7
UCLA Medical Plaza	G4
Ueberroth Building	G4
Unisys Building	I5
University Credit Union	I3
University Elementary School	B5
University Research Library	B6
University Residence	B5
Visitors Center (Ueberroth Building)	H4
Warren Hall	H2
West Alumni Center	E4
West Medical Center	I4
Westwood Center (Monty's Building)	I5
Weyburn Building	H4
Wight Art Gallery (Dickson Art Center)	B6
Wooden Recreation and Sports Center	D4
Young Hall	E6

Campus Libraries

	Grid No.
Archive of Popular American Music (B425 Schoenberg Hall)	D6
Arts (2250 Dickson Art Center)	B6
Biomedical (12-077 Center for the Health Sciences)	G5
Chemistry (4238 Young Hall)	E6
College Library (Powell Library Tent)	D5
East Asian (21617 University Research Library)	B6
Engineering and Mathematical Sciences (8270 Boelter Hall)	E5
Geology-Geophysics (4697 Geology)	E6
Law (1106 Law)	C7
Management (1400 AGSM)	C6
Map (A253 Bunche Hall)	C6
Music (1102 Schoenberg Hall)	D6
Physics (213 Kinsey Hall)	D6
University Research Library	B6

RIVERSIDE CAMPUS

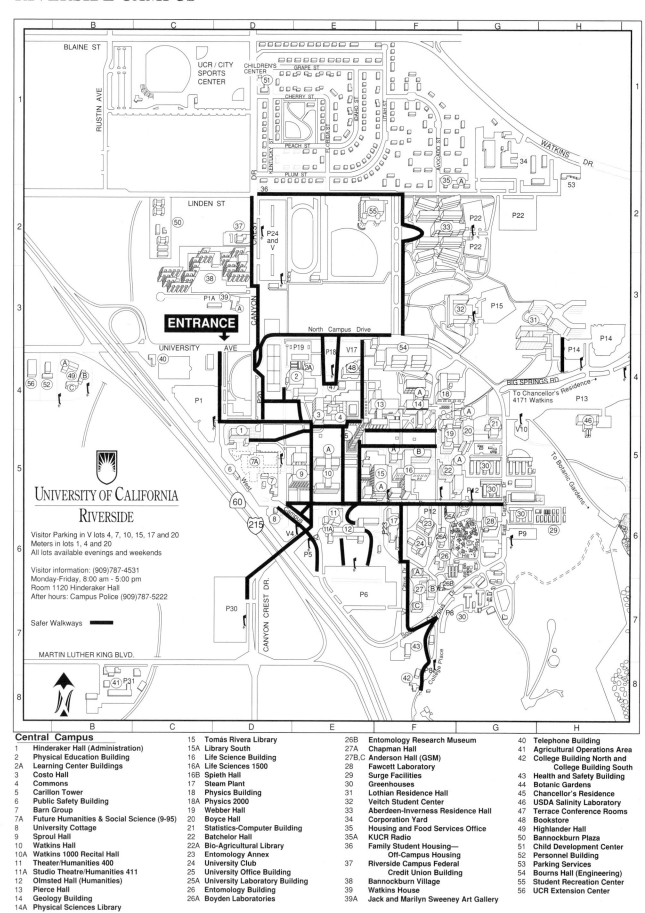

Central Campus

1	Hinderaker Hall (Administration)
2	Physical Education Building
2A	Learning Center Buildings
3	Costo Hall
4	Commons
5	Carillon Tower
6	Public Safety Building
7	Barn Group
7A	Future Humanities & Social Science (9-95)
8	University Cottage
9	Sproul Hall
10	Watkins Hall
10A	Watkins 1000 Recital Hall
11	Theater/Humanities 400
11A	Studio Theatre/Humanities 411
12	Olmsted Hall (Humanities)
13	Pierce Hall
14	Geology Building
14A	Physical Sciences Library
15	Tomás Rivera Library
15A	Library South
16	Life Science Building
16A	Life Sciences 1500
16B	Spieth Hall
17	Steam Plant
18	Physics Building
18A	Physics 2000
19	Webber Hall
20	Boyce Hall
21	Statistics-Computer Building
22	Batchelor Hall
22A	Bio-Agricultural Library
23	Entomology Annex
24	University Club
25	University Office Building
25A	University Laboratory Building
26	Entomology Building
26A	Boyden Laboratories
26B	Entomology Research Museum
27A	Chapman Hall
27B,C	Anderson Hall (GSM)
28	Fawcett Laboratory
29	Surge Facilities
30	Greenhouses
31	Lothian Residence Hall
32	Veitch Student Center
33	Aberdeen-Inverness Residence Hall
34	Corporation Yard
35	Housing and Food Services Office
35A	KUCR Radio
36	Family Student Housing— Off-Campus Housing
37	Riverside Campus Federal Credit Union Building
38	Bannockburn Village
39	Watkins House
39A	Jack and Marilyn Sweeney Art Gallery
40	Telephone Building
41	Agricultural Operations Area
42	College Building North and College Building South
43	Health and Safety Building
44	Botanic Gardens
45	Chancellor's Residence
46	USDA Salinity Laboratory
47	Terrace Conference Rooms
48	Bookstore
49	Highlander Hall
50	Bannockburn Plaza
51	Child Development Center
52	Personnel Building
53	Parking Services
54	Bourns Hall (Engineering)
55	Student Recreation Center
56	UCR Extension Center

SAN DIEGO CAMPUS

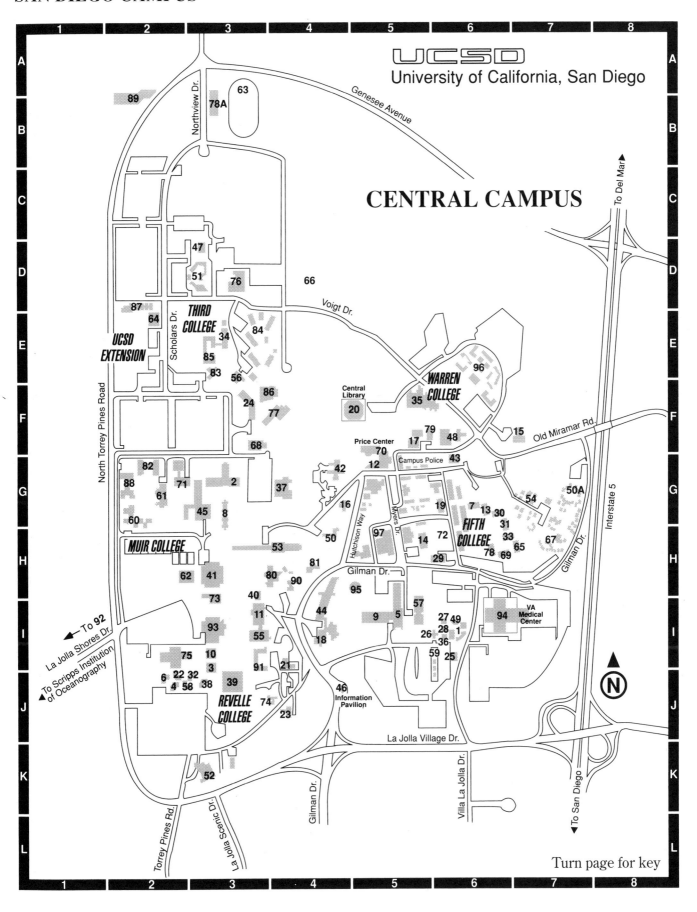

UCSD
University of California, San Diego

CENTRAL CAMPUS

Turn page for key

SAN DIEGO CENTRAL CAMPUS

SAN FRANCISCO CAMPUS

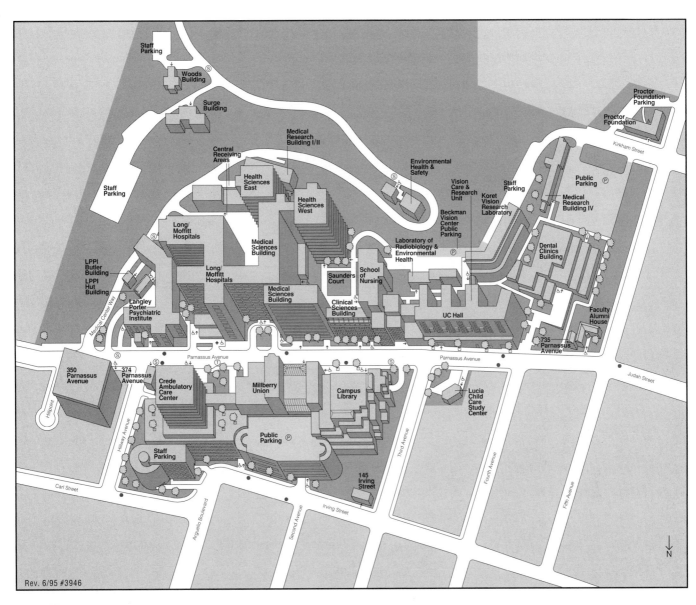

Rev. 6/95 #3946

Parnassus Campus

▨	UCSF Campus
Ⓟ	Public Parking
✚	Emergency Service
↑	Main Entrance
♿	Entrance for the Physically Disabled
•	Muni Stop
Ⓢ	Campus Shuttle Stop
Ⓣ	Taxi

Key

Crede Ambulatory Care Center (A)
400 Parnassus Avenue

Campus Library (CL)
530 Parnassus Avenue

Central Receiving

Clinical Sciences Building (C)
521 Parnassus Avenue
Dental Clinics

Dental Clinics Building (D)
707 Parnassus Avenue

Environmental Health & Safety (EHS)
50 Medical Center Way

Faculty Alumni House (FA)
745 Parnassus Avenue

Health Sciences East (HSE)

Health Sciences West (HSW)

Koret Vision Research Lab (K)
(Beckman Vision Center)
10 Kirkham Street

Laboratory of Radiobiology & Environmental Health (LR)

Langley Porter Psychiatric Institute (LPPI)
401 Parnassus Avenue
LPPI Butler Building
LPPI Hut Building

Long/Moffitt Hospitals (MC)
Patient Information
505 Parnassus Avenue
Joseph M. Long Hospital
Herbert C. Moffitt Hospital
Children's Medical Center

Lucia Child Care Study Center (CCC)
610 Parnassus Avenue

Medical Research Building I/II (MR I/II)

Medical Research Building IV (MR IV)

Medical Sciences Building (S)
513 Parnassus Avenue
Cole Hall
Graduate Division
School of Dentistry
School of Medicine
School of Pharmacy

Millberry Union (MU)
500 Parnassus Avenue
Bookstore
Conference Center
Recreation & Fitness Center

Proctor Foundation (PF)
95 Kirkham Street

Public Parking (P)
Millberry Union Garage
(enter on Irving or Parnassus)
Dental Clinics Building Lot (enter on Kirkham)

School of Nursing (N)

Surge Building (SU)
90 Medical Center Way

UC Hall (U)
533 Parnassus Avenue
Beckman Vision Center
Faculty Practice Offices
Toland Hall

Vision Care & Research Unit (VCRU)
(Beckman Vision Center)
8 Kirkham Street

Woods Building (W)
100 Medical Center Way

145 Irving Street

350 Parnassus Avenue
(Leased; fee parking available)

374 Parnassus Avenue

735 Parnassus Avenue

SANTA BARBARA CAMPUS

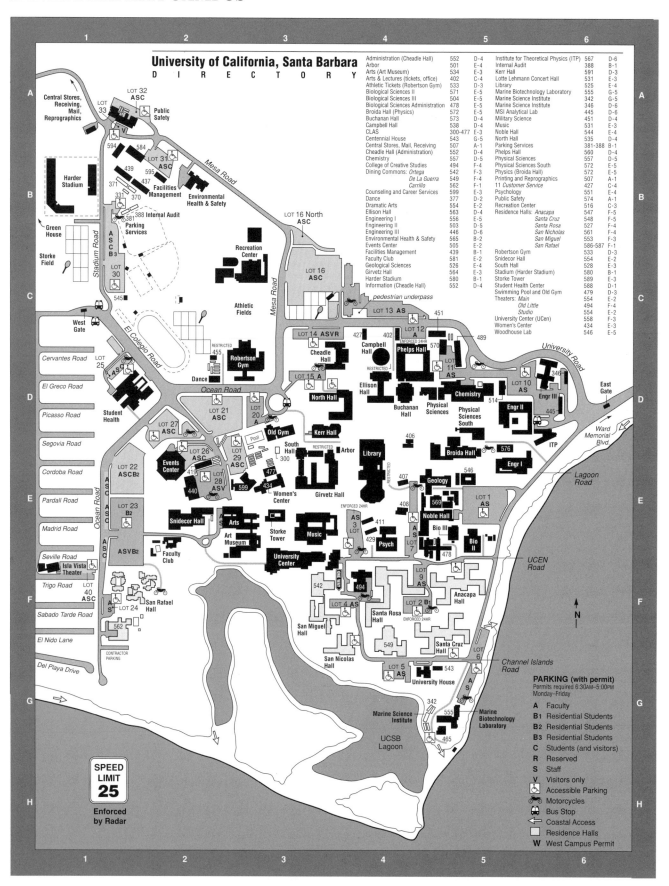

University of California, Santa Barbara
D I R E C T O R Y

Administration (Cheadle Hall)	552	D-4
Arbor	501	E-4
Arts (Art Museum)	534	E-3
Arts & Lectures (tickets, office)	402	C-4
Athletic Tickets (Robertson Gym)	533	D-3
Biological Sciences II	571	E-5
Biological Sciences III	504	E-5
Biological Sciences Administration	478	E-5
Broida Hall (Physics)	572	E-5
Buchanan Hall	573	D-4
Campbell Hall	538	D-4
CLAS	300-477	E-3
Centennial House	543	G-5
Central Stores, Mail, Receiving	507	A-1
Cheadle Hall (Administration)	552	D-4
Chemistry	557	D-5
College of Creative Studies	494	F-4
Dining Commons: Ortega	542	F-3
De La Guerra	549	F-4
Carrillo	562	F-1
Counseling and Career Services	599	E-3
Dance	377	D-2
Dramatic Arts	554	E-2
Ellison Hall	563	D-4
Engineering I	556	E-5
Engineering III	503	D-5
Engineering III	446	D-6
Environmental Health & Safety	565	B-2
Events Center	505	E-2
Facilities Management	439	B-1
Faculty Club	581	E-2
Geological Sciences	526	E-4
Girvetz Hall	564	E-3
Harder Stadium	580	B-1
Information (Cheadle Hall)	552	D-4

Institute for Theoretical Physics (ITP)	567	D-6
Internal Audit	388	B-1
Kerr Hall	591	D-3
Lotte Lehmann Concert Hall	531	E-3
Library	525	E-4
Marine Biotechnology Laboratory	555	G-5
Marine Science Institute	342	G-5
Marine Science Institute	346	D-6
MSI Analytical Lab	445	D-6
Military Science	451	D-4
Music	531	E-3
Noble Hall	544	E-4
North Hall	535	D-4
Parking Services	381-388	B-1
Phelps Hall	560	D-4
Physical Sciences	557	D-5
Physical Sciences South	572	E-5
Physics (Broida Hall)	572	E-5
Printing and Reprographics	507	A-1
11 Customer Service	427	C-4
Psychology	551	E-5
Public Safety	574	A-1
Recreation Center	516	C-3
Residence Halls: Anacapa	547	F-5
Santa Cruz	548	F-5
Santa Rosa	527	F-4
San Nicholas	561	F-4
San Miguel	553	F-4
San Rafael	586-587	F-1
Robertson Gym	533	D-3
Snidecor Hall	554	E-2
South Hall	528	E-3
Stadium (Harder Stadium)	580	B-1
Storke Tower	589	E-3
Student Health Center	588	D-1
Swimming Pool and Old Gym	479	D-3
Theaters: Main	554	E-2
Old Little	494	F-4
Studio	554	E-2
University Center (UCen)	558	F-3
Women's Center	434	E-3
Woodhouse Lab	546	E-5

PARKING (with permit)
Permits required 6:30AM–5:00PM
Monday–Friday

A	Faculty
B1	Residential Students
B2	Residential Students
B3	Residential Students
C	Students (and visitors)
R	Reserved
S	Staff
V	Visitors only
♿	Accessible Parking
🏍	Motorcycles
🚌	Bus Stop
⬅	Coastal Access
▢	Residence Halls
W	West Campus Permit

SPEED LIMIT **25**
Enforced by Radar

SANTA CRUZ CAMPUS

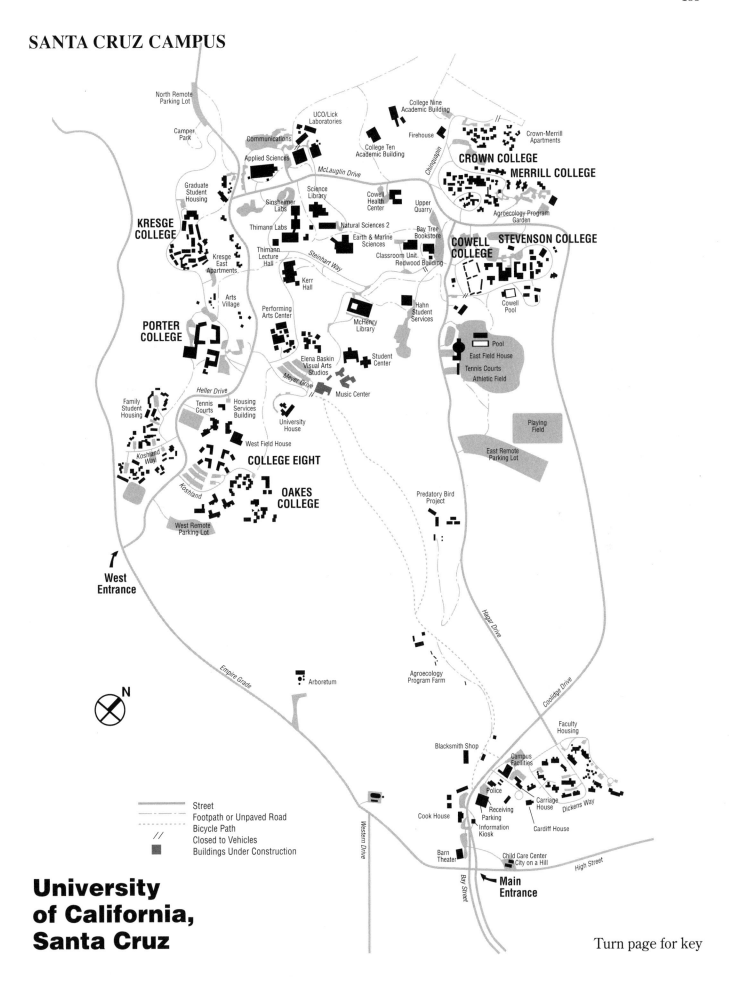

North Remote
Parking Lot

Camper
Park

Communications

Applied Sciences

UCO/Lick
Laboratories

College Nine
Academic Building

Firehouse

Crown-Merrill
Apartments

McLauglin Drive

College Ten
Academic Building

Chinquapin

CROWN COLLEGE

MERRILL COLLEGE

Graduate
Student
Housing

Sinsheimer
Labs

Science
Library

Cowell
Health
Center

Upper
Quarry

**KRESGE
COLLEGE**

Thimann Labs

Natural Sciences 2

Earth & Marine
Sciences

Bay Tree
Bookstore

Agroecology Program
Garden

Kresge
East
Apartments

Thimann
Lecture
Hall

Steinhart Way

Classroom Unit
Redwood Building

**COWELL
COLLEGE**

STEVENSON COLLEGE

Kerr
Hall

Cowell
Pool

Arts
Village

Performing
Arts Center

McHenry
Library

Hahn
Student
Services

**PORTER
COLLEGE**

Elena Baskin
Visual Arts
Studios

Student
Center

Pool

Meyer Drive

Music Center

East Field House

Tennis Courts

Athletic Field

Heller Drive

Family
Student
Housing

Tennis
Courts

Housing
Services
Building

University
House

Playing
Field

Koshland
Way

West Field House

COLLEGE EIGHT

East Remote
Parking Lot

Koshland

**OAKES
COLLEGE**

Predatory Bird
Project

West Remote
Parking Lot

↑
**West
Entrance**

Hagar Drive

Coolidge Drive

Empire Grade

Arboretum

Agroecology
Program Farm

⊗ N

Faculty
Housing

Blacksmith Shop

Campus
Facilities

Police

Carriage
House

Dickens Way

Cook House

Receiving
Parking

Cardiff House

Information
Kiosk

―――――― Street
―·―·―·― Footpath or Unpaved Road
·············· Bicycle Path
// Closed to Vehicles
⬛ Buildings Under Construction

Western Drive

Barn
Theater

Child Care Center
City on a Hill

High Street

University
of California,
Santa Cruz

Bay Street

← **Main
Entrance**

Turn page for key

134

SANTA CRUZ CAMPUS KEY

GENERAL FACILITIES

Admissions/Evaluation (Hahn Student Services)	C-4
Admissions/Outreach (Cook House)	I-5
Agroecology Program Farm	**H-4**
Alumni Office (Carriage House)	I-6
Applied Sciences Building	**B-2**
Arboretum	**H-3**
Arts Division (Porter College)	D-2
Baskin Center for Computer Engineering and Information Sciences (Applied Sciences)	B-2
Bay Tree Bookstore	**B-4**
Box Office (Redwood Building)	C-4
Cardiff House (Women's Center)	**I-6**
Career Services (Hahn Student Services)	C-4
Carriage House	**I-6**
Cashier (Hahn Student Services)	C-4
Center for Nonlinear Science (Natural Sciences)	B-3
Chancellor's Office (McHenry Library)	C-3
Child Care Center (YWCA-Granary)	**J-5**
City on a Hill (newspaper)	**J-5**
Classroom Unit	**B-4**
College Eight	**E-2**
College Nine Academic Building	**A-4**
College Ten Academic Building	**A-4**
Communications Building	**A-3**
Computer Center (Communications)	A-3
Conference Office (Housing Services)	D-2
Cook House (Admissions)	**I-5**
Cowell College	**C-5**
Cowell Student Health Center	**B-4**
Crown College	**B-5**
Development Office (Carriage House)	I-6
Disabled Student Services (Hahn Student Services)	C-4
Earth and Marine Sciences Building	**B-3**
Executive Vice Chancellor (McHenry Library)	C-3
Faculty Housing	**I-6**
Family Student Housing	**D-1**
Financial Aid (Hahn Student Services)	C-4
Firehouse	**A-5**

Garden (Agroecology Program)	**B-6**
Graduate Student Housing	**B-2**
Graduate Studies and Research (Applied Sciences)	B-2
Hahn Student Services Building	**C-4**
Housing Services	**D-2**
Humanities Division (Cowell College)	C-5
Institute of Marine Sciences (Applied Sciences)	B-2
Institute of Tectonics (Applied Sciences)	B-2
International Programs (Classroom Unit)	B-4
Kerr Hall	**C-3**
Kresge College	**B-1**
KZSC Radio (Crown College)	B-5
McHenry Library	**C-3**
Merrill College	**B-5**
Music Center	**D-3**
Natural Sciences Division (Applied Sciences)	B-2
Natural Sciences 2 Building	**B-3**
Oakes College	**E-2**
Parking Office (Police Office)	I-5
Personnel, Academic (McHenry Library)	C-3
Personnel, Staff (Communications)	A-3
Police Office	**I-5**
Porter College	**D-2**
Predatory Bird Project	**F-5**
Public Information/Publications (Carriage House)	I-6
Redwood Building	**C-4**
Re-Entry Program (Classroom Unit)	B-4
Registrar (Hahn Student Services)	C-4
SAA/EOP (Hahn Student Services)	C-4
Science Library	**B-3**
SCIPP (Natural Sciences)	B-3
Sinsheimer Laboratories	**B-3**
SOAR (Student Center)	D-3
Social Sciences Division (Kerr Hall)	C-3
Stevenson College	**C-6**
Student Center	**D-3**
Student Employment (Hahn Student Services)	C-4
Student Services (Hahn Student Services)	C-4
Summer Session Office (Classroom Unit)	B-4

Thimann Laboratories	**B-3**
Thimann Lecture Hall	**B-3**
UCO/Lick Observatory Offices (Natural Sciences)	B-3
UCSC Foundation (Carriage House)	I-6
University Advancement (Carriage House)	I-6
University House	**D-3**
Visitor Information	J-5
Women's Center (Cardiff House)	I-6

ARTS FACILITIES

Barn Theater	**J-5**
Baskin Visual Arts Studios	**D-3**
Performing Arts Center	**D-3**
Sesnon Art Gallery (Porter College)	D-2
Smith Art Gallery (Cowell College)	C-5
Upper Quarry Amphitheater	**B-4**

ATHLETIC FACILITIES

Field House East	**D-5**
Field House West	**E-2**
Physical Education, Recreation, Sports	**D-5**
Swimming Pool	D-5
Tennis Courts East (Field House East)	D-5
Tennis Courts West (Field House West)	D-2

RESTAURANTS AND COFFEEHOUSES

Banana Joe's (Crown College)	B-5
Cafe Oakes (Oakes College)	E-2
College Eight Cafe (College Eight)	E-2
Cowell Coffee Shop (Cowell College)	C-5
Howling Cow Cafe (Kresge College)	B-1
The Hungry Slug (Porter College)	D-2
Stevenson Coffee House (Stevenson College)	C-6
Taqueria Pacifico (Merrill College)	B-5
Togo's (Student Center)	D-3
Whole Earth Restaurant (Redwood Building)	C-4

C

The **California Business Higher Education Forum** is a nonprofit, nonpartisan organization made up of some 60 California business and higher education/foundation chief executive officers who are working in partnership to identify the problems facing the state's business and higher education institutions.

The California economy, business flight, and defense conversion are among the most immediate issues the Forum is addressing.

The purpose of the Forum is to promote understanding, communication and mutual support and to develop the means through which the state's business and higher education leadership can foster excellence in higher education and promote economic development in California.

Patterned after the American Council on Education's national Business-Higher Education Forum, the California Forum was conceived by UC President Jack Peltason in fall 1992.

To bring the organization together, Peltason was joined by the presidents of the California Institute of Technology, the University of Southern California, Stanford University and several other private California campuses, as well as the chancellors of the UC campuses and the chancellors and several presidents from The California State University and the California Community College system.

An equal number of representatives were invited to join from the business and financial community.

The California Business-Higher Education Forum held its inaugural meeting in February 1993. The meeting featured addresses by California's Governor and the Speaker of the Assembly.

From its inaugural meeting, the Forum has striven to be an action-oriented organization. At its fall 1993 meeting, the members developed agendas covered three areas of major importance for California: business flight and impediments, fiscal restructuring, and defense conversion jobs and retraining.

Because of its immediate importance to the state, the membership endorsed the formation of a task force charged with examining the need for fiscal reform for state and local government and with preparing a plan of action for California fiscal reform.

REFERENCES: "The California Business-Higher Education Forum," an information sheet, January 1994, and related materials.

CROSS-REFERENCES: Section of the Brief History relating to the Peltason initiatives.

California Council on Science and Technology: In 1988, the Legislature asked the University to establish a statewide council to conduct studies and issue reports on the state's urgent science and technology needs.

In response, the California Council on Science and Technology was formed in collaboration with the University of Southern California, the California Institute of Technology, Stanford University, and the California State University.

The 21-member Council is governed by a board of directors appointed by the presidents and chancellor of the founding universities. The membership consists of scholars and experts from both the universities and the private sector.

The Council held its inaugural session in November 1989.

The specific goals are to examine technical, social and economic issues related to science and technology in the state, to improve the competitiveness of the state's industries, and to increase collaboration between universities and industries.

Topics for studies may be proposed by the founding universities, the governor's office and other executive agencies, committees of the State Legislature, the advisory committee for the State Competitive Technology Program, other universities, nonprofit organizations, and appropriate industrial associations.

In addition, the Council may initiate studies.

REFERENCES: Fact sheets and news releases, Office of the President.

CROSS-REFERENCES: All subjects related to University-industry relations, technology transfer and science policy.

California Education Round Table: At a 1980 Regents' meeting, UC President David S. Saxon announced his intention to convene a California Round Table on Equal Educational Opportunity to bring together leaders from all levels of education in California along with civic and minority groups.

The Round Table was established as a public interest coalition dedicated to improving opportunity for low income and minority students.

Special emphasis was placed on improving elementary and secondary schools that served low income students and underrepresented students from minority groups in order to enhance academic achievement and provide them with new opportunities to succeed in post secondary institutions.

The original components of the Round Table were Instruction; Information; Remediation; Community and Parental Support; and Financial Support.

The Round Table functioned primarily to exchange information among participating institutions and organizations concerning efforts to improve educational achievement in California; to identify research questions relevant to policies for improving educational achievement and promote studies that illuminate such questions; to review outreach programs offered by postsecondary institutions and school improvement efforts at the secondary school level; to formulate policies that enhance the effectiveness and efficiency of such programs, including questions of coordination.

In March 1981, the members of the Round Table issued a "Statement of Purpose and Initial Agenda" which listed these goals:

1) Increase the percentage of students who graduate from high school

2) Improve the academic skills of high school graduates

3) Strengthen the teaching profession

4) Improve the coordination and effectiveness of postsecondary outreach programs

5) Strengthen the community college transfer function

In 1986, the Round Table changed its name to the California Education Round Table and expanded its focus to include the concept of intersegmental cooperation as an effective method of addressing statewide issues.

Intersegmental cooperation had taken on increased importance in the state as a way to enhance the outcomes of outreach and affirmative action programs and foster school improvement.

In 1987, the Commission for Review of the Master Plan recognized the Round Table as a logical choice to coordinate intersegmental programs to assure that individuals from all groups has full opportunity for quality education.

That same year, the Round Table established the Intersegmental Coordinating Council (ICC) as its administrative arm.

To this day, the Round Table continues as a voluntary organization committed to intersegmental cooperation.

The ICC is responsible for carrying out the Round Table's mandate for more effective intersegmental relations and for seeing that significant state policy issues are addressed by the educational community.

It serves as a forum for intersegmental policy discussion and proposals for action which are referred to the Round Table.

The Intersegmental Coordinating Council is composed of faculty, students and policy-level staff capable of fulfilling commitments made by California's educational segments.

In 1991, UC President David P. Gardner stated that "The Round Table is an effort on the part of educational leaders in California informally to share concerns and put on the table issues upon which they have a common interest, debate issues and help their respective institutions and responsibilities while affording the collective capacity to express views to the Executive and Legisla-

ture. With the changing situation of our state, we have even more occasion to come together."

The current membership of the Round Table includes the President of UC, the Chancellor of the California State University, the Chancellor of the California Community Colleges, the President of the Association of Independent Colleges and Universities, the Superintendent of Public Instruction and the Director of the California Postsecondary Education Commission.

REFERENCES: Information from Intersegmental Relations, Office of the President.

CROSS-REFERENCES: All subjects related to education.

The California Policy Seminar (CPS) is a joint program of the University of California and state government established in 1977 to apply the University's research expertise to the state's current and future policy concerns.

The need to draw upon UC research relevant to California's needs has become increasingly important in light of the state's growing economic, educational, environmental and health challenges.

CPS is a systemwide program administered through the division of Academic Affairs in the Office of the President. An 18-member Policy Steering Committee oversees the work of CPS.

The committee, which identifies priority topics for a yearly competitive grants program and makes resulting funding decisions, consists of representatives of the Governor, the Speaker of the Assembly, the President Pro Tempore of the Senate and the President of the University.

The California Policy Seminar conducts two programs, Policy Research and Technical Assistance, both supported by an active dissemination effort.

Through its Policy Research Program, CPS funds research by UC faculty on state priority issues identified by its Steering Committee. Research findings are published as *CPS Reports* and distributed to state officials, interested faculty and others.

In order to reach a broader range of public officials, academics and others interested in policy-related research, CPS inaugurated the *CPS Brief* series in November 1989.

Briefs summarize research funded by the Seminar, as well as feature the work of faculty sponsored by other sources of potential interest to state decision makers.

Each issue is distributed to nearly 1,500 readers, including California legislators, executive branch officials, public- and private-sector representatives and policy analysts, the state's congressional delegation, and selected UC faculty and administrators.

Approximately 12 *Reports* and 20 *Briefs* are issued each year describing the background, findings and policy implications of each research project.

To further inform policy debates, CPS has initiated a series of briefings in the state capitol. These briefings provide information about CPS-sponsored research, and enable the faculty to discuss their research and its implications with state officials and policy specialists.

In addition, CPS has convened a number of forums, roundtable discussions and other meetings in recent years to bring scholars and policy makers together to discuss specific issues.

Through its Technical Assistance Program, CPS offers immediate faculty assistance to policy makers on a wide range of state concerns.

In response to requests from legislative and executive branch officials, CPS identifies faculty experts; arranges and facilitates meetings, workshops, roundtable discussions, seminars, and conferences; or commissions data analyses and policy papers.

Under the auspices of the Technical Assistance Program, CPS has convened university specialists, governmental officials and other interested parties to discuss many critical issues, including the following:

Improving California's business climate, reducing neighborhood crime, managing the state's growth, preserving agricultural land and natural resources, improving the health of agricultural workers and extending health coverage to all Californians, improving transportation planning and reducing congestion, adapting to new workplace technologies, developing alternative energy resources, improving water quality and availability, and responding to natural disasters.

Findings of work conducted under the Technical Assistance Program are also issued in *CPS Reports* and *Briefs*.

Since 1990, CPS has also administered the Latina/ Latino Policy Research Grants Program as part of an Office of the President initiative on research related to the state's Latino population.

Under the direction of a faculty advisory committee, CPS funds policy-oriented research on California's Mexican, Central American and other Latin American origin populations.

This program was initiated as part of UC's response to a Senate concurrent resolution, which requested that the University address problems facing the state's Latino population.

Recognizing that a wide range of work potentially useful to state decision makers is under way throughout the University, CPS has been working to better coordinate its activities with those of other UC programs.

For example, CPS has cosponsored conferences on such topics as political reform, drug-exposed infants, taxation, the initiative process, and the proposed North American Free Trade Area (NAFTA) agreement.

California faced a host of challenges in the early 1990s as the state's fiscal health was threatened by nationwide economic restructuring and a resulting decline in revenues.

As a result, UC developed several initiatives facilitating cooperation between state government, private industry and the University to foster economic revitalization.

This effort draws heavily on the strengths and experience of the California Policy Seminar, ensuring that UC expertise is brought to bear on the critical issues of the day.

REFERENCES: California Policy Seminar Biennial Reports and Publication Lists.
CROSS-REFERENCES: Topics indicated in the text.

The California Postsecondary Education Commission was created by the California Legislature and the Governor in 1974.

The Commission is a citizen board of 17 members who receive no salary for their work as commissioners. The members meet at least six times a year to establish policies and direct the activities of the Commission's executive director and staff in Sacramento.

The Commission consists of nine representatives of the general public appointed by State officials, six representatives of California's major systems of education appointed by those systems, and two student representatives appointed by the Governor from nominees of the statewide student body associations of the systems.

One of the six representatives of California's major segments of education is a Regent of the University of California.

The others are representatives of the State Board of Education, the Board of Governors of the California Community Colleges, the Trustees of the California State University, and the Council for Postsecondary and Vocational Education. In addition, there is a representative of independent colleges and universities (appointment by the Governor).

The Commission is charged by law "to assure the effective utilization of public postsecondary education resources, thereby eliminating waste and unnecessary duplication, and to promote diversity, innovation, and responsiveness to student and societal needs."

Specifically, the Commission has three duties:

• To provide the Governor, the Legislature and educators with independent, non-partisan policy advice about major issues confronting higher education

• To coordinate the educational efforts of California's colleges and universities and their long-range planning activities

• To evaluate the success of California's higher education policies and practices in achieving State goals

The Commission fulfills its duties by working cooperatively with the state's educational systems and other state agencies. It develops its proposals for action with the advice of these systems and agencies, and it seeks to build consensus among all parties affected by the proposals.

The Commission is charged by statute to fulfill some 30 recurring responsibilities. In addition, each year it receives requests for policy analyses from the Governor, the Legislature and other agencies. It then develops an annual workplan based on its assigned duties, as limited by its available resources.

The Commission is provided with an annual appropriation in order to employ the executive director and the staff of 40, as well as to pay the costs of commissioners in connection with their attendance at meetings.

Each year, the Commission elects its chair and vice chair from among its nine members representing the general public. It conducts its business primarily through the work of three major committees on governmental relations, educational policy and programs, and fiscal policy and analysis.

It maintains cooperative relations with the state's educational institutions through its Statutory Advisory Committee, which consists of the chief executive officers of the state's six major systems of education or their designated representatives.

By law, the Commission's meetings are open to the public.

Almost every state has created an advisory commission like the Commission as a coordinating and planning agency for higher education, or else has had to form a single governing board to oversee its colleges and universities.

Under California's Master Plan for Higher Education, the State has not created a single governing board for its distinctive systems of colleges and universities. Instead, the Master Plan has directed the Commission to coordinate the activities of these systems of institutions in the public interest by "providing an integrated and segmentally unbiased view for purposes of State policy formulation and evaluation."

Prior to the Commission's creation, the Coordinating Council for Higher Education had been responsible for coordination of higher education in the state after California's Master Plan for Higher Education was approved in 1960.

REFERENCES: "New California Postsecondary Education Commission Officially Succeeds Coordinating Council for Higher Education on April 1," *University Bulletin,* Vol. 22, No. 26, March 25, 1974; Commission's informational material.

CROSS-REFERENCES: Master Plan for Higher Education; Regents; Site Selection; subjects related to education.

Campus Foundations. See Foundations.

Capital Improvement Program: For decades the University's programs of instruction, research and public service have been an important factor in both the society and economy of the state.

The University has been responsible for providing young men and women from all segments of society with the best of educational opportunities and accomplishments and preparing them for leadership in their communities, as well as in commerce, industry and science.

With knowledge and skills at the forefront of their fields, they have been key to creating and sustaining the state's economy, and they will be crucial to the state's response to the challenges ahead.

The University's capital program is designed to meet a variety of issues in order to sustain this educational mission.

First is change and obsolescence.

Instruction and research programs evolve, grow larger or smaller, change direction and fields diverge or converge. To prepare students properly, the academic programs responsible must themselves be at the frontiers of knowledge in those fields, developing and using innovative processes and technologies that generate discovery, expand knowledge and give competitive advantage to the state. Unless academic facilities are renovated and updated to meet continually changing program needs, those facilities become constraints to the capability and development of the programs and students.

Second is the wear and decline resulting from the age of many of UC's buildings and its infrastructure.

The importance of facility renewal is obvious at UC's older campuses, but even the newest campuses are now well into their third decade and are experiencing many of the same problems of deteriorating condition, service and operating cost.

In addition, many of UC's older buildings were designed to meet building, fire and life safety codes that have changed dramatically over the decades. Not only have society's understanding and expectations of proper design and safety changed, but the activities housed in the buildings (particularly science and engineering laboratory functions) have also become much more complex and problematic. As knowledge has grown about earthquake forces and building structural response, the University also has learned that many of its buildings have structural deficiencies that should be corrected.

The capital needs resulting from these factors were compounded by a period of very limited funding in the 1970s and early 1980s. The University's backlog of deferred maintenance and improvements grew dramatically, and the extent of facility deficiencies became a major constraint to program quality and innovation.

Starting in the mid-1980s, the State of California was able to increase capital funding substantially, from $17 million in 1982–83 to $233 million in 1992–93. During that same period, the University made every effort to expand non-State capital resources, and funding from sources other than the State grew from $145 million to about $400 million.

While expansion in financial support in the 1980s was most welcome, it occurred in a period of rapid enrollment growth that has continued to this time and for which many new facilities had to be provided.

The result is that the University has never caught up with its longstanding facility deficiencies. The pressure of supporting the growing numbers of new students meant that crowded classrooms, laboratories, offices and support facilities have been a continuing fact of life, and many deficiencies remain to be addressed, including problems of insufficiency, obsolescence, condition, code compliance and safety.

Funding arrangements have also become more complicated.

In the early 1980s the primary source of State capital outlay funding was tideland oil revenues appropriated through the Capital Outlay Fund for Public Higher Education; the basic source of non-State funding was a modest amount of debt financing for facilities that housed revenue-producing enterprises like student housing.

Now the mix of sources is much more complex.

General obligation bond measures are a primary source of State capital funds, but are dependent on approval by the voters at general elections every two years.

Also, three different revenue bond financing mechanisms have been approved by the State.

The University's private fund raising for capital projects has increased significantly, as has the level of debt financing, the use of lease-purchase mechanisms and land-lease arrangements with third-party developers.

And the University is seeing many more projects with multiple fund sources and creative funding approaches.

Because of this increasing complexity of both needs and funding arrangements, good planning is a necessity. The University's campuses have recognized this responsibility and have proceeded to update their long range development plans and conduct other planning studies to address individual campus issues.

A five-year capital program is now routinely prepared instead of the three-year program that was normal in the past. Projects proposed for State funding in the annual capital improvement budget are based on months of detailed planning and pre-design analysis that will enable the University to effectively explain the project during State review, and support project management during design and construction.

REFERENCES: "Overview: University of California Improvement Program," Budget for Capital Improvements, 1992–93, Office of the President.

CROSS-REFERENCES: Buildings.

Central Valley: The University has had a long history of service in California's Central Valley, even though it had no campus there.

The University's presence in the Valley began more than 100 years ago, when UC opened its first Valley research station at Tulare to study drainage and salinity problems. Since that time in 1888, the University's commitment to the Valley has continued to grow. UC now serves every major area in the region in a number of important ways.

Here is a summary of some of the programs that have been in place over the years.

• Cooperative Extension (CE). Operation of Cooperative Extension offices is a joint effort of UC, county governments and the U.S. Department of Agriculture. Every county in Central California has a CE office to help farmers put the latest advances in agricultural research to practical use. Each office specializes in agricultural development, the utilization of natural resources, and an understanding of community issues important to the county it serves. In their operations, these offices help growers in the selection of specialty crops, marketing, irrigation, weed control, safe pesticide use and other agricultural areas.

• 4-H. This popular program helps California youngsters between the ages of 9 and 19 develop into responsible, self-directed citizens and future leaders.

• Agricultural Field Stations and Research Centers. Three Valley centers, the Kearney Agricultural Center and the Westside and Lindcore Research and Extension Centers, work with growers, packers, and shippers of fresh market crops. Their purpose is to help improve handling, reduce marketing losses, and provide consumers with higher quality products. These facilities located in Parlier, Exeter and Five Points, conduct hundreds of ongoing scientific studies in soil and water conservation, pest and disease control, the development of new crop varieties, and other areas.

The Kearney Agricultural Center in Parlier is the largest off-campus agricultural research facility operated by UC. The center has increased the income of Valley farmers by more than $1 billion annually. In addition, UC researchers working in agriculture and natural resources experimental areas conduct field studies in cotton and other crops, as well as forestry, at a site near Sequoia National Park.

• Mosquito Control Research Laboratory. This laboratory, located at the Kearney Agricultural Center, pioneers new techniques to control mosquitos worldwide.

• The UCSF-Fresno Medical Education Program. This program has more than 125 fulltime UC faculty and 300 volunteer physicians teaching more than 220 resident and medical students at the center. It is a major clinical branch of UC San Francisco. It trains new doctors and provides San Joaquin Valley physicians with information about new medical research through continuing education. More than 10 percent of the Valley's doctors are graduates of this program.

- UCSF Central California Comprehensive Alzheimer's Center. This center provides comprehensive diagnosis and care for patients with Alzheimer's disease.
- UCSF Office of Post Graduate Education. This Fresno site offers classes and conferences for doctors, nurses and other health care professionals.
- The UC Fresno Regional Office. This office links Valley communities with the nine campuses.
- The UC Davis Transfer Opportunity Program. This program encourages community college students to transfer to UC Davis and other UC campuses.
- The UC Santa Cruz Early Academic Outreach Program. This serves 30 local middle schools and high schools to increase the number of underrepresented minority and low-income students who pursue higher education.
- The University Relations Office in the Office of the President. This office provides general information about UC to Central California residents. It also maintains liaison with other UC offices, alumni and legislators.
- Relations with Schools. Staff at this office provides UC admissions advising and coordination with area schools.

- UC Davis Veterinary Medicine Teaching and Research Center and Veterinary Diagnostic Laboratories. The center in Tulare is renowned for research in animal science. Three diagnostic laboratories in Tulare, Fresno and Turlock test for animal diseases
- UC Davis University Extension. This facility provides continuing education courses in agriculture and other subjects.
- UC Berkeley's Lawrence Hall of Science (LHS) has created an educational center in Fresno called the "GEMS" Center (for "Great Explorations in Math and Science"). It has recruited top Central California teachers and trained them in new ways to teach math and science, based on techniques developed at LHS. In addition, teachers in Fresno County have access to the latest science curricula, displays and interactive demonstrations from LHS.

REFERENCES: "UC Growth and Central California," informational leaflet, July 1990 and "UC Site Selection Update," Vol. 4, No. 2, July 1992, University Relations, Office of the President; "The University of California's valleywide presence," *UC Site Selection Update* newsletter, Office of the President, Vol. 4, No. 2, July 1992; "New UC Center Brings Innovative Science Teaching to the Valley," news release, September 24, 1992, University Relations.

CROSS-REFERENCES: Subjects cited in the text.

Chancellors: Men and Women of Distinction at UC

Each chancellor is the chief campus officer and executive head of all activities on his or her campus.

(These responsibilities do not extend to University-wide units and activities designated by the Board of Regents. With respect to their development and growth, however, the chancellor is consulted).

In all matters within the chancellor's jurisdiction, he or she has administrative authority within the budgeted items for the campus and in accordance with UC policies as determined by the president.

Within the provisions of both such budget and policy constraints, the chancellor's campus decisions are final.

The chancellor is responsible for the organization and operation of the campus, its internal administration and its discipline.

In addition, the chancellor nominates officers, faculty members and other employees on the campus in accordance with the provisions of the Regents' Standing Orders.

The University has had many outstanding chancellors in its 125-year history. They have been instrumental in ensuring the extraordinary growth and development of their individual campuses and in gaining for the University a reputation for academic distinction that is worldwide in scope.

During the past 25 years, four chancellors have earned a particularly important place in UC's history. The four, reading clockwise from top left on facing page: Tomás Rivera, Riverside; Rosemary S.J. Schraer, Riverside;

Barbara S. Uehling, Santa Barbara; and Chang-Lin Tien, Berkeley.

Rivera became the first minority chancellor of a UC campus when he took over the helm at Riverside in 1979. He died in 1984 at the age of 48 of a heart attack. The campus honored his memory in 1988 with the inauguration of the Tomás Rivera Archives, a collection of his novels, poetry, essays and public policy statements. In a daylong program that drew Hispanic scholars from across the country and from Mexico, the late chancellor was recognized for his scholarship and for his humanity.

Schraer and Uehling were the University's first women chancellors. Both were named chancellors at the same time in 1987; Schraer was the first to be inaugurated. Both committed themselves to high academic standards, to scholastic excellence, and to continued achievements in teaching, research and public service. Schraer passed away in office in 1992.

Chang-Lin Tien was the first person of Asian descent to become chancellor of a University of California campus. He was named Berkeley chancellor in 1990 following a highly successful period at the Irvine campus as executive vice chancellor. Born in China, he is now an American citizen. During his tenure as chancellor, he has continued to further Berkeley's reputation as an academic leader worldwide.

For further information about the chancellors and their achievements in office, see Campus Profiles.

REFERENCES: Regents' Standing Order 100.6, "Duties of the Chancellors."

CROSS-REFERENCES: Subjects cited in the above text.

Four Chancellors Who Made University History

TOMÁS RIVERA, *Riverside*
1979–84

ROSEMARY S.J. SCHRAER, *Riverside*
1987–92

BARBARA S. UEHLING, *Santa Barbara*
1987–94

CHANG-LIN TIEN, *Berkeley*
1990–

Childcare Issues: By the late 1980s, surveys showed that women were expected to account for almost half of the workforce by the year 2000.

Further studies began to show a substantial growth in the number of one-parent families in the U.S. While the majority of single parents were women, a growing number were men.

In view of the changing demographics, employers like the University have developed ways to address the increasing needs of faculty and staff who are parents.

By 1988, the University had in place a comprehensive set of policies related to childbearing and childrearing that covered issues such as leave (paid or otherwise), accrual and use of sick leave credit, and procedures for administrative approval.

(Policy also allowed a faculty member to stop the "tenure clock" for one year for childrearing purposes. A campus task force recommended that the provision be extended to one year per child.)

A 1989 report by the University showed that UC's campuses, all together, operated childcare centers that enrolled well over 1,000 children. However, the number of children served was far less than the demand.

The report, "The Challenge of Dependent Care," noted that childcare goes beyond providing direct care to such issues as "flex time" (flexible work schedules) and parental leave.

The document recommended establishment of a Universitywide task force to study what the Office of the President could do to assist the campuses, which have reported a widespread need to address the issues involved in childcare.

After the Universitywide task force was formed, it sought recommendations from the campuses. Recommendations prepared by various campuses in their own task force reports included the following:

• More campus-sponsored daycare for faculty and staff, including drop-in care and recovery care for temporarily ill youngsters.

• Direct financial subsidies for low-income parents.

• Better advertising of available daycare programs and dependent care programs which allow parents to deduct a monthly pre-tax amount to help pay childcare costs.

• Better leave policies, more flexible work schedules, and supervisory training to create a "family-friendly" environment that is sensitive to working parents' needs.

• Expanded options for holiday and summer care, including provision for full-time programs for children at certain types of UC facilities that have hands-on public programs.

After reviewing the campus input, the Universitywide task force developed a set of 36 Universitywide recommendations for review by the president of the University during 1992–93.

Among its recommendations, the Universitywide task force encouraged the development and enhancement of areas such as informational and support services, organizational flexibility and the availability and affordability of quality child care.

In addition, the task force recommended further development of supportive work places, better coordination and oversight of programs, and establishment of effective funding strategies.

Establishment of UC's child care programs began in the late 1960s and early 1970s as the outgrowth of student and staff co-operative movements and women's movements.

Each campus program developed in its own way and has provided programs suited to its own needs.

By 1989-90, each UC campus provided at least one on-site child care center (located on the central campus). These centers accommodated 613 children of faculty or staff parents and 776 children of student parents. The number has grown since then.

At some campuses, vendors have constructed and are operating child care centers. In all cases, UC provided the land, and the contractor or the developer built the facilities.

These vendors operate without UC subsidy and charge comparable prices to community and similar UC programs.

Campuses have exerted control over the vendor programs to varying degrees by means of contracts that attempt to specify levels of quality in each center's operation.

In general, faculty and staff pay market rates for campus child care.

For example, the 1989 full-time rates varied from a low of $270 a month at Riverside to a high of $515 at San Francisco, for children from two to five years old.

Fulltime infant and toddler care ranged from $336 a month at Davis to $540 at Santa Cruz.

(In general, costs have gone up a reasonable amount since then.)

UC locations have developed a variety of mechanisms to fund their dependent care programs (child care centers represent the single largest expenditure of funds for dependent care).

In 1989, the operating budget covering child care for children of faculty, staff and students amounted to $8.1 million.

Overall, parent fees accounted for half this total (the percent of parent fees varied by campus from 5 to 75 percent of the total budget).

The remainder was derived from direct UC support, student fees, State Department of Education and other subsidies, and support from other sources, including donations.

Some UC locations have sought to expand the supply of child care providers in the community to which they can refer faculty, staff and students.

These UC locations recruit and train potential family day care providers from the local community, as well as create family day care networks that bring together providers who wish to serve UC's affiliated families.

REFERENCES: University's Policies on Childbearing and Childrearing, July 1988; The Challenge of Dependent Care, 1989, Employee Relations, Office of the President; "Childcare may be the recruitment tool of the '90s," UC Focus, Vol. 4, No. 3, December 1989,; "Work and Family Strategies for the University of California," Final Report from the Universitywide Task Force on Dependent Care, September 1991.

CROSS-REFERENCES: Elder Care .

Collective Bargaining: The days when all University employees were covered by one set of UC staff or academic personnel policies became a thing of the past in 1978.

On September 13, 1978, a collective bargaining bill (AB 1091), also known as the Higher Education Employer-Employee Relations Act (HEERA), was signed into law.

Effective July 1, 1979, it authorized collective bargaining for employees of both the University of California and the California State University and Colleges.

Until passage of the bill, employees at UC and the California State University and Colleges were virtually the only state employees in California without the right to engage in collective bargaining.

The law is administered by the Public Employment Relations Board (PERB), which also administers the laws covering the state's K-14 and civil service employees.

The original version of HEERA was first introduced in the legislature in 1977.

It contained provisions on such key issues as the governance responsibilities of the Regents and the Academic Senate, the scope of issues that can be negotiated, and the determination of bargaining units.

The University initially opposed the bill, noting that certain provisions, such as an overly broad definition of negotiable issues, would impair UC's ability to serve students and the public.

The University's opposition was withdrawn when the legislation was substantially amended in response to UC's major concerns.

The University emphasized that withdrawal of its opposition did not mean endorsement of collective bargaining at UC. Its view was that collective bargaining was not inevitable, nor was it necessary for productive, rewarding work relationships.

However, UC believed that faculty and staff should not be denied a choice that the State Legislature had made generally available to comparable employees elsewhere.

After the measure's passage in 1978, UC continued to develop policies and programs to benefit employees that were based on consultative relationships with academic and staff employees as individuals and in groups.

The collective bargaining legislation contained a strong legal presumption that all UC employees in the same occupational group (except skilled craft employees) should be in one statewide bargaining unit.

For example, clerical employees at the nine campuses and the Lawrence Berkeley Laboratory would be in a single bargaining unit and would negotiate the terms and conditions of their labor contract at one bargaining table.

More than a decade after passage of HEERA, the role of collective bargaining continued to evolve at UC.

By the 1990s, however, the subject of labor relations was no longer totally mysterious to UC managers, supervisors and employees.

Instead, it had become accepted as part of UC's procedures in the areas of personnel and human resources (although improvements in the process were still being instituted).

As of 1993, UC had seven Universitywide collective bargaining agreements, eight local skilled craft bargaining agreements, and a local faculty unit at the Santa Cruz campus.

UC also had four separate staff personnel policy programs (Executive, Management and Professional, Administrative and Professional Staff, and Staff Personnel Policies), as well as policies and guidelines for most academic employees in the academic personnel manual.

The Office of Employee and Labor Relations in the Office of the President is charged with implementing HEERA and achieving consensus among the campuses regarding UC's labor relations objectives.

The Labor Relations unit translates these objectives and UC policy into labor agreements that meet the requirements of HEERA and, at the same time, preserve UC's ability to manage its employees and operations.

In so doing, Office of the President Labor Relations personnel interact with the large bargaining units that have been established, serving as UC's chief negotiators during bargaining with unions representing the employees.

Additionally, the Labor Relations staff perform the key function of systemwide contract and grievance administration.

The staff also are advocates and witnesses in representing UC in arbitration cases concerning the interpretation of contractual language.

The Labor Relations unit functions as a clearing house for UC labor relations issues and provides timely responses to changes in federal and state requirements regarding labor contracts.

The unit also provides advice and guidance to campus managers regarding interpretation and local administration of contractual provisions, and is responsible for

Collective Bargaining: The Important Terms

Here are a few terms explaining the collective bargaining process.

Arbitration: This is a method of settling disputes regarding the interpretation or application of the terms of the collective bargaining agreement (contract or memorandum of understanding) by having an impartial third party hold a formal hearing, take testimony and receive evidence, and render a decision which is binding upon both parties.

Employee Organization: This is what is commonly thought of as a union. The Academic Senate and its divisions are excluded from this definition.

Exclusive Representative: This means any recognized or certified employee organization or person authorized to act on its behalf.

Certified Organization: This means an employee organization which has been certified by the Public Employment Relations Board (PERB) as the exclusive representative of the employees in an appropriate bargaining unit as a result of a representation election conducted by PERB.

Meet and Confer: In the private sector, this is commonly called "collective bargaining." It refers to the obligation of both parties to try, in good faith, to reach an agreement on wages, hours and other terms and conditions of employment.

An impasse is reached when further meeting and conferring would be futile because of the differences in the positions of the parties. Once impasse has been reached the parties engage in the process of mediation and, if necessary, a formal fact-finding hearing.

Scope of Representation: This refers to those things over which UC and an exclusive representative must negotiate. In general, it excludes certain traditional management rights, including those delegated to the Academic Senate, and reserves to the employer all matters which are not wages, hours of employment or other terms and conditions of employment.

Additionally, it reserves to the Academic Senate its role in appointment, promotion, tenure, evaluation and grievances of its members (or those who are eligible for membership).

systemwide administration of unfair labor practice and representation issues before PERB.

The Labor Relations unit is UC's internal source for contract-costing information, official bargaining records employee demographics used in representation elections and other PERB proceedings.

As a result of the work of Labor Relations, UC has achieved standardized labor contracts acceptable to the campuses and has avoided fragmentation of benefit plans and other conditions of employment.

REFERENCES: "The Collective Bargaining Bill and UC's Role in the Process of Amending It," *University Bulletin,* December 4, 1978; "History of the University's Position on Collective Bargaining," "The University's Position on Collective Bargaining" and "The California Higher Education Employer-Employee Relations Act: the UC Experience 10 Years Later," informational papers, Office of Labor Relations, August 1989, Office of the President.

CROSS-REFERENCES: Academic Senate.

Conflict of Interest: California's Political Reform Act of 1974 requires that all public employees and officials disqualify themselves from making or participating in any governmental decision when that decision could result in a financial conflict of interest.

All UC employees and officials, except those at the Los Alamos National Laboratory, in New Mexico, are subject to the Act's provisions.

Under these provisions, every governmental agency in California, including the University, has had to adopt a Conflict of Interest Code.

The University adopted a Conflict of Interest Code in 1980. The code of employees is updated each year, in order to keep it current with amendments to the Act and to regulations as they occur.

In accordance with provisions in the Act, UC's code identifies a category of employees known as "designated officials," which refers to persons in positions having the potential for decision-making that could lead to a financial conflict of interest.

These "designated officials" at UC number about 1,500 (generally, they are executives, managers and others in similar categories).

In addition to being subject to disqualification requirements, designated officials are required by the University's Conflict of Interest Code and by state law to file financial disclosure statements upon assuming or leaving a designated position and annually while holding the position.

These statements are public documents.

Within the scope of the state act with regards to the disqualification requirements, an employee or official makes a "governmental decision" when, acting within the authority of his or her office, he or she does the following:

1) Votes on a matter.

2) Appoints a person.

3) Obligates or commits the University to any course of action.

4) Enters into any contractual agreement on behalf of the University.

5) Determines not to act in certain specified instances.

In addition to the restrictions on actually making a decision, an employee or official participates in making a decision when, acting with the authority of his or her University position, he or she negotiates, without significant substantive review, with a governmental entity or private person regarding the decision; or advises or makes recommendations to the decision-maker, either directly or without significant intervening substantive review by doing the following:

• Conducting research or making any investigation which requires the exercise of judgment on his or her part and the purpose of which is to influence the decision; or

• Preparing or presenting any report, analysis or opinion, orally or in writing, which requires the exercise of judgment on his or her part and the purpose of which is to influence the decision.

When does financial conflict of interest occur? Simply stated, it occurs when an employee has a financial interest in a University decision.

An employee has a financial interest if he or she can reasonably foresee that the decision will have a material financial effect, distinguishable from its effect on the public generally, as follows:

On himself or herself personally, on a member of his or her immediate family, or on a business entity in which he or she holds an investment or business position, or on property interests, or on a source of income including gifts as specifically defined and described in UC's Conflict of Interest Code.

After California's Political Reform Act was passed in 1974, there was concern that it might prohibit faculty, as well as other members of the University with teaching and research responsibilities, from making various decisions in the course of academic instruction and research.

Therefore, the State's Fair Political Practices Commission (FPPC) adopted a separate regulation covering academic decisions.

The University developed a Policy on Disclosure of Financial Interest in Private Sponsors of Research. In accordance with the regulation's provisions, under this current policy, governmental decisions are considered to be ones that are made in order to pursue research that is funded, in whole or in part, through the following:

A contract or grant with a non-governmental individual or entity in which the Principal Investigator (PI) has a financial interest, or a gift earmarked by the donor for a specific PI or to a specific research project in which the PI has a financial interest.

This means that a Principal Investigator must disclose whether he or she has a direct or indirect financial interest in the sponsor of research that is funded through a contract or grant (or other specified support) with a non-governmental entity.

The policy further states that a disclosure statement must be filed before final approval of any such research project is made. The statement will be available for public inspection.

When disclosure indicates that a financial interest exists, a committee consisting of faculty and administrators will conduct an independent, substantive review of the disclosure statement and the research, prior to acceptance of a contract, grant or gift.

A failure to make the required disclosure of financial interest, or to engage in the review process, subjects a Principal Investigator to possible civil and criminal liability.

In approving its Conflict of Interest Code, the University also developed guidelines to assist the University community in making decisions.

The guidelines state that traditional conflict of interest situations should continue to be avoided, research should be appropriate to UC, and the teaching and research environment should be open.

In addition, freedom to publish and disseminate research results should be preserved, licensing agreements should undergo thorough review, and UC facilities and resources should be used appropriately.

To further assist members of the University community, Conflict of Interest Code Coordinators have been appointed to provide information, answer questions, and help in the disqualification process.

The coordinators are located in the Office of the President, on each campus, and at the Lawrence Berkeley and Livermore Laboratories.

REFERENCES: State of California Political Reform Act of 1974; the following from the University Conflict of Interest Code Coordinator, Office of the President: University Conflict of Interest Code (revised annually); University of California Political Reform Act Disqualification Requirements; Business and Finance Bulletin G-39, Conflict of Interest Policy and Compendium of Specialized University Policies, Guidelines, and Regulations Related to Conflict of Interest; Policy on Disclosure of Financial Interest in Private Sponsors of Research, and related guidelines (Academic Personnel Manual Section 028).

CROSS-REFERENCES: Contracts and Grants; Technology Transfer.

Contracts and Grants provide a major source of funding for the University.

Together with private gifts, contracts and grants constitute what is known as "extramural support."

Extramural support assists scientists and scholars in conducting an array of research activities aimed at benefiting California and the nation.

Contracts and grants are awarded by local, state and federal agencies.

They also come from private sources, including business and industry, non-profit interest groups, and foundations and nonprofit organizations concerned with issues such as education and disease prevention.

(Private sources such as these also provide gifts to UC to support a wide variety of research and non-research activities. Gifts are different from contracts and grants, as described in the accompanying text to this section.)

All contracts and grants, as well as gifts, are subject to policies and review procedures established by each campus.

These must be in conformance with Universitywide policies and procedures.

For example, policies governing protection of human subjects, biosafety, occupational and environmental protection, and animal welfare apply to all Universitywide research-related activities, regardless of the source of funds used to support the project.

Research-related projects also must be conducted in conformance with equal opportunity and affirmative action policies.

In addition, UC has strict financial management and internal audit programs to ensure control and accountability of all expenditures.

In the area of contracts and grants, the Office of Research Administration in the Office of the President formulates and disseminates UC's policies regarding the administration of research funding agreements.

The office also develops policies and procedures to ensure that UC is in compliance with federal regulations regarding grants to academic research institutions.

The office oversees all contract and grant proposals exceeding $2 million, since these require Regental approval.

(Until 1992, the office also negotiated the University's major contracts with the three laboratories that UC manages for the U.S. Department of Energy. Those contracts are now negotiated by a new department within the Office of the President.)

In accepting contracts and grants from extramural sources, particularly commercial entities, the University seeks to recover direct and indirect costs in full, thus protecting UC against use of public funds for private gain.

However, in the case of nonprofit and federally sponsored research, UC may agree to share some costs, usually in the form of contributed effort.

And with regard to grants from independent philanthropic foundations, UC occasionally waives indirect costs through cost-sharing.

While initial discussions between industrial sponsors and UC faculty or senior research staff occur in a variety of ways, under University policy no program or project may be undertaken unless two conditions are met.

Initially, a carefully defined research proposal, including a budget, must be submitted through UC's internal review procedures, and then an acceptable funding agreement must be negotiated and signed by the authorized representatives of both parties.

Authority to solicit, negotiate and execute awards for research on behalf of the Regents is delegated by the chancellor to only a few officials on each campus.

REFERENCES: Presentation made to the Regents at their Consultation Hour, January 1973, and summarized in "Contracts and Grants: A Boon to California," *University Bulletin,* Vol. 21, No. 23, April 2, 1973; Contract and Grants Manual, Report of Activities Financed Through Contracts and Grants from Extramural Sources, University Policy on Review of Gifts/Grants for Research, and additional information from the Office of Research Administration, Office of the President.

CROSS-REFERENCES: All subject areas and references mentioned above .

A Grant or a Gift? There's a Difference

There is a distinction between gifts and grants for the purposes of UC's sponsored research program.

Here is a quick overview of the distinctions:

▶ Gift. Generally, if a faculty member receives funding from a donor who does not impose any contractual requirements and who provides the funds irrevocably, such funding is termed a gift.

▶ Grant. Funding is generally termed a grant if it involves (1) auditing provisions by the grantor, (2) directions to satisfy particular requirements, (3) a detailed technical report of results or expenditures or (4) other such conditions.

The appropriate category is determined by applying guidelines established by the Office of the President and in conformance with campus-based procedures.

Cooperative Extension is the most visible public service arm of the University of California.

Farmers, ranchers, fishermen, urban and rural youth, low-income families, teen parents and grandparents, homemakers, health professionals, government planning agencies and countless others receive help every day from this partnership of national, state and local resources working for the betterment of California.

Cooperative Extension is UC's window to every county in California. Through Extension offices from Alturas to San Diego, residents can receive advice and instruction from one or more of UC's farm, home, youth development, forest and marine advisors.

These researchers/educators also train scores of paraprofessionals and thousands of volunteers to extend UC's service to the community. In addition, they bring local research needs to the attention of campus-based specialists.

Cooperative Extension is supported through a funding partnership of federal, state and county governments, plus private contributions. It traces its beginnings back to 1913, when UC started an agricultural extension service to bring the results of agricultural research to California farmers. Today this mission is as important as ever.

California is the nation's leading agricultural state. Nearly 10 percent of the state's jobs depend on agriculture. Moreover, the challenges of modern agriculture are increasingly complex. They include a steady stream of new pests and diseases, global competition, the need to maintain profitability and protect the environment, and competing demands for limited natural resources.

Cooperative Extension helps solve agricultural and natural resource problems so that Californians can enjoy safe, affordable and sustainable supplies of food and fiber. Other Extension programs respond to changes in the state's social, environmental, economic and political landscapes.

Examples include research and educational outreach dedicated to the rural-urban interface, needs of youth and consumers in urban areas, special requirements of small farms, nutrition education for low-income households, and related public policy issues.

The county-based UC advisors are linked to University research programs through Cooperative Extension specialists, who are members of academic departments on three UC campuses: Berkeley, Davis and Riverside.

The county advisors and campus specialists are part of the Division of Agriculture and Natural Resources, which includes Cooperative Extension and Agricultural Experiment Station activities on those three UC campuses and in the county offices. The Division is widely regarded as the nation's most distinguished land-grant organization.

Cooperative Extension remains an energetic team of people investing in California's future. Here are some of their success stories.

• Rapid urban growth in Southern California in the 1960s forces many farms, ranches and orchards to move to newly irrigated lands up north. Extension solves serious problems on these lands related to water, drainage, and salt-and boron-affected soils.

• Dairy production continues to climb in the 1960s, due to Extension programs in genetic improvement, better feeding and milking techniques and the control of mastitis, a major bovine disease.

• A major informational campaign on safe handling of agricultural chemicals helps cut the number of pesticide-related deaths.

• Extension strengthens its focus on environmental issues, including research and outreach efforts to reduce air pollution caused by "agricultural burnings."

• Extension's role in mechanizing farming helps California crops remain competitive in the 1960s and 1970s, but also attracts criticism from those opposed to loss of agricultural jobs.

• In the 1960s, 4-H brings youth development programs to diverse, low-income urban communities and to youngsters with special needs. In the 1980s, federal funding permits the placement of more youth advisors in urban areas and the introduction of new subjects. By the 1990s more than 130,000 youngsters, half of them living in large cities or suburbs, participate in 4-H programs, with many programs accessible to disabled youth. And California-developed 4-H after-school, science and literacy programs are adopted nationally.

• The home economics program shifts in the 1960s from teaching homemaking skills to providing science-based information on nutrition, consumer economics and healthy family relationships. To reach a wider audience, Extension begins to work with "multipliers"— dietitians, public health workers, schoolteachers and others. In the 1980s, Extension adds multicultural programs on financial management for limited resource and military families, high school students, retirees and migrant workers. Other programs focus on the needs of young families. Among them are "Parent Express," a 15-part guide in English and Spanish on parenthood and baby care. Food safety education remains an important component of Extension outreach.

• An Expanded Food and Nutrition Education Program (EFNEP) is established in 1969 to improve the dietary well-being of low-income families in 17 counties. In its first 10 years, 100,000 California families, mostly from poor urban neighborhoods, learn how to provide nutritious meals within a limited budget. In the 1980s, the program begins to work with local agencies and emergency food centers to reach greater numbers of low-income families. It also surveys the extent of hunger in California communities and works with local agencies in an effort to reverse this disturbing trend.

• Taking on a wider range of issues, Extension revamps its communications programs to reach nonfarm audiences. Later, as more people from non-English-speaking backgrounds settle in the state, Extension provides materials in Spanish and other languages and makes special efforts to increase its outreach through multicultural media.

• Public policy relating to land use becomes another area for Extension activity in the 1960s, with Extension economists conducting studies to provide decision-makers with reliable, impartial information.

• In the 1970s, Cooperative Extension takes an international perspective, reflecting concerns over an adequate world food supply. In 1973, for example, an interdisciplinary task force of agricultural economists and scientists studies the implications of that year's worldwide food crisis. It also reviews the nation's ability to meet its food needs in the years to come.

• As the U.S. energy crisis of the early 1970s threatens farm productivity, Extension agricultural engineers explore major energy savings in areas such as cultivation, irrigation, greenhouse production, transportation and processing.

• In 1971, Extension implements a marine advisory program for California's seafood industry. The Sea Grant Extension program soon expands, encouraging the adoption of new technologies in areas such marine fisheries, port development, commercial and recreational fishing, aquaculture and coastal resource management.

• In 1974, Agricultural Extension changes its name to Cooperative Extension to reflect its wider-than-agriculture focus.

• Cooperative Extension hires its first woman county director in 1974 to lead the Contra Costa County office.

• In 1977, a Small Farm Program is established to focus on the specialized needs of small-scale and limited-resource farmers. Today, it offers assistance to California's 65,000 farms that gross less than $100,000 annually, in areas such as direct marketing, specialty crops, organic and sustainable farming. Special emphasis is placed on reaching Southeast Asian and Latino farmers unfamiliar with American farming methods.

• In 1977, Extension develops the nation's first extension program in farm personnel management to help farmers employ better management and farm safety practices.

• In 1979, the pioneering Integrated Pest Management (IPM) Program is formed to reduce farmer dependence on pesticides. The program soon earns an international reputation for excellence. In the 1990s, IPM techniques are used widely, thanks in part to the program's highly regarded IPM manuals, each detailing pest problems and management techniques for a specific crop.

• Extension creates a Water Task Force in 1982 to provide the public with information about water policy questions. Extension advisors and specialists bring together interested agencies and organizations to discuss policy controversies and possible resolutions. Extension is praised for facilitating public discussion on sensitive policy issues related to a prime natural resource such as water.

• An urban horticulture program makes UC plant science expertise available to city-based landscapers and gardeners. It also establishes the volunteer Master Gardener program, and through the media, disseminates drought and pest management related information to home gardeners.

• A Genetic Resources Conservation Program is created in 1985 to support biological diversity through conservation research and education.

• In 1986, UC receives State funds to launch the Integrated Hardwood Range Management Program in response to a serious decline in California's native oaks, an important habitat for wildlife. Extension hires specialists to work on long-term management of the state's native hardwood and rangeland vegetation species.

• The following year, again with State funding, UC appoints a sustainable agriculture specialist and estab-

UC Cooperative Extension And the Land-Grant System

Cooperative Extension was established 80 years ago, part of a national Extension System that is a cornerstone of one of the nation's most successful institutional innovations: the land-grant colleges and universities.

The roots of land-grant institutions are in agriculture. Legislation signed by President Lincoln in 1862 created a federal-state partnership to improve farming through science and help the nation meet its growing need for food and fiber. The land-grant campuses offered practical coursework in the application of scientific principles to agriculture.

Later, the demand for more and better scientific knowledge led to federal funding for full-scale research, the Agricultural Experiment Stations.

Still later, Agricultural Extension, the third component of the land-grant system, was added to bring the fruits of university research to the individuals, families and communities who needed it.

Over the years, land-grant institutions also focused on other critical issues, adding environmental concerns, natural resources management, and human and community development in both rural and urban settings to their research and extension responsibilities.

By virtually any standard, the results of this uniquely American approach to higher education in service to the public have greatly benefited the nation—and especially California.

lishes the Sustainable Agriculture Research and Education Program to work on strategies for minimizing the use of chemical pesticides and fertilizers, as well as non-renewable resources such as fossil fuels.

• In the drought of the late 1980s and early 1990s, Extension accelerates its research on water conservation and initiates statewide programs to help growers, nursery professionals, homeowners and others manage with less water.

• Extension plays a key role in a new UC multidisciplinary program to protect California's 1.2 million farm owners and workers from injury and illnesses. The federally funded program uses both research and outreach to provide practical solutions to health and safety problems in California agriculture.

• In a crippling freeze that throws thousands of agricultural workers out of work in 1990, Extension advisors help organize relief efforts that generate more than $5 million in housing, energy and food assistance and collect 10 million pounds of emergency food aid.

• In 1990, the nation's first Extension specialist in the rapidly expanding field of biotechnology is hired by the Berkeley campus.

• UC establishes the Center for Pest Management Research and Extension in 1991 to coordinate research and informational outreach activities involving more than 150 UC scientists and Extension advisors. Many of these programs explore biological and cultural options for replacing synthetic pesticides.

• In 1992, Cooperative Extension appoints the first political scientist to work fulltime as a public policy specialist. This researcher/educator focuses on revitalizing rural and small-city communities.

• Extension in 1993 develops an extensive public information campaign on the aggressive Africanized honey bee, expected to arrive in California in 1994. The program aims to replace wide-spread misinformation with research-based "do's and don'ts."

• Cooperative Extension affirmative action efforts receive national recognition from the U.S. Department of Agriculture. In 1991, CE is the recipient of the nation's first Award for Diversity, given for "developing a comprehensive program to ensure a new organizational environment that respects and values diversity." UC wins the national award again the following year, this time in the team category. In 1993, a member of the Los Angeles Cooperative Extension office is recognized for individual achievement in promoting diversity.

Under the leadership of Kenneth R. Farrell, UC vice president for agriculture and natural resources, Cooperative Extension continues to change to meet California's needs.

"The creation and application of knowledge and the development of human resources to enhance quality of life are as important today as at the founding of Cooperative Extension, perhaps more so," according to Farrell.

"Whether through programs to enhance opportunities for youth, women, and minorities, programs to address natural resource, environmental, food and nutrition issues or programs to enhance productivity in California's diverse and bounteous agriculture, Cooperative Extension has a rich, 80-year tradition to draw upon as it prepares to meet the challenges ahead."

REFERENCES: "Extending the Bounty of Research"—A Report from the University of California, Division of Agriculture and Natural Resources; "Cooperative Extension at 75", *California Agriculture,* Vol. 43, No. 3, May–June 1989; "A Sustaining Comradeship—The Story of University of California Cooperative Extension 1913–1988," Division of Agriculture and Natural Resources.

CROSS-REFERENCES: Subjects cited in the above text.

Cooperative Programs with Other Institutions:
The University and other academic institutions, in California as well as elsewhere, recognize that their cooperative efforts are important in advancing the goals and purposes of higher education.

As a result, they have cooperated in a number of important areas. Here are some of them that were put in place in recent years.

• The California Education Round Table regularly has brought together the heads of each of the academic segments to discuss state policy issues relating to education.

• The Intersegmental Coordinating Council was created by the California Education Round Table to foster collaboration on intersegmental programs.

• The University and the Community Colleges have designed programs to improve student transfer. Working through faculty-to-faculty collaboration on curriculum and through improved ways to advise students, these transfer agreement programs have raised dramatically the number of transfer applications to UC.

• The Berkeley campus library has a longstanding relationship with Stanford University's library, which has included reciprocal borrowing privileges, agreements to coordinate development of certain specialized collections, and operation of a shuttle service between the two institutions.

• The UCLA library has for many years maintained similar cooperative relationships with the libraries at the University of Southern California (USC), the California Institute of Technology, and the Getty Museum.

• UC's libraries also have established a variety of cooperative agreements with the California State University (CSU). These include special arrangements for fast retrieval of informational materials at the libraries.

• UC libraries provide support to other California libraries in less formal ways. For example, in the wake of the October 17, 1989 earthquake, the Berkeley campus library opened its doors to students from Stanford, San Francisco State University, and St. Mary's College of Moraga, until their damaged libraries could be reopened.

• The California Council on Science and Technology, established in 1989, provides advice to the Governor, the Legislature and others on urgent technical, social and economic problems with technological and scientific dimensions. It is a collaborative effort by UC, the California Institute of Technology, Stanford, USC and CSU.

• UC has been involved in the development and operation of the Keck Telescope, a history-making joint project. The California Institute of Technology has funded construction of the telescope and observatory, UC has helped with the costs of the initial complement of major instruments and the first 25 years of operation, and the University of Hawaii has provided the site atop nearby Mauna Kea.

• University-School Education Improvement (USEI) at UC works with other segments to help improve the preparation of teachers, strengthen the school curriculum, create new initiatives, and undertake related activities.

• The California Writing Project, a nationally recognized university-based school improvement effort, offers professional development to K-12 writing teachers. It has been a model for similar projects in math and science.

• The California Curriculum Consultant Project, another intersegmental initiative, has provided consultants from postsecondary and secondary campuses to help high school departments analyze and improve their curricula.

• UC's Lawrence Hall of Science at Berkeley sponsors an array of math and science education programs, providing such services as teacher education, children and adult instruction, school and community workshops, curriculum research and development, and other initiatives.

• The Mathematics, Engineering, and Science Achievement (MESA) program works with underrepresented minority students to encourage them to think about, and prepare for, careers in those three areas. MESA serves junior high, high school and university students and their parents by providing career advising, summer programs, admissions assistance, tutoring and other services.

(More information on some of these programs and other cooperative activities can be found throughout the book.)

REFERENCES: Text based on information in "Working Together: An Agenda for Joint Action," address by President David P. Gardner to the Western College Association, April 18, 1990.

CROSS-REFERENCES: Subjects cited in the above text.

Copyright Policy: The creation of copyrighted works is one of the ways the University fulfills its mission of contributing to the body of knowledge for the public good.

In keeping with this philosophy, the University encourages the creation of original works of authorship and the free expression and exchange of ideas.

The University revised its Copyright Policy of 1975 in 1992. The revision was undertaken because of the need to:

• Reexamine the document in light of changing circumstances and new technologies, particularly in view of the growing importance of computer software.

• Ensure that the language of the revised policy would be current and clear with regard to the Federal Copyright Act, which became law after UC's policy was first issued in 1975. (The law provides the University ownership of its employment-related works.)

• Establish a policy and a mechanism that would project copyright interests of the University and its employees under all provisions of contemporary copyright law.

The current policy is intended to embody the spirit of academic tradition, which provides copyright ownership to faculty for their scholarly and aesthetic copyrighted works.

Under the policy, UC's president has responsibility for all matters relating to intellectual property, including copyrights in which the University is involved.

The policy covers works produced at, by or through the University, its campuses and the Department of Energy (DOE) Laboratories. It applies to University employees, students and other persons or entities using UC facilities or acting under contract with UC for commissioned works.

The following covers some of the policy's major provisions.

For example, in keeping with academic tradition, the policy provides that ownership of copyrights to scholarly or aesthetic works which are prepared through independent academic effort, and not as part of a directed UC assignment, generally reside with the author.

Exceptions can be found if UC commissioned the work in question, or if the work was created under extramural support.

Scholarly or aesthetic works include, but are not limited to, books, articles, lectures, and computer software resulting from independent study.

They also include artistic works such as novels, videotapes, and musical compositions.

Otherwise, all rights in copyright arising from UC employment or the use of UC resources belong to the University.

Title to the copyrightable material developed under a contract or grant from a commercial sponsor normally belongs to UC.

Each campus has a designated official who is able to answer questions about applicability of the University Copyright Policy.

REFERENCES: Policy on Copyright Ownership, August 19, 1992, Office of the President; UC's Patent Policy.

CROSS-REFERENCES: Technology Transfer, as well as subject areas cited in the above text.

The Council of the University of California Emeriti Associations (CUCEA) was created by representatives of all the campus emeriti associations in October 1987.

The Council has a number of purposes, including the following:

• It provides two council representatives (Chair and Chair Elect) of the emeriti on the Academic Senate's Faculty Welfare Committee with an informed constituency

• It assists each campus to organize and maintain an active emeriti organization

• It fosters the scholarly study of faculty retirement

• It supports colleagues in their ongoing scholarly activities

• It maintains mutual supportive relations between the University and emeriti

In carrying out these purposes, the Council provides a number of services for UC emeriti.

It develops channels of communication, fosters relationships among campus emeriti associations, coordinates actions of these associations in addressing important issues, and engages in advocacy programs.

Issues crucial to emeriti include financial planning, pensions, health, dental and other benefits, Social Security, housing, investments, insurance, post-retirement employment, research opportunities, office space, and survivors' responsibilities.

The Council consists of one representative (or duly elected alternate) from each campus emeriti association.

A designated representative from the Office of the Associate Vice President for Academic Affairs serves as an ex-officio member of the Council.

The officers of the Council include the following (they are elected or confirmed by the members of the Council yearly): the Chair (who succeeds to the position after serving a year as Chair-elect), Secretary, Treasurer and Information Officer.

Additionally, UC campuses, Labs and the Office of the President have retiree associations for retired staff and administrators.

REFERENCES: "Council of University of California Emeriti Associations: Purposes" and "Council of University of California Emeriti Associations: Constitution and Bylaws."

CROSS-REFERENCES: Academic Senate.

Crime on Campus: On the nation's college campuses, violent crimes are committed daily.

As a result, crime has become a major issue at colleges and universities around the country, including the University of California.

In recent years, the number of major crimes increased as cities adjacent to campuses have grown in population and brought urban problems to academic settings.

Under a mandate of the California Education and Penal Codes, the University of California Police Department provides full police services to all UC campuses and the Lawrence Berkeley Laboratory (LBL).

As of 1991, a team of 345 sworn officers, supported by full and part-time staff, were serving an aggregate UC population of more than 293,000 students, staff and faculty.

This represented a ratio of 1.2 officers to 1,000 UC members of the UC community.

Campus police departments range in size from 80 officers at Berkeley (this includes Lawrence Berkeley Laboratory) to 15 at Santa Cruz.

The overall mission of each member of the UC Police Department is to provide a safe, orderly environment that is conducive to fulfilling UC's educational and research missions.

In recent years, colleges and universities, including UC, have gathered statistics about crime on campus, in order to understand the problems involved and to help address them.

The Federal Student Right-to-Know and Campus Security Act, together with similar California legislation,

FBI Crime Index Offenses, 1987–1991
Universitywide

Change**	1987	1988	1989	1990	1991	%
VIOLENT CRIME						
Homicide/Manslaughter	1	0	1	2	1	—
Rape:						
Rape by force	19	18	9	8	16	—
Attempt to commit rape	5	9	7	10	6	—
Robbery	54	38	50	69	57	−17%
Aggravated Assault	81	70	124	118	98	−17%
TOTAL VIOLENT CRIME	160	135	191	207	178	−14%
PROPERTY CRIME						
Burglary	960	942	1,054	1,012	1,276	26%
Larceny—Theft:						
Bicycle theft	1,859	1,969	2,181	2,249	2,577	15%
Other larceny—theft	5,177	5,127	4,661	4,751	4,969	5%
Motor Vehicle Theft	466	597	642	502	518	3%
Arson	39	27	40	30	48	—
TOTAL PROPERTY CRIME	8,501	8,662	8,578	8,544	9,388	10%
TOTAL FBI CRIME INDEX	8,661	8,797	8,769	8,751	9,566	9%

*New classification added in 1989 to provide more detail.
**Dash indicates percents not calculated because the base number is less than 50.

requires each UC campus to provide annual crime statistics, as well as safety policies and programs, to their community.

Statistics on campus crimes around the U.S. are gathered as part of the Federal Bureau of Investigation's Uniform Crime Reporting Program, which for 62 years has provided criminal statistics for use in law enforcement administration, operation and management.

In California, the program is administered by the Law Enforcement Information Center of the California Department of Justice.

As part of the program, the UC Police Department, as well as all other law enforcement agencies throughout the state, report summary information to this bureau on "selected" offenses.

These offenses are classified according to definitions designed to eliminate differences in those found in the penal codes of the various states.

The crimes counted are willful homicide, forcible rape, robbery, aggravated assault, burglary, larceny-theft, motor vehicle theft, and arson.

Misdemeanors and infractions are not counted, although the UC report lists other offenses such as vandalism and public drunkenness to indicate the range of offenses that typically occur on campuses.

(While statistics are valuable, caution some experts, they may not be complete if many crimes are not reported.)

Although crime at UC is a problem, statistics suggest that the rate of violent crime and property crime on its campuses continues to be lower than the rate of such crimes in the surrounding communities.

For example, between 1987 and 1990, violent crime per 100,000 population was 93.3 percent less than the overall California crime rate.

And the property crime rate at UC was 45 percent less than the overall California rate during the same period.

In addressing the problems of violence, theft and other crimes, UC has instituted programs and procedures to reduce the risks and dangers for its students on campus.

An overall drop in some crimes on campuses has been due, in large part, to steps taken to protect students.

These steps included heightening student awareness of campus crime and developing additional precautions, including increased use of crime prevention services.

These steps are based on the fact that, since each campus is a small city within a city, there generally is a strong sense of community and support.

As a result, members of the campus community are encouraged to report crimes and to be responsible for their own security and the security of others.

REFERENCES: California Education and Penal Code; Annual Report and Crime Statistics, University of California Police Department; and news releases, University Relations, Office of the President.
CROSS-REFERENCES: Police Services.

Crises: In recent years, the University community has lived through a number of major crises that have made national and international news.

Here are some notable ones.

Earthquake

Four UC employees died and 10 students and employees were injured (three seriously) in a 7.1 earthquake that struck much of Northern California at 5:04 p.m. on October 17, 1989.

The earthquake was second in magnitude only to the 1906 San Francisco temblor.

UC scientists said the quake released energy nearly 10 times more powerful than all the bombs dropped in World War II, including the atomic bombs.

However, it fell 30 times short of the power released by the 1906 quake.

This is a scene at one of UC's campuses showing the aftermath of a major quake.

Photo: Jim MacKenzie

Estimates soon after the quake indicated that UC suffered about $40 million in damages and losses. Nearly all of it occurred at the San Francisco, Santa Cruz and Berkeley campuses.

The University employees who died or were seriously injured were in a UCSF van pool vehicle. It was among several vehicles destroyed by the collapse of a section of freeway in Oakland.

The Santa Cruz campus was the most disrupted by the quake.

Seven minor injuries were reported there. Employees there were out for two days following the event, and classes were suspended for a period of time. Two buildings remained closed for more than a week following the disaster, and portions of the library were closed as well.

Classes also were suspended for a day at UCSF. Instruction continued as usual at Berkeley the day following the quake, although four campus buildings were closed at varying times to allow for structural inspection.

However, no UC buildings were destroyed or irreparably damaged.

Another major earthquake occurred in California in January 1994, causing damage at UCLA and elsewhere in the southern part of the state.

Gulf Crisis

On August 2, 1990, Iraq invaded Kuwait, and the United States elected to become massively involved in the conflict.

The U.S. did so through establishment of an economic embargo on Iraq and a worldwide diplomatic offensive, as well as the sending of American military forces to the region to serve with other forces.

These events, known as the Gulf Crisis, had an impact on the University community.

UC figures released in March 1991 showed that 80 employees in the military reserves (mostly medical personnel) were called to active duty.

The employees were located at seven UC campuses, all three national laboratories managed by UC, and the Office of the President.

Firestorm

A firestorm ravaged more than 3,000 homes in the Oakland and Berkeley hills on October 20, 1991.

It was the worst disaster of its kind in U.S. history.

About 650 UC students, faculty and staff were left homeless. A sophomore at Berkeley was among 24 victims who died in the fire.

The fire affected employees and students working or studying at the Berkeley and San Francisco campuses and at the Lawrence Berkeley Laboratory and the Lawrence Livermore National Laboratory. Some 16 staff members working in the Office of the President also lost homes.

In the case of crises of this nature, the University offered assistance programs, counseling and emergency and other services, as needed.

REFERENCES: "University Puts Earthquake Losses at $40 Million," *Notice*, Vol. 14, No. 2, November 1989; "UC shaken but undaunted," *UC Focus*, Vol. 4, No.2, November 1989, news releases, March 18, 1991 and October 24, 1991, and "Fire reduces research, writing to ash," *UC Focus*, January 1992, University Relations, Office of the President.

CROSS-REFERENCES: Earthquake Engineering Research.

D

Degrees: No one knew the exact moment when it happened or the campus where it occurred.

However, everyone agreed that a historic milestone had been reached in 1989.

That was the year the University awarded its millionth degree.

According to UC records, the first degrees were awarded in 1870.

In 1989, the University awarded 35,475 degrees. The figure brought the total number of degrees it had awarded throughout its history to well over the million mark.

The final tally for 1989 showed that UC had exceeded the million figure by nearly 3,000.

UC recognized this landmark in a way that reflected the diversity of its campuses and its students.

A special ceremony was held at Berkeley, UC's oldest campus, on April 27, 1990, at the annual Charter Day dinner sponsored by the California Alumni Association.

At that event, 10 seniors from throughout UC were collectively designated recipients of the One Millionth Degree.

As distinguished students, they exemplified the type of graduates UC produces: women and men, white and black, Latino, Asian and American Indian.

The 10 students were selected to demonstrate the diversity of academic, extracurricular and service activities that take place on each of the UC campuses.

The students, four of whom were also alumni scholars, included the following:

- A coordinator of an immigrant students project
- A co-chair of a disabilities support group
- A Rhodes scholar finalist
- A world-class athlete and holder of women's triple jump records
- A volunteer tutor at UC and in public elementary schools
- A mother who was active on the Intertribal Students Council
- A student body president active in the Asian-American Political Alliance
- A volunteer at the University YWCA
- A student Regent and student advisor for the California Postsecondary Education Commission
- A Warden of the Order of the Golden Bear who was a peer advisor and counselor on campus

REFERENCES: News release, April 23, 1990, University Relations, and "Opportunity . . . Service . . . Excellence . . . A Commitment from the University of California," *A Special Report to the People of California,* October 1990, Office of the President.

CROSS-REFERENCES: Alumni Associations; Student Regents.

A law school graduate expresses his joy at meeting a tough academic challenge.

What Happened to The Class of '42

In 1942, Japanese American students at the University were forced into internment camps along with many other Japanese Americans on the West Coast following the outbreak of World War II.

Fifty years later, their plight was remembered through a series of special events and activities at UC.

For example, at Berkeley nearly 100 Japanese Americans in their 70s attended a graduation ceremony to replace the one they were forced to miss as seniors a half century earlier. Some of them had received their Berkeley diplomas by mail in 1942 while housed in horse stalls at racetracks in the San Francisco area, but they were not allowed to be present for their graduation.

The 1992 ceremony occurred during the Berkeley campus convocation, an annual event held to welcome students, faculty and staff back to campus for the fall semester.

The class celebrating its 50th reunion traditionally leads the ceremonial procession. This time, the Japanese

American alumni in cap and gown, once held as prisoners in detention camps, led the official party into the campus auditorium to be recognized for their achievements as American citizens.

At UCLA, second-, third- and fourth-generation Japanese Americans from the campus and the community collaborated on a yearlong series of events commemorating the 50th anniversary of the signing of the U.S. executive order establishing the internment camps.

Coordinated by the UCLA Asian American Studies Center (AASC), the events drew together institutions, departments at UCLA. and groups within the Southern California Asian Pacific American community.

In connection with the commemoration, UCLA awarded the AASC a $100,000 Chancellor's Challenge Grant for the Arts and Humanities, a competitive grant to encourage the integration of arts activities, academic programs and faculty efforts in public arts programs.

The array of educational and commemorative activities, and the range of associated resources and talent involved in the enterprise, reinforced the deep commitment that UCLA has made to the Japanese American community over the years. The activities also focused on the importance of being vigilant in guarding the civil liberties of all citizens.

Sources: UC Berkeley news release, 9/2/92, and "A Year of Remembrance," *UCLA Magazine,* Winter 1992.

Dependent Care: See Child Care and Elder Care.

Disabilities Programs: The University provides special assistance and services to give students with disabilities the support they need to participate fully in campus programs and activities.

Each campus has an office that coordinates a variety of services for students with permanent and temporary disabilities.

The University has served an increasing number of students each year.

For example, in the 1979–80 academic year (the first year for which figures are available), the University served a total of 982 students.

Efforts to expand the representation of students with disabilities at UC campuses had succeeded in boosting this figure to 4,109 in 1991-92.

This represented an increase of more than 400 percent.

The University serves all students with qualified disabilities, including students with mobility, hearing, speech and vision impairments, as well as students who have learning disabilities.

The assistance provided allows students to participate fully, in the most integrated setting possible, in all of the University's services, activities and programs.

These services include the following:

Disability management counseling, assistance with registration and enrollment, orientation programs, accessibility tours and maps, on-campus van transportation, minor wheelchair repairs, and equipment loans.

In addition, federal and state law, as well as University policy, requires that UC provide specific academic support services to students with disabilities that are necessary to the pursuit of their studies.

As a result, academic support is available through readers for the blind, interpreters for the hearing-impaired, note-takers, special test-taking arrangements, and adaptive equipment such as voice synthesizers for students with vision-impairments.

In addition, UC has made special efforts to provide classrooms, laboratories and other facilities to accommodate students with disabilities.

For example, many campus buildings have ground-level or ramped entrances, automatic doors, wheelchair accessible restrooms, accessible drinking fountains, and elevators with lowered buttons, brailed numerals, and accessible emergency exits.

Central parking and accessible dormitory facilities are additional accommodations.

State funding for UC's program of services to students with disabilities began in 1979–80, although several campuses had programs in place for students with disabilities as early as the 1960s.

In the first year of state support, UC received funding based on approximately $465 for each student with a verified disability who enrolled at UC and received services.

This figure was based on the average per capita cost for disabled students at community colleges; however, it did not fund the different, and higher, costs of providing services to disabled students at UC.

One reason for UC's higher costs is the heavier course loads taken by disabled students, which increases the per-student need for auxiliary services such as note-takers and readers.

In 1982–83, the state raised the funding level to $566 per student and provided a workload adjustment associated with an increase in the number of students receiving services, as well as other support.

In 1987, State Assembly Bill 746 declared legislative intent to provide full state funding of the actual cost of providing services to students with disabilities.

This funding was to be based on a number of factors, including fixed and variable costs associated with providing these services, as well as one-time costs for equipment and auxiliary aids.

On the federal level, the Americans with Disabilities Act (ADA) was signed into law on July 26, 1990, and its provisions took effect in 1992.

The legislation prohibits discrimination against individuals with disabilities in private employment, public accommodations, state and local government services, transportation, and telecommunications.

Although disabilities advocates called the landmark legislation the most significant anti-discrimination decision since 1964, when Congress passed the Civil Rights Act, many of its provisions had already been implemented on UC campuses as a result of passage of the Rehabilitation Act of 1973.

Several provisions of ADA were taken directly from Section 504 of the Rehabilitation Act, which mandates many of the academic accommodations that UC extends to students with disabilities.

REFERENCES: Budgets for Current Operations, Office of the President; "Introducing the University, 1993-1994," Student Academic Services, Office of the President; information from the Universitywide Coordinator—Services to Students with Disabilities.
CROSS-REFERENCES: Affirmative Action.

Engineering students show their skills at designing an advanced type of wheelchair for disabled individuals.

Divestment: In September 1977, the Regents formally considered the issue of divesting its stock from companies doing business with South Africa.

This issue had been raised by some within the University community because of their belief that UC should not invest in companies with business ties to South Africa until that country's policy of apartheid was changed. Protests on the campuses eventually grew, calling for full and immediate divestment.

Although the Regents voted against divestment in 1977, it was the first step that eventually led to full divestment in 1990.

At the 1977 meeting, the Regents' Committee on Investments adopted an investment policy that included good corporate citizenship as one of the criteria to be reviewed within the objective of maximizing return consistent with prudent preservation of capital.

The Regents also adopted revisions to its Proxy Policies and Procedures, allowing individual Regents to "vote their conscience" on issues of social or public concern. The action required the Treasurer of the Regents to solicit individual Regental votes on all shareholder issues of public concern.

On April 24, 1984, a public forum was arranged by the Associated Students at Berkeley. Thirteen Regents were among the nearly 7,000 who attended the four-and-a-half hour session. Among the issues addressed by a series of speakers were the history of apartheid, fiduciary responsibility, potential conflict of interest, investment options, and student views on divestment.

In June 1985, following a full airing of views, a thorough study of the questions involved, and a detailed look at UC's investment portfolio, the Regents again considered the issue of divestment.

For the June meeting, the Treasurer of the Regents prepared a detailed investment study that had been commissioned by the Board.

It included a review of how UC investment decisions are made, what other universities were doing with respect to the South African issue, and various options open to the Regents if the Board chose to amend UC's current policy.

Figures in the report showed that UC was investing in 33 companies with subsidiaries in South Africa.

At the June meeting, the Regents rejected a proposal to divest UC holdings in American companies with ties to South Africa.

Instead, it agreed to monitor companies for adherence to principles of racial equality and to help improve educational opportunities for black South Africans.

Before voting, however, the Regents took several steps to become more informed about the issues. For example, in June 1985, Board members engaged in a number of meetings and extended discussions with students, staff, and faculty.

Although students and community groups were the most vocal on the issue, faculty input was also received at these public meetings, including a report from a special committee of the Academic Senate. In addition, UC's president met with an ad hoc group called Faculty for Full Divestment and gained the views of the Student Body Presidents' Council and others. He also met with South African Bishop Desmond Tutu, a leading opponent of apartheid.

During their deliberations, the Regents recognized that more information was needed in considering issues of social or moral concern before voting as a corporate stockholder. As a result, a review of the Regents' proxy voting policy was undertaken. The policy was subsequently revised in January 1986.

In addition, in June 1985 the University Advisory Committee for Investor Responsibility (UACIR) was established by the Regents. It was chaired by UCLA's chancellor and consisted of staff, faculty, and student representatives. The committee's duties included monitoring the corporate citizenship of companies in which UC invested that did business in South Africa. The group also was directed to consider ways of improving UC's exercise of its shareholding voting rights.

In 1986, UACIR began providing advice to the Regents in connection with the Board's new policy on the casting of proxy votes. Under the new policy, as amended in January 1986, only Regents actually submitting votes would be counted as voting on issues of social concern. (In the past, Regents who did not vote on proxy issues were counted as voting for management and against the stockholder issue.)

In addition, the Treasurer of the Regents was instructed to vote the proxy on the basis of the majority of those voting. However, as in the past, the Treasurer was instructed to vote for management on proxy issues of any business management nature.

In July 1986, the Regents voted again on the divestment issue.

This time the Board adopted a policy of phased full divestment of holdings in companies with business ties to South Africa. The Board's guidelines called for a three-year divestment program.

Holdings in companies doing business in South Africa were to be reduced by one-third of their total market value in each of the three calendar years, beginning in January 1988.

Under the Regents' policy, companies doing business in South Africa were defined as those with employees or assets in the country. The definition was consistent with that used by the Investor Responsibility Research Center, an independent, not-for-profit corporation that was compiling and analyzing the activities of business in society and related matters.

When the Regents adopted the investment policy in 1986, the University had investments in 29 companies that would have been subject to the policy. In 1988, when the phased divestment program began, 10 of those companies remained in UC's portfolio. The number was reduced in 1988 and 1989 as the result of withdrawal of companies from South Africa and routine investment decisions.

In December 1990, UC completed its South African divestment program with the sale of all holdings in three U.S. companies that continued to do business in South Africa.

When completed, the University's divestment was the largest by any educational institution in the world and, at the time, the second largest divestment in U.S. history.

In July of 1986, UC policy also specified that the Treasurer's Office would make no new investments in companies doing business in South Africa or with the South African government.

In 1992, however, the issue of UC reinvestment was revived as whites in South Africa voted to abolish apartheid and extend power to blacks. The University had no plans to recommend to the Regents that UC change its divestment policy at that time. Instead, the University planned to wait until it was certain that the evolving political situation in South Africa had stabilized.

While maximizing return and conserving principal remain the primary investment objective, the Regents' investment policy includes the evaluation of corporate citizenship as one of the criteria used in determining the suitability of an investment for inclusion in the Regents' portfolios.

This policy applies to both U.S.-based and foreign companies.

REFERENCES: Information from the Offices of the Treasurer and the Secretary of The Regents.

E

Earthquake Engineering Research: The Earthquake Engineering Research Center (EERC) was established as an Organized Research Unit (ORU) in 1967.

Originally the general objective of this ORU was to conduct research programs that ultimately would aid in the prevention of loss of life and damage to property resulting from future strong motion earthquakes.

The original programs placed major emphasis on the following:

• Predicting the characteristics and intensities of strong ground motions caused by earthquakes,

• Predicting their potential damage effects on existing structural, mechanical and soil systems,

• Improving seismically resistant design.

At present, the research and public service programs have expanded considerably to include new programs, such as the development of retrofit measures for upgrading hazardous existing structures, as well as the collection and dissemination of information on earthquake engineering.

During the first 10 years of the existence of EERC, most of the activities concentrated primarily on research in technical fields.

The greatest efforts involved researchers in the various disciplines of civil engineering and structural mechanics, soil mechanics, foundation engineering and fluid mechanics.

By the end of the 1970s, it was recognized that in order to carry out the above objectives of EERC effectively, an interdisciplinary effort was required.

Such an effort would involve researchers in the fields of materials, architectural engineering, geology and engineering seismology for developing technological concepts and procedures.

Other fields represented have been economics, social science, political science, city and regional planning and law.

Involvement of researchers in these disciplines has proven important in solving the many complex public policy issues related to the implementation of technological concepts and procedures.

Plans have been made to expand EERC's activities in a number of other technical disciplines.

At present, EERC's objectives are achieved through the following three major functions.

The first and primary function is to conduct academic research. This is performed by graduate students (primarily doctoral students), postdoctoral researchers and visiting scholars working with the center's faculty participants.

The second function is to provide research and testing capabilities to industry.

The third function is to disseminate knowledge.

This is accomplished through the activities of the EERC Library, through the publication and dissemination of EERC Reports, through the work of the EERC National Information Service for Earthquake Engineering, and through lectures, seminars and talks to engineering and scientific societies and other organizations in the U.S. and throughout the world.

REFERENCES: "Earthquake Engineering Research Center" annual report; information from Academic Affairs, Office of the President.

CROSS-REFERENCES: Technology Transfer.

Economic, Social and Cultural Impact of the University

In fulfilling its missions of teaching, research and public service, the University plays a vital role in sustaining the long-term economic, social and cultural health of California.

The state's strengths in fields ranging from aerospace to urban planning are directly affected by the quality of education provided California residents.

The state's future depends heavily on a workforce that is highly skilled and capable of adapting to change, as well as one that has a broad understanding of the international marketplace. UC graduates, whether physicists or teachers, help fill this growing demand for talented professionals.

In addition, research by UC scientists helps drive California's economy. University research has spawned entire new fields, such as biotechnology and nuclear physics, and has revolutionized others, including agriculture and microelectronics.

Trailblazing achievements by UC faculty, staff and students lead to new technologies that are essential to expanding California's industrial base and to maintaining the state's entrepreneurial climate.

This dynamic, pioneering work draws bright students and top notch faculty to California from throughout the world.

Moreover, UC draws more than a billion dollars annually in federal funds into the state, which it invests in research and teaching.

In addition, UC attracts millions of dollars more in private funds from corporations, foundations and individuals throughout the world to support programs, build classrooms and fund student scholarships.

Because of its commitment to diversity and to financial aid for needy students, the University's world-renowned academic programs are accessible to students from all backgrounds and income levels.

Student enrollment at UC's nine campuses encompasses the state's myriad of cultures, making it one of the most ethnically diverse universities in the nation. Ethnic minorities represent about 40 percent of UC's undergraduate and graduate students, and about half the students at the University's Berkeley, Irvine and Los Angeles campuses.

Based on demographic projections, UC enrollment could grow by 60,000 by the year 2005, reaching a total 226,000 students at UC's nine campuses.

Throughout, the University remains a gold mine for California.

For every $1 in state funds that UC receives, it generates another $2 in federal or private money, which supports teaching, research and public service programs.

However, UC's economic influence goes beyond the dollars it brings into the state or the number of jobs it provides.

The pioneering work of UC faculty has altered the shape of California business.

For example, the discovery of revolutionary gene-splicing techniques by UC and Stanford scientists launched what has become a multi-billion dollar biotechnology industry.

UC research also has led to better and greater quantities of agricultural produce, faster computers and more sophisticated computer software.

Higher education means a healthier state economy, including the higher incomes of college graduates.

For example, a worker with a B.A. makes twice as much as one with only a high school degree, according to a survey by the U.S. Census Bureau.

A bigger income means a bigger tax payment and more disposable income flowing through California businesses.

UC's contributions to the economy include the following:

• UC brings into the state about $975 million a year in federal funds that support research in fields ranging from AIDS to seismic safety. Through its management of the national laboratories at Berkeley and Livermore, UC oversees $1.2 billion in annual operating budgets funded by the U.S. Department of Energy.

• In private support, UC generates more than $470 million a year from donors to fund expenses such as classroom and laboratory equipment and student scholarships.

• Inventions developed and licensed by UC researchers yield about $40 million in royalties annually, a sum that has grown at double-digit rates in recent years. More than $10 million is distributed to UC campuses to help cover research and education costs. A portion of royalties goes to inventors and the remainder is returned to the state.

• UC campuses are forging university-industry joint ventures by building research parks near campuses, in part to strengthen relationships between academia and business and to shorten the time between scientific breakthroughs and their applications by industry.

• UC, including the two Department of Energy labs it manages in California, annually buys $2.7 billion in goods and services, and strives to support small, local businesses owned by minorities and women.

• Since the early 1980s, UC has spent more than $4 billion on construction projects, creating thousands of jobs in the design and construction industries. A majority of contracts have been awarded to California firms to build classrooms, laboratories and student housing as campuses replace outdated facilities and grow to keep up with increasing enrollment.

• UC's 130,000-member workforce includes groundskeepers, bookkeepers and professors, who earn a total $3.8 billion in annual wages, much of which is circulated back into local economies, generating additional income and jobs. UCSF, for example, is San Francisco's largest employer, outside of government.

• UC employees help stimulate California's economy through the goods and services they buy, as well as the sales taxes they pay.

• And University employees help support government services through taxes—about $520 million in federal and $140 million in state income taxes—paid each year.

UC graduates create works of art, eradicate disease, design safer freeways, build better computers, teach inner-city children and tackle social problems from drug abuse to racial discrimination.

Their accomplishments as business leaders, engineers and scientists help fuel California's economy, enhance our quality of life and improve our understanding of each other.

Among its distinguished faculty, there are 18 Nobel Prize winners, and more members of the National Academy of Sciences than any other college or university in the United States.

UC's curriculum is one of the broadest in the world with studies spanning more than 150 disciplines from agriculture to zoology.

The University's efforts in education, however, go far beyond its campuses.

As part of UC's Education Abroad Program, some 1,500 UC students study in more than 90 institutions in 32 countries, enabling students to experience different cultures and views. In exchange, more than 500 students from these foreign institutions study at UC campuses.

In communities statewide, UC coordinates a number of programs in public schools to encourage students, particularly low-income and ethnic minority students, to attend college. Activities include tutoring, academic counseling and summer workshops on UC campuses.

UC's Urban Community School Collaborative is providing support for programs both inside and outside the University to help restructure the curriculum of inner-city schools to make them more relevant to students and the social environment in which they live. The collaborative also is helping to train teachers to carry out new programs.

UC's educational contributions include the following:

• UC awards one out of every 10 Ph.D.s nationally, and is a major influence in filling the growing need for university professors, scientists and industry leaders.

• UC Berkeley alone awards more doctoral degrees to women and ethnic minorities, and more total doctoral degrees than any other university campus in the country.

• Each year, UC awards more than 41,000 degrees. Since the university was founded in 1868, it has granted more than one million degrees, a third of which were awarded in the last decade.

• The University operates five of the state's nine medical schools and trains more than half of California's medical students. The state's only school of optometry is at UC Berkeley and the only school of veterinary medicine is at UC Davis.

• Among UC's more than 800,000 alumni are numerous government and community leaders. California's governor and about a third of the state's legislators are UC alumni. From among California's 54-member congressional delegation, a third are UC graduates.

UC researchers have touched the lives of virtually all Californians with discoveries ranging from disease-fighting drugs to insights into social ills.

Using advanced technology, these researchers have forged advances that improve and save lives, whether it is fighting an epidemic or an economic recession.

The knowledge they bring to light has resulted in profound contributions to the well-being of Californians and to a better understanding of the world.

For example, University researchers worked with the California Institute of Technology to build the world's largest optical telescope in Mauna Kea, Hawaii.

The W.M. Keck Observatory and Telescope allows astronomers to probe distant reaches of space with unprecedented power and precision.

Others at UC are using the tools of genetics and molecular biology to unravel the complexities of heart disease and cancer, as well as Alzheimer's disease and other illnesses of aging.

In the early 1980s, when the AIDS epidemic exploded, a team at UC was among the first to identify the AIDS virus.

To help corporations and government plan for economic growth and declines, UC economists study issues, policies and events worldwide to form state and national forecasts on economic activity.

Through their analyses, they explain the ramifications of tax and trade policies, and their impact on government and business.

UC researchers have made many other contributions to ensure a better life for Californians.

For example, they have developed the first drug used to reduce the risk of organ rejection in organ transplants; performed the first in-utero operation, which has enabled doctors to undertake lifesaving surgery before infants are born; pioneered the science of nuclear physics and developed the first atom smasher; developed construction techniques to help buildings, bridges and highways better withstand earthquakes; designed safer, more fuel-efficient cars; and developed a heat process to eliminate the threat of botulism in canned foods.

(An extensive list of research breakthroughs can be found under Research Achievements.)

UC enhances the quality of life in California in other ways.

Through public education programs, cultural events and recreational facilities, UC provides a wealth of activities to those living in surrounding communities.

Hundreds of thousands of California residents attend events including music, athletics, dance, drama, film and lectures.

UC's museums, aquariums and academic centers offer exhibits, special seminars and training programs that extend University resources to the public.

For example, the Lawrence Hall of Science (LHS) at Berkeley is a center for teacher training and science education at the elementary, high school and junior college levels.

LHS developed a new course in high school chemistry that is used in thousands of high schools nationwide and other countries, and pioneered methods and materials for introducing science to children in primary grades.

And many UC students do their share as community volunteers, some as tutors for low-income junior high and high school youth. These UC students serve as role models, encouraging youngsters to continue their education.

Communities benefit in countless ways from UC's public facilities and resources.

• University Extension is the largest continuing education program of its kind, offering more than 15,000 self-supporting courses statewide. Student registrations total almost 390,000 a year.

• Researchers and educators of UC's Cooperative Extension reach out to California agricultural communities, sharing research results with the state's farmers and providing advice and educational programs. Among its other services, Cooperative Extension coordinates 4-H youth programs, and offers food and nutrition counseling for low-income families.

• UC is one of the largest single institutional providers of health services in the state. Its five teaching hospitals admit more than 110,000 patients annually. Patients make almost 1.5 million visits to UC clinics and emergency rooms for treatment.

• UC's 4,000 medical residents serve patients at county, community and Veterans Administration hospitals, in addition to UC hospitals and clinics.

• Dozens of public museums, art galleries, botanical gardens and arboretums are operated by UC throughout the state. Among them are the museum and aquarium at the Joseph M. Long Marine Laboratory at Santa Cruz and the California Museum of Photography at Riverside.

• The University also manages a Natural Reserve System, protecting more than 150,000 acres of California's most environmentally sensitive land in its natural state.

Whether faced with challenges posed by the Pacific Rim, Europe or concerns at home, UC explores new methods of teaching and new areas of research and technology that keep pace with emerging issues and trends.

UC offers programs such as the Graduate School of International Relations and Pacific Studies at UC San Diego, the nation's first school of international affairs to specialize in the Pacific area.

Other UC research centers address fields as diverse as robotics, laser technology, molecular genetics and social change.

Beginning in the mid-1990s, a new surge of students will be graduating from California's high schools, and many of them will turn to UC, triggering another wave in enrollment growth.

California's future depends on its tradition of excellence in education, as well as the intellectual capital it generates.

To those who look to the future, resources devoted to the University will continue to pay dividends that will enrich California's economic, social and cultural well-being.

REFERENCES: "UC: California's Gold Mine," informational brochure, Spring 1993, University Relations, Office of the President, based on official information provided by other UC offices.
CROSS-REFERENCES: Topics mentioned in the text.

Education Abroad Program (EAP): Since its inception in 1961, the University's Education Abroad Program has offered its students a chance for rigorous study amid settings and cultures that are worlds away from their usual lives.

UC juniors, seniors and graduate students pursue both studies in their major fields and electives in a vast array of subjects, from literature to ecology, international relations to chemistry, philosophy to psychology, engineering to anthropology. In countries where the native language is other than English, intensive language programs are provided, and most studies take place entirely in the host language.

In most cases, EAP students enroll for an academic year in regular university courses of the host institution, although there are a number of short-term opportunities and special focus programs as well.

By giving UC students a chance to learn a variety of academic subjects in these different settings, EAP also helps advance international understanding through educational exchange.

In addition, students gain an informal education in many instances by witnessing historic political, cultural and economic changes in countries where they are studying.

Home base for EAP's administration is at UC Santa Barbara, where the complex international enterprise is managed by the program's director and approximately 45 staff personnel.

In carrying out their responsibilities, the EAP staff works closely with participating faculty and administrators at each of UC's nine campuses.

Also playing a key role in the program is UCEAP, the Universitywide Academic Senate committee which oversees EAP's academic program, and UC faculty committees which advise EAP on the choice of program sites and curriculum.

It all began with EAP's approval in 1961, followed in 1962 with the opening of the first EAP study center in France at the University of Bordeaux. At that point, 80 students were enrolled in EAP.

Today EAP is a global program on a grand scale. In the 1992–93 academic year, some 1,450 UC students participated, attending courses at 90 host institutions in 32 countries.

EAP's first director was William H. Allaway, a world-renowned expert in international education, who retired in January, 1990 after serving 28 years. Earlier, he had been a special assistant to the chairman of the U.S. National Commission for UNESCO after earning degrees from universities both in this country and abroad.

Under Allaway's direction, more than 15,000 UC students had the chance to study in other countries. Through his leadership, the place of education abroad at the University was not only assured, but its EAP programs continued to grow in number and quality, particularly in countries of the Pacific Rim.

Allaway was succeeded by the current EAP director, John A. Marcum, an academic who is an eminent authority on international affairs.

Before assuming the directorship, Marcum had been a political science professor at UC Santa Cruz, a provost of Merrill College, the academic vice chancellor and the chair of International Programs and Activities. Earlier he had worked with councils, corporations, foundations and the U.S. government in areas of international relations.

Marcum's plans for EAP include maintaining its growth and quality and, by the end of the 1990s, having its activities fully integrated into UC's overall academic program of education.

By the beginning of 1993, Marcum headed a program that had 36 study centers, or administrative offices, in most of the 32 countries where EAP is located.

Continued following the photo spread

EDUCATION ABROAD

Education Abroad students may appear almost anywhere in the world as they pursue their studies.

Clockwise on this page: they can be spotted, for example, in a plaza in Spain or at a garden in Japan, as well as riding through a wildlife preserve in Africa.

Clockwise on the opposite page: they also can be seen in a schoolyard in China, studying outside a university building in Sweden, reading by the Prado in Madrid, visiting a marketplace in Africa and making friends in New Delhi.

Education Abroad *(cont'd)*

A study center usually is administered by a UC faculty member in residence, who serves as the center's director for a period of up to two years. Some centers are administered by a host university faculty member who serves as liaison to EAP.

At each study center, the director is responsible for assuring the academic and personal well-being of EAP students taking courses at one or more of the host institutions.

For example, the director and staff advise students on academic matters, assist with housing, plan field trips, provide information on cultural opportunities, and offer other assistance as needed.

An orientation program at each host institution helps students adjust to their new environment.

Here is what a student normally would expect if he or she studies abroad under EAP.

Academic-year programs in most non-English speaking countries presuppose at least two years of university-level study of the language and include an intensive language session of four to eight weeks. This takes place before the start of the academic year.

In some countries whose languages are little studied in the U.S. (for example, Sweden, Hungary, Thailand), no previous knowledge of the language is required, and language study during EAP participation is obligatory.

EAP students typically enroll in regular university coursework, studying side by side with local students at the host university. In many countries, they live in university housing.

While on EAP, most students make normal progress toward UC graduation. However, acceptance of credit toward major or graduation requirements depends on UC department or campus criteria.

The cost of studying abroad often is comparable to the cost of studying on a UC campus. Financial assistance offsets the higher cost of some locations.

For example, no overseas tuition is charged. At the same time, EAP students are responsible for UC registration and educational fees, campus fees, and room, board, books and personal expenses.

The only additional costs directly related to the Program are for round-trip transportation and on-site orientation and intensive language program (where applicable).

Most UC financial aid is available to EAP students, including grants, scholarships and loans.

In addition, a few specific scholarships and fellowships are available, along with special grants for minority and economically disadvantaged students.

Selection of UC undergraduate students is subject to these minimum qualifications:

A 3.0 cumulative GPA, or the equivalent, at the time of application and maintained until departure; junior standing by departure (84 quarter units or 56 semester units), except for specific short-term programs; support of the campus EAP selection committee; completion of language and other courses as required, with an overall GPA of 3.0 or the equivalent.

California community college transfer students may participate in the program as juniors if they are transferring to UC Irvine or UC Santa Barbara.

Graduate students may apply to study at most study centers, provided they have completed at least one year of graduate work prior to departure and have the support of their academic department and the graduate dean.

An integral component of EAP is the reciprocal exchange of students, which began in EAP's second academic year, 1963–64, when a small number of students came to UC from France, Italy, Germany, and Japan.

By 1980 the annual reciprocity student population was about 200 full-year students and 35 summer session students; by the end of the decade the number had doubled to over 400 full-year students, notably due to new programs in Pacific countries such as Australia, Japan, Korea, and New Zealand.

EAP's exchange agreements with affiliate host institutions typically allow coursework on a non-degree basis. In 1992–93 academic year, more than 500 full-year reciprocity students attended UC from 71 host universities in 20 countries, with another 60 students participating in a summer session at UC.

EAP also has a Faculty Exchange Program, instituted for the first time in 1987.

This program has two components: teaching exchange and research exchange. Both involve one-to-one exchanges between UC faculty and faculty from universities in Pacific Rim countries, Russia, and some other countries affiliated with EAP.

Today, the Education Abroad Program continues its historic role by looking to the 21st century and the benefits to be gained from a growing international community of students and scholars.

REFERENCES: "Undergraduate Education in the University of California: Off-Campus Learning Programs," Item 302 for Discussion, Regents' Committee on Educational Policy, November 6, 1991; EAP's "Frequently Requested Statistics on EAP; "Education Abroad Program Institutional Relationships: Lapsed Programs," EAP informational sheet; news releases, publication articles and other informational material, UC Santa Barbara and News and Public Affairs, Office of the President.

CROSS-REFERENCES: International Programs; Pacific Rim.

EAP Host Institutions: 1993–94

AUSTRALIA
The Australian National University, Canberra
Flinders University, Adelaide
La Trobe University, Melbourne
Monash University, Melbourne
The University of Adelaide
The University of Melbourne
The University of New England, Armidale
The University of New South Wales, Sydney
The University of Queensland, Brisbane
The University of Sydney
The University of Wollongong

AUSTRIA
University of Vienna

BRAZIL
Pontifical Catholic University of Rio de Janeiro

CANADA
University of British Columbia, Vancouver

CHILE
Pontifical Catholic University of Chile, Santiago
University of Chile, Santiago

CHINA
Nankai University, Tianjin
Peking University, Beijing

COSTA RICA
Monteverde Institute, Monteverde
University of Costa Rica, San José

DENMARK
University of Copenhagen

EGYPT
American University in Cairo

ENGLAND
University of Birmingham
University of East Anglia, Norwich
University of Essex, Colchester
University of Exeter
University of Hull
University of Kent at Canterbury
University of Lancaster
University of Leeds
University of London (Queen Mary and Westfield College)

* Programs suspended in 1993–94.

University of Sheffield
University of Sussex, Brighton
University of Warwick
University of York

FRANCE
Ecole Normale Supérieure, Paris
Ecole Normale Supérieure at Fontenay-Saint-Cloud, Paris Region
Ecole Polytechnique at Palaiseau, Paris Region
Paris Center for Critical Studies
University of Bordeaux
University of Grenoble, including Institut d'Etudes Politiques
University of Lyon
University of Pau*
University of Poitiers*
University of Toulouse

GERMANY
Georg-August University, Göttingen

GHANA
University of Ghana, Accra

HONG KONG
Chinese University of Hong Kong (CUHK)

HUNGARY
Eötvös Loránd University, Budapest

INDIA
Jawaharlal Nehru University, New Delhi
University of Delhi

INDONESIA
Gadjah Mada University, Yogyakarta
Indonesian Arts Institute (ISI), Yogyakarta

IRELAND
University College, Cork
University College, Galway

ISRAEL
The Hebrew University of Jerusalem

ITALY
Bocconi University, Milan
Il Bisonte International School of Graphic Arts
Scuola Normale Superiore, Pisa
University of Bologna
University of Padua
University of Venice
Venice Academy of Fine Arts

JAPAN
Doshisha University, Kyoto
International Christian University (ICU), Tokyo

Inter-University Center for Japanese Language Studies (IUC)
Meiji Gakuin University, Yokohama
Kyushu University, Fukuoka*
Kyushu Institute of Technology, Kitakyushu*
Nagoya University
Osaka University
Sophia University, Tokyo
The University of Tokyo
Tohoku University, Sendai
Tokyo Institute of Technology

KOREA
Yonsei University, Seoul

MEXICO
National Autonomous University of Mexico, Mexico City
San Nicolás de Hidalgo University of Michoacan

NEW ZEALAND
Lincoln University, Canterbury
Massey University, Palmerston North
University of Auckland
University of Otago, Dunedin
University of Waikato, Hamilton
Victoria University, Wellington

NORWAY
University of Bergen

RUSSIA
Financial Academy of the Russian Federation (*venue only*), Moscow

SCOTLAND
University of Edinburgh
University of Glasgow
University of St. Andrews
University of Stirling

SPAIN
Complutense University of Madrid
University of Alcalá de Henares
University of Barcelona
University of Granada

SWEDEN
University of Lund

TAIWAN
National Taiwan University, Taipei

THAILAND
Chiang Mai University
Chulalongkorn University, Bangkok

WALES
University College of Wales, Aberystwyth*

Former EAP Host Institutions/Programs

AUSTRALIA
Macquarie University, Sydney

BRAZIL
University of São Paulo

CHINA
University of Nanjing
Peking University of Science and Technology

COLOMBIA
University of the Andes, Bogota

ECUADOR
Catholic University of Ecuador, Quito

ENGLAND
King's College, University of London
University College, University of London
University of Cambridge
University of Oxford

FRANCE
Paul Valéry University (University of Montpellier III)
University of Aix-Marseille III

GERMANY
Eberhard-Karls University, Tübingen

GREECE
Ministry of National Education of The Kingdom of Greece, Athens/Delphi

HUNGARY
Budapest University of Economic Sciences (formerly Karl Marx University of Economics)

INDONESIA
Indonesian Dance Institute of Bandung (ASTI)
Padjadjaran University, Bandung
Advanced School of the Arts at Denpasar (STSI)

IRELAND
Trinity College, University of Dublin

ISRAEL
University of Haifa

ITALY
G.B. Martini Conservatory of Music
The Bisonte International School of Graphic Arts

KENYA
University of Nairobi

LEBANON
American University of Beirut

NORWAY
University of Trondheim

PERU
Pontifical Catholic University of Peru, Lima

PORTUGAL
University of Lisbon

RUSSIA
Alexander Herzen Russian State Pedagogical University
Leningrad State University
North-Western Personnel Centre

SIERRA LEONE
University of Sierra Leone, Freetown

TAIWAN
National Chengchi University, Taipei

TOGO
University of Bénin, Lomé
Village du Bénin, Lomé

WALES
St. David's University College of Wales, Lampeter

Education Abroad Program At a Glance: 1993–94

Academic-Year Programs Where There Is a Language Prerequisite:

Austria, Brazil, Chile, China, Costa Rica, France, Germany, Italy, Japan, Mexico, Spain, Taiwan.

Academic-Year Programs Where There Is No Language Prerequisite, But Language Study Is Required During the Year:

Denmark, Egypt, Hong Kong, Hungary, Indonesia, Israel, Korea, Norway, Sweden, Thailand

Academic-Year Programs Where There Is No Language Prerequisite:

Australia, Canada, Ghana, India, New Zealand, United Kingdom and Ireland

Short-Term/Special Focus Programs Where There Is a Language Prerequisite:

Brazil	Spring Semester
Chile	Spring Semester
China	Summer plus Fall Semester
Italy	Fall/Spring Semester (Bocconi only)
Mexico	Fall/Spring Field Study and Research Quarter/Semester Programs
	Summer Quarter Language and Society Program
Russia	Fall Semester
Taiwan	Summer plus Fall Semester

Short-Term/Special Focus Programs Where There Is No Language Prerequisite:

Canada	Fall Semester
Costa Rica	Fall/Spring Tropical Biology Quarter/Semester
Denmark	Summer Language Quarter
Hungary	Fall Semester
Indonesia	Fall Semester
Israel	Fall Archaeology Quarter
Japan	Spring Global Security Studies Semester
Korea	Summer plus Fall Semester
Thailand	Summer Quarter or Summer plus Fall Language and Society Programs

Education Improvement: The University-School Education Improvement unit (USEI) in the Office of the President coordinates several systemwide initiatives designed to improve the quality of pre-collegiate education.

Each of these programs is designed to enhance UC's understanding of issues facing public school educators, so that faculty research, teaching and public service responsibilities are effectively structured and focused.

USEI projects and staff focus on working with teachers and schools, especially with regard to addressing the challenges facing students historically underrepresented in higher education.

At the heart of USEI are the California Subject Matter Projects (CSMPs), a statewide network of professional development projects for teachers (K-16) in subject areas required for high school graduation.

The following provides some details.

• California Subject Matter Projects

The CSMPs are the foundation of California's professional development system for public schools and teachers.

The CSMPs support 94 discipline-based professional development sites statewide, most of which are located on university campuses (CSU and UC).

The network, administered by USEI, includes projects in the Arts, Foreign Languages, History-Social Sciences, International Studies, Literature, Mathematics, Science, and Writing, with Physical Education in the developmental stage.

Based on the Writing Project model of teachers-teaching-teachers, each CSMP offers intensive professional development institutes, school-year followup, and a wide range of activities and programs, both school- and university-based.

The projects seek to connect teachers to each others' knowledge and experiences, to university faculty and research, and to the principles and methodologies of their discipline.

Teachers involved with the CSMPs are part of a professional learning community (K-University) that supports the quest for new knowledge and skills to improve the quality of education for all children and the development of teachers as leaders of reform.

Other USEI programs include the Presidential Grants for School Improvement (PGSI), the Community Teaching Fellowship Program (CTF), the New Standards Project, and the Oakland Unified School District/UC Partnership for Mathematics Project.

Both PGSI and CTF are significant Universitywide efforts that represent the commitment of UC's Office of the President (UCOP) to, and interest in, K-12 education.

The Mathematics Partnership, funded by an Eisenhower Grant, is a collaborative effort of UCOP, UC Berkeley and the Oakland Unified School District.

• Presidential Grants for School Improvement

PGSI is a Universitywide program designed to stimulate ways in which UC researchers, in collaboration with K-12 educators, can improve the quality of pre-collegiate education.

Presidential grants are awarded to faculty through a competitive proposal process.

Since the inception of PGSI in 1987, more than 40 awards totaling some $800,000 have been made to faculty.

The proposals received over the past six years suggest that faculty are motivated with their K-12 colleagues by three inter-related commitments—commitments to learning, to the development of their discipline, and to the role of education in forging a better future.

The University believes that the presidential aegis of this effort not only elevates the prestige of the work, but gives strong visible evidence at the highest level of the organization of UC's commitment to K-12.

• Community Teaching Fellowship

CTF is a Universitywide initiative designed to enrich mathematics education and curricula in the public schools and to recruit talented UC mathematics students to public school teaching.

This grant-based program emphasizes efforts to strengthen the math education of students who historically have been underrepresented in mathematics and science fields.

To meet these purposes, campus CTF programs place UC graduate and undergraduate students with strong math backgrounds in schools with large numbers of low income, ethnic/language minority students.

CTF fellows introduce complex mathematical topics in ways that elicit new understandings and appreciation for mathematics by K-12 students. At the same time, the fellows gain valuable knowledge about teaching, especially in California's culturally diverse classrooms.

A majority of math undergraduate students who have participated in CTF have subsequently pursued K-12 teaching careers.

• The New Standards Project

New Standards is a joint effort of the Learning Research and Development Center of the University of Pittsburgh and the National Center for Education and the Economy.

New Standards is a partnership of these organizations and 19 states and six school districts that together enroll 50 percent of the nation's school children.

The goal is to build a voluntary assessment system that allows these states and districts to link their results to national standards that are benchmarked to international expectations for high performance.

California has provided substantial leadership to New Standards through the models of standard provided by the state's curriculum frameworks; models of assessment developed by the California Department of Education, supported by the California Subject Matter Project

teachers; and models of professional development created by the California Subject Matter Projects.

UC, through its University-School Education Improvement unit, provides a major portion of the intellectual leadership and organizational capacity required to produce new measures of student achievement.

The primary goal of the New Standards Project is to use a new system of standards and assessments as the cornerstone of a strategy to greatly improve the performance of all students, particularly those who perform least well now.

• Oakland Unified School District/ UC Partnership for Mathematics

The purpose of this partnership is to create professional development opportunities for teachers to improve the teaching and learning of mathematics in East Oakland area classrooms. The student enrollment is 6,948, with African American and Hispanic students comprising 75% of this population.

The project received a three-year grant from the California Postsecondary Education Commission's Eisenhower Math and Science program to support the project.

The project's goals are include the following:

(1) Enhancing professional development opportunities for Area III secondary mathematics teachers, (2)

Education at the University Receives High Marks

▶ A majority of UC graduates say they're happy with the education they received at UC, according to campus surveys. At UC Irvine, for example, 43 percent of the alumni surveyed said the quality of education was "more than satisfactory," and 29 percent said it was "excellent." At UC Davis, almost 90 percent of the recent graduates surveyed said they were "satisfied" or "very satisfied" with their academic experience.

▶ Californians in general say higher education has held its own or made gains. Statewide, 55 percent think the quality of higher education in the state is the same or better than 10 years ago, according to a survey commissioned by the California Higher Education Policy Center. In addition, investing in college pays off.

▶ In a recent survey by the California Higher Education Policy Center, 76 percent of those interviewed believe a college education is necessary to getting a better job.

▶ The U.S. Census Bureau estimates that a worker with a B.A. makes twice as much as one with only a high school degree.

▶ Economists predict that 68 percent of the new jobs created in California in the next five years will require some college education.

Source: University and External Relations, Office of the President.

strengthening Area III students' academic performance in mathematics, and (3) creating a model for the successful delivery of mathematics curriculum in urban schools.

The partnership is intended to help eliminate some of the isolation that teachers experience, while building content knowledge and developing teaching strategies known to be effective with underrepresented students.

The activities will allow teachers to come together on a regular basis to share ideas and collectively identify solutions.

REFERENCES: "University-School Education Improvement: Overview of Activities and Programs," informational material, Office of the President.

CROSS-REFERENCES: All subjects related to education.

Elder Care:

Elder Care: The graying of America had become a vital issue well before the 1990s.

As people began to live longer and to develop functional impairments because of advanced age, a new term for assisting them was coined.

It was "elder care."

The term refers to those services that can give older adults a chance to remain as independent as possible.

These include help with housekeeping, shopping or legal and financial matters, transportation to medical appointments, providing meals, and other adult care services.

However, working people at the University and elsewhere have found that providing such care can have a large impact on their own time-consuming personal and professional responsibilities.

To ease the burden, employees have said they would like University to offer such resources as extended insurance coverage, increased family sick leave, dependent-care assistance, an information and referral network, and flexible work hours.

As a result, the University has looked at ways to help its employees who need to care for elderly relatives.

At first, the issue was so new that little information was available on how many UC employees had, or were likely to have, elder care responsibilities, either locally or in another area of the state or the country.

However, some assumptions could be made in looking at the nation's demographic data.

For example, the average age of the UC workforce in 1991 (excluding student employees) was 41, significantly older than the U.S. average workforce age of 36.

The UC figures broke down as follows: the average age for ladder-rank faculty was 49, for campus management and staff, 39, and for the DOE Laboratories, 42.

Also projecting from national studies, UC analysts assumed that 20 percent of UC's employees, or most commonly those 40 or older, were providing assistance to elderly relatives.

The analysts concluded that UC employees had at least the same elder care needs as the general workforce, if not more.

The University believes that, for such employees, easy access to information about elder care will reduce time spent on the job locating care providers and will reduce stress.

As a result, in 1990–91, a Universitywide Dependent Care Task Force addressed a number of issues affecting elder care.

Among the issues studied were the dependent care needs of employees, personnel policies such as alternate work schedules and parental leave, a strategy for distributing dependent care information, and programs to provide assistance to employees whose elders do not live nearby.

Following the Universitywide review, more information has begun to appear, and more services have been developed.

For example, elder care resource guides have been developed by several campuses and DOE Laboratories.

Several campuses now have developed geriatric resource programs and referral and information services.

Alternative work schedules are becoming increasingly available to UC employees.

Policies have been adopted systemwide which provide most employees at least seven months unpaid leave in a 24-month period for a parent who has a serious health condition.

REFERENCES: "Workers seek services to care for elderly," *UC Focus,* Vol. 5, No. 3, January/February 1991; "Work and Family Strategies for the University of California," Final Report from the Universitywide Task Force on Dependent Care, September 1991, and information from the Office of Human Resource and Planning, Office of the President.

CROSS-REFERENCES: Child Care; Geriatric Resource Programs.

Emeriti Associations:

Emeriti Associations: See Council of the University of California Emeriti Associations.

Employee Assistance Programs:

Employee Assistance Programs: By the 1970s, employee assistance programs had taken hold in workplaces around the country. A decade later they had a attained high visibility.

The first employee assistance programs focused on the treatment of alcoholism (treatment had been identified as a way to address the problem of alcoholism in the work environment by the mid-1930s).

By the 1970s, the scope of employee assistance had expanded to what has been called the "broad brush" model of employee assistance, in which alcoholism and many other personal problems are addressed.

Employee assistance programs at many work sites, including the University, have enabled employees and employers to cope with the multitude of problems inherent in daily life and society generally that often interfere with productivity in the workplace.

Problems include chemical dependency and financial, family and personal problems.

Figures in 1990 showed that 70 percent of the Fortune 500 companies provided employee assistance programs;

figures also showed that 30 to 40 percent of the workforce nationwide had access to such programs.

Studies also showed there were dramatic decreases in employee and dependent health care claims, employee absenteeism, and employee attrition rates, when employee assistance programs were in place.

REFERENCES: "Summary of Proceedings of the Universitywide Symposium on Employee Assistance," jointly presented by the University Committee on Faculty Welfare and the Office of Employee Relations on April 27, 1990, Employee and Labor Relations, Office of the President.

CROSS-REFERENCES: Medical and Health Sciences.

Endowed Chairs, funded through private support to the University, are awarded to distinguished faculty members in support of their teaching and research activities only.

They may be used to recruit outstanding faculty members from another institution or retain UC faculty members.

An endowed chair is supported by income from an endowed fund established by gift or gifts from private sources: individuals, foundations, corporations or groups.

In addition, an endowed chair may be supported through a campaign.

A chair may be named in honor of the donor or honoree proposed by the donor.

The total amount required to establish an endowed chair shall not be less than $250,000, although higher minima may be established by the individual campuses.

Appropriate academic administrators are involved in the discussions with the faculty Senate committee concerning the establishment and naming of an endowed chair prior to Regental approval of the chair.

As of August 1993, there were 402 endowed chairs at UC.

REFERENCES: Regental Policy on Endowed Chairs and Administrative Guidelines.

CROSS-REFERENCES: Foundations; Private Support.

Endowed Chairs and Professorships

Revised August 31, 1993

KEY

Name

The designation "not yet disclosable" signifies that a chair is funded by a binding bequest provision that has yet to be realized.

Discipline

B - Business, Law, and Social Sciences

H - Humanities

M - Medicine

S - Theoretical and Applied Sciences

X - Miscellaneous or Multi-disciplinary

Endowment Held By

R - The Regents

F - Campus Foundation

Amount

The Policy on Endowed Chairs, approved by The Regents in May 1980, requires Regental approval for the establishing and naming of all endowed chairs. For chairs established after that date, the following listing indicates the chair funding level anticipated by the campus at the time of Regental approval. For chairs established before that date, the funding level indicated represents the actual book value of the chair endowment. The list does not include those faculty support entities that have not been established and named by The Regents.

An asterisk (*) after the amount signifies that the terms of the endowment provide for payment of base salary (applicable to pre-1980 chairs only), or, where the endowment is not sufficient for a full year's salary, for support of visiting professors.

SUMMARY

	Number of Chairs	*B*	*H*	*Discipline M*	*S*	*X*	*Total Amount*	*Endowment Held By Regents/ Foundation*	
Berkeley	161	59	25	3	37	37	$62,605,000	81.0	80.0
Davis	11			2	8	1	4,961,970	8.0	3.0
Irvine	18	5	1	8	1	3	11,213,783	1.0	17.0
Los Angeles	108	27	18	43	16	4	53,595,487	58.5	49.5
Riverside	15	2	4	1	5	3	4,850,000	1.0	14.0
San Diego	41		6	14	10	11	12,451,462	9.0	32.0
San Francisco	27			24	2	1	11,517,498	14.0	13.0
Santa Barbara	16	2	7		3	4	5,225,000	5.0	11.0
Santa Cruz	4				3	1	1,525,000	2.0	2.0
Office of the President	1					1	1,200,000	1.0	0.0
TOTALS	402	95	61	95	85	66	$169,145,200	180.5	221.5

Average Funding for Chair Endowments

1. $622,988 Irvine
2. 451,088 Davis
3. 496,255 Los Angeles
4. 426,574 San Francisco
5. 381,250 Santa Cruz
6. 388,851 Berkeley
7. 323,333 Riverside
8. 326,563 Santa Barbara
9. 303,694 San Diego

List of Endowed Chairs follows

Endowed Chairs and Professorships
Established and named by
The Regents of the University of California

BERKELEY

Name	Amount	Discipline	Date Estab-lished-	Endow-ment Held By
Agassiz Professorship of Oriental Languages and Literature	$ 762,869*	H	1872	R
All-Berkeley Class of 1950 Chair	500,000	X	1988	F
Alvarez, Luis W., Memorial Chair in Experimental Physics	400,000	S	1993	F
Arnold, Edward J. and Mollie, Chair in Business Administration	400,000	B	1990	F
Avenali, Peter and Joan, Chair in the Humanities	500,000	H	1987	F
Beckman, Mrs. William, Professorship of English Language and Literature	140,028*	H	1936	R
Berlin, A. Martin, Chair in Mechanical Engineering	300,000	S	1985	F
Bixby, Fred H., Jr., Chair in Population and Family Planning	500,000	B	1989	F
Boalt, John H., and Elizabeth J. Boalt Professorships of Law	448,175*	B	1928	R
Booth, Willis H., Professorship in Banking and Finance	300,000	B	1977	R
Braff, Solon M. and Pearl A., Chair in Clinical Optometric Science	400,000	S	1992	F
Bridges, Robert L., Chair of Law	400,000	B	1987	F
Burch, Robert D., Chair in Tax Policy and Public Finance	1,265,000	B	1993	F
Buttner, Edgar L. and Harold H., Chair of Electrical Engineering	469,000	S	1987	R
Byrne, Margaret, Professorship (American History)	468,677	H	1931	R
Cahill, Edward G. and John R., Chair for Civil or Mineral Engineering	400,000	S	1986	F
California Chair of Real Estate and Land Economics	525,721	B	1973	R
Carlson, Roy W., Chair in Engineering	500,000	S	1985	R
Chambers, Jerry and Evelyn Hemmings, Chair in Music	400,000	H	1983	F
Chernin, Milton and Gertrude, Chair in Social Welfare and the Social Services	300,000	B	1989	R
Chetkovich, Michael N., Chair in Accounting	300,000	B	1978	R
Chin Dook-Jow Chair in Letters and Science	400,000	X	1992	F
Cho, Choong Kun, Chair in Korean Studies	500,000	X	1990	R
Class of 1930 Chair in Letters and Science (rotating; indefinitely assigned to Latin American Studies)	301,008	X	1980	R
Class of 1932 Chair	300,000	X	1981	F
Class of 1933 Chair in Biological Sciences	300,000	S	1982	F
Class of 1934—Robert Gordon Sproul Chair in Agricultural Economics	250,000	S	1981	R
Class of 1935 Chair in Energy	250,000	S	1981	F

Name	Amount	Discipline	Date Estab-lished-	Endow-ment Held By
Class of 1936 Chair	$300,000	X	1984	R
Class of 1937 Chair	300,000	X	1985	F
Class of 1938 Chair	250,000	X	1984	F
Class of 1939 Chair (undergraduate education)	500,000	X	1984	F
Class of 1940 Chair (rotating)	400,000	X	1986	F
Class of 1941 World War II Memorial Chair (rotating)	300,000	X	1986	F
Class of 1942 Chair	500,000	X	1988	F
Class of 1943 Memorial Chair	500,000	X	1983	F
Class of 1944 Chair	440,000	X	1988	F
Class of 1951 Chair	510,000	X	1990	F
Class of 1954 Chair	400,000	X	1986	F
Class of 1955 Chair	400,000	X	1988	F
Class of 1956 Chair	400,000	X	1986	F
Class of 1957 Chair	500,000	X	1992	F
Class of 1958 Chair	250,000	X	1982	R
Class of 1959 Chair	300,000	X	1984	F
Class of 1960 Chair in Undergraduate Education	400,000	X	1985	F
Class of 1963 Chair	400,000	X	1988	F
Coffroth, James W. and Isabel, Chair in Jurisprudence	217,898*	B	1954	R
Coleman, Sylvan C., Chair in Finance	553,677	B	1977	F
Conner, Elizabeth and Edward, Chair (education)	400,000	X	1987	R
Corey, Evelyn Lois, Chair in Instructional Science	400,000	X	1987	R
Cortese, Paul J., Chair in Management	400,000	B	1988	F
Cox, E. Morris, Chair in Economics	300,000	B	1984	F
Crawford, William D., Chair in Taxation and Accounting	446,000	B	1988	R
Deutsch, Monroe E., Class of 1941 Chair (rotating)	300,000	X	1986	F
Dickinson, Fred E., Chair in Wood Science and Technology	400,000	S	1992	F
Ehrman, Sidney Hellman, Professorship of European History	285,808	H	1931	R
Elliott, Maxine J., Chair	526,000	X	1986	F
FANUC Chair in Mechanical Systems	500,000	S	1989	R
Fife, James, Chair (engineering)	400,000	S	1991	F[a]
Floyd, William S., Jr., Chair in Engineering	500,000	S	1990	F
Ford Foundation Professorship in Economics	252,925*	B	1957	R
Furst, Harold, Chair in Management Philosophy and Values	250,000	B	1989	R
Gardner, David Pierpont, Chair in Higher Education	400,000	X	1992	R
Gompertz, John L. and Margaret B., Chair in Integrative Biology	400,000	S	1990	F
Grether, Ewald T., Chair in Marketing and Public Policy	308,432	B	1979	R
Haas, Elise and Walter, Chair in East Asian Studies	300,000	H	1977	R

[a]Endowment is held by University of California San Francisco Foundation.

Name	Amount	Discipline	Date Estab-lished-	Endow-ment Held By
Hall, S. J., Chair in Forest Economics	$ 300,000	S	1985	R
Heller, Emanuel S., Professorship of Law	32,241[b]	B	1926	R
Helzel, Leo, Chair in Entrepreneurship and Innovation[c]	268,000	B	1986	F
Hildebrand, Joel H., Chair in Chemistry	250,000	S	1981	R
Hitchcock, Charles M. and Martha, Chair (for lectureships on general subjects)	160,440	X	1933	R
Horonjeff, Robert, Chair in Civil Engineering	300,000	S	1985	F
Hoskins, William Muriece, Chair in Chemical and Molecular Entomology	421,431	S	1992	F
Hotchkis, Preston, Chair in the History of the United States	250,000	H	1986	F
House, James H., and Hiram H. Hurd Chair of Environmental Regulation	400,000	B	1987	R
Hughes, Roscoe and Elizabeth, Chair in Mechanical Engineering	500,000	S	1990	F
Hunt, Thomas Forsyth, Chair in Agricultural Economics	300,000	S	1985	R
Hutto Patterson Charitable Foundation Chair in Child and Family Studies	300,000	B	1991	R
Indo-American Community Chair in India Studies	400,000	X	1991	F
Italian Culture, Chair of	299,083	H	1928	R
Jennings, Richard W., Chair of Law	500,000	B	1987	R
Johnson, Horace, Dorothy and Katherine, Chair in Engineering	500,000	S	1991	R
Johnson, Walter Perry, Professorship in Law	827,674*	B	1948	R
Kaiser, Edgar F., Chair in Business Administration	300,000	B	1982	R
Kaspin, Albert and Ruth McGovney, Chair in Slavic Languages and Literature	300,000	H	1986	F
Kleiner, Eugene and Rose, Chair for the Study of Processes, Practices, and Policies in Aging	400,000	B	1990	R
Koret Chair in Jewish History	500,000	H	1990	R
Koret Chair of Business Law	300,000	B	1983	R
Kragen, Adrian A., Chair of Law	500,000	B	1987	R
Leopold, A. S., Chair in Wildlife Biology	345,857	S	1984	F
Li, C. H., Chair of Biochemistry and Molecular Endrocrinology	1,500,000	S	1992	F
Lin, T. Y. and Margaret, Chair in Engineering[d]	500,000	S	1988	R
Mackay, John William, Jr., Professorship of Electrical Engineering	167,571*	S	1906	R

[b]In addition to the endowment administered by the University, an external trust produces about $15,000 annually for support of this professorship.

[c]Renamed by the Regents in September 1992 from the Leo Helzel Chair in Entrepreneurship and Business Development.

[d]Renamed by The Regents in June 1992

Name	Amount	Discipline	Date Estab-lished-	Endow-ment Held By
Malozemoff, P., Chair in Mineral Engineering[e]	$250,000	S	1986	R
Martin Sisters Chair in Medical Research and Public Health	250,000	M	1982	F
McAdams, William H., Chair in Physics	400,000	S	1986	F
McLaughlin, Donald H., Chair in Mineral Engineering	250,000	S	1985	R
Michelbacher, Abraham E. and Martha M., Chair in Systematic Entomology	400,000	S	1991	F
Mills Professorship of Intellectual and Moral Philosophy and Civil Polity	505,970*	H	1881	R
Mitchell, Lorraine Tyson, Chair in Leadership and Communication I	412,200	B	1986	F
Mitchell, Lorraine Tyson, Chair in Leadership and Communication II	700,000	B	1990	F
Mitsubishi Bank Chair in International Business and Finance	506,624	B	1988	F
Morrison, Alexander F. and May T., Professorship of American History and American Citizenship	443,815	H	1940	R
Morrison, Alexander F. and May T., Professorship of Municipal Law	304,746	B	1940	R
New, Il Han (Yu Il Han) Chair in Asian Studies	400,000	X	1990	F
Niemela, Emile R., Chair in Accounting	450,000	B	1984	F
Nishkian, Byron L. and Elvira E., Chair in Structural Engineering	250,000	S	1982	F
Pardee, E. H. and Mary E., Chair (rotating)	506,469	X	1987	R
Pardee, George C., and Helen N. Pardee Chair (rotating)	250,000	X	1987	R
Penney, L. H., Chair in Accounting	400,000	B	1980	F
Peyser, Jefferson E., Chair in Trial and Appellate Practice	400,000	B	1991	R
Power, William V., Chair in Biology	400,000	S	1991	F
Presidential Chair	250,000	X	1980	R
Quist, George, Chair in Business Ethics	500,000	B	1989	F
Ralston, Jackson H., Professorship of Law	[f]	B	1973	R
Rayner, Arno A., Chair in Finance and Management	400,655	B	1986	F
Real Estate Development, Chair in	400,000	B	1989	F
Riesenfeld, Stefan A., Chair of Law	500,000	B	1987	R
Robb, Agnes Roddy, Chair in Jurisprudence, Ethics and Social Responsibility	250,000	B	1983	F
Robbins, Milo Rees, Chair in Legal Ethics	300,000	B	1983	F
Robinson, George W. and Elsie M., Chair in Food and Agricultural Resource Economics	250,000	S	1982	F
Robson Research Professorships in Political Science	255,000	B	1980	R
Rocca, B. T., Jr., Chair in International Trade	400,000	B	1986	F

[e]Renamed by The Regents in June 1992

[f]External trust producing income of about $20,000 annually.

Name	Amount	Discipline	Date Estab-lished-	Endow-ment Held By
Royer, Herman, Visiting Professorship in Political Economy	$ 28,618*	B	1905	R
Saroyan, William, Chair in Armenian Studies	400,000	X	1992	F
Sarver, Morton D., Memorial Chair	418,344	S	1992	R
Sather, Jane K., Classical Chair	336,559	H	1912	R
Sather, Jane K., History Chair	222,577	H	1912	R
Sather, Peder, Chair of History	720,421	H	1991	R
Schlinger, William M. and Esther G., Chair in Systematic Entomology	400,000	S	1987	F
Schubert, Walter and Ruth, Family Chair	400,000	S	1991	F
Schutt, Henry and Julia Weisman, Chair in Music	300,000	H	1982	F
Selvin, Herman F., Chair (Law)	400,000	B	1990	R
Shansby, J. Gary, Chair in Marketing Strategy	300,000	B	1978	F
Shepard, A. D., Chair in History	264,661	H	1955	R
Shurtleff, Elizabeth H. and Eugene A., Chair in Undergraduate Education	500,000	X	1989	F
Simon, William G., Chair	400,000	B	1991	R
Simpson, John L., Chair in International Affairs I	415,554	B	1983	R
Simpson, John L., Chair in International Affairs II	400,000	B	1987	R
Simpson, John L., Chair in International Affairs III	400,000	B	1992	R
Simpson, John L., Chair in International Affairs IV	400,000	B	1992	R
Slusser, Clyde and Evelyn, Chair in English Literature Prior to the Twentieth Century	400,000	H	1992	F
Slusser, Willis S. and Marion, Chair in Philosophy	400,000	H	1986	R
Sonne, Muriel McKevitt, Chair in History	400,000	H	1991	F
Springer, Russell Severance, Professorship of Mechanical Engineering	183,318*	S	1954	R
Stephens, Paul H., Chair in Investment Analysis	250,000	B	1991	F
Stone, Irving, Chair of Literature	400,000	H	1991	F
Sullivan, Louise A., Professorship of Nuclear Medicine	20,473*	M	1975	R
Sweesy, King, and Robert Womack Chair in Medical Research and Public Health	252,445	M	1988	F
Taisei Chair in Civil Engineering	500,000	S	1993	R
Tamil Studies, Chair in	400,000	H	1993	R
Taubman, Herman P. and Sophia, Chair of Jewish Studies	724,380	H	1990	R
Transamerica Chair in Business Strategy	300,000	B	1982	R
Traynor, Roger J., Chair (Law)	400,000	B	1990	R
Trefethen, Eugene E. and Catherine M., Chair in Business Administration	729,000	B	1990	F
Turner, Shannon Cecil, Professorship of Jurisprudence	669,317*	B	1940	R
Warren, Earl, Chair in Public Law	190,899	B	1975	R

Name	Amount	Discipline	Date Estab-lished-	Endow-ment Held By
Wood, Gladys Rehard, Chancellor's Chair	$300,000	X	1984	R
Zellerbach Family Fund Chair in Social Policy, Community Change, and Practice	400,000	B	1992	R
Not yet disclosable	300,000	H	1982	F
Not yet disclosable	300,000	B	1984	R

DAVIS

Name	Amount	Discipline	Date Estab-lished-	Endow-ment Held By
Amerine, Maynard A., Professor of Enology and Viticulture	$ [g]	S	1978	R
Buck, Frank H., Jr., Chair in Agricultural Business	650,000	S	1990	R
Davis, L.D., Professorship in Pomology	325,000	S	1992	F
Hughes, John P., Chair in Equine Reproduction	500,000	S	1993	D
Lester, Will A., Chair in Pomology	650,000	S	1986	R
Presidential Chair	250,000	X	1980	R
Rowe, Albert Holmes, Chair of Genetics	1,000,000	S	1981	R
Sesnon Chair in Animal Science	400,000	S	1978	R
Shields, Peter J., Chair in Dairy Food Science	550,000	S	1983	R
Stowell, Robert E., Chair in Pathology	250,000	M	1990	F
UC Davis School of Medicine Alumni Association Endowed Chair in Bioethics	386,970	M	1993	F

IRVINE

Name	Amount	Discipline	Date Estab-lished-	Endow-ment Held By
Aldrich, Daniel G., Jr., Chair	$1,000,000	X	1984	F
Beckman, Arnold and Mabel, Chair in Laser Biomedicine	500,000	M	1988	F
Bell, Grace Beekhuis, Chair in Biological Chemistry	1,000,000	S	1984	F
Chair in Reproductive Biology	500,000	M	1991	F
FHP Foundation Chair in Health Care Management	1,000,000	B	1986	F
Gerken, Walter B., Chair in Enterprise and Society	263,783	B	1988	F
Gold Star Chair in Imaging Sciences	600,000	M	1988	F
Heinz, Clifford S., Chair[h]	300,000	B	1988	F
Leopold, Irving, Chair of Ophthalmology[i]	1,000,000	M	1981	F
Marsh, Dorothy J., Chair in Reproductive Biology	1,000,000	M	1987	F
Martin, Della, Chair in Psychiatry	1,000,000	M	1988	F
Presidential Chair	250,000	X	1980	R
Roosevelt, Franklin D., Chair in Rehabilitative Medicine	1,000,000	M	1988	F
Shepard, Danette (Dee Dee), Chair in Neurological Studies	500,000	M	1989	F
Taco Bell Chair in Real Estate Management	500,000	B	1992	F

[g] External trust producing income of about $35,000 annually.

[h] Renamed by the Regents as an intermim action in July 1991 from the Clifford and Elaine Heinz Chair in the Economics and Public Policy of Peace.

[i] Renamed by The Regents in July 1986 from the Marilyn and Richard P. Hausman Chair of Ophthalmology.

Name	Amount	Discipline	Date Estab-lished-	Endow-ment Held By
Teller Family Chair in Jewish History	$250,000	H	1991	F
Tierney, Thomas T. and Elizabeth C., Chair in Peace Studies	250,000	X	1986	F
Warmington, Drew, Chace, and Erin, Chair in the Social Ecology of Peace and International Cooperation	300,000	B	1989	F

LOS ANGELES

Name	Amount	Discipline	Date Estab-lished-	Endow-ment Held By
Adams, William, Chair in Medicine	$ 900,000	M	1990	R
Allstate Chair in Insurance and Finance	400,000	B	1980	F
Amado, Maurice, Chair in Sephardic Studies	500,000	H	1989	F
Andersen, Arthur/Andersen Consulting Chair in Business Economics	500,000	B	1986	F
Anderson, John E., Chair in Management	1,000,000	B	1993	R
Anderson, Marion, Chair in Management	500,000	B	1988	R
Armenian Educational Foundation Chair in Modern Armenian History	500,000	H	1986	R
Balter, Harry Graham, Chair in Law	500,000	B	1988	R
Beaumont, Louis D., Chair in Surgery	299,996	M	1978	R
Bixby, Fred H., Chair in Population Policy	242,878	B	1975	F
Boelter, L. M. K., Chair in Engineering	500,000	S	1984	F
Bowyer Professorship of Medical Oncology	980,000	M	1973	R
Braun, Judson, Chair in Biological Psychiatry	291,893	M	1978	F
Bruman, Henry J., Chair in German History	500,000	H	1990	F
Bunche, Ralph, Chair in International Studies	250,000	H	1981	F
California Chair of Real Estate and Land Economics	602,478	B	1973	R
Campbell, Joseph, Chair of Child Psychiatry	440,700	M	1976	F
Cantor, Iris, Chair in Breast Imaging	700,000	M	1992	R
Carter, Edward W., Chair in Business Administration	250,000	B	1982	R
Carter, Edward W., Chair in Internal Medicine	500,000	M	1982	R
Carter, Edward W., Chair in Netherlandish Art	250,000	H	1982	R
Cartter, Allan Murray, Chair in Higher Education	247,706	B	1978	R/F
Castera Chair in Cardiology	1,625,000	M	1977	R
Coelho, Tony, Chair in Neurology	896,783	M	1990	F
Coleman, James S., Chair in International Development Studies	500,000	H	1986	R
Collins, James A., Chair in Management	400,000	B	1984	F
Connell Professorship of Law	250,000	B	1975	R
Cordner, Warren C., Chair in Money and Financial Markets	340,000	B	1982	F
Courtaulds Chair in Chemistry	1,000,000	S	1990	F

Name	Amount	Discipline	Date Estab-lished-	Endow-ment Held By
Crump Chair in Medical Engineering	$ 407,804	M	1976	F
Crump, Marjorie, Chair in Social Welfare	500,000	X	1988	F
Davis, M. Philip, Chair in Microbiology and Immunology	1,000,000	M	1990	F
Dumont-UCLA Chair of Transplantation Surgery	500,000	M	1992	R
Ernst & Young Chair in Accounting[j]	250,000	B	1976	F
Factor, Max, Family Foundation Chair in Nephrology	475,000	M	1978	R
Feldman, Charles Kenneth, Chair in Ophthalmology	500,000	M	1982	R
Flint, Mr. and Mrs. C. N., Professorship of Philosophy	283,304	H	1928	R
Ford, Henry, II, Chair in International Management	500,000	B	1985	R
Friedmann, Norman E., Chair in Knowledge Sciences	500,000	S	1987	R
Green, Dolly, Chair in Ophthalmology	500,000	M	1980	R
Griffin, Gloria and Paul, Chair in Philosophy	500,000	H	1984	F
Guthman, Maud Cady, Chair in Cardiology	415,500	M	1990	R
Hammer, Armand, Chair in Leonardo Studies	500,000	H	1985	R
Hassenplug, Lulu Wolf, Chair in Nursing	325,000	M	1992	R
Hearsh, Goldyne and Irwin, Chair in Money and Banking[k]	250,000	B	1982	F
Hoffenberg, Marvin, Chair in American Politics and Public Policy[l]	500,000	B	1984	F
Hughes Aircraft Company Chair in Electrical Engineering	500,000	S	1989	F
Hughes Aircraft Company Chair in Manufacturing Engineering[m]	360,000	S	1981	F
IBM Chair in Computers and Information Systems	400,000	B	1980	R
Kawata, Chizuko, Chair in Cardiology	500,000	M	1989	F
Kneller, George F., Chair in Education and Philosophy	263,000	H	1981	R
Kneller, George F., Chair in Family Medicine	500,000	M	1992	R
Knight, Levi James, Jr., Chair in Engineering	500,000	S	1989	R
Kunin, Harry and Elsa, Chair of Business and Society	250,000	B	1978	F
Lantz, Grace and Walter, Endowed Chair (pediatric ophthalmology)	500,000	M	1991	F
Lee, S. Charles, Chair in Architecture and Urban Design	500,000	X	1986	R
Leonhard, William E., Chair in Management	400,000	B	1982	F

[j]Renamed by The Regents in June 1990 from the Arthur Young Chair in Accounting.

[k]Renamed by The Regents in May 1986 from the Irwin L. Hearsh Chair in Money and Banking.

[l]Renamed by The Regents in November 1990 from the Marvin Hoffenberg Chair in Political Science.

[m]Renamed by The Regents in January 1985 from the Hughes Aircraft UCLA Alumni Chair in Manufacturing Engineering.

Name	Amount	Discipline	Date Established	Endowment Held By
Leslie, Eleanor I., Chair of Neuroscience	$ 500,000	M	1975	R
Libby, Willard F., Chair in Physical Chemistry	500,000	S	1981	F
Longmire, William P., Chair in Surgery	900,000	M	1989	R
Martin, Della, Chair of Psychiatry	250,000	M	1977	F
Maxwell, Richard C., Chair in Law	500,000	B	1987	R
Medberry, Chauncey J., Chair in Management	400,000	B	1983	F
Mellinkoff, Sherman M., Distinguished Professor in Medicine Endowed Chair[n]	1,000,000	M	1986	R
Miller, Arjay and Frances Fearing, Chair in Law	500,000	B	1992	R
Modern European History, Endowed Chair in	350,000	H	1984	F
Murphy, Franklin D., Chair in Italian Renaissance Studies	500,000	H	1985	F
Narekatsi Chair of Armenian Studies	201,550	H	1969	R
Nicholson, James H., Chair in Pediatric Cardiology	247,570	M	1979	F
"1939" Club Chair (for studies of the holocaust)	300,507	H	1979	R
Nippon Sheet Glass Company Chair in Materials Science	600,000	S	1989	F
Northrop Chair in Electrical Engineering/Electromagnetics	500,000	S	1989	F
Paine Chair in Management	500,000	B	1987	R
Parsons, Ralph M., Chair in Chemical Engineering	350,000	S	1981	F
Pearlman, Samuel J., M. D., and Della Z., Chair in Head and Neck Surgery	500,000	M	1985	F
Perloff, Harvey S., Chair	350,000	X	1983	F
Pike, Thomas P. and Katherine K., Chair in Alcohol Studies	250,000	M	1977	F
Plott, Elizabeth R. and Thomas E., Chair in Gerontology	500,000	M	1992	R
President's Chair in Developmental Immunology	250,000	S	1990	R
Price, David G., and Dallas P. Price Chair in Law	500,000	B	1987	F
Reichenbach, Hans, Chair in Philosophy of Science	500,000	H	1989	F
Rigler, Leo G., Chair in Radiological Sciences	600,000	M	1992	R
Rockwell International Chair in Engineering	650,000	S	1988	R
Rose, Augustus S., Chair in Neurology	172,652	M	1977	R
Saxon, David S., Presidential Chair in Physics[o]	250,000	S	1980	R
Security Pacific Bank Chair (consumer law)	250,000	B	1981	R
Simon, Jennifer Jones, Chair in Biophysics	250,000[p]	M	1982	F
Slichter, Louis B., Chair in Geophysics and Planetary Physics	$1,000,000	S	1991	R
Speroni, Charles, Chair in Italian Literature and Culture	250,000	H	1985	R
Sprague, Norman F., Chair in Molecular Oncology	500,000	M	1982	R
Stark, Frances, Chair in Neurology	1,000,000	M	1992	F
Stark, Frances and Ray, Chair in Ophthalmology	500,000	M	1992	R
Stein, Jules, Chair in Ophthalmology	1,000,000	M	1982	R
Stern, W. Eugene, Chair in Neurosurgery	500,000	M	1989	F
Stotter, Ruth and Raymond H., Chair in Neurosurgery	500,000	M	1991	R
Straus, Dorothy and Leonard, Chair in Gastroenterology in Memory of Gussie Borun	500,000	M	1988	R
Streisand Chair in Cardiology	750,000	M	1980	R
Tiber, Leon J., M.D., and David S. Alpert, M.D., Chair in Medicine	1,000,000	M	1982	F
Times Mirror Chair in Management Strategy and Policy	400,000	B	1981	F
TRW Chair in Electrical Engineering	500,000	S	1988	F
UCLA Alumni and Friends of Japanese Ancestry Chair in Japanese American Studies	250,000	H	1980	R/F
UCLA Art Council Professorship in Art	250,000	H	1978	R
UCLA Foundation Chair[q] (rotating among departments, beginning with English, biology, physics, or history)	250,000	X	1980	F
Walter, Richard D. and Ruth P., Chair in Neurology	1,000,000	M	1992	R
Warren, William D., Chair in Law	500,000	B	1992	R
Wasserman, Fred W. and Pamela K. Chair in Health Services	500,000	M	1987	F
Wasserman Professor of Ophthalmology	626,166	M	1977	R
Winstein, Saul, Chair in Organic Chemistry	250,000	S	1981	R/F

RIVERSIDE

Name	Amount	Discipline	Date Established	Endowment Held By
Babbage, John, Chair in Environmental Engineering	$250,000	S	1992	F
Baker, James D., Chair in American Politics and the Economy	250,000	H	1991	F
Boyce, Alfred M., Chair in Entomology	500,000	S	1984	F
Boyd, Philip L., Chair in Finance	300,000	B	1983	F
Costo, Rupert, Chair in American Indian Affairs	300,000	H	1986	F
Field-Baker, Judy Anderson, Chair in the History of Art	250,000	H	1991	F
Holstein Family and Community Chair in Religious Studies	300,000	H	1991	F

[n]Renamed from the Distinguished Professor in Medicine Endowed Chair on the retirement of Dr. Sherman Mellinkoff in 1990, as approved by The Regents in September 1986.

[o]Renamed by The Regents in July 1986 from the Presidential Chair.

[p]External trust held by the Jennifer Jones Simon Foundation.

[q]Renamed by The Regents in November 1984 from the Chancellor's Associates Chair.

Name	Amount	Discipline	Date Established	Endowment Held By
Johnson, William R., Jr., Family Chair in Engineering	$400,000	S	1989	F
Jones, F. Burton, Chair in Topology	400,000	S	1987	F
Mouradick, Cy, Chair in Desert Agriculture	500,000	S	1990	F
Peloy Chair in Learning Disabilities of Children	350,000	X	1989	F
Presidential Chair	250,000	X	1980	R
Shevick, Murray M.D., and Patricia Shevick Francis/Tomas Rivera Chair in Cardiovascular Research	250,000	M	1993	F
Steffey, Albert O., Chair in Marketing	300,000	B	1989	F
University Honors Program Chair	250,000	X	1991	F

SAN DIEGO

Name	Amount	Discipline	Date Established	Endowment Held By
Alderson, Victor C., Chair of Applied Ocean Science	$ 250,000	S	1982	F
Bolivar, Simon, Chair in Latin American Studies	250,000	X	1983	F
Center for Magnetic Recording Research Chair I[r]	250,000	S	1985	R
Center for Magnetic Recording Research Chair II	250,000	S	1985	R
Center for Magnetic Recording Research Chair III	250,000	S	1985	R
Center for Magnetic Recording Research Chair IV	250,000	S	1985	R
Chancellor's Associates Chair I	300,000[s]	X	1983	R/F
Chancellor's Associates Chair II	300,000	X	1993	R/F
Gildred Chair for United States-Mexican Relations	250,000	X	1983	F
Hebrew Biblical Studies, Chair in	250,000	H	1986	F
Hsiu, Hwei-Chih and Julia, Chair in Chinese Studies	250,000	X	1986	F
Institute of the Americas Chair for Inter-American Affairs	250,000	X	1983	F
Isaacs, John Dove, Chair in Natural Philosophy	250,000	H	1982	R
Jacobs Irwin Mark and Joan Klein, Chair in Information and Computer Sciences	250,000	S	1981	F
Judaic Studies, Chair of	250,000	H	1981	F
Katzin Chair of Jewish Civilization	250,000	H	1993	F
Kuffler, Stephen W., Chair in Biology	500,000	S	1990	F
Levi, Estelle and Edgar, Memorial Endowed Chair in Aging	250,000	M	1988	F
Maas, Benard L., Chair in Inherited Metabolic Disease	250,000	M	1985	F
MacCracken, Nancy, Chair in Pediatric Pulmonary Medicine[t]	1,000,000	M	1987	F
Marston, Mary Gilman, Chair in Psychiatry	250,000	M	1988	F
Martin, Quinn, Chair in Drama	250,000	X	1981	F
Matthias, Bernd T., Chair in Physics	250,000	S	1989	R/F
Mori, Hajime, Chair in Japanese Language and Literature	250,000	H	1985	F

[r]Renamed the Stephen O. Rice Chair in Magnetic Recording Research
[s]Amount revised by The Regents in July 1993.
[t]Renamed by The Regents in March 1992 from the Chair in Pulmonary Medicine

Name	Amount	Discipline	Date Established	Endowment Held By
Pacific Economic Cooperation Chair in International Economic Relations	$250,000	X	1990	F
Perlman, Edith and William M., Chair in Clinical Cardiology	250,000	M	1988	F
Persons, W. R., Chair in Reproductive Medicine	250,000	M	1986	R/F
Powell, Charles Lee, Chair in Mathematics	250,000	S	1985	F
Presidential Chair	250,000	X	1980	R
Ranney, Helen, Chair in Medicine	250,000	M	1991	F
Rice, Stephen O., Chair in Magnetic Recording Research[u]	250,000	S	1992	R
Riford, Florence Seeley, Chair for Acquired Immune Deficiency Syndrome Research	500,000	M	1986	F
Riford, Florence, Chair in Alzheimer's Disease	841,462	M	1983	F
Ritter, William E. and Mary B., Memorial Chair	250,000	X	1992	R
Rohr Chair in Pacific International Relations	250,000	X	1988	F
San Diego County Heart Association Chair in Cardiovascular Research	250,000	M	1984	F
Tasch, Evelyn and Edwin, Chair in Cancer Research	250,000	M	1990	F
Trout, Sandra and Monroe, Chair in Pharmacology	250,000	M	1993	F
Urey, Harold Clayton, Chair in Chemistry	250,000	S	1983	F
Valtz Family Chair in Philosophy	250,000	H	1990	F
Walton, Sam M., Endowed Chair for Career Research	510,000	M	1993	F
Whitehill, Muriel Jeannette, Chair in Biomedical Ethics	250,000	M	1988	F

SAN FRANCISCO

Name	Amount	Discipline	Date Established	Endowment Held By
Aird, Dr. Robert B. and Mrs. Ellinor, Chair in Neurology	$499,531	M	1990	F
Bowers, Albert, Chair in Biochemistry	500,000	S	1990	F
Caygill, Theresa M., and Wayne M. Caygill, M.D., Chair in Ophthalmology	250,000	M	1990	R
Comroe, Julius H., Jr., M.D., Chair in Pulmonary Biology	250,000	M	1986	F
Diamond, Louis K., M.D., Chair in Hematology	500,000	M	1982	R
Dunphy, J. Englebert, M.D., Chair in Surgery	250,000	M	1986	F
Epstein, Leon J., M.D., Chair in Geriatric Psychiatry	500,000	M	1985	F
Fife, Betty Anker, Chair in Neurology	600,000	M	1991	F
Gellert, Fred, Chair in Reproductive Medicine and Biology	500,000	M	1989	F
Guggenhime, Berthold and Belle N., Professorship	330,098*	M	1957	R

[u]Renamed by The Regents in November 1992 from the Center in Magnetic Recording Research Chair I.

Name	Amount	Discipline	Date Established	Endowment Held By
Hahnemann, Samuel, Professorship of Medicine	$ 24,267*	M	1957	R
Herzstein, Morris, Chair in Biology	823,869*	S	1933	R
Kan, Tong-po, Chair in Neurological Surgery	250,000	M	1983	R
Kerr, William Watt, Professorship in Clinical Medicine	22,894	M	1933	R
Kroc, Robert L., Chair in Rheumatic and Connective Tissue Diseases	1,000,000	M	1985	R
Lange, Jack D. and DeLoris, Chair in Physiology	250,000	M	1982	R
Lee Hysan Chair of Oral Epidemiology	500,000	M	1992	F
Livingston, James P. and Marjorie A., Chair in Nursing	250,000	M	1986	F
Lucia, Salvatore P., Chair in Preventive Medicine	500,000	M	1985	F
Margulis, Alexander R., Endowed Chair in Radiology	918,000	M	1992	F
Nursing Education, Professorship of	169,112*	M	1933	R
Presidential Chair	250,000	X	1980	R
Shaw, Edward B., Chair in Pediatrics	250,000	M	1983	R
Sooy, Francis A., Chair in Otolaryngology	407,590	M	1990	F
Stern, Lucie, Chair of Cardiology	871,861	M	1974	R
Wood, David A., Chair of Tumor Biology and Cancer Research	528,818	M	1982	R
Wylie, Edwin J., M.D., Chair in Vascular Surgery	321,458	M	1987	F

SANTA BARBARA

Name	Amount	Discipline	Date Established	Endowment Held By
Abdul Aziz ibn Saud, King, Chair in Islamic Studies	$250,000	H	1984	R
ALCOA Chair in Materials	350,000	S	1986	R
Barandiarán, José Miguel de, Chair in Basque Studies	350,000	H	1993	F
Chancellor's Chair	$350,000	X	1986	F
Corwin, Dorothy and Sherrill, Chair in Music	350,000	H	1986	F
Dehlsen Chair in Environmental Studies	375,000	S	1986	F
Khashoggi, Essam, Chair	350,000	X	1985	F
Lancaster, Louis G., Chair in International Relations	350,000	B	1988	F
Leal, Luis, Chair in Chicano Studies	350,000	H	1989	F
Pellish, Maxwell C. and Mary, Chair in Economics	250,000	B	1989	F
Presidential Chair	250,000	X	1980	R
Raznick, Aaron and Cherie, Chair	250,000	X	1985	F
Rowny, J. F., Chair in Comparative Religions	350,000	H	1988	R
Rowny Chair in Religion and Society	350,000	H	1988	R
Takashima, Koichi, Chair in Japanese Cultural Studies	350,000	H	1993	F
Whittier, Donald W., Chair in Electrical Engineering	350,000	S	1985	F

SANTA CRUZ

Name	Amount	Discipline	Date Established	Endowment Held By
Baskin, Jack, Chair in Computer Engineering	$650,000	S	1988	F
Heller, Alfred E., Chair in Agroecology	375,000	S	1982	F
Presidential Chair	250,000	X	1980	R
Sinsheimer, Robert L., Chair in Molecular Biology	250,000	S	1987	R

OFFICE OF THE PRESIDENT

Name	Amount	Discipline	Date Established	Endowment Held By
MacArthur, John D., Chair (assignable among campuses at the discretion of the President; currently at Berkeley)	$1,200,000	X	1982	R

Energy Efficiency: The California Institute for Energy Efficiency (CIEE) was established in 1988 by the University in cooperation with California's electric and gas utilities, the California Public Utilities Commission, the California Energy Commission and the U.S. Department of Energy's Lawrence Berkeley Laboratory.

CIEE's mission is to coordinate, plan and implement a statewide program of medium- to long-term (5–15 years) applied research aimed at advancing the energy efficiency and productivity of all "end-use" sectors in California.

This research, conducted primarily at colleges, universities and university-affiliated research laboratories statewide, is designed to complement the research efforts of CIEE's sponsors.

CIEE's research and development (R&D) has the following goals:

1. To identify, develop and demonstrate efficient end-use energy technologies and processes that:

• Increase the security and sustainability of energy systems in California.

• Help assure continued access to reliable, affordable energy services for all California end-users.

• Enhance the productivity and competitiveness of California's agricultural, manufacturing and service industries.

• Contribute to improving the environment, including regional air and water quality and the quality of the indoor built environment, while remaining sensitive to global-warming issues.

2. To improve the data and analytical tools related to the end-use of energy so that utilities and the public sector can make sound planning decisions on the balanced development of demand- and supply-side energy resources in California.

In 1992, CIEE was planning, funding and managing $5 million in multiyear research, exploratory research, discretionary research and technology transfer activities.

In the near future, CIEE plans to continue conducting research and development activities that will help provide sustainable, affordable energy for California while improving the state's economy and environment.

REFERENCES: Information supplied and approved by Academic Affairs, Office of the president.

CROSS-REFERENCES: Energy Research.

Energy Research: The Universitywide Energy Research Group (UERG) was established in December, 1980 by UC's president.

It was formed in response to a perceived need to strengthen the energy-research programs on the nine campuses.

A universitywide planning committee, convened earlier to provide guidance for the new organization, adopted a mission statement that reads as follows:

"The systemwide University of California Energy Institute and its affiliates will:

"1) Foster and support distinguished research programs in the energy fields, complementing instruction at both the undergraduate and graduate levels.

"2) Serve as focal points for identification, initiation and execution of (a) interdisciplinary energy research, (b) policy-related studies on critical energy issues affecting California, the nation and the world, and (c) energy-related research in the natural and social sciences, engineering and environmental design areas of special interest to California.

"3) Serve as centers for discussion of energy issues and dissemination of energy information. These objectives will be accomplished through activities such as public lectures, conferences, extension services and studies.

"4) Cooperate with other research institutions and with state and federal agencies on studies aimed at solutions of energy problems."

The mission statement stresses both policy studies and technical research. It also emphasizes research on California energy problems.

Accordingly, the Universitywide Energy Research Group has attempted to develop research programs that stress these themes.

Policy research is embodied in the California Energy Studies (CES) Program, which emphasizes interdisciplinary and policy-oriented studies on a broad range of topics, and the Program on Workable Energy Regulation (POWER), which focuses narrowly on near-term issues.

Long-range technical research is the central focus of the Energy Science and Technology (EST) Program, which emphasizes goal-oriented basic science and engineering research related to development of energy technologies and understanding of energy systems.

Shorter-range technical research is conducted under the California Energy Studies Program.

Both CES and POWER are concentrated on problems of importance for the energy future of California.

During 1990–91, UERG provided grants of $296 thousand of UC funds to California Energy Studies, $162 thousand to POWER, and $278 thousand to Energy Science and Technology Research.

In addition to the above, the California Institute for Energy Efficiency (CIEE), a branch of UERG, was established in 1988.

It manages a statewide program of research on energy end-use efficiency funded by California utility companies.

REFERENCES: Information supplied and approved by Academic Affairs, Office of the president.

CROSS-REFERENCES: Energy Efficiency; Research Achievements; Technology Transfer.

Enrollment: The foundations for higher education planning that take place today at the University began in the late 1940s.

This planning period followed the wild gyrations in enrollments that took place as a consequence of the mobilization and demobilization of young men during and after World War II and the Korean War.

Fortunately, those responsible for higher education planning in California in the late 1940s and the 1950s saw beyond the extraordinary fluctuations of the time. They knew that the high birth rates following World War II and the large number of young families migrating into California would mean a huge increase in the demand for higher education in the 1960s.

Moreover, they agreed that the state should continue to be responsible for meeting that demand, accepting the longstanding principle that state institutions of higher education should accept all qualified applicants.

As a result, the 1950s were a decade of increasingly intense discussion and planning for the expected demographic surge.

These activities culminated in the 1960 Master Plan for Higher Education in California, 1960–1975, which guided the expansion of higher education in California in the 1960s. With some modification, the plan still provides the outline for major policy decisions in public higher education in California.

The central part of the Plan consisted of two sets of enrollment projections. Both assumed a slowly rising rate of attendance and the establishment of new campuses. Both used a straightforward grade progression methodology to project high school graduates and subsequent new entrants. In addition, both predicted unprecedented growth.

Their principal difference lay in certain policy assumptions concerning the imposition of ceilings at Berkeley and UCLA and diversion of lower division students to the community colleges (then called junior colleges).

Considering the time span, the projections were surprisingly good. In 1975, some 15 years after the projections were made, enrollments at the California State University and the University of California were only 2 percent and 4 percent lower, respectively, than the average of the two sets.

The Master Plan proved functional as well as accurate. The restructuring of higher education for which it laid the groundwork enabled the state to accommodate the tripling of enrollments it had predicted.

Among the recommendations relevant to undergraduate enrollment planning were:

• That campuses maintain enrollment ceilings. (While limits were later raised somewhat, the idea of ceilings based on academic considerations was retained.)

• That intrasegmental redirection procedures be developed to accommodate excess demand on individual campuses.

• That for reasons of economy and access a substantial portion of lower division students be accommodated at junior colleges and that transfer among all segments be facilitated.

• That the University draw its enrollment from the top one-eighth (12 1/2 percent) of all high school graduates, the criteria for selection to be determined by the University.

• That a small percentage of students be admitted in exception to the general eligibility rules, on the grounds of special talent or promise.

The authors of the Master Plan also recommended the establishment of three new campuses for UC and expansion of the existing campuses.

Subsequently, a basic addition was made to the policy framework of University undergraduate enrollment planning after approval of the Master Plan. That has been the policy of increasing the enrollment of hitherto underrepresented groups.

Efforts in this direction began in the mid-1960s with the creation of the Educational Opportunity Program (EOP) in 1964. EOP was and is targeted to low income students generally.

The Student Affirmative Action (SAA) Program, with particular emphasis on increasing the participation of underrepresented minorities, was established in the mid-1970s.

The two programs are now closely related on all campuses. In addition to EOP and SAA, several of the campuses sponsor other outreach programs designed to attract low income and minority students.

The very rapid growth of the 1960s encouraged considerable optimism among the state's higher education planners.

Enrollment growth in the early 1960s outpaced the Master Plan projections. In addition, by the middle 1960s, UC planners had raised their projected numbers for the 1970s above the Master Plan level, had extended the length of the projection to the end of the century, and were making plans accordingly.

However, the optimism of the 1960s did not outlast the decade. Among other indicators of a less exuberant future were the results of the 1970 Census, which showed a shrinking number of children under five and diminished migration into California.

By the middle 1970s, UC plans were based on the expectation of a diminished rate of increase in the 1970s and the possibility of "steady state," i.e., no growth, by the mid-1980s.

The possibility of decline in the late 1980s was discussed internally, but the late 1980s were beyond the 10-year planning period. The earlier projections were revised downward, but they still showed small increases from the mid-1970s to the mid-1980s. The expectation of slow and, finally, no growth in undergraduate enrollments was disrupted both by a surge in demand at the freshman level beginning in 1978 and by an increase in the retention rate starting around the same time. As a result, the early 1980s were years of burgeoning enrollment.

In October 1988, the University prepared revised undergraduate enrollment projections.

At that time, the University's enrollment feasibility analysis assumed that UC's assigned mission under the Master Plan would remain undisturbed, that the standards for freshman admission would continue to qualify the top 12.5 percent of California's high school graduates, and that the commitment to enroll eligible California residents seeking undergraduate admission would be honored.

The assumption was also made that the percentage of eligible California residents enrolling would continue to approximate current levels and that present limitations on State spending would be modified or that alternative arrangements for funding the University would be made so as to permit funding of projected growth with the same measure of support and consideration as had been accorded the University in the past.

By the late 1980s, California's dramatic population surge had contributed to steadily increasing demands for admission to the University. As a result, the Regents in November 1988 authorized UC's president to begin planning for new campuses in order to accommodate anticipated long-term enrollment growth. In early 1989, the president appointed a Site Selection Task Force, advisory to him, to undertake the search for and analysis of potential new campus sites. Over the next two years, the Regents took actions to approve the criteria and methodology for site selection and focus the search for the first new campus site in the central region of California.

By mid-1993, in light of changing of the state's fiscal situation, the University began to develop new enrollment projections.

Graduate enrollment planning was being studied as well, based on elements of societal need for advanced training and research. Other factors also are considered in such a process, including the balance of graduate to undergraduate students and affirmative action policies.

(Note: For further details, see enrollment figures accompanying this narrative.)

REFERENCES: "University of California Undergraduate Enrollment Plan, 1983–1988," January 1984, Office of the President: Minutes of Regents' Meeting of October 20, 1988; "Revised Undergraduate and Graduate Student Enrollment Projections," Item 306 for Discussion, Regents' Committee on Educational Policy, March 14, 1991; "Future of Graduate Education in the University of California: Changing Job Market Opportunities and Assessment of Needs for UC Graduate Enrollment Growth," March 1991, Office of the President.

CROSS-REFERENCES: Academic Planning and Program Review; Admissions; Master Plan; Site Selection.

Total Undergraduate Enrollment Systemwide	
1975	91,682
1976	90,318
1977	88,956
1978	90,166
1979	93,184
1980	96,472
1981	98,547
1982	100,381
1983	103,034
1984	105,765
1985	108,738
1986	112,113
1987	117,201
1988	121,745
1989	124,087
1990	124,245
1991	125,416

In 1992, according to UC's Corporate Student System Report CSS 346 for 1990 and 1992, undergraduate enrollment was 125,187. See REFERENCES for undergraduate, graduate and total enrollments, as well as related documents from the Office of the President.

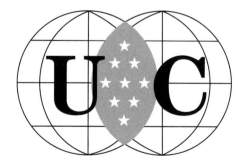

Expanded Food and Nutrition Education Program: Cooperative Extension's Expanded Food and Nutrition Education Program (EFNEP) celebrated its 20th anniversary in 1989.

EFNEP is a federally funded enterprise whose mission is to improve the dietary well-being of low-income families in California who have young children.

The U.S. Department of Agriculture provides the funding.

During its two decades of growth, EFNEP has changed some of its methods in order to reach more low-income families, even though its basic premise of "neighbors helping neighbors" has stayed the same.

Under the Adult EFNEP program, paraprofessional nutrition education assistants are recruited from low-income neighborhoods, trained, and then assigned to work with families in those areas. Nearly 13,000 families enroll annually.

Training is coordinated by Cooperative Extension home economists in each of the state's 16 EFNEP counties. The training covers basic nutrition and health practices; food planning, selection and buying; economical food preparation; and food storage, safety and sanitation.

By 1985 national and state studies had determined that group teaching, rather than traditional individual instruction, was a more effective, efficient way to reach low-income, ethnically diverse families.

Group teaching became the primary method for delivering EFNEP information in 1986.

Since then, the basic EFNEP program has been supplemented with new methods for reaching even greater numbers of the target population.

These methods include the following:

• Working with local emergency food distribution systems.

• Training staff and volunteers in related agencies that work with low-income groups to deliver EFNEP nutrition education information.

• Developing creative media approaches, such as Spanish-language radio tapes and videotapes to disseminate nutritional information.

Another component of EFNEP is the 4-H EFNEP program, also conducted by Cooperative Extension.

4-H EFNEP sponsors a variety of programs to deliver urgently needed quality nutrition education to youth at risk.

Popular formats where nutrition education is the focus include after-school programs and summer day-camps for inner-city children.

Currently operating in 10 California counties, 4-H EFNEP'S staff and volunteers serve more than 30,000 youngsters yearly.

Those who complete the program are able to improve significantly their eating habits and nutrition.

REFERENCES: "EFNEP makes a difference," *California Agriculture*, Vol. 43, No. 3, May–June 1989, and additional information from EFNEP office.

CROSS-REFERENCES: Agriculture and Natural Resources.

F

Faculty Housing Assistance Programs: In 1979, the University initiated a number of housing programs to enhance its efforts in recruiting and retaining key faculty and other designated employees, in order to help UC maintain its preeminent academic position.

UC's housing programs have been particularly important in this regard in the face of growing competition from other higher education institutions for a decreasing pool of candidates to fill their academic and administrative positions.

The University's housing programs also have been critical in addressing the problem of the large differential between the higher costs of housing surrounding UC locations and the costs at comparable institutions across the country.

The programs have expanded substantially since their inception in 1979. In July 1984, a significant development was the establishment of the Office of Faculty Housing Programs within the Office of the President.

The office's goals were to plan, develop and administer housing assistance programs for members of the Academic Senate and other designated classes of University employees.

In 1992, the name of the office was changed to Real Estate Management and Loan Programs Office in recognition of expanded responsibilities for managing a wide range of real estate transactions.

These include space leasing, acquisitions, sales and other real property related activities.

Housing assistance programs continue to remain targeted for members of the Academic Senate; however, the office also provides some assistance to the University's Executive Program members.

The office also provides policy overview for the Emergency Loan Fund (a non-housing loan program for all employees).

The housing and loan-related operations of the office are self-supporting.

These program components include:

• The Mortgage Origination Program, UC's major first deed-of-trust lending program

• Three tax-exempt bond financed single-family loan programs

• The Mortgage Credit Certificate Program

In addition to the direct administration of the above programs, the office also has policy and coordination responsibility for for-sale housing built on University-owned land at five campuses.

The office also administers the Supplemental Home Loan Program, which provides secondary financing to assist in home purchases.

In addition, the office has established a relationship with a major conventional lender to provide favorable financing terms for the acquisition and refinancing of housing at all UC locations.

Key policy components of the University's housing programs include the:

• Provision of a predictable source of mortgage financing for recruitment and retention of key faculty members and executives at each campus and laboratory

Summary of Housing Assistance Programs
(Cumulative as of June 30, 1992)

Program	Number of Loans/ Assistance	Dollar Value	Average Amount	Recruit- ment	Reten- tion
1979 Faculty Residential Mortgage Revenue Bond Program	196	$ 21,391,550	$109,141	158	38
1982 Home Mortgage Program	119	15,158,100	127,379	69	50
Short-Term Housing Loan Program	378	19,883,101	52,600	300	78
Salary Differential Housing Allowance Program	586	7,732,593	13,196	575	11
Mortgage Origination Program	882	185,785,645	210,641	702	180
1985 Mortgage Revenue Bond Faculty Loan Program	163	17,545,389	107,640	52	111
1987 Mortgage Revenue Bond Faculty Loan Program	168	20,772,990	123,649	104	64
Mortgage Credit Certificate Program	25	588,684*	23,547*	19	6
Wells Fargo Bank Home Loan Program					
First deed-of-trust mortgages	23	6,633,183	288,399	5	18
Second mortgages/ equity lines	8	774,000	96,750	0	8
Totals	**2,548**	**$295,676,551****	**N/A**	**1,984**	**564**

Campus For-Sale Housing Developments
(Cumulative as of June 30, 1992)

Location	Units Built	Units Sold	Units Unsold
Irvine	431	408	23
Los Angeles	110	102	8
Santa Barbara	65	65	0
Santa Cruz	61	61	0
Totals	**667**	**636**	**31**

* Figures do not represent the dollar value of the mortgage loans obtained to purchase the home, but rather the value of the mortgage credit certificates, which can range from 10% to 50% of the loan amount, with an average of 24.6%.

** Figure does not include the value of mortgage credit certificates.

• Provision of financing at short-term rates with qualification standards more liberal than those provided by conventional lenders, coupled with reduced down-payment requirements and no points or origination fees

• Utilization of existing University land and acquisition of additional land, where feasible, to develop for-sale and/or rental housing units to create affordable housing in proximity to work utilizing a broad range of design and pricing

• Continuation of supplements to University and conventional financing via the Supplemental Home Loan Program and Salary Differential Housing Allowance Program

• Development of programs of a one-time or short-term nature that supplement and/or complement existing University programs

REFERENCES: Annual Reports of the University of California Faculty Housing Assistance Programs.

CROSS-REFERENCES: Student Housing.

Faculty Representation on the Board of Regents: This question is frequently asked:

"Why doesn't the faculty have a voting membership on the Board of Regents, just as students and alumni do?"

The question is a valid one, since a constitutional amendment approved by the voters in 1974 stipulated that the Regents "may, at their discretion, appoint either or both a faculty or a student member to the Board."

This proviso also is in the Regents' bylaws. The bylaws also stipulate that a faculty Regent may be from UC or from another institution of higher education.

At the time the amendment was approved, the chair and vice chair of the Academic Council attended all Regents' meetings, but only as spectators.

They sat with the chancellors and UC executives close to the Regents' meeting table and had the privilege of coming up to the table to address the Board by pre-arrangement with the president of the University.

At the time the amendment was passed, the Academic Council discussed in detail the role the faculty might have as members of the Board.

The concern was not whether there should be a faculty Regent, but rather who that person should be. At the same time, there was no support whatsoever for a faculty Regent from another institution.

Moreover, the Council felt strongly that the selection of a faculty Regent should be made by the Academic Senate. Otherwise, the process might compromise the authority of the Academic Senate, as delegated by the Regents, to speak for the faculty.

In addition, appointment of a faculty Regent by an outside party could lead to situations in which the judgments of the faculty Regent and the Academic Senate might be in conflict.

Therefore, in 1975 the Academic Council recommended that the chair of the Academic Council be appointed to the Board.

However, the Council could not reach a consensus as to whether an appointment should carry full Regental status or nonvoting membership.

The argument against full Regental status, which ultimately prevailed, rested on the issue of trusteeship versus advocacy.

UC's president expressed the view that having a faculty member as a Regent would compromise the principal of "regency as trusteeship."

He felt, as did many faculty, that the trustee concept ruled out concurrent service as a Regent and as an officer of the Academic Senate.

In other words, a faculty Regent could not function both as a trustee of the institution as a whole and as a representative or advocate of faculty interests.

For example, a faculty Regent would have to withdraw from participating in matters where there was a conflict of interest, such as compensation, workload, promotion and tenure policies.

These were the very issues on which faculty would wish to see their representative exert strong leadership and influence.

The arguments were persuasive. The Regents adopted the recommendation of the Academic Council to seat the chair of the Council on the Board of Regents as a nonvoting participant (for an experimental two-year period).

In addition, in March 1975, another issue had been resolved. This related to ambiguity over whether nonvoting status removed the right to move or second motions.

An amendment passed by the Board stated that the privileges of the faculty representative include and are limited to being "seated at the meeting table with full participation in discussion and debate."

In September 1977, an amendment was adopted to include both the chair and the vice chair of the Academic Council as faculty representatives to the Board.

For two years after the Regents had voted to continue the arrangement of faculty representation, the Academic Council continued to discuss the pros and cons of what was eventually termed "regency versus representation"

The matter was referred to the divisions of the Academic Senate, which, after protracted debate, voted 6–2 in favor of full Regental status for the chair of the Academic Council.

Late in 1978, the Academic Council proposed this change in status to UC's president.

The ensuing consultation with the president evoked compelling arguments against such an arrangement, based again on the principle of trusteeship and on limited effectiveness of a faculty Regent.

The outcome was a reaffirmation of faculty representation and recognition that voting status would:

• Undermine the principle of trusteeship.

• Reduce the effectiveness of the faculty voice on the Board.

• Inevitably raise the specter of conflict of interest.

• Draw extensive criticism from faculty colleagues, students and administrators on voting issues of all kinds.

Since the current system has been in effect, parties have agreed on the value of faculty representation on the Board with no voting rights.

Faculty representatives are considered resource persons to the Board. They fill a need in the governance of the University to bring to the attention of the Regents the views of the Academic Senate on matters of concern to the faculty.

In addition, issues of importance can be discussed from a faculty perspective.

According to all parties involved, the benefits are reciprocal.

For example, the Regents provide the faculty, through their representatives to the Board, with perspective and insight into the governance of the University that could not be obtained in other ways.

This process strengthens communication and understanding between the Regents and the faculty that extends through the Academic Council, the Academic Assembly and the Divisions of the Academic Senate.

REFERENCES: "Commentary: Faculty and the Regents," reprint of remarks by Marjorie Caserio, former chair of the Academic Council, at the July 1986 meeting of the Regents, *Notice,* Vol. 11, No. 2, November 1986, and related information.

CROSS-REFERENCES: Academic Senate; Regents; topics mentioned in the text above.

Federally Sponsored Research and Indirect Costs:
By the beginning of the 1990s, there was heightened national interest in the issue of overhead costs charged to the U.S. government by universities for research contracts and grants.

In view of this interest, UC's president appointed a 26-member Universitywide task force to examine the issue.

The task force findings and recommendations were presented as part of a progress report on the indirect cost issue to the Regents at its November 1991 business meeting.

The recommended changes were then implemented through revisions to UC's accounting policy and procedures.

In a letter dated October 30, 1991, to UC's chancellors, the president summarized the work of the task force.

He said the task force, after an extensive review, concluded that UC's overall systems and procedures regarding indirect costs had "worked well."

However, as expected, the task force noted "variations from policy and some transaction errors." Some of these were in favor of the government, and others were in favor of UC.

(The UC task force said that if all the errors noted in its review of campus procedures were corrected, both those favoring the government as well as those favoring UC, current indirect cost rates negotiated by the campuses would be virtually unchanged.)

The variations that the task force found were mostly due to "errors in coding, interpretation of regulations, or omissions," the president explained.

He added that, although the task force had completed its overall review, individual campuses were continuing to review their indirect cost records.

"The results of the task force's work confirm that our indirect cost proposals have been developed and administered carefully and conscientiously, essentially consistent with federal regulations and pertinent University policies and procedures," the president said in the letter to the chancellors.

"The implementation of new procedures recommended by our task force will help us continue to meet our responsibilities in this area and to respond fully to both the letter and the spirit of new federal regulations and to the issues raised by the Congress," he stated.

The procedures developed by the task force provided for more detailed coding practices to clearly identify expenditures and reduce the risk of error.

To further ensure full compliance with all federal regulations, the University also decided it would exclude from any indirect cost reimbursement request all non-payroll costs incurred by the president's and chancellors' offices (even though most of these expenditures remained allowable under federal guidelines).

The task force was chaired by the University's senior vice president—administration. Its members included representatives from all UC campuses, the Office of the President, functional offices and members of the University auditor's staff and the University's external auditor.

In fiscal 1991, UC received about $900 million in federal grants and contracts, primarily in medicine, the physical and biological sciences, and engineering.

At that time, UC's overall accounting process encompassed roughly 20 million individual financial transactions, including those generated by more than 6,000 federal awards to the campuses.

University costs in connection with federal research are categorized as both "direct" and "indirect."

Direct costs cover costs directly attributable to the project, for example, laboratory equipment, project personnel, salaries and supplies.

Indirect costs are those incurred for purposes common to various projects, programs or activities of the institution.

As indicated earlier, indirect costs are those associated with space, such as building and equipment depreciation and maintenance and operation, as well as costs of administrative services such as accounting, purchasing, personnel and library services).

Indirect cost rates are negotiated for each UC campus with the U.S. Department of Health and Human Services. The negotiation process begins with a rate proposed by the University and results in a negotiated rate

Terms Used for Research That's Federally Sponsored

▶ Circular A-21: The U.S. Office of Management and Budget (OMB) issues Circular A-21 ("Cost Principles for Education Institutions"). This sets forth federal reimbursement policies for costs of federally funded projects.

The document prescribes basic cost accounting principles that are to be applied in determining total reimbursable cost (both direct and indirect) within an educational institution.

In part, it details how to determine the amount of indirect costs the federal government needs to reimburse an educational institution.

▶ Direct Costs: These include items such as laboratory equipment, salaries and wages, supplies and computer time identified solely for the conduct of the sponsored project.

All direct costs are charged against specific research projects.

▶ Indirect Costs: These are expenses not directly assigned to specific projects but are necessary for the operation of the institution. These costs are incurred for purposes common to a number of projects, programs or activities of an institution.

Such costs include (but are not limited to) building space, heating and janitorial services, as well as administrative services such as accounting, purchasing, personnel and library services.

▶ Indirect Cost Rate: From a very simplistic standpoint, this rate is the ratio, expressed as a percentage, between indirect costs and direct costs. The complexity of the process is in the classification of costs (direct vs. indirect) and in the allocation of indirect costs in conformance with Circular A-21.

▶ University of California Allocations: Administration by the Office of the President is part of UC's indirect costs. The portion of OP's administrative costs amounts to approximately $60 million (as of 1991).

This is allocated among the campuses for incorporation in their own calculations of indirect costs. The allocation to a given campus varies based on the relative size of campus operations (the allocations range from less than $2 million to nearly $15 million, as of 1991, based on the relative size of campus operations).

that remains in effect for periods ranging from one to five years.

As a result of negotiations with the federal government, campuses are reimbursed at rates below those proposed by the University (a rate considered by the University to be lower than its actual costs).

As of 1991, the average negotiated indirect cost rate (with regard to on-campus research) for UC campuses was 46.3 percent, compared with a national average of 52 percent for public institutions. (Rates for private institutions have been significantly higher than those for most public institutions.)

REFERENCES: Letter from UC president to chancellors, October 30, 1991; "Task Force Refines Accounting Procedures," news release, University Relations, November 7, 1991; "Progress Report on Indirect Costs," Item 904 for Discussion, Regents' Committee on Audit, November 14, 1991; UC Accounting Manuals.

CROSS-REFERENCES: Budgets.

Foundations: On October 20, 1978, the Regents adopted a Policy on University Support Groups, which at the time included campus foundations.

The Policy was developed in response to the perceived need for appropriate accountability for campus foundations and other groups associated with the University.

Formulation of the policy also was responsive to the State Auditor General's report of June 1978 requiring UC to formulate a clear and complete policy on permissible activities by affiliated fund-raising organizations.

Included in the 1978 support group Policy was an exemption for campus foundations to hold and invest endowments.

At the May 16, 1980 Regents' meeting, the Treasurer of the Regents was directed to obtain information pertaining to the foundations' investments and to make annual presentations to the Committee on Investments on this subject.

At the March 20, 1981 meeting, the Regents authorized and instructed the Committee on Investments to continue to review the investment policies, implementation, and investment results of the foundations.

The Committee on Investments also was directed to inform the foundations that the services of the Office of the Treasurer are available to any campus foundation requesting such services.

On May 15, 1987, the Regents adopted a separate policy pertaining only to campus foundations.

A new Policy on Campus Foundations was adopted by the Regents on September 15, 1989. A related set of Administrative Guidelines for Campus Foundations was issued by the Office of the President on October 13, 1989.

The 1989 policy and accompanying guidelines consolidated and updated the provisions of all former policies and guidelines relating to campus foundations.

The 1989 policy reads as follows:

"The Regents of the University of California recognize the tradition and importance of the Campus Foundations in fostering support for the University and its individual campuses.

"Each campus may have a single Campus Foundation designated by the Chancellor as the primary support group whose sole purpose is fund raising and providing support for that campus. A Campus Foundation shall be organized and operated as a separately incorporated tax-exempt, nonprofit, public benefit corporation. Because a Campus Foundation contributes to the furtherance of the University's mission, the Chancellor may grant the Foundation the use of the University's name and provide administrative assistance and other privileges of close association with the University of California. The Campus Foundations, in return, shall follow policies, guidelines, and procedures issued by the President or designee or the Chancellor to ensure appropriate financial controls.

"All Campus Foundations shall be audited annually by a firm of certified public accountants and, at the discretion of the President or Chancellor, also may be audited by the University's internal auditors."

The 1989 Administrative Guidelines for Campus Foundations state in part:

"A campus foundation shall make clear to prospective donors that:

1) The Foundation is a California nonprofit, public benefit corporation organized for the purpose of encouraging voluntary private gifts, trusts and bequests for the benefit of the campus.

2) Responsibility for governance of the Foundation, including investment of gifts and endowments, is vested in its governing board.

"A campus foundation may hold and invest endowments and funds functioning as endowments on a long-term basis. Such investments must be consistent with the terms of the gift instrument. Investment operations shall be conducted in accordance with prudent, sound

Campus Foundations

Here were the campus foundations as of June 30, 1992:

• The UC Berkeley Foundation, established in 1948

• The UC Davis Foundation, incorporated in 1959 as the Cal Aggie Foundation. It was given its present name in 1992.

• The UC Irvine Foundation, incorporated in 1967.

• The UC Irvine College of Medicine Foundation, incorporated in 1979. (As of July 1, 1992 this foundation merged with the UC Irvine Foundation.)

• The UCLA Foundation, the successor to the UCLA Progress Fund, which dates back to 1949.

• The UC Riverside Foundation, incorporated in 1974 (began active gift solicitation in 1980).

• UC San Diego Foundation, incorporated in 1972.

• UC San Francisco Foundation, incorporated in 1982.

• UC Santa Barbara Foundation, incorporated in 1973.

• UC Santa Cruz Foundation, incorporated in 1974.

practices to insure that gift assets are protected and enhanced and that a reasonable return is achieved, and with due regard for the fiduciary responsibilities of the Foundation's governing board . . ."

As of June 30, 1992, there were 10 recognized foundations supporting the nine UC campuses.

These foundations had a total of $501 million in assets at the end of fiscal 1992, versus $424 million the previous year.

The assets held by individual campuses ranged in size from $6 million to $167 million.

Of these assets, $302 million, or 60 percent, were classified and invested as endowments, compared to $247 million in fiscal 1991.

As of June 30, 1992, 61 percent of the foundations' endowment assets was being managed by external money managers, and 18 percent by the foundations.

Eight of the foundations used the Office of the Treasurer to manage a portion of their endowment assets, for a total of 21 percent of all foundation endowment assets.

REFERENCES: Policy on Campus Foundations, September 15, 1989, and Administrative Guidelines for Campus Foundations, October 13, 1989, Office of the President, and annual reports, University of California Campus Foundations.

CROSS-REFERENCES: Private Support.

4-H Program: The 4-H Youth Development Program is sponsored by the University's Division of Agriculture and Natural Resources.

4-H began in the early 1900s, offering a core of educational projects that promoted scientific methods of farming and home management and helped build character in young people.

For decades, it was highly regarded for its work with rural youngsters interested in raising crops and livestock, canning fruits and vegetables, or designing and sewing their own clothes.

But more varied experimental programs evolved in the late 1960s as 4-H and volunteer leaders responded to changing needs in a society rapidly growing more diverse and urban.

Today, 4-H sponsors activities relevant to interests, concerns and needs in keeping with the societal and personal challenges young people face in an increasingly complex world.

However, these activities still nurture self-esteem through the time-tested approach of learning-by-doing.

The activities fulfill a mission that remains the same after more than 75 years: to help young Californians develop and utilize their knowledge and skills in constructive ways.

Currently, youngsters engage in more than 65 4-H projects. Those related to agriculture, nutrition and resource management attract more than 120,000 participants each year.

Other projects explore areas such as cultural diversity, science and technology, outdoor adventure, citizenship and health.

For example, "Project 4-Health" teaches youngsters about the hazards of tobacco.

Young people also learn about alternatives to chemical dependence and ways to eliminate self-destructive behavior.

In addition, UC researchers have developed the "4-H After-School Program" for some of the 800,000 California children left alone each day. The program provides optional activities for so-called "latchkey kids".

Also, 4-H's childcare and education programs for at-risk school-age children have become national models. Areas with such programs include seven of Northern California's poorest counties and several low-income communities in Southern California.

And today's youth can gain positive, meaningful knowledge of science through a fun-filled program called Science Experiences and Resources for Informal Educational Settings (SERIES).

Through 4-H, Cooperative Extension specialists and advisors help more than 25,000 volunteer leaders apply UC's wealth of research-based knowledge to benefit youngsters in every corner of the state.

More than 130,000 young Californians up to 19 years of age are in 4-H programs. They come from a variety of ethnic, cultural and sociological backgrounds, and more than 50 percent live in large cities or suburbs. Minority membership has reached some 56,000.

REFERENCES: "4-H takes on new challenges," *California Agriculture,* Vol. 43, No. 3, May-June 1989; "A Sustainable Comradeship: The Story of University of California Cooperative Extension 1913-1988," Division of Agriculture and Natural Resources, 1988.

CROSS-REFERENCES: Agriculture and Natural Resources.

Fresno Regional Office:
In 1986, the University opened its Regional Office in Fresno.

The opening marked the first time that a University-wide office was available to provide extensive and much needed informational and other services directly to prospective students and the general public in the Central Valley.

UC's regional office works with California State University, Fresno, community colleges, private colleges and high schools in the area in offering an array of educational and cultural programs.

The regional office provides public affairs support to 30 UC programs in Fresno, Kern, Kings, Madera, Mariposa, Merced, Stanislaus, Tulare and Tuolumne Counties—representing a population of approximately 3 million people.

The office's goals are to ensure students in the Central Valley have ready access to information about academic programs at all the UC campuses, to educate the public about UC's academic programs, and to increase public awareness of the University and its programs in the Valley.

In addition, the emphasis on improving University advocacy and alumni affairs in the Valley has spurred the building of stronger relationships with area legisla-tors and provided support for new alumni programs in the region.

The opening of UC's regional office in 1986 actually was the latest manifestation of a long-standing University—Valley relationship.

UC agricultural stations have been working with farmers there for more than a century, and three such UC programs are available in the Valley.

The UC Kearney Agricultural Center in Parlier is the largest off-campus agricultural research facility operated by the University.

Other major programs in the Valley are the UC San Francisco—Fresno Central San Joaquin Valley Medical Education Program, the UC Davis—Tulare Veterinary Medicine and Research Center, and the UC Santa Cruz Early Outreach Program which recruits low income and minority students interested in higher education.

In addition, about 8,000 UC alumni live in the Valley.

Beginning in 1986 the new regional office brought a special UC function into the Valley for the first time, by providing information and services about UC's campuses to all potential college candidates.

The new move into the Valley was important.

At the time, studies had shown that San Joaquin Valley students were underrepresented at UC for a variety of reasons, despite a general feeling of goodwill toward the University and the belief that it offers an outstanding education.

For example, less than 2.7 percent of the high school graduates in the Valley chose UC, according to data current at the time. That compared to 7.5 percent in all the other counties.

Instead, it appeared that a large percentage of the area's college-eligible high school seniors were opting for a local community college or Fresno State University or not going on to college at all. The reasons given for not choosing UC were cultural, financial or academic.

The regional office has been successful in building important relationships in the Valley and informing students of their options in higher education.

In carrying out its responsibilities, the office has merged the missions of two branches of the University's Office of the President: Relations with Schools and University Relations.

Regional office staff members work to make high school and community college counselors more fully aware of UC programs and the type of student preparation needed for admission to the University, and keep the general public informed about UC's activities in the Valley.

REFERENCES: "Plans Announced for Opening of University Regional Office in Fresno," *University Bulletin,* Vol. 34, No. 18, Week of January 20–24, 1986; "A New Chapter to the University's History in the San Joaquin Valley," *University Bulletin,* Vol. 34, No. 37, July 28–August 1, 1986; descriptive material from Mark Aydelotte, head of UC's Regional University Relations Office.

CROSS-REFERENCES: Central Valley; Medical and Health Sciences; Site Selection.

G

Genetic Research at the University seeks answers to life's basic scientific riddles. Scientists at the University's campuses and Laboratories are engaged in the quest to solve these riddles. Some of their outstanding work is described in sections related to research and research achievements in this book and in Campus Profiles. The following provides some background.

The Special Language Used In Genetic Research

Here are some of the more commonly used terms UC scientists use in the study of genetics.

Amino acid: Any of the 20 organic molecules containing amino and acidic carboxyl groups that, when linked together, form proteins in living things.

Cell differentiation: The process by which once-identified cells specialize according to their form and function (liver, nerve, muscle cells, etc.).

Chromosomes: Individual strands of DNA within the nucleus of cells that contain the genetic information of the cell and organism.

Clones: A group of genetically identical cells that came from the same ancestor.

Cloning: The process of reproducing such identical cells.

DNA (deoxyribonucleic acid): The long molecule within the nucleus of cells in which all genetic information is coded and which carries this information from generation to generation.

DNA sequencing: The process of determining the order of base parts in a segment of DNA from a chromosome.

Gene: Any portion of the DNA molecule that contains the instructions, as determined by a specific sequence of nitrogen bases, for making a particular protein.

Gene expression: The process by which a gene's coded instructions on the DNA molecule are actually used.

Genetic code: The rules for reading messenger RNA and inserting specific amino acids into a protein chain.

Genetics: The scientific field of study that explores the genetic composition, heredity and variation of organisms.

Gene regulation: The process by which gene activity is switched on and off within cells.

Gene splicing: A technique that separates and then recombines genes.

Gene mapping: The process of identifying the location of specific genes on a chromosome and the distance between them.

Gene sequencing: The process of determining the order of base pairs in a gene.

Genetic engineering: The laboratory techniques that enable scientists to manipulate and modify genes to produce new proteins or rapid malfunctioning ones.

Genome: All of the genetic material on all of the chromosomes of a particular living organism.

Gene therapy: An approach to medical treatment that attempts to correct abnormal protein production by cutting out, replacing or turning off a defective gene.

Junk DNA: Portions of the double helix that do not code for any particular protein and whose function still is unclear.

Messenger RNA: A particular type of ribonucleic acid that provides instructions for production of a specific protein (messenger RNA is a copy of DNA).

Mitosis: The process of cell division (in all but the sex cells) during which chromosomes replicate once and send identical copies of themselves to each new cell.

Mutation: A spontaneous or induced change in the DNA sequence of new cells.

Nucleus: The cellular compartment of nigher cells such as those of humans that contains the cell's genetic material.

Nucleotide: A unit of DNA or RNA that consists of a nitrogen base, a sugar and phosphate.

Nucleic acids: Long molecular strands (DNA, RNA) consisting of nucleotide subunits.

p53: A protein believed to influence growth and cell differentiation; errors in the gene that codes for this protein have been found in more than half of all types of human cancer.

P element: A jumping gene of the fruit fly DNA that, because it can insert itself in different places in the fly, can be manipulated by scientists to reveal gene activity.

Proteins: Large molecules, made of specific sequences of amino acids, that carry out many molecular activities of cells and organisms.

RNA (ribonucleic acid): A long molecule found inside and outside the nucleus that is very similar in structure to DNA; several different types of RNA play different roles in protein synthesis.

Source: UCSF Magazine. Also see Campus Profiles and sections on DOE Laboratories.

Sunlight, Skin Cancer and the Repair of DNA

The incidence of skin cancer is increasing epidemically because of today's sun-seeking lifestyles.

The rate probably will soar even higher if the protective ozone layer of the Earth's atmosphere declines as predicted.

Many factors influence the development of skin cancer, including skin pigmentation, genetic constitution, and the elevation at which one lives.

However, scientists generally believe that damage to a cell's DNA is caused primarily by ultraviolet radiation.

(DNA is the carrier of genetic information found at the cell level in all living organisms.)

Scientists at the University and elsewhere are continuing to learn more about the complex processes that cause skin cancer, as well as the DNA-repair mechanisms that protect the body from the harmful effects of ultraviolet radiation.

The accompanying cartoon illustrates what they have learned about the DNA-repair mechanism.

In the cartoon, letters indicate different kinds of nucleotides, or chemical elements that form the DNA's genetic code.

In (1), a strand of DNA molecule containing certain nucleotides has been damaged by ultraviolet light.

In (2), DNA-repair proteins (in the form of the "demolition workman") cut and (3) remove the damaged nucleotides.

In (4), the proteins regenerate the excised section of DNA by using an undamaged DNA strand as a template.

Scientists have learned that the way the body deals with the damage, as well as with the resulting mutant cells, is an inherited characteristic. There is no doubt, they explain, that inborn errors in a person's DNA can mean the difference between healthy and cancer-prone skin cells.

With this basic knowledge in mind, the scientists continue their search to learn more about how different individuals can prevent the damaging, and sometimes fatal, effects of skin cancer.

Cartoon and text adapted from Los Alamos National Laboratory Research Highlights.

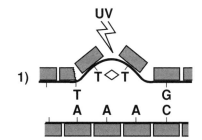

1)

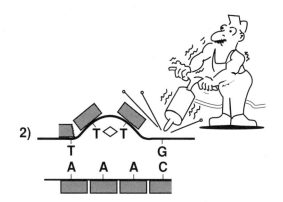

2)

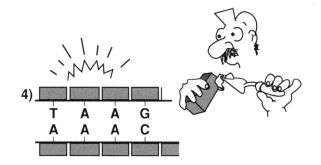

3)

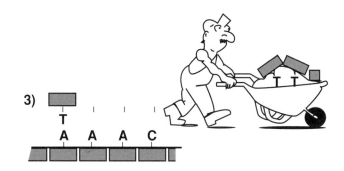

4)

Geriatric Resource Programs: In September 1984, Assembly Bill 2614 was enacted into law. It authorized $1 million a year to the University to establish multidisciplinary academic geriatric resource programs at its health sciences campuses.

Specifically, the legislation established the Academic Geriatric Resource Program (AGRP), which provided a stimulus for geriatrics education, training and research at UC.

The program is intended to influence the education and training at UC of health professions students, residents and fellows, health care practitioners, and faculty in the behavioral and social sciences, dentistry, medicine, nursing, optometry, pharmacy, public health and social welfare.

AGRP also is intended to respond to recent demographic trends in California and to increased awareness around California and the U.S. of the need to provide specialized health care to the elderly.

According to the 1990 census, the population of California is estimated to be 30 million.

The elderly population (those 65 and older) in California is estimated to be 3.1 million persons; 10 percent, or approximately 300,000 persons, are over age 85.

The most recent California Department of Finance study projects that the number of elderly can be expected to increase to 3.7 million by the year 2000 and to 6.1 million by 2020.

Additionally, the population over 65 that represents approximately 10 percent of California's total population presently is expected to represent 11.5 percent of the population by the turn of the century and 15.5 percent by the year 2020.

In response to these shifting demographic trends, the health care professions will need to reassess the types of service required by the elderly.

A 1990 study on health care costs in the *Journal of the American Medical Association* reported on the anticipated impact increases in life expectancy and the projected growth in our older populations will have on the nation's health care system.

The study estimates that by 2020, Medicare expenditures for those 65 and older could approach $125 billion, and that there could be as many as 3 million nursing home residents whose care could cost in excess of $40 billion dollars.

The University's Academic Geriatric Resource Program and other programs across the state and the nation have committed themselves to address these kinds of issues and needs in the years ahead in a variety of ways.

AGRP is intended to provide:

1) Preclinical, clinical or postgraduate educational programs in geriatrics for health sciences students.

2) Continuing education in geriatrics for health care providers and the general public.

3) A teaching nursing home program to research nursing home health care practices and to instruct and train health sciences students about geriatric care.

The program staff and its advisory committee have a number of goals in mind.

These include finding ways to:

• Provide adequate, secure funding for new, innovative approaches to geriatrics education, services and research.

• Develop an adequate core of faculty, in terms of appropriate numbers and range of disciplines and specialty interest.

• Expand the range and number of multidisciplinary institutional and community sites (such as teaching nursing homes and geriatric assessment units) that can be used for training and research.

• Involve the formal academic course review and approval processes to integrate geriatrics content into the health sciences curricula.

• Create an environment in which geriatrics is encouraged, in order to help attract students and to contribute to an increase in the number of graduates seeking careers in geriatrics-related services.

Through FY 1992, AGRP has made 337 awards totaling $9 million to the six UC campuses with health sciences schools in such areas as:

Geriatric preventive medicine, vision care in nursing homes, geriatric psychiatry and rheumatology, drug therapy in elderly outpatients, Alzheimer's disease assessment, improved quality of care in nursing homes, family nurse practitioner training in an eldercare setting, health promotion, and the prevention of disease and injury.

REFERENCES: "The University of California Academic Geriatric Resource Program," Progress Reports, Office of the Vice President—Health Affairs, the Academic Geriatric Resource Program Staff, and the Academic Geriatric Resource Program Advisory Committee , Office of the President; 1990 Census of Population and Housing PL94-171 Data, California and New York. Compact Disc issued February, 1991, UC Bureau of Census; State of California, Department of Finance. Population Projections for California Counties, 1980–2020, with Age/Sex Detail to 2020. Report No. 86-P-3, December, 1986; Schneider, E. L. and Guralnik, J. M. The aging of America: impact on health care costs. JAMA 1990, 263(17):2335-40.

CROSS-REFERENCES: Health Sciences.

Gifts and Endowments: See Private Support.

Global Conflict and Cooperation: The University's Institute on Global Conflict and Cooperation (IGCC) was founded in 1983 as a multicampus research unit serving the entire UC system.

The institute's purpose is to study the causes of international conflict and the opportunities to resolve it through international cooperation.

During IGCC's first five years, research focused chiefly on the issue of averting nuclear war through arms control and confidence-building measures between the superpowers.

Since then the research program has diversified to include international security consequences of such common-enemy problems as global ecological changes, international economic imbalances and regional security issues.

In addition to projects undertaken by the central office, IGCC supports research, instructional programs and public education throughout the UC system.

The institute receives financial support from the Regents of the University of California and the State of California, and has been awarded grants from such foundations as Ford, MacArthur, Rockefeller, Sloan, the Carnegie Corporation, the United States Institute of Peace, W. Alton Jones and Ploughshares.

Susan L. Shirk, a professor in UCSD's Graduate School of International Relations and Pacific Studies and in the Department of Political Science, was appointed director of IGCC in June 1992 after serving for a year as acting director.

Former directors of the institute include John Gerard Ruggie, who served from 1989 to June 1991, and Herbert F. York, who served from the institute's founding in 1983 until 1989 and now serves as director emeritus.

IGCC is headquartered at UC San Diego, at the Graduate School of International Relations and Pacific Studies.

Its core staff includes a director, three faculty research directors, a coordinator of policy research, and a coordinator of campus programs.

This staff is augmented by postdoctoral fellows and by visiting as well as local faculty associates.

A steering committee composed of UC faculty and representatives of the Livermore and Los Alamos National Laboratories advises the director on ongoing program activities and allocates fellowships and grants.

An international advisory board composed of leading figures from the public and private sectors provides overall policy guidance and helps enhance the voice of the University of California in national and international policy debates.

IGCC's core research program comprises both policy studies and basic research.

Policy research combines insights gained from academic analysis with the knowledge and experience of policy specialists to examine the feasibility of creative solutions to contemporary international problems.

The basic research projects are focused on longer-term trends in the determinants and forms of global conflict and cooperation.

IGCC's current policy studies include the following:
• Space Monitoring of Global Change
• Reconceptualizing U.S. Policy Toward East Asia: Trade, Environment and Security
• Arms Control and Security in the Middle East
• Pacific Security Relations After the Cold War
• Regional Security After the Cold War
• Security in South America
• Future French, Chinese and British Nuclear Weapons Policies

One of the primary purposes of IGCC is to stimulate and encourage basic research throughout the UC system on international security, broadly defined.

To that end, IGCC sponsors or supports a number of systemwide research workshops.

Current topics for these intercampus workshops have included the following:
• The Domestic Politics of Post-Soviet Foreign Policies
• Reconceptualizing Regional Relations
• Redefining Global Security
• Social Stratification in Eastern Europe After 1989 and the Circulation of Elites
• Sustaining American Leadership: Domestic Politics, Foreign Policy and the New World Order
• International Relations Theory After the End of the Cold War

In addition, IGCC supports research and teaching projects by UC faculty members through annual competitive grants.

Collaborative projects involving more than one discipline or more than one campus are encouraged.

IGCC offers graduate dissertation fellowships on a competitive basis to University of California graduate students.

Doctoral candidates in the final stages of their graduate careers can apply for dissertation fellowships of up to two years.

Every UC campus has an IGCC-supported program that focuses on international security issues.

Campus program activities include interdisciplinary courses, seminars, visiting lecturers and community forums.

Every year, IGCC organizes several teaching seminars for faculty and advanced graduate students from the University system, the California State University system and the community colleges.

These seminars are designed to help faculty introduce international security issues and materials in their courses.

Recent teaching seminar topics include the following:
- Managing Nuclear Weapons in a Changing World
- The Middle East in the Post-Cold War World
- The Curricula of Peace Studies

IGCC incorporates public outreach into its activities through its UC campus offices, public forums, briefings for journalists and government officials, study groups for civic leaders, and the distribution of institute-sponsored policy papers, reports and books.

Many of the campus programs also organize town-gown seminars to enhance public understanding of international affairs.

REFERENCES: Information supplied and approved by Academic Affairs, Office of the President.

CROSS-REFERENCES: Organized Research Units.

Global Environment: The National Institute for Global Environmental Change (NIGEC) was established by congressional mandate, the Energy and Water Act of 1989.

The University of California hosts NIGEC through a Cooperative Agreement between the Department of Energy (DOE) and UC's Office of the President.

The purpose of NIGEC is to conduct through Regional Centers a research program supportive of DOE's mission related to global environmental change.

This major national research program provides a unique opportunity to increase understanding of global environmental and climate change.

In carrying out its responsibilities, the Institute has these research goals:
- Improved scientific understanding of the mechanisms of global environmental and climate change,
- The reduction of key scientific uncertainties surrounding environmental and climate change,
- Improved assessments of the potential impact of regional environmental and climatic conditions projected for the next century.
- Development of innovative experimental or observation programs to enhance our understanding of regional, or ecosystem scale processes contributing to global change,
- Development and application of tools for policy and decision making that are more appropriate for the global environmental and climate change issue than those currently in use,
- Education and training opportunities to increase the flow of talented young researchers into global environmental change research areas,
- Focused contributions to the education of the public, and development of new curriculum materials for educational purposes at all levels.

NIGEC has six regional centers, where research projects originate. These centers are located at host academic institutions, which represent geographic areas with defined research goals.

Recently, NIGEC sponsored three major conferences: the Methane Conference, in January 1992, "Reducing Scientific Uncertainty," in April 1993, and a conference on ultraviolet radiation in the biosphere, in June 1993.

REFERENCES: Information supplied and approved by Academic Affairs, Office of the President.

CROSS-REFERENCES: Organized Research Units.

Graduate and Professional Education: The University is renowned for its academic and professional programs at the graduate and postgraduate levels.

Qualified college graduates may continue their studies in most academic fields at the graduate level. All campuses offer master of arts, master of science, and doctor of philosophy degree programs.

The University's many graduate professional schools offer programs of study leading to professional degrees, such as the Master of Business Administration, Master of Public Health, Doctor of medicine, and Juris Doctor (law).

Some professional programs are open to qualified upper division undergraduates, but most accept only qualified students who have completed their undergraduate work.

The accompanying table shows examples of professional programs offered at UC.

REFERENCES: "1994–1995, Introducing the University," Student Academic Services, Office of the President; Campus General Catalogs.

CROSS-REFERENCES: All subjects related to education and degrees.

UC Graduate and Professional Programs

Field	Campuses
Architecture	Berkeley, Los Angeles, San Diego
Business Management	Berkeley, Davis, Irvine, Los Angeles, Riverside
Dentistry	Los Angeles, San Francisco
Education	Berkeley, Davis, Irvine, Los Angeles, Riverside, Santa Barbara
Forestry	Berkeley
Journalism	Berkeley
Law	Berkeley, Davis, Los Angeles, Hastings (San Francisco)
Library Science	Berkeley, Los Angeles
Medicine	Davis, Irvine, Los Angeles, San Diego, San Francisco
Nursing	Los Angeles, San Francisco
Optometry	Berkeley
Pharmacy	San Francisco
Physical Therapy	San Francisco
Public Health	Berkeley, Los Angeles
Public Policy	Berkeley
Social Welfare	Berkeley, Los Angeles
Veterinary Medicine	Davis

Source: "1994–1995, Introducing the University," Student Academic Services, Office of the President.

H

Hastings College of the Law in San Francisco was founded in 1878 as the original law department of the University.

The College was made possible by a gift from the first Chief Justice of the California Supreme Court, Serranus Clinton Hastings.

The University also has law schools at Berkeley, Davis and Los Angeles. However, Hastings is unique among UC professional schools as the only law school that operates independent of an undergraduate campus.

Hastings College of the Law is located in the heart of California's legal community—near the California Supreme Court, federal and state appellate courts, and San Francisco's financial district.

Degrees are granted under the authority of the University's Board of Regents, while administration of the campus is governed by a separate Board of Directors appointed by the Governor and confirmed by the State Senate.

Here are basic facts about Hastings:

• Hastings College of the Law, founded in 1878 by Chief Justice Serranus Clinton Hastings, is the oldest law school in California and the oldest in the Western U.S.

• Hastings prepares students for legal careers with a goal of providing the profession with responsible men and women to meet the needs of society for legal service and the administration of justice.

• Hastings is the second largest public law school in America. As of 1992, it enrolls nearly 1,300 students and grants about 425 law degrees a year.

• Almost 14,000 Hastings alumni are serving the legal community as lawyers, judges and elected officials. Some 85 percent of those alumni live and work in California.

• In addition to legal practice that covers the entire spectrum of law, Hastings alumni service to California is a particular hallmark, with Hastings graduates sitting as judges on the State bench by a 3–1 margin over any other California law school.

• The student body is comprised of about half men and half women. One of every four students is from a minority group.

• The two undergraduate universities from which the largest numbers of Hastings students come are UC Berkeley and UCLA.

• In both 1991 and 1992, U.S. News and World Report ranked Hastings in the top seven public law schools and in the top 20 of all U.S. law schools, public and private.

• Located in San Francisco's Civic Center, Hastings gives students unparalleled access to the legal community. The California Supreme Court, State Court of Appeal, and U.S. Court of Appeals for the Ninth Circuit are nearby. Two blocks away is City Hall, housing civil departments of the Superior and Municipal Courts. Within three blocks is the U.S. District Court.

REFERENCES: Information from Hastings College of the Law.
CROSS-REFERENCES: Law Schools.

Hazardous Materials Management: The University's teaching, research and medical facilities utilize a wide variety of hazardous materials that produce a relatively small volume of hazardous waste.

However, UC continues to seek ways of reducing the volume still further.

Hazardous wastes, such as acids, pesticides, solvents and low-level radioactive waste, are a natural byproduct of certain teaching, research, and medical support programs in the health sciences, chemical and biological sciences, nuclear sciences and other high-tech disciplines.

In the past, UC's campuses and research centers had, independently, managed the means of handling, transporting and disposal of hazardous materials at off-campus sites throughout the country. No central policy guided them.

As student enrollment and graduate research programs increasingly shifted to high-tech studies, and as methods of resulting instruction and research have changed, increased production of hazardous wastes has occurred.

Simultaneously, materials once considered benign by federal and state regulatory agencies have been newly defined as hazardous and have contributed to the volume of waste at research institutions throughout the country.

The changes have meant that laws have imposed tighter mandatory restrictions on ways to dispose of hazardous waste.

In addition, these increasingly stringent requirements have added to the cost of hazardous materials handling, treatment, and disposal.

As a consequence, costs associated with the disposal of hazardous wastes have risen sharply in recent years, and the University has had to divert funds from other UC programs to meet these costs.

In light of the changing laws, the volume of hazardous waste, and the exponential increase in related expenses, UC continues to study its current waste management procedures and to implement new ones where possible.

It is in the process of developing and implementing uniform Universitywide policies and procedures covering hazardous materials management, modernizing steps required for handling such materials, and working on new ways of reducing volume.

Environmental health and safety at the three national laboratories managed by the University is a critical issue of the 1990s.

While the three laboratories utilize a wide variety of hazardous materials, they produce a relatively small volume of hazardous waste.

Nevertheless, they continue to seek ways to further ensure the safe handling and storage of hazardous, radioactive and mixed wastes and to maintain and enhance its treatment, storage and disposal in accordance with national, state and local regulations.

REFERENCES: Environmental Protection Services Facilities, Design, Construction, and Maintenance, Office of the President.

UC Extension's Continuing Education and Training

University Extension is one of the nation's leading providers of continuing education and training for environmental and hazardous materials managers.

As part of the University's programs of training and education for professionals, University Extension surveys developing fields and moves to meet its constituents' needs for current information.

In this rapidly changing society, research, regulation and information develop with such speed that practicing professionals need continuing education to remain competitive.

Environmental management has been one of the most rapidly developing fields in the last decade. In response, the Extension offices at UC's eight general campuses and three Extension statewide entities have developed a number of programs to meet evolving needs.

The three entities are Continuing Education of the Bar, the Center for Media and Independent Learning, and the Institute of Transportation Studies Extension Programs.

In providing education and training, Extension offers classes, certificate programs, short courses, workshops, public policy conferences, correspondence courses, and on-site training.

Source: "University Extension: A Resource for Professional Development," which describes programs in environmental management.

Health Sciences' Clinical Facilities: A number of clinical facilities support health sciences programs at the University.

These facilities include:

• Two dental clinics, at Los Angeles and San Francisco, along with off-campus community dental clinics

• Veterinary medicine clinical teaching facilities at Davis and in the San Joaquin Valley

• Two neuropsychiatric institutes, at Los Angeles and San Francisco

• An optometry clinic at Berkeley.

In addition, occupational health clinics in the north and south, a number of demonstration schools, vivaria and other activities provide academic support to health sciences and general campus programs.

Most of these facilities provide experience for students, as well as valuable community services. Their support is derived from a combination of State funds, patient revenue and other income.

The following are descriptions of programs.

The on-campus and community dental clinics at Los Angeles and San Francisco serve primarily as teaching laboratories in which dental students and graduate professional students enrolled in the schools of dentistry organized clinical curricula practice under the supervision of dental school faculty.

The community dental clinics at Los Angeles and San Francisco provide a spectrum of teaching cases that are generally unavailable in the on-campus clinics.

The dental clinics give students practical clinical experience and a broader perspective in determining treatment plans, thereby enhancing the required training in general and pediatric dentistry.

While providing valuable clinical experience for students, the clinics also serve thousands of low-income patients, many of whom would not otherwise receive dental care.

The two veterinary medicine clinical teaching facilities, one at Davis and the other in the San Joaquin Valley, are specialized teaching hospitals and clinics that support the School of Veterinary Medicine.

Students enrolled in veterinary medicine are trained at these facilities by faculty of the School of Veterinary Medicine in the clinical aspects of diagnosis, treatment, prevention and control of diseases in animals.

The two neuropsychiatric institutes are among the state's principal resources for the education and training of psychiatric residents and other mental health professionals and for the provision of mental health services.

The primary missions of the institutes are to treat patients with diseases of the nervous system and to strive for excellence in the development of approaches to problems associated with mental retardation and neurological disorders.

The optometry clinic at Berkeley serves primarily as a clinical teaching laboratory for the School of Optometry, while providing a complete array of visual health care services to many patients.

At the clinic, optometry faculty supervise students in the clinical aspects of the prevention, diagnosis and remediation of problems of the visual system.

In addition, students receive clinical experience at various Bay Area community health centers which exposes them to a broad range of cases and provides a much needed public service to the community.

Vivaria are centralized facilities for the ordering, receiving and care of all animals essential to instruction and research.

REFERENCES: "1993–94 Budget for Current Operations," Office of the President.

CROSS-REFERENCES: Health Sciences Instruction.

Health Sciences Instruction: Under the provisions of the 1960 California Master Plan for Higher Education, the University has two basic responsibilities in the health sciences.

One is to develop new basic knowledge in a variety of health science disciplines. The other is to train students, residents and fellows in professional health sciences programs, and to train graduate students who will become teachers and researchers in the biomedical sciences, including molecular biology, cell biology, genetics, immunology, and neuroscience.

Instructional programs in the health sciences are conducted in 14 schools at the University.

These provide education in various health fields to students preparing for careers in health care, teaching and research.

The health sciences schools are located on six campuses and include the following:

• Five schools of medicine (Davis, Irvine, Los Angeles, San Francisco, San Diego).

• Two schools of dentistry (Los Angeles, San Francisco).

• Two schools of nursing (Los Angeles, San Francisco).

• Two schools of public health (Berkeley, Los Angeles).

• One school of optometry (Berkeley).

• One school of pharmacy (San Francisco).

• One school of veterinary medicine (Davis).

In addition, four programs in medical education are conducted at Berkeley, Fresno, Riverside and the Charles R. Drew University of Medicine and Science in Los Angeles.

Faculty requirements for the instructional programs are determined in accordance with student-faculty ratios that have been developed for each type of school and for each of the categories of students enrolled by these schools.

As examples, a student-faculty ratio of 3.5:1 is provided for medical students, a ratio of 4:1 for dentistry students, and a ratio of 11:1 for pharmacy students.

Faculty salary costs constitute approximately one half of the total budget for the health sciences instructional program.

Instructional support costs represent approximately one quarter of the program's budget.

These costs include staff personnel, equipment and supplies which are provided for each faculty position based on support levels determined for each school.

The remaining one quarter of the program's budget provides funding for other expenses including employee benefits, partial support of stipends paid to interns and residents and a portion of malpractice insurance premiums.

A major step in planning for health sciences instruction took place in 1970, when UC submitted to the State of California a document entitled "Planning For The Health Sciences, 1970–1980: A Ten Year Plan."

The plan recommended doubling the number of health sciences graduates over the next decade and strengthening programs for training future academicians in the health sciences.

In 1975, UC submitted a revised plan based on an extensive reevaluation of health sciences programs and resource requirements.

The revised plan attempted to provide a reasonable balance between the state's need for health care professionals and its ability to finance the projected growth, given the uncertain fiscal climate of the late 1970s.

The revised plan would guide health sciences planning efforts into the 1980s.

During the 1980s the University had to make significant enrollment reductions in health sciences programs in order to accommodate a series of budget cuts.

For example, in 1981–82, loss of federal capitation funds resulted in a health sciences enrollment reduction of 140 students.

From 1981–82 through 1985–86, UC health sciences programs were reduced by $12.6 million, resulting in enrollment reductions totaling 1,193 students.

The University's health sciences programs experienced a modest gain of 188 graduate academic students from 1986–87 through 1988–89.

In 1991–92, state funding fell more than $300 million dollars short of meeting UC's essential needs.

As a result, UC was forced to take painful actions to accommodate this shortfall, including an enrollment reduction of 5,500 budgeted FTE undergraduate, graduate, and health sciences students.

As the state's budget problems continue to grow in the early 1990s, and its impact on UC intensifies, UC plans only a moderate expansion of graduate academic programs in the health sciences.

REFERENCES: UC's Operating Budgets; *Health Sciences Planning: The Context and Issues For the 1990s.* Office of Health Affairs June 1989; Report of the Subcommittee on Support Funds For the Health Sciences. Universitywide Health Sciences Committee, September 1991; Internal Analysis of Health Science Enrollments. Office of Health Affairs.

CROSS-REFERENCES: All sections relating to the health sciences.

HEALTH SCIENCES

Medical scientists, physicians and other health science specialists at the University are dedicated to helping Californians live longer, healthier lives. In so doing, they conduct highly delicate operations and pursue knowledge through the latest computer and laboratory techniques.

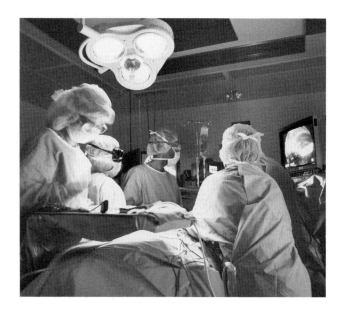

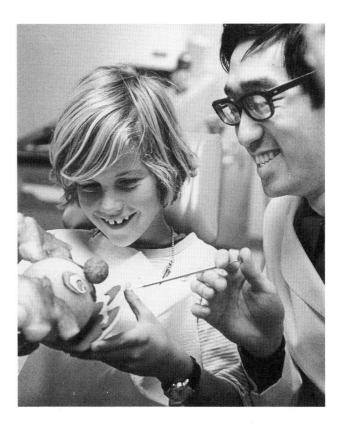

Some of their greatest achievements lie in helping newly born children, toddlers, pre-teens and older youngsters grow up to be fit and energetic adults.

Honorary Degrees: A moratorium on honorary degrees has been in effect at the University since the 1972–73 academic year.

The Regents had agreed, for a number of reasons, to the plan proposed by UC's president to call the moratorium.

For example, some Board members had questioned the rather substantial number of honorary degrees that UC was awarding each year.

Concerns also were expressed about the criteria being used for selecting candidates and about the process involved in determining the proper time and place for awarding such degrees.

In addition, questions were raised about whether or not the awarding of honorary degrees served any useful purpose for the University.

In September 1986, the moratorium was reviewed by the Regents.

Among the objections to reinstating honorary degrees were these:

• The degree sometimes was awarded to people who did not enhance the prestige of the institution granting the honor.

• The decision to award an honorary degree to particular individuals might invite unnecessary argument and controversy.

• In order to avoid such dissension, those making decisions about the awards often narrowed the field of candidates, thus limiting the possibility of selecting outstanding individuals.

According to one suggestion, if honorary degrees were to be restored, their conferral should be administered by UC's president rather than by the various campuses.

However, after further discussion, the Regents agreed that the moratorium should continue.

REFERENCES: "University Policy on Awarding Honorary Degrees," Minutes of the Regents' Committee on Educational Policy, September 18, 1986 and attachment, "University of California Honorary Degrees"; Regents' Bylaw 29.1 and Standing Order 100.4(b).

Human Remains and Cultural Items: In the early 1990s, the University addressed issues relating to its collections of human skeletal remains and artifacts.

UC's internationally recognized collections constitute the largest pre-agricultural series of Homo sapiens in existence, and thus provide a vital record of early human life.

For example, the remains and artifacts in the collections document the following:

The arrival, diversity, demographics, health, disease patterns, medical practices, burial customs, diet, nutrition, social status, trade networks and lifestyles of prehistoric California.

Curators and researchers familiar with campus collections believe that approximately 95 percent of the skeletal remains and associated artifacts of California origin at

UC are from the pre-European contact period ranging from 500 to 7,000 years old.

In April 1990, UC's president appointed a special committee to review issues related to these collections.

The appointment took place after representatives of Native American groups in California expressed an interest in acquiring some of UC's skeletal remains for reinterment or other disposition.

At about the same time, legislation was proposed or enacted at the federal and state levels regarding the disposition of such collections.

The major federal law is the Native American Graves Protection and Repatriation Act, enacted November 16, 1990, covering federal agencies and all museums and other institutions receiving federal funds, including UC. It requires affected institutions to inventory their collections and to return skeletal remains and associated items to Native American groups who request them, under stated conditions.

The UC committee, consisting of 13 academicians and administrators from within the University and nationwide, began to assess the adequacy of UC policies and practices affecting human skeletal remains and associated artifacts.

The committee also considered policies, practices and legal issues pertaining to the preservation, use and disposition of human bones and artifacts being held by UC's campuses and museums.

The group was called the Joint Academic Senate-Administration Committee on Human Skeletal Remains.

Its members had expertise in such fields as Native American studies, religious studies, law, anthropology, archaeology, sociology and natural and forensic sciences.

Two of the members were employed by anthropological museums, and five were Native Americans.

The committee consulted widely with a number of individuals and groups, including Native American organizations and leaders, both in California and outside.

The committee's final report recognized the need for a Universitywide policy to provide for the transfer of human skeletal remains and burial artifacts, under specified conditions, to individuals and tribes requesting such action.

On April 1, 1991, the University established its "Policy and Procedures on the Repatriation of Human Remains and Cultural Items," which was consistent with federal law and was responsive to many of the points recommended in the committee's report.

UC was the first university in the country to establish a repatriation policy since passage of the federal Native American Graves Protection and Repatriation Act of November 1990.

The policy enables both federally- and California-recognized Indian tribes and groups to make repatriation claims (the federal law applies only to federally-recognized tribes).

UC considers its policy to be a balanced approach to the repatriation issue, taking into account the concerns of many Native Americans about the holdings of museums, as well as a recognition of the scholarly value of the collection.

The policy requires campus and other sites that have Native American human remains and cultural items to establish a process to transfer, under specified conditions, items in its collections to descendants and Indian tribes.

The policy clarifies the manner in which UC will comply with federal law and sets forth the differing responsibilities between the Office of the President and the campuses.

In addition, the policy includes requirements for the inventory, identification, notification and repatriation of remains and cultural items that will fulfill the provisions of the federal law.

The policy required museums with Native American human remains to begin to inventory their collections in July 1991.

According to the policy, evidence to establish cultural affiliation may include biological, geographical, kinship, archeological, historical or other relevant information.

Each museum must notify possible descendants and/or Indian tribes and transfer Native American remains and funerary objects to requesting descendants and/or Indian tribes, under specified conditions. However, partial results are to be released as they become available.

The inventory and notification process is to be completed by January 1996, as required by the federal law.

The campuses have primary responsibility for the inventory of their collections and notification of potential descendants.

Human remains, as well as funeral items and other cultural objects, will be repatriated upon request to those who have been identified under campus procedures as descendants or by Indian tribes which qualify under the policy.

Native American representatives are to be consulted in all aspects of the total process. At the same time, the policy encourages dialogue and mediation among all parties involved.

The Office of the President is responsible under federal law for providing information to the Department of the Interior about the steps being taken.

In addition to all these steps, the University is to establish a standing Advisory Committee on Repatriation.

The committee will consist of seven members, three of whom are to be Native Americans. It is responsible for reviewing the administration of UC's policy. It also may review campus repatriation decisions.

REFERENCES: Report of University of California Joint Academic Senate-Administration Committee on Human Skeletal Remains," August 1990, and "Policy and Procedures on Repatriation of Human Remains and Cultural Items," Office of the President, 1991; "Status Report on the University's Policy and Procedures on Repatriation of Human Remains and Cultural Items," Item 306 for Discussion, Regents' Committee on Educational Policy, June 20, 1991; news releases, University Relations, Office of the President.

Humanities Initiative: In 1987, the University enhanced research and graduate education in the humanities by developing the Humanities Initiative.

Its purpose was to help instill in UC students a better appreciation of history and culture.

Development of the initiative followed a 1986 report by the National Endowment for the Humanities (NEH) that showed widespread lack of knowledge by young people in these areas.

The four-part, $3.5 million initiative, which included a Universitywide Humanities Research Institute at Irvine, was the most comprehensive of its kind in the nation.

It was developed in response to President David P. Gardner's call to invigorate the humanities and its disciplines in the UC curriculum.

The lack of attention to the humanities went beyond UC, Gardner pointed out.

He cited a 1980 report by the Rockefeller Commission on the Humanities that noted the declining quality of humanities education and research around the nation.

At the same time, funding support nationally for humanities research was low. For example, the 1987 budget for the National Science Foundation was $1.6 billion compared to $139 million for NEH.

"The health and vigor of the humanities are indispensable if we are to offer students the broad liberal education they will need to function in a dramatically changing world," Gardner said.

The Humanities Initiative grew from ideas of an ad hoc committee of faculty representatives convened by the president in 1986 and chaired by Stanley Chodorow, dean of arts and humanities at San Diego.

The initiative adopted the NEH concept of the "humanities," which covered the study of the following:

Modern and classical languages, linguistics, literature, history, jurisprudence, philosophy, archaeology, comparative religion, ethics, the history, criticism and theory of the arts, and those aspects of the social sciences that have a humanistic content and employ humanistic methods.

A keystone of the initiative has been the UC Humanities Research Institute, which features successive groups of scholars-in-residence who study humanistic themes and publish the proceedings of conferences, seminars and workshops.

The institute is intended to be a center for scholarly work where the world's leading humanists can learn from one another, as well as a place where an understanding and appreciation of the humanities can be advanced.

UC and other scholars come there for extended periods up to a year, receiving partial or full salary support.

The concept for the institute was based on similar models at Santa Barbara (for theoretical physics) and Berkeley (for mathematical sciences).

Irvine was chosen to house the institute after a review of competitive proposals from several UC campuses.

Murray Krieger, University Professor of Humanities, was selected as the founding director of the institute. He was succeeded in 1989 by Mark Rose, professor of English at UC Santa Barbara.

During the 1987-88 planning year, conferences were held on a variety of topics, including art history, medieval studies, German literature, and philosophical problems in medical genetics.

The institute was budgeted to receive an annual $800,000 from the Office of the President and $300,000 from UCI.

Other important elements of the Humanities Initiative:

• Annual core support of $800,000 was provided for new organized research activities in the humanities.

• Another $800,000 annually was earmarked to support faculty research fellowships. Grants of $15,000 to $25,000 for six months to a year would provide individual faculty members with paid leave in which to pursue research projects.

• Another $800,000 annually was budgeted to support predoctoral humanities fellowships, which were offered to graduate students as part of four-year support packages. Two years of fellowship support were to be supplemented by at least two years of campus support, most commonly in the form of teaching assistantships.

In each of the above three programs, OP annually contributes $600,000 of the total, and the campuses another $200,000.

The Humanities Research Institute publishes a newsletter at least twice a year which includes notices of conferences, publications and residential groups. In addition, campus humanities centers at various UC campuses publish newsletters containing up-to-date information.

REFERENCES: "UC Unveils $3.5 Million Humanities Initiative; Includes Institute at UCI, Faculty Fellowships," *Notice,* Vol. 12, No. 1, October 1987; "Humanities Research Initiative: Restoring 'the soul of education,'" *UC Focus,* October 1987; news releases, University Relations, Office of the President; information from Academic Affairs, Office of the President, and the Humanities Research Institute.

CROSS-REFERENCES: Arts.

The Campus is Full of Noises: Sounds and Sweet Airs at UC

Since 1980, Shakespearean scholars among the faculty, students and staff of the University have met regularly under the aegis of the Shakespeare Forum.

The Forum is a multi-campus research unit devoted to the teaching, study and performance of Shakespeare.

It originated with the development of a collection of leased feature films of Shakespeare's plays at the UC Berkeley Extension Media Center under the title of the UC Shakespeare Media Library.

The Shakespeare Media Library has encouraged development of Shakespeareans' interest in performance which became a major element in the Forum's programs.

Thus, the annual meetings, which rotate among the nine UC campuses, have been closely coordinated with significant productions organized by the host campus.

Alternatively, the Forum has focused its meetings on professional productions, such as "King Lear," by Kenneth Branagh's Renaissance Theatre Company.

The Forum recently has joined in the sponsorship of a new initiative, "Shakespeare and the Classroom," in cooperation with the Globe Centre in London, academic institutions and schools. The initiative is designed to aid in the effective teaching of Shakespeare.

The Forum's 1993 conference took place at UC San Francisco. Lectures there were held on the theme of "Shakespeare and Medicine," and members attended a performance of the California Shakespeare Festival Production of Hamlet at the Festival's new theatre in Orinda.

The current chair of the Shakespeare Forum is Hugh Richmond, professor of English, Berkeley, who has held that post since 1980.

I

Improper Governmental Activities, Policy and Procedures for Reporting: The subject of "whistle-blowing," or the reporting of improper governmental activities, has become a particularly sensitive issue in the workplace.

Effective January 1, 1990, the University issued a policy and accompanying procedures for reporting improper governmental activities.

The policy and procedures also provide protection against retaliation for reporting such activities.

The provisions apply to all employees and, in some situations, to students, applicants for employment, and members of the public.

The policy responds to requirements of the "Reporting of Improper Governmental Activities Act" in the California Government Code, certain sections of which apply specifically to the University.

The policy provides for establishment of internal University procedures for employees and others in reporting improper governmental activities.

It also provides for development of an internal University process for hearing complaints concerning interference or retaliation in filing such reports.

The policy was developed through extensive review with the campuses and the DOE Laboratories. Employees and employee organizations also submitted comments.

UC's policy is to encourage its employees and others to disclose improper governmental activities, as defined in the Government Code, and to address written complaints alleging acts of reprisal or intimidation due to disclosure of such activities.

At the same time, UC management has the responsibility to seek out and correct abuses regarding improper activities.

Any person may file a confidential report alleging improper activity under the established procedures of their respective jurisdictions.

"Any person" includes, but is not limited to, UC academic and staff employees, students, applicants for UC employment, and members of the public.

Improper activity is defined as any activity by a UC department or by an employee that is undertaken in the performance of the employee's official duties, whether or not such action is within the scope of his or her employment and which:

- Is in violation of any state or federal law or regulation including, but not limited to, corruption, malfeasance, bribery, theft of UC property, fraudulent claims, fraud, coercion, malicious persecution, misuse of UC property and facilities, or willful omission to perform his or her duty.

- Is economically wasteful.
- Involves gross misconduct, incompetency or inefficiency.

Reports alleging improper activity are investigated, if warranted, and reported according to specific UC procedures.

Under the policy, a UC employee may not directly or indirectly use or attempt to use the official authority or influence of his or her position or office to interfere with:

1) The right of a person to file a report in accordance with the law, or

2) The right to file such a report with the University Auditor, the Auditor General of the State of California or other public official designated to receive required reports of improper activity.

UC's policy stipulates that a retaliation complaint officer (RCO) be appointed to investigate, or oversee the investigation of, complaints from employees or applicants for employment alleging such interference or retaliation.

The policy further spells out how a complaint may be filed, what is involved in the RCO's investigation and in the final decision at the chancellor's or equivalent level, and the steps taken in the processes of discipline and appeal.

REFERENCES: "Policy and Procedures for Reporting Improper Governmental Activities and Protection Against Retaliation for Reporting Improper Activities," January 1, 1990, Office of the President; "Reporting of Improper Governmental Activities Act" (Sections 10540-10551 of the California Government Code).

Integrated Pest Management: In the 1950s, 1960s and early 1970s, synthetic pesticides were often the first choice of farmers and growers for control of pests in their fields.

Widespread use of pesticides in agriculture brought benefits, in the form of increased production, improved product quality, extended seasons and more reliable economic returns.

At the time, alternatives to the scheduled spraying of pesticides on a weekly or biweekly basis had not been well developed for California's modern production systems.

However, today's successful farmer or grower knows that synthetic pesticides have significant limitations.

Some pests develop resistance to chemicals, pesticides have grown increasingly costly, and spraying them can have a deleterious impact on the environment and on worker health.

Because of these concerns, farmers in recent years started looking at a wider range of options for pest management.

That was when integrated pest management (IPM) appeared on the scene.

Actually, ever since the 1950s, the University has been a national leader in advancing integrated pest management. The steps it has taken have been pioneering and innovative.

IPM represents a comprehensive approach to the challenges of farming by calling on many different disciplines. It seeks links and relationships among these disciplines rather than seeking to establish a separate science.

As an environmentally-based pest control strategy, it provides an array of practices as part of an overall crop production system that can be used to fight farm pests in an economically and environmentally efficient manner.

By adopting a season-long or even a multi-season perspective, IPM takes maximum advantage of naturally occurring factors to increase pest mortality, such as biological controls and favorable environmental and climatic conditions.

Some IPM practices introduce, conserve or enhance predators and parasites to control pests. Others depend more on modifications of cultural practices such as adjustments in planting/harvesting times, new planting techniques, selective pruning or changes in irrigation regimes.

An integrated approach does make use of pesticides when they are warranted; however, the philosophy also considers pesticides to be a last resort and advocates the use of selective pesticides less harmful to nontarget organisms (e.g., microbials). That view can, and often does, lead to reduced pesticide use.

Increased IPM research accelerated in the 1970s, and the need for crop consultants who could implement IPM systems became apparent.

The need for properly trained professional crop consultants who would advise growers in IPM strategies was formally recognized in 1971 when California first required the licensing of pest control advisers.

Throughout the mid-1970s, individuals in state government, the University and various agricultural interest groups called for increased development and awareness of IPM. Organized IPM research was conducted nationally and in California through federally supported programs.

In 1978, the California Department of Food and Agriculture's Environmental Assessment Team called for, among other things, expanded research in IPM. The following year, the President of the United States renewed a call for the development and adoption of IPM systems.

In 1978, the vice president—agriculture and natural resources appointed an Advisory Committee for the Development and Implementation of a Statewide Integrated Pest Management Program in California.

In 1979, the University of California Statewide IPM Project was approved as a special UC budget appropriation.

The UC IPM Project's goals are to:

1) Reduce the pesticide load in the environment, 2) increase the predictability, and thereby the effectiveness, of pest control techniques, 3) develop economically, environmentally and socially acceptable pest control programs, 4) marshal agencies and disciplines into an integrated pest management program, and 5) increase the utilization of natural pest controls.

Major research and extension activities were initially limited to eight commodities: alfalfa, almonds, citrus, cotton, grapes, rice, tomatoes and walnuts.

In 1987, IPM workgroups were restructured to emphasize areas of research that were more focused (e.g., studies emphasizing biological control).

IPM celebrated its 10th anniversary in 1990 with the support and encouragement of the legislature. In its first decade, the research arm had funded 222 projects in 35 different commodities involving over 220 scientists throughout the state. By 1990, its diverse research and education program was supported by a state budget of $2.1 million.

The UC Integrated Pest Management Project is considered a national leader in its area, having developed approaches and disseminated information regarding alternatives to total dependence on synthetic pesticides.

IPM's research and educational programs have brought new methods to thousands of California growers.

They provide access to IPM information through a sophisticated computer system, 11 nationally acclaimed IPM manuals, and annual training conferences for pest management professionals.

In recent years IPM began educational programs in the important areas of farm worker pesticide safety and pesticide applicator safety. IPM Area Advisors work in all regions of the state with other UC Cooperative Extension Farm Advisors, with professional pest control advisors, and directly with farmers.

Now into its second decade, IPM continues to evolve as growers confront a multitude of pest challenges.

New approaches are being studied, developed and tried for the array of pests threatening California's 250 different crops. Using IPM techniques, California growers can thrive in the 1990s, without many of the risks associated with the use of synthetic pesticides.

REFERENCES: "IPM: reshaping the approach to pest management," "Integrated pest management in California," *California Agriculture,* Vol. 44, No. 5, September–October 1990. *Beyond Pesticide Report,* Agriculture and Natural Resources, Office of the President.

CROSS-REFERENCES: Agriculture and Natural Resources; Cooperative Extension.

International Programs: For many decades, the University has played a leading role in the international arena as part of its missions of teaching, research and public service.

In recent years, many economic, socio-political and technological issues have assumed greater global importance than in the past. As a result, the University has expanded its programs of international interest.

In its academic programs, the University seeks to provide its students with the knowledge, skills and understanding needed to become productive citizens in the emerging and increasingly interdependent world environment.

The University also affords its faculty greater opportunities to engage in the international exchange of knowledge, and it has extended its public service mission worldwide.

The University recognizes that the following aspects of international education and programs help support its missions of teaching, research and public service, as well as California's economic, political and cultural well-being:

• Offering rigorous courses of study at all academic levels and in as many fields as possible, in order to increase students' understanding of global issues and cultural differences

• Maintaining vigorous foreign language programs to train students to communicate more effectively in other cultures and to enhance their understanding of other nations' values

• Providing opportunities for students to have direct contact with other cultures in overseas educational programs sponsored by UC, in order to give these students special academic training as well as broadened personal experience

• Enrolling qualified students from other countries at the undergraduate, graduate and professional levels in sufficient numbers and geographic diversity to inspire in all students an appreciation for differences among cultures, as well as a deeper understanding of the values and perspectives of other peoples

• Establishing faculty exchange and collaborative research programs with overseas institutions

• Providing forums for the discussion of world issues

• Extending UC's public service mission to the international level through overseas programs designed to help developing countries meet some of their critical needs

REFERENCES: Informational material from Academic Affairs, Office of the President.

CROSS-REFERENCES: Education Abroad; Missions of the University; Pacific Rim.

J

Joint Doctorates: The California Master Plan for Higher Education recognizes that research and doctoral education are inextricably bound together.

As a result, the Master Plan designates the University as the state's principal academic agency for conducting research. It gives UC sole authority among public higher education institutions to grant the doctorate.

The view is that the state's educational resources are more efficiently utilized if one institution is primarily responsible for these dual missions.

At the same time, the Master Plan provides for the University to offer the doctorate jointly with the California State University (CSU) in certain selected fields.

The belief is that joint doctorates can serve the state well in areas where CSU exercises special strengths, such as in education, as well as in certain other designated fields.

The University has pledged itself to make the joint doctorate an effective avenue for new program planning to meet state needs for advanced training.

In taking this stance, UC believes that development of joint doctorates are important for a number of reasons.

These include improved access to doctoral education, more effective use of faculty and other resources of higher education, and opportunities for UC and CSU to offer programs together that neither could provide alone.

To encourage and facilitate effective development of joint doctorate programs, a Joint Graduate Board, established in 1963 and reorganized in 1987, has redesigned the by-laws governing joint graduate degrees.

The changes have given the board a more active role in the process of planning and development.

Currently, the board is co-chaired by senior UC and CSU officials. It includes both graduate deans and faculty leaders from the two systems.

UC's Universitywide Senate Coordinating Committee on Graduate Affairs is the principal faculty review body for the programs.

Developing a program can take several years because of the need for careful planning. For example, each program has to fit within the institutions' two different structures of governance and administration.

Despite the complexities involved, progress continues to be made. For example, by the end of 1991, approximately 226 joint doctoral degrees had been granted since passage of the 1959 Donahoe Act, which had authorized the Master Plan.

Thirteen programs currently offer joint doctorates.

Here are examples:

• UCLA in cooperation with Los Angeles State University, and UC Berkeley in cooperation with San Francisco State University, have joint doctoral programs in special education. These programs have been in place for nearly a quarter of a century.

• Joint doctoral programs in biology, chemistry and clinical psychology between UC San Diego and San Diego State University

• A program in ecology between UC Davis and San Diego State University

• A joint doctorate in geography between UC Santa Barbara and San Diego State

• A program in engineering and another in public health-epidemiology conducted by UC San Diego and San Diego State University

• A master's program in physical therapy between UC San Francisco and San Francisco State University

In fall 1991, the University and California State University systems initiated their latest joint doctoral program.

The program in educational leadership is administered by UC Davis. It is located at California State University-Fresno, and is designed and taught by faculty from Davis, Fresno State and other UC campuses.

Classes are conducted at CSU Fresno. The majority of doctoral candidates work in school districts in the San Joaquin Valley.

This is the first joint doctoral program in educational administration between universities in the two California public university systems.

The program's principal goal is to prepare school leaders who can address the challenges of the ethnic, economic and intellectual diversity of students in the Central Valley, particularly the Fresno region.

The Central Valley is considered a critical site for such a program, because it is experiencing a rapid growth in population which is highly diverse, socially, culturally and economically.

For example, between Sacramento and Fresno, 70 ethnic groups are represented. Latino and Indochinese populations are increasing most dramatically, and as many as eight different language groups may be represented in a single valley classroom.

The valley also presents great variety in school settings, from Fresno, the third largest district in the state, to tiny rural districts.

In 1991–92, 13 experienced educators, including principals, psychologists, directors and assistant superintendents of instruction and a teacher, were enrolled in the program for four years of part-time studies. In 1993, enrollment totaled 27.

A third cohort of 13–15 students was being selected to begin the program in fall 1993.

REFERENCES: Information from Academic Affairs, Office of the President.

CROSS-REFERENCES: Sections relating to California education; Master Plan.

K

The **Kearney Agricultural Center** was founded in 1962 as the Kearney Horticultural Field Station.

The 330-acre center is UC's largest off-campus agricultural research facility.

Situated in the geographic center of the fertile San Joaquin Valley, the center serves the region's agricultural industry.

It is dedicated to M. Theodore Kearney, a 19th-century pioneer who helped develop the Fresno region. It began with the help of funds raised by area growers, packers and shippers and with support from the Kearney Foundation.

The facility's name was changed to the Kearney Agricultural Center in the early 1980s. Since then, it has grown greatly in both breadth and stature, attracting an international cadre of agricultural researchers.

In 1989, a $5 million building was completed to allow for more sophisticated research by greater numbers of scientists. There are now 35 laboratories and over 120,000 square feet of facilities dedicated to the research programs at Kearney.

Some 26 researchers from UC Davis, Berkeley and Riverside are permanently assigned to pursue research and extension responsibilities full time. Other faculty members commute routinely to conduct studies on the site.

More than 100 research projects are under way involving 120 scientists on over 40 different crops.

The center is internationally recognized for research that has resulted in new fruit, nut and grape varieties, innovative irrigation practices, better pest and disease management, and more efficient fertilization methods.

The center also works with growers, packers and shippers of fresh market crops to improve handling, reduce market losses and provide consumers with higher quality products.

New advanced postharvest research facilities will enable UC scientists to make new discoveries in the critical area of increasing concern to the agricultural industry.

Kearney has been long involved in environmental issues and, for 20 years, has been a pioneer in air pollution and water quality studies in California.

The center also is home base for the UC Mosquito Research Laboratory.

As of January 1991, 26 academic staff from three campuses and the Division of Agriculture and Natural Resources were assigned to the center.

REFERENCES: "New era for agricultural research in the San Joaquin Valley," *California Agriculture,* Vol. 43, No. 3, May–June 1989; information from the Kearney Agricultural Center and Agriculture and Natural Resources, Office of the President.

CROSS-REFERENCES: Agriculture and Natural Resources; Cooperative Extension; Integrated Pest Management.

W. M. Keck Observatory: Since Galileo, astronomers have sought ever-larger telescopes to allow them to peer deeper into the heavens—and farther back toward the dawn of the universe.

The larger the mirror, the greater a telescope's capacity to detect the most distant objects in space, whether they emit light in the part of the spectrum we can see or in longer, infrared wavelengths invisible to the naked eye.

Infrared explorations can also pierce dense shrouds of galactic gas and dust to the very birthplace of stars.

A massive mirror scoops up enough faint light to allow astronomers to identify the atomic elements and molecules of luminous objects in space. By "reading" the telltale wavelengths, or spectra, of light, scientists can learn the composition, physical conditions, velocity, distance and age of everything from stars, like the sun, to vastly distant quasars, which burn with the firepower of more than a million suns.

In 1977, a University committee met to consider building a large ground-based telescope powerful enough to allow astronomy to advance well beyond the limits of the world's reigning telescopes.

It had been nearly 30 years since Palomar Observatory's five-meter Hale Telescope had come on line, and this "eye on the sky," operated by the California Institute of Technology, was still the world's premier instrument for optical and infrared discovery.

Jerry Nelson, a young Berkeley astronomer on the UC committee, urged his colleagues to sidestep the impos-

ing challenges of building a still larger and heavier single-mirror telescope—essentially a scaled-up version of the Hale Telescope.

The mirror for such an instrument would be physically vulnerable if it could be built at all, he argued, and the telescope to support it would be prohibitively expensive. Instead, he proposed creating a giant new mirror out of many thin, and therefore light, reflecting segments: a mosaic mirror.

Once the technology was mastered, he predicted, there would be no inherent limit to the size a segmented mirror could be built; its overall dimensions could far exceed what was possible with a single piece of glass. In addition, a lighter, segmented mirror could be the key to large space-based telescopes of the future.

In 1978, the Regents provided $500,000 as seed money to develop a telescope that would go beyond conventional technology, and the UC committee invited Nelson to pursue his idea.

While the segmented mirror approach had advantages over the physical limits of single mirrors, it posed at least two entirely new—and daunting—challenges.

First, a new way would be needed to sculpt the surface of the mirror segments. In conventional mirror polishing, the goal is always to create a symmetrical shape. Although the overall mirror Nelson proposed would be symmetrical, each individual segment would not. It was as if a potter were being asked to create a smooth bowl by first making dozens of oddball-shaped shards.

In addition, a highly sensitive and reliable computer-controlled system would be needed to keep the indi-

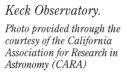

Keck Observatory.

Photo provided through the courtesy of the California Association for Research in Astronomy (CARA)

vidual mirror segments aligned with one another so that together they would always serve as a single giant surface. Accuracy finer than a millionth of an inch was required.

In 1978, Nelson headed a team at UC's Lawrence Berkeley Laboratory to move the segmented mirror concept beyond the drawing board. Less than two years later, in late 1979, his team had figured out how to solve both problems, (see related text on how to build a giant telescope).

After he demonstrated the ingenious solutions to the UC committee of senior scientists, the group chose the segmented mirror approach to produce what was to become the world's largest telescope.

Nelson proposed a mosaic of 36 hexagonal mirrors, each six feet across but only three inches thick. Arrayed together, they would create a record-breaking 10-meter-wide (33-foot) parabolic shape needed to focus light from distant sources. The proposed mirror would be twice as big, and have four times the light gathering capacity of the Hale Telescope. Yet it would weigh no more.

In October 1980, the Regents allocated $1.1 million for the group to develop the telescope design, as well as to work up a technical demonstration of the optical system with a full-scale mirror segment and part of an adjacent segment.

UC astronomers reviewed possible sites for the new telescope and selected Mauna Kea, a dormant volcano on the island of Hawaii, and at well over 13,000 feet, the highest mountain in the Pacific Basin.

Mauna Kea is considered the world's best post for viewing the heavens and is the site of more than a half dozen other observatories. The cold mountain air is extraordinarily clear and dry. Turbulence is slight, and the night sky is the black of coal.

By 1984, scientists and engineers at LBL, Berkeley's Space Sciences Laboratory and Lick Observatory had contributed to the design, development and technical demonstrations of the segmented mirror telescope.

During this time, Caltech astronomers had been independently pursuing ideas for a large optical telescope to supplement the Hale Telescope. In 1984, Caltech made the decision to join UC in searching for donors for the 10-meter segmented-mirror telescope conceived by Nelson.

In January, 1985 Caltech announced a $70 million grant from the W. M. Keck Foundation to help build the telescope. UC and Caltech formed the partnership known as the California Association for Research in Astronomy, and that same month, glass was poured for the first mirror segments. These were the first optical facets of what is now the W. M. Keck Telescope.

As construction atop Mauna Kea was nearing completion in the fall of 1991, UC and Caltech scientists, engineers and officials journeyed to Hawaii to participate in a mountaintop ceremony dedicating the Keck Telescope.

In the Hawaiian tradition, a chanter invoked the Island's gods to bless the new window on the universe.

Also in the Hawaiian tradition, the ground beside the Keck was blessed in preparation for building a second 10-meter telescope—an identical twin, dubbed Keck II. An evening banquet the next night celebrating the dual achievements was hosted by Walter Cronkite.

Like Keck I, construction funds for Keck II came largely from a grant to Caltech given by the W. M. Keck Foundation—this time for up to $74.6 million. UC is to fund most of the operating costs for both telescopes.

To those who have ever teamed up to build a world-class telescope, there are a few major mileposts: the first night starlight hits the mirror's surface; the day the instrument is physically completed; its first discovery; and the official commissioning date, when the telescope is ready to be pointed skyward routinely for decades of discovery.

Keck has passed the first three mileposts, and is well on its way to the fourth. But there have been years of daunting technical challenges and more than a few moments of total bewilderment.

One in particular captures well the mix of insight and surprise that comes with any new large-scale technical project.

Keck's novel giant eye was readied for "first light" just before Thanksgiving 1990. Although only nine of its 36 mirror segments were yet in place, the mirror's potential light-gathering area already matched that of the Hale Telescope.

First light was the first chance to literally see if Keck's massive computer-controlled mosaic mirror might truly push back the limits of the visible universe.

For the telescope's first target, the team chose a spiral galaxy 65 million light years deep into space, and called, inelegantly, NGC 1232. Sensors continually monitored the orientation of each mirror segment, relaying to motor drives just how many millionths of an inch to nudge each segment so that they could maintain the shape of a single, huge, smooth-surfaced mirror.

With all systems ready, operators punched instructions into another bank of computers to point the telescope's eye toward its first celestial target.

Nothing happened.

The telescope wouldn't move. The scientists just stared at a spot in the sky. As the earth rotated, they sat there and saw streaks zip by on their screens.

As it turned out, the problem wasn't the optics, even though the Keck's was an untested, pioneering system.

The problem was simply mechanical: the drive system which moves the telescope wasn't operating. Two days later, when the glitches in the telescope drive control system were corrected, the astronomers achieved a first-light image of the distant galaxy proving both the revolutionary telescope's mechanical and optical potential.

One scientist figured out that the resolution of the first light image was roughly the same as being able to distinguish between a car's two headlights 250 miles away.

Jerry Nelson, who 13 years earlier had dreamed up the idea for the segmented mirror telescope, said simply of the first-light success, "I'm ecstatic."

Two other milestones followed. The 36th and final mirror segments was installed on April 14, 1992, ushering in a full year of optical testing.

Almost exactly one year later—and eight years after Keck construction had begun—astronomers released to the world in April, 1993, an unprecedented image of the most-distant known galaxy in the universe.

The infrared image required a half-hour exposure, but it faintly reveals several previously unseen objects near a galaxy 12 billion light years away, born near the dawn of time.

To the scientists and engineers of UC and Caltech who created the Keck Telescope, the April achievement demonstrated its full power. In that "stellar" moment, the Keck emerged as the new leader, poised to explore the edges of time and space in the search for our ultimate origins.

REFERENCES: "Keck Foundation Proposes $70 Million Grant to Caltech To Build World's Largest Optical Telescope," news release, W. M. Keck Foundation, January 3, 1985; news release, Office of the President, University of California, January 3, 1985; CARA's "Fact Sheet for the W. M. Keck Observatory," rev. November 1990; "Ancient Light from a Young Galaxy," news release, CARA, April 17, 1993.

CROSS-REFERENCES: Astronomy.

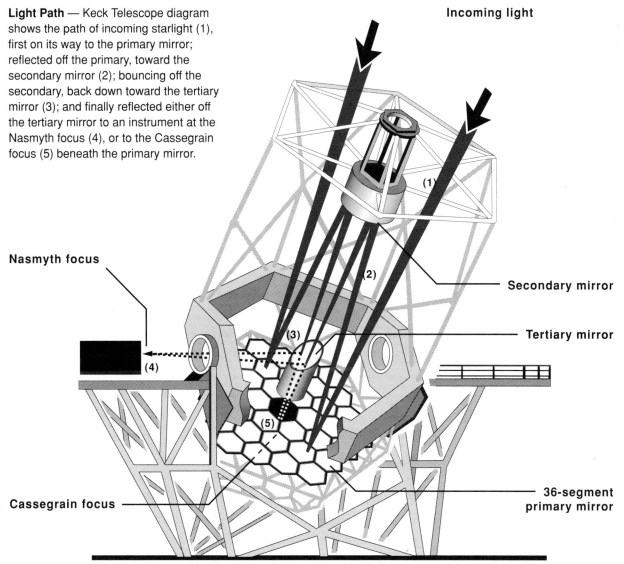

Light Path — Keck Telescope diagram shows the path of incoming starlight (1), first on its way to the primary mirror; reflected off the primary, toward the secondary mirror (2); bouncing off the secondary, back down toward the tertiary mirror (3); and finally reflected either off the tertiary mirror to an instrument at the Nasmyth focus (4), or to the Cassegrain focus (5) beneath the primary mirror.

Incoming light

Nasmyth focus

Secondary mirror

Tertiary mirror

36-segment primary mirror

Cassegrain focus

Credit: California Association for Research in Astronomy

Building a Giant Telescope: It's Done With Mirrors

Only a little more than a generation ago, astronomers began to recognize the true scale of the universe, and the fact that our Milky Way Galaxy is but one of many in the universe.

To probe the universe, powerful new instruments have shown the way. The heart of any telescope is its mirror to focus light from distant sources, and the size and precision of the mirror's light-collecting surface determines the quality of astronomical viewing.

Despite a call for larger telescopes, a practical limit seemed to have been reached in 1948.

That was the year when the Hale Observatory was completed on Mt. Palomar. The Hale's mirror, then the world's best and largest, measured a full five meters (approximately 16 feet) in diameter, and led the way for nearly half a century of optical and infrared astronomy.

Traditional mirror design dictates that the larger the mirror, the thicker it must be in order to hold its parabolic shape. That means many tons of glass, and an increasingly expensive physical support structure within the observatory dome.

More than 10 years ago, a young professor of astronomy at Berkeley, Jerry Nelson, found a way out of this bind. His solution led to the giant mirror for the Keck Telescope.

Instead of a mirror made of a single, thick monolithic slab of glass, Nelson conceived of a segmented mirror.

He proposed a mosaic of 36 hexagonal mirrors, each six feet across but only three inches thick. Arrayed together, they would create a 10-meter-wide (33-foot) parabolic shape, twice as large as the Hale Telescope's mirror, but weighing no more.

To achieve his goal, Nelson and the other telescope designers in the UC-Caltech scientific partnership, known as the California Association for Research in Astronomy (CARA), surmounted technical challenges never before seriously considered, let alone solved, on this scale.

The first challenge was to sculpt the individual mirror segments. Conventional mirror polishing creates a nearly perfectly symmetrical bowl of glass. But only the final mosaic array of Keck's 36 mirror segments is symmetrical. Like shards of a broken bowl, the individual mirror segments that make up the mosaic mirror are irregular in shape.

Nelson concocted a novel scheme.

He realized that if the disks of glass were forced into a slight twist before they were conventionally polished, they could later be released from the twist and would relax into a slightly asymmetrical shape.

With Berkeley engineering professor Jacob Lubliner, Nelson calculated precisely how much to contort each disk of glass before sending it to an optics factory for conventional polishing. After each mirror segment was polished to apparent symmetrical perfection, it was allowed to relax into the desired asymmetric shape.

The technique, refined by Nelson, Terry Mast, George Gabor and a team at the Lawrence Berkeley Laboratory, is called "stressed mirror polishing." It has been used in creating the six sets of six differently contoured mirror segments which fit together like a giant jigsaw puzzle to form the Keck Telescope's mirror.

That was one problem solved.

However, when the 36 mirror segments were in place, the Keck Telescope would also need a system of unprecedented sensitivity and precision to maintain the overall shape as the mosaic mirror swept the sky to peer at celestial objects.

Nelson's team calculated that each observation, each slight movement of the entire mirror, would require that each of the 880-pound mirror segments be moved in a choreography accurate down to millionths of an inch.

To accomplish this task, scientists developed electrical position sensors that would continually monitor each segment's three-dimensional position and relay this information to computer-controlled and motor-driven devices. These, in turn, prod the segments the required microscopic fraction of an inch.

Once these problems were solved, the six-year job of constructing the telescope—one of the world's most complex instruments—still remained.

Keck Observatory Facts

Participating Organizations

Operators: California Institute of Technology and the University of California

Project management: California Association for Research in Astronomy

Major donor: W.M. Keck Foundation

Site provider: University of Hawaii

Observatory Information

Observatory location: Mauna Kea, Hawaii

Headquarters location: Kamuela (Waimea), Hawaii

Start of operations: 1993

Getting the telescope built within budget, and without compromise to the brain-numbing effect of the 13,600-foot site, has been the task of the "other" Jerry: Jerry Smith.

One of the world's top space science project managers, Smith came to the Keck project in 1985, fresh from leading the highly successful Infrared Astronomical Satellite project conducted by the space agencies of the U.S., Britain and the Netherlands.

Today, the pioneering Keck Telescope works as planned. Its success, despite many setbacks along the way, is demonstrated by the fact that its design and construction are being closely mimicked in the effort now under-way to build its next-door twin, the 10-meter Keck II, due for completion in 1996.

Keck Observatory Timeline

1977–78: Initial design studies

1981–85: Technical demonstration

1985: Gift from W. M. Keck Foundation

　　　Formation of California Association for Research in Astronomy (CARA)

　　　Glass poured in Germany for first mirror segments

　　　Groundbreaking at observatory site on Mauna Kea

　　　Observatory dome fabrication begins on mainland

1986: Delivery of mirror blanks, beginning of development of mirror manufacturing processes

Gift from Richard Smart Trust of land for observatory headquarters, Kamuela, Hawaii

1987: Beginning of production of mirror supports, mirror control hardware

　　　Beginning of installation of observatory dome

　　　Beginning of work on telescope structure

　　　First cut of mirror segment to hexagonal shape

1988: Groundbreaking, beginning of construction of headquarters

　　　Completion of dome

　　　Transition from development of mirror-making processes to full-scale manufacturing

1989: Moving of project office to Hawaii from California

　　　Telescope structure arrives for installation in dome

1990: Installation of first mirror segments, and start of "debugging" process for mirror control system

　　　Achievement of "first light" using nine mirror segments

1991: Continuation of process to align mirror

　　　Grant from W. M. Keck Foundation for construction of second Keck telescope

1992: Installation of final primary mirror segments; Installation of secondary mirror

　　　Optical testing

1993: Beginning of installation and testing of scientific instruments

　　　Final testing of telescope and observatory support

　　　(tentative) Start of full operations

K–12 EDUCATION

A sound education for youngsters in kindergarten through the 12th grade is critical to their success in school and beyond.

The University of California reaches out to young people around the state through a variety of educational programs.

These programs stimulate youngsters' minds, develop their interest in learning new ideas and help them grow up to be adults who remain curious about the world around them.

L

The **Laboratory of Biomedical and Environmental Sciences (LBES)** was established April 1, 1947 at UCLA.

Financial support was provided by the U.S. Atomic Energy Commission (AEC) under one of the four major management and operating contracts administered by the University.

Initially called the Atomic Energy Project, LBES was the first active operational unit of the new School of Medicine at UCLA.

The Project's original purpose was to provide biomedical and environmental support to the AEC's mission of evaluating hazards and effects of nuclear testing at the Nevada Test Site and the development of peaceful applications of nuclear technology.

In the 1950s, the Project was reorganized as the Laboratory of Nuclear Medicine and Radiation Biology. In functioning under the Department of Biophysics, it strengthened its ties to academic departments related to its interests.

In the 1960s, research programs were refined and focused, guided by the long-range missions of the U.S. Department of Energy, the successor to the Atomic Energy Commission.

As part of its reorganization in 1980, the Project was renamed the Laboratory of Biomedical and Environmental Sciences. It was divided into three operational units: the Division of Biomolecular and Cellular Sciences, the Division of Environmental Biology, and the Division of Nuclear Medicine.

In 1987, DOE modified its funding arrangement with the Laboratory to a cooperative agreement. Shortly thereafter, UC oversight for the Laboratory devolved from the Office of the President to UCLA.

LBES is an Organized Research Unit (ORU) of the UCLA School of Medicine. All of the principal investigators hold academic appointments and participate in teaching at all levels. Research also is conducted by graduate and postgraduate students, visiting scientists and faculty colleagues.

Currently research is conducted on the following: (1) fundamental cellular processes which control gene expression—particularly the events leading to cancer induction, (2) physiological ecology of arid land plants, (3) the exploitation of positron emission tomography (PET) for studying basic biochemical and physiological processes in man in both health and disease and related phenomena such as the mechanisms of drug action, and (4) programs in structural and computational biology and genetics.

REFERENCES: "Historical Background: UCLA Laboratory of Biomedical and Environmental Sciences," informational material, Office of Laboratory Affairs, Office of the President.

CROSS-REFERENCES: Laboratories.

Laboratory Management: The University manages three laboratories under separate contracts with the U.S. Department of Energy (DOE). The contracts are renewable every five years.

The three are the Lawrence Berkeley Laboratory (LBL) and the Lawrence Livermore National Laboratory (LLNL), both in California, and the Los Alamos National Laboratory (LANL), in New Mexico. Unlike LLNL and LANL, Lawrence Berkeley Laboratory does not engage in any classified activities.

The story of the relationship between the University and the laboratories began more than half a century ago.

Early History

By the late 1930s, physicists around the world, including UC's Ernest O. Lawrence, inventor of the cyclotron, and J. Robert Oppenheimer, had begun research on the newly discovered phenomenon of nuclear fission.

Numerous scientists, both in the U.S. and elsewhere, concluded that fission might be used to create bombs of unprecedented destructive capacity. Several nations explored this possibility during World War II.

When the American bomb project was established after Pearl Harbor, Lawrence was given responsibility for work on electromagnetic separation of uranium-235 and on plutonium, and Oppenheimer was recruited to the bomb-theory group.

Consequently, they were strategically placed to counsel General Leslie Groves as he took charge of the Manhattan Project during the Fall of 1942. In particular, it was on Oppenheimer's advice that Groves selected remote Los Alamos, New Mexico, as the laboratory site for bomb research and production.

Early in 1943, Groves and Oppenheimer, who would be directing Los Alamos, persuaded UC Treasurer Robert Underhill to arrange for the University to operate the laboratory. This arrangement became public in August 1945 shortly after Los Alamos's uranium-235 and plutonium bombs devastated Hiroshima and Nagasaki, respectively.

The Immediate Postwar Years

Following World War II, the University's Regents and UC administrators tried to disengage from Los Alamos. The original contract contained, at the insistence of Underhill who was concerned about UC's control over purchasing and exposure to liability claims, a clause specifying termination 90 days after hostilities ended.

UC agreed to two or three short-term extensions on the grounds that doing so would facilitate an orderly transition to postwar management.

In 1947, however, Lawrence's group threw its support behind regularization of the Los Alamos contract. UC President Robert Gordon Sproul soon ordered the negotiation of what turned out to be the first of an ongoing series of multi-year contracts for University operation of the laboratory.

In 1948, far earlier than had been predicted by the U.S., the Soviet Union detonated its first nuclear explosive. In fall 1949, Lawrence and nuclear theorist Edward Teller, then at the University of Chicago, led the way in arguing that the best American response to this event was to begin a program to develop a thermonuclear explosive, or fusion bomb.

The 1950s and Beyond

Despite opposition from the AEC's General Advisory Committee and a majority of the Commissioners, President Harry Truman decided early in 1950 to order the development of the vastly more powerful thermonuclear weapon.

Soon, spy scandals and the Korean War intensified the sense of urgency that many felt about the program.

In the early 1950s, Lawrence secured AEC funding to construct a prototype accelerator at an abandoned Naval Air Station at Livermore. The project was managed by the California Research and Development Corporation, a subsidiary of Standard Oil of California.

The purpose of this accelerator (whose full-scale version was to be built at Weldon Springs, Missouri) was to produce plutonium using a relatively small amount of uranium feed material.

Wide-scale uranium prospecting in the U.S. soon revealed that there was adequate uranium to make the plutonium using conventional reactors, and the accelerator project was abandoned.

During this same time, Teller was advocating the creation of a second laboratory that would focus exclusively on designing a fusion explosive. With the abandonment of the accelerator project, the Livermore site became available, and Lawrence decided that this would be the ideal place for the second laboratory.

The idea soon won approval from the AEC and the Regents, and the laboratory at Livermore started operations under UC management in 1952.

For 30 years, beginning in the early 1950s, both laboratories experienced substantial overall staff and budget growth. Much of this growth was motivated by Soviet-American rivalry. However, a good deal of the growth, especially in the 1970s, was also motivated by the energy crisis.

UC Action and New Committees

Since 1980, the Laboratories have been affected by drastic cuts in energy programs and increases in non-nuclear weapons programs. They have had continued growth in their staffs but not in their constant-dollar budgets.

While World War II, the Korean War and the Cold War provided favorable political contexts for the establishment and subsequent growth of the Los Alamos and Livermore laboratories, the Vietnam War engendered numerous questions concerning U.S. military policies and posture.

At the meeting of the Assembly of UC's Academic Senate in May 1969, UCB Professor Andrew Imbrie secured unanimous consent to present, under new business, a motion calling on the Academic Council to create a committee to consider "the appropriateness of the present relationship between the University and the research laboratories at Livermore and Los Alamos." After discussion, the motion passed.

In just two weeks, Council Chair Randolph Wedding appointed the "Special Committee on University Research at Livermore and Los Alamos," with UCD political scientist Paul Zinner as chair.

The Zinner Committee completed its report in March 1970. It recommended that continuation of UC management "would be appropriate only with substantial modifications" in the relationship with the laboratories.

The committee wanted the University to exercise greater administrative control, to enlarge its role in policy formulation and to increase the educational benefits.

A lone dissent came from UCLA geophysicist George Wetherell who argued that "the development of nuclear weapons is an unfit business for the University of California" and urged severance of the relationship.

Later that year, UC's faculty endorsed the Zinner Committee's report. It voted against severance by 2,278 (57%) to 1,712 (43%) and for the recommended contract modifications by 2,810 (74%) to 984 (26%).

The impact of the Zinner Committee's report and the faculty's subsequent vote was modest. In particular, the 1972 contract was not modified in any substantial way.

Some Changes Made

The President's office did use its existing discretion to make various changes. Most notably, it increased the openness of the searches for Laboratory directors and established the Scientific Advisory Committee to monitor the laboratories and give advice to UC's president regarding their operations.

But the next major review committee would find that there was very little difference between the current relationship of the University to the Laboratories and that which existed when the Zinner Committee was appointed.

In July 1975, UCLA's David Saxon succeeded Charles Hitch as the University's president. At least two forces soon impelled him to seek a fresh review of the laboratory relationship.

First, California's new governor Jerry Brown was frequently articulating doubts about the appropriateness of University management. Second, a new organization in Berkeley, the UC Nuclear Weapons Lab Conversion Project, was advocating the complete conversion of the laboratories to non-military research.

As early as December 1976, President Saxon promised that he would appoint a committee to make recommendations for the 1982 contract.

Six months later, he created the "Committee to Examine the University's Relationship with the Los Alamos and Livermore Laboratories," naming UCLA Senior Vice

Chancellor and political scientist William Gerberding as chair.

The Gerberding Committee submitted its report in February 1978. It unanimously recommended "continued management of the Laboratories by the University of California." But the majority endorsed "continuation *only* if . . . significant changes" were implemented (emphasis in the original).

The committee's most important recommendation was that, within a year, the Regents should constitute a committee to serve as "a board of overseers with trusteeship functions."

Consisting of Regents, faculty and others, this board would

> . . . continually survey all aspects of the Laboratories' programs and policies so as to discharge the University's obligations to itself and the public by ensuring that the Laboratories' participation in the formulation and conduct of their programs be of the highest quality and greatest objectivity, and that the laboratories not be isolated from the larger world of thought and action.

In short, Gerberding and his colleagues believed that UC, by taking on a new and much more active role in the relationship, could play a part that was "constructive and in the public interest."

The Gerberding Committee was only slightly more successful than the Zinner Committee. The President's office seems to have had some liking for the proposed board of overseers, but the Department of Energy opposed any involvement of the University in nuclear weapons policy matters. The reasoning was that policies related to nuclear weapons were matters within the purview of the federal government.

Congress backed DOE's view strongly, and pointedly passed legislation placing the word "National" in the official names of the laboratories at Los Alamos and Livermore. At the same time, DOE Secretary James Schlesinger instructed the Energy Research Advisory Board, chaired by Solomon J. Buchsbaum, to review the agency's management options, if agreement could not be reached between DOE and the University.

Faced with this situation, the President's office abandoned the idea of a board of overseers. Instead, it responded to the concerns expressed by the Gerberding Committee with a series of more limited measures. For instance, the position of Special Assistant for Laboratory Affairs was established in the President's office.

The Scientific Advisory Committee and the Regents' Committee on Special Research Projects were reconstituted as the Scientific and Academic Advisory Committee and the Regents' Committee on Oversight of the DOE Laboratories. Two other review and oversight committees also were established; these were subsumed sometime later into a council established by UC.

These and related measures have resulted in some increase in UC's involvement in managing the Los Alamos and Livermore Laboratories.

Recent Events

The following lists major actions and decisions related to UC's management of the three DOE laboratories in recent years.

In September 1987, the Regents voted to renew contracts with DOE for management of the labs.

In November 1988, in a continuing effort to strengthen laboratories management, UC announced plans to appoint three senior liaison officers to monitor programmatic and administrative activities at the labs. Two officers would be based at Livermore and Los Alamos, respectively, and one at UC's Office of the President.

In 1989, an advisory committee established by the Academic Council issued a report about UC's relations with the Labs.

The panel was named the Advisory Committee on the University's Relations with the Department of Energy Laboratories. It was chaired by Malcolm D. Jendresen, UCSF professor of dentistry, and as a result was often called the Jendresen Committee.

The committee's report responded to the general charge from the Academic Council "To provide a thoughtful and independent evaluation of the role of the University in managing DOE Labs," as well as to several more specific charges.

The committee also responded to the Academic Council's statement that "the public service function of the University is central to the argument justifying the University's role in managing the Labs."

In so doing, the committee proposed five general criteria for public service appropriate to the University:

(1) The activity is supportive of the University's primary mission of teaching and research, (2) the activity is consistent with the University's essential commitment to freedom of expression, (3) the activity can be performed at least as effectively by the University as by other institutions, (4) the activity has no serious adverse effects on the University, and (5) the activity contributes to human well-being.

All but one member of the eight-member committee found that UC's operation of the Labs failed to satisfy these criteria. Six members concluded that UC should, in a timely and orderly manner, phase out its responsibility for operating the Labs while maintaining its cooperative relationship with them in teaching and research. Two members believed that it was not yet clear that a total contractual break was required and suggested consideration should be given to a separate corporate body to operate the Labs within UC's structure.

On May 18, 1990 the University's Scientific and Academic Advisory Committee (SAAC) issued its own report after examining a broad range of arguments for and against continued management at the Lawrence Livermore and Los Alamos National Laboratories.

While SAAC acknowledged the concerns raised by those in opposition to continued University management, its members felt that, overall, the positive influences which UC brought to the Labs' operations were important and substantial and outweighed the concerns and negatives associated with them.

SAAC also believed that continued UC management was particularly desirable in light of major changes in the thrust of the Labs' efforts that could be anticipated because of changing world events affecting the U.S. and the USSR.

If these world events were to continue on course, the committee believed, the Labs could evolve from institutions whose main purpose had been to support national security to institutions that would increasingly use their scientific and technical expertise and facilities to address a much broader range of goals.

SAAC concluded that UC involvement, with its long tradition of broad-based research excellence and its ideals of openness and free inquiry, should be integral to significant redirections in the Labs' scientific programs.

In its report, SAAC unanimously endorsed continued University management of the Labs. In addition, the committee offered recommendations to strengthen that management in order to give added assurance that the values that could derive from UC management were realized.

In September 1990, the Regents voted to negotiate renewal of the lab contracts and to endorse several objectives for the negotiations. Of 19 Regents present for the voice vote, three voted "no" with regard to the Labs, and one abstained.

In January 1991, UC announced further changes in laboratory management, pending successful negotiations for contract renewal. These called for establishment of a new administrative unit within the Office of the President and formation of a new advisory group, the President's Council on the National Laboratories. The group's work would incorporate that performed by three long-standing UC advisory committees.

In July 1991, DOE announced it would begin negotiations with the University to renew UC's management of the three labs, and in August, contract negotiations began between teams representing UC and DOE. In September 1992, the Regents approved a 60-day extension to the current lab management contracts so that negotiations could be completed.

In November 1992, the Regents approved contracts for the three laboratories by a vote of 16–1. The new five-year contracts expire September 30, 1997.

In acting on the contracts, the Regents also certified environmental impact reports prepared for the two California labs under the state's Environmental Quality Act.

Unlike previous contracts, the current contracts may be terminated without cause by either party upon one year's written notice.

The Regents' action provided an opportunity not only to continue UC's role in managing the labs, but to strengthen and broaden it.

Under UC management, the labs had been considered vital in meeting national defense goals and contributing to the safeguarding of world peace. Now the labs could be increasingly effective in a wide range of other areas of benefit to the nation, under UC leadership.

The contracts represent a new and innovative approach to the University's management of the three laboratories that stresses performance-based management. The contracts are intended to serve the best interests of the University, the federal government and the nation as the laboratories adapt to changing times.

Through the contracts, UC and DOE have sought to balance the scientific and technological excellence that distinguished UC's lab management with the provision for enhanced management oversight.

Approval of the contracts came after more than a year of negotiation between UC and DOE, during which the previous five-year management contracts were rewritten and restructured.

The new contracts contain a number of fresh elements common to all three labs, such as a preamble defining the role and objectives of UC and DOE and a detailed listing of principles of operation of the contracts.

The agreement provides for significantly expanded and enhanced UC management oversight of the labs and allows for UC-directed research and development by the labs.

At the same time, it preserves the fundamental principles of UC's status as a non-profit contractor. Chief among these is the provision that UC manages the labs for no loss and no gain.

One major aspect of the University's expanded laboratory management was the establishment of a new administrative unit within UC's Office of the President. Named to head the new administrative unit was Robert W. Kuckuck, a physicist and former associate deputy director at LLNL. Management areas under his oversight at the three labs include facilities management, environmental health and safety, procurement and property management, human resources, financial systems, and safeguards and security.

Another aspect of the new contracts was the formation of a new high-level advisory council to advise UC on lab management. The advisory group, called the University of California President's Council on the National Laboratories, has 21 members and 7 ex officio members. The members have experience in academic and research institutions, private industry and government. Approximately one-third of the council are UC faculty members.

REFERENCES: Report of the Advisory Committee on the University's Relations with the Department of Energy, November 1989, Academic Senate and reports of other committees cited in the text; "Fact Sheets," September and November 1992, and "New DOE Laboratory Contracts Approved," news release, November 20, 1992, Office of the President; information from laboratory sources.

Management Agreement Between The University and DOE

Key features of the latest management agreement between the University and DOE include the following:

• A performance-based management system using objective standards to assess UC's overall performance of its contract obligations. Performance measures in the areas of environment, safety and health, financial management, human resources, property management and procurement, and safeguards and security are included in the contracts and are renegotiated annually.

• Mechanisms for the effective analysis, implementation and coordination of existing and new DOE orders and directives.

• A process for addressing and resolving differences that might arise between UC and DOE over policy, operational, management or procedural issues associated with lab management.

Designated UC and DOE representatives will conduct the first level of the issues resolution process, with two other levels consisting of senior officials from both parties and, ultimately, the U.S. Secretary of Energy and the President of the University.

• Improved means for efficient and vigorous technology transfer, including the passing of ideas, inventions and discoveries from the labs to private industry and the public as a means of enhancing state and national competitiveness.

• Preservation of intellectual and scientific freedom for lab scientists and engineers. This accords them the equivalent rights and obligations of UC faculty in publishing research findings, engaging in open debate, and participating in scientific, educational or professional meetings and conferences.

• Procedures for the timely, accurate release of information related to the labs and their work to the news media and the public.

Compensation of the University for managing the Laboratory for DOE is provided in part through a $6 million per year fixed payment in lieu of indirect costs from which the State's traditional share is to be paid.

In addition, for the first time the contracts provide for payment of $5 million annually to the University for the ground lease of the Lawrence Berkeley Laboratory real property which is owned by the University.

The contracts include a provision for full funding of the University's new administrative management oversight unit, estimated at approximately $5 million for the first year of the contract year.

The contracts also provide for the payment of $14 million annually to the University as a program performance fee which is for use at the University's discretion.

These funds will be available for risk management costs associated with the University's laboratory management, including establishment of a contingency reserve fund on which interest may be earned and accrued.

To the extent that is possible to do so, the University intends to apply these funds for support of the Laboratories—for example, by funding enhanced complementary and beneficial activities and fostering increased collaborative activities between University campuses and the Laboratories, as well as supporting University-directed Laboratory research.

LBL is set in the hills above the Berkeley campus.

LAWRENCE BERKELEY LABORATORY

LAWRENCE BERKELEY LABORATORY is a multiprogram laboratory that provides national scientific leadership and technological innovation through its mission to:

• Perform leading multidisciplinary research in the energy sciences, general sciences and life sciences in a manner that ensures employee and public safety and the protection of the environment

• Develop and operate unique national experimental facilities for use by qualified investigators

• Educate and train future generations of scientists and engineers

• Transfer knowledge and technological innovations and foster productive relationships between LBL research programs and industry

LBL was established in 1931 as the UC Radiation Laboratory. It was located on the Berkeley campus. During the early 1940s, it moved to its present location above the campus in order to construct the 184-inch cyclotron.

The cyclotron was used in the Manhattan project to test methods for isotope separation. The government contract under which this work was done was renewed in 1947 with the newly-established Atomic Energy Commission, and LBL became a government-owned, contractor-operated national laboratory.

The University was chosen as the contractor, and the contract has since been renewed every five years. The current contract commenced in Fall, 1992.

The name Lawrence Berkeley Laboratory was adopted in 1971.

LBL is managed by the University for the U.S. Department of Energy (DOE). The budget for fiscal 1993 was $251.5 million. Total of full-time personnel was 2,420.

LBL has research programs in the Energy Sciences, the General Sciences, the Biosciences, and Resources and Operations.

Energy Sciences consists of Chemical Sciences, Earth Sciences, Energy and Environment, and Materials Sciences. The following shows the areas of studies under each.

• Chemical Sciences: chemical physics and the dynamics of chemical reactions; structure and reactivity of transient species; electron spectroscopy; surface chemistry; catalysis; chemistry of the actinide elements, and atomic physics

• Earth Sciences: structure; composition and dynamics of the continental lithosphere; geophysical imaging methods; chemical and physical transport of geologic systems; isotopic geochemistry; and physicochemical processes

• Energy and Environment: building-energy efficiency; environmental effects of technology, energy storage and distribution; fossil-energy conversion; industry and utility energy use; and national and international energy policy studies

• Materials Sciences: advanced ceramic, metallic and polymeric materials for catalytic electronic, magnetic and structural applications; superconductivity; instrumentation for surface science; microstructural analysis by electron microscopy; x-ray optics; electronic structure of solids and interfaces

General Sciences includes Accelerator and Fusion Research, Nuclear Science, and Physics. The following shows the areas of studies under each.

• Accelerator and Fusion Research: fundamental accelerator physics; accelerator design and operation; advanced accelerator technology development; accelerator and ion-source research for heavy-ion fusion and magnetic fusion; construction of the Advanced Light Source

• Nuclear Science: relativistic heavy-ion physics; medium- and low-energy nuclear physics; nuclear theory; nuclear astrophysics; nuclear chemistry; studies of transuranium elements; nuclear-data evaluation; detector development

• Physics: experimental and theoretical particle physics; advanced detector development; particle data base for the high-energy physics community; astrophysics; applied mathematics

The Biosciences include Life Sciences and Structural Biology. The following shows the areas of studies under each.

• Life Sciences: gene expression and molecular genetics; cellular differentiation and carcinogenesis; hematopoiesis; DNA repair and recombination; radiation biology at the cellular and molecular levels; diagnostic imaging, radiotherapy and radiosurgery; biochemical mechanisms of disease; medical instrumentation; LBL's Human Genome Center

Scientists carry out vital research in major laboratory buildings like this at LBL.

• Structural Biology: structural biology; structural and molecular biology of nucleic acids and proteins; genetics and mechanisms of photosynthesis; photochemistry; mechanisms of mutagenesis

Resources and Operations includes Engineering, Environment, Health and Safety, and Information and Computing Sciences. The following shows the areas of studies under each.

• Engineering: engineering design, planning and concept development; shops and technical support for scientific programs and research facilities; advanced accelerator components; electronic and mechanical instrumentation systems; fabrication of detectors and experimental systems

• Environment, Health and Safety: technical support for safety and environmental protection; radiation associated with accelerator technology; advanced dosimeters; dispersion of radionuclides; waste management

• Information and Computing Sciences: advanced software engineering; information management; scientific imaging and visualization tools; computation tools for the human genome project; biostatistics

Major research facilities at LBL include the Advanced Light Source, the 88-inch Cyclotron, the National Center for Electron Microscopy, the Tritium Labeling Facility, the Human Genome Center, the Surface Science and Catalysis Laboratory, the Advanced Materials Laboratory.

Among LBL's issues and activities are the following.

Education

• Graduate and undergraduate programs: More than 200 LBL staff members are also members of the faculty of UC Berkeley. These faculty members use LBL facilities to train their graduate students, who can number up to 700. The Lab also provides more than 80 postdoctoral appointments. About 100 doctoral dissertations and masters theses, based on research performed at LBL, are completed each year. Nearly 400 undergraduate students work at LBL as research assistants or guests. They come from UC Berkeley and other surrounding colleges during the academic year and from across the nation during the summer.

• BASTEC: LBL is working with three other national laboratories and 18 colleges, universities and other organizations under the Bay Area Science and Technology Education Collaboration (BASTEC) to assist the Oakland, California, Unified School District in restructuring and revitalizing mathematics and science education. BASTEC has been adopted by the District, which serves more than 50,000 students and has 3,000 teachers and administrators and coordinates teacher advancement opportunities in science and mathematics. BASTEC has also been asked to help redevelop curriculums in math and science for the District.

• SEABA: LBL is a participant in the Science Education Academy of the Bay Area (SEABA), an "academy without walls" designed to bring bay area teachers the latest information in math and science. SEABA's goal is to equip some 40,000 teachers with up-to-date technical knowledge and appropriate methods for teaching math and science to Bay Area students. A one-stop shopping catalog of educational opportunities for teachers is being established along with attempts to streamline applications and funding processes for existing programs and workshops. SEABA will also create a database to keep track of professional development opportunities.

• Other educational programs: These include providing community college, high school and junior high school teachers of science and math with summer research positions; the annual High School Honors Program in the Life Sciences; two undergraduate programs, the Laboratory Co-op Program and the Science and Engineering Research Semester (SERS); and the long-established consortium with Jackson State University and the Ana G. Mendez University System of Puerto Rico.

University Collaborations

In addition to the teaching and research relationship with UC Berkeley, LBL has collaborations with other UC campuses.

For example, LBL is working on a design for a proton therapy accelerator to be built at the UC Davis Medical Center. Researchers at LBL and UC Santa Barbara have a long-running experiment under the Oroville Dam near Sacramento that began as a hunt for neutrinos and has recently been involved in the search for weakly interacting massive particles. Two UC Davis faculty members have been appointed to professorships at LBL's Advanced Light Source.

Idea-sharing and sophisticated equipment pay off in making scientific advances.

Technology Transfer

LBL has developed methods to support the development and use of LBL technology by industry and to strengthen the value of the Laboratory's research programs for the nation. This includes improving access and dissemination of information, including training, personal exchanges, publications and conferences. It also includes extending intellectual property rights by reducing barriers and improving information acquisition. And it includes the development of research programs and Collaboration Research and Development Agreements (CRADAs) with U.S. industry. Examples of CRADAs include:

• Methane conversion: LBL signed its initial CRADA with ORION, A.C.T., Inc. based in Wilmington, Delaware, to jointly develop a technology that converts methane to ethylene, propylene and other valuable hydrocarbons without the production of unwanted carbon dioxide. The technology to be developed through this CRADA involves a catalyst and operating conditions for methane conversion which was discovered by a team of scientists from LBL's Center for Advanced Materials.

• Lithium/polymer batteries: These are batteries to be developed for use in electric automotive vehicles. Funds are to be provided by the United States Advanced Battery Consortium (USABC) which is composed of GM, Ford and Chrysler, with EPRI providing a minor part of the funding. Lithium/polymer batteries promise to provide a very favorable weight to stored-energy ratio.

• SQUIDS: A CRADA is anticipated to be issued with Conductus, a small business partner of LBL, which is developing commercial applications for an extremely low-noise detector, the superconducting quantum interference device (SQUID). Funding currently comes from DOE and the California Competitive Technology Program.

• CIEE CRADA: The California Institute for Energy Efficiency is an organized research unit of the University of California for which LBL performs research. The goals are to produce new hardware or software that contributes to end-use energy efficiency and new information useful for energy decision-making by consumers, and government, corporate and utility leaders. The CRADA allows LBL to provide administrative support to manage and operate CIEE.

• The Laboratory Technology Transfer Program of DOE's Office of Energy Research has allocated funds to LBL to carry out CRADA's for a number of projects.

Environmental Restoration and Waste Management

LBL environmental management site projects supported through the DOE Office of Environmental Restoration and Waste Management are essential to correct and restore environmental conditions at the Laboratory and to improve the management of waste handling operations in support of DOE's national environmental objectives. The corrective actions achieve and maintain required low exposure and risk levels; the environmental restoration program includes the assessment and characterization of contamination and the closure of the existing Hazardous Waste Handling facility and the construction of a new one.

Tiger Team Action Plan

A Tiger Team assessment of LBL was conducted in January-February 1991. No Category I (imminent danger) and 10 Category II (major nonconformance) findings resulted.

LBL's Tiger Team Corrective Action Plan was approved by the Secretary of Energy on February 20, 1992. The first Quarterly Report on Corrective Action Plan Status was submitted to DOE/SF on January 31, 1992.

Major tour sites at LBL include the following:

• The Advanced Light Source: LBL's Advanced Light Source (ALS), scheduled to go into operation in 1993, will provide brilliant coherent radiation in the vacuum ultraviolet and soft x-ray parts of the spectrum. Investigators from universities, industry and national laboratories will use the ALS's unique capabilities of high spectral brightness and very short pulse length. It will permit new studies in basic and applied science in physics, chemistry, materials sciences and the life sciences.

• The Human Genome Center: LBL's Human Genome Center is one of three DOE centers working on the Human Genome Project, which involves the deciphering of the genetic code contained in human DNA. New mapping and sequencing technologies and new database management techniques are being developed at LBL to speed the efforts and to make the knowledge gained readily accessible.

• Center for Advanced Materials: CAM focuses on fundamental research in areas of interest to industry. Current programs include advanced polymers, semiconductors, catalysts and ceramics as well as high-performance metal alloys and high-temperature superconductors. CAM researchers interact with industry through workshops, advisory boards and reciprocal visits.

• The National Center for Electron Microscopy: NCEM houses two powerful microscopes: the High Voltage Electron Microscope, which permits the probing of sample thousands of atoms deep; and the Atomic Resolution Microscope, which can resolve objects only 1.6 angstroms apart. A third microscope, the Analytical Electron Microscope, is used to analyze the chemical composition of samples.

• Center for Building Science: Research is aimed at saving energy and energy costs through energy-efficient windows, lighting, appliances and controls. Other research areas include analysis and control of indoor air quality, building systems analysis, appliances standards, least-cost utility planning and international energy use.

Directors

Ernest O. Lawrence, 1936–58
Edwin McMillan, 1958–73
Andrew M. Sessler, 1973–80
David A. Shirley, 1980–89
Charles V. Shank, 1989–

The square mile of the Lawrence Livermore National Laboratory from the air.

LAWRENCE LIVERMORE NATIONAL LABORATORY

LAWRENCE LIVERMORE NATIONAL LABORATORY was established September 2, 1952, to function as a national resource of scientific and technical capability for the nation's defense programs and, as appropriate, for other programs of national interest. It is managed by the University for the Department of Energy (DOE).

The Laboratory has evolved into a multidisciplinary, multiprogram laboratory which has designed and developed 22 nuclear weapons, including the most safe and secure to remain in the enduring stockpile.

The Lab also has developed strong technological support for arms control and nonproliferation, as well as conceived and developed strategic defense technology, including satellite technology.

LLNL operates two high-performance supercomputer centers, including the National Energy Research Supercomputer Center. It has developed the world's most powerful laser, Nova, for inertial confinement fusion research, and has developed and prepared for commercial deployment Atomic Vapor Laser Isotope Separation for uranium enrichment for reactor fuel.

The Laboratory is a national Human Genome Research Center, and has cloned and mapped most of chromosome 19. It has developed and operates the national Atmospheric Release Advisory Capability, and it has developed and demonstrated large-scale coal gasification, nuclear waste storage, and environmental cleanup technology.

In addition, the Lab has in place or in negotiation more than 80 CRADAs (Collaboration Research and Development Awards) with U.S. industry for the development of advanced commercial technology. The Lab also has received 41 "RD 100" awards for the invention of exceptional new technologies.

The Laboratory's mission is to serve as a national resource in science and engineering, focused on national security, energy, the environment, biomedicine, economic competitiveness, and science and mathematics education, with a special responsibility for nuclear weapons.

The Laboratory is considered preeminent in the application of science and technology to important societal needs. It directs research and development toward the solutions of large-scale, high-payoff, multidisciplinary problems that would be difficult for others to execute because of the size, complexity, risk, and long-term commitment.

The Lab also provides advanced capabilities in terms of its core competencies and distinctive facilities. It focuses on partnerships with industry, with other laboratories and with universities to gain access to their strengths and to increase the effectiveness and accessibility of its capabilities.

Throughout all its endeavors, the Laboratory is committed to quality management, diversity, excellence and the highest standards of health and safety for its workforce and the community.

As the nation downsizes defense from the Cold War priority level and increases economic priorities based on industrial strength, the Department of Energy and its laboratories are changing focus and method of operation to meet new challenges.

The impact of these changes within DOE is to create an environment for the Lab which encourages innovation, measured risk-taking and a more entrepreneurial approach in bringing science and technology to bear on national needs.

Changes within the "defense sector" are profound, and there is no requirement for new nuclear weapons. However, there remain responsibilities which are emerging as extremely important to the national security.

For example, the verified, balanced dismantlement of the U.S. and former Soviet weapons stockpiles is considered a high priority for the nation, and one that needs to be accelerated, and the diversion of these weapons and abundant special nuclear materials must be prevented. In addition, effective errant weapon detection and disablement methods are needed, and nuclear proliferation must be slowed down and, if possible, reversed, through improved intelligence, enforceable international agreements and the effectiveness of "super-brilliant," stealthy, accurate conventional weapons.

In the "civilian sector," LLNL is continuing to pursue clean, fuel-abundant fusion power, support the safe and beneficial use of nuclear power, support a hydrogen technology initiative, and provide technology for more efficient energy use and for exploitation of fossil energy resources in as environmentally benign ways as possible.

The environment has emerged as both a national value and a pervasive constraint. In previously closed parts of the world, environmental catastrophes that threaten habitation or use of large land and water areas are being found. World resources, critical ecologies and the global climate are threatened by on-going practices of resource use and waste disposal. While the development and evolution of environmentally sensitive national and global economies is a long-range dream, the near-term concentration is on cleaning up past mistakes and understanding the implications of current practices.

Health care is the fastest growing segment of the nation's economy, and universal health care is one of its major objectives. While genetics and genomics programs are developing diagnostics and therapies that have immediate application and commercial value, the real objective is the fundamental revolution in medicine that will accompany thorough knowledge of the human genome. LLNL is moving ahead on both the basic biology and molecular structure of human life and the biotechnology needed to access and exploit this basic knowledge.

"Commercial sector" activities are increasing rapidly at the Laboratory and are intended to comprise about one fifth of its work within five years. These industrial partnership activities include licensing of the Lab's patents and copyrights, cooperative research and development agreements, and enduring technology centers that support the development and commercialization of economically important advanced technologies.

In addition, the Lab is forming more complex alliances with other laboratories, universities, state and federal agencies, and private industry, such as the Cali-

A technician stands amidst the laser bay of the Nova laser.

fornia Environmental Enterprise, directed at the cleanup of environmental contamination in the region and commercialization of the relevant processes and systems.

In support of commercial, defense, and civilian programs, the Laboratory has developed a broad base of expertise and special facilities. It has approximately 8,000 UC career employees. About 50 percent have scientific and technical degrees and about one in three of these (1,300) has a doctorate. Their fields include physics, chemistry, materials science, biology, environmental science, earth science, mathematics, computer science, electrical, mechanical, aeronautical, metallurgical and civil engineering, and technician specializations.

In addition, the Laboratory has a research and development complex with replacement value of about $5 billion. This complex includes world-class lasers, including laser fusion and isotope separation facilities, supercomputers, accelerators, chemistry and materials laboratories, energetic materials laboratories and field test facilities, radio chemistry and heavy element laboratories, biology, biotechnology, and environmental laboratories and field test facilities, magnetic fusion facilities, equipment reliability test facilities, and precision fabrication facilities.

Although the Laboratory was originated to develop nuclear weapons and to harness thermonuclear energy for civilian power, its facilities as a multiprogram, multidisciplinary national resource provide a demonstrated ability to respond to a wide range of national needs.

Specific areas of competency include the following:

Nuclear Science and Technology.

High-Performance Computation.

High-Performance Lasers.

Advanced Sensors and Instrumentation.

Plasma Physics and Technology.

Accelerator Physics and Technology.

Energy Science and Technology.

Biology and Biotechnology.

Environmental Science and Technology.

Atmospheric Science.

Earth Science.

Space Technology.

Materials, Processing, and Fabrication.

LLNL also excels in the area of Large-Scale Science Systems. In the past two decades, the Lab has built and operated six major laser systems, four magnetic fusion systems, five linac and Van de Graff accelerators (two of which were used to drive large free-electron lasers), and two supercomputer centers.

It has conducted large-scale demonstrations of isotope separation, underground coal gasification, underground nuclear waste storage, and oil shale recovery.

These systems ranged in value up to about $500 million (FY 1992 dollars). Generally, the systems were

A scientist at LLNL loads a set of samples into an accelerator mass spectrometer for measurement.

specified by Laboratory scientists, designed, assembled and operated by Laboratory engineers, and fabricated by industry. In most cases, U.S. industrial partners participated in all phases of these projects.

In carrying out its responsibilities in all the areas described above, the Lab has a number of technical goals and objectives. These include:

• To develop marketable technology in collaboration with U.S. industry and make a significant contribution to the economic strength of the nation: specifically, to double its technology transfer activities in the next two years

• To provide the scientific and technological base for critical national defense capabilities: specifically, to gain approval for critical research facilities, the National Ignition Facility and the Contained Firing Facility; to use these and other national facilities to support the core defense technologies; to demonstrate technologies for the long-range detection of nuclear, biological and chemical weapons; and to demonstrate methods for the disablement of terrorist weapons

• To improve energy efficiency and develop new energy sources that are clean, abundant, safe, and economical: specifically, to achieve ignition with inertial confinement fusion, to support the development of advanced magnetic fusion systems and the International Thermonuclear Reactor, and to develop new, clean transportation systems and fuels

• To develop the environmental science and technology needed to assess and predict environmental effects, to clean up past contamination, and to move toward an ecologically and economically healthy future: specifically, to develop methods for treating mixed waste, to apply "smart" clean-up technology, like dynamic stripping, to national remediation problems, like the DOE complex and the closing military bases, to commercialize these technologies with U.S. industry, and to provide global, regional and risk models for the assessment of environmental hazards and the response to environmental threats and accidents

• To understand human life, health and pathology at the genetic level

Additional technical goals and objectives of growing importance to the Laboratory are:

• To enhance science, engineering, and mathematics education: specifically, to concentrate on high-leverage programs, like teacher training and environmental worker training

• To serve as a source of computation/information science and technology to meet a broad range of national needs: specifically, to participate in the development of high performance computer systems, of high volume information storage (the National Storage Laboratory), and of wide-band networks (Energy Research Network), and to contribute to the development of the national information infrastructure

• To support the missions of other national agencies in the areas of environment, health, energy, defense, space, education and economic competitiveness: specifically, to develop more effective partnerships with the Departments of Defense, Commerce, Transportation and Education, the National Aeronautics and Space Administration, the National Institutes of Health, the Nuclear Regulatory Commission, and the Environmental Protection Agency, the comparable agencies at the state level

The Lab also has several institutional management goals and objectives essential to its long-term viability and success, namely:

• To promote policies and a work environment that attract a diverse and excellent work force, an environment in which people are productive and thrive: specifically, to continually increase the diversity of the Lab's workforce and management at all levels to reflect the diversity of the nation

• To enhance the environment, health and safety of Lab employees and the community: specifically, to comply with all applicable regulations governing Lab operations and to continuously improve on its health and safety record

• To conduct Lab operations and programs in accordance with the principles of total quality management and continuous quality improvement: specifically, to extend the use of these methods from the Lab's operations, where they are already used extensively, to all areas of the Laboratory

The goals and objectives stated here represent the Lab's current best articulation of what it sees as its commitments to the University, the Department of Energy and its other sponsors and partners. These goals will continue to evolve through an ongoing process of redefining changing needs and expectations, as well as new understanding of what can be done. Throughout, the Lab is committed to respond to the technical and scientific needs of the nation as defined by its own vision and by the leaders and institutions invested with the responsibilities to meet these national needs.

Directors

Herbert F. York, 1952–58
Edward Teller, 1958–60
Harold Brown, 1960–61
John S. Foster, 1961–65
Michael M. May, 1965–71
Roger E. Batzel, 1971–88
John H. Nuckolls, 1988–94

View of the Los Alamos National Laboratory.

LOS ALAMOS NATIONAL LABORATORY

The Los Alamos National Laboratory (LANL) is one of the world's largest multidisciplinary, multiprogram research centers. It is managed by the University for the U.S. Department of Energy.

The Laboratory offers challenges and discoveries in a setting of great natural beauty, about 35 miles northwest of Santa Fe. It covers 43 square miles of mesas and canyons at a 7,300-foot site in the Jemez Mountains of northern New Mexico, surrounded by pinon and ponderosa pine.

Scientists at the Lab investigate a multitude of phenomena that extend from the earth's interior through its atmosphere and magnetosphere into outer space, from subnuclear particles to galaxies, from events occurring in trillionths of a second to those that take thousands of centuries, and from temperatures near absolute zero to those measured in tens of millionths of degrees.

LANL has about 7,300 employees and a budget amounting to approximately $1 billion. It is home to 2,134 scientists and engineers. Of these, about one-third are physicists, and one-third are engineers. The rest hold degrees in chemistry, computer science, materials science, biosciences and other disciplines.

The site was established in 1943 as Project Y of the Manhattan Engineer District, the secret World War II effort to develop the first atomic weapons.

J. Robert Oppenheimer, a Berkeley physics professor, was selected to head the scientists who would conduct the research, develop the technology and produce the weapons.

To maintain the tradition of free inquiry and open debate cherished by Oppenheimer and his colleagues, the University, rather than industry or government, was chosen to manage to laboratory.

The wartime mission was successfully completed in 27 months.

A number of people strongly urged that the Los Alamos site be abandoned and a large laboratory be established in Southern California.

However, the federal government believed that the Los Alamos laboratory should continue so that the nucleus of a staff for future weapons development would be available.

From that beginning, Los Alamos has grown into today's research complex.

In 1980, the Lab was designated by Congress as the Los Alamos National Scientific Laboratory, in recognition of its contributions to the nation's scientific strengths.

In 1993, the Lab celebrated its 50th anniversary.

From its beginning, the Lab has concentrated on designing and developing nuclear devices, a responsibility it shares with the Lawrence Livermore National Laboratory.

Today, Los Alamos continues its mission of ensuring the nation's security through research and development into nuclear weapons technology and nonnuclear defense programs.

In addition, the Lab pursues extensive research into energy and related technologies, chemistry and materials science, biomedicine, advanced computing and basic science.

Work at Los Alamos bridges the gap between the basic research orientation of universities and the applications and manufacturing focus of industry. The Lab's strength lies in its ability to conduct large, complex technology projects where science makes a difference.

Increasingly, Los Alamos is turning its multidisciplinary capabilities toward domestic and economic needs, such as clean and abundant energy, a clean environment and a refurbished national infrastructure, that in the long run may affect national security as much as they do military needs. Technology continues to be the engine that will drive economic growth in the future and improve the quality of life.

With the end of the Cold War, Los Alamos' traditional security role is focusing on four areas:

(1) Stewardship of the nation's enduring weapons stockpile, (2) countering the proliferation of nuclear weapons around the world, (3) the safe dismantlement and final disposition of weapons returning from the stockpile, and (4) helping to clean up the effects of 50 years of weapons production.

In addition, the Lab has been working on ways to accommodate the U.S. strategic defense initiative of the 1990s.

This initiative has shifted from national defense against massive nuclear attacks to local defense and protection of the nation against limited nuclear strikes that might occur through terrorist and accidental launches.

A researcher prepares superconducting material.

While nuclear weapon technology currently accounts for about half the Lab's research effort, its original mission entailed a venture into uncharted territory that has demanded a multidisciplinary approach to research. As a result, research at the Lab spans most of the disciplines of science. This means that the Lab's mission has expanded over the years to include non-nuclear defense programs, and a broad array of non-defense programs, allowing the Lab to address major issues that have an impact on national security in the broadest sense.

For example, capabilities developed for the Lab's nuclear weapons work allow it to contribute to research involving conventional weapons and strategic defense.

The Lab also seeks to develop technologies to ensure a secure supply of energy, including nuclear fusion, fossil and geothermal electricity transmission and storage, regional energy assessment and policy analysis, development of alternative fuels, and enhanced recovery of domestic oil.

In addition, the Lab has fostered significant research in fields such as astrophysics, biomedicine, computational science, materials science, molecular biology, and public health. Scientists also have been heavily involved in biological research. While studies originally focused on understanding the health effects of radiation, programs now span the entire range of the life sciences.

To conduct its many research activities, LLNL has a number of major centers, including:

• The Confinement Physics Research Facility, which allows scientists to study the energy potential of nuclear fusion, the process that powers the sun and stars, to determine new ways for nuclear reactors to be fueled.

• Los Alamos, General Motors and the University of Wisconsin are working together on a manufacturing technology to make material surfaces harder and more resistant to wear and corrosion. Ion implantation is not a coating, but a way to transform near-surface layers of such products as machine tools, ball bearings and automobile and aerospace components into an integrated, protective layer.

• The Center for Human Genome Studies, which scientists utilize to learn more about the genome, the complete set of genetic instructions encoded in each human being's DNA. Understanding the genome, once achieved, will provide an essential tool for future biology and offer a new approach to treating more than 4,000 genetic diseases.

• GenBank, an international data base of DNA sequences that helps handle the vast amounts of genetic information produced by researchers worldwide.

• The Integrated Computing Network, located in the Central Computing Facility at Los Alamos, is one of the leading scientific computing centers in the world. The network utilizes the Lab's supercomputers and an array of other computers and associated systems.

• The Clinton P. Anderson Meson Physics Facility, which is used to study nuclear and elementary particle physics, atomic physics, nuclear chemistry, radiobiology, and condensed-matter physics. Research will be useful in medicine, isotope production, defense science, and materials structure.

• The Manuel Lujan, Jr. Neutron Scattering Center, which produces neutrons at thermal energies to conduct basic and applied research of value to condensed-matter physics and structural biology.

• The Superconductivity Pilot Center, established by DOE as one of three in the nation. LANL's role is to synthesize new high-temperature superconducting materials and compounds to investigate ways for materials to conduct electricity without energy loss.

• The Center for Materials Science, which enhances Lab programs in condensed-matter physics, metallurgy, ceramics, and materials chemistry. Materials engineering programs supported by the center include the processing of plutonium and other elements, the fabrication and analysis of advanced materials, and the study and preparation of high explosives.

• The Center for Nonlinear Studies, which investigates the dynamics of nonlinear systems. Such systems are characterized by (1) chaotic features, (2) the abrupt appearance of natural factors such as tornadoes, hurricanes, vortices and the like, or (3) both types of phenomena together.

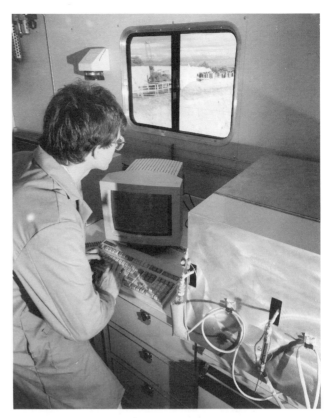

A technician uses a gas chromatograph mass spectrometer to analyze soil.

• The Institute of Geophysics and Planetary Physics (Los Alamos branch), which fosters scientific collaboration between UC and the Lab. The institute supports joint research projects that include work in geophysics, atmospheric and space sciences, and related specialties.

• The Light Detection and Ranging (Lidar) uses pulses of light in much the way that radar uses radio waves. Because of the way light interacts with particles and gases in the air, lidar can be used to detect and measure atmospheric pollution and also to track some of the key physical and chemical processes in the atmosphere.

• Los Alamos and Lockheed Environmental Systems and Technologies Co. are working together in the area of magnetic soil remediation. This involves a physical separation process for removing radioactive actinides such as plutonium, uranium and americium from contaminated soils.

• The Oil Recovery Technology Partnership is an alliance among the Department of Energy, Los Alamos and Sandia national laboratories and the petroleum industry to increase domestic oil production.

• The KIVA computer code was developed in response to the energy crisis of the 1970s. Now it is used by nearly every automaker worldwide to simulate the behavior of gases in internal combustion engines. The code models the turbulent and explosive events inside engines, such as air flow, fuel spray, combustion and exhaust.

• Los Alamos and General Motors have been working on a fuel cell system that could power passenger cars of the future cleanly and efficiently. Fuel cells will reduce the nation's dependence on petroleum by increasing the use of alternative fuels. They also can improve air quality by substantially reducing automobile pollution. A fuel cell engine can attain twice the overall efficiency of a gasoline engine.

• The Institutional Collaborative Research Program, which fosters scientific collaborations between Los Alamos and UC campuses in areas such as high-temperature superconductivity, nonlinear science and global climate modeling.

• The Center for National Security Studies, which lets political scientists and technical experts exchange ideas on questions of national security.

• Exploratory Research and Development Center, which works with industry on a variety of research areas.

• The J. Robert Oppenheimer Study Center, which has one of the most significant technical collections in the country, including 300,000 volumes and journals and more than half a million reports from around the world.

Since basic research is crucial to the Lab's mission, it makes a concerted effort to encourage collaborative research through formal mechanisms established at certain of its centers.

The purpose is to encourage scientific collaboration with UC faculty and graduate and postdoctoral students.

In addition, the Lab tries to be a good neighbor by fulfilling its civic responsibilities.

For example, Los Alamos employees are activity involved in a number of community organizations. The Lab itself promotes educational outreach, technical assistance and volunteer programs.

Each year, the Lab's outreach programs touch 20,000 students from grade school through high school. Special programs focus on teachers and college students.

The Lab also supports small and disadvantaged businesses by ensuring that they have an opportunity to bid on supply and service contracts.

In undertaking all its important activities, Los Alamos carries on a proud scientific tradition. Its community and its natural setting are unique, and opportunities—both professional and personal—abound. Most important, those who contribute to the success of the Lab believe that their efforts can make a positive difference in the world.

Directors

J. Robert Oppenheimer, 1943–45
Norris Bradbury, 1945–70
Harold Agnew, 1970–79
Donald Kerr, 1979–85
Sigfried Hecker, 1985–

Laboratory-Campus Collaborative Research Projects: The University has received a management allowance from the U.S. Department of Energy (DOE) for managing the three national laboratories at Berkeley and Livermore in California, and Los Alamos, in New Mexico.

Part of that allowance was used to fund a program of collaborative research among UC's campuses and the three DOE laboratories. With the new contracts signed effective 1992, a Complementary and Beneficial Activities fund has been established to continue these collaborative research efforts.

The collaborative funds are used predominantly to support graduate students and postdocs and to provide travel funds to the laboratories.

Collaboration between the labs and the campuses covers an array of different research topics.

The largest and oldest program supported by these funds is the Institute for Geophysics and Planetary Physics (IGGP).

IGGP is an interdisciplinary Multicampus Research Unit of the University. Branches are located at three campuses and at the Livermore and Los Alamos laboratories.

The goals of the laboratory branches are to:

• Promote expanded exchange and interaction of scientists among the campuses and the national laboratories and expedite shared use of special facilities at the labs.

• Promote excellence in scientific research at LLNL and LANL in those fields related to the institute's mission.

• Provide organizational support for intellectual centers in special areas of research related to the institute's mission.

The institute's primary scientific emphases are space physics, planetary physics, geophysics, geochemistry, high-pressure sciences, and calculational and experimental astrophysics.

Following an increase in the University's management allowance that was part of the 1987 contract renewal to manage the labs, UC initiated an expanded effort to foster collaborative research.

The Institutional Collaborative Research (INCOR) Program was created to fund large research projects that involve multiple disciplines, campuses, or laboratories.

The program was designed to support projects for a minimum of four years of funding. Research projects that have received INCOR funding study scientific topics of current national importance, including global climate change, analytical cytology, high temperature superconductivity, and nonlinear phenomena.

The Campus-Laboratory Collaborative Research (CALCOR) Program was also created to foster increased interaction between campus and laboratory researchers.

CALCOR was designed to facilitate research between a lab scientist and an individual researcher and his or her students at a campus.

A moratorium was placed on the CALCOR program in 1989 because the interest in the program far surpassed the available funds. While there continues to be an inter-est in its renewal, it has remained suspended until additional or reallocated funds for collaborative research are identified.

In addition to INCOR and CALCOR, the collaborative research fund provides support for special, one-time research projects of particular merit.

REFERENCES: Annual Reports to the Department of Energy on Complementary and Beneficial University Activities Related to the Department of Energy Laboratories, Office of the President.

CROSS-REFERENCES: Topics related to the Laboratories; Organized Research Units.

Latin American Studies: The University is a national leader in the number and scope of programs focusing on Latin American research and teaching.

For example, approximately 400 faculty members at UC devote their time to the study of Latin America, and specialists in Latin American studies have won hundreds of prestigious fellowships and numerous awards for teaching, research and service.

In addition, the UC faculty includes four past presidents of the international Latin American Studies Association.

Four major centers of research and teaching on Latin America exist at three UC campuses as Organized Research Units (ORUs). Four other campuses offer degree programs in Latin American studies.

Moreover, the University operates three federally funded National Resource Centers on Latin America.

These are UCLA's Center for Latin American Studies, the UC San Diego-San Diego State University Consortium on Latin America, and the joint UC Berkeley-Stanford National Resource Center for Latin American Studies.

Each of these centers is supported by the Department of Education as part of the National Defense Education Act. They develop research programs, support graduate student and faculty research, and foster collaboration among scholars and students working on Latin America.

There are 11 National Resource Centers for Latin American Studies in the U.S. The University is the only institution with more than one.

A number of Universitywide programs focus to some extent on areas related to Latin America. They include the California Policy Seminar, the Education Abroad Program, the Institute on Global Conflict and Cooperation, the Linguistic Minority Research Institute, the Pacific Rim Program, and UC MEXUS.

As a result of all these efforts, UC faculty in Latin American studies are able to work closely with centers and programs outside the University that concentrate on Latino populations. These faculty experts contribute to an understanding of the many roles of Latino communities in both the state and the nation.

REFERENCES: "Latin American Studies, University of California," brochure, Coordinator of Research Issues, Office of the President.

CROSS-REFERENCES: California Policy Seminar; Education Abroad Program; Institute on Global Conflict and Cooperation; Latino Eligibility Task Force; Organized Research Units; Pacific Rim; UC MEXUS.

Latino Eligibility Task Force: In August 1992, the University's Latino Eligibility Task Force was established by UC's president to study a problem that has serious implications for California's future.

The task force set out to learn why only 3.9 percent of Latino high school students are eligible for UC, compared to 12.3 percent of all California public high school graduates.

In March 1993, the task force issued its first report, addressing the issues associated with the low level of Latino student participation and recommending ways to deal with the situation.

Eugene Garcia, task force chair and dean of the Division of Social Sciences at UC Santa Cruz, said his group was working with a sense of urgency because Latino children are a rapidly growing segment of California's education system.

"By 2005, Latino children are projected to represent 42 percent of California K-12 student enrollment and 38 percent of California high school graduates—the single largest ethnic group among high school graduates. California cannot afford to have higher education bypass these children."

Garcia said that while the first report's recommendations do not directly address eligibility, "they do set the tone and direction even as the task force addresses the larger eligibility issues."

According to the report, Latino student participation can be increased if certain changes are made in outreach, financial aid, related policies, and college counseling at the high school level.

The changes would help encourage those who meet admissions requirements to enroll at UC, the report stated.

Specifically, the report recommended that UC:

• Structure financial aid for needy students in the form of grants and scholarships rather than loans, particularly in the first year, and insure that there is enough aid to cover the basic financial needs of these students.

• Provide eligibility, admissions and financial aid information to Latino parents in Spanish and English, and address issues relevant to them, such as housing and campus safety.

• Encourage campuses to coordinate outreach efforts with K-12 schools, community colleges, community organizations and businesses.

• Direct some university programs and research units that address Latino concerns to focus on improving Latino student eligibility, especially by concentrating on K-12 teaching and curriculum for Latino students.

• Change specific UC policies and practices that may negatively affect Latino students.

The changes in policies and practices would provide a number of benefits, according to the report.

For example, the changes would allow English as a Second Language (ESL) or other bilingual-content courses to meet A–F course requirements, help in better

coordinating the student admission, financial aid and housing processes, and provide for earlier admission of community college transfers.

The task force report also attacked myths about Latinos, including the belief that many Latino students admitted to the University are not qualified.

Garcia said that the myths addressed in the report were as important as the recommendations.

"Too often myths are used as the basis for understanding this complex issue. Popular misunderstanding of Latino student eligibility and participation is a case in point," he said, adding: "We can't allow these myths to continue."

Among the 10 myths cited and refuted in the report was the claim that over the last few years many Latino students had been admitted under a Universitywide policy to accept a limited number of students who showed potential to succeed even though they did not meet the requirements.

Asian American Journals Created at Two Campuses

In 1992, students at UCLA and Berkeley created the nation's first two Asian law journals.

Law students at UCLA and Berkeley produced the publications because increasing numbers of Asian Americans are becoming lawyers.

Law journals at academic institutions have met the needs of professionals interested in specific fields by focusing on issues concerning, for example, African Americans, Hispanics, women, ecology, Pacific Rim trade, technology and industrial relations.

However, there had been no law journals concerned with Asian American interests and issues before the two were created at UC.

The first issue of UCLA's Asian American and Pacific Islands Law Journal was published in February 1993.

In its first issue, the publication examined how the federal Immigration/Marriage Fraud law affects domestic violence among mail-order brides.

It also looked at the racial tensions that surfaced between Korean and African American residents in Los Angeles during the 1992 riots.

UC Berkeley's Asian Law Journal planned to address issues that included anti-Asian discrimination and immigration laws in the United States, U.S. trade policy toward Asian nations, and legal histories and biographies of prominent Asian Americans.

Unlike the approach in traditional law journals, the articles appearing in the two new publications often will cover controversial issues involving the interplay of law and racism.

The report stated that less than 5 percent of Latino applicants, on average, had been offered admission under special-action provisions in the previous four years. Almost all Latinos who are admitted are fully eligible.

Another myth is the belief that Latinos' lack of achievement in higher education is a result of their lack of interest in education.

However, as evidence of strong interest, the report cited a survey conducted by UCLA's Chicano Studies Research Center.

The survey found that 88 percent of the respondents agreed special measures should be taken to ensure that the same percentage of Latinos as other groups are admitted to college.

Parents of Latino students reported an extremely high interest in having their children attend the university and a high regard for education generally.

The Latino Eligibility Task Force consists of 15 faculty members and administrators from the nine UC campuses. It is continuing to examine the eligibility issue by analyzing existing information, conducting original research, and sponsoring conferences in order to highlight problems and identify solutions.

The task force's plans have included a spring symposium on Latino eligibility and a study of transcripts of freshmen entering UC, California State University and the community colleges. In addition, the task force will conduct mini-studies whose results can be quickly implemented.

REFERENCES: "Latino Task Force Leader Eager to Make a Difference," news release, August 12, 1992, and "UC Latino Report Makes Recommendations and Rebuts Myths," news release, March 11, 1993, University Relations, Office of the President, and Latino Student Eligibility and Participation in the University of California, Report Number One of the Latino Eligibility Task Force, March 1993, Division of Social Sciences, UC Santa Cruz.

CROSS-REFERENCES: Latin American Studies.

Law Schools: The University has four law schools.

Three are located on UC campuses, at Berkeley, Davis and Los Angeles. The fourth school, affiliated with UC, is Hastings College of the Law, located in downtown San Francisco.

At Berkeley, the Department of Jurisprudence was created in 1894. The name was changed to the School of Jurisprudence in 1912 and to the School of Law in 1950.

In 1963, provision was made for a law school at Davis. Instruction began in 1966.

In 1947, the California State Legislature appropriated funds for the construction of a law school on the Los Angeles campus. The law school accepted its first class in 1949.

In 1992, the three campus law schools gained national recognition.

In a profession historically dominated by men, three women had risen to the top as deans of the three schools. UC then had the distinction of being the only university system in the nation with women heading all of its campus law schools.

(At the time, there were just 14 women deans among the 177 law schools accredited by the American Bar Association.)

The three women deans at UC were Herma Hill Kay, School of Law (Boalt Hall), Berkeley; Ellen Rausen Jordan, School of Law, Davis; and Susan Westerberg Prager, School of Law, UCLA.

The fourth law school affiliated with UC, Hastings College of the Law, was founded in 1878 in San Francisco as the original law department of the University. It is unique among UC professional schools as the only law school that operates independently of an undergraduate campus.

REFERENCES: Centennial Record; UC's General Catalogs; "UC Heads the Dean's List," UC Focus, June/July 1992, University Relations, Office of the President.

CROSS-REFERENCES: Hastings College of the Law.

Libraries: The University's libraries are a vital academic resource, They provide books, documentary materials and information required by students and faculty for effective study and research.

In addition, the libraries provide services to students and faculty of other California colleges and universities and to citizens in the surrounding communities.

UC's library budget is divided into the following three categories representing major activities:

• Acquisitions-processing, which represents 60 percent of the budget and includes all staffing activities related to acquiring library materials and preparing them for use, such as ordering, receiving and cataloging. This category also includes expenditures for books and binding (representing 25 percent of the total library budget).

• Reference-circulation, which represents 36 percent of the budget. It includes activities which provide users with information and materials. It involves managing circulation of materials, shelving and reshelving books, maintaining periodical and document collections, providing reference services and instructing students in the use of the library.

• Activities of the systemwide library automation unit of Information Systems and Administrative Services, which represent 4 percent of the total budget. These activities provide Universitywide access to the resources of UC's libraries through the MELVYL online system.

In 1977, the University adopted a comprehensive library plan with the goals of improving library service and reducing the rapid rise in library costs.

To achieve these goals, the plan recommended increased cooperation among UC's libraries and creation of a library system that would serve all University users, regardless of campus or location.

Since 1977, the State has provided most of the operating and capital budget resources called for in the library plan.

By 1992, implementation of the plan had proceeded on schedule, and many of the benefits foreseen by the plan were being realized.

For example, the following had been accomplished:

1) The budgeted acquisitions rate had been increased to 614,000 volumes

2) A Universitywide Shared Acquisitions Program had been implemented to acquire materials that, because of their high cost or anticipated level of use, should not be duplicated but should be shared among the campuses

3) An online union catalog, part of the MELVYL system, had been developed to provide users with convenient bibliographic access to the library material of all UC campuses

4) A union list of periodicals and other serial publications received by the University, the California State University, the California State Library and other institutions of higher education in California, was available online through the MELVYL catalog

5) An Intercampus Exchange Program had been established and included funds for photocopying of materials for intercampus use, as well as for daily intercampus jitney bus service between Los Angeles and other UC campuses in the south, and between Berkeley and other UC campuses in the north

6) Computerized systems had been implemented on all UC campuses to catalog and process books

7) Automated circulation systems had been installed at all UC campuses, allowing more efficient handling and recordkeeping

In addition, the State of California had provided $200,000 in 1986-87 to begin a program of preservation and conservation of library materials in recognition of one of the most serious problems facing UC's libraries: books that are literally falling apart.

Many library books have been decomposing at an alarming rate because they were printed on acid paper; as a consequence, they react adversely to such factors as heat, light and humidity.

As funds permit, the University is continuing a preservation program which includes such elements as microfilming, monitoring developments in deacidification techniques, maintaining and repairing collections, and installing environmental monitoring controls in the libraries.

REFERENCES: "Budget for Current Operations," Office of the President.

CROSS-REFERENCES: MELVYL; Telecommunications.

Library Collections: See Campus Profiles.

Lick Observatory: People have an age-old fascination with the beauty and mystery of the night-time skies.

In their enthusiasm, many of them head for the hills—in this case, the Diablo Range at the eastern edge of California's Santa Clara Valley, near San Jose.

Up a narrow, two-lane, twisting ribbon of a road lies their destination: Lick Observatory, at the top of 4,200-foot Mount Hamilton.

It is one of astronomy's premier observatories. While more than a dozen telescopes are larger than Lick's largest, its stature worldwide remains undiminished after 100 years and then some.

In 1988, the world-famous observatory celebrated a birthday. On June 1, it was exactly a century old. The centennial marked the moment in 1888 when the private Lick Trust gave UC the deed to the scientific facility.

Since then, UC astronomers have continued to make major discoveries in all parts of the light spectrum, as well as to make important advances in the theoretical work they do. In so doing, they continue to develop a more cohesive understanding of the universe.

In their work, they have helped push back the limits of the observable universe.

For example, they and other scientists have detected galaxies and other luminous sources so distant that their light has been traveling toward our own galaxy for three quarters of the time since the birth of the universe itself.

The observatory's tales of achievement start with James Lick, a wealthy, eccentric bachelor who lived in San Francisco and later moved to a plot of land almost in the shadow of Mount Hamilton.

Eventually he provided $700,000 to a board of trustees to build a 36-inch telescope "superior to and more powerful" than any in history, and the associated observatory at a site on the mountain.

Lick further stipulated that the entire observatory be transferred to the University to be used for research and astronomy.

The observatory was the first to be built on a wilderness mountain, where viewing would be at its best.

James Lick's gift to the University proved beneficial to science almost from the beginning. Astronomers began making major discoveries in looking at the glints of light they caught from distant space. As they made their discoveries, they helped change, forever, human perceptions about the universe.

In 1966, after nearly 80 years as an isolated mountaintop research station, Lick Observatory underwent a metamorphosis when its staff astronomers moved their headquarters to UC's new Santa Cruz campus.

With them came the technical personnel and shop equipment necessary to design and construct the optical, mechanical and electronic instruments used with the telescopes. During a week-long move, 67 tons of equipment, books and photographic plates were brought down from the mountaintop.

Advances in the science of astronomy had made it unnecessary for Lick's staff astronomers to stay continually at their observation posts. From that time on, they were teachers as well as researchers. When required, they travel back up the mountain to search the skies.

Their star-gazing activities take place along a knife-edged ridge where eight domes loom against the sky.

One dome houses the old 36-inch telescope. Scattered nearby are other instruments of different sizes and ages.

The biggest dome on the ride arches 10 stories high over the massive Shane Telescope, named for the late C. Donald Shane, former director and internationally renowned UC Santa Cruz astronomer.

The telescope has a mirror diameter of 120 inches. For nearly two decades after it began operating in 1959, it was the world's second largest telescope, after Palomar's 200-inch.

UC Astronomers Keep Letting The Stars Get in Their Eyes

The research by astronomers at Lick and at UC's general campuses and laboratories literally covers the skies.

Here is just a hint of their many and diverse research programs.

In addition to learning more about how galaxies are born and evolve, they are investigating supernovas (giant "exploding stars") and using computers to simulate the "Big Bang," which, many believe, created the universe.

Other UC scientists are hunting for the origin of gamma ray bursts, or pulses of high energy radiation emitted from space where no obvious sources seem to exist.

Still others keep an eye on red giants (dying stars) and an occasional white dwarf (the hot remnant of a star).

UC astronomers also are studying explosion-like releases of energy on the sun, or using arrays of radio telescopes to detect waves of sound emitted during the birth and death of stars.

In recent years, Lick and other astronomers have joined in a study of something brand new: quasars.

A quasar (quasi-stellar radio source) is an oddity in the remote fringes of observable space. Unlike other stellar objects, quasars were first spotted because some emit powerful radio energies.

In addition to all of this activity, astronomers from UC and elsewhere travel over to Hawaii, where they use the giant 10-meter Keck Telescope.

To use it, one first enters a control room filled with electronic panels and computers showing a myriad of dials, switches, buttons, glowing numbers and blinking lights.

To one recent visitor, it all looked like "a giant control panel on Captain Nemo's submarine."

Light-tight doors lead to the inner dome, where the telescope is angled against the evening sky.

Because the telescope is fully automated, an astronomer sets its controls from a console in a nearby room and observes the flow of information with the help of computers, TV monitor and data displays.

Actually, none of an astronomer's time is spent peering through eyepieces, and little is spent on top of the mountain. The electronic gear attached to the telescopes automatically stores all the light-borne information on tape, allowing researchers to spend most of their time on campus.

They use that time to develop and study the incredibly clear images taken by the telescope's cameras, feed information to computers, evaluate stacks of data and puzzle through physical theories to explain what they have found.

And they do all this using high-tech equipment that can greatly amplify incoming light for sharper display, convert photons into digital signals for closer study, measure an object's brightness to high accuracy, and even separate light rays into colors like a rainbow to find the temperature and composition of stellar objects.

Lick scientists have pioneered the development of such highly advanced, complex instruments, which vastly extend the ability of their telescopes to peer deeper into the skies. With their extended scientific capabilities, these scientists are pushing the technology to the limit, to better decipher and understand the enigmas they find far out in space.

REFERENCES: *Centennial Record;* "At the University of California: New Horizons for Lick Observatory," Special Report to the Regents, February 1967; "Lick turns 100: Still gazing after all these years," *UC Focus,* Vol. 2, No. 8, June 1988; "Astronomy at the University of California," news release, April 1991, University Relations, Office of the President; "Lick Observatory, University of California," observatory booklet.

CROSS-REFERENCES: Keck Telescope.

At Lick: Looking Forward In Order To Look Backward

Lick Observatory has the 14th largest telescope in the world, and it is located at a good site atop Mount Hamilton (except for light pollution from nearby San Jose).

In utilizing their scientific expertise, Lick faculty and technical staff have sought truly innovative ways of making the most of the light collected by its large Shane Telescope.

To this end, in the early 1970s, Lick astronomers pioneered in the conversion usage of military hardware (image intensifiers and disectors) to capture and analyze light too faint to be recorded on photographic plates. A system called the image-intensifier image-disector scanner was copied for use at many other telescopes around the world.

The Lick staff also were early developers in the use of computers to collect data on the object of interest with minimum interference from urban light pollution. This technique, called automatic sky-subtraction, has become a standard routine used at all major observatories.

In the 1980s, Lick astronomers advanced the science of high resolution spectroscopy with the development of the high resolution echelle spectrograph.

This was the first modern instrument to be designed around the next generation of low-light level detectors, the charge-coupled device (CCD), with its generally square rather than linear format. By using a second prism, the Hamilton Spectrograph stacks the otherwise linear rainbow spectrum of the object into a roughly square shape.

This innovation permits the astronomer to record nearly the whole spectrum in a single exposure rather than multiple ones.

The result is a great increase in the productivity of the telescope, since in an equal amount of time an astronomer can collect data on many more subjects.

(The Hamilton Spectrograph pays tribute to the man for whom Mount Hamilton is named, the Rev. Laurentine Hamilton. It was provided by a gift from Clara-Belle Hamilton, his granddaughter.)

A similar advance was made in low resolution spectroscopy with the development of the W.G. Kast Double Spectrograph (named for another donor).

This instrument enables the astronomer to record data simultaneously at both the red and blue ends of the rainbow spectrum. It was designed to work on very faint objects, and uses two highly innovative, multi-element optical cameras. The cameras utilize unusual materials for the lenses, including calcium fluoride and salt.

These developments and designs have been exported to other observatories. With such knowledge at their disposal, these observatories now have the ability to look at the whole spectrum more effectively than in the past. It is like having a second telescope of the same aperture.

The 1980s and 1990s also saw the beginnings of dramatic advances in detector technology at Lick.

While the CCD became the standard light detector at all observatories, their very small size (about a quarter-inch square) proved to be a major handicap to instrument designers and astronomers. Also, their availability was limited, and they were very expensive.

Working with industry, Lick astronomers have been able to produce CCDs of about two inches square with more than 250 times the number of collecting nodes. Many other observatories have sought Lick's help in obtaining these experimental devices for their own use.

All of this technical innovation resulted in Lick's initiative in the building of the world's largest telescope. This instrument, the W.M. Keck Telescope in Hawaii eventually will have a twin 10-meter telescope alongside. (The Keck Telescope is described in another section of this book.)

In 1993, Lick astronomers and technicians completed a six-year project to deliver another high-resolution spectrograph, this one for use at Keck. It is a sort of "son-of-Hamilton."

In addition, CCDs developed at Lick figure to play a prominent role in the Keck instruments. The Keck low-resolution spectrograph was conceived and optically designed at Lick, an extension of the innovations found in the Kast spectrograph. And automatic sky subtraction is built into the data-taking routines at Keck, in this case to combat the natural background light of the night sky rather than any possible future urban light pollution.

In sum, Lick Observatory's successes are rooted in its long and technically sophisticated heritage. Such innovation will go on as Lick continues to look to the future in order to find better ways of looking at the past.

Source: Lick Observatory.

Lick Observatory at nightfall.

The **Linguistic Minority Research Institute** (LMRI) is a Universitywide research unit.

It started in 1984 in response to a request by the State Legislature for increased UC attention to language minority educational issues.

The institute stimulates, supports, undertakes and coordinates faculty research on education topics and related activities that improve the understanding and chances of school success of language minority students, as well as their access to UC and other institutions of higher education.

LMRI places an emphasis on collaborative research with schools and school districts, and on developing long-term relations between UC faculty and schools with high enrollments of language minority students.

Since its inception, the institute has sponsored more than 34 Small Grant (one-year) research projects, and five Thematic (three-year) research projects.

In addition, it helped found the federally funded National Center for Research on Cultural Diversity and Second Language Learning at UC Santa Cruz.

UC faculty are encouraged to seek extramural funding for continuation of research with schools.

As of early 1993, UC's investment has been parlayed into substantial extramural support, resulting in an approximate 1:16 rate of return for every UC dollar provided for research.

LMRI conducts a Research Grant competition providing modest seed-grants for the conduct of projects lasting up to one year, as well as multiple-year thematic research projects involving faculty from one or more campuses investigating a common research problem related to educational practice.

These thematic grants are expected to develop into long-term relationships with schools and school districts.

While the funded research topics have been varied, there has been a concentration of support in several focused areas:

• Strategies for improving instruction and instructional outcomes

• Acquisition of language, literacy and cognitive skills

• Policy analyses and administrative practices of language minority education issues

LMRI-affiliated faculty are nationally recognized as leading research scholars in the area of language minority students' education and language development.

In addition to the LMRI involvement with The National Center for Research on Cultural Diversity and Second Language Learning at UCSC, LMRI contributes to the research programs of other national research centers.

For example, LMRI research projects based at UC Santa Barbara are conducted for the National Center for Effective Education of Disadvantaged Students at Johns Hopkins University and for the National Center for Adult Literacy at the University of Pennsylvania.

The institute, which involves a large number of nationally and internationally recognized faculty, is coordinating the development of extramural support of bilingual education pre-doctoral fellowships throughout the system.

LMRI has successfully coordinated the solicitation of 17 competitively awarded federally funded pre-doctoral fellowship programs at UCSB and UCSC, with the objective of including such support at each of the UC

Linguistic Minority Research Institute: An Overview

Throughout 1984–92, LMRI was supported by the Office of the President as a Project (LMRP).

In 1992, its status was upgraded to a Multicampus Research Unit, and the name was changed to the Linguistic Minority Research Institute, to reflect this new, permanent status.

In 1987, the administrative headquarters was moved from the President's Office to UC Santa Barbara.

While the LMRI is a systemwide activity, the substantive academic research and training concerns of the institute are an integral component of the long-range academic plan of UCSB and the UCSB Graduate School of Education.

As a research unit involving all the campuses, LMRI has also involved UC faculty from many disciplines, including education, anthropology, medicine, psychology and sociology, in addressing the effective education of language minority students in California.

A steering committee is the primary intercampus advisory group to LMRI.

Members of the steering committee represent each of the nine campuses.

The steering committee provides oversight to LMRI activities and is responsible for setting long-term goals for the unit and for reviewing the annual plan and progress of the institute.

These accomplishments and activities attest to the growing prominence of LMRI at the state level and as a national resource contributing to the education of language minority students.

LMRI faculty and staff are available to work with local school districts, schools of education, the State Department of Education and other education agencies on interpreting research findings for the purpose of implementing effective schooling and teacher training practices.

campuses where there is currently a viable doctoral program related to linguistic minority education.

These fellowships are funded by the U.S. Office of Bilingual Education and Minority Languages Affairs.

The objective of this pre-doctoral program is to continue the development of creative and qualified research professionals and practitioners.

In addition, the institute is currently coordinating resources with various campuses and departments to host U.S. and international visiting and post-doctoral scholars with specializations and interests in linguistic minority research.

This program promotes the interaction between UC and non-UC scholars and the sharing of research undertaken in California and other parts of the world.

While stimulation, support and conduct of original research are LMRI's primary goals, it has also undertaken various research dissemination activities.

LMRI holds an annual conference addressing the education of language minority students.

Conference presentations have included the results of basic, applied and policy research.

Six conference proceedings have been published and disseminated by LMRI.

Other dissemination activities include compilation and publication of an inventory of research on language minority students by UC faculty; research findings are communicated to school practitioners, school district administrators and legislative staff and state educational agency staff.

In addition, LMRI, in collaboration with the Chicano Studies Research Center Library at UCLA, is in the process of establishing an electronic network to bring information resources to researchers, students and staff inside and outside UC in education, language, Chicano/ Latino studies and cultural issues.

This system, expected to be fully on-line by 1994, will provide for specific and easy access, maintenance and development of an electronic newsletter, user group forums and access to selected bibliographic and statistical data sets around these topics.

REFERENCES: Information from the UC Linguistic Minority Research Institute.

CROSS-REFERENCES: All subjects related to Education Organized Research Units.

M

Master Plan for Higher Education: Prior to the development of California's Master Plan for Higher Education, policy was set by the Legislature, the Governor and a Liaison Committee.

The Liaison Committee was made up of representatives of the State Board of Education, which oversaw the state colleges and junior colleges, and The Regents of the University of California.

In 1959, the Legislature asked the Liaison Committee to develop a long-range plan for higher education in the state. Clark Kerr, then UC president, was a member of that Committee.

Under the direction of the Liaison Committee, a Master Plan Survey Team produced a document titled "A Master Plan for Higher Education in California, 1960–1975," which was approved in principle by the Regents and the State Board in December 1959 and submitted to the Legislature in February 1960.

A special session of the 1960 Legislature passed the Donahoe Higher Education Act, incorporating most of the Master Plan recommendations, and approved additional legislation to implement the plan.

The developers of the Master Plan attempted to achieve two major objectives: (1) "guard the State and State funds against unwarranted expansion and unhealthy competition among the segments of public higher education" and (2) "provide abundant collegiate opportunities for qualified young people and give segments and institutions enough freedom to furnish the diverse higher education services needed by the State."

The 1960 Master Plan made recommendations covering structure, function and coordination; selection and retention of students; institutional capacities and area needs; faculty demand and supply; adult education; and the costs of higher education. The Plan endorsed universal access to higher education in California for all qualified and motivated students.

The major recommendations that shaped the state's higher education system include:

1) The establishment of three segments of postsecondary education in California, each with a defined mission or function. The three are:

• The University of California, the state's primary academic agency for research, providing undergraduate, graduate and professional education. UC was granted the exclusive jurisdiction in public education over instruction in law and graduate instruction in medicine, dentistry and veterinary medicine, and in the awarding of the doctoral degree. Provision also was made for providing doctorates through joint programs with CSU.

• The state colleges, later renamed California State University (CSU), which focus on undergraduate education and graduate education through the master's degree. Faculty research was authorized consistent with the primary function of instruction.

• The junior colleges, now known as California Community Colleges (CCC), authorized to provide the first two years of undergraduate education, as well as vocational and technical courses and classes in general education. The academic classes were to prepare students for admission to a four-year institution.

2) The establishment of the principle of universal access and choice.

Under this provision, the segments were to select students from defined pools. UC was to select from among the top 12.5% of the high school graduating class, CSU was to select from among the top one-third of the high school graduating class, and the community colleges were to admit any student capable of benefiting from instruction.

The transfer function was seen as an essential component of the commitment to access. UC and CSU were to strive to establish a lower division to upper division ratio of 40:60 in order to provide transfer opportunities for community college students.

3) The reaffirmation of the principle of tuition-free education to residents of the state, and the recommendation that provision be made for student aid and loans.

4) The establishment of a governance structure for the segments, reaffirming the role of the UC Regents and establishing a Board of Trustees to oversee CSU.

Initially, the community colleges continued to be governed by the State Board of Education; however, in 1967 a separate Community College Board of Governors was established.

5) The establishment of a statutory coordinating body, the Coordinating Council for Higher Education.

6) In recognition of the demographic growth in the state, the Plan gave priority to community college expansion.

No new campuses of UC or CSU were to be built until all regions of the state were adequately served by a community college.

The Master Plan has been reviewed twice in subsequent years, and additions and modifications made.

A review in 1971–73, conducted by the Legislature's Joint Committee on the Master Plan for Higher Education, focused on the following four issues:

1) Access and Educational Opportunity: The Committee reaffirmed the State's commitment to find a place somewhere in the system for every student willing and able to benefit. It recognized that certain groups were underrepresented in postsecondary education, and recommended that the segments address barriers to college attendance posed by ethnicity, gender, income level, geographic location, age, and inadequate information about student choice.

2) Coordination and Planning: The Coordinating Council for Higher Education was replaced by the California Postsecondary Education Commission (CPEC).

The new body included representation from the independent sector and the private postsecondary schools, and was charged with coordination of long-range planning, evaluating the success of higher education policies and practices, and advising the Governor and the Legislature on major issues facing higher education.

3) Governance: The review reaffirmed the tripartite system of public higher education, and recommended that faculty and students be added to the governing boards of each system, that the terms of UC Regents be shortened from 16 years to 8 years, and that there be enhanced coordination via CPEC.

4) Diversity: The review reaffirmed the basic missions of each segment, recommended that each produce a mission statement, and advocated that UC provide for excellence in teaching as well as research.

In addition, the review took note of the role of the independent colleges and universities, recommending that they be encouraged to participate voluntarily in statewide cooperative programs.

A second review of the Master Plan took place in 1985–88.

The review began with an assessment of the community colleges and was then expanded into a review of the overall Master Plan and state postsecondary education in general.

The initial review was conducted by a Commission of 16 lay people, and its recommendations published in a July 1987 report, *The Master Plan Reviewed: Unity, Equity, Quality and Efficiency in California Postsecondary Education.*

The Commission's work was reviewed by a Joint Legislative Committee, which made recommendations to the Legislature. The Joint Committee issued its report in March 1989, *California Faces . . . California's Future: Education for Citizenship in a Multicultural Democracy.*

The reports focused on four issues: unity, equity, quality and efficiency.

• Unity: The commission reaffirmed the basic missions of the public segments, but called for greater clarification of the responsibilities of the segments, including the independent and private postsecondary and vocational segments.

The reports stressed the need for strong structural links between the segments in all areas, to be provided by the Education Round Table, a body composed of the heads of all the public higher education segments, the independent colleges and universities, and the California Department of Education.

The Commission reaffirmed the admissions policies established by the 1960 Master Plan and the central role of transfer; stressed the importance of revitalizing the community colleges and of implementing the 40:60 ratio of lower division to upper division students at UC and CSU; and recognized the need to strengthen governance at the community colleges.

• Equity: The Commission recognized that members of minority groups are underrepresented in postsecondary education, and stated that the achievement of educational equity must be a priority for the Governor, Legislature, governing boards and the Education Round Table.

In addition, the Commission noted that student financial assistance was increasingly provided in the form of loans rather than grants or employment, and recommended that the State provide financial aid in a manner which favored grants and employment and optimized student choice.

The Commission recognized the increasing number of part-time and older students, and gave primary responsibility for these students to CSU, with both four-year segments asked to make accommodations to ensure equity for those students; recommended that governing boards be held accountable for retention; and permitted UC and CSU to offer remedial courses as needed.

• Quality: The Commission stressed the importance of quality in education, especially at the K-12 level, and made teacher education a high priority.

It emphasized the importance of quality undergraduate education and made governing boards and faculty responsible for the coherence and quality of the undergraduate curriculum. The Commission also recommended a new commitment to excellence in teaching and advocated systematic, rigorous review of graduate programs to ensure quality.

The Commission instructed UC, CSU and the community colleges to develop campus infrastructures to take advantage of new educational technologies, and made recommendations concerning the improvement and oversight of private postsecondary and vocational education.

The Commission also recommended that the segments work with accrediting bodies to ensure that adequate attention is paid to student outcomes in evaluating institutions.

• Efficiency: The Commission gave CPEC the responsibility for reviewing the segments' long-range plans, and assessing whether plans for growth were consistent with mission. It recommended that CPEC, in cooperation with the Department of Finance, the Legislative Analyst and the segments, pursue efforts to avoid unnecessary duplication and contain rising costs, and examine the formulas used to budget State support of each system.

In addition, the Commission reaffirmed the State's responsibility to be the primary source of funding for postsecondary education, with students paying a portion of the cost. Student charges should not be changed substantially in a any single year, and fees should be maintained in a constant relationship to State support. Differential fees, by level or discipline, would be permitted at the discretion of the governing boards, and nonresident tuition set at the average cost of instruction and related services at each of the segments.

In general, the recommendations uphold and reaffirm the following: (1) the differential missions of the public segments of postsecondary education, while offering some refinements, (2) the pools from which the segments were to select their students, (3) the concepts of access and student choice, broadening access to include specifically social and economic equity as well as geographic access, (4) the centrality of transfer as a keystone of the Master Plan, and (5) the importance of cooperation and coordination among the segments.

In addition, the review addressed, for the first time, the issue of quality in education, at all levels, and underscored the importance of teacher preparation and curriculum planning. It also noted the importance of a reasonable student-faculty ratio, urging the State to stem the trend to an increased ratio.

Despite the reaffirmation of the basic principles of the Master Plan as recently as 1989, California's worsening economic situation in the early 1990s resulted in a substantial loss of funding to postsecondary education, which led to further reconsideration of the basic precepts of the Plan.

As in the 1960s, California faces enrollment pressures—the numbers of eligible students are expected to increase dramatically after 1997—and the Master Plan's educational equity goals take on added importance in the face of California's changing demographic profile and increasingly diverse population.

The need to accommodate increasing numbers of students is confounded by the prospect of slow economic recovery for California, and the situation is further complicated by State budgeting procedures that allow flexibility in only 15% of the budget. Postsecondary education is included in that 15% along with government services and corrections.

In confronting these difficult economic circumstances, and in keeping with California's strong commitment to provision of accessible and affordable education to the people of the state, the postsecondary institutions—together with CPEC and other branches of State government and policy experts—are seeking new ways to carry out their missions.

All segments are working to streamline operations and maximize efficient use of personnel, facilities and available technologies. All are rethinking academic program and curriculum, as well as focusing attention on increasing cooperation between the segments. Finally, new ways of funding higher education and the potential for additional sources of revenue are being explored.

REFERENCES: Centennial Record; information from Educational Relations, Office of the President; "The Master Plan, Then and Now: Policies of a Master Plan for Higher Education 1960–1975, in Light of 1993 Realities," April 19, 1993, California Postsecondary Education Commission; Master Plan reviews.

CROSS-REFERENCES: Budgets; California Postsecondary Education Commission; Enrollment; Student Fees; Student Financial Aid; all subjects related to education, teaching, the Regents and other subjects mentioned in the above text.

UC's Responses to Master Plan Review and Recommendations

In accordance with the Master Plan, the University:

• Maintains dual entitlement by finding a place somewhere in the system for all eligible freshmen and transfer students who wish to attend

• Has achieved and sustains a lower division-upper division ratio of 40–60

• Facilitates transfer through course articulation, Transfer Centers on the community college campuses, and ASSIST, a computerized information system

• Has implemented and participates in numerous programs with the K-12 schools to improve student preparation; disseminates information about UC eligibility requirements to junior and senior high school students and counselors; works with schools to increase the eligibility rates of underrepresented students (e.g., through the Early Academic Outreach Program); and promotes professional development for K-12 teachers through the Subject Matter Projects

• Designs and implements successful strategies to increase the proportion of underrepresented minorities in all sectors of the University (students, faculty and staff)

• Constantly examines and strives to improve the quality of undergraduate education, conducting a number of studies and working to implement the recommendations resulting from these studies

• Works cooperatively with CPEC and the other segments to facilitate statewide planning and maximum efficiency in the use of resources

Medical and Health Sciences: See information in Health Sciences section of this book and in Campus Profiles.

Medical Schools: See Campus Profiles (Davis, Irvine, Los Angeles, San Diego, San Francisco).

Melvyl® Catalog, UC's Online Union Library Catalog, Development of: The University's online public access catalog contains the bibliographic records of all of UC's campuses.

It also contains records from the California State Library, the California Academy of Sciences in San Francisco, and the Center for Research Libraries based in Chicago.

The catalog is part of the Universitywide approach to library automation, which includes fully automated systems for campuses and conversion of all campus collections to machine-readable form.

August 1991 marked the 10th anniversary of the catalog's implementation.

The original online union catalog was first deployed on August 17, 1981, with the name "MELVYL," after Melvil Dewey of Dewey Decimal fame.

This prototype catalog contained 733,412 book titles representing 1.3 million holdings. It was accessible from 100 terminals in 32 UC campus libraries.

Since that time, growth has been rapid.

The catalog now contains more than seven million titles representing more than 14 million holdings.

In addition to books, the catalog contains records of audiovisual materials, sound and video recordings, motion pictures, government documents, dissertations, music scores, computer files and maps.

Users can access the catalog through library terminals, personal computers with telephone modems and campus networks.

It also is available through the Internet.

Internet is a series of interconnected local, regional, national and international networks that provide electronic mail, remote login and file transfer functions for about five million people worldwide, mainly in the research and education community.

Since its inception, the catalog has evolved into a system that provides access to additional databases mounted locally, as well as Internet access to a number of library systems and other information resources throughout the U.S. and internationally.

Although online library catalogs are commonplace today, it is hard to remember how radical a notion it once was to have an online union catalog for public access.

A look back to the 1970s shows how it all began.

By 1970, it was clear that previous growth plans for UC libraries had become outmoded.

In 1971, the State Department of Finance published a report that encouraged increased cooperation among UC libraries and less duplication in acquisitions, with a recommendation that "budgetary restraints be used to insure compliance."

A series of task forces and plans ensued.

Eventually, a Universitywide Library Planning Office was established, and an executive director for library planning was appointed to direct and coordinate the library planning process.

This responsibility involved overseeing the writing of a plan for future development.

Dozens of staff personnel researched the history of the University and its libraries, and gathered and analyzed data on library users and their information needs, circulation procedures, loan methods and reference services.

Personnel also developed computer models and formulas for facilities planning and book acquisitions, and explored the feasibility of various automation projects.

Input came from numerous administrators, librarians, faculty members and staff.

In July 1977, the Office of the Executive Director of Universitywide Library Planning issued *The University of California Libraries: A Plan for Development, 1978–1988.*

The plan's major premise could be summed up in these words: "One university, one library."

The plan mapped out library evolution at UC over the next 10 years, from capital projects, to acquisitions, to access, to establishment of the regional storage facilities.

	Prototype Catalog	MELVYL System
Number of records	733,412 representing 1.3 million holdings	Over 6.6 million titles, representing over 13 million holdings
Contents	Book titles only	Books, periodicals, audiovisuals, computer files, maps, music scores and recordings, videos, archives and manuscripts, dissertations, and government documents.
Contributors	Nine UC campuses Hastings Law Library Lawrence Berkeley Lab	All UC and affiliated libraries California State Library California Academy of Sciences Center for Research Libraries
Number of databases	1	7
Number of indexes	10	27
Number of commands	19	27
Total number of searches in one week	No stats available	Over 500,000 (in November 1991)
Number of terminals	100	Over 600 in campus libraries; indeterminate number through dial-up and internet access
Access to remote systems	None	30 remote systems

In addition, the plan was the first step in the funding, development and implementation of the Universitywide MELVYL online union catalog.

Although implementation of library automation at the Universitywide level generally proceeded according to the plan, changes in available technology and campus needs raised new issues.

In February 1986, a Universitywide Library Automation Review Committee was appointed to assess the significance of such changes.

In its report the committee addressed the importance of campus systems, campus flexibility and responsibility, Universitywide library policy, Universitywide access, and the development of a complete Universitywide database.

The committee found that no campus had achieved full automation of library operations and services.

It noted that deficiencies in campus automation could threaten UC's competitive position as a major library resource.

In the committee's words, "university libraries throughout the country are now installing automated systems, and users of research collections are even now coming to expect the advantages of automation . . .

"The University of California must meet this expectation if it is to maintain its leadership in instruction and research and to attract the best faculty and students."

The committee supported most existing library policies, noting that UC should build on existing policy and the considerable financial investments that the State of California and UC had made in library automation.

The committee recommended that automation be implemented in all campus libraries and that a Universitywide union catalog be maintained.

The report emphasized the following:

Users should be able to "use the same commands and procedures" for both campus and Universitywide systems, campus and Universitywide systems should support one another in case of system failures, and data should be updated and synchronized in both systems.

In addition, the report supported conversion of all library materials to machine-readable form.

Over the next six years, Universitywide library automation changed in response to many of the issues raised in the 1986 report.

Campuses created machine-readable records for 86 percent of their collections (as of July 1992), with some

Databases Available Through the MELVYL® System

As of 1992–93, databases available through the MELVYL system included:

1) The UC union catalog database of books, recordings, maps, etc.

2) The California Academic Libraries List of Serials (CALLS), which includes more than one million serials holdings from the following:

UC's nine campuses; the California State Library; the 19-campus California State University system; the Center for Research Libraries; the California Academy of Sciences; Stanford University; the University of Southern California; the Getty Center for the History of Art and the Humanities in Southern California.

3) The MELVYL MEDLINE database, a file of the National Library of Medicine's MEDLINE database, which includes more than six million article citations indexed from more than 4,000 health sciences journals from 1966 to the present.

4) The MELVYL Current Contents database, which contains more than 5.6 million article citations from more than 6,500 journals indexed by the Institute for Scientific Information.

5) The Magazine and Journal Articles Index, the Newspaper Articles Index, and the Computer Articles Index (the online equivalent of Expanded Academic Index, National Newspaper Index, and Computer Database, respectively).

Together, these contain more than three million article citations indexed from journals and newspapers by Information Access Company.

6) INSPEC, which contains more than four million citations in the fields of physics and electrical engineering. Citations are indexed by the Institution of Electrical Engineers from more than 4.200 journals and 1,000 conference proceedings, reports and books from 1969 to the present.

7) PsycINFO, which contains more than 840,000 citations indexed from more than 1,300 journals by the American Psychological Association.

8) ERIC, a database of educational materials collected by the Educational Resources Information Center of the U.S. Department of Education.

The database, which contains about 767,000 citations from 1966 to the present, is available through Stanford University as part of a reciprocal sharing agreement between Stanford and UC.

9) GeoRef, which contains more than 1.7 million citations indexed from more than 3,500 journals, conference papers, government publications and other materials by the American Geological Institute. This database also is available through Stanford University as part of the reciprocal agreement.

campuses actually converting up to 100 percent of their holdings.

Campuses also automated their circulation and acquisition functions, and many installed local online catalogs.

Library Automation in the Office of the President increased access to information resources by adding new article databases to the MELVYL system and opening connections to library catalogs throughout the world.

The original network created for the MELVYL catalog expanded and evolved into a multipurpose, high-speed network for the entire University.

Today, the University's Library Automation unit continues to explore new information resources and new ways to access information for the UC community.

In keeping with a goal of the 1986 report, it is designing a system based on the Z39.50 protocol for computer-based information retrieval to allow patrons to search distant catalogs using familiar commands.

It also is conducting experiments in making full text available through the catalog, and allowing users to request documents electronically from library document delivery services.

New features are added regularly and old features are enhanced to meet the needs and expectations of library patrons.

In summary, information access remains central to UC's mission of promoting education and research. Everyone involved knows that UC's continuing exploration of the frontiers of library automation will help it remain competitive in an age in which information represents a highly potent force.

MELVYL is a registered trademark of The Regents of the University of California. The following are also registered trademarks or service marks: Computer Database, Expanded Academic Index and National Newspaper Index (Information Access Company); Current Contents (Institute for Scientific Information, Inc.); MEDLINE (National Library of Medicine); and PsycINFO (American Psychological Association).

REFERENCES: Office of the Executive Director of Universitywide Library Planning. *The University of California Libraries: A Plan for Development, 1978–1988.* (Berkeley: University of California, 1977); Library Automation Review Committee. *Library Automation in the University of California, 1987–1992.* (Berkeley: University of California, 1986); Office of the Associate Vice President—Academic Affairs and Office of the Associate Vice President—Information Systems and Administrative Services. *Guidelines for Coordinating Library Automation in the University of California.* (Oakland: University of California, 1989).

Also, "In-Depth: University of California MELVYL," Parts 1 and 2. *Information Technology and Libraries:* 1:4, 2:1 (December 1982 and March 1983); "Special Section: Happy Birthday to MELVYL," Parts 1, 2 and 3. *Information Technology and Libraries* 11.2; 3, 4 (June, September and December 1992); Mary Jean Moore. "Also Present at the Creation." *DLA Bulletin* 12.1 (Spring 1992), pp. 12–23; information and handouts, Library Automation, Office of the President.

CROSS-REFERENCES: Libraries; Telecommunications.

MESA (Mathematics, Engineering, Science Achievement Program) is an intersegmental program of the University. It is a partnership between California public schools, universities and private industry.

MESA provides students with academic workshops and peer tutoring, career counseling, professional mentors, leadership workshops—all the educational enrichment, experience and practical help they need to prepare for university-level programs.

The program reports to Student Academic Services in the Office of the President and is housed at the Lawrence Hall of Science.

Since the year it was formed, MESA has become a national model.

In 1968, a Berkeley engineering professor, a secondary school science teacher and other professionals shared their concerns about the small proportion of engineers from historically underrepresented minority groups, African American, Latino American and American Indian students.

These groups, they found, constituted 15 percent of the nation's population.

Based on their observation of student preparation and understanding of the requirements to successfully compete in the engineering environment at Cal, the MESA project was formed in 1970.

At that time, 25 students enrolled in additional MESA enrichment classes at Oakland Technical High School.

Recognizing that preparation for these science-related careers should begin early, MESA's founders had designed a program encouraging minority-group students to take the college-preparatory courses they need to major in mathematics, engineering and the physical sciences at the university level.

Today, MESA works with underrepresented minorities in elementary and secondary schools, community colleges and baccalaureate degree granting institutions, serving nearly 17,000 students.

Pre-College Program

In the pre-college program, about 11,500 students receive MESA services, such as academic workshops, counseling, career development, tutoring, field trips and scholarship awards. They participate in many hands-on science and math activities which supplement their in-class learning.

Almost 80 percent of MESA's students go to college after they graduate from high school, compared with 57 percent of all California high school graduates.

Students' activities are coordinated at the school site by math and science teachers who act as MESA Advisors. They work with MESA Center Directors who are housed on college campuses in schools of engineering. In 1991–1992, 253 schools representing 20 school districts were served in the pre-college program.

MESA Minority Engineering Program

The college program, called the Minority Engineering Program, involves about 5,500 college students at public and private university campuses who participate in activities such as study sessions, summer internships and counseling.

These students are clustered in key introductory course, i.e., calculus, physics and chemistry. They participate in academic excellence workshops based on a model developed by Uri Treisman, former UC Berkeley faculty member.

The 23 campuses involved include UC, California State University and private institutions such as University of the Pacific and the University of Southern California.

Community College Program

Over the past several years, several corporations, private and federal agencies have shown significant interest in providing a better mechanism for the matriculation of underrepresented students to 4-year institutions.

During the past year, five Community Colleges have sustained MESA programs on their campus, one, focusing on engineering students exclusively.

In 1993–1994, 11 Community Colleges will be supported, many with Proposition 98 funding, ensuring an even larger number of California's historically underrepresented students complete baccalaureate degrees in the sciences, mathematics and engineering.

In addition to assisting students in their education, MESA has a number of other educational goals, as well.

These include parent participation in the education process and increased awareness of mathematics-based career opportunities.

Teacher training in mathematics and the sciences, as well as improved teacher morale also are critical to the educational achievement of students.

For example, MESA is involved in the development of a mathematics curriculum and is supportive of the Robert Moses Algebra Project in Los Angeles and Oakland.

With the continued support of all of MESA's "stakeholders," the program plans to continue providing enhanced academic support to its students leading to an increased number of college graduates in mathematics-based fields.

REFERENCES: Annual reports, newsletter and additional information from MESA.

CROSS-REFERENCES: All subjects related to Education.

MICRO (Microelectronics Innovation and Computer Research Opportunities) was established in 1981 by the State of California to support "innovative research in microelectronics technology, its applications in computer information sciences, and its necessary antecedents in other physical science disciplines."

The objective of the MICRO program is to help the California electronics and computer industries maintain their leadership by expanding relevant research and graduate student training and education at the University.

Under the research part of the program, UC faculty members submit proposals for research projects which will be at the forefront of technology and which may lead to products some years in the future.

The State and industry jointly fund the research projects. The UC funds are supplemented by industrial contributions on a project-by-project basis.

In carrying out their research, UC faculty members maintain a close liaison with the industrial donors. Each faculty member is responsible for obtaining a prior commitment from an industrial firm to support at least half the cost of the project.

Graduate student education is supported both through research assistantships funded by the projects and through fellowships granted directly to students in the fields covered by MICRO.

The MICRO program is under the overall guidance of a Policy Board of nine members consisting of three representatives each from industry, the State Government and the University.

The operation of the program is conducted by an Executive Committee consisting of six faculty members, one each from six of the participating UC campuses.

MICRO has almost quadrupled in the level of State funding from its inception in 1981–82. This growth is seen as well in other aspects such as industrial contributions, number of participating industries and the number of research projects funded each year.

In addition, funds earmarked for the award of fellowships have steadily increased, from approximately $100,000 in 1981–82 to nearly $800,000 in 1992–93.

By the beginning of 1993, it was clear that MICRO continued to be a very strong program, despite the economic recession.

The operation of the MICRO program is based on the philosophy that the choice of topics for research, as well as the garnering of support from industry for the proposed research, should be made by the individual faculty member.

This approach is based on the belief that the researcher and his or her technical counterpart in industry are best able to judge what topics are ripe for investigation.

In making their judgments, they take into account the faculty researcher's expertise and the interests of industry and its willingness to support the project.

The Executive Committee determines the merits of the proposal based on a peer-review process before a funding decision is made.

After the proposal has been funded, the faculty member supervises and participates in the research, while maintaining a close liaison with the supporting industry.

The program has been well received by industry. It also has proven to be one of the most successful programs for linking State government, industry and the University in support of advanced research and education in high technology.

The three constituent segments of the MICRO program benefit equally.

The University obtains urgently needed financial support for its research and educational missions. The faculty members and students are exposed to the technical issues important to industry, and they gain access to expensive equipment and facilities available only in the sponsoring industry.

In addition, industry gets fresh, innovative ideas from the research and recruits graduate students who are well trained in the frontiers of microelectronics and computer science.

As a result of MICRO, industrial sponsors have reported unprecedented, fruitful cooperative efforts with University researchers, leading to interaction between industry and UC in ways that would not have been possible under other circumstances.

REFERENCES: MICRO Progress Report, December 1992, Academic Affairs, Office of the President.
CROSS-REFERENCES: Economic, Social and Cultural Impact of the University; Research Achievements; Technology Transfer.

Missions of the University: The University's fundamental missions are teaching, research and public service.

Undergraduate instructional programs are available to all eligible California high school graduates who wish to attend the University.

The Master Plan for Higher Education in California has designated UC as the primary State-supported academic agency for research, with exclusive jurisdiction in public higher education over instruction in law, as well as graduate instruction in medicine, dentistry and veterinary medicine.

Sole authority also is vested in the University to award doctoral degrees in all fields, except that joint doctoral degrees with the California State University may be awarded.

The Master Plan was most recently reviewed beginning in 1985. A first review was by a blue-ribbon citizen's committee. Later it was reviewed by a Joint Committee of the Legislature.

Subsequently, legislation has reaffirmed the University's missions.

REFERENCES: "1993–94 Budget for Current Operations," Office of the President.
CROSS-REFERENCES: All sections relating to education, public and community service, research, and teaching and instruction.

N

Naming University Properties, Programs and Facilities: In 1993, the Regents approved the current policy on the naming of University properties, programs and facilities.

The policy states that the Regents "retain authority for naming University land reserves, buildings, major centers of activities and other highly visible properties, and major or multicampus programs or facilities.

"Naming of streets and roads, portions of buildings, small outdoor areas and other minor properties, and single-campus programs or facilities may be approved by the President."

Each proposal for naming an individual shall be considered on its merits. The following criteria shall apply.

• Proposal for naming for an individual, in recognition of a gift

1) No commitment for naming shall be made prior to Regental or Presidential approval of the proposed name

2) In reviewing requests for approval of naming for a donor or for a person whose name is proposed by a donor, consideration shall be given to:

a) the significance of the proposed gift as it relates to the realization and/or success of the project or to the enhancement of the project's usefulness to the University;

b) the urgency of need for the project or for support funds for the project;

c) the eminence of the individual whose name is proposed; and

d) the individual's relationship to the University.

UC Buildings, Channel Islands and Scottish Regions

Residence halls at UC campuses usually are named after two categories of individuals.

One includes important donors. These include distinguished faculty or administrators whose careers have included active concern with student welfare.

However, the names of some residence halls at UC are a bit more exotic.

For example, residence halls at Santa Barbara have been named after the Channel Islands along the southern California coast.

And those at Riverside have been named after Scottish regions, in keeping with UCR's identification as "the Highlanders."

---

3) The gift shall be in an amount that will either fund the total cost of the project to be named or provide funding for that portion of the total cost which would not have been available from any other source (such as federal or state funds or appropriations, student fees, bond issues), the latter to constitute a significant portion of the total cost of the project to be named, as determined on the merits of each individual case

• Proposal for naming in honor of an individual, no gift involved

1) A proposed honoree shall have achieved distinction in one or more of the following ways:

a) while serving the University in an academic capacity, demonstrated such high scholarly distinction as to have earned a national or international reputation in the individual's field(s) of specialization;

b) while serving the University in an important administrative capacity, rendered distinguished service to the University warranting recognition of the individual's exceptional contributions to the welfare of the University;

c) although not having served the University as an academician or administrator, contributed in truly exceptional ways to the welfare of the institution or achieved such unique distinction as to warrant recognition.

2) If an individual has served the University in an academic or important administrative capacity, a proposal shall not be made for naming in honor of the individual:

a) prior to or less than one year after retirement, nor while the individual is still involved with the University in a decision-making capacity; or

b) within one year after the person's death.

REFERENCES: Regents' Policy on Naming University Properties, Programs, and Facilities, approved July 16, 1993.

CROSS-REFERENCES: Bond Issues; Budgets; Buildings; Foundations; Private Support.

Native American Education and the Sherman Intertribal Academy: In 1988, a milestone was reached in the history of Native American education.

That year, the University joined with other academic institutions in the development of a college preparatory school for American Indians.

At that time, UC's Irvine and Riverside chancellors signed a letter of commitment to aid in the development of the Sherman Intertribal Academy.

The academy enrolled its first class of freshmen (9th graders) in fall 1988, as an adjunct to the Sherman Indian High School in Riverside.

In 1988, the Sherman Indian High School was one of 184 Bureau of Indian Affairs (BIA) schools in the U.S., of which six were off-reservation boarding schools.

It was the only Indian boarding school in California and the only one to develop a college preparatory school like the Sherman Intertribal Academy.

Currently, it draws its students from five southwestern states. The high school had 459 students enrolled in 1988 in its basic high school curriculum.

Indicative of the progress made in curriculum and instruction at Sherman is the fall 1992 enrollment of 265 students in higher level mathematics classes (Algebra I and beyond).

The 1992–93 academic year also saw a 150 percent increase in student participants in the Gifted and Talented Education program (GATE) over the prior year. Sherman is now becoming a magnet school for GATE students.

Establishment of the Sherman Intertribal Academy followed approval of its advanced placement concept by the U.S. Office of Indian Education.

Development of the academy was intended to help increase academic success for American Indian students by opening up opportunities for them at colleges and universities like UC, where Native Americans traditionally have been underrepresented.

For example, in fall 1987, some 299 American Indians had enrolled as entering freshmen at UC (or one percent of the entering class), making a total of 810 in the UC system (or 0.7 percent of the entire student body).

While this was a small percentage, the enrollment of American Indians at UC still was nearly double that of 1980, when there were 483.

Kogee Thomas, co-director of the Office of Relations with Schools at UC Irvine and one of the leaders in helping to establish the Sherman Intertribal Academy, called the partnership between UC and the prep school "the most important development in American Indian education in 200 years."

She noted: "While some BIA schools specialize in vocational and occupational training or special education, none has focused on excellence in preparation for higher education."

The first American Indian treaty signed with the U.S. War Department in 1794 included an educational provision in its terms of agreement, she explained.

In later years, 119 treaties made between various tribes and the government contained educational provisions.

However, the approval of the Sherman Intertribal Academy was the first educational agreement of its kind to be recognized.

In 1987, the Sherman Indian High School had asked UC Irvine to help in the development of a curriculum plan for the new academy.

The UCI Academic Excellence Fellows, a body consisting of high school principals, UCI administrators and county education specialists, were called upon to assist.

The group developed a plan stressing the importance of establishing a curriculum that would include all courses needed for UC admission, so that all Sherman Academy graduates could be eligible to attend the University.

UCI administrators also helped develop grant proposals, and UC Riverside staff assisted in recruiting freshmen students to the academy and in developing a brochure on the school.

REFERENCES: News release, April 22, 1988, University Relations, Office of the President; Sherman Intertribal Academy brochure.

CROSS-REFERENCES: Affirmative Action.

An Important Bit of History And the Sherman Academy

A bit of history underscores the importance of the Sherman Academy.

The first American Indian treaty signed with the U.S. War Department in 1794 included a provision to establish links between Indian secondary schools and higher education.

In later years, 119 treaties made between various tribes and the government contained similar educational provisions.

However, because government and higher education didn't provide much encouragement, Indian education came to be called "a national tragedy" and "a national challenge."

The development of the Sherman Academy, with UC's help, is considered one of the most important developments in American Indian education in nearly 200 years.

Natural Reserve System: High in the Sierra, a snowshoe-clad chemist collects water samples from an ice-covered lake to measure acid precipitation.

Two hundred miles to the west, on a tiny island off California's central coast, biologists observe the mating strategies of a bull elephant seal.

Meanwhile, in the Mojave Desert, students in a course on passive solar architecture discuss energy-efficient designs for remote research facilities.

What do these far-flung scholars have in common?

All are working on sites in the University's Natural Reserve System (NRS).

The Natural Reserve System is a Universitywide academic support unit, central both to UC's teaching and research goals and to California's environmental future.

The overall mission of the NRS is to contribute to the understanding and wise management of the Earth and its natural systems by supporting university-level teaching, research and public service at protected natural areas throughout the state.

NRS lands represent a cross section of California's natural habitats. They are reserved for research and instructional use by faculty and students from all UC campuses and many other educational institutions.

The Natural Reserve System includes more than 150,000 acres in 32 reserve sites across 12 ecological regions, all protected from public intrusion and habitat degradation. More than 500 faculty regularly use NRS reserves for research and teaching. Currently, students in more than 150 UC courses regularly use the reserves.

These outdoor classrooms and laboratories offer unparalleled opportunities for both short- and long-term study of a wide range of ecological, environmental and natural resource management issues critical to the state and the nation.

Taken together, the sites represent a distinctive subset of California's ecosystems, stretching from the coast across the mountains to the deserts. No other university system in the world encompasses such a valuable set of natural lands.

However, as the state's population continues to swell, many of these ecosystems are threatened, and various species are endangered. At the same time, California's natural resources are becoming scarcer, and global environmental problems seem ever more ominous.

Consequently, the value of the NRS continues to grow, helping to ensure California's environmental health for generations to come.

Established by the Regents in 1965, the NRS has for many years been administered by the Division of Agriculture and Natural Resources (DANR) in the Office of the President.

The Division has been strengthening its research and extension programs in natural resources, specifically in integrated resource management. The NRS staff is playing a key role in this process, and by so doing, it is becoming more fully integrated into DANR programs than ever before.

The campuses also play a key role.

For example, each reserve is assigned to a campus, which is responsible for its daily operations, as well as for the design and conduct of research and instruction programs at the reserve. These responsibilities are coordinated with the systemwide NRS office.

An NRS Universitywide Advisory Committee, consisting of both faculty and staff, works closely with the NRS director in formulating systemwide programs and plans.

In 1989, UC's president and DANR's vice president appointed an external review committee to develop a consensus paper that would identify the needs of the system, set its direction and guide its development.

The consensus paper became the *Final Report of the Natural Reserve System Steering Committee on Long-Range Planning*. It proposed NRS development through full integration into UC's research, teaching and public outreach programs.

The committee's vision was that the reserve system would one day be part of the educational and research experience offered to all UC students.

This fox, an endangered species, is protected and studied at an NRS site.   Photo by Dawnn Menendez

The NRS long-range plan (LRP) was completed and widely distributed in 1991 and presented to the Regents in 1992.

The LRP advances many specific recommendations, both functional and fiscal, to help the system realize its full potential. Several of these recommendations have already been completely or partially implemented.

For example, a mission statement has been adopted, the advisory committees have been reconstituted, an academic director has been appointed, and land holdings have not been expanded further without consideration for their stable financial support.

By early 1993, the Natural Reserve System was poised to continue a number of other tasks, including creation of an accurate inventory, database and monitoring systems, as well as to seek physical development.

However, at a time when answers to questions about the state's environmental future have been desperately needed, financial support for the reserves was limited.

For example, the NRS had only 50 percent of the recurring funds needed to operate the system at a reasonable level. Because UC's budget declined, campus fiscal support for reserves either was cut or, at best, remained stable.

Therefore, as 1993 proceeded, the Natural Reserve System focused its efforts on outside fundraising, while continuing to seek ways to balance and increase funding from University sources in order to follow through on many of its plans.

In particular, the NRS directed its energies toward three major efforts:

• It was increasing private funding for undergraduate course use and research opportunities at the reserves.

• It was working to create and maintain a readily accessible reserve database.

This effort to collect and widely disseminate information of interest to reserve users began a decade earlier with the creation of the NRS Publications Program and the startup of a biannual newsletter entitled the *NRS Transect* and an ongoing NRS reserve brochures series.

A new initiative developed at the systemwide NRS office has been the creation of geographic information systems (GISs) for the reserves. A GIS is a set of interactive, geo-referenced maps and data files that instructors, students, researchers and managers can use to obtain information, generate questions and test ideas.

• The systemwide NRS office also has initiated the development of new courses to use at the reserves, following discussions among select Universitywide advisory committees.

As the NRS community of scientists, staff and students look to the future, they seem guided by the statement of philosophy that appeared in a recent UN environmental report. The statement read, in part: "We have not inherited the earth from our fathers, we are borrowing it for our children."

In heeding these words, the Natural Reserve System will continue in the years ahead to provide valuable opportunities for scientific research and training essential to the understanding and wise management of California's irreplaceable environmental heritage.

REFERENCES: NRS Annual Reports and related publications.

CROSS-REFERENCES: All sections relating to teaching and instruction, public and community service, and research.

Sites in the University's Natural Reserve System

The following is a complete list of Natural Reserve System sites, as of January 1993, organized by the UC campus that administers each site.

BERKELEY

(1) Chickering American River Reserve

Placer County (1,699 acres).

Located in the subalpine headwaters basin of the north fork of the American River. Has diverse topography, soil and moisture regimes on sedimentary, igneous, and metamorphic substrates. Supports approximately 1,000 plant species and a variety of large mammals.

(2) Hastings Natural History Reservation

Monterey County (2,253 acres).

Contains a representative sample of California's interior coast ranges, with annual and perennial grasslands, oak woodlands, chaparral, and running streams. Hs 620 vascular plant species and 166 bird species. Is noted for a history covering more than 50 years of research on vertebrate ecology and oak woodland biology. Important research on native grassland restoration in progress.

(3) Northern California Coast Range Preserve (NCCRP)

Mendocino County (7,520 acres).

Is one of the most diverse sites, with 26 terrestrial and 4 aquatic habitat types. Location is along a belt of highly deformed, well-defined coastal ridges cut by the south fork of the Eel River. Contains the largest virgin Douglas-fir community left in the state, as well as four undisturbed watersheds. Is part of the UNESCO California Coast Ranges Biosphere Reserve Cluster. Land currently owned by The Nature Conservancy is being deeded to the University.

(4) Hans Jenny Pygmy Forest Reserve

Mendocino County (70 acres).

Supports elfin forests of endemic pygmy cypress, stand of bishop pine, and unusual evergreen shrub species on highly podsolized, old marine terrace soils.

DAVIS

(5) Bodega Marine Reserve

Sonoma County (416 acres).

Located on graniticx peninsula separated from mainland by the San Andreas fault zone. Contains broad range of coastal habitats, including harbor mudflats, dunefields, coastal uplands, and exposed and protected sandy beach and rocky shore. Is adjacent to UC's Bodega Marine Laboratory and the Bodega Marine Life Refuge. Geographic information system (GIS) available for research and teaching.

(6) Eagle Lake Field Station

Lassen County (62 acres, adjacent to large tracts of BLM land).

Contains very diverse habitats along shores of a highly productive, 30,000 acre oligotrophic lake, which is a remnant of Pleistocene Lake Lahantan. Located at the juncture of four major geologic provinces: Sierra Nevada, Cascades, Great Basin, and Modoc Plateau. Harbors more than 180 bird and 70 mammal species. Owned by California State University, Chico, and jointly operated by the University.

(7) Jepson Prairie Reserve

Solano County (1,566 acres).

Contains one of the best remaining vernal pool habitats in California, native bunchgrass prairie, and numerous endemic species of plants and animals. GIS being constructed to aid the management of sensitive species.

(8) Donald and Sylvia McLaughlin Natural Reserve

Napa and Lake counties (330 acres).

Region of highly altered marine sedimentary rocks, including serpentine colonized by unusual plant communities containing many endemic species. Woodlands, grasslands, and shrublands possess rare animal species. Aquatic systems also present. Excellent database and monitoring systems present.

(9) Quail Ridge Reserve
Napa County (2,000 acres).

An isolated peninsula projecting into Lake Berryessa, with outstanding examples of diverse, native grasses and oaks, including oak hybrids. An important link in the series of reserves in the Putah Creek drainage of the Vaca Mountains, which includes the McLaughlin, Stebbins, and Putah Creek (campus) reserves.

(10) Stebbins Cold Canyon Reserve
Solano and Napa counties (579 acres).

Offers a representative sample of inner coast range canyon, encompassing high diversity of slope, exposure, and moisture regimes. Has abundant and varied flora, including oaks, mixed evergreen forest, and aquatic species.

IRVINE
(11) Burns Piñon Ridge Reserve
San Bernardino County (306 acres).

Is a south-facing desert slope on rugged, granitic terrain in the transition zone between Sonoran, Mojavean, and Transverse Range floras. Contains Mojavean pinyon-juniper woodland with elements of Joshua tree woodland and desert dry-wash woodland.

(12) San Joaquin Freshwater Marsh Reserve
Orange County (202 acres).

Contains low-lying wetlands in an ancient river-cut channel at the head of a coastal estuary. Is located along the Pacific Flyway. Harbors 212 bird species, more than 50 percent of which are migratory. A GIS has been constructed to aid restoration and management activities.

LOS ANGELES
(13) Santa Monica Mountains Reserve
Los Angeles County (760 acres).

Is a diverse, relatively pristine segment of the Santa Monica Mountains. Harbors varied flora, including one endangered species, that comprise chaparral and coastal sage communities. High energy stream systems available for study.

RIVERSIDE
(14) Box Springs Reserve
Riverside County (160 acres).

Contains rugged granitic terrain in a transition zone between coastal sage scrub and chamise chaparral. Harbors two listed species.

(15) Philip L. Boyd Deep Canyon Desert Research Center
Riverside County (16,461 acres).

Is a large reserve containing a major portion of an entire drainage system from montane forest to Sonoran desert on the north flank of the Santa Rosa Mountains. Deep Canyon transect harbors 42 reptile, 210 bird, and 46 mammal species, including bighorn sheep. Is part of the UNESCO Mojave and Colorado Deserts Biosphere Reserve Cluster.

(16) Emerson Oaks Reserve
Riverside County (215 acres).

Offers excellent examples of Southern Californian coastal sage scrub, chaparral, and oak woodland habitats, with several permanent springs, located along steep elevational gradients.

(17) Granite Mountains Reserve
San Bernardino County (8,920 acres).

Is an isolated mountain mass in the eastern Mojave Desert, with creosote bush scrub, enriched desert scrub, pinyon-juniper woodland, sagebrush scrub, and yucca woodland. Contains permanent springs, rich archaeological sites, a herd of bighorn sheep, and more than 400 vascular plant species, including six listed taxa.

(18) James San Jacinto Mountains Reserve
Riverside County (29 acres).

Contains a mixed conifer and oak forest with alder/willow montane riparian woodland and a small anthropogenic lake. Additional desert and montane sites (900+ acres) within 30 miles of the reserve. Oasis de los Osos, a satellite reserve, is located nearby, at the base of the San Jacinto Mountains, north of Palm Springs, and is a mixture of desert and coastal species.

(19) Motte Rimrock Reserve
Riverside County (622 acres).

Located on a low granitic plateau at the western edge of Perris Valley. Contains rich archaeological resources, including some of best-preserved pictographs in Southern California. Has mostly coastal sage scrub, with a suite of endangered and candidate species, but also occasional seeps and springs. Contains permanent plots and transects for fire-succession studies, as well as a GIS.

(20) Sacramento Mountains Reserve
San Bernardino County (591 acres).

Located on a south-facing rocky desert slope. Associated bench and alluvial slope feature is moderately developed desert pavement and desert varnish with exceptionally dense stand of jumping cholla cactus.

SAN DIEGO
(21) Dawson Los Monos Canyon Reserve
San Diego County (219 acres).

Consists of young east/west-trending, stream-cut valley through coastal terrace/foothill valley province of Southern California. Contains perennial stream and springs, with southern coastal oak woodland, coastal sage scrub, and south coastal mixed chaparral.

(22) Elliott Chaparral Reserve
San Diego County (107 acres).

Located on a flat, narrow ridge of Kearney Mesa, bounded on the north and south by broad, flat-bottomed valleys and associated arroyos. Supports chamise chaparral intermixed with elements of coastal sage scrub.

(23) Kendall-Frost Mission Bay Marsh Reserve
San Diego County (16 acres).

Preserves the last remnant of Mission Bay salt marshlands. Contains open water, subtidal mudflats, and low silty salt marsh cut by well-developed tidal channels. Harbors 107 species of birds, including two listed taxa. A GIS is available for research, teaching, and management use.

(24) Scripps Coastal Reserve
San Diego County (943 acres).

Encompasses coastal mesa and canyon, sea cliffs, exposed sandy beach, open water, intertidal zone, and nearshore continental shelf at La Jolla Bay. Includes tributary slopes of Scripps and La Jolla submarine canyons. Harbors a wide variety of intertidal and benthic invertebrates, as well as 90 fish species.

SANTA BARBARA
(25) Carpinteria Salt Marsh Reserve
Santa Barbara County (120 acres).

Part of south coastal estuary at the base of the Santa Ynez Mountains. Includes salt marsh, tidal channels and mudflats, transitional and high marsh, exposed sandy beach, and offshore rocky reef. Harbors endangered plants and birds. A GIS is being developed to aid marsh management and study.

(26) Coal Oil Point Natural Reserve
Santa Barbara County (117 acres).

Encompasses coastal terrace and seasonally flooded tidal lagoon-mudflat estuarine system, featuring largely undisturbed coastal dunes an experimental vernal pools.

(27) Santa Cruz Island Reserve
Santa Barbara County (54,488 acres).

Largest, most topographically and geologically diverse of the California Channel Islands, including 15 geologic formations with coastal terraces and major fault system; supports woodlands, annual grasslands, chaparral, and mixed evergreen forests. Harbors more than 500 plant species, including 46 species endemic to northern Channel Islands, 165 bird species, and diverse bat fauna. Contains well-preserved archaeological sites. A GIS is being developed.

(28) Valentine Eastern Sierra Reserve: Sierra Nevada Aquatic Research Laboratory (SNARL)
Mono County (51 acres).

Located on an alluvial plain at the eastern base of Mt. Morrison, on the edge of the Sierra Nevada Great Basin. Encompasses the former U.S. Fish and Wildlife Service laboratory (established 1935), including chemistry and radio-isotope laboratories, controlled-environment chambers, a snow science lab, and a series of manmade, experimental stream channels. Site is also the center for research on Mono Lake and the high Sierra Nevada.

(29) Valentine Eastern Sierra Reserve: Valentine Camp
Mono County (136 acres).

Contains an unusually diverse sample of eastern Sierra Nevada located in climatic ecotone between the sagebrush desert of Great Basin and the coniferous forests of the Sierra Nevada. Relatively minor changes in topography, exposure, soil, and moisture regimes have produced strongly differentiated plant communities, including 247 species of vascular plants, of which 94 percent are native. Outstanding meadow and stream systems.

SANTA CRUZ
(30) Año Nuevo Island Reserve
San Mateo County (8 acres).

Encompasses Miocene shale and marine terrace island, with associated low rocky islets and intertidal shelf of gently dipping dune deposits. Serves as breeding grounds for elephant seals, Stellar sea lions, California sea lions, and harbor seals, with occasional fur seals and sea otters. Contains sea bird nesting colonies and historic buildings.

(31) Landels-Hill Big Creek Reserve
Monterey County (3,848 acres).

Contains diverse habitats, including coast redwoods, coastal chaparral, mixed evergreen forest, oak woodland, mixed conifer stands, and annual grasslands. Offers perennial streams and rocky shoreline with access beach. Unusual mixture of species, including many endemic, disjunct, or near limit of their range. Rich archaeological resources. Is part of the UNESCO California Coast Ranges Biosphere Reserve Cluster. A GIS has been developed for research use.

(32) Younger Lagoon Reserve
Santa Cruz County (26 acres).

Contains a small coastal wetland on an open coast immediately north of Monterey Bay, including a Y-shaped lagoon, barrier sandbar, and backdune pickleweed flat, steep bluffs with dense coastal scrub, pocket beach, and dense willow thickets. Supports some 217 resident and migratory water birds.

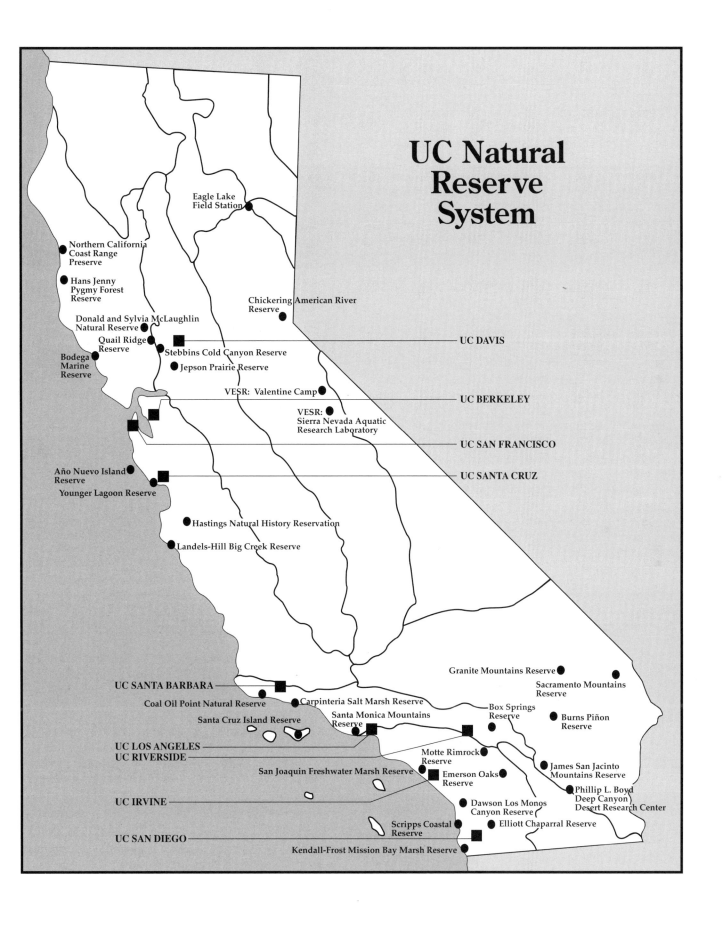

UC Natural Reserve System

Eagle Lake
Field Station

Northern California
Coast Range
Preserve

Hans Jenny
Pygmy Forest
Reserve

Donald and Sylvia McLaughlin
Natural Reserve

Quail Ridge
Reserve

Bodega
Marine
Reserve

Chickering American River
Reserve

Stebbins Cold Canyon Reserve

Jepson Prairie Reserve

UC DAVIS

VESR: Valentine Camp

VESR:
Sierra Nevada Aquatic
Research Laboratory

UC BERKELEY

UC SAN FRANCISCO

Año Nuevo Island
Reserve

Younger Lagoon Reserve

UC SANTA CRUZ

Hastings Natural History Reservation

Landels-Hill Big Creek Reserve

Granite Mountains Reserve

Sacramento Mountains
Reserve

UC SANTA BARBARA

Coal Oil Point Natural Reserve

Santa Cruz Island Reserve

Carpinteria Salt Marsh Reserve

Santa Monica Mountains
Reserve

Box Springs
Reserve

Burns Piñon
Reserve

UC LOS ANGELES
UC RIVERSIDE

San Joaquin Freshwater Marsh Reserve

Motte Rimrock
Reserve

Emerson Oaks
Reserve

James San Jacinto
Mountains Reserve

UC IRVINE

Dawson Los Monos
Canyon Reserve

Phillip L. Boyd
Deep Canyon
Desert Research Center

Scripps Coastal
Reserve

Elliott Chaparral Reserve

UC SAN DIEGO

Kendall-Frost Mission Bay Marsh Reserve

O

Oceanography and Marine Sciences draw researchers from a variety of disciplines in the basic sciences, from biology and geology to mathematics and physics.

Oceanographers and marine scientists at a number of the University's campuses and at other academic institutions are conducting studies that are critical to knowing more about such concerns as natural resources, food, energy, national security, marine biotechnology, and the environment.

Specifically, some scientists are examining the use of oceans as dumping grounds for waste products; many are looking at the relationship of this use to global warming or global change. Other researchers are studying marine biodiversity, food chain ecology, and environmental degradation.

Still other scientists are studying the patterns of ocean currents and circulation to help determine if safe retrieval of mineral and energy resources on the ocean floor is feasible. In addition, a number of investigators are looking at environmental impacts on coastal areas.

Some of UC's scientific achievements are noted in the sections on research which are found elsewhere in this book, as well as the section on Sea Grant.

Specific campuses where research in oceanography and marine sciences is conducted are indicated in those particular sections. Additional details may be obtained from each campus.

UC research goes on everywhere, even in the ocean's depths.

Scripps Institution of Oceanography: Achievements

Scripps is the oldest oceanographic institution in the U.S.

It was the first to offer doctoral training programs in oceanography.

Since the 1950s, Scripps' vessels have steamed more than four million nautical miles in pursuing oceanographic research.

Research achievements have been many. For example, Scripps' scientists have:

• Discovered the deep-scattering and thermal inversion layers of the oceans, two features critical to submarine operations and underwater warfare.

• Made the first measurements of atmospheric carbon dioxide and confirmed the rise of CO_2 in the atmosphere from pre-industrial levels.

(These continuing measurements are the basis upon which all current analysis of increasing CO_2 are founded.)

• Developed a host of oceanographic tools and instruments.

(These have included the torque balanced wire rope, expendable bathythermographs, ocean bottom seismometers, and many others. Among the ocean devices is FLIP, for Floating Instrument Platform, a 355-foot-long buoy that rises to a vertical position in the water.)

• Discovered the mid-Pacific mountain range and numerous other seafloor features throughout the Pacific Ocean.

• Explained and confirmed aspects of seafloor spreading and the theory of plate tectonics through drilling operations of the Deep Sea Drilling Project, a 25-year program of collecting deep-sea sediment cores.

252

- Conducted the first major U.S. oceanographic expeditions into the Pacific Ocean, including MidPac Expedition and the expeditions of the International Geophysical Year, known as GEOSECS.

- Developed reliable forecasting techniques for El Niño, a tropical Pacific air-sea phenomenon that affects weather worldwide.

- Found the deepest known part of the ocean, the Challenger Deep, located in the western Pacific.

- Developed a technique to utilize mussels and oysters to monitor a wide range of pollutants, including heavy metals and pesticides, in the marine environment.

- Discovered a chemical compound, manoalide, from a marine sponge that is being used by more than 20 companies as a tool for understanding the process of inflammation.

(For example, manoalide shows promise as a new way to treat the biochemical process that causes inflammation and pain.)

- Developed techniques of collecting satellite data on ocean temperatures and circulation and supplying that information to commercial fishermen to determine sites where ocean conditions would attract fishes of various kinds.

Office of the President: From the University's founding in 1868 until 1951, the president of the University directly supervised the campuses, overseeing business management, accounting, non-academic personnel functions and public information on the campuses.

Agriculture, public health, the graduate division and several research institutes were also considered statewide departments, outside the control of campus officers.

Robert Gordon Sproul, who served as UC president for 28 years (1930–58), divided his time among the campuses. He spent about half his time at Berkeley, a third at Los Angeles, and the remainder divided between the other campuses.

But as the University grew, it became increasingly difficult for the president to oversee all operations.

In 1951, the first chancellors were appointed at UCLA and Berkeley and chief campus officers were designated at the other campuses.

They had authority over all but statewide activities on their campuses, although Sproul kept his hand in campus affairs.

In 1958, the size of centralized administration staff was reduced. Many functions were placed under the chancellors, who were also given more authority over budget affairs and personnel actions.

The decentralization and reduction in Universitywide administrative staff continued through the first half of the 1960s, resulting in a greater autonomy for the campuses.

In the late 1970s and early 1980s, the size of the Universitywide headquarters began to grow in response to the increasing volume of state and federal laws and regulations in such areas as affirmative action and collective bargaining.

Through all these years, the headquarters had been alternately called Statewide, Universitywide or Systemwide Administration. In 1983, it was renamed the Office of the President.

As the 1990s proceed, further changes in the administrative structure of the Universitywide headquarters have been studied to determine the best means of meeting the increasingly complex demands facing UC during the remainder of the decade.

REFERENCES: *Centennial Record;* "A Historical Look at the Office of the President, *Intercom,* Newsletter for the Office of the President, October 1991; *The University of California 1868–1968* by Verne A. Stadtman.

Oral History is, as one scholar noted, "history out loud."

This is one way of describing a modern research technique for capturing and preserving first-hand accounts of important events in history through tape-recorded recollections of people who observed or participated in them.

These eyewitness accounts fill in gaps in the written record and make history come alive with personal and anecdotal material.

Such material illustrates how and why decisions are made, what factors motivate achievers, how individuals influence the course of history, and other information that may otherwise be lost to historians.

Recorded conversations of oral history interviews have proven of inestimable value to scholars. These conversations provide a distinctive view of major events or trends in the state, the West and the nation over the years, as recollected by leading public figures or well-placed observers.

Such interviews are extensively quoted in books, journals, magazines, monographs, dissertations and catalogs. The typescripts or audio- or videotapes also are used in developing exhibitions and in creating documentaries, multimedia presentations, television and films.

While specific procedures may vary from campus to campus, the following gives some sense of how an oral history is developed.

In determining subjects and selecting people to interview, an oral history office considers recommendations by many sources, within UC and community-wide. The office also consults with faculty advisers.

In addition to UC funding, many projects are supported by outside gifts and grants. With funds in hand, an office signs an agreement with each prospective interviewee to participate and release the material. The office then assigns a skilled interviewer with particular subject matter expertise.

Careful research precedes the interview, to elicit the most useful information. The interviews are unrehearsed, tape-recorded sessions of one to two hours in length, in a relaxed atmosphere. The narrator is encouraged to speak candidly.

An oral history interview may last one session or as many as 20 sessions. The tapes are transcribed verbatim.

The interviewee has the option to review a draft transcript and close any sensitive material for a specified period. Most interviewees, however, choose to allow immediate access.

After an interviewee's review and additions or clarifications are incorporated, the typescript is indexed, reproduced and bound.

The transcripts and tapes are placed in the special collections departments of UC campus libraries. Copies are made available to other research libraries nationwide. They are cataloged electronically on campus and on two national databases.

Regional oral history offices were established a number of years ago at Berkeley and Los Angeles, and since then UC's other campuses have developed important oral history programs of their own.

REFERENCES: Regional oral history informational material.

Citrus research is conducted at one of the University's ORUs. Research is described in the next section.

Organized Research Units: The growth of organized research at the University, as at other major academic research institutions in the U.S., expanded rapidly as a result of World War II.

This was a time when federal agencies began to invest heavily in university-based research.

A second period of expansion came about in the post-Sputnik era in the 1950s, after the Soviet Union had launched its first spacecraft ("sputnik," in Russian) before the U.S. was able to do so.

This immediate postwar federal support of research by the U.S. primarily benefitted the sciences.

By the 1960s, federal support for the humanities, arts and social sciences became significant. However, in the 1970s, federal support leveled off. Then in the 1980s, support picked up again, but slowed at the end of the decade.

The University benefitted from all this federal support, particularly with the growth of its Organized Research Units (ORUs) and Multicampus Research Units (MRUs).

Today, there are some 200 ORUs/MRUs at UC, reflecting the faculty's research excellence and their competitive success in winning federal contracts and grants.

The large number of ORUs/MRUs also reflect the commitment of the state government to finance organized research at UC.

ORUs and MRUs manage interdisciplinary research programs that cut across departmental, college, and in the case of MRUs, campus boundaries.

Although they do not administer courses, they contribute to graduate student training through involvement of such students in faculty research and through direct sponsoring of graduate student research.

In addition, with core budgetary support from the University, ORUs and MRUs leverage extramural funds from governmental agencies, private and corporate foundations, and industry.

Organized Research Units are established by the Regents to contribute to UC's general goals and to strengthen its interdisciplinary programs of research, teaching and public service.

ORUs frequently administer research projects when substantial extramural funds and extensive facilities are required in the support of interdisciplinary projects that cut across departmental, college and campus boundaries.

University research capabilities are not confined to ORUs, however.

There are faculty, student and staff research capabilities within UC's academic departments, University Extension courses, and professional schools and colleges.

Other research programs are administered through the Division of Agriculture and Natural Resources and the Office of Health Affairs in the Office of the President.

ORUs are established by the Regents, on the recommendation of UC's president, who seeks the advice of chancellors and the Academic Senate.

REFERENCES: Directory of Organized Research Units, Senior Vice President—Academic Affairs, and University of California Administrative Policies and Procedures Concerning Organized Research Units, Office of the President.

CROSS-REFERENCES: Arts; Contracts and Grants; Humanities; Private Support; Research Achievements.

What are MRUs?

▶ Multicampus Research Units (MRUs) include all units with facilities and personnel on two or more campuses or locations associated with campuses.

▶ They also include all units with facilities at a single location on or near a campus if the participation of staff members from other campuses is so extensive as to give such a unit a Universitywide character.

▶ MRUs report to UC's president through the chancellor of the campus housing the MRU administration. The president retains ultimate responsibility for matters of general policy and intercampus coordination.

▶ In the case of the Agricultural Experiment Station, the Water Resources Center, the Kearney Foundation for Soil Science, and the Giannini Foundation for Agricultural Economics, their directors report to the vice president—agriculture and natural resources, but maintain administrative liaison with the chancellors.

There Are Different Kinds of ORUs

"Institute," "Laboratory" and "Center" are used most often as designations for an ORU, but other titles may be employed in particular situations.

In addition, an Institute may comprise several Centers, or a Station may consist of several facilities.

The designations of some long-established units may not always conform to the definitions that follow. Also, some ORUs have names such as Bureau, Division, Foundation or Organization that cannot be conveniently changed.

Here are examples of ORUs.

▶ An Institute coordinates and promotes faculty-student research that extends across department, school, college and perhaps even campus boundaries.

▶ A Laboratory maintains facilities for research in several departments.

▶ A Center furthers research in a designated field or engages primarily in providing research facilities for other units and departments.

▶ A Station provides physical facilities for interdepartmental research in a broad area (e.g., agriculture), sometimes housing other units and serving several campuses.

Designations of units similar in function but of more narrow interest are Facility, Observatory, Arboretum, Botanical Garden, Vivarium.

University of California ORUs and MRUs

BERKELEY:

Agricultural Experiment Station
(Branch)
MRU. 1874

Archaeological Research Facility
ORU. 1961

Cancer Research Laboratory
ORU. 1950

Center for Chinese Studies
ORU. 1957

Center for Environmental Design
Research
ORU. 1962

Center for Japanese Studies
ORU. 1958

Center for Korean Studies
ORU. 1964

Center for Latin American Studies
ORU. 1958

Center for Middle Eastern Studies
ORU. 1965

Center for Pure & Applied Mathematics
ORU. 1966

Center for Real Estate and Urban
Economics
ORU. 1961

Center for Research in Management
ORU. 1961

Center for Slavic & East European
Studies
ORU. 1957

Center for South Asia Studies
ORU. 1957

Center for SE Asia Studies
ORU. 1959

Center for Studies in Higher Education
ORU. 1956

Center for the Study of Law and Society
ORU. 1961

Laboratory of Chemical Biodynamics
ORU. 1961

Earl Warren Legal Institute
ORU. 1966

Earthquake Engineering Research Center
ORU. 1967

Electronics Research Laboratory
ORU. 1963

Engineering Systems Research Center
ORU. 1961

Environmental Engineering and Health
Sciences Laboratory
ORU. 1949

Field Station for Behavioral Research
ORU. 1966

Giannini Foundation for Agricultural
Economics
MRU. 1928

Institute of Business & Economic
Research
ORU. 1941

Institute of Cognitive Studies
ORU. 1989

Institute of East Asian Studies
ORU. 1978

Institute of Governmental Studies
ORU. 1921

Institute of Human Development
ORU. 1927

Institute of Industrial Relations
ORU. 1945

Institute of International Studies
ORU. 1955

Institute of Personality & Social Research
ORU. 1949

Institute for the Study of Social Change
ORU. 1969

Institute of Urban & Regional
Development
ORU. 1962

Radio Astronomy Laboratory
ORU. 1958

Lawrence Hall of Science
ORU. 1958

Phoebe Hearst Museum of Anthropology
ORU. 1901

Museum of Vertebrate Zoology
ORU. 1908

Environmental Engineering & Health
Sciences Laboratory
ORU. 1949

Seismographic Stations
ORU. 1887

Space Sciences Laboratory
ORU. 1959

Survey Research Center
ORU. 1958

Theoretical Astrophysics Center
ORU. 1985

Virus Laboratory
ORU. 1948

DAVIS:

Agricultural Experimental Station
MRU. 1909

Agricultural History Center
ORU. 1964

Bodega Marine Laboratory
ORU. 1961

California Regional Primate Research
Center
ORU. 1962

Center for Consumer Research
ORU. 1965

Center for Geotechnical Centrifuge
Modeling
ORU. 1983

Center for Image Processing &
Interactive Computing
ORU. 1988

Crocker Nuclear Laboratory
ORU. 1965

Institute of Ecology
ORU. 1966

Institute for Toxicology and
Environmental Health
ORU. 1956

Institute of Governmental Affairs
ORU. 1965

Institute for Theoretical Dynamics
ORU. 1985

Institute of Transportation Studies
ORU. 1991

Intercampus Institute for Research at
Particle Accelerators (Branch)
MRU. 1977

IRVINE:

Cancer Research Institute
ORU. 1980

Center for the Neurobiology of Learning
& Memory
ORU. 1981

Center for Research on Information
Technology and Organizations
ORU. 1966

Critical Theory Institute
ORU. 1987

Developmental Biology Center
ORU. 1969

Institute for Mathematical Behavioral
Sciences
ORU. 1992

Institute for Surface & Interface Science
ORU. 1987

Institute of Transportation Studies
(Branch)
MRU. 1974

Public Policy Research Organization
ORU. 1966

LOS ANGELES:

American Indian Studies Center
ORU. 1971

Asian-American Studies Center
ORU. 1969

Brain Research Institute
ORU. 1959

Center for Afro-American Studies
ORU. 1969

Center for Medieval & Renaissance
Studies
ORU. 1962

Center for Russian & East European
Studies
ORU. 1957

Center for the Study of Comparative
Folklore & Mythology
ORU. 1961

Center for the Study of Women
ORU. 1984

Center for 17th & 18th Century Studies
ORU. 1985

Chicano Studies Research Center
ORU. 1969

Crump Institute for Biological Engineering
ORU. 1976

Dental Research Institute
ORU. 1966

Institute of American Cultures
ORU. 1972

Institute of Archaeology
ORU. 1973

Institute of Industrial Relations
ORU. 1945

Institute of Plasma and Fusion Research
ORU. 1986

Institute for Social Science Research
ORU. 1974

James S. Coleman Center for African
Studies
ORU. 1959

Jules Stein Eye Institute
ORU. 1961

Laboratory of Biomedical &
Environmental Sciences
ORU. 1947

Latin American Center
ORU. 1958

Mental Retardation Research Center
ORU. 1970

Molecular Biology Institute
ORU. 1963

Gustave E. Von Grunebaum Center for
Near Eastern Studies
ORU. 1957

WMRS
MRU. 1950

IGPP (Universitywide), IGPP (Branch)
MRU. 1946

RIVERSIDE:

Agricultural Experiment Station (Branch)
MRU. 1907

Center for Social and Behavioral Science
Research
ORU. 1970

Dry Lands Research Institute
ORU. 1963

Kearney Foundation for Soil Science
MRU. 1951

IGPP (Branch)
MRU. 1967

SAPRC
MRU. 1961

UC Mexus
MRU. 1961

Water Resources Center
MRU. 1957

SAN DIEGO:

Cancer Center
ORU. 1979

Center for Astrophysics & Space Science
ORU. 1979

Center for Energy & Combustion
Research
ORU. 1974

Center for Human Information
Processing
ORU. 1967

Center for Iberian & Latin American
Studies
ORU. 1975

Center for Molecular Genetics
ORU. 1974

Center for Magnetic Recording Research
ORU. 1987

Center for Research in Computing and
the Arts
ORU. 1973

Center for Research in Language
ORU. 1969

Center for US-Mexican Studies
ORU. 1983

Institute for Biomedical Engineering
ORU. 1991

Institute for Neural Computation
ORU. 1967

Institute for Nonlinear Science
ORU. 1986

Institute for Pure & Applied Physical
Science
ORU. 1967

Intercampus Institute for Research at
Particle Accelerators (Branch)
MRU. 1977

Sam and Rose Stein Institute for Research
on Aging
ORU. 1983

Laboratory for Mathematics & Statistics
ORU. 1982

Scripps Institution of Oceanography
ORU. 1912

CalSpace
MRU. 1980

IGCC
MRU. 1985

IGPP (Branch)
MRU. 1960

IMR
MRU. 1954

SAN FRANCISCO:

Cancer Research Institute
ORU. 1948

Cardiovascular Research Institute
ORU. 1958

Francis I. Proctor Foundation for
Research in Ophthalmology
ORU. 1947

Hooper Foundation
ORU. 1913

Hormone Research Laboratory
ORU. 1950

Institute for Health Policy Studies
ORU. 1981

Laboratory of Radiobiology &
Environmental Health
ORU. 1949

Metabolic Research Institute
ORU. 1950

Reproductive Endocrinology Center
ORU. 1977

Institute for Health & Aging
ORU. 1985

SANTA BARBARA:

Center for Chicano Studies
ORU. 1969

Community & Organization Research
Institute
ORU. 1967

Computer Systems Laboratory/Center for
Remote Sensing and Environmental
Optics
ORU. 1972

Institute for Crustal Studies
ORU. 1987

Institute for Interdisciplinary Application
of Algebra & Combinatorics
ORU. 1973

Institute for Polymers & Organic Solids
ORU. 1983

Intercampus Institute for Research at
Particle Accelerators (Branch)
MRU. 1977

Linguistic Minority Research Institute
MRU. 1992

Marine Science Institute
ORU. 1969

Neuroscience Research Institute
ORU. 1964

Quantum Institute
ORU. 1969

SANTA CRUZ:

Institute of Marine Sciences
ORU. 1976

Center for Nonlinear Science
ORU. 1987

Institute for Particle Physics
ORU. 1980

Institute of Tectonics
ORU. 1986

University of California Observatories
(Lick)
MRU (MRF) 1988 (Lick: 1888)

DEPARTMENT OF ENERGY LABORATORIES

Center for Accelerator Mass
Spectrometry
MRU. 1988

Institute of Geophysics and Planetary
Physics
Los Alamos National Laboratory (Branch)
MRU. 1980

Lawrence Livermore National Laboratory
(Branch)
MRU. 1982

OFFICE OF THE PRESIDENT:

Natural Reserve System
ORU. 1965

Agricultural Experiment Station
MRU. 1909

In addition to formally-established ORUs and MRUs, there are two other types of research entities: campus-based federally-funded research centers and nonformal multicampus and campus organized research programs.

Federally-funded research centers are established through competitive peer review by federal agency grants for a specific period of time, generally five years; these centers may also receive renewed funding through a competitive renewal process.

Nonformal multicampus and campus research programs have not received formal Universitywide Academic Senate approval; they receive support from a combination of campuses, Office of the President (in the case of multicampus programs), and extramural sources.

Like ORUs and MRUs, federally-funded research centers and nonformal multicampus and campus research programs contribute importantly to graduate student training; some also offer programs to introduce undergraduate students to the research experience. For details on all these types of research endeavors, consult the Organized Research Unit Directory, Division of Academic Affairs, Office of the President.

P

Pacific Rim: Today, scores of men and women at the University are at the edge of the continent, looking out over the Pacific.

They are looking at a vast region known as the Pacific Rim, which is bringing great changes to California.

The University's people by the sea are researchers and teachers whose curiosity about this area of the world will help the University and the state reach the 21st century equipped with knowledge and insights about an international community that is unlike any other in history.

At times, UC scientists and scholars can be found, as one of them said, "out on the Rim," gathering information for their research somewhere in the Pacific.

They then hurry back to gleaming computers and to laboratories crowded with the latest scientific gear to assess their findings.

Just what is meant by "the Pacific Rim"?

It's a term new in time for a region deep in history.

One look at a map shows that it consists of the wide sweep of nations ringing the largest and deepest ocean in the world.

It extends from the Pacific coast to China and from the Aleutians to the western edges of South America.

Australia is part of it, too, and so is a bit of the Soviet Union that pokes itself into the cold waters off Siberia.

This interdependent community of nation-states is one of the most dynamic regions of the globe.

More than half of the world's people live there. In addition, the region contains a sizeable share of the world's natural resources.

Issues of cultural and scientific significance are being decided there.

The rapid economic, strategic and political changes have produced an explosion in trans-Pacific trade.

For example, U.S. exports to the Far East have grown some 1200 percent since 1960, and since 1978

The Pacific Rim Area Is a Vast Oceanic Community

A line of restless volcanoes curves around the edge of the Pacific, and more of them rise out of the ocean floor.

Their tremors are an uneasy reminder that many of the lands sharing this immense seascape live within a huge Ring of Fire.

Now another name is being used to describe this oceanic community in the last years of this century.

It's called the Pacific Rim.

The Pacific consists of 70 million square miles of the largest and deepest ocean on the globe.

It occupies one third of the earth's surface, extending from the top of the world across the belt of the Equator to the antarctic and from the Western Hemisphere to faraway Asia.

The countries of the west lie 16 hours from those of the east, and the 6,000 miles between them are split by the slightly zig-zagging International Date Line so that today becomes tomorrow in the blink of an eye.

Spotted throughout the vast ocean are a score of nations and some 20,000 islands, once isolated but now neighbors in the age of supersonic jets.

Who first came to this huge expanse?

As researchers sift through clues left by time, they discover evidence of Pacific islands populated centuries ago by Asians who first tested the waters by crossing long distances of open sea in primitive boats.

Europeans got a hint of this great ocean when Marco Polo heard about it in his travels and came home with the news when the 14th century had dawned.

Columbus missed seeing it, and trading ships in the late 15th century sailed around Africa to its edge but thought it was part of the Atlantic.

Finally in 1513 Balboa stood on its western shore (unfortunately he missed poetic immortality when Keats miscast him as "stout Cortez"), and Magellan came hard after to give the ocean its name.

In the 16th century, supremacy in the Pacific was shared by Spain and Portugal; in the next century, the English and Dutch established a hold, followed by France, Russia, Germany and the United States.

By then the names of latter-day explorers became legends, Drake and Cook among them.

By the 18th century, the Pacific was home to sealers, whalers and clipper ships, and its map had finally taken shape.

Now the Pacific has become a tourist haven reached by ships and planes criss-crossing the ocean in a vast peace-time armada.

However, some spots face political, economic or social troubles of volcanic proportions.

Trade, instead of exploration or war, has become a hot issue as Japan, once an enemy, is both a staunch ally and a fierce economic competitor; China grapples with ways to join the modern age; the Philippines faces turmoil in the midst of its newly won democracy; and along with these countries, other places and events are shaping the final years of the 20th century.

People around 1900 could never have envisioned the modern era, but Secretary of State John Hay hit the mark when he called the Pacific "the ocean of the future."

more American trade has crossed the Pacific than the Atlantic.

Today, this community is a three trillion dollar consumer market, and California sits on its edge.

Everything in it—commerce, technology, science, finance, culture, education, health, agriculture—affects the state and the nation.

By the turn of the century, its growth will bring about dramatic changes.

Six of the world's 10 largest urban centers will probably be within the Pacific Rim.

Among them will be Mexico City and Shanghai.

The era of the Pacific Rim reached a major milestone in 1985 when more than 40 state leaders from around the U.S. attended a conference at Berkeley to discuss the region's growing importance.

The gathering, sponsored by UC and the State Legislative Leaders Foundation of Boston, was the largest such meeting ever held to discuss the subject.

The University's presence was important to the conference because of the expertise it could offer, through its array of highly distinguished teaching, research, library and instructional programs concerned with the Pacific Rim.

REFERENCES: "University's Pacific researchers go out on the rim," *UC Focus,* Vol. 1, No. 1, May 1987.

CROSS-REFERENCES: Education Abroad; International Relations and Pacific Studies; Pacific Rim Research Program.

Pacific Rim Research Program:

The University's Pacific Rim Research Program was inaugurated in 1986–87 to help UC scientists and scholars learn more about an increasingly prominent region of the world.

The Pacific Rim (sometimes termed the Pacific Basin) includes the states and nations that border both sides of the Pacific Ocean, as well as the island nations in between. It stretches from Canada to South America and from Australia to Japan.

The goal of the University's Pacific Rim Research Program is to encourage studies that will contribute to a further understanding of the entire region.

The knowledge gained can be useful to California as it seeks a major role in the growth and development of the region. In addition, it will help the University in planning ways to help advance education throughout the area.

The program encourages interdisciplinary studies, as well as scholarly collaboration across national boundaries.

UC faculty engaged in such studies work with colleagues at other California universities and at foreign universities. They have also developed relationships with researchers in governments and private corporations throughout the Pacific Rim.

Research has been wide-ranging.

For example, scientists and scholars have studied trade, finance, economic development, public policy, cross-cultural communication, changing technology, geology, ecology, linguistic issues, film, and religion.

The UC program is administered by an executive committee consisting of faculty from the nine campuses.

Assistance is provided to the committee by the Office of the Associate Vice President—Academic Affairs within the Office of the President.

The committee provides grants for research projects and for pilot projects intended to develop future research proposals. Grants may go to researchers qualified for principal investigator status on their own campuses and are intended for projects involving two or more collaborators.

By 1992, the Pacific Rim Program had funded 93 projects involving more than 200 UC faculty and more than 100 scholars from institutions on both sides of the Pacific and in both the northern and the southern hemispheres.

In 1992–93, the Office of the President provided $496,250 in grants to support some 28 research programs at UC's nine campuses. In addition, the State provided $516,100.

REFERENCES: "University of California Pacific Rim Research Program: Request for Proposals" and other information, Academic Affairs, Office of the President.

CROSS-REFERENCES: Education Abroad; Organized Research Units.

Parking Policy:

Over the past 25 years, the University's parking and transportation operation has become a major service to the faculty, staff, and students.

The current focus of that operation is substantially different from what it was during the first half of the century.

From the time private vehicles became a popular mode of transportation, UC's policy was to provide as much parking as possible in the most convenient locations.

In the main, this policy was carried out through the construction of surface lots, ranging in size from a few spaces to several hundred. These were located throughout the campuses wherever space could be found.

Through the 1970s, this policy met the needs of the University community at a minimum cost to the user.

By 1980, the nine campuses operated a total of approximately 72,000 parking spaces to serve an average daily population in excess of 220,000 faculty, staff, students, and visitors.

Parking fees at the various campuses ranged from $3.50 to $18 per month, and from 10 cents to $1.00 per hour.

The period of the 1980s was one of dramatic growth for the University. Enrollments increased and projections for the 1990s indicated further expansion.

To meet demand, construction of new academic, administrative, and student service facilities was required.

However, most of the land to be occupied by the new facilities was being used for parking; therefore, many of the parking spaces in the core of each campus were demolished as construction began.

It became apparent that a new approach to parking was needed. Because each campus was in the process of developing its Long Range Development Plan, the time for change was ideal.

Additional incentives were provided by the increasing awareness of the effects of pollution on the environment, as well as the federal and state regulations that were promulgated to reduce the use of the single-occupant vehicle.

The policy for the foreseeable future sets aside the core of each campus for academic, administrative and student support purposes and relegates all but a small number of parking spaces to the campus fringe or to remote areas.

In some instances, parking structures are being built in order to avoid assigning a disproportionate amount of land to parking while still providing a necessary level of accessibility.

In the future, it is not expected that the ratio of parking spaces to campus population will remain at the pre-1990s level.

Major efforts are under way to provide a variety of alternative transportation modes to faculty, staff, and students. Vanpools, buspools, transit subsidies, flexible work hours, and emergency rides home are a few of the program components.

The expectation is that, by the year 2000, the University will meet or exceed the federal average vehicle ridership requirements.

REFERENCES: Information from the Office of Business Analysis, Office of the President.

CROSS-REFERENCES: Enrollment.

Patent Policy: Since 1926, the University has required certain employees to report patentable inventions to the University.

Initially the patent program's focus was limited to meeting contractual obligations to research sponsors, and the University had no mandatory assignment policy.

Authority over intellectual property was under the Regents at this time.

In 1963, the University adopted a mandatory assignment policy which required all University employees or researchers using University funds or facilities to assign their inventions to the University.

At the same time, the University established that inventors would share in royalties.

In 1983, the Regents approved Standing Order 100.4 which delegated "the Authority to execute documents necessary for the administration of intellectual property" to UC's president.

The patent policy was amended in April 1990 to modify the share of royalties going to inventors.

The UC Patent, Trademark and Copyright Office (PTCO) was founded in 1979.

It was responsible for meeting the regulatory compliance requirements of sponsoring agencies, primarily the federal government, and for assisting individual faculty members in the commercialization of their patentable ideas.

From 1979 to 1985, PTCO reported to the Regents, who were advised by the Board of Patents. The Board consisted of administrators and faculty.

In 1985, the Patent Policy was issued as a Presidential Policy. That Policy also established the Intellectual Property Advisory Council (IPAC), replacing the policy functions of the old Patent Board.

In 1985, shortly after the Patent Policy became a Presidential Policy, the Office of the President asked an outside auditing firm to assess PTCO operations and make recommendations for improvements. Their recommendations were later implemented.

In 1987, the same auditing firm was again asked to review the PTCO operations and recommend further improvements.

In 1989, recognizing the necessity to address the unique needs of the individual campuses regarding technology transfer, the University developed three alternative models for campus involvement. Each campus was given the opportunity to adopt the model best suited to its individual needs.

In 1991, PTCO's name was officially changed to the Office of Technology Transfer, reflecting a more assertive marketing and licensing approach to the University's technology portfolio.

REFERENCES: Information from Academic Affairs and Campus Liaison, OTT (OP).

CROSS-REFERENCES: Technology Transfer.

Photographic Collections: The University has gathered together, for the first time, information about a treasure trove of photographic collections throughout UC.

The effort was part of a Universitywide photographic project started in July 1984 with funding from the Office of the President.

The project is called the University Survey of Photographic Resources. It was overseen by the California Museum of Photography at Riverside, which had proposed the idea.

As part of the project, the museum made suggestions for improved access to UC's array of photographic resources and encouraged their preservation.

This responsibility is in addition to the museum's role as custodian of its own photographic collections, which are available for research and for public displays.

One of its accomplishments is the publication of a directory identifying accessible photographic collections throughout UC.

The directory introduces scholars and other interested parties to UC's range of photographic resources.

These resources are available in academic and administrative departments, research centers, and specialized and general interest collections.

Photographic images cited in the directory are significant in one of two ways.

For example, an image may contain information of importance to a researcher, or it may be so unique that it warrants preservation.

The number of images identified for the project now stands at more than 17.5 million.

These holdings include:

1) Photographic records of important research.

2) Useful tools for current and future scholars in the humanities and the sciences.

3) Archival materials that document the history and contributions of the University itself.

4) Important objects in the history of photography.

The information gathered about each collection details its purpose, organization, storage facilities and procedures and current use.

By using the directory, scholars can assess the usefulness of a collection for research purposes before actually going to the images themselves; in this way, the images can be preserved from unnecessary handling.

Despite its extensive information, the directory does not contain a complete inventory of all UC collections, for two reasons.

Either a number of identified collections may not be accessible to scholars, or some collections may not have come to the attention of those directing the project.

REFERENCES: Directory of Photographic Collections, California Museum of Photography, UC Riverside; "University Survey of Photographic Resources Newsletter," published quarterly by the museum, 1984–86.

CROSS-REFERENCES: Libraries.

Photography Museum Reaches Out To Schools and to the Public

In 1990, the California Museum of Photography moved from quarters on the Riverside campus to a newly renovated 23,000-square-foot building in the downtown area.

Since then, the museum has continued to enhance a number of programs in connection with its survey of UC's photographic resources.

For example, the museum has developed a more systematic way of organizing and cataloging its vast holdings. At the same time, it continues to provide better access to its collections.

Through a number of private grants, the museum has begun a series of systematic conservation and cataloging projects using the descriptive format of the Library of Congress.

Together with the Office of the President's Division of Library Automation, the museum will provide access to catalog records through the Melvyl library catalog system.

In addition, the museum has received private support to prepare digital image representations from historical photographs.

The museum also has expanded its exhibition program. In the largest exhibition space devoted to photography west of Rochester, N.Y. (home of a vast photography museum), the Riverside site presents contemporary art, studies of the history of photography, and community programs for a diverse audience.

Using UC's sophisticated computer networking capabilities, the Riverside museum also has made plans to mount a series of special exhibitions. These will be organized with the K-12 curriculum in mind.

In carrying out this activity, the museum is working with regional school districts that have access to the Internet research computer network, which UC utilizes on an ongoing basis.

By using the network, students will be able to review digital images from the museum's collections in their classrooms. The digital images can be used in papers, collaborative projects and other educational exercises.

All these continuing projects represent just a few examples of the museum's long-term contributions to a substantial number of educational and public service programs.

Police Services: In 1947, the Regents established the University of California Police Department, within provisions of the State of California's Education Code.

Under this authority, UC appoints police officers with full peace officer status for the enforcement of law and the maintenance of security in and about areas controlled or administered by the Regents.

The Office of the President is responsible for the Universitywide coordination of certain functions relating to UC police services.

This responsibility is carried out through the Office of the Coordinator of Police Services, who is appointed by the Senior Vice President—Administration from among the police chiefs at each campus for a specified period of time.

The Coordinator of Police Services is responsible for:

• Coordinating development and dissemination of UC policies, procedures and professional standards for police services.

• Establishing and maintaining standards for training and performance.

• Coordinating employee selection.

• Providing for dissemination and intercampus exchange of information about police and security services, including the collection and dissemination of crime prevention information.

• Planning for intercampus mutual assistance.

• Serving as liaison with community, state and other law enforcement agencies.

At each campus, responsibility for security and law enforcement is assigned to the chancellors, who also are responsible for campus organization, operation, internal administration and discipline.

Each chancellor has established a police or public safety department with responsibility for law enforcement and the protection of the lives and property of the students, faculty, staff and the public.

The jurisdiction of campus police officers is shared with local law enforcement agencies.

REFERENCES: Education and Penal Codes of the State of California; The Standing Orders of The Regents, 100.4 and 100.6; University of California Manual on Police Policies and Procedures, rev. July 1988, Senior Vice President—Administration.

CROSS-REFERENCES: Crime on Campus.

Coordinators of Police Services at the University

• William P. Beall Jr. (B) 1969–81
• John C. Barber (LA) 1981–86
• E.M. McEwen (D) 1987–91
• John A. Anderson (SD) 1991–

Printing Services: See UC Printing Services.

The **President's Postdoctoral Fellowship Program** was initiated in 1984 by the Office of the President.

It is designed to enhance the competitiveness of outstanding women and minority Ph.D. degree recipients for faculty appointments at the University and other major institutions of higher education

The program currently offers up to two years of sponsor support for postdoctoral research for up to 26 new fellows per year. Each fellow has a faculty sponsor who provides mentoring and guidance and who helps promote the fellow's visibility among colleagues on other campuses.

Awards to the postdoctoral fellows include a stipend of $26,000–$29,000, health benefits and up to $4,000 for research-related expenses. Each award is for a 12-month period, renewable for a second year pending demonstration of satisfactory progress. Fellowships are awarded for research conducted under faculty sponsorship on any of the UC campuses and at the three DOE labs.

Fellowships are awarded through annual competitions open to citizens and permanent residents of the United States. Preference is given to minority and women candidates historically underrepresented in their disciplines of higher education.

Applications are encouraged from African Americans, American Indians, Asian Americans, Filipino Americans, Latinos, Mexican Americans and Puerto Ricans, as well as from white women in physical sciences, mathematics and engineering. Only those individuals who anticipate completion of their Ph.D. degrees by July 1 of each year are eligible to apply.

REFERENCES: "The President's Postdoctoral Fellowship Program," informational text provided in January 1992, Academic Personnel and Affirmation Action, Office of the President.

CROSS-REFERENCES: Subjects related to affirmation action.

The President's Postdoctoral Fellowship Program: An Overview

Some 1,894 individuals had applied to the program as of 1992–93.

• Of these, 162 received fellowships.

• Approximately half the applicants had received a Ph.D. degree from UC.

• By 1992–93, some 121 fellows completed the program.

Distribution of these 121 by discipline was as follows:

• The program has included 35 fellows from the life sciences, 30 from the social sciences, 25 from the physical sciences, 20 from mathematics or engineering, and 11 from the humanities.

• Participants have included 34 African Americans, 23 Chicanos, 11 Latinos, 5 American Indians, 3 Filipino Americans, 4 Asian Americans, and 41 white women.

From the program's beginning until 1992–93:

• Fellowships had been awarded to 100 women, and of these, 79 had completed the program; they included 12 African Americans, 3 American Indians, 10 Chicanos, 4 Latinos, 2 Asian Americans, 1 Filipino American, and 41 white women.

• Seventy-five fellows who completed the two-year program obtained tenure-track faculty positions at major universities.

By 1992–93, some 46 fellows were either pursuing additional postdoctoral opportunities, holding temporary faculty appointments at UC, or had taken research positions with private industry or government.

Privacy of and Access to Information: Heated debate continues in this country about two fundamental and opposing rights.

On one hand, there are the basic rights of all individuals to privacy.

On the other hand, there is the right of the public to be informed about the operations and practices of public agencies and institutions.

Laws dealing with privacy of and access to information attempt to deal with this delicate balance between an individual's right to privacy and the public's right to know.

To address the issues that are involved, Congress has passed various laws that apply to federal agencies, and it has strengthened other laws.

The State of California has laws on privacy of and access to information similar to a number of laws at the federal level.

These state laws affect all public academic institutions.

At the University, the application or implementation of these two rights is twofold.

First, how should information or records be collected about any individual at the University, and, second, what records maintained by UC should be made available to the public?

The following is a summary of federal and state laws on privacy of and access to information that have a bearing on such policy interpretations and implementation.

• The Federal Privacy Act of 1974

This is primarily directed to federal agencies for the purpose of protecting the privacy of individuals identified in federal records.

The act applies to UC with regard to the use of Social Security numbers. It puts restrictions on the collection and use of these numbers.

In addition, the act applies in rare instances when a contract obligates UC to operate a system of records on behalf of a federal agency in order to accomplish a function of that agency.

• The United States Freedom of Information Act of 1966, amended 1974

This applies only to records maintained by federal agencies. It requires federal agencies to make their records available to the public.

It applies to the University only in the rare instances when a contract obligates UC to operate a system of records on behalf of a federal agency in order to accomplish a function of that agency.

• The Federal Family Educational Rights and Privacy Act (the Buckley Amendment) of 1974, dated July 17, 1976, and State of California Education Code Section 67100 et. seq. (The Donahoe Higher Education Act)

While these two laws apply to the University, they relate only to the privacy of and access to student records. "Student records" are those records that pertain to students directly in their capacity as students.

Such records include, but are not limited to, academic evaluations, transcripts, test scores and other academic records, disciplinary records, and financial aid records.

Students have a right of access to their own records and have a right to refuse permission for public access to their records. Unless access is so denied, the public may have access to a limited amount of student information.

Such information includes the following:

The student's name, address (campus and/or permanent), telephone numbers, date and place of birth, major field of study, dates of attendance, degrees, honors, the most recent previous educational institution attended, and participation in officially recognized activities, including athletics.

Records maintained for purposes unrelated to a student's status as a student, such as medical, psychological or employment records, are not considered to be "student records."

Also not considered are records of applicants who have not enrolled in any UC academic program. Once applicants become students, however, their admissions records become "student records."

• The California Public Records Act of 1968

This act applies to the University.

It states that access to information concerning the conduct of the public's business is a fundamental, necessary right of every person in the state, that public records are open to inspection at all times during regular office hours, and that they are subject to inspection and copying by any citizen, except as provided otherwise in the act.

The law covers all types of records, whether handwritten, typed, printed, photographed, or recorded by any means. Only a few records are exempt from public disclosure, including but not limited to:

Litigation records prior to final adjudication or settlement; personnel, medical or similar files, the disclosure of which would constitute an unwarranted invasion of personal privacy; certain police records; text questions and other examination data used for employment or in an academic examination.

Also, library circulation records; certain records related to activities governed by the Higher Education Employee-Employer Act; records of Native American graves, cemeteries and sacred places; and home addresses and home telephone numbers of UC employees.

In addition, records can be withheld from public access when it can be demonstrated that the public interest served by not making the record public clearly, not minimally, outweighs the public interest served by disclosure of the record.

In summary, the interest of the public and not just the interest of the University is to be considered.

• The California Information Practices Act of 1977

This act also applies to the University.

It is based on the concepts that (1) the right to privacy is a personal, fundamental right protected by Section I, Article I of the Constitution of California and by the U.S. Constitution and (2) all individuals have a right of privacy in information pertaining to them.

This complex, lengthy law establishes certain requirements for the collection, maintenance and dissemination of any information that identifies an individual; however, it does not apply to student records, as described above.

It establishes the conditions under which information maintained about individuals must be released to anyone without restrictions and upon request, can be released only to the subject of the data, but not to others, and cannot be released to the subject of the information or to third parties except under carefully controlled conditions.

By UC policy, and in accordance with the act, all information about individuals is classified as confidential, confidential academic, nonpersonal, or personal.

Access rights to such information vary by the type of information and by whether or not the requestor is the subject of the information, a UC employee whose position requires access, or someone else.

The act further requires that only information about an individual that is relevant and necessary to accomplish a purpose of the University shall be collected and maintained.

It further requires that information about an individual shall be collected to the greatest extent practicable directly from that individual and that all records shall be maintained to the maximum extent possible with accuracy, relevance, timeliness and completeness.

In addition, it requires that the University not modify, transfer or destroy a record for the purpose of avoiding compliance with these legal requirements, and in particular shall not do so once access to that particular information has been requested.

The California Information Practices Act is an extremely complex law, and before the principles stated above are applied in any set of circumstances, reference should be made to the pertinent Business and Finance Bulletins and Policies of the University.

• University Policies

In any specific case pertaining to students, staff or faculty, reference should be made to the appropriate University policies and guidelines.

It is not unusual, given the complexity and amount of legal and policy guidelines in existence, that interpretation will be necessary.

This should be obtained from a campus or laboratory Information Practices Coordinator, the Coordinator of Information Practices and Special Projects in the Office of the President, or the Office of the General Counsel.

REFERENCES: "A Compilation of State and Federal Privacy Laws," Robert Ellis Smith, Privacy Journal, 1988; "Legal Requirements On Privacy of and Access to Information," UC Business and Finance Bulletin, July 1, 1992, Office of the Senior Vice President—Administration; information from the Office of Information Practices and Special Projects, Office of the President; pertinent UC policies and guidelines.

CROSS-REFERENCES: Conflict of Interest.

Private Support: Public universities recognize that private support is critical to building and sustaining institutional standards of excellence in teaching, research and public service.

Such support can make a difference between a good university and a great one, by helping an institution attract and retain exceptional faculty and students and by providing additional facilities needed for academic advancement.

Through the years, the State of California normally has funded most of the University's core operating costs, such as basic faculty salaries, equipment, libraries, operation of facilities and other critical activities important to sustaining its academic missions.

Further funding, primarily in the form of financial aid, contracts and grants, is provided by the federal government.

However, funding from private sources is needed for a wide range of programs and activities not normally funded by the state or federal government, but still critical to academic advancement.

Such support helps the University maintain its competitive edge as a major academic institution; it becomes especially important during hard financial times when state and federal is cut.

From 1868 to the present, income from private support has grown steadily in real terms. However, income from governmental and non-governmental sources such as teaching hospitals and auxiliary enterprises has increased even more dramatically as a proportion of UC's total operating income.

Nevertheless, while the proportion of private funding to public funding has declined, the rate of growth, the number of fund-raising activities and the total dollars received from private sources have increased dramatically.

In its early years income from private sources constituted UC's entire annual operating income three times during the 1860s and 1870s. In 20 of UC's first 25 years, private support accounted for more than half of all its operating income. It averaged 65 percent annually. And, during UC's first 50 years, private support averaged 48 percent of the total operating income.

One of the periods in UC history when private support dipped occurred in the late 1960s.

As a carefully worded statement in Universitywide report for 1969–70 noted:

"The effects of campus unrest on gift totals eludes quantification, lacking reliable statistical evidence of donor disenchantment."

But while 1969 was a troubled time for the University, as well as for other colleges and universities around the nation, overall private support continued to increase.

In the next decade, support to the Regents showed overall gains significantly above the rate of inflation.

In addition, support to campus foundations increased 572 percent (this figure covers the time since records had first been reported in 1971–72.)

The 1980s saw further generous growth in private support.

Private Support: Who Gives, And What They Give

Private support comes primarily from individuals, who may be alumni, friends of UC or education-minded philanthropists attracted to University programs or projects.

Considerable private support also comes from foundations, business and industry.

Private support takes different forms, as outright gifts, trusts and other deferred gifts, bequests, gifts-in-kind, endowed funds and private grants (nongovernmental grants which entail specific contractual requirements).

Donations are usually in the form of cash, securities, remainder interests, personal and real property and other kinds of non-monetary contributions, including prized personal possessions.

Private support has enabled UC to start new campuses and add vitally needed buildings and other facilities to meet growing academic demands. It also has provided scholarships and fellowships to assist students in their academic careers.

Gifts often reflect the interests and concerns of the era in which they are made.

For example, in the 1980s and 1990s, there have been gifts to support AIDS research, advanced communication technologies, Pacific Rim studies, research into space, UC-industry liaisons, and projects to learn more about how to serve the needs of the homeless and individuals displaced by economic change.

In other years, the University has been the beneficiary of art objects, rare books, mineral rights, undeveloped land for natural reserves, palm trees, commercial real estate, a land cruiser and even model steam locomotives. Some items UC has sold, and others it has used to good academic purpose.

This is the bottom line for the University:

With all this support through more than a century of service to California, many programs at UC have gained an extra margin of excellence.

During that decade, annual giving to UC grew more than threefold, from $121.2 million in 1980–81 to $436.1 million in 1989–90.

Capital support rose to $117.8 million in 1989–90, almost six times the $20.2 million in 1980–81.

A trend that emerged during the decade was the interest of foreign donors in the University, as many individuals and corporations in other countries pledged their support in recognition of UC's importance to the worldwide community.

In 1991–92, despite a prolonged recession, the University received $430,048,173 in private donations. However, the level of private support did drop from the previous year's all-time high of $436,074,049.

Through several decades, UC's approach to raising money from private sources was rather informal but reasonably effective. As more students enrolled, and the multi-campus model was embraced, then the costs of operating an expanding university grew.

The Regents elected to establish a more formal program to further stimulate the awarding of gifts to the University. In 1959, Development Offices were established at each campus to engage in fund-raising activities, and a Universitywide Gifts and Endowments Office was formed.

The purposes of this office (later the Office of Development Policy and Administration in the Office of the President) have been to ensure that all fund-raising activities conform to policies and procedures established by the Regents, report on UC's private support program, ensure that gifts are used in accordance with donor wishes, and conduct associated activities.

Development Policy and Administration and its counterparts on the campuses are responsible for private support as differentiated from contracts and grants. However, together these two non-state government sources constitute what is known as "extramural support." All extramural support is subject to policies and review pro-

UC Systemwide Performance
(Five-Year Comparison)

Source	1987–1988	1991–92
Alumni	$ 47,772,317	$ 41,830,939
Other Individuals	54,198,472	111,089,150
Sub Total	101,970,789	152,920,089
Campus-related Organizations	9,933,064	13,288,681
Corporations	95,427,371	96,334,772
Foundations	62,685,100	116,633,883
Other Nonprofits	43,143,542	50,870,749
Totals	313,159,866	430,048,174

Source: Annual Reports.

cedures established by each campus in conformance with Universitywide policies and procedures.

Research-related projects also must be conducted in conformance with equal opportunity and affirmative action policies.

In addition, UC has strict financial management and internal audit programs covering all private and other extramural support.

UC's program of fund-raising is a decentralized operation in which considerable authority and accountability is held by each chancellor. Day-to-day responsibility for actual fund-raising normally resides in a campus Development Office.

At the same time, the President and Regents, through the Office of the President, exercise oversight responsibility and have the ultimate accountability for all Regents-held gift funds.

REFERENCES: Annual reports and other information, Office of Development Policy and Administration, Office of the President; Regents' Bylaws and Standing Orders; *Centennial Record.*
CROSS-REFERENCES: Budgets; Contracts and Grants; Foundations; Research Achievements; Support Groups.

The Miner Who Gave UC A Golden Opportunity

The world of private support for the University is a fascinating place, sometimes filled with surprises and a bit of mystery.

One particular surprise came from someone known in University folklore as "the grubstake man."

As the story goes, a traveler drifted down from the gold country in the early days of this century, on horseback over the first primitive miles of dirt road and in a dusty flivver in the later stages of his journey.

He bounced along a narrow winding highway until he reached his destination in Berkeley: the office of UC President Benjamin Ide Wheeler.

The visitor handed the president a sack of gold coins worth $750 and disappeared.

With the sack was an unsigned note from a mine owner in the Sierra foothills.

He told the president he wanted to repay the University for the outstanding education he received and for the help it gave him in starting his highly successful career.

He asked that the gold be used to start a loan fund for needy students.

It would be, he said, their "grubstake."

That was the beginning of an extensive loan program that, to this day, has proved invaluable to thousands of UC students.

Public Service Activities: Webster's dictionary defines a university in part as "an institution of higher learning providing facilities for teaching and research...."

But a university is more than that. It also serves the public in a variety of direct ways.

For example, each year tens of thousands of people visit the campuses of the University of California to take in the museums, art galleries and libraries and to enjoy numerous other attractions.

While interesting and entertaining to visit, the museums and galleries provide an extra-special public service as resource centers offering basic information, educational programs and academic research opportunities.

At these sites, visitors can, for example:

• Catch feeding time for octopi, sharks and other marine life at the Scripps Aquarium at UC San Diego. The aquarium is the educational and interpretive center of the Scripps Institution of Oceanography, and one of the area's most popular public attractions.

• Visit the Lawrence Hall of Science at Berkeley, a regional center for innovative and entertaining displays in astronomy, biology, chemistry, computer science, mathematics, physical science and robotics.

• Look through a collection—the world's largest—of stereographic negatives and prints chronicling an entire century of world history at Riverside's California Museum of Photography.

UC's campuses also offer a variety of programs geared toward elementary, junior and senior high school students. Some open their doors to youngsters interested in learning about physics.

At campuses such as Santa Barbara and Santa Cruz, which have facilities in the marine science, schoolchildren can learn about the natural ocean habitats of many animals.

In addition, art museums abound throughout the UC system.

At these museums, as well as in office buildings and libraries, visitors can enjoy all kinds of art forms, from classical and contemporary to the exotic and the esoteric.

Among the largest and best known of the art facilities at the University is UCLA's Frederick S. Wight Art Gallery.

It features a variety of work from 20th century prints to ancient Chinese ceramics. It also includes the Grunwald Center for the Graphic Arts, with its permanent collection of 30,000 prints, drawings, photos and artists' books.

In addition, UCLA's Fowler Museum of Cultural History contains ethnographic objects and specimens representing contemporary, historic and prehistoric cultures.

Another major facility is Berkeley's University Art Museum, whose modernistic fan-shaped structure is artistic in itself. Also at Berkeley is the Lowie Museum of Anthropology, where visitors can see a wide assortment of artifacts from the museum's large research collection.

The San Diego, Irvine, Riverside, Santa Barbara, Santa Cruz and Davis campuses also maintain art galleries and museums—several per campus in some cases.

Permanent collections and visiting exhibits at these sites include ethnic art and artifacts, Renaissance medals, Old Masters paintings, crafts, clothing and furniture, architectural drawings and models, contemporary works by noted artists, student art, "folk art" by untrained artists, and offbeat items such as historical toys.

But formal museums or galleries are not the only places around the UC system to find interesting cultural and educational sights and activities.

Libraries commonly display rare books, photographs, writings by famous authors and other rare or historical pieces. The library at UC San Francisco offers something particularly worth seeing: changing displays of medical equipment, artifacts and writings, some of them geared to local history.

For those interested in earthquakes, there is the UC Berkeley Seismographic Station with its battery of recording devices. The station is in the Earth Sciences Building, whose halls are home to extensive exhibits in geology and paleontology.

And often available to the public are the University's lecture halls and open spaces around campus, which will feature renowned scholars, writers and musicians as speakers.

For example, at UC San Francisco there may be noontime lectures on a variety of subjects, such as AIDS, alcohol and drug abuse, the values of exercise, and the dangers of stress.

The general public also makes up a large part of the audience attending UC's many cultural events, including performances of dance, theater and music.

And the list goes on, but the message is clear.

At the University of California, there is no shortage of sights and activities, both for the general public and for UC's community of students, faculty and staff.

REFERENCES: UC's General Catalogs; "UC campuses offer the public a bounty of treasures" and "From old bones to Old Masters, UC's exhibits show the wealth," *UC Focus,* Vol. 2, No. 4, January 1988.

CROSS-REFERENCES: All subjects cited in this text.

Publications: Since its inception, the University has engaged in a wide variety of publishing activities.

In 1868, its first administrative announcements were issued.

In 1873, UC's Printing Department, then part of University Press, was established.

It provided printing services for administrative publications that were difficult to obtain from the small printing industry of San Francisco or the State Printing Office in Sacramento.

(Eventually, the Printing Department was separated from University Press and became a separate entity. It is now UC Printing Services.)

Publications may be categorized as follows:

(1) Those that serve teaching programs and are used by faculty and present or prospective undergraduate, professional and graduate students ("official" administrative publications), (2) those that serve the day-to-day internal administrative needs of the University, (3) public service publications designed to extend UC programs to extramural audiences, and (4) professional or scholarly publications.

The following are some examples.

Publications that serve UC's teaching programs consist of catalogs, school and college announcements, schedules, directories of classes, and other written materials.

Publications serving day-to-day, internal administrative needs include campus telephone directories and the Universitywide Directory, as well as various materials at the medical centers and other UC entities.

Public service publications include material produced by various University Extension and Cooperative Extension programs.

Professional publications include scientific, agricultural and other research information, as well as the proceedings of various on-campus meetings.

Many of UC's campus and Universitywide administrative and research units also provide annual or occasional reports.

Audiences for all UC's publications are widespread and varied.

For example, campus newspapers or magazine-style publications are published for faculty, staff, alumni, donors, parents, the campus community, legislators or other important external recipients.

Some campuses produce magazine-format publications of science, engineering and medical news for the campus and for the wider campus community. In addition, newsletters may be published to keep the community surrounding a campus informed of specific on-going issues.

Each campus has an independent or semi-independent student newspaper, which is read by members of the wider campus community.

The national laboratories managed by UC for the federal government also produce a number of publications for employees, managers, retirees or other audiences.

The Office of the President generates a number of publications. Among them are *UC Focus,* a newspaper-format publication for Universitywide faculty and staff, and the President's Report to the Regents, a compendium of news and other informational items from throughout UC for the Board of Regents.

The Universitywide Academic Senate publishes Notice, a newsletter for its members.

In many instances, departmental publications are produced throughout the University for readers within specific areas of interest.

Faculty and staff associations and retiree associations also have publications for their members.

REFERENCES: *Centennial Record;* University Relations files, Office of the President.

CROSS-REFERENCES: President's Report to the Regents; UC Bulletin Board; UC Clip Sheet; UC Printing Services; University Bulletin; University Press. (Also see individual campus and laboratory publications.)

The **Puente Project,** sponsored by the University of California and the California Community Colleges, is an academic and leadership program to help Chicano/Latino students stay in school, obtain a college degree, and return to their community as mentors and leaders.

Puente ("bridge," in Spanish) was established in 1981 at Chabot College, Hayward, to help increase the number of Chicano and Latino community college students transferring to four-year institutions. Puente recently received private funding to pilot the program in 18 high schools over the next four years.

The project became an administrative part of UC's Office of the President in 1985.

As part of the project, teachers, counselors and mentors from local communities work with motivated but underachieving students in order to help them succeed. The project integrates a one-year writing course with academic counseling and mentoring provided by over 1,800 professionals from the Mexican American/Latino community.

Puente's innovative training model provides the teacher/counselor site teams with the tools they need to implement Puente in their communities.

Over 100 educators have been trained in Puente's ten-day institute and continue to receive ongoing training while in the Program.

Corporate grants and other funding help support the project's services.

More than 3,500 students have enrolled in Puente since its inception.

Some 66 percent of the students who complete the program transfer to four-year colleges and universities.

Puente currently has programs in 29 California Community Colleges, serving more than 2,300 students a year.

REFERENCES: Information from the Puente Project.

CROSS-REFERENCES: All subjects related to Education.

R

Recognition: Many distinguished scholars and scientists at the University have been recognized for academic excellence over the years by highly prestigious national associations.

In large part because of the outstanding awards and honors that its teachers and researchers have earned, the University ranks as one of the nation's major academic institutions.

Members of the University's faculty are recognized for their contributions and achievements on the national and international scene in a number of ways—for example, through elections and appointments to leading professional societies and through the receipt of major grants and fellowships.

The accompanying tables help tell the story of UC's achievement.

The figures and other information in these lists obviously were compiled earlier than the date of publication of this book. Updated information may be obtained from the individual UC campuses or from the University Relations Office in the Office of the President.

Further background on recognitions of various kinds may be obtained from the Centennial Record of the University of California by Verne Stadtman and from other publications about the University that were produced during UC's 100th and 125th anniversaries.

Figures Tell the Story

Following are figures showing the number of living scholars and scientists at UC's campuses and laboratories who have been elected or appointed to organizations or who have received other honors (the figures are those available in Spring 1993).

National Academy of Sciences	236
American Academy of Arts and Sciences	339
National Academy of Engineering	59
Institute of Medicine	64
American Philosophical Society	47
Guggenheim Fellowships	973
(Figures available since 1964 when records started being kept)	
National Medals of Science (Since 1962)	31

Recognitions at the Campuses: See Campus Profiles.

Living Nobel Prize Winners

(As of March 1993)

Name	Field of Prize	Year of Prize	UC Campus	Year Joined UC
Alfven, Hannes	Physics	1970	San Diego	1967
Bishop, Michael J. (shared w/Varmus)	Medicine	1989	San Francisco	1968
Calvin, Melvin	Chemistry	1961	Berkeley	1937
Chamberlain, Owen (shared w/Segre)	Physics	1959	Berkeley	1948
Cram, Donald J. (shared w/Lehn and Pedersen)	Chemistry	1987	Los Angeles	1947
Crick, Francis	Chemistry/ Biology	1962	San Diego	
Debreu, Gerard	Economics	1983	Berkeley	1962
Dulbecco, Renato	Medicine	1975	San Diego	1977
Glaser, Donald A.	Physics	1960	Berkeley	1959
Guillemin, Roger	Medicine	1977	San Diego	
Holley, Robert W.	Chemistry	1968	San Diego	
Lee, Yuan T.	Chemistry	1986	Berkeley	1974
Milosz, Czeslaw	Literature	1980	Berkeley	1960
*Schrieffer, Robert J.	Physics	1972	Santa Barbara	1979
Schwinger, Julian	Physics	1965	Los Angeles	1972
Seaborg, Glenn T. (shared w/McMillan)	Chemistry	1951	Berkeley	1937
Townes, Charles H.	Physics	1964	Berkeley	1967
Varmus, Harold E. (shared w/Bishop)	Medicine	1989	San Francisco	1970

*Moved to Florida State University, 1993   3/9

Deceased Nobel Prize Winners

Alvarez, Luis (died 1988)	Physics	1964	Berkeley	1938
Giauque, William F. (died 1982)	Chemistry	1949	Berkeley	1922
Lawrence, Ernest O. (died 1958)	Physics	1939	Berkeley	1936
Libby, Willard F. (died 1980)	Chemistry	1960	Los Angeles	1959
*Mayer, M. Geoppert (died 1972)	Physics	1963	San Diego	1960
McMillan, Edwin M. (shared w/Seaborg)	Chemistry	1951	Berkeley	1935
Northrop, John H. (died 1987) (shared w/J.B. Summer and Stanley)	Chemistry	1946	Berkeley	1935
Segre, Emilio G. (died 1989)	Physics	1959	Berkeley	1939
Stanley, Wendell M. (died 1971) (shared w/J.B. Summer and Northrop)	Chemistry	1946	Berkeley	1948
Urey, Harold C. (died 1981)	Chemistry	1934	San Diego	1958

*First woman in USA; second in the world

The **Regents of the University:** The University is governed by a Board of Regents.

More than 400 individuals have held the position of Regent in the University's 125-year history.

Currently, the Board consists of 26 members: 18 are appointed by the Governor for 12-year terms, one is a student appointed by the Board to a one-year term, and seven are ex officio Regents.

The ex officio Regents are the Governor, Lieutenant Governor, Speaker of the Assembly, Superintendent of Public Instruction, the President and Vice President of the Alumni Association of the University, and the President of the University.

The Governor is officially President of the Board of Regents; however, in practice, the presiding officer is the Chairman, elected from among its body for a one-year term (the Vice Chairman is elected in the same manner).

The Board operates through seven standing committees: Audit, Educational Policy, Finance, Grounds and Buildings, Hospital Governance, Investments, and Oversight of the Department of Energy Laboratories.

The Board meets nine times a year: seven two-day meetings and two one-day meetings.

Standing committees meet as required, usually on the day preceding the Board's business meetings.

The Board has delegated a broad range of authority and responsibility to the President of the University and has delegated authority to the faculty in matters relating to academic programs.

With few exceptions, all matters requiring Board action are first considered by the appropriate committee, with authority only to recommend or report to the Board.

The President of the Board, the Chairman of the Board (or, in the Chairman's absence, the Vice Chairman of the Board), the immediate past Chairman of the Board, and the President of the University are ex officio members of all Standing Committees, except that the President of the University is not a member of the Committee on Audit.

The Superintendent of Public Instruction is an ex officio member of the Committee on Educational Policy, as is the Regents' representative to the California Postsecondary Education Commission. CPEC is the advisory body established by the California Legislature to plan and coordinate all of the state's educational activities beyond high school.

REFERENCES: "Regents and Officers, University of California," informational folder. Secretary of The Regents.

CROSS-REFERENCES: All subjects related to Regents and the Board's Standing Committees.

Regents' Meetings: During the 1960s, the Board of Regents reviewed the question of appropriate locations for its meetings, as well as the number of meetings to be held each year.

Until the late 1960s, the Board of Regents held its meetings at each of the University's campuses.

In 1969, a Regents' special committee found that some Board members favored the practice of meeting on the campuses.

However, other Board members proposed that the next several meetings be held at University Hall, the Universitywide headquarters across the street from the Berkeley campus.

Still others suggested that meetings be held, alternately, somewhere else in the San Francisco Bay Area and in Los Angeles.

In the 1970s, a new general structure for locations of Regents' meetings was established.

Meetings were held in the north at the San Francisco Extension Center (the meeting site later was moved to UC San Francisco's Laurel Heights) and in the south at the Los Angeles Convention Center (the meeting site later was moved to UCLA).

During this time, the Regents also approved a flexible annual program of campus visits, in addition to their regular Board meetings. The plan would give Regents an opportunity to learn more about the campuses firsthand, as well as allow members of each campus community to meet the members of the Board. (The formal scheduling of campus visits was discontinued in 1975. However, informal visits by Regents continued to be encouraged).

In 1973, the Board began once more to meet on the campuses, as it had done in the 1960s. However, by 1976, the Regents' meetings returned to a San Francisco/ Los Angeles schedule. The Regents did not meet on campuses again until 1985.

Regents' meeting schedules also underwent a number of changes over the years.

During the 1960s, regular Board meetings were held every month except August and December. In 1971, the regular April meeting was eliminated.

Beginning in 1983–84, the Regents decided on a revised schedule.

Then in 1986, the Regents established a format allowing for six business meetings a year and three policy meetings.

The policy meetings were designed to provide a forum for discussing University issues and programs in greater depth.

In 1993–94, following that general format, the Regents approved this meeting schedule:

• Seven two-day business meetings in September, November, January, March, May, June and July.

• A one-day meeting in October for consideration of the Regents' annual budget and other policy issues.

• A one-day policy meeting in February.

In the midst of working out meeting sites and schedules, Regents also have had to confront another, and larger, set of corporate responsibilities.

For example, the growth in size and scope of UC's activities in recent years has created substantial complexities in the decision-making process, both for the University administration and for the Board.

Between 1983 and 1990, more than 50 changes in policies and Regents' Bylaws and Standing Orders were approved to mitigate some of this complexity.

However, by 1990, the Board still was reviewing, discussing or acting on a large number of business items annually (for example, in a single year, there might be more than 500 items on its agenda).

By early 1993, it was apparent that the business conducted by the Board was becoming more complex, as UC's administrative procedures, reflecting its large size and scope, tended to burden the Regents' agenda with an increasing number of items of business.

This meant that the Board had too little time to devote to major policy and long-range planning issues.

As a result, the Board began to examine and articulate its priorities, in order to ensure that both time and resources were used to best effect in discharging the responsibilities it has for governing the University.

It seemed to be a particularly appropriate time for the Board to take a hard look at its practices and procedures. During this period, the University administration itself also was reexamining all campus and Office of the President operations to see if they could be streamlined or improved.

REFERENCES: "Feasibility of Holding Meetings of The Regents in Campus Facilities," Item for Discussion, Special Committee on Regents' Procedures, July 7, 1982; "Dates and Locations of Regents' Meetings for 1993–94," Item 1 for Action, Special Committee on Regents' Procedures, and Item SP-1 for Discussion, "Review of Board Practices and Procedures," January 14, 1993; information from the Secretary of the Regents.

CROSS-REFERENCES: All sections relating to the Regents.

Regents' Meetings, Closed Sessions of: Regents' meetings are open to the public, except in certain instances defined by State law and the Regents' Bylaws.

In those instances, the Regents can meet in closed session.

The Board of Regents may conduct closed sessions when it meets to consider or discuss the following:

1. Matters affecting the national security.

2. The conferring of honorary degrees or other honors or commemorations.

3. Matters involving gifts, devises, and bequests.

4. Matters involving the purchase or sale of investments for endowment and pension funds.

5. Matters involving litigation, when discussion in open session concerning those matters would adversely affect, or be detrimental to, the public interest.

6. The acquisition or disposition of property, if discussion of these matters in open session could adversely affect the Regents' ability to acquire or dispose of the property on the terms and conditions it deems to be in the best public interest.

7. Matters concerning the appointment, employment, performance, compensation or dismissal of University officers or employees, excluding individual Regents other than the president of the University. (This provision does not include meetings of the nominating committee held to propose officers of the Board and members of its various committees.)

8. Matters relating to complaints or charges brought against University officers or employees, excluding individual Regents other than the president of the University, unless the officer or employee requests a public hearing.

While a witness is being examined during any open or closed session, any or all other witnesses in the investigation may be excluded from the Regental proceedings.

The nominating committee of the Regents may conduct closed sessions held for the purpose of proposing officers of the Board and members of the Board's various committees.

Committees of the Regents may conduct closed sessions held for the purpose of proposing a student Regent.

The Regents shall not be required to give public notice of meetings of special search or selection committees held for the purpose of conducting interviews for university officer positions.

The Regents also may hold closed sessions with respect to matters within Government Code section 3596, a part of the Higher Education Employer-Employee Relations Act (HEERA).

Such matters include consideration or discussion of UC's position about meeting and conferring or about any matter within the scope of representation or instructing UC's designated representatives.

Committees of the Regents may conduct closed sessions on Medi-Cal contract negotiations.

The great majority of closed session actions fall within (2) through (7) in the above list.

According to Regents' Bylaw 14.7:

"(a) The confidentiality of closed sessions of the Board and its Committees shall be maintained, subject to the provisions of this Bylaw.

"(b) Actions taken in closed session normally shall be released to the public following final action by the Board or a Committee of the Board empowered to act. Actions may be withheld from release or release may be delayed if disclosure would constitute an invasion of privacy of individuals or would adversely affect the interests of the University. Actions taken in closed sessions to appoint, employ, or dismiss University employees and any roll call votes thereon shall be reported at subsequent public meetings of the Board.

"(c) Release of actions shall be determined by the President of the University and by the Secretary, the Treasurer, and the General Counsel of The Regents in their respective areas of responsibility and in accordance with procedures established by the Board.

"(d) Information from closed sessions other than final actions may be released only as follows:

"(1) The President of the University, the Secretary, the Treasurer, and the General Counsel of The Regents in their respective areas of responsibility may release from closed session background information as required for the conduct of ordinary business of the University.

"(2) The President, in consultation as appropriate with the Chairman of the Board and General Counsel of The Regents, may release information for scholarly purposes when the substance would not presently be considered in closed session, would be scheduled for release to the public subsequent to the closed session, or when the information is twenty-five years or more old."

REFERENCES: Regents Bylaws 14.6 and 14.7; "Change in Bylaws and Adoption of Procedures Pertaining to Release to the Public of Information from Executive Sessions of Meetings of The Regents," Item 2 for Action, Special Committee on Regents' Procedures, June 10, 1981; California Education Code Section 92030; Government Code Section 3596.

CROSS-REFERENCES: All matters related to the Board of Regents

Bylaws and Standing Orders: What's the Difference?

The Regents' Bylaws and Standing Orders serve two distinct purposes.

▶ The Bylaws set forth the following, in addition to other matters:

The composition and power of the corporation and the Regents' committees.

The responsibilities of the Board's standing committees.

The duties and responsibilities of the corporation's officers.

Matters relating to procedure.

▶ The Standing Orders set forth:

Duties of the University's officers.

Provisions relating to faculty members, the Academic System and academic units.

Matters concerning employees.

Provisions covering the retirement system.

Article IX, Section 9: Changes Over the Years

Here is a quick summary of how the membership and composition of the board of Regents changed over the years.

1868: Provisions under the Organic Act (these provisions were maintained under Article IX, Section 9, of the State Constitution as ratified in 1879):

- Composition of the Board
    8 Gubernatorial Appointees
    6 Ex Officio Members: Governor, Lieutenant Governor, Superintendent of Public Instruction, Speaker of the Assembly, President of the State Board of Agriculture, President of the Mechanics Institute of San Francisco
    8 "Honorary" Members, elected by appointee and ex officio members of the first Board only; successors to the original 8 became appointed Regents chosen by the Governor
    Total: 22

- Length of Terms:
    For the first Board: 2–16 years (determined by lot)
    For subsequent Boards: 16 years

1918: Amendments to Article IX, Section 9 added the President of the University and the President of the Alumni Association as ex officio members

- Composition of the Board:
    16 gubernatorial appointees
    8 ex officio members
    Total: 24

- Length of Terms: 16 years

1972: Amendments to Article IX, Section 9, reinstated the requirement of Senate approval of appointed Regents (it had been deleted in the 1918 amendment)

1974: Amendments to Article IX, Section 9:

Reduced the length of terms of appointed members from 16 to 12 years

Increased the number of appointed members from 16 to 18

Reduced the number of ex officio officers from 8 to 7 by eliminating the Presidents of the State Board of Agriculture and the Mechanics Institute and adding the Vice President of UC's alumni association

Provided for the appointment of a faculty and a student Regent (UC faculty chose not to exercise the right to appoint a faculty Regent, but students elected to appoint a student Regent; the faculty does have representation at Regents' meetings, however, as described elsewhere in the book)

Established a 12-member committee to advise the Governor on Regental appointments

Added the requirement that the Regents be broadly reflective of the diversity of the state

- Composition of the Board:
    18 gubernatorial appointees
    7 ex officio members
    1 student Regent
    Total: 26

- Length of Terms:
    1 year for student and alumni Regents
    12 years for appointed Regents

1976: Amendments to Article IX, Section 9 made the following additions

- Added provisions on compliance with competitive bidding procedures

- Added the requirement that no person be "debarred admission to any department of the University on account of race, religion, ethnic heritage, or sex"

Appointed Regents Who Served the Longest Terms

During the past 25 years, two appointed Regents, Edwin W. Pauley and Edward W. Carter, completed more than three decades of service on the Board.

They were among the 10 appointed Regents in UC's history who have served the longest terms.

The 10 Regents and their terms of service were:

Edward A. Dickson, 1913–1956 (43 years)
Garrett W. McEnerney, 1901–1942 (41 years)
Isaias W. Hellman, 1881–1918 (37 years)
James K. Moffitt, 1911–1948 (37 years)
Edward W. Carter, 1952–1988 (36 years)
Chester H. Rowell, 1914–1948 (34 years)
Charles A. Ramm, 1912–1944 (32 years)
Guy C. Earl, 1902–1934 (32 years)
Mortimer Fleishhacker, 1918–1950 (32 years)
Edwin W. Pauley, 1940–1972 (32 years)

Women on the Board of Regents From 1897 to 1992

In 1868, the Board of Regents was organized in accordance with provisions of the Organic Act, which had created the University that same year.

The Regents' membership was all-male until 1897.

In that year, Phoebe Apperson Hearst was appointed. She served until 1919.

After the turn of the century, other women began serving as appointed members of the Board. Still others have served as student Regents and as alumni Regents.

Here is a list of women who have served on the Board of Regents, as of January 1993, with their dates of service and, as applicable, dates as Board chair (in parentheses).

Appointed Regents:

Phoebe A. Hearst, 1897–1919
Minna Sherman, 1913
Margaret Sartori, 1919–1937
Eleanor MacFarland, 1937–1940
Dorothy Chandler, 1954–1968
Catherine Hearst, 1956–1976
Elinor Heller, 1961–1976 (7/1/75–3/1/76)
Vilma Martinez, 1976–1990 (7/1/84–6/30/86)
Theodora Kroeber-Quinn, 1977–1978
Yvonne B. Burke, 1978–79; 1982–93
Meredith Khachigian, 1987– (7/1/91–6/30/93)
S. Sue Johnson, 1990–
Alice Gonzales, 1990–

Student Regents:

Carol Mock, 1975–1976
Daryn Peeples, 1976–1977
Renee Turkell, 1978–1979
Leslie Lurie, 1980–1981
Linda Sabo, 1982–1983
Janice Eberly, 1985–1986
Jacquelyn Ross, 1987–1988
Deborah Thorpe, 1988–1989
Jenny Doh, 1990–1991
Diana Darnell, 1991–92

Alumni Regents

Cheryl Biles, 1978–1979
Lois Weeth, 1981–1982
Shirley Conner, 1982–1983
R. Marilyn Lee, 1987–1988
Beatrice Mandel, 1987–1988
S. Sue Johnson, 1988–1989
Martha Newkirk, 1990–1991
Gail Anderson, 1991–1992

Also see list of Regents on a subsequent page for later members in these categories

Regents of the University of California

First Row, Front, Left to Right:

Regent Jacques S. Yeager, Regent Frank W. Clark, Jr., Regent S. Stephen Nakashima, Alumni Regent Paul J. Hall, President J. W. Peltason, Board Chairman Meredith J. Khachigian, Governor Pete Wilson, Lieutenant Governor Leo T. McCarthy, Regent Alice J. Gonzales, Faculty Representative Arnold Binder

Second Row, Left to Right:

Regent S. Sue Johnson, Regent Yvonne Brathwaite Burke, Regent Glenn Campbell, Regent Leo S. Kolligian, Regent Clair W. Burgener, Board Vice Chair William T. Bagley, Student Regent Alex Wong, Regent Tirso del Junco

Third Row, Left to Right:

Regent John G. Davies, Alumni Regent-designate Robert E. Murphy, Faculty Representative W. Elliot Brownlee, Regent Harold M. Williams, Alumni Regent-designate Roy L. Shults, Regent Dean A. Watkins, Regent Roy T. Brophy, Alumni Regent Carl J. Stoney, Jr.

Not present: Speaker Willie L. Brown, Jr., Regent Jeremiah F. Hallisey, Superintendent Bill Honig, Regent Howard H. Leach

Photograph as of January 1993

The Regents of the University of California Through the Years

Appointed Regents

Name	Years
Ahlport, Brodie E.	1941–1957
Ainsworth, George J.	1883–1895
Andelson, Sheldon	1982–1987
Anderson, Alden	1922–1932
Archer, Lawrence	1868–1880
Ashburner, William	1880–1887
Bagley, William	1989–
Bard, Thomas R.	1907–1911
Barnes, William H.L.	1899–1902
Bartlett, Columbus	1887–1896
Bateson, Gregory	1976–1980
Beale, Truxton	1911–1913
Beard, John L.	1876–1891
Bidwell, John	1880
Bowles, Philip E.	1911–1922
Boyd, Philip L.	1957–1970
Britton, John A.	1903–1923
Brophy, Roy T.	1986–
Brown, Willie L., Jr.	1980–1981
Budd, John E.	1896–1913
Burgener, Claire W.	1988–
Burke, Yvonne B.	1979; 1982–1993
Campbell, W. Glenn	1968–
Canaday, John E.	1958–1974
Carter, Edward W.	1952–1988
Casserly, Eugene	1876–1880
Chandler, Dorothy B.	1954–1968
Clark, Frank W., Jr.	1980–
Coblentz, William K.	1964–1980
Cochran, George I.	1919–1946
Connerly, Ward	1993–
Crocker, Charles F.	1888–1897
Crocker, William	1908–1937
Curtis, Nathaniel G.	1880–1883
Davidson, George	1877–1884
Davies, John G.	1992–
del Junco, Tirso	1985–
Delmas, Delphin M.	1885–1892
Dickson, Edward A.	1913–1956
Dohrmann, Frederick W.	1903–1914
Doyle, John T.	1868–1872
Dutton, Frederick	1962–1978
Dwinelle, John W.	1868–1874
Earl, Guy C.	1902–1934
Ehrman, Sidney M.	1930–1952
Ellinwood, Charles N.	1901–1908
Fenston, Earl	1948–1958
Fleishhacker, Mortimer	1918–1950
Foote, Henry S.	1892–1900
Forbes, William	1962–1977
Foster, Arthur W.	1900–1930
Gallwey, John G.	1932–1938
Geffen, David	1980–1987
Giannini, Amadeo P.	1934–1949
Giannini, Lawrence M.	1949–1950
Gonzales, Alice J.	1990–
Griffiths, Farnham P.	1948–1951
Hagar, Gerald H.	1951–1964
Haggerty, Cornelius J.	1950–1966
Haight, Henry H.	1872–1876
Haldeman, H.R.	1968–1969
Hallidie, Andrew S.	1876–1900
Hallisey, Jeremiah P.	1982–1993
Hamilton, J.M.	1874–1876
Hammond, Richard P.	1868–1873
Hansen, Victor R.	1946–1962
Harman, Willis W.	1980–1990
Harrison, Maurice E.	1944–1951
Hayes, Jay O.	1923–1928
Haynes, John R.	1922–1937
Hearst, Catherine C.	1956–1976
Hearst, Phoebe A.	1897–1919
Heller, Edward H.	1942–1958; 1960–1961
Heller, Elinor R.	1961–1976
Hellman, Isaias W.	1881–1918
Henning, John F.	1977–1989
Higgs, DeWitt A.	1966–1982
Hope, Frank L., Jr.	1984–1988
Houghton, James F.	1888–1903
Johnson, Frank S.	1908–1911
Johnson, S. Sue	1990–
Jordan, Fred M.	1937–1954
Kennedy, Laurence J., Jr.	1964–1968
Khachigian, Meredith	1987–
Kolligian, Leo J.	1985–
Kroeber–Quinn, Theodora	1977–1978
Lawrence, John H.	1970–1983
Leach, Howard H.	1990–
Lee, Lester	1993–
MacFarland, Eleanor B.	1937–1940
Martin, James W.	1871–1899
Martinez, Vilma	1976–1990
Marye, George T., Jr.	1883–1898
McEnerney, Garret W.	1901–1942
McKee, Samuel B.	1868–1883
McKinley, James W.	1903–1918
McLaughlin, Donald H.	1951–1966
Meek, William	1874–1878
Merritt, Ralph P.	1923–1930
Merritt, Samuel	1868–1874
Miller, Albert	1887–1900
Miller, Azariel B.	1938–1941
Mills, Darius O.	1874–1881
Mills, James	1914–1942
Moffitt, James K.	1911–1948
Mohn, Einar O.	1966–1968
Moore, Joseph A.	1974–1990
Mosher, Samuel B.	1956–1968
Mosk, Stanley	1940–1941
Moss, Joseph M.	1874–1880
Naffziger, Howard C.	1952–1961
Nakashima, S. Stephen	1989–
Neylan, John F.	1928–1955
Nimitz, Chester W.	1948–1956
Noyce, Robert	1982–1988
Olson, Gus	1951–1960
O'Melveny, Stuart	1937–1940
Orr, Verne	1976–1981
Pardee, George C.	1899–1903
Pauley, Edwin W.	1940–1972
Phelan, James D.	1898–1899
Phelps, Timothy G.	1880–1899
Pixley, Frank M.	1875–1880
Ramm, Charles A.	1912–1944
Redding, Benjamin B.	1880–1882
Reinstein, Jacob B.	1895–1911
Reynolds, Robert O.	1969–1986
Rhodes, Augustus	1880–1888
Rodgers, Arthur	1883–1902
Roman, Frederick W.	1940–1948
Rosencrans, William S.	1884–1885
Roth, William M.	1961–1977
Rowell, Chester A.	1891–1912
Rowell, Chester H.	1914–1948
Sartori, Margaret R.	1919–1937
Sheinbaum, Stanley K.	1977–1989
Sherman, Minna E.	1913
Simon, Norton	1960–1976
Slack, Charles W.	1894–1911
Sloss, Louis, Jr.	1890–1891
Smith, William French	1968–1990
Sprague, Norman	1942–1952
Stanford, Leland	1882–1883
Stebbins, Horatio	1868–1894
Steinhart, Jesse H.	1950–1962
Storke, Thomas M.	1955–1960
Sullivan, Jerd F., Jr.	1958–1964
Swift, John F.	1872–1888
Taussig, Rudolph J.	1906–1907; 1913–1922
Teague, Charles C.	1930–1950
Wada, Yoritada	1977–1992
Wallace, William	1875–1902
Watkins, Dean A.	1969–
Watt, William	1868–1871
Waymire, James A.	1891–1908
Wheeler, Charles S.	1902–1906; 1911–1923
White, Stephen M.	1899–1901
Williams, Harold M.	1982–
Wilson, William A.	1972–1988
Winans, Joseph W.	1873–1887
Yeager, Jacques S.	1988–
Yorke, Peter	1902–1912

Appointed Student Regents

Mock, Carol	1975–1976
Peeples, Daryn S.	1976–1977
Salerno, Michael	1977–1978
Turkell, Renee	1978–1979
Lozano, Hector C.	1979–1980
Lurie, Leslie K.	1980–1981
Neuman, David A.	1981–1982
Sabo, Linda R.	1982–1983
Anderson, Richard E.	1983–1984
Gaines, Fred N.	1984–1985
Eberley, Janice	1985–1986
Hoffman, David	1986–1987
Ross, Jacquelyn	1987–1988
Thorpe, Deborah	1988–1989
Rodriguez, Guillermo, Jr.	1989–1990
Doh, Jenny J.	1990–1991
Darnell, Diana K.	1991–1992
Wong, Alex	1992–1993
Morrisoe, Darby	1993–1994

Governors
Ex Officio Regents

Haight, Henry H.	1867–1871
Booth, Newton	1871–1875
Pacheco, Romualdo	1875
Irwin, William	1875–1880
Perkins, George	1880–1883
Stoneman, George	1883–1887
Bartlett, Washington	1887
Waterman, Robert W.	1887–1891
Markham, Henry H.	1891–1895
Budd, James H.	1895–1899
Gage, Henry T.	1899–1903
Pardee, George C.	1903–1907
Gillett, James N.	1907–1911
Johnson, Hiram W.	1911–1917
Stephens, William D.	1917–1923
Richardson, Friend W.	1923–1927
Young, Clement C.	1927–1931
Rolph, James, Jr.	1931–1934
Merriam, Frank F.	1934–1939
Olson, Culbert L.	1939–1943
Warren, Earl	1943–1953
Knight, Goodwin J.	1953–1959
Brown, Edmund G.	1959–1967
Reagan, Ronald W.	1967–1975
Brown, Edmund G., Jr.	1975–1983
Deukmejian, C. George	1983–1991
Wilson, Pete	1991–

Lieutenant Governors
Ex Officio Regents

Holden, William	1868–1871
Pacheco, Romualdo	1871–1875
Irwin, William	1875
Johnson, James A.	1875–1880
Mansfield, John	1880–1883
Daggett, John	1883–1887

Waterman, Robert W.	1887
White, Stephen M.	1887–1891
Reddick, J.B.	1891–1895
Millard, Spencer G.	1895
Jeter, William T.	1895–1899
Neff, Jacob H.	1899–1903
Anderson, Alden	1903–1907
Porter, Warren R.	1907–1911
Wallace, Albert G.	1911–1915
Eshleman, John M.	1915–1916
Stephens, William D.	1916–1917
Young, Clement	1919–1926
Fitts, Buron	1926–1928
Carnahan, Herschel L.	1928–1931
Merriam, Frank F.	1931–1935
Hatfield, George J.	1935–1939
Patterson, Ellis E.	1939–1943
Houser, Frederick F.	1943–1947
Knight, Goodwin J.	1947–1953
Powers, Harold J.	1953–1959
Anderson, Glenn M.	1959–1967
Finch, Robert H.	1967–1969
Reinecke, Ed	1969–1974
Harmer, John L.	1974
Dymally, Mervyn	1975–1978
Curb, Mike	1978–1983
McCarthy, Leo T.	1983–

Speakers of the Assembly
Ex Officio Regents

Ryland, Caius T.	1868–1869
Rogers, George H.	1870
Shannon, Thomas B.	1871–1872
Estee, Morris, M.	1873–1874
Carpenter, Gideon J.	1875–1877
Berry, Campbell P.	1877–1879
Cowdrey, Jabez F.	1880–1881
Parks, William H.	1881–1882; 1885–1886
LaRue, Hugh M.	1883–1884
Jordan, William H.	1887–1888
Howe, Robert	1889–1890
Coombs, Frank L.	1891–1892; 1897–1898
Gould, Frank H.	1893–1895
Lynch, John C.	1895–1896
Anderson, Alden	1899–1900
Pendleton, Cornelius	1901–1902
Fisk, Arthur G.	1903–1904
Prescott, Frank C.	1905–1906
Beardslee, Robert L.	1907–1908
Stanton, Philip A.	1909–1910
Hewitt, Arthur H.	1911–1912
Young, Clement C.	1913–1919
Wright, Henry W.	1919–1922
Merriam, Frank F.	1923–1926
Levey, Edgar C.	1927–1933
Little, Walter J.	1933–1934
Clowdsley, Forsythe C.	1934–1935

Craig, Edward	1935–1937
Jones, William M.	1937–1939
Peek, Paul	1939–1940
Garland, Gordon	1940–1943
Lyon, Charles	1943–1947
Collins, Samuel L.	1947–1953
Silliman, James L.	1953–1955
Lincoln, Luther H.	1955–1959
Brown, Ralph M.	1959–1961
Unruh, Jesse M.	1961–1968
Monagan, Robert T.	1969–1970
Moretti, Bob	1971–1974
McCarthy, Leo T.	1974–1980
Brown, Willie L., Jr.	1981–

Superintendents of Public Instruction
Ex Officio Regents

Fitzgerald, Oscar P.	1868–1871
Bolander, Henry N.	1871–1875
Carr, Ezra S.	1875–1880
Campbell, Fred M.	1880–1883
Welcker, William T.	1883–1887
Hoitt, Ira G.	1887–1891
Anderson, J.W.	1891–1895
Black, Samuel T.	1895–1898
Meredith, Charles T.	1898
Kirk, Thomas J.	1899–1907
Hyatt, Edward	1907–1918
Wood, William C.	1919–1927
Cooper, William J.	1927–1929
Kersey, Vierling	1929–1937
Dexter, Walter F.	1937–1945
Simpson, Roy E.	1945–1962
Rafferty, Max	1963–1970
Riles, Wilson	1971–1982
Honig, Bill	1983–1993

Presidents of the State Board of Agriculture
Ex Officio Regents

(In the earlier years, these were Presidents of the Agricultural Society)

Reed, Charles F.	1868–1872
Carey, R.S.	1873–1876
Biggs, Marion	1877
Boruck, Marcus D.	1878
LaRue, Hugh M.	1879–1880; 1882
Shafter, James M.	1881
Finigan, P.A.	1883–1884
Carr, Jesse D.	1885–1886
Shippee, Lodowick U.	1887–1888
Green, Christopher	1889–1891
Cox, Frederick	1891–1892
Boggs, John	1893–1894
Chase, Charles M.	1895–1898
Spreckels, Adolph	1898–1904
Rush, Benjamin F.	1904–1909
Jastro, Henry	1909–1910
Scott, A.L.	1911–1913

Perry, John M.	1914–1916
Roeding, George C.	1917–1919
Jastro, Henry A.	1921–1925
Condee, Robert A.	1925–1930
Miller, Azariel B.	1931–1938
Meigs, Stewart	1939–1943
McFadden, Arthur J.	1943–1959
Watson, John S.	1959–1963
Tapp, Jesse W.	1964–1967
Grant, Allan	1967–1974

*Presidents of the Mechanics Institute
Ex Officio Regents*

Hallidie, Andrew S.	1868–1878
Scott, Irving M.	1878–1880
Cornwall, Pierre B.	1881–1889
Kerr, David	1889–1891
Stump, Irwin C.	1892
Hallidie, Andrew S.	1893–1895
Denicke, Ernst N.	1896–1900
Irving, Samuel C.	1901
Taussig, Rudolph J.	1902–1906; 1908–1912
Mead, Lewis R.	1906–1908
Jenks, Livingston	1913–1918
Mauzy, Byron	1918–1928
von Geldern, Otto	1929–1932
Scott, Arthur W.	1932
Cumming, Joseph M.	1932–1937
Steiger, Charles D.	1937
Hodgen, Joseph D.	1938–1941
Hind, George U.	1941–1946
Stoddard, Elgin	1946–1949
Merchant, William G.	1949–1961
Wilkens, Arthur E.	1961–1962
Meyer, Theodore R.	1962–1969
Brett, James Q.	1968
Moore, Joseph A., Jr.	1969–1974
McDaniel, David J.	1974

*Presidents of the Alumni Association
Ex Officio Regents*

Creed, Wiggington E.	1919–1920
Gregory, Warren	1920–1922
Miller, Clinton E.	1922–1924
Merrill, Charles W.	1924–1925
Wangenheim, Julius	1926–1928
Brown, Everett J.	1929–1930
Raskins, Samuel	1930–1932
Olney, Warren	1932–1934
Hotchkis, Preston	1934–1936

Fisher, Ralph T.	1936–1938
Masser, Harry L.	1938–1940
Wheeler, Charles S., Jr.	1940–1942
Yost, Paul	1943–1944
Witter, Jean C.	1945–1946
Barnes, Stanley N.	1947–1948
Hutchinson, Paul R.	1948–1949
Hale, William M.	1949–1950
Canaday, John E.	1950–1951
Toll, Maynard J.	1951–1952
Crowell, Warren H.	1952–1953
Symes, John P.	1953–1954
Cunningham, Thomas J.	1954–1955
Harbach, Edwin L.	1955–1956
Nigg, Cyril C.	1956–1957
Majors, O. Cort	1957–1958
Vaughn, John V.	1958–1959
Smith, Mortimer	1959–1960
Forbes, William	1960–1961
Archer, James	1961–1962
Alshuler, Robert E.	1962–1963
Nash, Norris	1963–1964
Davis, William T.	1964–1965
Mage, John R.	1965–1966
Haldeman, H.R.	1966–1967
Hudson, William	1967–1968
Pettitt, Roger C.	1968–1969
Witter, Wendell W.	1969–1970
Farrer, William C.	1970–1971
Markey, Christian	1971–1972
Smith, Bert L.	1972–1973
Keene, William B.	1973–1974
Link, George H.	1974–1975
Morris, Edward A.	1975–1976
Collins, James	1975–1976
Willens, Earl P.	1976–1977
Field, Charles D.	1976–1977
Reithner, Donald G.	1977–1978
Pendergast, Gene E.	1977–1978
Biles, Cheryl F.	1978–1979
Plant, Forrest A.	1978–1979
Wenzel, Lee B.	1979–1980
Kieffer, George D.	1979–1980
Rosston, John W.	1980–1981
Goodman, Allan J.	1980–1981
Wainer, Stanley A.	1981–1982
Weeth, Lois W.	1981–1982
Conner, Shirley B.	1982–1983
Phillips, Frank S.	1982–1983
Thayer, James N.	1983–1984
Schmidt, Douglas E.	1983–1984

Milliken, William	1984–1985
Pennebaker, George	1984–1985
Farrell, John B.	1985–1986
Cusumano, Gary	1985–1986
Hutchison, Claude	1986–1987
Toledano, James	1986–1987
Lee, R. Marilyn	1987–1988
Mandel, Beatrice	1987–1988
Heggie, Richard	1988–1989
Johnson, S. Sue	1988–1989
Luke, Sherrill	1989–1990
Enomoto, Ron	1989–1990
Newkirk, Martha	1990–1991
Hoadley, Walter E.	1990–1991
Ochoa, Ralph	1991–1992
Anderson, Gail G.	1991–1992
Stoney, Carl	1992–1993
Hall, Paul	1992–1993
Robert E. Murphy	1993–1994
Roy L. Shults	1993–1994

*Presidents of the University
Ex Officio Regents*

(UC Presidents were not ex officio members of the Board prior to David P. Barrows)

Barrows, David P.	1919–1923
Campbell, William W.	1923–1930
Sproul, Robert G.	1930–1958
Kerr, Clark	1958–1967
Wellman, Harry R.	1967 (Acting)
Hitch, Charles J.	1968–1975
Saxon, David S.	1975–1983
Gardner, David P.	1983–1992
Peltason, Jack W.	1992–

Honorary Regents

Bowie, Augustus J.	1868–1880
Butterworth, S.F.	1868–1873
Felton, John B.	1868–1877
Friedlander, Isaac	1868–1869
Hager, John S.	1868–1890
Haight, Henry H.	1872
Hallidie, Andrew S.	1873
Low, Frederick F.	1868
Moss, Joseph M.	1868–1874
Moulder, Andrew J.	1868
Ralston, William C.	1868–1875
Sachs, Louis	1869–1875
Tompkins, Edward	1868–1872

Chairmen and Vice Chairmen of the Board of Regents

The following are lists of chairmen and vice chairmen of the Board of Regents.

According to the minutes, prior to 1920, a chairman was elected for each meeting of the Board to preside at that particular meeting.

The position of vice chairman was added to the Bylaws and Standing Orders in 1964.

Chairmen

Guy C. Earl. 1920–22
Arthur W. Foster, 1922–27
William H. Crocker, 1927–37
Garret McEnery, 1937–42
James K. Moffitt, 1942–48
Edward A. Dickson, 1948–56
Edwin Pauley, 1956–58
Donald McLaughlin, 1958–60
Edwin Pauley, 1960–62
Gerald Hagar, 1962–64
Edward Carter, 1964–66
Theodore R. Meyer, 1966–68
DeWitt A. Higgs, 1968–70
William French Smith, 1970–72
Dean A. Watkins, 1972–74
William French Smith, 1974–75
Elinor Heller, 1975–76
William French Smith, 1976
William K. Coblentz, 1976–78
Robert O. Reynolds, 1978–80
Joseph A. Moore, 1980–82
W. Glenn Campbell, 1982–83
Yori Wada, 1983–84
Vilma Martinez, 1984–86
Frank W. Clark, 1986–88
Leo S. Kolligian, 1988–89
Roy T. Brophy, 1989–91
Meredith J. Khachigian, 1991–93
Howard H. Leach, 1993–

Vice Chairmen

Donald McLaughlin, 1964–65
William M. Roth, 1965–66
Dorothy B. Chandler, 1966–67
Philip L. Boyd, 1967–68
Elinor Heller, 1968–69
William French Smith, 1969–70
DeWitt Higgs, 1970–71
Elinor Heller, 1971–72
Edward A. Carter, 1972–73
William K. Coblentz, 1973–74
DeWitt Higgs, 1974–75
William French Smith, 1975–76
William M. Roth, 1976
Edward A. Carter, 1976–77
Robert O. Reynolds, 1977–78
DeWitt Higgs, 1978–79
Joseph A. Moore, 1979–80
Edward Carter, 1980–81
W. Glenn Campbell, 1981–82
Vilma Martinez, 1982–83
Stanley K. Sheinbaum, 1983–84
Frank Clark, 1984–85
Robert Noyce, 1985–86
Yvonne B. Burke, 1986–87
Roy T. Brophy, 1987–88
Harold M. Williams, 1988–89
Meredith J. Khachigian, 1989–90
S. Stephen Nakashima, 1990–91
Jeremiah Hallisey, 1991–92
William T. Bagley, 1992–93
Harold M. Williams, 1993–

Source: Office of the Secretary of the Regents

Officers of the Regents

President of the Regents—The Governor of the State of California

Chairman of the Regents

Guy C. Earl	1920–1922
Arthur W. Foster	1922–1927
William H. Crocker	1927–1937
Garret McEnergy	1937–1942
James K. Moffitt	1942–1948
Edward A. Dickson	1948–1956
Edwin Pauley	1956–1958
Donald McLaughlin	1958–1960
Edwin Pauley	1960–1962
Gerald Hagar	1962–1964
Edward W. Carter	1964–1966
Theodore R. Meyer	1966–1968
DeWitt A. Higgs	1968–1970
William French Smith	1970–1972
Dean A. Watkins	1972–1974
William French Smith	1974–1975
Elinor Heller	1975–1976
William French Smith	1976
William K. Coblentz	1976–1978
Robert O. Reynolds	1978–1980
Joseph A. Moore	1980–1982
W. Glenn Campbell	1982–1983
Yori Wada	1983–1984
Vilma Martinez	1984–1986
Frank W. Clark	1986–1988
Leo S. Kolligian	1988–1989
Roy T. Brophy	1989–1991
Meredith J. Khachigian	1991–1993
Howard H. Leach	1993–present

Treasurer of the Regents

Regent William C. Ralston	1868–1875
Regent Darius O. Mills	1875–1883
James C. Flood	1883–1885
Louis Sloss	1885–1902
Lewis Gerstle	Aug.–Nov. 1902
Isias W. Hellman, Jr.	1903–1916
Regent Mortimer Fleischhacker	1916–1930
George Tourny	1930–1933
*Robert M. Underhill	1933–1963
Owsley B. Hammond	1963–1978
Herbert M. Gordon	1978–present

*Underhill was Secretary and Treasurer of the Regents and Land Agent (1933–60; Treasurer of the Regents and Land Agent (1960–63).

Secretary of the Regents

Andrew J. Moulder	1868–1873
Regent J. West Martin	Jan.–Apr. 1874
Robert E. C. Stearns	1874–1881
J. Harmon C. Bonte'	1881–1896
William A. McKowen (acting)	1896–1897
Edward W. Davis	1897–1898
William A. McKowen (acting)	1898–1903
William A. McKowen	Feb.–Dec. 1903
Victor H. Henderson (acting)	1903–1907
Carl C. Plehn	May–Nov. 1907
Victor H. Henderson (acting)	1907–1909
Victor H. Henderson	1909–1918
Robert G. Sproul (acting)	Jan.–June 1918
Ralph P. Merritt	1918–1920
Robert G. Sproul (acting)	Mar.–June 1920
Robert G. Sproul	1920–1930
Luther A. Nichols(acting)	July–Nov. 1930
Robert M. Underhill	1930–1960
Marjorie J. Woolman	1960–1982
Bonnie M. Smotony	1982–1993
Leigh Trivette	1993–Present

Counsel of the Regents

Henry H. Haight	1877–1878
John B. Mhoon	1878–1903
Charles E. Snook	1903–1905

Title changed to **Attorney for the Regents**

Charles E. Snook	1905–1908
Fletcher A. Cutler	1908–1911
Warren Olney, Jr.	1911–1919
James M. Mannon, Jr.	1919–1923
Jno. U. Calkins, Jr.	1923–1941
**Ashley H. Conrad	1941–1946
Jno. U. Calkins, Jr.	1946–1955

In 1955, the title of the office was changed to General Counsel of the Regents.

Thomas J. Cunningham	1955–1973
Donald L. Reidhaar	1973–1985
James E. Holst	1986–present

In 1993, the title was changed to General Counsel and Vice President—Legal Affairs.

**Acting while incumbent on leave

Land Agent

Horace A. Higley	1869–1873
James W. Shanklin	1875–1876
J. Hamilton Harris	1876–1888

This office was made an additional appointment held by the Secretary of the Regents in 1873–74 and 1889–1918. It was made an additional appointment of the Comptroller between 1918 and 1931, an additional appointment held by the Secretary (1931–33), by the Treasurer (1933–52), and ex officio by the Treasurer after 1952.

Comptroller

Ralph P. Merritt	1911–1920
Robert G. Sproul (acting)	Mar.–June 1920
Robert G. Sproul	1920–1930
Luther A. Nichols	1930–1940
James H. Corley	1940–1949

In 1949, the title of this office was changed to Vice President—Business Affairs. Its accounting functions were assumed by a chief accounting officer.

Vice President—Business Affairs

James H. Corley	1949–1959

In 1959, this office was placed under the jurisdiction of the President of the University.

Chief Accounting Officer of the Regents

Olaf Lundberg	Jan.–June 1950

The title of this office was changed to controller in July, 1950.

Controller

Olaf Lundberg	1950–1953
George E. Stevens(acting)	1953–1955
Raymond Kettler	1955–1959

The office of controller was placed under the jurisdiction of the President of the University in a newly-established office of Vice President—Finance.

Research: How UC Has Improved People's Lives

People's lives constantly are touched by UC's discoveries and inventions.

For example, UC architects and engineers design the buildings people live and work in, and the roads they travel. UC scientists develop new varieties of fruits and vegetables, and they pioneer medical advances that fight disease.

UC researchers and scholars also help write laws, solve social problems and provide new insights that help people understand the world around them.

The list below is a sampling of UC's research contributions that it has made through its agricultural, scientific, medical and other research programs. These discoveries resulted from work over the years at the UC's Berkeley, Davis, Irvine, Los Angeles, Riverside, San Diego, San Francisco, Santa Barbara and Santa Cruz campuses and at the three federal laboratories that the University manages at Berkeley, Livermore and Los Alamos.

Feeding the World

In the late 1800s, researchers discovered how to remove salts from the "alkali" soils in California's central valley, thus turning barren land into the world's most productive farming region.

In 1915, UC studies led to new, less severe fruit tree pruning techniques, which increase yields and maintain fruit quality.

In 1920, a UC bacteriologist developed a heat process to kill the organism that causes botulism, the deadliest form of food poisoning. The discovery led to the modern canning industry.

In the 1940s, California's strawberry industry was saved when UC scientists developed a hybrid plant resistant to a devastating virus. UC has since developed about 40 strawberry varieties grown worldwide. Today, California accounts for 75 percent of the U.S. strawberry production.

In 1946, UC scientists stopped the "tristeza" virus from wiping out California's citrus industry by creating a hybrid resistent to the virus. Much of the citrus in South America and South Africa had been killed by the virus before the hybrid was developed.

UC was the first to use bacteria, rather than pesticides, to control insects. A bug "pathogen" was used in 1951 to combat a caterpillar that destroyed alfalfa. Today, bacteria is commonly used against pests.

From 1956 to 1982, at least a half dozen varieties of tomatoes were developed by UC. They represent as much as 85 percent of the nation's production.

In 1958, UC scientists created four new varieties of asparagus that produce larger spears and grow beyond the normal harvest season.

In the 1960s and 1970s, UC scientists modernized farming with new machinery, such as tree-shaking devices for harvesting fruit and nuts, and the mechanical tomato harvester. Work to fine-tune equipment and develop new machines continues today.

More than a million people in Africa were fed and famine was averted by a black-eyed bean developed by UC in the 1980s. The bean, which thrives in drought-stricken Senegal, tripled crop productivity in one of the world's harshest environments.

Scientists discovered that a gene in a common bacterium triggers frost damage in crops. In 1988, they altered the bacterium to prevent freezing and found that crops coated with the so-called "ice minus" bacterium reduces frost damage.

The ash whitefly, which ruined crops in the West, was controlled by UC scientists by the early 1990s, using a tiny stingless wasp that feeds on the flies. The fly was eradicated without pesticides.

A new avocado variety, developed by UC in 1991, outproduces the industry mainstay by 2 to 1. The "Gwen" avocado equals the quality of the Hass, currently the most common, but the Gwen is larger and more uniform.

Tomatoes, genetically altered by UC scientists, turn ripe on cue, and remain ripe for as long as three months without spoiling. This discovery in 1992 may help consumers, especially those in Third World countries, store fruit longer without refrigeration.

Ensuring Better Health

In 1922, two UC scientists discovered vitamin E, which is needed to protect against damage to DNA, the molecules that contain the genetic blueprint for life.

In 1935, Vitamin K, a factor necessary for blood to clot properly, was discovered by a UC scientist.

In 1946, a minimum requirement of vitamin A for humans was identified by UC scientists studying growth and reproduction.

In 1967, a potent form of Vitamin D, critical to metabolism, was discovered by UC. This work led to new approaches to manage diseases, particularly of the bone and kidney.

In 1969, a UC scientist developed a blood test for the genetic defect that causes Tay-Sachs, a disease that causes mental retardation, crippling and death. This led to prenatal tests and parental screening.

In 1974, UC epidemiologists discovered that the organism Chlamydia trachomatis can cause pneumonia and lung damage in newborns. Expectant mothers now can be tested and treated.

UC scientists were the first to identify the lack of a gene as a cause of disease. In 1975, they discovered that a missing gene results in a blood disease called alpha-thalassemia, causing anemia and sometimes death. A prenatal test was developed.

In 1979, the gene for human growth hormone was first cloned by UC for mass production. Today, the synthetic hormone treats thousands of children whose growth otherwise would be stunted.

In 1981, the first human vaccine, created by genetic engineering, was developed by UC scientists who cloned the gene for the hepatitis B virus.

An eye test, developed by UC optometrists in 1982, detects an inability of diabetics to see blue. Patients are shown green, red and blue spots of light flashed against a yellow background. If detected early, treatment can prevent severe vision loss.

A procedure developed by a UC doctor in 1982 restores hearing by replacing damaged middle ear bones with sculpted cartilage.

UC scientists in 1982 discovered "prions," an infectious pathogen believed to cause degenerative brain diseases. The discovery is providing insight into diseases such as Alzheimer's disease, the fourth leading cause of death among Americans.

In 1984, the first "bladder pacemaker," now in clinical trials, was developed by UC urologists to restore continence for paraplegics, quadriplegics and others.

UC pediatricians in 1984 were first to find a link between Accutane, a widely used anti-acne drug, and birth defects.

In the mid-1980s, a UC ophthalmologist developed a way to transplant corneas in infants suffering from a blinding disease called Peter's Anomaly, characterized by a cloudy, opaque covering over one or both eyes.

In 1987, a hormone called human chorionic gonadotropin, a marker for Down's syndrome, was discovered by a UC researcher. He developed a blood test to determine the risk for having a Down's baby.

UC scientists in 1987 developed a high-speed cell sorter that analyzes 50,000 cells or chromosomes a second, 5–10 times faster than other instruments. The technology is used to help fight diseases such as AIDS and leukemia.

Men who have had vasectomies are able to father children with a procedure developed by UC in 1990. Doctors developed a technique to remove sperm, then place them in "test tubes" for fertilization.

An inner-ear implant, developed by UC in 1991, enables the deaf to recognize tones to understand speech. The device stimulates the auditory nerve via an electrode, inserted into the inner ear.

A nicotine skin patch, worn on the upper arm to wean smokers off cigarettes, was developed in 1991 by UC researchers.

UC scientists in 1991 discovered chromosome 19, responsible for atherosclerosis or hardening of the arteries.

In 1991, UC scientists developed a way to "paint" or "stain" human chromosome with fluorescent dyes to highlight abnormalities that may cause inherited diseases or cancer.

A test for lead in pottery was developed by UC scientists in 1991 to determine if and how much lead pottery contains.

UC researchers were the first in 1992 to link low levels of vitamin C to increased genetic damage in sperm, which could mean greater risk of birth defects in embryos.

UC researchers in 1992 found a way to screen chicken eggs for salmonella bacteria, using technology originally developed to detect chemical and biological weapons.

In 1991, UC researchers found that eating yogurt containing living organisms increases levels of gamma interferon, which strengthens the immune system.

Saving Lives

The three most common radioisotopes used in nuclear medicine for testing and treatment were discovered at UC in the late 1930s.

In 1947, UC developed a life-saving technique to re-establish the drainage of bile from the liver to the intestine when the bile duct is damaged. The condition can be fatal if bile is not drained.

In 1964, a standard test for tissue typing was developed by a UC doctor. Today, patients throughout the world undergo this test before receiving an organ transplant.

In 1967, UC researchers developed a way to maintain organs for transplant for up to 72 hours, making it possible to transport organs from distant hospitals.

UC doctors developed two treatments for premature infants whose lungs are not fully developed, the most common cause of death among newborns. The treatments, developed between 1969 and 1990, increased survival for afflicted babies worldwide from 50 percent 25 years ago to more than 90 percent today.

The "Ames test," developed by a UC scientist in the early 1970s, is the most widely used measure for chemicals that may cause cancer. The test led to the removal of chemicals in children's pajamas, photocopying toner and hair dyes.

A procedure to temporarily relieve failing hearts was developed by UC in 1976. The "venoarterial bypass" removes blood, processes it through bypass equipment and pumps it back into an artery.

In 1980, a UC research team was the first to show that organ rejection could be significantly reduced by a series of three blood transfusions from the organ donor before surgery.

In 1981, UC doctors were the first to successfully operate on an infant while still in the womb. Today, UC specialists alone perform "open fetal surgery," during which the fetus is partially removed from the uterus and then returned to the womb.

A UC researcher in 1981 developed a technique that enables labs to make a prenatal diagnosis in less than two weeks rather than a month.

Continued following the photo pages

SCIENCE AND TECHNOLOGY

Faculty, researchers and students in science and engineering at the University all share in a common pursuit: the search for knowledge in highly technical fields that require equal amounts of intellectual discipline and personal dedication.

While the challenges that they face can be formidable, their efforts often prove both stimulating and rewarding. They know that they are contributing to knowledge that can help meet the future needs of society.

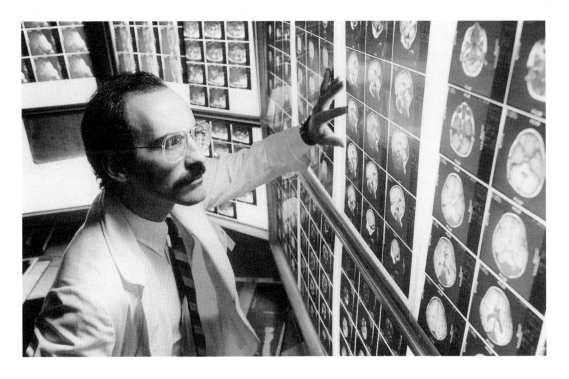

Research *(cont'd)*

A gene marker that detects the Huntington's disease gene, an inherited fatal neurological disorder, was discovered in 1989 by UC scientists.

Easing the Pain

In 1970, UC doctors developed a plastic and metal artificial knee, the first to replicate the motion of the entire knee joint.

Debilitating pain from nerve damage can be relieved with a technique developed by UC in 1973 called "deep brain stimulation." A platinum wire is inserted into the brain to electrically stimulate the brain and relieve pain.

In 1974, an artificial ankle was developed by UC doctors to replace joints damaged by arthritis. Today, the "UCI ankle" remains one of the most widely used in orthopedic medicine.

A method to inject medication under the tongue, when other veins are not accessible, was developed in 1982 by a UC doctor.

In 1989, UC researchers adapted a heart pump implant to pump insulin in diabetics. It eliminates the need for daily insulin injections.

In 1992, UC doctors discovered that aspirin relieves pain in part by blocking communication between spinal cord nerves. This reversed the belief that aspirin works at the place of injury and could lead to injection of drugs like aspirin into the spinal column.

Fighting AIDS

The first national report on AIDS was written in 1981 by a UC immunologist. It was the first warning of what was to become a worldwide epidemic.

In 1983, UC scientists were among the first three groups in the world to isolate the AIDS virus.

UC opened the nation's first AIDS outpatient clinic in 1983 at UC-affiliate San Francisco General Hospital.

UC opened the nation's first AIDS patient hospital ward in 1983 at UC-affiliated San Francisco General Hospital.

In 1984, UC doctors first warned that AIDS could be transmitted through blood. This led to the UC development of a heat treatment to kill the virus for blood transfusions.

In 1993, UC researchers found a quick method to determine if infants are infected with the AIDS virus. The test separates the mother's and infant's antibodies to obtain accurate results.

Clearing the Air

An electrical "precipitation" device, which cleans smokestack emissions, was developed by UC chemists in 1907 and is still used today. High voltage draws out toxic particles from polluting gases.

In the 1950s, UC engineers were the first to identify the photochemical process that creates Los Angeles smog. They also designed a carburetor that led to fuel injection for cleaner-running cars.

Global warming, now known as the "greenhouse effect," was first recognized by UC scientists in 1957. They found that carbon dioxide from fossil fuels, such as coal and petroleum, traps solar heat in the atmosphere, much as a greenhouse.

In 1974, a UC chemist co-discovered that chlorofluorocarbons are depleting the earth's ozone layer. The finding led to a 1976 ban in the United States and other countries on CFC propellants, including those used in aerosol cans.

Protecting the Environment

In 1947, UC foresters developed cultivation practices that today are the standard for reseeding forests.

UC scientists helped save the gray whale from near-extinction in the 1950s by persuading the Mexican government to preserve a major breeding lagoon in Baja California.

Energy-saving measures that are saving billions of dollars a year worldwide have been developed by UC physicists since the 1970s. Contributions include energy-efficient windows and a "compact" fluorescent bulb.

In 1972, a UC professor of natural history founded UC's Natural Reserve System, which today preserves more than 100,000 acres of pristine California land for teaching and research.

Car engines are more efficient and less polluting, due to computer software developed in 1973 by UC scientists. The software, used to design engines, simulates an engine's cylinder to project factors such as fuel efficiency, pollution emissions and power.

A campaign that brought attention to dolphins drowning in tuna-fishing nets was spearheaded by UC scientists during the mid-1970s. The campaign led to the prohibition of the nets by U.S. fisheries.

UC's Predatory Bird Research Group nursed California's peregrine falcons back from the brink of extinction from 1975 to 1992. The birds were nearly wiped out in the 1960s by DDT. Now, there are at least 120 nesting pairs.

UC overturned the belief that stable environments are essential for the survival of diverse species in tropical rainforests and coral reefs. They found in 1978 that disturbances, such as hurricanes, keep the most competitive species from dominating.

In 1987, UC scientists found a way to remove toxic levels of selenium in soil using microbes that consume the trace element. Previously, soil microbes were too slow to be practical. UC scientists sped-up the process by adding activators.

A process to clean contaminated soil by injecting steam into the ground and flushing out pollutants was developed in 1991 by a team of UC researchers.

Safer, Faster Travel

A geometric runway design, developed by UC engineers in 1957, enabled planes to take-off faster than ever before and allowed airports to boost capacities. The design is still used today.

"Centerline" runway lighting, the standard at airports worldwide, was developed by UC engineers in 1959. Lights in the center, rather than on the side, help pilots land more accurately. A UC engineer also wrote the first book on airport engineering.

In 1966, UC researchers developed and tested highway signs, warning "wrong way, do not enter," which became the standard for highways nationwide.

UC research led to a federal law in 1966 that established safety standards for new cars including lap seatbelts. Other innovations prompted by UC are shatterproof glass for windshields and headrests to prevent "whiplash." Traffic moves faster through some toll booths now, thanks to an invention by UC scientists. The system, developed in 1972, reads electronic tags on windshields and "bills" drivers as cars pass.

In the Stars

Since the 1960s, UC scientists pioneered studies of the masses and dynamics of galaxies. They were the first to recognize explosive events in galaxies as well as the characteristics of star-like quasars.

In the 1970s, a UC geochemist used the radioactive decay system to date rocks and minerals, calculating a more accurate date for the "age" of the earth and solar system at 4.5 billion years.

UC scientists in the late 1970s designed power generators for the deep-space missions of the National Aeronautics and Space Administration.

In 1979, a UC physicist was the first to suggest that an asteroid or comet struck the earth 65 million years ago, altering the earth's environment and causing the extinction of dinosaurs.

In 1987, UC physicists discovered the neutrino, a chargeless subatomic particle.

In 1992, UC astronomers designed and co-constructed the world's largest telescope, the W.M. Keck Telescope, atop the dormant Mauna Kea volcano on the island of Hawaii.

UC scientists in 1992 discovered "ancient seeds" that grew into today's galaxies. They showed that slight temperature fluctuations in radiation left by the "big bang," the explosion believed to have created the universe some 15 billion years ago, evolved into galaxies and space.

Innovative Devices

A UC scientist invented the rectilinear scintillation scanner to locate tumors and to study liver, kidney and lung function. The machine, developed in 1950, pinpoints radioisotopes injected into the body.

The first wetsuit was invented in 1952 by a UC physicist. From a crude rubber prototype, wetsuits have evolved into a $100 million annual business.

In 1959, UC scientists invented the first practical process to turn salt water into fresh water. The discovery has created rivers of fresh water in the Middle East and North Africa.

The ground-fault interrupter, found in virtually every electrical outlet to protect people from electric shocks, was invented in 1965 by a UC engineer.

In 1974, a UC pharmacologist invented the positron emission tomography (PET) scanner, which shows a cinematographic view of organs such as the brain or heart.

In 1975, UC doctors created a device to determine when "brain death" occurs.

In 1976, a method of detecting radioactivity to date archaeologic and geologic materials was invented by a UC physicist.

In 1988, an electrically powered microscopic motor, no larger than the width of a human hair, was developed by a UC engineer and graduate students for uses such as surgical equipment.

In 1990, UC researchers performed the first robot-assisted surgery, using a device they developed called "Robodoc" that cuts bone for hip implants.

New Frontiers

UC scientists set up the first earthquake recording network in California from 1887 to 1898, creating a data base still used today. UC researchers also mapped and named the San Andreas Fault.

In 1924, a helium and oxygen mixture was developed by a UC chemist, enabling deep sea divers to delve deeper in the sea than ever before. The mixture prevents the "bends," a painful condition that can be fatal to divers when surfacing.

In the 1930s, a UC professor was one of the founders of modern statistical theory.

UC scientists in the 1930s discovered plutonium and eight other transuranium elements. The discovery of plutonium revolutionized science and medicine, leading to the nuclear bomb, nuclear energy and nuclear medicine.

In 1931, UC scientists helped open the door to the "Atomic Age" when they invented the first cyclotron, or atom smasher.

In 1954, the photosynthetic process, by which plants use sunlight to change carbon dioxide and water into sugar, was discovered by a UC scientist.

In 1956, a UC researcher founded "fuzzy logic" technology, which enables machines to respond to changing conditions. When a "fuzzy" vacuum cleaner moves from carpet to bare floor, for instance, it changes power accordingly. Manufacturers now are incorporating fuzzy logic into appliances.

In 1965, a UC scientist pioneered "biogeology," which merged geology with biology, chemistry and cosmology. The field brought attention to environmental problems society is coping with today.

In 1968, a UC biologist proved that RNA drives the activity of ribosomes, which manufacture proteins in every living cell. It was one of the first indications of RNA's importance to life.

A UC scientist was the first to identify the reaction center in photosynthesis. Research, conducted from 1972 to 1992, found that the reaction center is responsible for light absorption and energy transfer.

In 1973, a UC biochemist and a Stanford colleague invented gene splicing techniques, which launched the multi-billion dollar biotechnology industry.

In 1974, the mechanism that activates gene expression, to determine for instance why a cell is a liver or a kidney cell, was discovered at UC. This work furthered the understanding of cell growth, such as in embryonic development and cancer.

UC virologists discovered that cancer-causing genes exist in healthy cells. In 1976, they showed that environmental, hormonal and other factors can alter cell structure and result in cancer.

In 1984, a UC research team used genetic engineering to decode genes from a 20-million-year-old fossil magnolia leaf. By comparing old and new DNA, far-reaching conclusions are being made about evolution.

In 1990, UC researchers developed a way to study small amounts of cancer-causing chemicals, as little as a single molecule. An accelerator mass spectrometer monitors carcinogens in quantities that more closely approximate realistic situations.

UC scientists analyzed the oldest piece of genetic material ever found: DNA from a bee dating back as long as 40 million years. They proved in 1992 that DNA could survive longer than believed.

Other Notable Achievements

Since the 1930s, UC researchers helped make California wines among the best in the world by developing new high quality grape varieties and new winemaking techniques.

A half dozen types of cement, developed by UC engineers during the 1930s, made possible landmarks including the Hoover Dam and the Bay Bridge between San Francisco and Oakland.

In the late 1950s, UC scientists developed a chemical treatment for fabric that prevents moths and carpet beetle larvae from eating wool fiber.

California's no-fault divorce law, the first of its kind, was co-drafted by a UC law professor. The law eliminated the need for blame in a failed marriage. Since it became California law in 1970, every U.S. state enacted some version of no-fault divorce.

In 1972, UC established the Thesaurus Linguae Graecae, which has recorded more than 9,500 works by nearly 4,000 ancient Greek authors, representing virtually all the surviving texts from 750 B.C., the time of Homer, to A.D. 600.

A computer program, developed in 1976 by UC scientists to study stress on weapons systems, was adapted to simulate car crashes and the handling of products to improve their design.

Techniques to avoid potential failures in computer software were identified in 1980 by UC researchers. The systems are applied to operations such as nuclear reactors and space flights.

In 1981, two UC scientists and their graduate students designed a cheaper, faster approach to computer design that has been adopted by virtually every major U.S. computer maker.

A technique, developed in 1988 by UC scientists, helps criminal investigators obtain fingerprints on surfaces where conventional dusting powder and chemicals fail. The process uses gold particles to bind to proteins left by fingerprints.

"Smart" glass, which changes colors in response to chemical compounds, was developed in 1992 by UC. The glass could be used in medicine to analyze blood for calcium and oxygen.

Material, believed to be the world's lightest, was developed by UC scientists in 1992 using agar, a seaweed derivative. Called Seagel for "safe emulsion agar gel," the biodegradable material is lighter than air and could have numerous uses such as packaging foam or insulation.

Research Supported by Special Regents' Programs: Special Regents' Programs are established by action of the Regents and are financed by the University Opportunity Fund.

The University Opportunity Fund is derived from UC's share of indirect cost recovery on federal contracts and grants supporting faculty research.

Campuses receive block allocations from the University Opportunity Fund in four major areas: research, instruction, institutional support, and deferred maintenance.

Separate allocations are provided for Student and Faculty Affirmative Action.

UC's long-term goal is to use the University Opportunity Fund primarily for projects that improve the quality of research and instructional programs.

REFERENCES: "1993–94 Budget for Current Operations," November 1992, Office of the President.

Retirement Incentive Programs: In 1990, "Plus 5" was a popular term around UC.

On October 18, the Regents approved a workforce reduction plan under a Voluntary Early Retirement Incentive Program called VERIP or "Plus 5."

It was offered to UCRP members who met certain age and service requirements.

Eligible members were offered five additional years of service credit and a one-time lump-sum payment as incentives to retire earlier than they had planned.

The hope was that VERIP would be a cost-effective way of achieving substantial savings to help offset the effects of drastic state budget cuts on the University.

More than 3,000 employees eventually "VERIPed." Figures showed 59 percent of the estimated 4,100 eligible staff and 33 percent of the 2,000 eligible faculty retired under the program.

As a result, UC saved an estimated $75 million and helped reduce its permanent workforce by nearly 2,000 people.

A generally equivalent retirement incentive program not funded by UCRP was offered to PERS members.

Then along came "Take 5."

In 1992, in the face of increased budget cuts by the state, the Regents approved a new voluntary program that enabled faculty and staff to retire early.

The program, called VERIP 2 or "Take 5," was similar to the one offered the previous year.

Some 2,277 members accepted the offer to retire under the second program.

A second voluntary program called TRIP also was approved in 1992 to help meet the budget crisis.

This allowed employees to reduce their work hours over the short term. Some compensation to be given at a later time was approved, in order to balance the temporary drop in salary.

In 1993, a third voluntary early retirement program was approved.

REFERENCES: "With VERIP Numbers In, Administration and Faculty Count up Gains, Worry About Losses," *Notice,* Vol. 15, No. 7, May 1991; "Early retirement, work reduction plans offered," *UC Focus,* Vol. 6, No. 7, July 29, 1992; information from University Benefit Programs and from University Relations, Office of the President.

CROSS-REFERENCES: Retiree Associations; Retirement Age; Retirement Plan.

Retirement Plan: Faculty and staff throughout the entire University system receive a comprehensive benefits package as members of the University of California Retirement System (UCRS).

The package includes UCRP, a defined benefit pension plan, called the Basic Plan, which provides retirement, survivor and disability income to members and beneficiaries.

UCRP is funded by the University through employer contributions, as well as by an assessment from a growing membership.

The investment objective is to achieve a rate of return that ensures that the plan can meet its financial obligations to members, survivors and beneficiaries.

With its conservative funding policies and successful investment performance, the plan in the mid-1960s gained the financial stability necessary to meet its obligations.

Features of the Basic Plan continue to change, both through liberalization of UC requirements and through legislative amendments to the governing statutes in the Internal Revenue Code.

Benefits under the Basic Plan are determined by specific formulas rather than by accumulation of contributions and earnings.

The formulas are based on an individual's years of service, age and highest average three-year salary at retirement.

A member may retire as early as age 50 with at least five years of service credit.

Also available as part of the University of California Retirement System (UCRS) are two defined contribution plans: one for mandatory employee assessments, and one for voluntary savings.

These allow participants to accumulate additional retirement benefits through salary deduction and to invest monies among five UC-managed common trust funds.

When UC introduced its first employee pension plan back in 1904, it was much more modest than at present.

At that time, UC purchased annuities for only one specific group of employees: retiring professors at Berkeley and San Francisco.

However, from that time to 1937, the pension plan for UC faculty was enhanced.

Then in 1937, all nonacademic employees were included in the newly established State Employees' Retirement System, now known as the Public Employees' Retirement System (PERS).

In 1961, the Regents established the University of California Retirement System (UCRS), extending coverage to all full-time UC employees.

Also in 1961, PERS integrated with Social Security. At that time, continuing PERS members, including UC employees, were given the option of electing Social Security coverage. New members were automatically covered.

However, the Regents chose not to offer Social Security coverage to UCRS members.

In 1967, a defined contribution plan was first offered on an after-tax basis only. Savings and Equity Funds were the initial investment alternatives.

In 1969, another plan was established that allowed contributions on a pretax basis.

In 1971, annual automatic cost-of-living adjustments (COLAs) were first applied to benefits in UCRP. The maximum COLAs were 2 percent. Prior to this, members had received cost-of-living increases only on an ad hoc basis.

Survivor and disability benefits also were greatly improved, principally to match those offered by Social Security.

In 1976, plan members were offered the option of joining Social Security. Since then, all new employees have been automatically covered with Social Security.

Both members and UC contribute to the retirement plan and to Social Security, and members can be eligible for benefits from both programs.

Both retirement and survivor benefits are reduced by a portion of the Social Security benefit payable at age 65.

In 1985–86, investment options in UC's defined contribution plans were further expanded to include a number of other types of investments, such as an externally managed, socially responsible mutual fund.

Between 1986 and 1988, plan changes and statutory reporting and full disclosure policies were adopted and implemented as part of a concentrated effort to bring UCRP into compliance with governing provisions of the Internal Revenue Code.

In 1989, UCRP was restructured into a separate plan document and trust. This replaced the plan approved much earlier by the Regents, which had been in the form of a corporate resolution.

REFERENCES: UC's Financial Reports; Faculty Manual; UC Retirement Plan, Regents' Items for Action, October 18, 1990; "Comparison of Retirement Benefits," Item 509 for Action, Regents' Committee on Finance, November 18, 1992; information from University Benefit Programs and University Relations Offices, Office of the President.

CROSS-REFERENCES: Budgets.

Risk Management: In 1970, the Regents adopted a policy to guide the University in determining the programs it might need to cover property or liability risks.

Within the Office of the President, the Office of Risk Management is charged with developing and maintaining programs of self-insurance, insurance, and loss prevention to protect assets of the Regents and UC from unanticipated losses.

The office administers risk management programs that include (1) professional medical and hospital liability, (2) property and casualty loss, (3) risk financing, (4) contract and resource management, and (5) workers' compensation.

In carrying out its responsibilities, the risk management office provides uniform interpretation, operation and administration of the program, manages UC's self-insurance programs, negotiates and purchases insurance, and coordinates matters relating to loss prevention.

In addition, the office provides systematic risk analysis, develops techniques to reduce potential exposure to loss, maintains a constant overview of the economy, the insurance market and the risk management profession, and adjusts liability and property claims.

The risk management office coordinates its programs with UC's campuses, teaching hospitals, national laboratories, corporate offices, and outside entities which have a relationship with the University.

REFERENCES: Annual reports, Office of Risk Management, Office of the President; UC's Business and Finance Bulletins.

CROSS-REFERENCES: Environmental Health and Safety.

Roundtable on Educational Opportunity. See California Roundtable On Educational Opportunity.

S

Sea Grant Program: In 1966, the concept of land grant colleges took to the seas.

At that time, a new national program called Sea Grant was enacted by Congress.

It brought together universities from around the country to promote the sustainable use of marine resources.

Since then, these institutions have been furnishing technical information and assistance in marine science and technology to researchers and administrators in academia, industry and the government.

The network now consists of 30 programs at more than 300 universities and affiliated institutions throughout the U.S.

The University became a Sea Grant College in 1973. Today, the California Sea Grant College is the largest of the 30 programs that make up the national program.

California Sea Grant has its headquarters at the Scripps Institution of Oceanography at UCSD. It is administered by the Universitywide Institute of Marine Resources.

California Sea Grant scientists conduct research, education and extension programs at UC's eight general campuses and at various California State University campuses and private universities.

How Sea Grant Works To Help Californians

A sea urchin fisherman needs to know how government regulations will affect his profits.

A schoolteacher wants the latest information on marine mammals.

A coastal county planning committee seeks information on the effectiveness of wetland mitigation.

A supermarket manager wants to know how to keep seafood fresh and safe.

To get the information they need, they go to the Sea Grant Extension Program, a marine advisory program established in 1971.

It is the principal provider of advisory services for the California Sea Grant Program.

Administered by UC Cooperative Extension, its role is to furnish up-to-date technical information and assistance to industry, government and academia so that the results of ocean research and technological development can reap the widest benefit to society.

These scientists study an array of subjects, such as ocean engineering and instrumentation (which encompasses, for example, the safety of ships and offshore platforms and the development of acoustic techniques for remote sensing of fish stocks); coastal ocean research, including water quality and wetland mitigation; development of new marine products, such as marine pharmaceuticals; improvement of seafood quality; and the health of California fisheries and aquaculture industry.

Advisory services for UC's Sea Grant are provided by the Sea Grant Extension Program.

REFERENCES: *California Ocean Research: A Sea Grant Sampler,* 1978, booklet produced by the Sea Grant College Program, Institute of Marine Resources, UC San Diego; "The California Sea Grant connection," *UC Focus,* Vol. 2, No. 3, November 1987, University Relations, Office of the President; Scripps Institution of Oceanography annual reports.

CROSS-REFERENCES: Oceanography and Marine Sciences.

Seismology: See Berkeley Campus Profile.

Site Selection Process for a New Campus: By the late 1980s, California's dramatic population surge had contributed to steadily increasing demands for admission to the University.

In November 1988, the Regents authorized UC's president to begin planning for new campuses in order to accommodate anticipated long-term enrollment growth.

In early 1989, the president appointed a Site Selection Task Force, advisory to him, to undertake the search for and analysis of potential new campus sites.

Over the next two years, the Regents took actions to approve the criteria and methodology for site selection and focus the search for the first new campus site in the central region of California.

Including the sites which had been identified by the initial consultant plus later sites submitted by interested communities and owners, the staff eventually visited over 85 sites throughout the region and prepared preliminary reports on each of them.

On the basis of the executive staff reports the Task Force designated 20 of these sites as candidate sites in March 1990.

The Task Force designated eight of these sites as preferred sites on June 8, 1990.

In July 1990, the Regents approved these eight sites for further study.

The designation of the eight preferred sites represented a major milestone in the selection process.

Subsequent to the Regents' action, the University informed the general public about the location of the sites under consideration, and the executive staff initiated discussions with site owners and local governments.

In October 1990, the Task Force visited each of the eight preferred sites and held public meetings in Modesto and Fresno to receive public comment about the sites.

In March 1991, the Regents approved the reduction of the number of sites under active consideration to three.

The three sites, all in the San Joaquin Valley, were Lake Yosemite in Merced County, Table Mountain in Madera County, and Academy in Fresno County.

At the same meeting the Regents endorsed the President's recommendation that the new campus be given the working title of the "San Joaquin Campus."

Between March 1991 and early 1993, the efforts of the task force focused on additional analyses of the three sites and continued negotiations with property owners to acquire the sites.

In March 1992, UC's president was scheduled to recommend to the Board which of the three sites should be advanced for further study and the preparation of an Environmental Impact Report, preparatory to selection of the final site for the prospective San Joaquin campus.

However, the presentation of this recommendation was postponed several times because of uncertainty about UC's budget situation.

In June 1992, the Task Force visited the Academy and Lake Yosemite sites and observed the proposed Table Mountain site.

In connection with each of these visits representatives of the local site committees and local governments briefed the Task Force on local plans for the sites and surrounding areas.

The Site Selection Task Force met in October and November 1992 to consider options for the site selection process, in light of forecasts of long-term financial concerns for the state and the increased uncertainty about the level of UC enrollment that the state would support in the future.

The task force recommended that the site selection process continue with the preparation of an Environmental Impact Report (EIR).

In addition, the task force added a new requirement that UC have the right to control a site for up to 10 years following its selection as the final site, in order to deal with the uncertainty about when the campus might be developed.

The task force also recommended that two sites, Lake Yosemite and Academy, be advanced and that site representatives be asked to present a proposal to the University by March 31, 1993 which provided UC with the right to acquire the site at nominal cost during a 10-year period following selection as the final site.

UC's president concurred with these recommendations.

The Task Force met in October 1992 and voted to recommend that ownership discussions be continued for the Academy and Lake Yosemite sites.

The Task Force again discussed and reconfirmed this recommendation prior to the November 1992 meeting of the Regents.

The Regents, however, voted to continue consideration of all three sites, setting March 31, 1993 as a deadline for completion of ownership discussions by which time the University should have the right to acquire the site, subject to its being selected as the final site, for a 10-year period.

However, after the Regents took action in November 1992 to move the site selection process forward to completion, the University's fiscal circumstances further worsened.

Following a visit in early April to the San Joaquin Valley (which included site visits and consultation with site representatives), and in light of the further deterioration in the state's fiscal situation, the president asked the Site Selection Task Force once again to consider the reasonable options for the site selection process.

The task force met on May 12 and recommended that the site selection process be suspended.

By May 1993, the future level of state support was unknown, and it was not possible to estimate UC's long-term enrollment capacity, when a 10th campus might be needed, or whether such a need might reasonably occur within the next 10 years.

Given this degree of uncertainty, the task force believed that it was not reasonable for UC to expend additional resources to continue the site selection process or to ask communities in the San Joaquin Valley to continue to spend time, effort and money on the process.

The task force also recommended that, while it might not be reasonable (given the state's fiscal circumstances) to continue planning for a 10th campus, UC should continue to explore ways to improve and expand services in the San Joaquin Valley as a part of planning for the future of the University as a whole.

These steps led to the Regents' decision at their May 1993 to approve the President's recommendation to suspend the site selection process for the prospective San Joaquin campus.

However, in July, in light of subsequent positive indicators of budget improvement and the State Legislature's encouragement, the Regents decided to resume the site selection process, subject to approval by the State of funds for preparation of an EIR.

UC's president had made the recommendation to the Board based on two significant factors: actions by the Legislature and the Governor to reduce the University's anticipated 1993–94 budget cut by $50 million, and preliminary indications from the Governor of a 3 percent budget augmentation for UC in its 1994–95 budget.

In order to support continuation of the site selection process, the 1993–94 Budget Act as approved by the Legislature included a capital budget appropriation of $1.5 million for the "purpose of preparing an environmental studies report for a proposed new campus of the University of California in the Central Valley region of California."

This appropriation was to be funded from 1990 general obligation bonds for higher education facilities approved by the voters.

With a view toward avoiding an action in conflict with a decision already made by the Regents, the Governor vetoed this $1.5 million appropriation.

Subsequently, the Governor wrote to the President indicating that if the Regents decided to proceed with the site selection EIR he would support the appropriation of State funds for the purpose. On September 10, 1993 the Legislature again appropriated funds. Under the assumption that the Governor would sign this appropriation, the University again proceeded with preparation of the site selection Environmental Impact Report.

At the same time, it was acknowledged that UC's long-term budget prospects were still unclear, and consequently the timetable for actual development of the 10th campus remained uncertain.

In view of the different circumstances now facing the University, the availability of a 10-year option for acquisition of a site—an earlier consideration for advancing a site—may no longer be appropriate. In any case, it is believed that the EIR should contain an analysis of all three sites, in order to provide a reasonable range of alternatives.

Property agreement issues, as well as size and configuration, compatibility with adjacent areas, status and funding commitments for highways, potential water sources, and other considerations will be among the factors considered as criteria for a final site selection.

REFERENCES: "Approval of the President's Recommendation Concerning the Site Selection Process for the Tenth Campus," Item 102 for Action, May 20, 1993, Regents' Committee on Grounds and Buildings (approved by the full Board); "San Joaquin Valley Campus Search To Be Suspended," news release, May 21, 1993, and "Regents Decide To Renew Site Selection process," news release, July 16, 1993, News and Public Affairs, Office of the President, and related Regents' item for action (July 16, 1993).

CROSS-REFERENCES: Subjects noted in the text.

Space Research: The California Space Institute (CalSpace) conducts and supports space and planetary science, education and technology research within the University.

CalSpace is a multicampus research unit. Administrative offices are at the Scripps Institution of Oceanography on the San Diego campus.

Through collaborative research and joint faculty appointments, CalSpace has developed close ties with many departments within UC.

These associations, promoted by CalSpace director Dr. Sally K. Ride and associate director Dr. David P. Rogers, have strengthened the institute's in-house research and its role in education.

Today, the CalSpace research staff comprises approximately two dozen scientists who conduct pure and applied scientific research in the broad interdisciplinary fields of space science and engineering, as well as in the areas of climate and global change.

Research at CalSpace is currently focused primarily in two areas: space plasmas and their interaction with

DR. SALLY K. RIDE

Photograph courtesy of NASA

celestial bodies and other ionized gases, and remote sensing and global change.

CalSpace achieves these goals by selectively supporting and participating in a mixture of workshops, conferences, research programs and educational activities.

For example, during 1991–92, CalSpace continued its management of the NASA-sponsored California Space Grant Consortium, helped establish two new research centers, supported two workshops, and conducted a graduate student summer school in global change.

The California Space Grant Consortium is sponsored by NASA's Space Grant Program, which is dedicated to providing space-related information to achieve national goals in research, education and public outreach. It uses the space program as a vehicle to improve scientific and technical literacy and knowledge at all levels of education.

In addition to its other activities, CalSpace administers a mini-grant program to support astrophysics, space science, engineering and global change research in the UC system through the disbursement of small research grants.

The CalSpace mini-grant program, open to all UC principal investigators, solicits proposals for one-year investigations.

These small grants are designed to provide seed money to explore and develop innovative areas of space-related research.

The program encourages proposals supporting graduate students and postgraduate researchers.

Sally K. Ride was best known as the first American woman to go into space. Her first Space Shuttle flight was in 1983. She flew on two space shuttle missions (the 7th shuttle flight, June, 1983, and the 13th flight, Oct. 1984) and was in charge of their scientific experiments.

In 1989 she was named professor of physics at UC San Diego and director of the California Space Institute. The institute was created in 1979 by the California Legislature to coordinate space-related research at UC's eight general campuses.

Three women associated with the University have been space pioneers: Sally Ride (SD) Kathryn Sullivan (SC) and Millie Hughes-Fulford (SF). Kathryn Sullivan and Sally Ride were on the same shuttle flight (Ride's second, Sullivan's first). Other astronauts also have had connections to UC.

REFERENCES: CalSpace annual report.

CROSS-REFERENCES: Education; Keck Telescope.

Staff Assemblies

Staff Assemblies are local campus advisory groups interested in discussing and advising management on a broad range of issues affecting staff employees at the University.

The assemblies focus on issues affecting employees who are not exclusively represented by unions.

The purpose is to provide a forum for employees to exchange information, network, and increase their awareness of the contributions they make to the University.

All campuses and the Office of the President now have staff assemblies.

Each staff assembly sends two representatives to serve on the Universitywide Council of UC Staff Assemblies (CUCSA), formed in 1975.

The council's purposes are to establish, maintain and enhance communication among the staff on the campuses and within the UC administration and to provide advice to administrators on matters that have an impact on UC staff.

The council meets quarterly on one of the campuses on a rotating basis. During their two-day meetings, council members discuss a wide range of topics that affect non-represented staff.

In addition, the council meets with UC administrators to discuss areas of interest.

REFERENCES: "The Council of UC Staff Assemblies Reaches Out to a Systemwide Community," *University Bulletin*, Vol. 30, No. 27, April 26, 1982; "Intercom" memo to Office of the President staff, October 3, 1990; "UC Assemblies Are Not Unions," *UCOPA Banner*, Vol. 2, No. 1, Winter 1993, Office of the President.

Student Fees: A basic policy of the University from its inception has been that tuition shall be free to all residents of California.

Although the policy has been subject to review by both the Regents and the State Legislature on several occasions, tuition was charged state residents only during the first three months of the University's existence.

While the University continues to extend tuition-free education to state residents, out-of-state residents are required to pay tuition (a term which signifies, in general, classroom expenses). Students who are not residents of California have paid, over and above UC's usual fees, an additional $7,699 in tuition fee each year.

There are two fees at the University which all students must pay: an educational fee and a registration fee. Other fees and expenses vary from campus to campus. The accompanying table provides figures showing undergraduate student fees in recent years.

In addition to these fees, students must pay other costs. Here were typical costs for an undergraduate California resident living in a UC residence hall in 1993–94 (these varied campus by campus): books and supplies, $600–$827, room and board, $5,355–$6,313, and miscellaneous expenses, $957–$1,582.

REFERENCES: *Centennial Record:* "1994–1995: Introducing the University," publication produced by Student Academic Services, Office of the President.

Undergraduate Student Fees

Year	Total Fees*	Percent Change
1982–83	$1,300	30.4
1983–84	1,387	6.7
1984–85	1,324	-4.5
1985–86	1,326	0.2
1986–87	1,345	1.4
1987–88	1,492	10.9
1988–89	1,554	4.2
1989–90	1,634	5.1
1990–91	1,820	11.4
1991–92	2,486	36.6
1992–93	3,044	22.4
1993–94	3,727	22.0

*Includes average miscellaneous fees. These are assessed by student vote and may vary by campus.

Resident Student Fees for 1992–93: Some Comparisons

UC Undergraduate Fees vs. 23 Public Institutions

1. Cornell University $7,056
2. Pennsylvania University 4,618
3. University of Michigan 4,584
4. Michigan State University 4,041
5. University of Virginia 3,890
6. State Univ. of New York (Buffalo) 3,485
7. University of Illinois 3,458
8. University of Minnesota, 3,200
9. University of California 3,044
10. University of Missouri 2,812
11. Ohio State University 2,799
12. Indiana University 2,794
13. University of Maryland 2,778
14. University of Oregon 2,721
15. University of Colorado, 2,540
16. Purdue University 2,520
17. University of Wisconsin 2,346
18. University of Washington 2,274
19. Iowa State University 2,228
20. University of Iowa 2,228
21. University of Nebraska 2,187
22. University of Kansas 1,798
23. University of Texas 1,372
24. University of North Carolina 1,284

UC Graduate Professional Fees vs. Four Public Institutions

Medical

1. University of Michigan $12,843
2. Sate Univ. of New York (Buffalo) 9,305
3. University of Virginia 7,944
4. University of Illinois 7,170
5. University of California, 3,376

Dentistry

1. University of Michigan $10,833
2. State Univ. of New York (Buffalo) 9,215
3. University of Illinois 5,584
4. University of California 3,292

The University of Virginia does not have a dentistry school

Law

1. University of Michigan $10,553
2. University of Virginia 6,170
3. State Univ. of New York (Buffalo) 5,744
4. University of Illinois 5,008
5. University of California 3,737

Source: Communications Services, Office of the President.

Student Financial Aid: Large-scale student financial aid programs at academic institutions are a relatively recent development in the history of higher education.

Such programs have evolved in all their complexity in response to changing perceptions of the value of higher education.

Today, there is a general recognition that society benefits most when the broadest possible spectrum of the population is represented in higher education.

Student financial aid began in earnest right after World War II, when the GI Bill provided federal support for the massive numbers of veterans who entered higher education.

In the 1950s, in response to the space race, the federal government created the National Defense Student Loan Program (NDSL).

At that time, the government poured funds into fellowships, traineeships and research assistantships for graduate students, particularly in the sciences.

By 1965, society generally recognized the benefits of an educated populace across the board, believing that the greatest possible number of people should get a college education, if necessary with federal and state assistance.

This concept of student financial assistance led to the passage of the Higher Education Act of 1965, which was designed to promote college attendance from all segments of society, especially from those previously disenfranchised.

However, between 1986 and 1992 a significant change took place.

The federal government began to reduce its support for financial aid because of the high cost of funding post-secondary education as a public benefit for a student population that was growing ever larger.

In 1986 and 1992, the Higher Education Act of 1965 was amended. Federal programs were maintained, but money was saved by reducing student eligibility for financial assistance.

In addition, those students who remained eligible under the amended act received slightly smaller grant awards, but markedly higher loan awards.

As the federal government's approach to student financial aid evolved in recent years, UC's approach also took on a new shape.

Until the 1960s, UC's primary means of subsidizing students had been its tuition-free policy. Modest private support provided additional aid for selected categories of students. Most financial aid, regardless of the source, was based largely on merit, not need.

In the 1960s, the University began offering increasing amounts of financial aid to help students meet the costs associated with their education.

In particular, UC sought to attract certain categories of students by providing specific types of financial aid.

For example, such aid included nonresident tuition fellowships for foreign students (1960), Regents Scholarships for outstanding undergraduates (1962) and Regents Fellowships for exceptional graduate students (1963).

Eventually, in response to the growing number of low-income students admitted to UC, institutional grants, loans and work-study programs were established.

Today, financial assistance for University students comes from four sources.

Ranked from highest to lowest in terms of total support, these sources are:

(1) The federal government through direct and subsidized programs, (2) the University, (3) the State of California, and (4) private and outside agencies.

In developing and enhancing its aid programs, UC has continued to examine issues such as the balance between merit- and need-based aid and between graduate and undergraduate aid, proper funding sources of UC's programs, and the appropriate relationship between federal and UC aid. For example, UC has supported a nationwide call for increases in federally subsidized student aid, which has not kept pace with rising costs in students' living expenses.

UC's programs are designed primarily to supplement the support that students receive from federal, as well as from state, sources, and to allow UC the flexibility to support certain types of students that are not supported by government programs.

In providing assistance, UC seeks to increase student aid whenever it has to impose higher fees and whenever the cost of housing, food and other student expenses escalate because of inflation.

Unlike the federal government, UC focuses its aid on needy low-income and middle-income students. In so doing, it emphasizes grants, rather than loans.

In contrast, as much as 65 percent of all federal aid has taken the form of loans.

Data available at the beginning of 1993 showed that financial aid appeared to have been a key factor in preserving access to UC for qualified students at a time when fees were rising dramatically because of the fiscal crisis faced by the State of California.

Information at that time showed that trends in application rates by income level had not shown any major changes through fall 1992 that could be attributed to costs.

In addition, there was no evidence that UC had lost low- or middle-income students during the period 1988–89 and 1991–92. (These were the latest years for which UC had income data.)

In analyzing the data, UC administrators found that the Fee Grant Program, established in 1991–92 to help needy low- and middle-income students, was successful in mitigating the impact of the $650 fee increase that year.

Low-income financial aid recipients received an average of $813 more in grants and scholarships in 1991–92 than a year earlier. Their loan amounts increased an average of only $68 a year per low-income borrower.

Needy middle-income students received additional grant aid, but as planned, not to the same degree as low-income students.

As a result, borrowing by these students increased an average of $133 a year.

The fee grant program is for all needy students whose fee increases are not covered by some other source.

Grants are provided to cover fee increases according to a sliding scale tied to income.

Needy middle-income students receive a fee grant along with additional loan funds to cover the fee increase.

Low-income students have the entire fee increase offset by a grant.

As fees have risen, UC has continued to increase the amount of funds available for grants. It anticipated doing so again in 1993–94.

Overall, from 1990–91 to 1992–93, the amount of Universitywide need-based grant aid grew from $49 million to $92 million, an increase of 88 percent.

However, in 1992–93 and possibly in 1993–94, outside factors threatened to continue adversely affecting UC students despite the University's commitment to provide adequate financial aid.

For example, in 1992–93, funding for the state's primary need-based grant program (Cal Grant) failed to keep pace with rising fees.

In addition, the final state budget cut Cal Grants by 15 percent.

The University partially compensated for some of the shortfall by redirecting funds from other programs.

However, because of the size of the cut in Cal Grants and UC's own budget crisis, UC could make up only a small portion of the entire gap.

There would be no additional funding for Cal Grant in 1993–94, and the legislature was hard-pressed to restore funding cuts made to the Cal Grant programs in 1992–93, much less provide additional funds to cover the increase needed for the 1993–94 fees.

Thus, Cal Grant recipients and low-income students have been bearing the brunt of the state's inability to fund financial aid the way it has in past years.

As of the beginning of 1993, several other external factors were affecting students:

• Non-fee expenses such as housing, food and books were rising faster than income during the recession.

• Federal grant funding was expected to decline, even though loan programs had been expanded.

• More students would be eligible for financial aid because of Congressional changes in the definition of financial need.

In recent years, financial aid has become increasingly important as the costs of attending college continue to soar.

Fees make up about one-fourth of a student's total educational cost.

For example, in 1992–93, the average total cost of education for an undergraduate was approximately $11,103.

That total included room and board, books and supplies, personal expenses and transportation, as well as fees of $3,036 a year.

The University has been taking a variety of actions to help its students deal with both the rising fees and climbing non-fee expenses.

For example, some campuses have begun pilot programs using database services that supply information on a wide variety of sources for grants and fellowships. In addition, campuses and the Office of the President have increased their efforts to publicize financial aid information to schools, parents and students.

REFERENCES: "Student Financial Aid," background information from University Relations, Office of the President, for the news media, June 20, 1986; Financial Aid Packet, 1990–91; "Report on Student Financial Support," Item 304 for Discussion, Regents' Committee on Educational Policy, and "More Students Receive Financial Aid," news release, University Relations, Office of the President, March 19, 1992; "Financial Aid Helping Preserve Access to UC," news release, January 14, 1993, University Relations; UC's Fees and Tuition Schedules, Budgets for Current Operations, and Financial Reports.

CROSS-REFERENCES: Budget; Student Fees.

Student Financial Aid: The Basics

These two terms are used when evaluating financial aid:

• Merit-based aid (also known as nonneed-based aid), which is student aid based on academic achievement and promise.

• Need-based aid, which is based on demonstrated financial need.

Basis of Awards

Student financial aid is awarded on one of two bases:

1) Academic achievement and promise (non-need or merit aid).

(Although such aid is awarded without regard for financial need, the amount may be influenced by need.)

2) Demonstrated financial need (need-based aid).

"Demonstrated" means that the student provides financial information that is analyzed according to national standards, and the amount of the parents' and student's contribution is determined.

The student's aid is usually provided in a "package" consisting of scholarship or grant, a loan and, for some, a work-study authorization.

How the Process Works

Here is how financial aid is awarded:

• Each year, financial aid offices at UC formulate standard budgets that reflect average expenses for students during the nine-month academic year.

• UC considers the amount the student can contribute and the amount the student's parents can contribute if the student is a dependent. This contribution is established by a federally mandated process that considers income, assets, family size and other factors.

• To determine financial need, UC subtracts the expected parent and student contributions from the student budget formulated by campus financial aid offices. The result is the student's need, i.e., the amount of the student budget that is not covered by the parental and student contributions.

Types of Financial Aid

There are several types of financial aid, including:

1) Scholarships and Fellowships: These are awarded on the basis of academic achievement, and repayment is not required.

2) Grants: These are awarded on the basis of financial need and do not have to be repaid.

3) Loans: A wide variety are available, some awarded on the basis of financial need and some not, and repayment is required.

4) Work-study: This provides support to students in return for work either on- or off-campus.

(Off-campus employers contribute part of the funds. Money comes from federal sources and UC. On-campus jobs include teaching and research assistantships, work in libraries and administrative offices and similar employment.)

Recent Studies

Recent studies of financial assistance for undergraduates have shown the following:

• While UC recognizes academic achievement and promise in its scholarship programs, the amount of an award usually depends upon financial need. Consequently, virtually all undergraduate student aid requires a financial need analysis.

• Awardees without financial need generally receive a nominal award, such as the $500 Regents Scholarship honorarium.

• The proportion of undergraduate students receiving financial aid has changed very little over the past few years, with two out of five claiming some form of aid.

• Sixty-two percent of undergraduate aid is awarded in the form of "gift" aid (scholarships and grants) rather than "self-help" aid (loans and work-study).

• Almost all low-income, dependent, underrepresented minority, California resident undergraduates received some grant support.

• Almost three-fifths of UC's dependent undergraduate need-based aid recipients came from families with incomes of less than $30,000.

• Low-income, dependent, needy undergraduates are more likely to receive grant support and less likely to borrow than their moderate- to higher-income counterparts.

Recent studies on financial aid for graduate students have shown the following:

• In contrast to undergraduates, graduate students receive a significant proportion of their financial aid based on merit.

• Borrowing also comprises a large share of the graduate student aid portfolio; for example, 21 percent of graduate aid is provided in the form of a loan.

• Almost all graduate students receive some form of financial assistance (including assistantships), averaging $11,788 per recipient.

• UC-funded programs, excluding assistantships, provide $152 million in support for undergraduate and graduate students, almost exclusively in the form of scholarships, fellowships and grants.

• Three-quarters of the support for graduate students is in the form of fellowships and assistantships.

REFERENCES: Information from the Office of Student Financial Support, Office of the President.

CROSS-REFERENCES: Budget; Student Fees.

Student Aid: Types of Support

A large portion of UC's own Universitywide student aid budget comes from the State General Fund and is statutorily restricted to need-based financial aid.

The merit-based programs are funded entirely from Educational Fee income.

Additional University-funded aid is provided from endowment income, current gifts, repayments from UC loans, and campus discretionary funds.

UC continues to commit more than 95 percent of its own financial aid resources to fellowships, scholarships and grants, while also maintaining small loan and work-study programs.

The following constitute major types of financial aid from all sources.

Federal

• Federal Family Educational Loan Program (formerly Stafford and Guaranteed Student Loan Program)

This is the largest source of financial aid funds for UC students. It is made up of a variety of federally authorized and guaranteed loans for students and parents, and repayment is required.

• Health Education Assistance Loans (HEAL)

This program provides larger federally guaranteed loans to health professional students. Repayment is required.

• Pell Grants

This federal program provides more grant support to more undergraduates than any other federal program.

• Campus-Based Programs

These include College Work-Study, Supplemental Educational Opportunity Grants and Perkins Loans.

• Federal Fellowships

These include awards to graduate students from federal agencies (examples: National Institutes of Health, National Science Foundation).

State

• Cal Grants A, B, and C

The Cal Grant programs, which together accounted for 97 percent of State aid, are "portable" financial aid programs, meaning that awards are made directly to students, who carry the awards to their institution of choice.

Cal Grants are the primary sources of state aid to UC undergraduates. Cal Grant A awards are based on a combination of academic merit and financial need. Cal Grant B awards are based on high academic potential, financial need and a disadvantaged background. Cal Grant C awards provide a few UC students with support for technical studies, such as the Physician's Assistant Program at UC Davis.

• State Graduate Fellowship Program

This is a state program that awards aid to needy graduate students who have high potential, are from disadvantaged backgrounds, and plan to enter a career as a faculty member.

• State Work-Study Program

Three UC campuses participate in this program, which funds work-study placements in career- or major-related fields.

University

A large portion of the University's student aid budget is funded from the State General Fund and is statutorily restricted to need-based financial aid.

The merit-based programs are funded entirely from Educational Fee income. Additional University-funded aid is provided from endowment income, current gifts, repayments from University loans, and campus discretionary funds.

The University continues to commit more than 97 percent of its financial aid resources to fellowships, scholarships, and grants, while also maintaining loan and work-study programs.

Types of support include the following.

• President's Undergraduate Fellowships.

This UC program awards grants for undergraduate research projects.

• Regents' Fellowships.

These are awarded from UC funds. They provide stipends of $8,500 plus fees and nonresident tuition, if applicable, to graduate students pursuing academic degrees.

• Regents Scholarship Program.

This is UC's most prestigious scholarship program. It provides stipends to undergraduate students with financial need, or a $500 honorarium to scholars without financial need.

• Student Affirmative Action Grants.

This University-funded program awards grants to needy underrepresented minority undergraduate students.

• University Scholarships.

These are awarded to students on the basis of financial need and academic merit.

• University Student Aid Program

This is the largest of the UC-funded aid programs. Aid is awarded by grant, loan and work-study assistance to undergraduate and graduate students solely on the basis of financial need.

• Graduate Opportunity Fellowships.

These are awarded from UC funds. They provide stipends of $8,500 plus fees and nonresident tuition, if applicable, to women and minority graduate students who are underrepresented in academic graduate departments and who are pursuing academic degrees.

- In-Candidacy Fee Offset Grants.

Under this program, UC covers the educational fee of all graduate students who have advanced to doctoral degree candidacy, regardless of financial need.

Alumni Scholarships

UC matches funds from alumni and donor contributions to provide scholarships to students entering from high schools and community colleges.

Private

In 1991–92, approximately $26 million was awarded to University students from private and outside agency sources. This represented 5 percent of the financial support students received during that year.

Support in this category includes:

- Small scholarships from, for example, a student's local PTA or Rotary Club.

- Traineeships and fellowships from private companies.

- Funding from associations and foundations (e.g., the National Merit Scholarship Foundation and the American Cancer Society).

- Support that foreign governments provide for their students.

University of California
Student Financial Support 1991–92

	Undergraduate	Graduate	Total
Scholarships/ Fellowships			
State	$234,500	$644,930	$879,430
UC	$14,160,510	$66,541,077	$80,701,587
Federal	$0	$27,402,287	$27,402,287
Private	$3,440,577	$2,091,691	$5,532,268
Grants			
State	$54,932,277	$0	$54,932,277
UC	$50,073,747	$16,497,969	$66,571,716
Federal	$57,152,207	$712,023	$57,864,230
Private	$6,153,319	$10,150,860	$16,304,179
Loans			
UC	$1,667,353	$1,634,302	$3,301,655
Federal	$100,973,113	$83,237,350	$184,210,463
Private	$684,023	$3,301,960	$3,985,983
Work-Study			
State	$153,602	$137,018	$290,620
UC	$858,950	$611,879	$1,470,829
Federal	$11,643,284	$2,859,815	$14,503,099
Teaching Assistantships	$0	$91,787,441	$91,787,441
Research Assistantships	$0	$99,614,530	$99,614,530
Grand Total	$302,127,462	$407,225,132	$709,352,594

Student Financial Support Facts, 1991–92

	Undergraduate	Graduate	Total
Number of Financial Support Recipients	55,577	34,545	90,122
Percent of Students	44%	94%	56%
Average Award	$ 5,436	$11,788	$ 7,871

Data for graduate students includes teaching and research assistantships.

Source: Report on Student Financial Support, 1991–1992, University of California, Office of the President, Student Academic Services, Student Financial Support, March 1993.

Median Parental Income, Undergraduates Only

Financial Support Recipients	$39,100
All Undergraduates	$55,019
Students Not Receiving Aid	$77,288

Source: Student Expenses and Resources Survey, 1991–1992, University of California, Office of the President, Student Academic Services, Student Financial Support, November 1992.

Packaging Aid for Students Is An Exacting, Complex Task

To assist eligible students, UC offices develop individual financial aid packages consisting of a combination of grants, loans, scholarships and work-study employment.

A student's financial aid package varies from year to year, depending on available resources and student needs.

The pool of money available for the University's financial aid comes, in part, from a portion of student fees it charges all students and from endowment funds.

However, in recent years, dwindling federal and state revenues, as well as an emphasis on other priorities for society, have meant that college students must carry a greater share of the expenses to cover their education.

At the same time, the federal and state governments have provided for grant, loan and other support programs to assist students who have significant financial need.

Over the years, the number of student aid recipients at UC has continued to grow, as fees keep rising and the associated costs of attending a campus burgeon.

For example, in 1991–92, the number of UC students receiving financial aid increased by 9 percent over the previous year.

Figures for 1991–92 showed that 90,122 UC students, or 56 percent, received $709 million in student support.

In comparison, 82,805 students, or 51 percent, received $600 million the year before.

In 1991–92, UC and the federal government, together, provided 88 percent of the financial aid for students. UC provided 41 percent, and federal sources 47 percent. State and private sources provided the rest.

The University's efforts to increase grant support in 1991–92 helped forestall any marked increase in borrowing among needy undergraduates. In 1991–92, as in 1990–91, the percentage of need-based aid recipients who borrowed was 70%.

As of 1991–92, the cost of attending the University had increased at a rate faster than inflation over the previous decade.

This increase was determined by measuring the factors in what UC calls "the student budget."

The student budget is the total of fees and a specified allowance for living and personal expenses, books and transportation.

In 1991 constant dollars, the average total cost to attend UC as an undergraduate in 1991–92 was $10,233, as opposed to $7,075 a decade earlier.

Living expenses represented the largest part of the increase, accounting for 46 percent. Overall, non-fee expenses made up 78 percent of the increase.

Student Health Services: The University began a campus-based health care in 1906 when the Berkeley campus opened the nation's first student infirmary.

Now, Student Health Services on each campus provide students with primary care and ancillary programs to help keep students healthy.

The scope of services varies by campus and is defined by campus size, funding, student interest and special local need.

Services include general outpatient medical care, specialty medical care, health education and health promotion and health insurance.

Programs are integrated into campus life and coordinated with community services.

Each campus provides a student health program that is a combination of on-and-off campus services. On-campus services are supported through registration fees, fees-for-service and other sources of funding. Off-campus care is supported primarily through students' insurance policies (private, Graduate Student Health Insurance Plan, etc.).

This combination of primary care services supported by registration fees and major medical plans together enable Student Health Services to provide a comprehensive medical package to students at a reasonable cost.

In 1990–91, figures for the nine UC Student Health Services showed that there were 447,403 outpatient clinic visits. In addition, 261,845 laboratory tests and 23,044 x-ray procedures were carried out, and 200,080 pharmacy prescriptions were filled.

In addition, health education programs at the campuses made 121,651 contacts with individuals in their respective communities.

REFERENCES: Special Report on Student Health Services, UC Advisory Committee on Student Health, Office of the President.
CROSS-REFERENCES: Health Sciences, Student Fees.

Student Housing: The University has a variety of on-campus housing for undergraduates, including housing specifically designated for student families.

Overall, approximately 26 percent of student enrollment can be accommodated; students are therefore advised to investigate other housing options, including student cooperatives, rooming houses, and privately-owned apartments and houses.

Some fraternities and sororities provide housing for members, but it is usually not available to freshmen or other new students.

Most student housing is coeducational, meaning that men and women live in the same building, sometimes on the same floor. However, some facilities are just for women or men. A number of facilities include non-smoking floors/areas.

At some campuses, there are designated facilities for students with special academic interests, such as art, social science or a foreign language.

Several campuses also have an international house, where programs are specifically designed to accommodate students from other countries.

At Santa Cruz and San Diego, each undergraduate college has its own housing community.

All campuses guarantee on-campus housing to freshmen who meet application and contract deadlines and certain other requirements.

The Davis, Irvine, Los Angeles, Riverside and San Diego campuses guarantee residence hall housing to new transfer students who meet established requirements.

Some campuses use a random drawing, or lottery, to make specific room assignments. Others do it on a first-come, first-served basis as applications are received.

The purpose and objectives of University-operated housing are different from those for housing operated by the private sector.

Generally speaking, the purpose of University-operated housing is to enhance educational development, recruitment and retention of students by providing self-sustaining facilities and activities in support of campus academic programs.

The methods of financing and the philosophy of management are also different.

From 1957 through June 1993, student housing facilities were part of one of the following categories established by the Regents in May 1957:

• Group A Housing System. This was a University-wide system which included facilities at all campuses, and was financed primarily from the sale of Group A Housing System Revenue Bonds, other revenue bonds, Regents' loans and appropriations of Regents' Equity Capital that was reserved for this System in 1971.

• Group B Housing System. All other facilities.

In May 1993, the Regents rescinded the Group A and B designations and authorized the establishment of a new system—the University of California Housing System (UCHS). All facilities not part of the UCHS are operated as campus facilities.

For UCHS facilities, student housing operations will be administered in accordance with the terms of the University of California Housing System Revenue Bond Indenture of 1993.

The Indenture contains covenants that are legally binding on the University and constitute much of the basis for establishing housing fees.

In addition, in March 1967 the Regents adopted a rate structure policy, which continues to be applicable to UCHS operations and which states in part that:

(1) The [UCHS] must be entirely self-supporting, (2) occupancy of student housing is to be voluntary, (3) fees are to be set at levels intended to maintain a 95 percent occupancy level (per academic year for residence halls, per calendar year for student family apartments), and (4) operating services and their costs could vary in accordance with individual campus conditions.

The rate structure policy also states that capital costs (debt service, sinking fund, major maintenance reserves) are to be allocated equitably across the Housing

Housing for UC students under construction.

System on the basis of construction costs adjusted to a common index.

(This provision provides for appropriate distribution of the capital debt among facilities at all campus locations.)

As projects are added to the Housing System, each one must, within the context of all campus UCHS facilities, be financially feasible in terms of demand, anticipated fee levels, operating expenses and capital costs. Because the UCHS is universitywide, the Office of the President has central administrative responsibility to insure the System's financial viability.

Campus housing facilities are not administered as universitywide system and responsibility for operations is a campus matter. In general, however, these operations are managed in a manner very similar to UCHS.

REFERENCES: "Comparison of Rental Rates for Typical University of California Student Housing Facilities with Similar Housing Facilities in the Private Sector," Item 510 for Information, Regents' Meeting, May 15, 1980; "Introducing the University, 1993–1994," Student Academic Services, Office of the President.

CROSS-REFERENCES: Admissions; Student Fees; Student Financial Aid.

Student Organizations: Each campus has an official campuswide student organization.

In general, the goals of each organization include serving the needs of students, increasing the avenues for student participation in education and campus operations, and directing a large variety of student activities.

Graduate students also may be represented in their own official organization.

Official student organizations support ethnic, cultural and social activities, hobbies, sports, entertainment, recreation, food services, travel arrangements, assistance programs (through clinics and special projects), individualized student services (such as check cashing), and Student Union activities.

In addition, the University of California Student Association (UCSA) serves the Universitywide interests of students.

REFERENCES: Campus Catalogs.

CROSS-REFERENCES: All subjects related to students.

University of California Undergraduate Student Housing

	Students Housed in Residence Halls & Apts.	Student Family Apts. (No. of Units)	Guaranteed for Freshmen	Guaranteed for Transfers
Berkeley[1]	5,000	1,022	X	
Davis	4,462	676	X	X
Irvine[2]	3,487	1,066	X	X
Los Angeles	3,939	774	X	X
Riverside	2,225	268	X	X
San Diego	4,665	1,086	X	X
Santa Barbara[3]	3,572	592	X	
Santa Cruz[2]	4,242	199	X	

[1] Berkeley guarantees housing to freshmen who enroll in the fall. Berkeley also houses 600 students in its International House.

[2] Irvine and Santa Cruz have parks with limited space for students with their own RVs and trailers.

[3] An additional 2,000 Santa Barbara campus students are housed in three private residence halls adjacent to campus.

Student Orientation is offered by each University campus during the summer or in the beginning of the fall term for newly admitted freshmen and transfer students who will begin school in the fall.

Such programs help students become more familiar with the campus, obtain assistance with course planning and scheduling, and meet other new students.

Orientation programs vary in length from one to several days. During two- or three-day programs, students stay in campus residence halls. In many cases, parents are invited to attend.

In early summer, each campus mails information to its new students, providing details about the orientation program, information about required fees, and instructions about registering in advance.

REFERENCES: Campus catalogs.

CROSS-REFERENCES: All subjects related to students.

Student Participation in Governance: As members of the campus community, students have a substantial interest in the governance of the University.

Their participation has increased significantly in the last two decades, and the University has benefitted from it. In developing its policy in this area, the University has reaffirmed its commitment to the principle of student involvement in governance in both administrative and academic areas.

The University's commitment is based on the premise that student participation is vital to a vigorous intellectual exchange and the furtherance of the objectives of University education and research. Appropriate, effective and productive student involvement, consistent with the development of policies that reflect the total needs of the University, is the goal.

The governance of the University involves more than the process of making decisions. The process of governance provides a forum for group interaction, expression of concerns, exploration of feasible solutions and reconciliation of diverse viewpoints.

Within this context, student participation serves several functions.

First, it is important to the sound development of policy.

Student views and advice, often from special perspectives, provide for more informed University decision-making. The University believes that participation should be encouraged and strengthened through the involvement of all levels of student representation.

Second, there is a recognition that students have a vital interest in decisions directly related to policies and programs affecting their academic and non-academic experience at the University.

Clear procedures are required at UC to ensure that students are afforded access to needed information, an opportunity to share ideas, and encouragement to express concerns, both formally and informally.

Third, student participation is crucial to ensure that student viewpoints are considered on issues of importance to the University community.

This communication provides opportunities for testing assumptions, understanding the attitudes of others, sharing information and developing understanding and mutual trust among constituencies. The special nature of the University requires a sense of community; while the University recognizes that not every decision can be wholly satisfactory to all parties, the governance process should provide a forum for candid discussion.

The University has experienced rapid development in the area of student participation in governance over the past several years. At the same time, there have been some problems and ambiguities. In seeking a resolution of these, efforts continue to be directed toward improving the extent, the quality and the effectiveness of student involvement.

In order to further these efforts, each campus has a plan for student participation. These plans, developed under the direction of the chancellors, focus on administrative matters.

In developing these plans, there was broad consultation with the campus community, including formal consultation with student governments and the Academic Senate. The type and extent of student participation in the administrative areas of governance were examined and defined.

Essential to the success of such plans was a review of the procedures used by student governments and other student organizations.

Matters delegated by the Regents to the Academic Senate have been beyond the scope of these campus plans; however, UC's president encouraged direct discussions between students and the Academic Senate on student participation in the Senate's deliberations.

The development of plans for student participation in institutional governance provided the campuses with an opportunity not only to develop formal procedures where they did not exist, but also to review existing participation.

In developing their plans, campuses considered the research data and analysis of the staff and task force reports on "The Evaluation of Student Participation in the Governance of the University of California" (August 1977). Each campus plan provides for periodic review and evaluation of progress toward implementation of the plan.

REFERENCES: "The Evaluation of Student Participation in the Governance of the University of California," 1977 report, Office of the President; Policies Applying to Campus Activities, Organizations, and Students, Student Affairs and Services, Office of the President.

CROSS-REFERENCES: All subjects related to students and UC administration and governance.

Student Regents: Each year since 1975 a student Regent has been appointed by the Board of Regents to serve on the Board for a one-year term.

During the two years prior to this first appointment, the Board addressed the matter on a number of occasions.

The intense discussions during this time reflected many of the complex issues facing higher education.

In 1973, the State Legislature's Joint Committee on the Master Plan for Higher Education recommended that: "A governing board must have credibility with its constituency.

"In higher education students and faculty are a part of that community. Therefore, one student and one faculty member, each peer-selected, should be added to the three statewide boards and each community college district board."

An advisory group of Regents on the Master Plan for Higher Education, proposed that they oppose Recommendation 7.

Some members of the advisory group noted that changes in the Board's membership would require a constitutional amendment. When discussed in the Legislature, it was argued, these would raise other issues threatening UC's independence.

However, members of the advisory group also noted that the Student Body President's Council (SBPC) and the Student Lobby were very much in favor of having some type of student representation on the Board.

During the deliberations, one Regent argued that the Board had been effective in the role of trustee, with no Regent being representative of any special interest.

He said he believed that a student, and to some extent a faculty member, would feel a greater responsibility to their respective constituencies than to the overall interests of the University.

Partly because of such concerns, the Joint Committee on the Master Plan for Higher Education recommended that the student and faculty representatives not be voting members of the Board.

Legislation subsequently was adopted that called for an amendment to Article IX, Section 9 of the State Constitution relating to membership, terms and method of selection of the Regents.

In November 1974, the constitutional amendment was approved by the voters.

The approved amendment (Proposition 4) included the following language:

(c) the members of the board may, in their discretion, following procedures established by them and after consultation with representatives of faculty and students of the university, including appropriate officers of the academic senate and student governments, appoint to the board either or both of the following persons as members with all rights of participation: a member of the faculty at a campus of the university

or of another institution of higher education; a person enrolled as a student at a campus of the university for each regular academic term during his service as a member of the board. Any person so appointed shall serve for not less than one year commencing on July 1.

The implementation of this amendment was referred to the Regent's Special Committee on Reorganization, which held several discussions over the several months following its adoption.

Appearing before the Special Committee, the president of the Student Body Presidents' Council said that a student Regent could give new direction and perspective on subjects with which that individual was particularly familiar, such as financial aid and affirmative action. He assured the Special Committee that a student Regent would act as "trustee," having no affiliation with the SBPC.

UC's president stated that he agreed with the constitutional provision, even though originally he had opposed the appointment of faculty and student Regents. At that time, he had believed strongly in the "trustee", as contrasted with the "representational," concept of Regency.

Questions were then raised as to possible conflicts of interest.

In this connection, the Regents' General Counsel advised that specific provisions of the law having to do with conflict of interest would bear upon a student or faculty Regent to the same degree as they bear upon all other Regents.

Also applicable would be the Regents' policy on conflict of interest.

On January 15, 1975, at the meeting of the Regents' Special Committee on Reorganization, the General Counsel further advised that the Political Reform Act of 1974 would not preclude a UC student from serving as a Regent.

However, he stated, if the student Regent had received $250 or more of student financial aid in the preceding 12 months, the individual would be required to refrain from participating in financial aid matters affecting him or her.

At its February 1975 meeting, the Special Committee recommended that on an experimental basis for a two-year period, a student be appointed to the Board.

The appointment was to be made by the Board upon the recommendation of a special committee appointed by the Board for that purpose. The special committee was to make its recommendation from a panel of three names submitted by the SBPC.

Two nominating commissions, one from the four northern campuses and one from the five southern campuses, would be established with one graduate and one undergraduate representative from each campus.

Four candidates from the northern commission and five from the southern commission would be selected to be interviewed by the SBPC.

From these nine candidates, three nominees would be selected. Not all Regents in attendance were in agreement with the proposal.

One Regent expressed concern that the appointment of a student Regent would "downgrade" the chancellors, who are, after all, the leaders of their respective campuses.

In agreeing with him, another Regent offered a substitute motion. It proposed that a student representative be appointed to attend all meetings and to be seated at the meeting table with all rights and privileges of participation other than voting.

Other Board members disagreed with these suggestions, stating that the intent of Proposition 4 was that there be a student Regent (not merely a "student representative").

During the discussions, one Regent expressed earlier concerns that, because of the manner of selection and the realities of a student's relationship with a campus, a student Regent, in effect, would become an extension of a student organization.

He felt that the proposed selection process was contrary to Proposition 4, because it delegated the selection function to a student government organization.

A Regent who disagreed said it was important that a selection procedure be adopted under which the student Regent would have credibility with the student community, but not stigmatized by the manner in which he or she was selected.

To help assure a fair process, UC's president recommended that the nominee could not be an officer of the student government. Also, the nominee would be selected by an outgoing Student Body President's Council and not the Council that would serve during the new student Regent's tenure.

When the Special Committee's recommendation went forward to the Board, amendments to the procedure for selecting the student Regent were then offered.

The Governor (an ex-officio Regent) suggested the following amendment to the recommendation before the Board:

"The Chair of the Student Body President's Council shall sit as an ex officio member of the special committee with all rights and privileges except voting."

This amendment was adopted, as was the recommendation of the Special Committee on Reorganization to appoint a student Regent, on an experimental two-year basis.

In June 1975, the Regents appointed the first student Regent, Carol Mock.

The next year, the procedures approved for appointment of a student Regent were reviewed as part of the Regents' determination about whether or not to continue the appointment of a student Regent each year.

The review was again delegated to the Special Committee on Reorganization.

UC's president told the Special Committee that the presence of a student at the Regents' table had provided new insights and information and a new type of resource to the Board.

He felt the program should continue on an experimental basis for a five-year period.

The Special Committee recommended to the Board that the appointment of student Regents be continued on an experimental basis for five more years.

The procedures for selection remained basically the same.

Amended procedures stated that a student body president, or equivalent, or a member of the SBPC shall not be eligible for appointment as a student Regent.

Also, while serving on the Board, a student Regent could not hold any appointive or elective student government position.

In addition, a student who is or has served as a student Regent shall not be eligible for reappointment as a student Regent.

The Board of Regents approved this recommendation in January 1977.

In 1981, 1984 and 1987, the Board of Regents reviewed the continuation of appointment of a student Regent.

Over the years, minor amendments were made, but the procedure for selection remains basically the same.

REFERENCES: Information from the Office of the Secretary of the Regents.

CROSS-REFERENCES: All topics relating to the Board of Regents; Conflict of Interest; Master Plan.

Substance Abuse: Society's understanding of the social costs of alcohol and substance abuse began to grow by the 1970s.

By the beginning of the 1980s, the medical community, legislators and the general public showed grave concern about the problems resulting from such abuse.

College and university administrators shared this concern and began developing programs to discuss the nature and extent of alcohol and drug abuse on campuses.

In 1988, the federal Drug-Free Workplace Act of 1988 was enacted, and on March 18, 1989, UC issued a policy on substance abuse in the workplace, in compliance with the new law.

After UC's policy was implemented, further legislation in the war against drugs continued to be proposed at the national and state levels.

On November 1, 1990, UC's policy was revised in response to the following:

(1) Changes in the final regulations for the Drug-Free Workplace Act, (2) issuance of U.S. Department of Education regulations to the Drug-Free Schools and Communities Act of 1989, and (3) passage of the state Drug-Free Workplace Act of 1990.

In its policy, the University recognizes alcohol and drug dependency as a treatable condition and offers programs and services for UC employees and students with substance-dependency problems.

Employees (including student employees) and students are encouraged to seek assistance, as appropriate, from employee support programs, health centers, and counseling or psychological services available at UC locations, or through referral.

Information obtained regarding an employee or student during participation in such programs or services will be treated as confidential, in accordance with federal and state laws.

UC strives to maintain campus communities and worksites free from the illegal use, possession or distribution of alcohol or controlled substances, as defined by federal codes.

Unlawful manufacture, distribution, dispensing, possession, use or sale of alcohol or controlled substances by UC employees and students in the workplace, on University premises, at official UC functions, or on UC business is prohibited.

In addition, employees and students shall not use illegal substances or abuse legal substances in a manner that impairs work performance, scholarly activities or student life.

Employees found to be in violation of the policy, including student employees if the circumstances warrant, may be subject to corrective action, up to and including dismissal, under applicable UC policies and labor contracts.

As an alternative, they may be required, at UC's discretion, to participate satisfactorily in an employee support program.

Students found to be in violation of the policy may be subject to corrective action, up to and including dismissal, as set forth in official UC policy statements and regulations.

Alternatively, they may be required, at UC's discretion, to participate satisfactorily in a treatment program.

In addition, the federal Drug-Free Workplace Act of 1988 and the state Drug-Free Workplace Act of 1990 require that UC employees directly engaged in work on a federal or state contract shall abide by the policy as a condition of employment.

Such employees shall notify the University within five days if they are convicted of any criminal drug statute violation while in the workplace or on UC business.

This requirement also applies to all indirect-charge employees who perform support or overhead functions related to a federal contract or grant and for which the federal government pays its share of expenses, unless the employee's impact or involvement is insignificant to the performance of the contract or grant.

UC is required to notify the federal contracting or granting agency within 10 calendar days of receiving notice of such conviction.

UC also must take appropriate corrective action or require the employee to participate satisfactorily in available counseling, treatment and approved substance-abuse assistance or rehabilitation programs within 30 calendar days of having received notice of such conviction.

The University's campuses now offer a variety of services directed toward helping with the problems of alcohol and drug abuse.

These include informational programs, crisis intervention, counseling, development of guidelines and rules for student organizations, courses in academic departments, and conferences and workshops for staff who administer drug and alcohol programs.

The University is sensitive to state and national concerns about drug abuse. Its personnel policies and procedures address performance issues arising from substance abuse, and it continues to be diligent in providing counseling and rehabilitation for employees experiencing substance abuse difficulties.

REFERENCES: Proceedings of the University of California Student Affairs Conference on Students and Substance Abuse, May 12-14, 1985, Student Affairs and Services Office, Office of the President; "Report on Alcohol and Drug Education Programs for University Students," Item 308 for Information, Regents' Committee on Educational Policy, September 17, 1987; "University Policy on Substance Abuse in the Workplace," Office of the President, March 18, 1989; "UC Substance Abuse Policy Update: Implementation, Drug Testing," *HR Currents*, Human Resource Newsletter for University Administrators, Vol. 1, No. 1, November 1989, Employee Relations, Office of the President; "University of California Policy on Substance Abuse, November 1, 1990, and Implementing Guidelines, December 10, 1990, Office of the President; University of California Policies Applying to Campus Activities, Organizations, and Students (Part A); campus regulations and pertinent federal and state laws.

Support Groups: A Policy on University Support Groups was adopted by the Regents on October 20, 1978, and Systemwide Administrative Guidelines Governing University Support Groups were issued by the President on October 31, 1978.

The Policy and Guidelines were applicable to Campus Foundations as well as to other types of support groups, typically smaller organizations formed by volunteers to raise funds for a UC department or program.

In September 1989, the Regents approved a new Policy on Campus Foundations, and relevant procedural details were placed in Administrative Guidelines for Campus Foundations issued by the Office of the President on October 13, 1989.

In November 1990, the Regents adopted a new Policy on University Support Groups. Administrative Guidelines for University Support Groups were issued by the Office of the President on December 14, 1990.

• Policy: The 1990 Policy on University Support Groups reads as follows:

"The Regents of the University of California recognize the commitment and service of University Support Groups in fostering support for the University and its individual campuses.

"University Support Groups, which are in addition to the University of California Campus Foundations and Alumni Associations, provide valuable assistance through fund raising or other support for the benefit of the University. Status as a University Support Group is achieved by official recognition as such by the President or a Chancellor.

"Granting official recognition establishes the privileges and responsibilities of the relationship between a University Support Group and the University, including use of the University's name and its facilities and services.

"Recognized University Support Groups shall comply with applicable policies, guidelines, and procedures issued by the President or a Chancellor to insure proper organizational and financial controls.

"Without such recognition, no group may (a) represent itself as raising funds or otherwise providing support on behalf or for the benefit of the University, (b) use the name of the University or any of its campuses, facilities, or programs, either expressly or by implication, in connection with such activities, or (c) use University facilities, equipment, or personnel in connection with such activities."

• Guidelines: The Administrative Guidelines for University Support Groups incorporated into a single document the substantive details of the 1978 policy and the 1981 Systemwide Administrative Guidelines Governing University Support Groups.

In addition, the 1990 Guidelines made two changes:

1) Provisions specific to Campus Foundations were removed because separate Policy and Guidelines applied to Campus Foundations.

2) Provisions for compliance with conflict of interest regulations were added to the Guidelines to reflect those in the Administrative Guidelines for Campus Foundations.

In 1991, Administrative Guidelines for University Support Groups were issued in revised form, superseding previous Guidelines issued in 1990.

REFERENCES: Policy on University Support Groups, November 1990, and Administrative Guidelines for University Support Groups, April 24, 1991, Office of the President.

CROSS-REFERENCES: Foundations; Private Support.

T

Tanner Lecture on Human Values: The University was named as a host institution for the Tanner Lecture on Human Values in 1988.

The Tanner lectureship was established in 1978 at the University of Cambridge by American scholar, industrialist and philanthropist Obert Clark Tanner.

The purpose was to broaden and strengthen the understanding of human values.

Presented yearly by host institutions, the public lectures are international in scope, transcending ethnic, national, religious or ideological distinctions.

The purpose of these lectures is "to advance and reflect upon the scholarly and scientific learning relating to human values and valuation. . . . [embracing] the entire range of values pertinent to the human condition, interest, behavior, and aspiration."

The cosmopolitan spirit of the lectureships is in keeping with the intent of the founders to develop a program that is international and intercultural in scope, transcending ethnic, national, religious or ideological distinctions.

Invitations to present the Tanner Lectures are extended only to those whose extraordinary accomplishments merit the highest accolades of their profession.

In establishing the lectureship, Tanner said: "I hope these lectures will contribute to the intellectual and moral life of mankind.

"I see them simply as a search for a better understanding of human behavior and human values. This understanding may be pursued for its own intrinsic worth, but it may also eventually have practical consequences for the quality of personal and social life."

The Tanner Lectures on Human Values is a non-profit corporation administered by the University of Utah, and the Tanner Trust funds the lectures.

David P. Gardner, who had served as president of the University of Utah before assuming the presidency of the University of California in 1983, was a founding trustee.

As of 1992, permanent Tanner Lectureships had been established at eight institutions in the U.S. and England.

In addition to UC, host institutions for the Tanner lectureship are the following:

Clare Hall, the University of Cambridge; Brasenose College, Oxford University; Harvard University; Yale University; Princeton University; the University of Michigan; the University of Utah; and Stanford University.

One-year lectureships have been funded at a number of other universities.

These include the Hebrew University of Jerusalem, the Australian National University, Nehru University, the University of Helsinki, the University of Madrid, the

University of Buenos Aires, the University of Warsaw and the Chinese University of Hong Kong.

REFERENCES: Informational material, University Relations, Office of the President.

CROSS-REFERENCES: International Programs; Recognitions.

Tanner Lecturers at the University: From Confucianism to Civic Forum

1988: Columbia University historian Wm. Theodore de Bary, internationally acclaimed authority on the role of Confucianism in East Asian societies, spoke at Berkeley on "The Trouble with Confucianism."

At the time of his lecture, de Bary was the John Mitchell Mason Professor of the University at Columbia University. He had earned numerous honors and awards as a distinguished historian of the complex civilizations of China and East Asia.

His Tanner Lecture traced Confucianism in East Asia from classical through contemporary times.

It was based on studies showing that the teachings of Confucius have greatly influenced East Asian societies through the centuries.

Today, according to the lecture, Confucianism remains influential in the political, cultural, educational and economic life of China, Taiwan, Japan, Korea, Hong Kong and Singapore, and thus presents a particular challenge in the international arena.

1989: Sociologist S. N. Eisenstadt, the Rose Isaacs Professor of Sociology at The Hebrew University of Jerusalem, gave two Tanner lectures at Berkeley on "Cultural Traditions, Historical Experience and Social Change—The Limits of Convergence."

In his lecture, he addressed the question of whether a "culture of modernism" is spreading throughout the world, even to lesser developed nations.

He discussed whether this trend will lead to the convergence of societies and social structures, despite political and cultural differences.

He also discussed aspects of both Western and Eastern civilizations, with particular emphasis on ancient and modern Japan.

Eisenstadt has been internationally recognized as an authority on the study of the history and social structure of major civilizations and the recipient of numerous awards and honors. These included the Balzan Prize in sociology, the Italo-Swiss award that is one of the world's highest academic honors,

1990: No speaker was scheduled.

1991: Two speakers of international renown gave lectures, one at Berkeley and one at UCLA.

• Amid a swarm of media representatives, tight security and a combined UC and German entourage, Helmut Kohl, chancellor of the Federal Republic of Germany, delivered the Tanner Lecture at Berkeley's sixth annual Convocation.

Kohl's speech represented the first on the West Coast by a chancellor of the Federal Republic of Germany since 1960, when Konrad Adenauer visited Berkeley.

Kohl had played a key role in the historic unification of Germany, completed in 1990.

"We now have the chance to redress a little the problems of the past," he told his audience at the Convocation.

". . . Try to look back at the history of this century and learn from the experiences we have had . . . that peace, freedom, the rule of law, and democracy are essential for personal happiness."

• At UCLA, Vaclav Havel, then president of the Czech and Slovak Federal Republic (which was separated into two nations in 1993), delivered the Tanner Lecture.

Havel was the dissident playwright who led the 1989 "Velvet Revolution" that overturned his country's Communist leadership.

In 1977 he helped found the Charter 77 human rights movement, creating the Civic Forum. This was the non-violent, non-partisan organization that ultimately toppled the Communist regime.

In his Tanner Lecture at UCLA, Havel said the political pattern in his country demonstrated "the arrogance of modern man, who styles himself master of nature and the world, the only one who understands them, the one everything must serve, the one for whom our planet exists.

"Intoxicated by the achievements of his mind, by modern science and technology, he forgets that his knowledge has limits, limits beyond which there stands a great mystery, something higher and infinitely more sophisticated than his own intellect."

1992: No speaker was scheduled.

1993: Plans were under way early in the year for UC's next Tanner Lecture.

Teaching: Although the University is internationally renowned as a major research institution, it places a high value on the importance of teaching.

Students who attend its campuses have the benefit of learning from world-renowned theorists and researchers who are intent on passing their knowledge on to future generations.

Excellent teachers may be encountered in all departments and all disciplines, in large classes and in seminars. However, teaching styles are as varied as the courses.

Nevertheless, a set of high standards guides each teacher.

For example, he or she seeks to encourage the free pursuit of learning in each student by acting as an intel-

Continued following photo pages

TEACHING

Teaching is one of the University's traditional missions. UC's scholars, scientists and their undergraduate and graduate students extract new information and uncover secrets of the world around them.

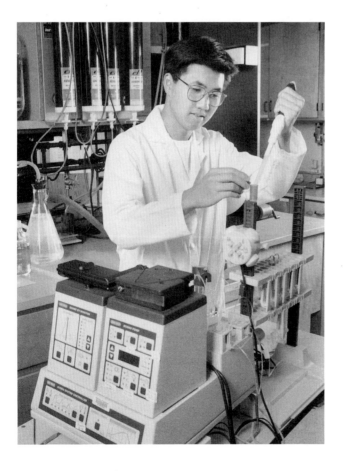

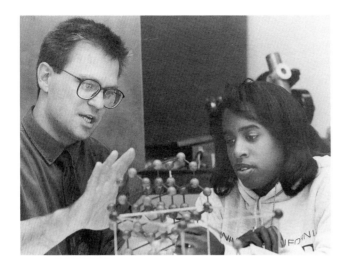

They can be found in classrooms and laboratories, as well as in the outside world where even such natural features as massive rocks and fragile tidepools can yield a wealth of knowledge.

Teaching (cont'd)

lectual guide and counselor and by upholding high scholarly standards.

Good teachers do more than convey knowledge in a field.

They try to clarify for students the relationships between their subject and other fields of knowledge; they ignite in their students a desire to learn; and, as a consequence, they often have a lifelong impact on their students' lives and careers.

Department chairs are charged with gathering evidence of a candidate's teaching ability at all levels of instruction, from lower division to graduate courses and dissertation supervision.

Teaching is considered an essential criterion to appointment or advancement.

Campuses honor a number of their outstanding faculty members each year by presenting them with awards for distinguished teaching.

In addition, departments annually nominate many of their faculty as distinguished teachers.

Examples of important teaching programs can be found in the Campus Profiles.

In February 1992, the University's president took another major step to improve the quality of education received by undergraduates at UC.

In a letter to chancellors at the eight general campuses, President David P. Gardner called for a phasing in of additional courses and sections over the next three years, within existing resources, in order to accelerate UC's ongoing efforts to improve the education of its undergraduates.

He asked the chancellors to submit a plan of action to him by July 1, and to report once a year on campus progress.

His four objectives, which had the full support of the Universitywide Academic Senate and of the chancellors, included provisions to:

• Increase the number of freshman and sophomore seminars.

• Reduce class size when and wherever possible.

• Increase the range and number of opportunities UC's undergraduates have for supervised research.

• Increase the number of courses and sections offered by the campuses so that students can more easily make normal progress toward their degrees.

The president referred to his comments at the January meeting of the Regents, in which he emphasized the interest in and dedication of the faculty to their students and cited their previous and continuing efforts to enrich the undergraduate experience.

He also called for a "renewed and vigorous" collaboration between the campus Academic Senates and administrations to accomplish those objectives.

"The faculty of the University of California is as hardworking, as creative, as talented and as dedicated to their work and students as any faculty in the world," Gardner told the Regents. "Does all this mean that we cannot do better or that we should stop striving to improve? Of course not."

The chair of the Academic Council told the Regents that the Council endorsed and supported the president's statement on the improvement of undergraduate education at UC, adding that the Council would support faculty and administration efforts in implementing the increase wherever the educational gains were demonstrable, and the changes in scheduling policies fair. The council chair stated further that the increase in teaching contribution would represent the faculty's commitment to enhancing the quality of education even in the face of UC's current financial difficulties.

UC's latest interest in this area was stimulated in 1985 when the president asked Berkeley Professor Neil Smelser to chair a major study of UC's lower division programs.

The recommendations from this study resulted in improved, monitored and reported changes in teaching programs for freshmen and sophomores.

The Smelser Report was followed in 1991 by another committee study chaired by Santa Cruz Chancellor Karl Pister.

This study examined UC's faculty rewards system, including specifically the role and place of teaching in assessing faculty performance. Debate on and review of the report was continuing within the Academic Senate as 1992 began.

In the meantime, new teaching departments and programs were created, others were dropped, and the curriculum continued to receive ongoing scrutiny.

In spring 1992, the president convened an All-University Faculty Conference on Undergraduate Education, which focused on the role of the academic department in shaping and delivering undergraduate education.

In his February 1992 letter to the chancellors, the president said he expected that campus plans would include "specific objectives and schedules for phasing in . . . improvements.

"The plan should be tailored to your campus's particular needs and, of course, may include activities built on your initiatives of recent years as well as new ones.

"Your goals and plans will need to be expressed in ways that will permit the gathering of both quantitative and qualitative data so that these may be shared throughout the University, with the Regents, and with others having an interest in this matter."

And he told them, "Your active personal oversight, together with the full cooperation of the Academic Senate, is indispensable if we are to be successful in carrying this program forward."

Some years before the current interest in the enhancement of undergraduate education, the University was seeking improvements in the teaching process, beginning most particularly in 1979–80 following issuance of a report by a Universitywide Task Force on Teaching Evaluation and subsequent support of UC's president.

REFERENCES: "Saxon Announces Two-year Program To Enhance UC's Commitment to Teaching" and "What Is in the Task Force Report on Teaching Evaluation," *University Bulletin,* Vol. 29, No. 11, November 17, 1980; The Report of the Task Force Report on Teaching Evaluation, Spring 1980; "President Tells Chancellors of Teaching Objectives," news release, February 12, 1992, University Relations, Office of the President.

CROSS-REFERENCES: All-University Faculty Conferences; subjects related to education.

Teaching Hospitals:

The University operates five teaching hospitals (academic medical centers).

Their primary mission is to support the clinical teaching programs of UC's health professional schools, including five Schools of Medicine, two Schools of Nursing and one School of Pharmacy.

The schools are located on the Davis, Irvine, Los Angeles, San Diego and San Francisco campuses.

Many University health sciences students, as well as students from community programs, receive instruction in patient care at the teaching hospitals.

The core clinical learning experiences in the health sciences takes place, to the extent possible, in hospitals where programs are under the control of the University.

Coinciding with their teaching mission, the teaching hospitals provide a full range of health care services and are the sites for testing the application of new information and the development of new diagnostic and therapeutic techniques.

With their tripartite mission of teaching, research and service, the five UC teaching hospitals are a major resource for California and the nation.

For example, they train tomorrow's health professionals and provide educational opportunities for community health professionals.

In addition, they provide care to thousands of patients each day, who generally have severe illnesses and limited financial resources.

Their research products serve all people. The research is supported by nearly $500 million of National Institutes of Health awards to the University. This research core attracts some of the best scientists in the world and stimulates California's biotechnology industry.

Effective July 1, 1990, an important addition was made to one of the hospitals. At that time, the Mount Zion Hospital and Medical Center, a not-for-profit community hospital in San Francisco, was integrated with the UC San Francisco Medical Center. The integration made possible the expansion of UC clinical programs at the Mount Zion site and assured the continued operation of that facility in the community.

In 1992–93, the five University teaching hospitals, including the Mount Zion facility, had a combined licensed bed capacity of 3,146 acute care beds. They were expected to generate more than 720,000 patient days and more than 1.6 million out-patient visits.

Because of this high volume, the University hospitals constitute one of the largest health care systems and one of the two largest Medi-Cal providers in the state.

(In July 1993, another hospital, the Thornton Hospital, opened at UC San Diego.)

Each of the UC hospitals is distinctive, with its own set of traditions, spectrum of services, centers of excellence, referral patterns, planning challenges, contractual arrangements, and organizational dynamics.

And each, with its own missions of teaching, service and research, and its need to balance its resources among the competing demands generated by these missions, represents a complex entity of its own.

At the request of the State of California, the University assumed the operation of former county hospitals in Sacramento, Irvine and San Diego in the 1960s and 1970s, rather than constructing teaching hospitals of its own.

As a result, these three hospitals historically have had a disproportionately high percentage of medically indigent patients. These patients are most likely to be sponsored by the State's Medi-Cal program, or by county programs or have no payors.

The responsibilities of the governing body for each teaching hospital are delegated by the Regents to UC's president, who in turn delegates these responsibilities to the chancellor of the individual campus.

Each chancellor is responsible, under policies established by the Regents and the president, for the academic, operational and financial performance of the particular medical center.

The director of the medical center is, in turn, responsible, to the chancellor for the operation of the hospital.

The medical staff of each of these hospitals is a separately organized entity, comprising UC faculty physicians, with its own medical staff bylaws.

Within the parameters of these bylaws, each physician staff member is responsible to the hospital for adhering to policies and procedures governing his or her patient care and related activities.

Over the past several decades, the Regents have utilized a variety of standing and ad hoc committees in the exercise of their governance and oversight responsibilities, including the establishment of the Committee on Hospital Governance in 1982.

REFERENCES: UC's Budgets for Current Operations; information from Health Sciences, Office of the President.

CROSS-REFERENCES: Health Sciences Instruction.

Technology Transfer: From 1989 to 1993, the University dramatically increased its interaction with industry to meet the public responsibility it has in getting its technology into the marketplace.

Up until 1989, UC's Technology Transfer Program had focussed mainly on protecting University technology by patent prosecution. A relatively small amount of effort was devoted to the licensing of technology, and this was primarily in response to industry requests for access to specific technology.

As a result of various administrative reviews in the late 1980s, new goals and models were established that reorganized the technology transfer operation.

The major goal of these changes was to meet UC's public responsibility to transfer its technology, developed largely with federal research funding, into the marketplace.

The goal was to be achieved by changes that included the following:

1) Enhanced service to the faculty, aimed at generating more disclosures of technology advancements (a "disclosure" is the filing of information by a faculty or staff member of a potentially patentable idea)

2) Active marketing and industrial liaison strategies aimed at generating interest in UC-developed technology.

In 1989, the plan was put into effect with the recruitment of new management and a commitment to support expansion and upgrading of the staff.

Using fiscal year 1989 as a benchmark, here are a few comparisons to indicate the rapid progress made in the following four years.

• In 1989, there were 355 disclosures. In 1993, 571 disclosures were made. This represented a 68% increase.

• In 1989, 29 initial agreements with industry were executed. These agreements, termed "secrecy agreements" in the technology transfer world, are the forerunners of full disclosure of technology and subsequent licensing agreements. In 1993, 732 such agreements were executed, a 25-fold increase, and a strong indication that the marketing strategy was working.

• In 1989, licenses, options and letters of intent numbered 70. In 1993, 149 such agreements were put in place, representing a more than two-fold increase. Income from this activity also enjoyed a marked increase during those four years, rising from less than $9 million in 1989 to more than $44 million at the end of the 1993 fiscal year.

• The actual filing of U.S. patent applications had kept pace with disclosures during the four-year period, while patents filed overseas had increased more than 50%. This was the result of a larger number of companies licensing UC technologies, then requesting and paying for worldwide protection.

• While the cost of patent applications increased from $2.8 million in 1989 to $4.9 million in 1993, the net cost to the University actually decreased as more and more companies were willing to underwrite patent costs either through direct reimbursement or by paying option and license fees calculated to include these legal costs.

Thus, the primary goal for the University's technology transfer program is not to make money on the results of the University's research, but to further UC's mission of serving society.

This public service is effected through the transfer of knowledge which ultimately leads to the development of new products and processes that enhance the quality of life, as well as economic vitality.

Nonetheless, income is one measure of how successful the University is in transferring its research results to the public.

After expenses, this income is shared with the inventor, the State and the campuses. Of the $8.9 million generated in 1989, $1.9 million was shared with inventors. In 1993, $10.5 million of the $44 million generated was shared with inventors.

The State's share rose from $1.1 million in 1989 to approximately $4.5 million in 1993.

Similarly, in 1989, $1.6 million was distributed to the campuses of origin, while in 1993 they received $9.4 million.

As a general rule of thumb, it is assumed that average royalty payments equal about 2% of gross sales. Accordingly, the University's income of $44 million represented more than $2 billion in product sales during 1992–93. This figure was generated by UC technology for products used beneficially by the public, which has supported UC's organized research efforts, primarily through Federal and State funding.

Thus, the University has made substantial progress over a four-year period in getting University-developed technologies out to the public. At the same time, UC officials have been taking steps to determine the best way to further the University's technology transfer program.

In late July 1993, UC President Jack W. Peltason delegated to Senior Vice President—Business and Finance V. Wayne Kennedy responsibility for the management of UC's intellectual property matters, including the Office of Technology Transfer.

Kennedy subsequently was asked to convene a technology transfer advisory group consisting of faculty and administrators. The group membership includes one representative from each campus and Laboratory, designated by the chancellor/Laboratory director, and three faculty members designated by the Academic Council.

The group was to undertake two responsibilities.

First, it would review various studies, recommendations, analyses and plans regarding technology transfer from both UC sources and other major research universities. This review is to result in advice to the president on the most appropriate objectives for a University program and on the most effective organizational structure to implement such a program systemwide and at the campus and Laboratory level.

Second, the group would recommend an on-going mechanism to ensure Universitywide consultation in the area of technology transfer, so that the University can respond in a timely way as issues arise in this vital link between UC, industry and the State.

The advisory group's first meeting was held in mid-October 1993. It intended to complete its work by February 1994.

The group included one representative from each campus and laboratory, designated by the chancellor or laboratory director, and three faculty representatives designated by the Academic Council.

In addition, as part of his examination of the University's technology transfer program, Vice President Kennedy stated his intention to review business relationships and practices of the management of the UC Office of Technology Transfer (OTT). OTT, which administers the technology transfer program, is funded by a portion of the income it generates.

Finally, while plans moved forward to enhance UC's technology transfer efforts, the Office of the President decided to defer action on a proposal to develop a nonprofit and/or a for-profit corporation to increase such efforts. The decision followed wide-ranging consultation and discussion throughout the University over a several month period.

REFERENCES: "An Update on the University's Recent Progress in Technology Transfer," presentation by Senior Vice President—Business and Finance V. Wayne Kennedy to the Regents, September 24, 1993.

CROSS-REFERENCES: Community and Public Service; Research Achievements; subjects cited in the text.

Teleconferencing: Over the years, the University has developed teleconferencing capabilities by utilizing telephone hookups connecting many UC sites hundreds of miles apart.

Such hookups have allowed conferees to "meet" and discuss their agendas, while cutting the expense and time involved in traveling hundreds of miles.

By 1992, some teleconference participants actually began to see the individuals they were talking to, in a form of TV called "video teleconferencing," or VTC.

By May 1992, video teleconferencing equipment was operational at the Davis, Los Angeles, Riverside and San Diego campuses and the Office of the President's Harbor Bay Isle offices in Alameda.

All of the sites' systems are identical, consisting of:

• A control panel at the conference table (seating a minimum of six people) to allow a user to regulate the system's functions.

• Two 35-inch monitors, one for viewing conferees at a single distant site, and the other for displaying graphics.

• A camera which allows a user to push a button on the control panel and pan to any one of the people at the conference table.

• Microphones on the conference tables.

• An auxiliary camera for times when a speaker to be viewed is not sitting at the conference table.

• A graphics stand, with camera, for displaying documents.

In addition, a multipoint control unit (MCU) is located within the Office of the President at the Kaiser Building in Oakland, to be used when holding conferences between three or more sites.

By early 1993, video teleconferencing had been successfully used at conferences involving UC libraries, campus administrators, college deans, auditors and project managers.

In addition, several additional University campuses and the three national laboratories managed by UC have been studying ways to implement VTC use.

There also has been a strong interest in using the technology for long-distance education, which includes college-level courses. A number of academic institutions across the country already have used VTC for this purpose.

REFERENCES: "Video Teleconferencing Comes to UC," Summer 1992, No. 3, and "Video Teleconferencing Update," Fall/Winter 1993, No. 4, *IS&AS Connections,* Information Systems and Administrative Services, Office of the President.

Tobacco-Related Disease Research Program: In passing Proposition 99, the Tobacco Tax and Health Protection Act of 1988, the people of California specified that five percent of the revenue from a new tobacco tax be earmarked for research on tobacco-related disease.

The State Legislature requested the University to establish and administer a research program to facilitate the elimination of smoking in California because "The elimination of smoking is the number one weapon against four of the five leading causes of death in California" [Health and Safety Code, Article 8.7, Section 424.10(a)(6)].

The goals of the research supported by these funds are to enhance understanding of the causes of tobacco-related disease and to develop more effective interventions for prevention and treatment of such disease.

Though scientific research on tobacco-related disease has the short-term benefit of increasing knowledge, changes in standard prevention and treatment practices based on this new knowledge typically take a sustained effort over many years.

The expected gain in knowledge is occurring and, moreover, there is promise that knowledge gained from ongoing and future research will lead to improved prevention and treatment.

The Tobacco Related Disease Research Program (TRDRP) established by UC in 1989 entered its fourth year of operation in 1992.

In 1992, TRDRP awarded 92 new research grants for a total of $24,626,594 to investigators at 26 public and private nonprofit research institutions in California.

Since 1990, TRDRP has awarded $116,950,433 in 378 grants to investigators at 43 California institutions.

Research supported by TRDRP grants has yielded important findings which have been reported in hundreds of presentations at scientific conferences and in science publications.

These publications include the influential *Journal of the American Medical Association, New England Journal of Medicine, American Journal of Public Health, Science, Nature,* and *Proceedings of the National Academy of Sciences U.S.A.*

Scientists conducting research with the support of the TRDRP grants have contributed directly to statewide and local tobacco control activities, enhancing the state's efforts to ameliorate the effects of tobacco-related disease by:

• Providing advice to local tobacco use prevention programs and technical assistance to Department of Health Services and State Department of Education.

• Initiating programs to reduce tobacco use in Vietnamese, Chinese and Latino communities, especially by pregnant women.

• Providing data and technical assistance pertinent to the establishment of State and local policies that restrict smoking, including effects of tobacco tax, cost of smoking to California, and effectiveness of anti-smoking legislation.

TRDRP has facilitated the exchange and dissemination of research findings by organizing or co-sponsoring the following:

(1) Meetings of scientists, (2) meetings of researchers and key persons making and implementing tobacco control policies, (3) workshops on the health effects of exposure to environmental tobacco smoke and analysis of surveys of tobacco use in California, and (4) an Institute of Medicine study of efforts to prevent nicotine addiction among youth.

TRDRP also has institutionalized policies and procedures for soliciting, evaluating, awarding and managing research grants.

These policies and procedures are documented in printed materials and reports that have been widely distributed throughout California's research and tobacco control communities.

TRDRP has been nationally recognized in the Journal of the American Medical Association, the American Journal of Public Health and Science.

REFERENCES: Tobacco-Related Disease Research Program: Abstracts of Funded Research Projects, and Tobacco-Related Disease Research Program, Annual Reports, Office of Health Affairs, Office of the President.

CROSS-REFERENCES: Health Sciences.

TRDRP Highlights: Some of its Research Results

Costs of Smoking: One in five deaths in California is attributable to smoking; the total economic burden of smoking in California is $7.6 billion annually or $256 per Californian per year; one year after Proposition 99 went into effect, cigarette sales in California were reduced to 9.5 percent below the pre-tax trend, a reduction that was sustained throughout 1991.

Prevention of Smoking: Tobacco education that emphasizes personal coping skills is more effective in preventing youth smoking than conventional health education.

Environmental Tobacco Smoke: Creation of smoke-free workplaces both protects nonsmokers from environmental tobacco smoke and reduces total cigarette consumption; ten years of exposure to environmental tobacco smoke at work increases the risk of asthma by 50 percent; accumulation of fat in the coronary and pulmonary arteries (atherosclerosis) was nearly double in animals exposed to a high level of environmental tobacco smoke and a high-fat diet; exposure to sidestream smoke significant alters the growth of neonatal lungs.

Nicotine Addiction: Nicotine addiction appears to be the result of the reduction of activity of neurons in the nucleus accumbens regions of the brain caused by the administration of nicotine; one reason that Black male smokers have higher rates of lung cancer than White male smokers, despite smoking fewer cigarettes, may be that Blacks are three times more likely to smoke menthol cigarettes; new biochemical markers of tobacco use will enable nicotine patch or gum users who have quite smoking to be distinguished from those who have not.

Causes of Tobacco-Related Diseases: Children born to smoking women had lower birthweight and gestational age and experienced more neonatal infections; smoking increases the risk of bladder cancer through genetically determined differences in metabolism of particular carcinogens present in cigarette smoke; chronic nicotine exposure appears to predispose the heart muscle to a higher frequency of ventricular arrhythmias; free radicals in cigarette smoking damage key cells in the immune system that are believed to be a factor in tobacco-related disease; nicotine exposure can interact synergistically with high blood pressure to alter the antioxidant defense system and lead to cardiovascular disease.

Also, nicotine interferes with normal regulation of an enzyme (tPA), which may increase the likelihood of blood clot formation; a deficiency of the enzyme LCAT is linked with increased risk of heart disease; this enzyme is inhibited by cigarette smoke; nicotine decreased the effect of a natural substance (bradykinin) that reduces inflammation in diseases such as bronchitis and arthritis; a single exposure to cigarette smoke led to a three-fold higher formation of a highly carcinogenic compound in the lungs of developing animals.

Treatment of Tobacco-Related Diseases: Illudins are natural products derived from Jack O'Lantern mushrooms that appear to be effective against a variety of smoking-related cancers; a new variety of anti-cancer drug appears to be more active against human lung tumor cells and more selective against tumor cells than normal cells; the drug pentoxifylline partially inhibited the increased number of inflammatory cells induced in the lung by inhaling tobacco smoke.

U

The **UC Clip Sheet** was started in the mid-1920s as a "service for the press of California."

Originally, as the Clip Sheet, it provided a weekly clipping service for newspaper editors around the state interested in printing articles about UC's growth, research and accomplishments in their newspapers.

Stories were based on material prepared by the University's campuses and by the laboratories managed by UC for the federal government.

Topics in early issues of the Clip Sheet included, for example, the need for funding support, the quest for intelligent life in the universe, education for Californians, high medical standards in UC's hospitals, agricultural service to the state, the increase of women in higher education.

All these remained subjects of interest through the years.

However, after its topography was modernized, the UC Clip Sheet covered other subjects that no one could have envisioned in earlier times, including AIDS, radioactive waste, jet lag, environmental concerns, and supercomputers.

Over the years, the UC Clip Sheet was prepared by University Relations in the Office of the President.

The mailing list included newspapers, radio and TV stations and free-lance writers in every state. Copies also were posted throughout UC to help keep the University community informed.

With the November 1990 issue, the UC Clip Sheet discontinued publication.

It returned in 1991 in an electronic format that continues to serve media and free-lance outlets by providing a quick, complete source of information on what is happening at UC. The electronic format is called "UC Newswire."

REFERENCES: University Relations files, Office of the President.

CROSS-REFERENCES: Publications; "UC Newswire."

"UC Newswire" is a computerized service that transmits news and other information from offices throughout the University to electronic and print media, as well as to free-lance writers and other subscribers.

The service is available to recipients in California and in other states and countries.

It began service in 1991 in the University Relations Office in UC's corporate headquarters in Oakland. The successful and expanding enterprise is now located in the Fresno Office of University Relations.

The electronic "bulletin board" was designed to enhance and expedite communications between UC sources and the media by supplementing mail, FAX and telephone communications.

A staff member at the Fresno Office receives news and other information from the campuses and from the DOE Laboratories managed by the University and sends it out via a specialized computer system.

News items in the system are listed under more than 20 topic categories, ranging from agriculture to veterinary medicine. In addition, background information on the UC administration, the Regents and other UC sources is available on a continuing basis.

The system provides a special number for subscribers to call 24 hours a day, seven days a week. Information is updated daily.

Subscribers can gain access to the system through the use of a personal computer equipped with a modem and any commercial communications software program.

REFERENCES: "UC news on-line and available byte-by-byte," Newsline, May 8, 1991, and additional information, News and Public Affairs, Office of the President.

CROSS-REFERENCES: UC Clip Sheet.

The **University Bulletin** served faculty and staff for 36 years (1952–88) as UC's weekly publication of record and the only Universitywide publication of news and information.

A notice on the front page of the first issue of May 12, 1952 explained its purpose. Under the headline "FOR YOUR INFORMATION—AN EXPERIMENT," the notice read:

"An information bulletin for all staff members of the University of California is under consideration. This is one in a series of experimental issues distributed for suggestions and emendations.

"As contemplated, this bulletin would publish reports of Regents' meetings and Academic Senate meetings, announcements of the President and other University officers, statements of administrative policy and procedure, and other official actions affecting the conduct of University affairs.

"It would also publish news items concerning academic and non-academic personnel features about the University and its activities, and a statewide calendar of events of general interest."

And so it did, for more than three decades.

During all this time, the publication included articles about UC's major contributions and achievements in teaching, research and public service, policy announcements, official information, and other items of Universitywide interest and importance.

In so doing, it performed a number of services.

It provided a sense of institutional continuity and tradition, helped develop an understanding of UC as a single university, kept faculty and staff aware of the importance of their daily tasks and the contribution each was making to the University, provided a medium for sharing ideas about UC's missions, and furnished vital information to UC personnel for the successful exercise of their duties and responsibilities.

In 1976, the *University Bulletin* won national recognition as one of the several best publications of its type in the U.S.

The award came from a national professional organization, the Council for the Support and Advancement of Education (CASE), representing professionals in the fields of publications, public information, development, alumni affairs and other areas.

The *University Bulletin* ceased publication in 1988. It was replaced by *UC Focus*, a newspaper-format publication.

REFERENCES: Files, University Relations, Office of the President.

CROSS-REFERENCES: Publications.

UC MEXUS, the University of California Institute for Mexico and the United States:

Since the early 1900s, scholars at the University have contributed significantly to knowledge about Mexico and its relationship with the United States.

By the middle of the century, UC scientists were working actively with their Mexican colleagues, especially in agricultural topics. In the last two decades, the importance of Mexico within the University's educational, research, and public service missions has become increasingly clear.

Externally, Mexico has become the most dynamic, influential, and unpredictable of California's neighbor's. Internally, the Mexican-origin population is the largest of California's ethnic minority groups, and the fastest-growing population in California's society. Together, California and Mexico are integrating rapidly into a single region. Individually and jointly, they are key players in the economic, social, and political associations of the Pacific Rim countries.

Recognizing both the strength of the faculty's interests in Mexico and the importance of Mexico to the future of California, the University in 1980 began a fund to begin focusing its resources in Mexico-related topics.

This step led to the establishment in 1981–82 of the UC Consortium on Mexico and the United States. The UC MEXUS Universitywide Headquarters was opened at the Riverside campus in 1984. Professor of Botany Arturo Gómez-Pompa, a tropical ecologist, was named director in 1986. In 1992, the consortium was formally established as a University of California Multicampus Research Unit and its name changed to the University of California Institute for Mexico and the United States.

The Institute's broad objectives are to increase the quantity, visibility, and effectiveness of Mexico-United States projects in the University; to strengthen and develop research, exchange programs, and teaching; to support and coordinate interdisciplinary and inter-campus projects; to encourage and enable collaborative approaches by UC and Mexican scholars to the issues which affect both nations; to act as a source for information about all University-sponsored United States-Mexico activities; to develop new resources for support of research and instructional programs; and to promote a better understanding between the two countries.

In support of these objectives, UC MEXUS conducts competitive grants programs for the development of international collaborative research and/or education projects; literary, artistic, or other creative activities that are Mexican or Chicano in subject or style, research in Mexico-related or Chicano topics; and dissertation research in the Institute's areas of interest. The UC MEXUS program, Critical Issues in United States-Mexico Relations, brings together scholars, public officials, and representatives of the media from both countries in dialogue directed toward resolution of binational challenges.

The Institute's Universitywide headquarters contributes to interests in Mexican and Chicano topics at all campuses through sponsorship of guest lecturers and performances, conferences, library collections, publications, and exhibitions. UC MEXUS issues a regular newsletter, *UC MEXUS NEWS*, and sponsors the bilingual, international academic journal, *Mexican Studies/ Estudios Mexicanos*, which is published by UC Press. In 1989, UC MEXUS published the report, *The Challenge: Latinos in a Changing California*, in response to California Senate Concurrent Resolution 43, concerning the status of the Hispanic population in California.

Since the establishment of UC MEXUS, more than 500 members of the University of California faculty have participated in its programs, along with nearly 400 scholars and scientists from Mexican institutions and some 150 UC graduate students.

REFERENCES: "New Consortium Formed on Mexico and U.S.," University Bulletin, Vol. 30, No. 27, April 26, 1982; *UC MEXUS: Report of Activities, 1991–1992*, UC MEXUS Universitywide Headquarters; *UCR General Catalog 1993–1994*, University of California, Riverside; Regents' Item 303, "Establishment of UC MEXUS . . .," Committee on Educational Policy, May 14, 1992; Regents' Item 301G, "Name Change . . .," Committee on Educational Policy, September 17, 1992.

CROSS-REFERENCES: International Programs; Organized Research Units.

UC Printing Services (UCPS)

is a high-volume, non-profit, self-supporting enterprise, within the Office of the President for many years and now part of the Berkeley campus.

Some 84 professionals at its printing plant in Berkeley engage in a $9 million-a-year business that offers an array of production services for the entire UC community.

In addition, UCPS maintains a large paper stock and supply warehouse in nearby Richmond and operates two library book binderies in Oakland and Culver City, each with 35 employees and generating $2.6 million in combined recharge sales.

UC Printing Services is not funded by the University's annual state budget. Instead, it is completely self-supporting. This means the money it earns from its customers must meet all its operating, equipment, administrative and payroll expenses.

In recent years, UCPS has installed technologically advanced printing and other equipment capable of providing professional quality materials that meet the competitive demands of the printing marketplace in terms of efficiency, quality and price.

For example, it has installed modern electronic pre-press equipment, including advanced image-setters, digital scanners, computerized cameras, and other automated devices.

Also in use are a number of high-speed, multi-color printing presses.

UCPS also has developed advanced bookbinding techniques, including an innovative brittle-book replacement program and cost-effective adhesive binding for library preservation.

In addition, each of the two library binderies in Oakland and Culver City is installing a highly sophisticated machine called the Ultrabinder, which has electronic sensors.

The Ultrabinder was developed specifically for library bookbinding, and is based on technical recommendations contributed by the bindery managers.

As a result of the new technologies, single color or complex multi-colored books, catalogs, newsletters, posters, leaflets and brochures have become the printing plant's specialties.

These products often are printed on acid-free paper or recycled stock.

UCPS can receive material to be printed in any of a number of ways. For example, manuscript copy can be submitted directly, sent via word processing or desktop publishing diskettes, or transmitted over a UC network.

In addition, UCPS has a computer-controlled management information system to monitor all its work. With this system, a job planner can follow any project through every step of its production.

Beginning in 1976, in response to serious operational problems, commitments were made to get new equipment and to institute advanced printing technologies. Training issues became of paramount importance.

As a result, in a few short years, UC Printing Services became a financially solid, modern and thriving enterprise, ready to serve the needs of the entire University.

REFERENCES: "UC's Printing Department," *While You Were In,* September 1983, University Relations; "The successful Don Bell years leave a lasting impression," *Intercom,* Vol. 2, No. 3, December 1988, University Relations; "Do You Know About UC Printing Services?", *IS&AS Connections,* Spring 1992, Information Systems and Administrative Services (all offices within the Office of the President).

Soybean Inks and the Environment

UC Printing Services entered the modern age when it switched to soybean-based inks.

These contain less than 1 percent VOCs (volatile organic compounds), which are believed to be harmful to the environment. (Conventional petroleum-based inks contain 25–30 percent VOCs.)

Soybean inks can be used on all kinds of coated or uncoated papers. The rub resistance and durability are good.

In addition to being environmentally favorable, soybean inks cost the same as petroleum-based inks.

UCPS also offers a wide variety of recycled and other papers.

Although recycled paper is more costly than other types of paper (because of a special process it must go through), it has been increasingly in demand.

University Extension celebrated its centennial in 1991.

It all began when three Berkeley professors crossed San Francisco Bay by ferry to offer courses in the Palace Hotel in 1891.

Eventually, more than 800 people attended their classes, which dealt with Shakespeare, history and mathematics.

From that point in time, Extension's programs grew rapidly, and the term "lifelong learning" became its watchword.

In 1902 the Regents made University Extension an autonomous department.

In 1915–17, the first legislative appropriation was made, amounting to $40,000 for the biennium.

Through World War I, the Jazz Age, the Great Depression, World War II, and the postwar expansion of higher education, University Extension continued to reach out to thousands of adult students.

In 1968, Extension was administratively decentralized so that Extension units at each of UC's eight general campuses were given more autonomy.

Today, an Extension unit on a campus typically is headed by a dean who reports to the chancellor or his designee. The change has made it possible for Extension units to respond more quickly and effectively to local and regional needs.

Two other important, but related changes took place in the 1960s. In 1963, all state funding for Extension was withdrawn, and in 1968, it became completely self-supporting.

Today, University Extension is entirely supported by the fees of those who enroll in its courses, as well as by grants, contracts, and publication sales.

Extension has remained a success story, even in tough economic times.

In 1991–92, for example, 389,780 persons enrolled in UC Extension's offerings (an increase of 9,400 over the previous year), making it one of the largest extension operations in the U.S.

These enrollments brought in approximately $120 million as income.

In the same period, 15,018 courses, programs, seminars, conferences and field studies were provided throughout California and in several foreign countries.

All of Extension's courses and programs are designed and taught by recognized academic and professional experts and overseen by carefully selected advisory committees.

By offering high-quality education and training at convenient times and locations throughout the state, Extension has become a major statewide provider of professional development and an essential complement to UC's regular curriculum.

As a result, Extension makes it possible for adults to keep abreast of the latest developments in their fields, to pursue new careers, to acquire new skills, and to enrich their lives.

Two-thirds of the offerings are designed to serve the continuing educational needs of professionals. The remainder are in the arts, humanities and behavioral sciences.

More than 75 percent of the registrants have at least a bachelor's degree.

Today, Extension certificates are granted in more than 50 professional fields. The largest enrollment areas are business and management, computers and information systems, engineering, environmental sciences, education, English language programs, and law. In addition, UC Extension offers a variety of community affairs programs and public service activities.

When Extension began more than a century ago, its founders decided it would not simply follow traditional models of extended learning of the late 19th century. Instead, it would adapt itself to California's special circumstances and needs.

In recent years, its role became increasingly important, as economic and social changes have forced many individuals to undertake new careers or to seek specialized instruction that will enhance their professional skills.

Extension has been diverse enough to respond quickly to these changes and flexible enough to devise practical ways to meet an escalating statewide demand for training in a number of new areas.

For example, to help meet the increasing demand in the job market for specialization, Extension has developed certificate programs for people who seek employment or advancement, but who also need training.

These programs are planned sequences of courses designed under the guidance of advisory committees of campus faculty and top professionals.

Extension historically has offered programs dealing with major social issues. To help address these issues, Extension has brought together in a neutral setting corporate executives, politicians, government officials, and experts from various fields to explore solutions.

The issues have focused, for example, on the use of hazardous materials, alcohol and drug abuse, transportation, water quality, and biotechnology.

Other issues have included bioethics and the law, the Constitution and human rights, homeless youth, the social concerns of AIDS, child abuse, computer technology, moral issues in modern medicine, and teacher training, and immigration policy in California.

Specific to California and its economy are programs to help the state maintain the health of its high-technology fields, such as biotechnology, engineering, computer technology, traffic management, telecommunications and telecomputing.

In addition, programs and courses relating to California's ethnic and cultural diversity are being emphasized, and as the Baby Boom generation grows older, the role of the elderly will continue to be given special concern.

University Extension has long been involved in meeting the needs of Californians who wish to learn more about the world at large. Extension offers programs for individuals from other countries, including courses in languages, business, environmental management, and advanced technology and research.

All these activities, both current and planned, are a far cry from University Extension's small start in the 19th century, and they demonstrate one important point.

University Extension is meeting the 21st century head-on.

REFERENCES: "'The Uncommon School' and Lifelong Learning," University Bulletin, July 16, 1973; "University of California Extension, 1891-1991: A History of Service," UC Extension centennial publication; letter to history project editor from Statewide Dean of University Extension, September 16, 1992; University Extension Annual Report; UC's Budget for Current Operations.

CROSS-REFERENCES: Cooperative Extension.

UNIVERSITY EXTENSION
Fiscal Year 1991–1992

Registrations

Total Registrations	389,780
Degree Credit	26,990
Professional Credit	169,901
Professional and Non-Credit	189,102
Single Admissions	3,787

Registrations and Programs by Campus and Statewide Units

	Registrations	Programs
Berkeley	48,166	1,955
Davis	54,676	2,451
Irvine	28,323	1,424
Los Angeles	112,427	4,545
Riverside	30,688	1,342
San Diego	26,533	1,447
Santa Barbara	13,403	633
Santa Cruz	24,769	1,120
Continuing Education of the Bar	50,795	101

Statewide Extension Programs Offer Education Services

In addition to campus Extension operations, there are other statewide programs involving leading academic and professional teachers and other specialists.

They include the following.

▶ Continuing Education of the Bar (CEB), jointly sponsored by the Regents and the State Bar of California.

This is a comprehensive statewide program providing continuing legal education for California's legal profession. Founded in 1947 and headquartered at Berkeley, CEB is one of the largest continuing legal education enterprises in the country.

▶ The Center for Media and Independent Learning (CMIL).

Initiated in 1913 and located in Berkeley, CMIL offers more than 200 college and continuing education courses and 65 high school courses. CMIL has two components:

1) Independent Study (IS), which provides students with a flexible alternative to classroom instruction, including those who need courses not offered locally, those with scheduling conflicts, and those living in areas remote from educational institutions.

2) Media Distribution, which is a major activity whose mission is to make available the latest film and video resources to any classroom, library, museum, training facility, or home in the world where audiovisual and electronic media are employed for educational purposes.

▶ Continuing Education in Transportation Studies.

This is a complement to ITS research units at Berkeley, Davis and Irvine. (ITS refers to Institutes of Transportation Studies.) Located in Berkeley, it is designed to provide continuing education programs on its own or in conjunction with University Extension units at other campuses.

University Extension Looks to the Future

As University Extension's centennial publication noted in 1991, "it's fun to imagine where Extension might go in the 21st century."

The publication went on to explain:

"Perhaps it will offer the first virtual college, where students from all over the world will attend class, not by traveling to California, but by entering a computer-constructed three-dimensional world where they can see and talk to the instructor and to each other as if they were together in a real room.

"Perhaps Extension will prepare people to live on other planets or teach them how to rebuild entire cities quickly and inexpensively using nanotechnology.

"Perhaps Extension will become a critical interpretive or filtering hub in the massive data exchange that will take place among unified economic communities, giant multinational corporations, and integrated multinational university systems.

"Human innovation and invention will take many directions. Whatever they may be, University Extension will endeavor to prepare Californians to succeed, to live fully, and to enjoy the lifelong pursuit of learning."

University of California Press celebrated its 100th anniversary in 1993.

The Press is among the top academic presses in the nation. Its publications have won numerous awards for scholarship and literary excellence, as well as for graphic design.

With offices in Berkeley, Los Angeles, New York and London, it is UC's not-for-profit publishing arm.

It publishes 180 new books annually, as well as about 90 paperbook reprints and 30 scholarly journals. Approximately 3,600 titles are included on its active backlist.

The Press attracts manuscripts from all over the world. About one-third of its books are written by UC faculty. Its annual sales have reached the $12 million mark.

The Press publishes primarily in the humanities and social and sciences, with a small program in the natural sciences as well.

Special subjects in these areas include history, literature, art, music, film, the classics, sociology and anthropology, as well as Asian, Latin American, Middle Eastern and African studies.

Other major subjects have focused on agriculture, water issues, and the natural history of the state.

The Press's fundamental mission is to disseminate scholarship within the academic community and to the general public, through books, journals and, increasingly, electronic media.

By increasing the number of books published in paperback, the Press is particularly well equipped to serve undergraduate needs.

Specific publishing landmarks in recent years have included the following:

Ishi in Two Worlds by Theodora Kroeber (1961), *The Plan of St. Gall* by Walter Horn and Ernest Born (1979), *French Gothic Architecture* by Jean Bony (1983), *Spanish Cities of the Golden Main* by Richard Kagan (1989), and *The Papers of Martin Luther King* (Volume I, 1992, and future volumes to come).

In 1990, anticipating its 100th anniversary celebration, the Press established the Centennial Books program, to include 100 titles to be published between 1990 and 1995, including the King papers.

A pamphlet that sold for 25 cents a copy signalled the beginning of the Press in 1893. It was M.W. Shinn's "Notes on the Development of a Child."

Established on the German model, the Press functioned primarily as a print-and-exchange organization for more than 50 years.

By 1925, one might purchase written material for 75 cents on a variety of topics, including "Two New Owls from Arizona," "Factors Contributing to the Delinquency of Defective Girls," and "Nocturnal Wanderings of the California Pocket Gopher."

In 1943, a complete catalog of the Press's previous publishing was issued. Only a handful of books was included on this list. The remainder of the list was devoted to research reports, papers and monographs.

During this period, President Robert Gordon Sproul changed the Press's mandate.

He adopted a plan prepared by Samuel T. Farquhar, the first non-faculty manager of the Press, who earlier had been a printer and advertising executive.

The plan established a book program much like those at other major universities, such as Oxford, Cambridge, Harvard, Princeton and Chicago.

In addition, books of great anthropologists, such as Alfred Kroeber, appeared on the list, and important new translations of Isaac Newton and other major scientists were published.

And in 1945, the Press printed and published the United Nations Charter in several languages for the organization's historic conference on June 26, 1945.

(The effort was a complicated and frantic one, as copies were typeset and proofread through the night in Berkeley and then delivered to the Civic Auditorium in San Francisco barely minutes before the conference began.)

Farquhar's successor, August Frugé, moved the Press toward the premier position it now holds in scholarly publishing.

He separated the publishing side of the Press from the University printing plant, sought printers and binders the world over, and formed sales offices in New York and a distribution company in London.

In addition, during his tenure, he established the renowned programs that the Press has in Asian studies, classics, literary criticism and the social sciences.

James H. Clark, the current director, who has held the position for 16 years, has confirmed the Press's commitment to scholarly publications.

At the same time, he has broadened the publishing program to include books of scholarly merit that appeal to general readers.

Even with that modification, however, UC Press still devotes a larger percentage of its list to scholarly monographs than do other academic presses in the U.S.

Acquisition and editing functions are performed both at the Berkeley office headquarters and in the editorial office at UCLA (which is responsible for one-third of the Press's publishing program).

In April 1992, the Press formed a joint venture with Princeton University Press to handle the job of fulfilling domestic orders.

The Press also has formed a consortium with Princeton and Columbia University for overseas sales.

Although the Press's basic operation is self-sustaining, UC has invested funds to support portions of its publishing program.

For example, an annual appropriation enables the Press to subsidize some publications of UC faculty. The interest from a UC endowment fund set aside for the Press is added to the equity account each year to support the Press's capital base.

The total of all these UC funds amounts to approximately 10 percent of the Press's budget.

REFERENCES: "The University of California Press," *UC Focus*, Vol. 2, No. 2, September 1987, University Relations, Office of the President; "Authorization to Negotiate and Execute a Joint Venture Agreement for Order Fulfillment Services, UC Press," Regents' C Report, approved September 20, 1991; "Report on the University of California Press," Regents' Item 304 for Discussion, January 14, 1993; "University of California Press Celebrating Centennial," January 14, 1993, University Relations; catalogs and related information from UC Press; *The University of California Press: The Early Years, 1893-1953,* by Albert Muto, and *August Frugé, A Skeptic Among Scholars; August Frugé on University Publishing* (both UC Press, 1993).

CROSS-REFERENCES: Academic Senate; UC Printing Services; University of California Press and The Martin Luther King, Jr. Papers Project.

Here's How UC Press Began

One day early in 1893, when the University was just a generation old, a Mr. J. H. Bonte sat down at his rolltop desk and carefully typed out one of UC's most historic letters.

That century-old letter, now framed and still looking crisp, hangs on a wall in the building in Berkeley that houses the University of California Press.

The letter is both a birth certificate, of sorts, and a historic testament to a publishing house of outstanding quality and stature.

As secretary of the Regents, Mr. Bonte imparted the following in his letter to UC's president, Martin Kellogg, following a UC committee report:

"Your Committee, believing that it is often desirable to publish papers prepared by members of the Faculty, begs leave to submit the following recommendations:

"The sum of $1,000 shall be appropriated in the annual budget for the printing of monographs, etc., prepared by members of the Faculty. . . ."

In 1893 dollars, this represented a solid commitment to publish the University's research findings and to share them with scientists and scholars far beyond the walls of UC itself.

University of California Press and The Martin Luther King, Jr. Papers Project: The struggle to end racial injustice in this country is being extensively documented through a landmark undertaking called The Martin Luther King, Jr. Papers Project.

In 1987, the University of California Press was selected as the publisher of the papers by King's widow, Coretta Scott King, the center's president and chief executive officer.

Stanford University historian Clayborne Carson was named project editor.

The project will produce the first definitive scholarly edition of King's life and legacy as seen through his speeches, sermons, letters, articles and other writings. The 14-volume edition of these works represents one of the most important publishing projects in this country.

Now well under way, the massive project will be completed in the early part of the next century. (Volume I was published in February 1992. Volume II was to be published in January 1994.)

The project is under the general direction of the Martin Luther King, Jr. Center for Nonviolent Social Change, based in Atlanta.

Publish or Perish?

▶ UC Press is an academic unit of the University.

▶ In keeping with a basic principle of university press publishing, the Press is governed by an academic board.

▶ Known as the Board of Control, it consists of top UC administrators, the director of the Press, the faculty co-chairs of the editorial committee, and two past executive officers of other presses.

▶ The editorial committee reviews and approves every manuscript for publication. The committee consists of 20 faculty members appointed by the Academic Council from all nine UC campuses.

▶ The Board of Control makes the final decisions about any work submitted to the Press. Its judgments are based on each work's scholarly, intellectual and literary merits, not on commercial, political or social considerations.

▶ Walter E. Massey, UC's senior vice president—academic affairs and provost in the Office of the President, chairs the Board of Control. The director of UC Press is James H. Clark.

The selection was based on the Press's reputation as a highly successful publisher of important scholarly books, including other multi-volume scholarly editions and works on black history and politics.

Among these publications are seven volumes of the writings of black activist Marcus Garvey; an award-winning 50-volume series called Perspectives on Southern Africa; and a multi-volume UNESCO General History of Africa.

The King papers will include a significant amount of material that has never been published.

As a result, readers will gain a picture of the civil rights leader that goes much deeper into his family background and intellectual development than people know at present.

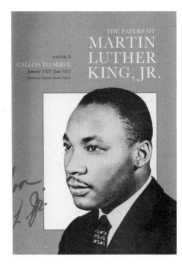

The 14-volume edition of the King Papers, including this volume, represent one of the most important publishing projects in this country.

The papers also will reveal, in detail, more about events such as:

The dynamiting of King's home in Montgomery during the bus boycott, the freedom rides and sit-ins around the South, the tensions within the protest movement, the mood of student activists, the attack of savage police dogs in Birmingham, the rock-throwing during a Chicago march, and King's selection to receive the Nobel peace prize.

Throughout, readers will discover more about King's theological and philosophical views of nonviolence, his role as spokesman for blacks in the South, and his growing opposition to the war in Vietnam.

REFERENCES: "Martin Luther King Papers: UC Press wins major publishing project," *UC Focus*, Vol. 2, No. 2, September 1987, University Relations, Office of the President; additional information from UC Press.

CROSS-REFERENCES: University of California Press.

W

Washington, D.C. Programs: The University has been active in Washington, D.C. for over 125 years.

Its establishment as a Federal Land-Grant Institution and its preeminence as a research university have given UC a long and important presence in the nation's capital.

UC was one of the first universities in the nation to engage a resident federal relations officer in Washington. A fulltime director and office have been in place since 1966.

In recent years, UC resident activity has broadened into a number of areas. For example, undergraduate academic programs are now carried out under the direct supervision of faculty from three campuses. These programs complement the ongoing student internship programs sponsored by eight UC campuses.

The University believes that expanding its presence in Washington, D.C. is a natural and desirable step for an institution with growing national and international interests. Expansion involves strengthening existing programs and developing others.

Here are brief descriptions of UC/DC programs.

• Campus Academic Programs

The Davis, Los Angeles and Santa Barbara campuses currently offer regular courses in Washington, D.C. for undergraduates. Several other UC campuses have been preparing similar programs.

These courses enable students to progress toward their degrees while conducting internships in the nation's capital.

Graduate students also participate in these programs as teaching assistants, research assistants, and mentors for undergraduates while working toward completing theses and research projects.

UC faculty serve in these programs through their home campuses and departments.

Visiting and guest lecturers from Congress, executive agencies, media and local research institutes regularly take part in the classes.

The undergraduate programs also include UC seminars and tele-courses available to students in both California and Washington, D.C.

Also available is a UC President's Scholarship program, designed to enhance student participation in the Washington academic and internship programs by providing funding support to students who otherwise could not afford to participate in an off-campus program.

• Student Internships

In addition to the academic programs described above, campuses also offer undergraduate intern programs.

These programs enable students to participate in internships in the Washington area by facilitating placements and housing.

In some instances, students can make arrangements for independent study credits through their departments. These programs, which operate throughout the year, are particularly active in the summer.

• Faculty Research Opportunities

UC faculty who teach courses in Washington draw upon the extensive intellectual resources available in the area.

Faculty also come to Washington to pursue their short- and long-term research interests. These interests include political science, public policy, history, journalism, art, the sciences and a variety of other fields.

• Federal Governmental Relations

UC has a long-standing and important policy, fiscal and public service relationship with the federal government.

As a national and international university, and with a large California Congressional Delegation, UC's federal relations operations have become an increasingly important link with Washington, D.C. policymakers.

The University's Office of Federal Governmental Relations is responsible for serving as UC's eyes and ears in the capital.

As such, the office does the following:

1) Represents UC's interests or position on pending legislation or regulations.

2) Provides information and service to the California Congressional Delegation.

3) Monitors the actions of federal executive agencies.

4) Analyzes initiatives that may affect UC or its campuses.

5) Provides casework support for dealing with the federal government. For example, the San Diego campus received a license from an on-campus TV station with support through the Washington office.

6) Serves as a partner with the various national higher education associations.

7) Serves as an information resource to the higher education community.

In addition to its fulltime staff, the UC office also has an arrangement for a student intern from each campus to serve in the office during the course of a year.

The office also prepares and circulates a weekly report reflecting the range of interests and issues of importance to the UC community.

• UC Visitors Center

The UC office also serves as a visitors and information center and as a meeting site. Visiting faculty and administrators are encouraged to use space and facilities there while in Washington.

• Related UC Programs in Washington

Other programs are also housed in the Washington office. They include:

1) Lawrence Livermore National Laboratory, one of the three federal laboratories managed by the Uni-

versity; it has an information-gathering office in Washington.

2) Professional Development Fellowships, which provides facilities for administrators from throughout UC who wish to spend varying lengths of time in the Washington office gaining a better understanding of the people and processes at the federal level of government.

• National UC Alumni Network

UC's alumni base broadens with every graduating class. There are now several thousand UC alumni in the Washington, D.C. area, and there are alumni chapters organized in the D.C. area for every campus.

Washington alumni chapters have been organized for each campus of the University under the guidance of the Alumni Association of the University of California (AAUC).

These chapters organize a variety of activities, social events, subject matter conferences, receptions for visiting UC officials, and an annual UC Alumni Day on Capitol Hill. The Alumni Day activities include meetings with Members of Congress, panel discussions on topical and timely subjects, and Washington-area Alumni of the Year awards.

REFERENCES: News release on possible establishment of a Washington, D.C. center, University Relations, Office of the President, June 15, 1989; "A helping hand in the nation's capital" and "Plans go forward for UCDC," *UC Focus,* December 1989; "Undergraduate Education in the University of California: Off-Campus Learning Programs," Item 302 for Discussion, Regents' Committee on Educational Policy, November 24, 1991; "The University of California Washington, D.C. Programs," brochure, January 1992, and additional information, Federal Governmental Relations, Office of the President.

CROSS-REFERENCES: Alumni Associations; Federal Governmental Relations; International Programs.

Water Resources: Much of the problem-solving expertise of the University's Division of Agriculture and Natural Resources (DANR) is directed toward helping agriculture stay competitive globally while protecting the state's precious water resources.

The Division's Water Resources Center, with a 180,000-volume archive at its disposal, may have the most comprehensive collection of references on the subject in the world.

The archive provides valuable information in support of the center's primary mission of stimulating research on the wise, environmentally sound use of water resources in the western United States.

Research focused toward the improvement of water conservation technology and irrigation practices and procedures by agriculture is a major effort. One approach being investigated by DANR scientists involves new irrigation schemes for plants which have been identified as relatively drought tolerant. The goal is to supply the plants with less than their potential water use during the growth period while minimizing the negative impact on the sustained use of the marketable product.

Recent work in this area indicates that controlled deficit irrigation (CDI) on pistachio trees appears promising. The most successful CDI regimes to date show seasonal water savings of between 20% and 30% from fully irrigated orchards, with no significant reduction in the yield of marketable product.

Another water-saving option has been tested for onion farmers in Riverside County, where a UC farm advisor introduced drip irrigation as an alternative to sprinkler and furrow systems.

This method shows promise of reducing water use, disease problems and the levels of nitrates leaching into ground water.

UC scientists also are working to remove unintended side effects of modern irrigation practices. These are particularly troublesome in the San Joaquin Valley's West Side, a major producer of the nation's fruits, nuts and vegetables.

The area has experienced high salt levels in soils, a rising ground water table that encroaches on crops' root zones, and potentially toxic concentrations of natural trace elements, like selenium, in drainage water.

Forging solutions to these problems is the pursuit of a Divisionwide Salinity/Drainage Task Force. Among the promising alternatives they have tested is a system of growing salt-tolerant shrubs and trees to act as sponges for salty drainage water.

The task force also is seeking ways to reduce concentrations of selenium and other potentially harmful trace elements in soil. One experiment has used microbes and plants to convert selenium into a harmless gas.

Recent research by other UC scientists is disclosing how soils capture pollutants. This knowledge could improve soil management practices used to halt the seepage of pesticides and other pollutants into water supplies.

Still other UC scientists have developed a new approach to safely using municipal sewage sludge on soils. Their work has provided new insights into ways to improve environmental quality and natural resources management.

The University's Division of Agriculture and Natural Resources is engaged in an array of other programs aimed at understanding and improving the quality of water, as well as air and soil.

In so doing, they know that water, air and soil are the irreplaceable building blocks on which food supply depends. Their work is intended to ensure that the state's resources are used prudently and that its agriculture remains productive and strong.

REFERENCES: "Extending the Bounty of Research," informational booklet, Division of Agriculture and Natural Resources, and related information.

CROSS-REFERENCES: Agriculture and Natural Resources.

Wellness became an important word by the mid-1980s.

It refers to the improvement of personal health through prevention and other health promotion activities.

During the next few years, the concept of wellness began to grow in popularity.

The University, particularly the Berkeley campus, engaged in a number of health promotion activities designed to encourage people to lead healthier lives.

In 1991, Health Net, California's second largest health maintenance organization, made a gift to the University of California to support a series of UC faculty lectures on wellness.

This marked the beginning of the UC/Health Net Wellness Lecture Series.

The purpose of this program is to encourage UC faculty to conduct research in critical health promotion areas, provide opportunities for them to present public lectures on their research results, and disseminate copies of their lectures in notebook form to a wide audience.

Proposals are solicited annually from UC faculty and a competitive peer-review process is used to select the most meritorious proposals.

A Universitywide Steering Committee selects six UC faculty to receive awards to support their research in health promotion, present public lectures, and distribute their lectures in written form.

These lectures are presented on UC's six health sciences campuses, including Berkeley, Davis, Irvine, Los Angeles, San Diego and San Francisco.

In addition, Health Net's gift supports an annual symposium and roundtable discussion among selected California and national health policymakers and the UC faculty who receive these awards.

Copies of the lectures are compiled in "Wellness Notebooks" and are distributed widely to UC faculty, California's health policy leaders, national health care leaders, and many health care providers. These notebooks are updated annually.

Video and audio tapes of the talks are also available and have been distributed to universities and colleges throughout this country.

This program is administered by the Office of Health Affairs in the Office of the President.

REFERENCES: News releases, University Relations, Office of the President; "Wellness: One Million and Counting," UC Focus, March 1990; "University of California, Berkeley Wellness Letter," School of Public Health, Berkeley; "Wellness Notebook" Office of Health Sciences, Office of the President.

CROSS-REFERENCES: AIDS Research and Treatment; Health Sciences; Teaching Hospitals.

Whistleblowing: See Improper Governmental Activities, Policy and Procedures for Reporting.

White Mountain Research Station: White Mountain Research Station, founded in 1950, has been fully operated as a Universitywide facility since 1978.

Before 1978, it had been operated by the Berkeley campus as one of its research facilities. The facility now serves as a research station for all campuses of the University and for five dozen or more other universities, colleges and institutions.

It is located at Bishop, 260 miles north of Los Angeles, on the eastern side of the Sierra Nevada.

It comprises four sites, which represent a unique transect from the high desert to the alpine zones. They are located largely within the Inyo National Forest.

Although White Mountain has become well known for research on hypoxia and physiology, past and ongoing studies have continued to address many of today's serious environmental concerns.

For example, a principal goal is to support research by faculty, advanced students and visiting investigators who focus on the following:

• Ecological, behavioral and physiological studies of land vertebrates, insects and plants.

• Geological, geomorphological and biogeographical studies

• Archaeological and anthropological studies,

• Astronomical, astrophysical and cosmological research.

Other goals include:

• Supporting student training in conjunction with ongoing research and instruction at both the graduate and undergraduate levels.

• Providing facilities for federal and state research groups.

• Encouraging the protection of the delicate alpine region in the White-Inyo Range.

REFERENCES: White Mountain Research Station annual reports; information from Academic Affairs, Office of the President.

CROSS-REFERENCES: Organized Research Units.

Women's Resource Centers: Each of the University's campuses has a Women's Resource Center.

Such centers are intended to help enhance the academic achievement and personal development of women and provide them with a chance to advocate changes in campus policies or practices which have an adverse impact on their opportunities and aspirations.

Centers are committed to promoting understanding of diversity and creating a supportive, inclusive campus community.

The centers address a wide range of critical issues, including social, political and economic issues, multicultural awareness, and creativity, as well approaches to addressing major problems such as sexual harassment, rape, and physical abuse. In addressing these issues, the centers offer a number of programs and services, including workshops, counseling, and self-defense classes.

The centers also offer skill-building internships, re-entry programs, assertiveness training, career planning, and support groups.

In addition, the centers provide listings of campus and community services, such as health care, child care, legal assistance, and counseling.

Each center maintains a library specially devoted to women's issues. Films, performances, lectures and art exhibits about women are also offered on a regular basis. In addition, many of the centers publish a newsletter.

REFERENCES: Women's Resource Centers; UC General Catalogs.

CROSS-REFERENCES: Affirmative Action.

Women's Studies:
The discipline of women's studies was initiated at American colleges and universities in 1969–70 as an outgrowth of the women's movement.

Since then, such programs have multiplied throughout the U.S., growing from approximately 100 courses in 1970 to tens of thousands today.

In the past few years, in response to the growing body of feminist theory, the number of programs and the motivation of their students have changed.

For example, students initially took courses in women's studies because of an interest in the subject. However, by the 1980s, women's studies had been accepted as academic majors, and research on women and gender has continued to expand on all UC campuses.

Today, women's studies programs explore options available in a woman's professional and personal lives and provide an understanding of what these options offer.

Such studies have brought to research and teaching a greater knowledge of women's experience and culture within the total human culture.

In addition to Women's Study Centers, campuses also have Women's Resource Centers, as well as separate units devoted to research on women and gender.

In 1985–86, in an effort to strengthen research on women and gender-related topics within the University, the UC Council of Women's Programs was created. Its missions have been to carry out the goals of teaching and research on women and gender issues within UC and to facilitate the exchange of knowledge, the growth and coordination of programs and activities, and the co-operation of scholars at all levels in research and teaching about women at the campuses.

The Council sponsors systemwide conferences and promotes intercampus cooperation on referrals of speakers, library and film resources, and exchanges of scholars. Each campus sends delegates from its women's studies programs and research centers to the Council's annual business meetings and research retreats.

REFERENCES: "Women's studies: A need to remain autonomous," *UC Focus,* Vol. 2, No. 8, June 1988; "Research on Women and Gender: A Directory of UC Scholars," 1991, UC Council of Women's Programs and the UCLA Center for the Study of Women; information from Women's Centers and UC General Catalogs.

CROSS-REFERENCES: Affirmative Action; Women's Resource Centers.

Work-Learn Programs:
Each campus offers a variety of special work-learn programs for undergraduates.

These include internships, field study, cooperative education, experiential learning, and community service.

A work-learn experience can help a student assess his or her skills and abilities, explore career options, and gain on-the-job experience.

Placements are available in government agencies, industry, political offices, health care facilities, professional businesses such as accounting and architectural firms, non-profit and community service organizations, farms, and research institutes. (The University encourages student involvement in public service activities.)

At some campuses, a student may design a placement to meet his or her specific educational and career interest.

A work-learn situation may be full-time or part-time, for credit or not for credit, voluntary or salaried. It may last a quarter or up to two years. The situation depends on a students needs and interests and the availability of placements at the campus.

All programs include professional supervision and emphasize learning rather than routine activities.

Different programs have different requirements, but most are open only to qualified juniors and seniors.

REFERENCES: "1994–1995, Introducing the University," Student Academic Services, Office of the President.

CROSS-REFERENCES: All subjects related to education and student financial aid.

Many Thanks

Deep appreciation is extended to the following for their kind assistance and warm support.

Marc Aarens, State Legislative Issues (OP)
Joe Acanfora, Campus Liaison, OTT, University Controller's Office (OP)
Mary Beth Acuff, Public Affairs (LLNL)
Christopher Adams, Long Range Planning (OP)
Jo Agustin, Academic Affairs (OP)
Sandra Ahn, Benefits Programs (OP)
Michael Aldaco, Admissions and Outreach Services (OP)
Gwen M. Allamby, Health Affairs (OP)
Mary Jane Alpaugh, Regents' Office
Donald Alter, Corporate Accounting (OP)
Michael Alva, News Media (OP)
Tommy Ambrose, Laboratory Affairs (OP)
John A. Anderson, Universitywide Police Services (SD)
Rosemary Amidei, SEAGRANT (SD)
Adele Amodeo, Health Affairs (OP)
Patricia Anaya, Health Affairs (LA)
Willie C. Archie, Research Administration (OP)
Randy Arnold, Education Abroad Program (SB)
Lynn Atwood, Public Information Office (B)
Jo Augustin, Academic Affairs (OP)
Mark Aydelotte, University Relations Regional Office (Fresno)
Paul Y. Bagasao, Faculty and Graduate Student Affirmative Action (OP)
Becky Bainbridge, Institutional Planning (R)
William B. Baker, Budget and University Relations (OP)
Diane Banegas, Public Information (LANL)
Ronald B. Banister, UC Printing Services (B)
Philip C. Bantin, Archives (LA)
Rose Barksdale, University Relations (OP)
Willa K. Baum, Oral History (B)
David Belk, Hazardous Materials Project (OP)
Ricki Bennett, Student Academic Services (OP)
Michael J. Bocchicchio, Facilities Administration (OP)
Rita B. Bottoms, Archives (SC)
Elizabeth Branstead, Employee and Labor Relations (OP)
Carroll Brentano, Center for Studies in Higher Education (B)
Doras Briggs, Physical Planning and Construction (OP)
Molly Brown, California Policy Seminar (OP)
Adolph Brugger, Academic Affairs (OP)
Jim Burns, Public Information (SC)
George Cage, Budget (OP)
Joseph Calmes, Lick Observatory (SC)
Sherry M. Carletta, Risk Management (OP)
Gregory Carr, Facilities Design, Construction and Management (OP)
William A. Carroll, Continuing Education of the Bar (OP)
Marjorie C. Caserio, Academic Affairs (SD)

Susie A. Castillo-Robson, Student Affairs and Services (OP)
Joanne Cate, Budget and University Relations (OP)
Mary Chaitt, Academic Planning and Budget (LA)
Jack Chappell, University Relations (R)
Norm Cheever, Employee Relations (OP)
Grace Choi, Public Information (LA)
Denise Cicourel, University of California Press
Jacqueline Cisneros, Budget and University Relations (OP)
Cindy Clark, Scripps Institution of Oceanography (SD)
James H. Clark, University Press (OP)
William Clipson, UC Printing Services (B)
Charles Colgan, Scripps Institution of Oceanography (SD)
Theony Condos, Academic Affairs (OP)
Clive Condren, Education Relations (OP)
Gloria Copeland, Office of the President
Barbara Correia, Personnel Services (OP)
Winifred Cox, University Communications (SD)
George W. Craig, UC Printing Services (B)
Edwin M. Crawford, University Relations (OP)
Barbara Cronin, Communications Office (I)
Afton Crooks, Information Practices and Special Projects (OP)
Philip Daro, California Mathematics Project
Nirmal K. Das, Health Affairs (OP)
Tom Debley, Community Relations (Hastings)
Anthony De Bone, Administrative Policies (OP)
Jill Dillard, Capital Planning and Budgeting (SD)
Roger G. Ditzel, Business and Finance (OP)
Deborah Dobin, University Extension (B)
Doris Doner, Personnel Services (OP)
Alvan J. Donner, Agricultural and Natural Resources (OP)
Sandra B. Douglas, Intersegmental Relations (OP)
Madeline Drake, Natural Reserve System (OP)
Dian Duryea, Development Policy and Administration (OP)
Troy Duster, Department of Sociology (B)
Edward Earle, California Museum of Photography (R)
Wilfred O. Easter, MESA Statewide
Georgina Edwards, University Relations (OP)
Deborah Elliot-Fisk, Natural Reserve System (DANR)
Judith Ellis, Educational Relations (OP)
Gay Englezos, Development Policy and Administration (OP)
Andrea Estrada, News & Communications Office (SB)
Carmen A. Estrada, Business and Employment Affirmative Action (OP)
Robert Eustachy, Designer and Graphic Artist
Sherilyn Evans, Information Systems and Administrative Services (OP)
Dorothy Everett, Office of the President

F. Louis Fackler, Facilities and Services (SC)
Elizabeth Falor, Budget and University Relations (OP)
Lucie Faulknor, News and Public Information (SF)
Carla Ferri, Student Academic Services (OP)
Harriet Fishlow, Academic Affairs (OP)
Harriet Fleischer, University Relation (R)
Mary Louise Flint, IPM Education and Publications (D)
William P. Foley, Police Department (B)
Amy Foster, University Relations (OP)
Sandria B. Freitag, Intersegmental Relations (OP)
Hardy T. Frye, Academic Affairs
Loren Furtado, Budget (OP)
Marian L. Gade, Center for the Study of Higher Education (B)
Dennis J. Galligani, Academic Affairs (OP)
Thomas M. Gaona, University Relations (OP)
Eugene E. Garcia, Latino Eligibility Task Force (SC)
David P. Gardner, President of the University
Jeanne Gardner, Administration (OP)
Saul Geiser, Budget and University Relations (OP)
Barbara Gerber, Academic Affairs (OP)
Huda Gontkon, University Communications (SD)
Jane Gonzalez, Academic Personnel and Affirmative Action (OP)
Julie Gordon, Academic Affairs (OP)
Linda Granell, Communications (I)
Susan Greer, Institute on Global Conflict and Cooperation (SD)
Charles L. Gruder, Tobacco-Related Disease Research Program (OP)
Linda Guerra, Budget and University Relations (OP)
John Gustafson, University Relations (OP)
Sarah Gustafson, Agricultural and Natural Resources (OP)
Stephen Handel, Student Academic Services (OP)
Stephanie Hauk, Public Information (SC)
Ruth Haynor, Health Affairs (OP)
Trudis Heinecke, Long Range Resource Planning (OP)
Harvey Z. Helfand, Planning and Design (B)
David W. Heron, Council of the University of California Emeriti Associations
Lawrence C. Hershman, Budget (OP)
Kief Hillsbery, Administrative Communications (SB)
Mark S. Hooper, Alumni Advocacy (OP)
Cornelius L. Hopper, Health Affairs (OP)
Sondra Hopson-Smith, Budget and University Relations (OP)
Rose Hsu, Alumni Advocacy (OP)
Susanne L. Huttner, Systemwide Biotechnology Research and Education Program (LA)
Laurie Itow, Communications Services (OP)
Patricia JaCoby, Institutional Outreach (SD)
Lynn Javier, Architecture and Project Management (I)
Kate Jeffrey, Student Academic Services (OP)
Andres Jiminez, California Policy Seminar (OP)
Helen M. Johnson, Public Information (I)
Joan Johnson, Budget and University Relations (OP)
Johnetta Jones, Benefits Programs (OP)
Jaime Jue, Planning and Design (B)
Joyce B. Justus, Educational Relations (OP)
Marcia Kai-Kee, Budget and University Relations (OP)
James S. Kane, Academic Affairs (OP)
Gabriele Kassner, External Relations (DANR)
Pamela Kast, Business Analysis (OP)
Louis Katz, UCSB Publications (SB)
Maureen Kawaoka, Institute of Industrial Research (OP)

James P. Keenan, Astronomy (B)
Lonnie Keith, Development Policy and Administration (OP)
Clark Kerr, President of the University, Emeritus
Ann B. Khayat, Loan and Property Management (OP)
Kerry Klayman, Communications Office (I)
Janet H. Kodish, Puente Project (OP)
Ronald Kolb, News and Public Affairs (OP)
Judy Kowarski, Student Academic Services (OP)
Gregory Kramp, Personnel Programs (OP)
Davis Krauter, University Relations (OP)
R. David Krogh, Academic Council
Robert Kuckuck, Laboratory Administration (OP)
Carol Kummer, UCSF Publications (SF)
Lillian Kurosaka, News Media (SB)
Jeanne Lance, Publications (SC)
Suzie Lascurettes, Office of Budget and Planning (SB)
Michael B. Lassiter, University Relations (OP)
Eleanore Lee, Academic Affairs (OP)
Linn Lee, University Relations (OP)
Lubbe Levin, Employee and Labor Relations (OP)
Martha Levy, Budget and Planning (SB)
Mary Limosner, Campus Planning (SF)
James Litrownik, Academic Affairs (OP)
Cherly Lofton-Brown, Academic Affairs (OP)
Ernest A. Lopez, Public Affairs (SB)
Owen Lunt, Laboratory of Biomedical and Environmental Sciences
Kay MacFarland, Facilities Administration (OP)
Reynaldo F. Macías, Linguistic Minority Research Institute (SB)
Karen Mack, Public Information (LA)
James A. MacKenzie, University Advancement (SC)
Rob Maddock, Publications (D)
Joan Magruder, News Media (SB)
Rick Malaspina, News and Public Affairs (OP)
Susan L. Mandilag, Facilities Design, Construction and Management (OP)
Pat Mann, Office of the President
John Marcum, Education Abroad Program (SB)
Hallie Masler, University Relations (LA)
Janet Mason, Capital Planning (I)
Niall J. Mateer, Academic Affairs (OP)
Steven M. Mathews, Loan and Property Management (OP)
Deborah Maxon, University Relations (OP)
Kevin R. McCauley, Health Affairs (OP)
Carol McClain, Academic Affairs (OP)
Judy McConnell, Employee Relations Programs (OP)
Beverly P. McDonald, Telecommunication Projects and Building Services (OP)
Roy McJunkin, California Museum of Photography (R)
Jennifer McNulty, Public Information (SC)
David F. Mears, Research Administration (OP)
Bonnie Mediano, University Relations (R)
Jesus Mena, Public Information (B)
Bobbie Mendoza, Budget and University Relations (OP)
Karen Merritt, Academic Affairs (OP)
Fran Miller, Public Information (SD)
Jeff Miller, Public Information (SF)
Calvin C. Moore, Academic Affairs (OP)
Mary Jean Moore, Information Systems and Administration Services
Nina Moore, Educational Relations (OP)
Elmo Morgan, Physical Planning and Construction (OP)

Evelyn Murphy, Public Affairs (LLNL)
Ralph K. Nair, Council of the University of California Emeriti Associations
Nancy Nakayama, Office of the President
Steven P. Nation, Governmental and External Relations (DANR)
Cici Nickerson, Regional Oral History Office (B)
Karen Nikos, Law School (LA)
Janet Norton, Institutional Relations (SF)
Suzanne Oatie, Public Information (LA)
Verna Osborn, Budget and University Relations (OP)
Donald E. Osterbrock, Lick Observatory (SC)
Fran Owens, Capital Planning (SC)
Thomas O'Leary, Public Information (SC)
Shirley Odorico, California Space Institute (SD)
Jorge Ohy, University Controller's Office (OP)
Cynthia Pace, Office of the President
Beverly D. Pachner, Health Affairs (OP)
Camille Parker, Employment and Business Affirmative Action (OP)
Joseph A. Pastrone, University Controller (OP)
Patricia A. Pelfrey, Office of the President
Jack W. Peltason, President of the University
Robert Peyton, Agriculture and Natural Resources (OP)
Sally Philbin, Personnel Services (OP)
James W. Phillips, Employee and Labor Relations (OP)
Robert Polkinghorn, Educational Relations (OP)
Sharon Pugsley, University Library (I)
Carla Rafetto, Information Systems and Administrative Services (OP)
Elizabeth C. Rajs, University Relations (OP)
Wallace Ravven, California Association for Research in Astronomy
Michela Reichman, Communications, News and Public Information Services (SF)
Debra Reynolds-Lowe, Budget and University Relations (OP)
Hugh M. Richmond, Department of English (B)
Sally Ride, CAL SPACE (SD)
Kathryn L. Roberts, UC MEXUS (R)
William M. Roberts, Archives (B)
Linda Rodden, Public Communications (D)
Joan Rogin, Coordination and Review (OP)
Celeste E. Rose, University Relations (OP)
Edwin F. Rosinski, Office of Medical Education (SF)
Sheldon Rothblatt, Center for Studies in Higher Education (B)
Susan Gee Rumsey, Natural Reserve System (OP)
Janet Ruyle, Center for Studies in Higher Education (B)
Georgette Salazar, UC Printing Services (B)
J. Roger Samuelson, Natural Reserve System (OP)
Lori Sanchez, Benefits Programs (OP)
Robert L. Sanders, Public Information (B)
Richard Santee, Budget and University Relations (OP)
David S. Saxon, President of the University, Emeritus
Linda Scheffer, University Controller's Office (OP)
Rick Schlee, Information Practices and Special Projects (OP)
Murray L. Schwartz, Academic Affairs (OP)
Adrienne B. Sciacca, Linguistic Minority Research Institute (SB)
Charles F. Scribner, UC Printing Services (B)
Lucy Sells, Information Practices and Special Projects (OP)
Keith Sexton, University Extension (OP)
Pat Shand, UCO/Lick Observatory (SC)
Michael M. Shannon, Telecommunications Services (OP)
Theda Shapiro, Education Abroad Program (SB)
Jesse Shaw, Budget and University Relations (OP)

Anne L. Shaw, Secretary of the Regents Office
Susan Shea, Development Policy and Administration (OP)
Julie Shearer, Regional Oral History Office (B)
Mohan W. Sitlani, Academic Affairs (OP)
Darlene Skeels, Public Information (LA)
Patricia A. Small, Office of the Treasurer of the Regents
Dennis E. Smith, Library Affairs (OP)
Dianne A. Smith, MESA Statewide
June B. Smith, Development Policy and Administration (OP)
Ross Smith, Information Practices and Special Projects (OP)
Bonnie M. Smotony, Secretary of the Regents
Verne Stadtman, Editor, *The Centennial Record of the University of California*
Elizabeth K. Stage, California Science Project (OP)
Elaine Stamman, Academic Affairs (OP)
Jeffrey A. Steindorf, Campus Planning (SD)
Linda Steiner-Lee, Public Information (LA)
Mary E. Stephens, Information Systems and Administrative Services (OP)
Maril Stratton, Public Communications (D)
Tamra Suslow-Ortiz, Student Financial Support (OP)
Frederick Swanson, Kearney Agricultural Center
Valerie Swanson, Education Abroad Program (SB)
Carole A. Swartz, University Benefits Program (OP)
Paul E. Sweet, Federal Government Relations (OP)
Ellen S. Switkes, Academic Personnel and Affirmative Action (OP)
Judith Talley, Budget and University Relations (OP)
Kogee Thomas, Relations with Schools (I)
Patricia Thomas, Statewide Academic Senate
Patricia A. Tilley, Information Systems and Administrative Services (OP)
Dale Treleven, Oral History Program (LA)
Arthur Tressler, Lawrence Berkeley Laboratory
Lee Trivette, Secretary of the Regents
Yasuko Umemoto, Information Services and Administrative Services (OP)
Rodney C. Umscheid, Risk Management (OP)
Debbie Vacca, Secretary of the Regents' Office
Robert Walen, Physical Planning and Construction (OP)
Myrna Walton, Personnel Planning and Executive Programs (OP)
John Webster, Public Information (LANL)
Tati Wennekamp, Public Programming (LA)
Donna Wentzel, Budget and University Relations (OP)
Paul West, Budget and University Relations (OP)
Richard P. West, Information Systems and Administrative Services (OP)
Mark Westlye, Academic Affairs (OP)
Janet White, Agricultural and Natural Resources (OP)
Toby R. Winer, Agriculture and Natural Resources (OP)
Martha Winnacker, Academic Affairs (OP)
Lynne Withey, UC Press
Judith Woodard, Public Affairs (SF)
Neila M. Woods, News and Public Affairs (OP)
Rex Woods, Water Resources Center (D)
Anne Wright, Expanded Food and Nutrition Education (OP)
Lynn Yarris, Public Information (LBL)
Barbara Yoder, Contracts and Grants (OP)
Lynda Yon, Laboratory Administration (OP)
Janet Young, Office of the President
Nancy W. Zinn, Special Collections (SF)

Index